Communications in Computer and Information Science 2534

Series Editors

Rationale

The CCIS series is devoted to the publication of proceedings of computer science conferences. Its aim is to efficiently disseminate original research results in informatics in printed and electronic form. While the focus is on publication of peer-reviewed full papers presenting mature work, inclusion of reviewed short papers reporting on work in progress is welcome, too. Besides globally relevant meetings with internationally representative program committees guaranteeing a strict peer-reviewing and paper selection process, conferences run by societies or of high regional or national relevance are also considered for publication.

Topics

The topical scope of CCIS spans the entire spectrum of informatics ranging from foundational topics in the theory of computing to information and communications science and technology and a broad variety of interdisciplinary application fields.

Information for Volume Editors and Authors

Publication in CCIS is free of charge. No royalties are paid, however, we offer registered conference participants temporary free access to the online version of the conference proceedings on SpringerLink (http://link.springer.com) by means of an http referrer from the conference website and/or a number of complimentary printed copies, as specified in the official acceptance email of the event.

CCIS proceedings can be published in time for distribution at conferences or as post-proceedings, and delivered in the form of printed books and/or electronically as USBs and/or e-content licenses for accessing proceedings at SpringerLink. Furthermore, CCIS proceedings are included in the CCIS electronic book series hosted in the SpringerLink digital library at http://link.springer.com/bookseries/7899. Conferences publishing in CCIS are allowed to use Online Conference Service (OCS) for managing the whole proceedings lifecycle (from submission and reviewing to preparing for publication) free of charge.

Publication process

The language of publication is exclusively English. Authors publishing in CCIS have to sign the Springer CCIS copyright transfer form, however, they are free to use their material published in CCIS for substantially changed, more elaborate subsequent publications elsewhere. For the preparation of the camera-ready papers/files, authors have to strictly adhere to the Springer CCIS Authors' Instructions and are strongly encouraged to use the CCIS LaTeX style files or templates.

Abstracting/Indexing

CCIS is abstracted/indexed in DBLP, Google Scholar, EI-Compendex, Mathematical Reviews, SCImago, Scopus. CCIS volumes are also submitted for the inclusion in ISI Proceedings.

How to start

To start the evaluation of your proposal for inclusion in the CCIS series, please send an e-mail to ccis@springer.com

Maxim Bakaev · Radomir Bolgov · Anna Chizhik · Andrei Chugunov · Yury Kabanov · Roberto Pereira · Elakkiya R · Wei Zhang
Editors

Internet and Modern Society

Human-Computer Communication

27th International Conference, IMS 2024
St. Petersburg, Russia, June 24–26, 2024
Selected Papers

Springer

Editors
Maxim Bakaev
Novosibirsk State Technical University
Novosibirsk, Russia

Radomir Bolgov
St. Petersburg State University
St. Petersburg, Russia

Anna Chizhik
St. Petersburg State University
St. Petersburg, Russia

Andrei Chugunov
ITMO University
St. Petersburg, Russia

Yury Kabanov
HSE University
St. Petersburg, Russia

Roberto Pereira
Federal University of Paraná
Curitiba, Paraná, Brazil

Elakkiya R
BITS Pilani, Dubai
Dubai, United Arab Emirates

Wei Zhang
Huazhong University of Science
and Technology
Wuhan, China

ISSN 1865-0929 ISSN 1865-0937 (electronic)
Communications in Computer and Information Science
ISBN 978-3-031-96176-2 ISBN 978-3-031-96177-9 (eBook)
https://doi.org/10.1007/978-3-031-96177-9

This Springer imprint is published by the registered company Springer Nature Switzerland AG
The registered company address is: Gewerbestrasse 11, 6330 Cham, Switzerland

Preface

On June 24–26, 2024, the International Conference "Internet and Modern Society" (IMS 2024) was held in St. Petersburg (Russia), preceded by its Dubai (UAE) section. This was the 27th edition of the conference, which has been held without interruptions since 1998.

The current proceedings contain the 29 papers in the field of Human-Computer Communication that were selected by the IMS 2024 Program Committee and presented at the conference. In total there were 75 submissions from over 10 countries, which were evaluated by about 50 reviewers,and on average each submission received 2.07 reviews. The double-blind review process was supported by licensed EasyChair software. Overall, there were over 300 registered participants in the conference. Another volume of the conference proceedings is to be published with Springer Geography, containing the 22 papers related to Urban Studies, Smart Cities, Digital Sustainability, etc.

This proceedings book addresses the topical issues of computer and information science and engineering, providing experts in the related fields with a platform for discussion and collaboration. In it, authors from all over the world consider the impact of the recent drastic changes in human-computer communication posed by the introduction of the AI-supported "intent-based" interaction paradigm and its lasting effects on the social, economic, educational, and technological aspects of human life. The main areas of the conference this year included Human-Computer Interaction, Natural Language Processing, Collaborative and Social Computing, E-Governance, Interactive Systems, Cyber Psychology, etc. The papers of the current proceedings were presented within the two major sections of IMS 2024:

- Interactive Systems & Information Society Technologies (InterSys);
- Computational Linguistics (CompLing).

The conference also involved several keynote talks, including:

- The "Gosuslugi" platform as an eco-system for digital interaction with the citizens (Oleg Yu. Kachanov, Deputy Minister, Ministry of Digital Development, Communications and Mass Media of the Russian Federation);
- Digitalization vs. well-being: how to ensure balance in the development of smart cities (Tatiana A. Momotova, Candidate of Political Sciences, Director of the Competence Centre for Cooperation with International Organisations at the HSE University);
- Digital technologies in managing urbanized territories (Sergey A. Mityagin, Candidate of Technical Sciences, Director of the Institute of Design & Urban Studies at ITMO University);
- A human as a weak side in the digital world: the problems of legal protection (Viktor B. Naumov, Doctor of Law, Managing Partner of Nextons, Chief Researcher at the Institute of State and Law of the Russian Academy of Sciences).

Overall, the content of the book may be of interest both to academics working in the related fields and to IT industry practitioners.

ITMO University was the main organizer of IMS 2024 held in cooperation with the partner universities:

- Birla Institute of Technology and Science, Pilani – Dubai Campus, United Arab Emirates;
- Federal University of Paraná, Curitiba, Brazil;
- Huazhong University of Science and Technology, China.

We would like to thank those who made this event possible and successful. We especially express our gratitude to the Program Committee members for their contribution to the selection of the papers. We thank the authors for submitting their manuscripts. We are proud of having attracted a great team of scholars from different countries and disciplines and will work further to sustain and expand the IMS community through joint research and collaboration.

June 2024

Maxim Bakaev
Radomir Bolgov
Anna Chizhik
Andrei Chugunov
Yury Kabanov
Roberto Pereira
Elakkiya R
Wei Zhang

Organization

General Chair

Dmitry Prokudin	St Petersburg University, Russia

Program Committee Chairs

Maxim Bakaev	Novosibirsk State Technical University, Russia
Radomir Bolgov	St Petersburg University, Russia
Anna Chizhik	St Petersburg University, ITMO University, Russia
Andrei Chugunov	ITMO University, Russia
Yury Kabanov	HSE University, Russia
Roberto Pereira	Federal University of Paraná, Brazil
Elakkiya R	BITS Pilani Dubai Campus, United Arab Emirates
Wei Zhang	Huazhong University of Science and Technology, China

Steering Committee

Nikolay Borisov	St Petersburg University, Russia
Andrei Chugunov	ITMO University, Russia

Program Committee

Anton Alekseev	Steklov Mathematical Institute, Russia
Mikhail Alexandrov	Universitat Autònoma de Barcelona, Spain
Olga Babina	South Ural State University, Russia
Olga Blinova	St Petersburg University, Russia
Alfiya Galieva	Kazan Federal University, Russia
Anna Glazkova	University of Tyumen, Russia
Olga Kamshilova	Herzen University, Russia
Margarita Kirina	HSE University, Russia
Marina Kogan	Peter the Great St Petersburg Polytechnic University, Russia

Antonina Laposhina	Pushkin State Russian Language Institute, Russia
Tatiana Litvinova	Voronezh State Pedagogical University, Russia
Olga Mitrofanova	St Petersburg University, Russia
Dmitry Morozov	Novosibirsk State University, Russia
Anna Moskvina	St Petersburg University, Russia
Olga Nevzorova	Kazan Federal University, Russia
Aleksandr Raikov	Kennan Institute of Supercomputing Technology, China
Svetlana Sheremetyeva	South Ural State University, Russia
Mariya Timofeeva	Novosibirsk State University, Russia
Lyudmila Vidiasova	ITMO University, Russia
Yulia Zherebtsova	ITMO University, Russia

Additional Reviewers

Sergey Alekseitsev
Thiago Campos
Caio Carvalho
Wei Dai
Valeriia Demareva
Ashish Gupta
Angel Jothi
Deógenes Junior
Natalia Loukachevitch
Olga Lyashevskaya
Sujatha M.
Bharathi Mohan
Radka Nacheva
Kumaran P
Shanthi P
Anton Pashkov
Alexander Piperski
Ashok Rajan
Prasannakumar Rangarajan
Gustavo Rossi
Olga Razumnikova
Gustavo Yuji Sato
Olga Scrivner
Yuan Tao
Subramaniyaswamy Vairavasundaram
Valeriia Viakhireva
Zizhao Zhao

Contents

Computational Linguistics and Machine Learning

Computational Linguistics and Machine Learning

Multiple Personalities by Order: Can ChatGPT Simulate Personas for User-Centered Design?

Maxim Bakaev[1], Svetlana Gorovaia[2], and Olga Mitrofanova[2](✉)

[1] Novosibirsk State Technical University, Novosibirsk, Russia
bakaev@corp.nstu.ru
[2] Saint Petersburg State University, Saint-Petersburg, Russia
st094316@student.spbu.ru, o.mitrofanova@spbu.ru

Abstract. AI technologies facilitated by Large Language Models (LLMs) are increasingly used in Software Engineering, particularly to support developers in writing, understanding and testing programming code. Meanwhile, UI/UX engineers remain somehow detached from this revolutionary automation, as the cornerstone of the User-Centered Design (UCD) is involvement of real and representative users. We believe that while this approach is primarily justified, certain Human-Computer Interaction (HCI) aspects could be polished based on AI-supported tests. In our paper, we explore the capabilities of LLM-based ChatGPT service to simulate personas that represent different user groups, identified by gender, age, and education level. For this end, we ask ChatGPT in English and Russian to generate short textual associations after contextually prompting it to "be" one of the 4 specially devised persons. We further perform linguistic analysis of the 200 association units, relying on TTR (Type-Token Ratio) measure. We find that the difference in associations for different stimuli is much higher than for different personas, which suggests that ChatGPT is relatively poor at simulating them. The outcome of our study might be a step towards the development of LLM-based user behavior models (UBMs) that can facilitate testing automation in the UCD process.

Keywords: Large Language Models · Prompt Engineering · Human-Computer Interaction · Type-Token Ratio

1 Introduction

The advent of ChatGPT in 2022 marked the start of a new era in human interaction with computer systems. People widely began to employ LLM-based chatbots and generative services in their professional activities, seeking to increase the work productivity and the quality of the output. These gains, however, had been uneven for different tasks – less for the ones that are further from search and summarization of information. In particular, there is an ongoing debate on whether AI-based technologies can be effectively employed in a sort of their "know thyself" task – that is, in human-computer interaction (HCI) engineering [1].

M. Bakaev et al. (Eds.): IMS 2024, CCIS 2534, pp. 3–12, 2026.
https://doi.org/10.1007/978-3-031-96177-9_1

The two iterative activities of a UI/UX (user interface/user experience) engineer are *design* and *evaluation.* The generative models have already demonstrated high utility in *ideation*, which is sometimes identified as a distinct stage in design, but their adoption for generation of final UIs so far remains limited. It is rather a common knowledge that LLMs are more lacking the more context-specific the task is, particularly due to their still constrained capabilities to grasp contextual descriptions. We argue that evaluation of UIs might be more favorable, since it can get along with less context specification and more common sense than UI design. This is actually confirmed by the considerably larger number of LLM-based tools that are in use for software testing vs. for design [2].

Of the two most effective UI/UX direct (i.e., non-expert) evaluation methods, A/B Testing and User Testing, the former sees more practical usage in the industry, particularly due to the need of the latter to employ costly and capricious human subjects [3]. Naturally then, an area where LLM/GPT technologies could aid with their robust knowledge of "common sense" is simulation of real users' preferences and behaviors. Since one of the HCI principles is "no UI is perfect for every user" the obvious caveat here is that "Your actual customers are not "average humans" [4]. However, there seems to be no reason why the "common sense" cannot be differentiated by target user groups, like it is done e.g. with design guidelines for specific populations. The resulting method would not belong to User Research, but rather would be on the edge with the expert-based ones, a sort of enhanced Heuristic Evaluation (call it *AIstic Evaluation*, if you will).

Another well-established qualitative method in HCI, suggested by A. Cooper, is development and application of "Personas" throughout the UI/UX engineering process. At the same time, existing research offers good evidence that models can imitate not just different writing styles, but even diverse personalities – foremost with contextual prompts [5]. Moreover, there are reports that people already try ChatGPT's capabilities in creating personas [6]. The question is, however, could LLM-based chatbots grasp the personality-defining context to the extent of reliably imitating a specific behavior.

There are many dimensions to a personality, and different disciplines propose their own views on what makes us Us. In our current work we decided to take a rather high-level view on this, relying on ontological approach, which is shared by Philosophy, Linguistics, and Informatics. Previously, it has been demonstrated that even complex objects and processes can be described by a set of concepts from a domain ontology, for subsequent comparison with a similarity measure [7]. Moreover, since ontological concepts are represented in textual form, the approach should be native to LLMs. Thus, for the sake of the experiment performed in our paper we assume that the difference in a set of ontological concepts used to describe an object corresponds to a difference in personalities. The research problem deals with detection of personified features texts generated by LLM.

The remainder of our paper is structured as follows. In Sect. 2, we provide a brief overview of the research background related to the methods applied in our study. Section 3 describes the experiment we undertake with 4 personas and 5 stimuli words from the academic/educational domain. Section 4 presents the linguistic analysis of the outcome, mainly based on TTR (Type-Token Ratio). In the final section of the paper, we summarize and discuss our findings and outline the plan for further work.

2 Research Background

Sociolinguistic and psychological profiling implies extraction of text features which correlate with certain aspects of personality: age, gender, social status, geographical location, interests, psychological traits, emotional state, etc. [8]. It turns out that such lexical, morphological, syntactic, pragmatic features as lexical divergence, lexical preferences, POS distribution, phrase structure, clause types, syntactic complexity, discourse markers are relevant in speaker profiling [9, 10]. Natural language texts convey latent features of speakers' idiostyle and individual semantic differences in the use of words and lexical constructions [11]. Individual features intrinsically stored in contexts form associative meanings which are represented in associative lexical databases, cf. Russian data in [12–14], etc. In most cases lexicographic resources store associations annotated as regards speakers' age, gender and social status[1], although such information as psycho-emotional background poses certain difficulties in observation and registration that is why it often falls out of sight. e same time, high-level modelling of human communication requires both personal traits annotated corpora such as RusNeuroPsych[2] and a comprehensive description of associative fields and association type markup within the lexicon [15].

Development of LLMs gives rise to a new challenge which concerns personality (characters, personas) identification in the AI's behavior. Technological and linguistic aspects of human-machine interaction have reached an unprecedented height [16]. On the one hand, it is clear that LLMs can reveal human-like strategies in communication, on the other hand, there are no precise linguistic criteria allowing to evaluate personalized traits in user interaction with LLMs. Recent advances in investigations of LLM personalities deal with LLM control [17]; personality prompting in inducing identity features in LLM behavior [18], evaluation of personality consistency and linguistic alignment of LLMs and their users in conversational interaction [19], etc. In our study we focus on lexical associations which correlate with LLM personified linguistic features.

3 The Experiment Description

In our study, we have developed a novel scheme of the associative experiment, taking the classical methodology as a basis [20, 21] and adapting it to the situation of interaction between the human user and LLM. It is expected that in the course of experiments the model should reproduce human behavior as a participant of the educational or research process. First, we selected lexical stimuli which are frequent in the given communicative settings, second, we invented fictional personas and adjusted their profile as regards age, gender, personal name, marital status, location, education, current job, plans for future, etc. Restrictions on the model output deal with lexical type of reactions (unigrams) and their number in a set (10).

[1] URL: https://smallworldofwords.org/ru.

[2] URL: https://rusidiolect.rusprofilinglab.ru/.

3.1 Stimuli

The stimuli words for the associations were extracted using Advego[3], an online service for frequency analysis, from the official websites of the two universities: St. Petersburg State University (https://spbu.ru) and Novosibirsk State Technical University (https://nstu.ru)[4]. The Russian versions of the websites' homepages (as of 7th of March 2024) were used.

First, the stop-words were removed, e.g., the universities' names, the current month name, etc.). Ultimately, we found that the following 5 words were the most frequent in the texts:

1) *center/центр*: 51 occurrences,
2) *university/университет*: 44 occurrences,
3) *scientific/science/научный/наука*: 58 occurrences,
4) *educational/education/образовательный/образование*: 65 occurrences,
5) *program/программа*: 23 occurrences.

The validity of this set is confirmed by the following facts:

1) the stimuli and their derivatives are frequently used in the PolyLing Corpus developed at Saint Petersburg Polytechnic University and includes texts from the websites of leading Russian universities [22],
2) the stimuli and their derivatives can be found in associative dictionaries [13].

3.2 Subjects (Personas)

There were no human subjects in the study. The 4 personas representing common target users for university websites were simulated using ChatGPT (see Table 1). The descriptions of the personas, which we used as the context prompts, can be found in the online Appendix A[5].

Table 1. The "characteristics" of the personas devised for the study.

PersonaID	Persona name	Gender	Age (group)	Education (level)
1	"Enrollee"	Female	18 (0)	High school (0)
2	"Graduate"	Male	25 (0)	Bachelor (1)
3	"Parent"	Female	40 (1)	Bachelor (1)
4	"Post-Doc"	Male	34 (1)	Graduate/PhD (2)

[3] https://advego.com/text/seo/.

[4] The authors of the current paper are affiliated with these two universities.

[5] https://github.com/gorovuha/personGPT/tree/main.

3.3 The Experimental Procedure

The prompts corresponded to the conditions of an associative experiment. The experimental trials with ChatGPT were performed sequentially. We used the default settings for our experiments, to ensure replicability and consistency across different sessions.

In each session, we would first reset the chat, so that the context is nullified. Then we would use the context prompts in the following format:

"Hello! Imagine that you are <Persona name>…, the description is given below. Answer the following requests on behalf of …"
"Здравствуйте! Представьте, что вы …, описание приведено ниже. Ответьте на следующие запросы от имени …. "

After that, we would provide the description for each of the four personas, and then ask ChatGPT to come up with associations for the five stimuli words:

"Come up with 10 one-word associations for the next five words …".
"Придумайте 10 ассоциаций для следующих пяти слов. "

In each chat session, ChatGPT would respond with polite confirmations referring to the described personas (both in Russian and English), such as:

"Alright, as Olga, I'm here to respond to your requests! How can I assist you today?",
"Here are ten one-word associations for each of the given words, from my perspective as Anton",
"As Artyom, focusing on my experiences and aspirations, here are my associations for each word".

3.4 Derivations

Model replies generated in our experiments form the associative field which transmits the network of relations linking stimuli and reactions. Traditionally associations may be differentiated as syntagmatic and paradigmatic, and further labeled as synonymy, antonymy, hyponymy, meronymy, conversion and other varieties of semantic proximity in paradigmatic case, or as collocability, lexical functions or some types of semantic compatibility or adjacency in syntagmatic case [23].

The relevance and specificity of associations can be assessed by analyzing their lexical variety using TTR (Type-Token Ratio), which is calculated by dividing the number of unique words by the total number of words in a group, cf. an overview of approaches to lexical diversity in [24]. In quantitative respect TTR has certain limitations as it gives distortions in case of long texts, but its use as a measure for evaluating associative groups of limited size seems to be justified. As a qualitative variable, TTR corresponds to the range and variability of the vocabulary that speakers manifest in their utterances.

As the dataset considered in our research contains associative groups of lemmatized reactions that are limited in number, the standard approach to TTR, which is applied in processing textual data, needs revision. In our analysis we treated TTR as V/N, where N is the total number of reactions in a group, while V is the number of distinct reactions (i.e.

unique reactions and repetitive reactions are counted once). Thus, high TTR corresponds to variability of reactions within groups, while low TTR indicates stereotyping and hidden trends in associative groups.

4 Results

4.1 Descriptive Statistics for the ChatGPT Output

Ten LLM associations were generated for each persona and each stimulus, so a total of 200 = 10 * 5 * 4 lexical units were collected, forming the associative field. The online Appendix B[6] presents the outcomes of the association experiments in English and Russian languages.

4.2 Qualitative Analysis of the Associations

The features characterizing the structure and content of the associative field were as follows:

1) these are mainly topic-related nouns which maintain paradigmatic associations of contiguity; as for other parts of speech, there are adjectives such as *образовательный/educational, исследовательский/research, инновационный/innovative* (Rus), attributive modifiers in noun phrases *training, learning, software, online*, etc. (Eng), as well as adverbs *дистанционно/remotely* (Rus), *scholarly* (Eng); there is also a complex noun *мастер-класс/master class*, one collocation *учебный план/curriculum* (Rus), two named entities *Java* and *Python*;
2) morphological fluctuations in number were recorded in the following cases: *инновация – инновации/innovation – innovations, исследование – исследования/research (sing, pl), курс – курсы/course – courses, педагог – педагоги/teacher – teachers, проект – проекты/project – projects, эксперимент – эксперименты/experiment – experiments* (Rus), *degree – degrees, student – students, theory – theories, scholarship – scholarships* (Eng), etc.; these options were considered equivalent;
3) as far as derivational relations are concerned, the following derivational chains can be distinguished: *исследование – исследовательский/research (noun, adjective), инновация – инновационный/innovation – innovative, класс – мастер-класс/class - master class, преподавание – преподаватель/teaching – teacher, специальность – специализация/specialty – specialization, учеба – учебник – учебный – учебный план/study – textbook – educational – curriculum – research* (Rus), *school – scholar – scholarship* (Eng), etc.

4.3 Type-Token Ratio (TTR) Analysis

The TTR values for the groups associations per personas were calculated as follows: for each of the four personas, a group of 50 associations was obtained for each of the five stimuli. Repeated reactions were identified and their impact on the results of the

[6] https://github.com/gorovuha/personGPT/tree/main.

experiment was assessed. In total, six repetitive Russian associations were identified: *инновации/innovation, исследования/research, развитие/development, курс/course, квалификация/qualification, студенты/students.* The association *исследования/research* has been repeated for all the personas. Among English associations, we found the following iterative reactions: *curriculum, development, innovations, learning, research,* of which *curriculum* and *research* turn out to be common for all personas. Figure 1 presents the TTR values for the two languages per the personas.

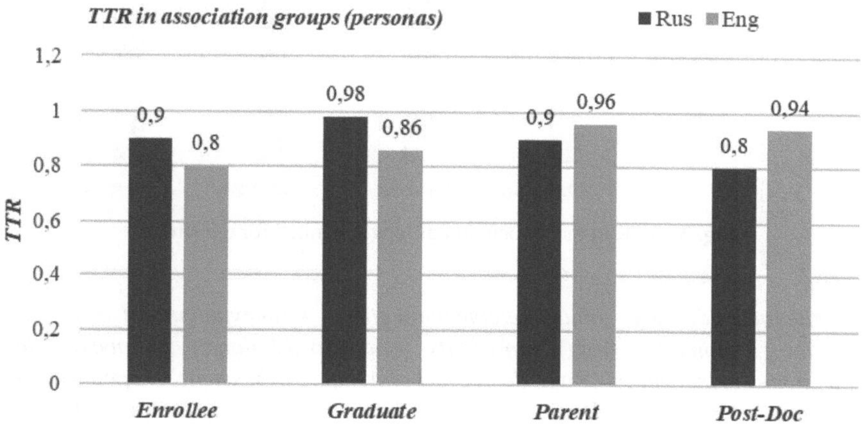

Fig. 1. TTR in the association groups generated for the personas.

The TTR values for the association groups per the stimuli were calculated as follows: for each of the five stimuli, a group of 40 reactions was obtained from four personas. As in the previous case, repeated reactions were defined and their effect on the outcome of the experiment was evaluated. Figure 2 presents the TTR values for the different stimuli in Russian and English.

Unlike the lists of repeated reactions obtained as regards personas, the associative field formed by reactions to the stimuli was significantly wider and contained 41 lexical units in Russian and 49 in English. Considering the importance of repetitions in the results of the associative experiment, we assume that additional categories are identified in the associative field clarifying the set of stimuli being first-order categories. Both experiments share Russian associations *инновация/innovation, исследование/research, развитие/development, курс/course,* English associations *curriculum, development, innovations, learning, research, scholarship* forming second-order categories. The remaining reactions are treated as third-order categories.

We considered parallel repetitive reactions as prototypical markers of association groups, e.g.: *university – academy/академия, library/библиотека, campus/кампус, lectures/лекции, professors/профессора, students/студенты; program – algorithms/алгоритмы, training/обучение, project/проект; science – analysis/анализ, discovery/открытие, experiment/эксперимент, laboratories/лаборатории,* etc. Language specificity of associations is exhibited by such reactions as *center*

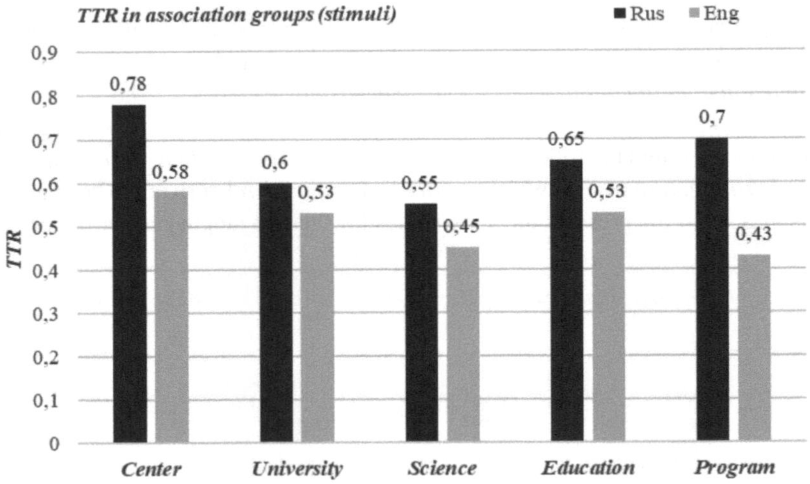

Fig. 2. TTR in the association groups generated for the stimuli.

– *активность/activity*, *общение/communication*, *культура/culture* (Rus), *collaboration*, *community* (Eng); *university* – *диплом/diploma*, *знания/knowledge*, *специальность /speciality* (Rus), *degree*, *scholarship* (Eng); *science* – *гранты/grants*, *публикации/publications* (Rus), *Biology*, *Chemistry*, *Physics* (Eng); *education* – *стипендия/scholarship*, *учеба/study*, *учебник/manual* (Rus), *diploma*, *knowledge*, *skills* (Eng); *program* – *практика/practice*, *сертификат/certificate*, *технологии/technology* (Rus), *code*, *application*, *software* (Eng), etc.

5 Discussion and Conclusion

In our project we introduced and tested the experimental procedure aimed at personalized interaction with ChatGPT. We invented four personas corresponding to the most probable addressees – visitors to university websites, and selected five words as stimuli in requests to ChatGPT. Associative experiment was designed and performed in order to collect and analyze personalized responses to the stimuli which deal with science and education. The comparison of the Russian and English data suggests the unity of core reactions and their specificity with respect to personas and languages. The comparison of TTR for the association groups for personas and stimuli allows us to draw the following conclusions:

1. In the group of associations to stimuli per personas the TTR is significantly higher (Rus: 0.8 … 0.98, Eng: 0.8 … 0.94) compared to the group of associations for personas as regards stimuli (Rus: 0.55 … 0.73, Eng: 0.43 … 0.58).
2. The increase in the number of repetitions in the second experiment compared to the first one suggests that LLMs are able to handle individual variations in stimuli more effectively than in personas.
3. In English associations TTR turns out to be lower than in Russian, therefore English ChatGPT is more sensitive to stimuli and personas than Russian.

Of the three types of personas simulated by Role-Playing Language Agents that are specified in a recent review of the field [25], ours belong to Demographic Personas. The negative LLM personification results that we obtained for the UX domain are consistent with the up-to-date findings for Character Personas. For instance, in [26] they concluded that ChatGPT failed to reach human-level performance in fiction literature characters-aligned conversations.

Our research was aimed to prove the necessity of supplementing, but not replacing human-to-human usability testing. No one says that automated tests in software engineering have replaced human testers, but neither would deny the gain in programmers' productivity, when these tests were introduced into the development process. If some bugs (and UI/UX problems) might be detected automatically in simulated or hypothetical contexts and environments, then human experts should not spend time on such relatively trivial issues.

The experiments discussed in our paper had certain limitations as they involved only one LLM-based service (ChatGPT) and only one particular domain (university websites), while the personas were not drastically different (on the other hand, different target users rarely are). Out further research plans include comparing the associations provided by ChatGPT with real people's ones that had been registered in lexical databases for Russian and English.

Acknowledgements. The study is performed with partial support of SPbSU research project 124032900006-1.

References

1. Nielsen, J.: What AI Can and Cannot Do for UX (2024). https://jakobnielsenphd.substack.com/p/ai-can-cannot-do-ux. Last accessed 18 Apr 2024
2. Hou, X., et al.: Large Language Models for Software Engineering: A Systematic Literature Review (2024). https://arxiv.org/pdf/2308.10620.pdf. Last accessed 18 Apr 2024
3. Bakaev, M. et al.: We Don't Need No Real Users?! Surveying the Adoption of User-less Automation Tools by UI Design Practitioners. In: Web Engineering. ICWE 2022. Lecture Notes in Computer Science. Vol. 13362. Springer, Cham. (2022)
4. Nielsen, J.: User Research with Humans vs. AI. https://jakobnielsenphd.substack.com/p/research-humans-ai (2024). Last accessed 18 Apr 2024
5. Wang, H., et al.: Cue-CoT: chain-of-thought prompting for responding to in-depth dialogue questions with LLMs. In: Findings of the Association for Computational Linguistics: EMNLP 2023, pp. 12047–12064. Singapore (2023)
6. Nielsen, J.: Top AI Tools Used by UX Professionals (2024). https://jakobnielsenphd.substack.com/p/top-ai-tools-for-ux. Last accessed 18 Apr 2024
7. Bakaev, M., Avdeenko, T.: Indexing and comparison of multi-dimensional entities in a recommender system based on ontological approach. Computación y Sistemas **17**(1), 5–13 (2013)
8. Dehghani, M., Boyd, R.L.: Handbook of Language Analysis in Psychology. Guilford Press, New York (2022)
9. Panicheva, P. et al.: Predicting subjective well-being in a high-risk sample of Russian mental health app users. In: EPJ Data Science, vol. 11, pp. 1–42. (2022)

10. Pronoza, E., Panicheva, P., Koltsova, O., Rosso, P.: Detecting ethnicity-targeted hate speech in russian social media texts. Inform. Process. Manage. **58**(6), 102674 (2021). https://doi.org/10.1016/j.ipm.2021.102674
11. Litvinova, T.A., Panicheva, P.V.: Individual differences in the associative meaning of a word through the prism of the language model and the semantic differential. In: Scientific result. Questions of theoretical and applied linguistics, vol. 10, no. 1, pp. 61–93 (2024). (in Russian)
12. Karaulov, Y.N., Cherkasova, G.A., Ufimtseva, N.V., Sorokin, Yu.A., Tarasov, E.F.: The Russian associative dictionary. In: 2 volumes, vol. 1. From Stimulus to Reaction. 784 p. Vol. 2. From Reaction to Stimulus. 992 p. M.: Astrel; AST (2002). (in Russian)
13. Shaposhnikova, I.V., Romanenko, A.A.: The Russian regional associative dictionary: Siberia and the far East. In: 2 volumes; Institute of Philology SB RAS; Novosibirsk State University. CPI NSU, Novosibirsk (2022). (in Russian)
14. Ufimtseva, N.V., Cherkasova, G.A.: Associative lexicography and studies of linguistic consciousness. Philology Cult. **4**(38), 193–199 (2014). (in Russian)
15. Litvinova, T.A., Lyubova, S.G.: Marking up Associative reactions by types of "stimulus-associate" relationships as a stage in creating an annotated multicomponent corpus of associative reactions of an individual. In: Problems of Studying the Living Russian Word at the Turn of the Millennium: Materials of the XI International Scientific Conference, Voronezh, 27–28 Oct 2023, pp. 49–58 (2023). (in Russian)
16. Kotov, A.A.: Mechanisms of Speech Influence. Moscow (2022). (in Russian)
17. Weng, Y., et al.: ControlLM: crafting diverse personalities for language models (2024). arXiv 2024. https://arxiv.org/abs/2402.10151. Last accessed 18 Apr 2024
18. Jiang, G. et al.: Evaluating and Inducing Personality in Pre-trained Language Models. In: Advances in Neural Information Processing Systems 36 (NeurIPS 2023). arXiv 2023. https://arxiv.org/abs/2206.07550. Last accessed 18 Apr 2024 (2013) (2023)
19. Frisch, I., Giulianelli, M.: LLM Agents in Interaction: Measuring Personality Consistency and Linguistic Alignment in Interacting Populations of Large Language Models. In: arXiv 2023. https://arxiv.org/abs/2402.02896. Last accessed 18 Apr 2024 (2023)
20. Pishchalnikova, V.A., et al.: Associative Experiment: Theoretical and Applied Perspectives of Psycholinguistics: Monograph/Ed. V.A. Pishchalnikova, Moscow (2019). (in Russian)
21. Ufimtseva, N.V.: Linguistic Consciousness: Dynamics and Variability. Institute of Linguistics of the Russian Academy of Sciences, Moscow, Kaluga (2011). (in Russian)
22. Kogan, M.S., et al.: On Determining the complexity of multimodal texts of sites of Russian universities (based on the PolyLing corpus). In: International Journal of Open Information Technologies, vol. 11, no. 12, pp. 62–72 (2023). (in Russian)
23. Antipenko, A.A., Mitrofanova, O.A.: Comparative analysis of associations in social network corpora based on distributive semantic models for the Russian language. Int. J. Open Inform. Technol. **8**(1), 27–33 (2020). [in Russian]
24. Zakharova, E.Y., Savina, O.Y.: Lexical diversity measures' review and classification. TSU Herald. Hum Res. Humanitates **6**(1), 20–34 (2020). https://doi.org/10.21684/2411-197X-2020-6-1-20-34
25. Chen, J.. et al.: From Persona to Personalization: A Survey on Role-Playing Language Agents (2024). arXiv preprint arXiv:2404.18231
26. Chen, N., et al.: Large language models meet harry potter: a dataset for aligning dialogue agents with characters. In: Findings of the Association for Computational Linguistics: EMNLP 2023, pp. 8506–8520. Singapore. (2023)

On Automated Creation of Gold-Standard Corpus for Multi-Aspect Sentiment Analysis

Svetlana Sheremetyeva(✉) and Olga Babina

South Ural State University, 76, Lenin Pr, Chelyabinsk 454080, Russia
{sheremerevaso,babinaoi}@susu.ru

Abstract. Data annotation is the cornerstone of sentiment extraction processes within practically all technological approaches: rule-based, statistical, machine learning, neural or hybrid. The article presents a methodology for automated creation of a gold-standard corpus for multi-aspect sentiment analysis as well as results of the methodology application to a collection of general public evaluative opinions about the activities of medical institutions found on online platforms. The specificity of such online reviews as compared to literate media published texts and its influence on the annotation procedure is investigated.

Described are the stages of a) review corpus acquisition and lexicon extraction b) conceptualization of lexical knowledge into sentiment and aspect related classes, whose label codes are used as a tagset, c) developing program tools to digitalize and store the linguistic knowledge, as well as to automate knowledge acquisition and annotation processes. The tools reused, updated and newly developed include a lexical extractor, grammar checker, annotation platform which, in turn, consists of an e-lexicon and a tagger that can produce coarse and fine levels of tagging. The research results, both the gold-standard corpus and tools are to be further used for aspect sentiment analysis at the following stages of our research. They may also deserve the attention of both computational linguists and sociologists.

Keywords: Multi-Aspect Sentiment Annotation · Gold Standard Corpus · Russian · General Public Data · Computer Tools

1 Introduction

Sentiment analysis and related to it more refined aspect sentiment analysis are indispensable for improving the quality of production and/or services in all spheres of society, and therefore, have come in focus of many NLP areas. Sentiment-only analysis assesses the judgments about an object as being "negative", "positive" or "neutral", advanced models going further to identify different levels of the sentiment intensity. However, even advanced sentiment analysis doesn't show people's opinions on different characteristics of objects (products or services), which is critical for improvements. What gives the information about the user attitude to the components of an object i.e., object "aspects" is multi-aspect sentiment analysis where every aspect can be characterized by its own sentiment tonality. The latter does not exclude the possibility to generalize aspect sentiment

M. Bakaev et al. (Eds.): IMS 2024, CCIS 2534, pp. 13–24, 2026.
https://doi.org/10.1007/978-3-031-96177-9_2

calculations to get the tonality of the object as a whole. There exist various sentiment and aspect sentiment calculation methodologies based on rule-based, machine learning, neural net, and hybrid approaches, each involving establishing a correspondence between corpus texts and hidden factors (tone scores and assessment aspects), all based on annotated data.

Data annotation (or "labeling") is the process of adding metadata, or tags, to raw data and is a corestone of most information processing projects that contributes essentially the accuracy of the analysis results. It is extremely effort and time consuming, and the need to automate the annotation process is obvious. However, in many sentiment related research, the stage of data annotation is often overlooked or lacks the description of annotation.

The current paper is meant to attend to the above mentioned issues and describes the methodology of constructing resources for automatic multi-aspect sentiment analysis that can be used in the frames of different aspect sentiment extraction technologies: rule-based, statistical, neural or hybrid. Described are the stages to create a gold-annotated task-oriented corpus including a) data acquisition and formalization, and b) development of program tools to automate linguistic knowledge acquisition and corpus annotation. The linguistic knowledge acquisition stage consists of corpora formation followed by qualitative analysis of its conceptual structure with subsequent digitalization. The sentiment and aspect conceptual class labels form the annotation tagset. The tool development includes creating a) an e-lexicon that serves both to store the digitalized linguistic knowledge, and to automate its acquisition, b) a grammar checker, and c) an aspect-sentiment tagger that can be configured to output annotations at coarse or fine levels. The methodology is used to create a gold-annotated corpus of Internet discourse texts in the domain of patient opinions about the activities of medical institutions in the Ural region.

The rest of the paper is organized as follows. Section 2 gives an overview of related work. In Sect. 3, the methodology of the current research is presented. Data analysis and tagset definition are given in Sect. 4. Aspect sentiment annotation tools are presented in Sect. 5. Section 6 describes the gold standard annotation process. Conclusions summarize the research results and outline our future work.

2 Related Work

Literature attending to data/corpus annotation relevant for our research covers both, sentiment and aspect-sentiment analysis, and, in general, share all or a combination of the following stages: corpus acquisition, preprocessing, extraction of sentiment/ aspect relevant lexica and annotation proper. The annotation schemes differ from work to work depending upon the type of corpus and analysis task. For data annotation in conducting particular projects, some researchers rely on, if possible (which is far from being the case), existing annotated resources, such as RuSentiTweet, – a sentiment analysis datasets of general domain tweets [1], RuSentiment, – an enriched sentiment analysis dataset for social media [2], or on domain-tuned resources [3]. In reality, the most popular annotation approaches are.

a) in-house manual or automated mark-up, either with computer interfaces like BRAT [4], or based on some heuristics, as tag assignment, based on emoticons [5];

b) crowdsourcing through platforms, like Yandex.Toloka (https://toloka.ai/);
c) outsourcing annotation to freelancers.

The main problem here is that, if annotated manually, the annotators' inter-rater agreement score is often neglected [1]. Corpus sentiment or aspect sentiment annotation can be done at different levels (sometimes called annotation granularity): words/phrases, sentences, or documents/texts [6]. Apart from methods mentioned above, assigning tags to the whole document can be based on a) the evaluation marks, provided by the document authors, e.g., on 1–10 or 1–5 scale [7], or by summarizing annotations of each word/sentence in the document [8]. Before the actual annotation process, collected corpora are often preprocessed[1], as a rule, includes removal of stop word, controversially user-marked documents [5] and/or stemming, tokenization, part of speech tagging and parsing with NLP techniques [9].

The most problematic stage of the annotation process shared by both, sentiment, and aspect sentiment analysis research is extraction and classification of textual fragments (words and phrases) that express authors' sentiment and/or aspect. In the works that rely on existing annotated resources, sentiment and aspect lexica extraction, classification and annotation depends on the resource annotation schemes and is normally performed by matching corpora against a preexisting resource, that is, by preexisting resource look-up. In other cases, the collected corpora is processed (automated or manually) resulting in lists of sentiment/aspect related words and expressions that are further classified into polarity-related classes and aspect categories, the number and content of which vary from project to project. The coarse polarity proper classification includes sorting lexical items into "negative" and "positive", or "negative", "positive" and "neutral". More advanced polarity annotation schemes go further and account for the sentiment intensity and include such classes as "most positive", "most negative" and "modifiers/operators", – lexical items that can further be divided into subclasses of those that change the sentiment intensity, revert the polarity of a text token from "positive" to "negative" or vice versa, or make the sentiment of the token "irreal" [10]. More lexical sentiment analysis related classes are sometimes added to those listed, like, e.g., "speech act"(greetings, congratulations, etc.) "skip" (phrases of unclear sentiment) [1] or (what is the same)"phrases of mixed tonality" [7], all of which are in fact sentiment noise and are normally deleted from the corpus before annotation. Most often, annotation comes in the form of numerical values (scores or weights) showing discrete or gradual degrees of sentiments [9, 10].

Aspect terms can be coarse-grained, like, e.g., FOOD, PRICE, SERVICE, etc. in the restaurant reviews dataset presented in [11, or can be subdivided into several categories. For example, in [12], aspects are classified into three subtypes: explicit aspects, implicit aspects and sentiment facts. Explicit aspects refer to some parts or characteristics of an object. Implicit aspects are sentiment words that are stereotypically associated with a certain aspect class: "tasty" (positive + food). Sentiment facts are phrases that indirectly convey both the sentiment and the aspect category. The annotation schemes of political review corpus described in [13] takes categories of named entities (GEOPOLIT, LOC), etc., as coarse aspects that are further subdivided into source, target, current and past

[1] Preprocessing can also be done after the corpus has been annotated before actual aspect/sentiment calculation but it is out of this paper scope.

subcategories, while polarity mark-up being binary. In the Swedish corpus annotated for aspect-based sentiment analysis [14], the entity-based annotations are text, sentiment value, target, entity. In much fewer works other approaches to formalize and annotate aspect sentiment data are used. For example, a domain and task oriented ontological formalism can be suggested to complement numerical weights [15].

3 Methodology

The methodology of automated creation of a gold-standard annotated corpus for multi-aspect sentiment analysis conducted in this research is data-driven, domain-tuned and includes several stages: the first one involves corpus acquisition and analysis of its specifics. At the second stage, corpus is analyzed at the conceptual level, resulting in creating several lexicons classified into aspect and sentiment conceptual (in fact ontological) categories. The specificity of our methodology is as follows:

- the set of sentiment and aspect categories covers the domain of patient opinions on the services of medical institutions;
- the set of corpus lexical units (tokens) which fall into particular conceptual categories are called 'annotation units' and include one- and multicomponent phrases;
- the tagset is designed to strike a balance between those features that are relevant to conceptual annotation and realistic expectations for their automatic detection;
- An important aspect of our research methodology is its focus on saving time, research effort and, as a consequence, finances, which involves the maximum possible reuse and adaptation of previously developed tools in addition to those developed in-house in the process of the current research.

Based on the outlined above methodological principles, our research includes several interconnected automated and manual steps, the main of which are.

- preparation and formalization of linguistic knowledge to specify the aspect sentiment annotation tagset and
- development of computer tools to digitalize and store the annotation knowledge as well as to automate both the knowledge acquisition, and annotation procedure.

4 Initial Data Specificity

Our initial data is a Russian language corpus of 3247 patient reviews on 27 private clinics in the Ural region totaling to more than 200,000 word usages. It was collected by continuous sampling from the 2GIS website. The specificity of the linguistic features of this corpus is not only conditioned by its domain but also by the fact that it is a collection of general public produced texts found on on-line platforms to which people of all levels of education eagerly contribute.

This, contrary to literate media texts, makes general public "raw" reviews full of spelling and grammar mistakes that could easily be seen even at first glance. Apart from spelling mistakes, surprisingly many people do not know how and which prefixes or particles should be used. Especially often, such mistakes are found in adjectives and adverbs, but other parts of speech also suffer. For example, you can see such pearls as

**не мало важно* (немаловажно), **не в коем случае* (ни в коем случае) **на изнанку* (наизнанку), **ни куда* (никуда) **не дорогая* (недорогая), **не правильное лечение* (неправильное лечение), *идти *на встречу* (идти навстречу) **не воспитанность* (невоспитанность), **ни первый год* (не первый год), **недоверяйте* (не доверяйте), etc., etc. These linguistic failures of course influence negatively on the correctness of annotation procedure, especially, if automated tools are used. In our research, we do attend to the illiteracy problem, which is often neglected. As for spelling mistakes, they can be corrected interactively with any online available spellchecker. Other types of mistakes are more problematic and we extracted all wrongly written lexical items concerning the usage of "*ни*"' and "*не*" semi-automatically passing the raw corpus with the "search" function. More mistaken phrases were collected on the fly. The resulting list was then used as knowledge for an in-house developed tool meant to correct such mistakes, which we conditionally call grammar checker. It is described in Sect. 6.

5 Tagset Specification

The compiled corpus was first automatically processed with an extractor of typed lexical phrases permitting flexible relevance settings [16] that was previously configured by the authors of the paper to the Russian-language domain of medical reviews.

The extractor interface can be configured to sort output lists of every extracted lexical group (NPs, VPs, ADJPs and ADVPs) in alphabetic or reverse order, according to absolute frequency in the corpus of "patient opinions" as a whole or relevancy that can be set as a combination of different parameters. To facilitate lexical analysis and not to omit any important lexical items, especially multicomponent annotation units, we used frequency, alphabetic and relevancy lists for every part of speech lexical group. Figure 1 shows the setup page of the extractor tuned to output noun phrases ranked by relevancy (shown in square brackets) that was calculated by the formula $n * 10 + F + T * 5 + M$, where n is the number of lexeme word-components, F – absolute frequency, T – number of word-components in a lexeme that are found in the list of the corpus top 30% most frequent single words, M – total absolute frequency of lexeme word-components; 10 and 5 are the weights of the parameters n and T. Such output ranking prioritizes multi-component lexemes containing top-frequency components. From the POS lists of thus extracted typed lexical phrases, aspect and sentiment relevant units where manually identified and further classified into conceptual classes following special guidelines (starting with an intuitively prescribed class set). The concept labels that were worded in English but the meaning of each concept is set by its definition. Throughout the research, weekly discussions were held by the project participants to provide for inter-conceptualization consistency and brush up.

The codes of the conceptual (in fact, ontological) classes thus defined formed the annotation tagset that includes 7 sentiment related tags further classified into sentiment proper and modifier tags, 19 aspect related tags and 2 sentiment/aspect irrelevant tags (OTHER and UNK). The sentiment proper tags refer to the concepts of positive (POS), extremely positive (POSX), negative (NEG), extremely negative (NEGX). Text units of neutral sentiments are neglected. The sentiment modifier tags signal of strengthening (MAG), weakening (ANT) or reversing the sentiment (REV) coded by the sentiment proper tags. The aspect tags code the subjects of patient sentiment, such as decease treatment quality (Q), doctor qualification (CH), technical equipment (EQ), etc. Apart from that such phrases that contain sentiment words but are not sentiment relevant as a whole (e.g., «добрый вечер (good evening)» similar to what is called "SpeechActs" in"Skip" (phrases of unclear sentiment) [1]. Such tokens in our research are put in one class and are marked up with the tag OTHER, while the rest of the tokens are tagged UKN.

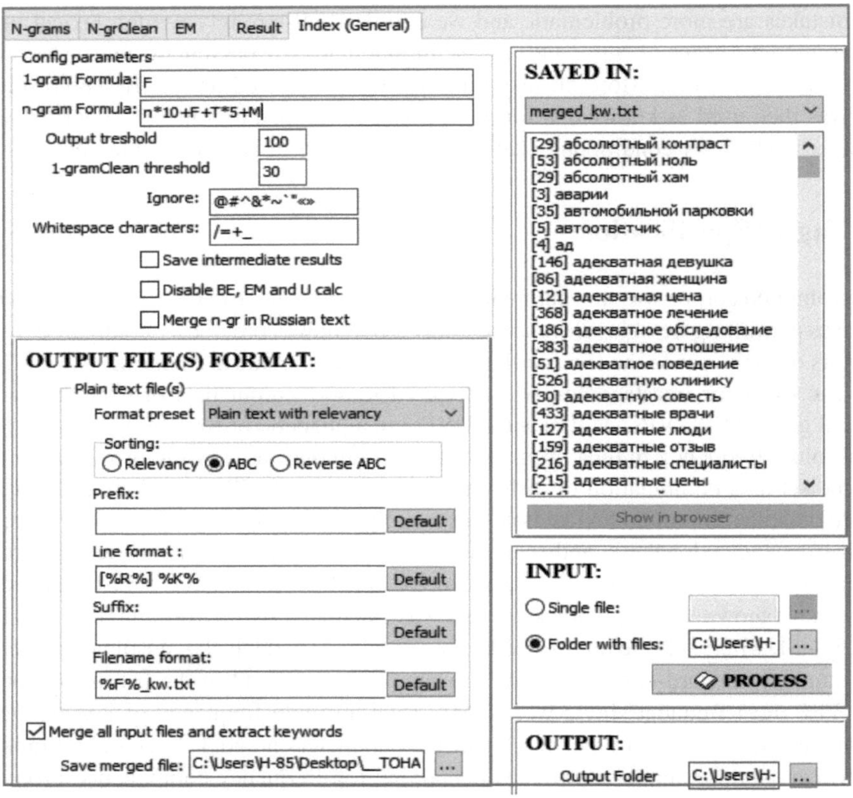

Fig. 1. A screenshot of the lexical extractor setup page. In the top of the right pane,

a fragment of the extracted NPs sorted on relevancy calculated by the formula typed in the top interactive window on the left pane.

In addition, the corpus is annotated with metadata, such as the clinic name, review source (2GIS service), and assessment of a medical center by the review author on the scale from 1 to 5.

The list of lexemes included in different conceptual classes can overlap which is mostly the case with adjectives and adverbs whose tone is conditioned by the context.

For example, the adjective *высокий* (*high*) is included in POS, NEG and OTHER conceptual classes that can easily be seen in such phrases as *высокая квалификация (high qualification), высокая цена (high price) и высокое давление (high pressure),* correspondingly. We call such lexemes conceptually ambiguous. That means that the stand-alone lexeme *высокий* in automatic annotation will be labeled with three tags and we can expect the disambiguation problem. This is the main reason for our annotation units to preferably be multicomponent tokens, which are normally not ambiguous. There are also lexemes that in [10] are called "implicit aspects" (sentiment words stereotypically associated with a certain aspect class: "tasty" (positive + food), and "sentiment facts", (indirectly convey both the sentiment and the aspect). In fact, both such text phrases simultaneously convey a non-contradictory aspect and sentiment information. We call such tokens conceptually syncretic, in our annotation they are labeled with an ASPECT and POLARITY tags with no need for disambiguation.

The annotation team included the developers of the tag set (4 highly qualified computational linguists and 10 students of the SUSU linguistic department whose work was closely supervised by the project manager).

6 Annotation Tools

The main tools directly used for aspect-sentiment annotation are three program components that combined into an annotation platform: an e-lexicon, aspect-sentiment tagger and grammar checker. The program shells of these tools are strongly updated versions of the modules described in [17], while the knowledge for all the tools is new and acquired in the process of the current research.

The e-lexicon is the heart of the platform that serves as digitalized linguistic knowledge storage with a powerful environment for the automated knowledge acquisition and administration. All effort saving functions can be accessed through the e-lexicon user interface. Every entry is meant for one sense of a lexical unit described as a tree of features:

$$[\text{semantic class/concept } [\text{language}[\text{part - of - speech}[\text{other morphology}[\text{tag}]]]]]$$

One of the main specificities of the e-lexicon is that its morphological zone is programmed to contain a full paradigm of a lexeme, where each member (wordform) is associated with a supertag that codes conceptual and fine morphological knowledge. This allows skipping the necessity of using extra NLP module for morphological analysis at the preprocessing stage. All information can be assigned to a textual token by a simple lexicon look-up. The e-lexicon program was configured to and filled with the medical review domain aspect/sentiment knowledge as described in Sect. 5.

The screenshot of the main e-lexicon interface is given in Fig. 2. The interface buttons are self-explanatory. On the left pane (from left to right), shown are the interactive list of the lexical units, corresponding concept class codes (SC) and parts-of speech (PoS). All fields are interactive and can be edited. As every entry is meant for one sense (conceptual class) of a lexical unit, in case a lexeme belongs to several conceptual classes, a corresponding number of entries is created. See, for example, Fig. 2, where the lexeme *черствый и бесчеловечный сотрудник (hard-hearted and inhuman employee)* is put in two entries, one corresponding to the ASPECT conceptual class PERSONEL(S) and another – to the POLARITY class EXTREMELY NEGATIVE (NEGX). In the center of the screenshot, shown is the morphological zone of the highlighted entry containing the whole paradigm of the lexeme wordforms, each provided with a supertag (on the right) coding rich linguistic information. For example, the supertag Npersnegxg in the morphological zone filler *черствого и бесчеловечного сотрудника* codes the features "PERSONEL(S), noun, masculine, singular, genitive. The supertags are created automatically through the acquisition interface where the acquirer is to simply select a conceptual class and POS from two consequent pop-up menus which calls a corresponding entry template with preset supertags. The e-lexicon currently contains 15741 entries.

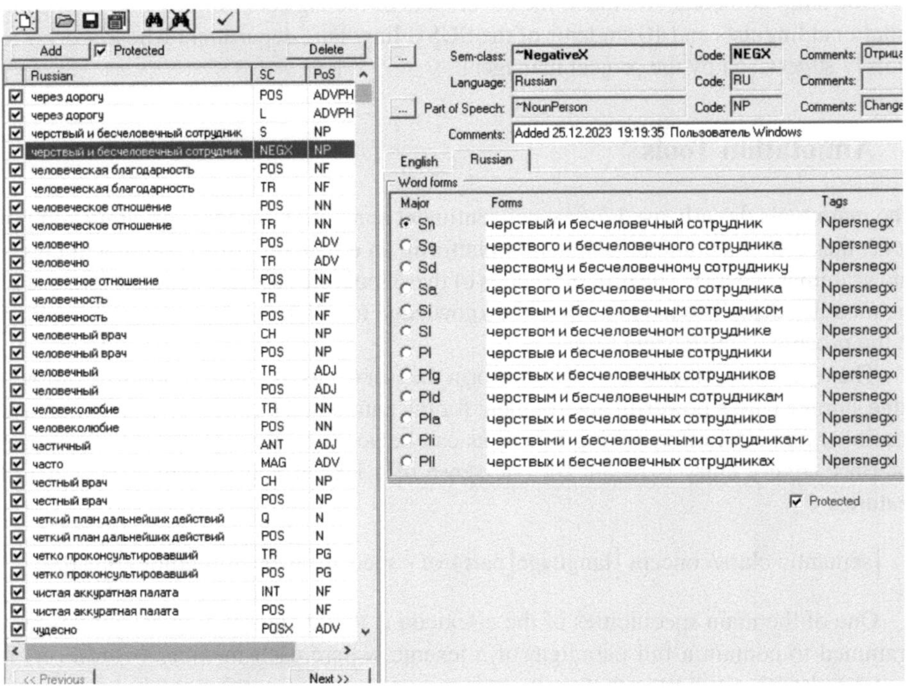

Fig. 2. A screenshot of the main e-lexicon interface with displayed morphological zone of the highlighted lexeme.

To provide for a collaborative setup for sharing knowledge acquisition tasks, the e-lexicon is programmed in two versions: the MASTER version with the full range of activated built-in tools and the LIGHT version, – an empty e-lexicon program shell configured as MASTER but with the Configuration block disabled for consistency of the acquired knowledge. Acquirers can individually fill LIGHTs with new lexical knowledge, which is then automatically imported into MASTER on a regular basis.

The e-lexicon is pipelined to the tagger and grammar checker. The tagger can be configured to annotate textual units on the fine-grain (supertags) level or on the coarse-level (conceptual tags only). The tagging procedure is carried out by a simple lexicon look-up and does not require any morphological preprocessing, e.g., lemmatization, due to the specificity of the e-lexicon morphological zone that contains the whole lexeme paradigm (see Fig. 2).

The grammar checker has a rule-acquisition compiler and a front-end control interface with a lot of effort saving functionalities, – it is possible on a mouse click to automatically get rule templates, transfer tag notations from the displayed list of tags to a curser position and check the consistency of tags and rule syntax (See Fig. 3).

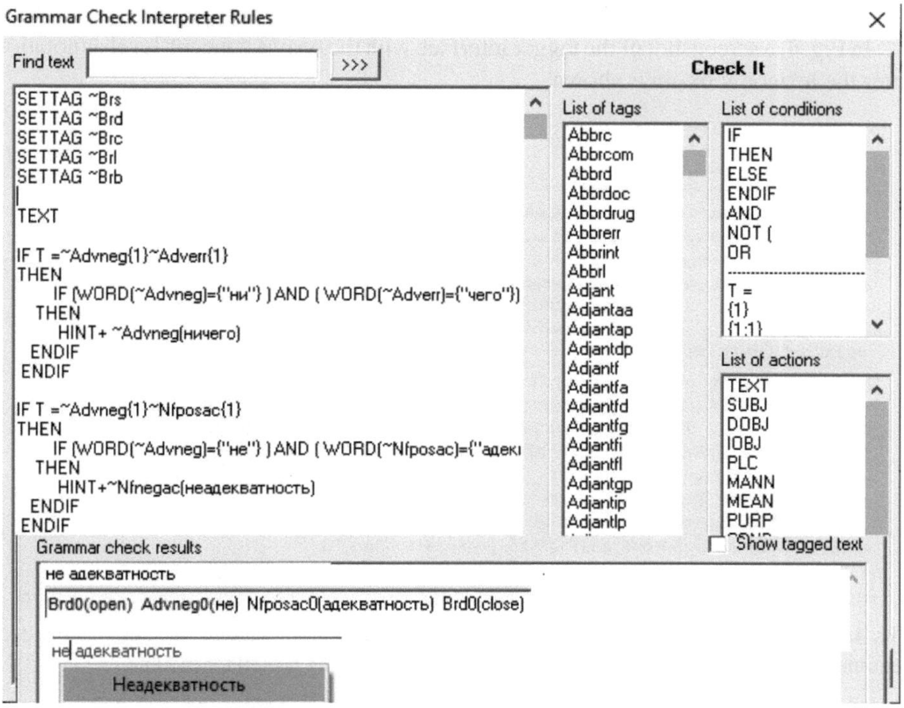

Fig. 3. Fragments of the grammar checker rule-acquisition compiler and front-end control interface

7 Creating Gold-Standard Corpus

The gold standard corpus has been built by annotating 1601 medical review texts broadcast by clinic patients in the Ural region. It contains reviews on 8 medical institutions totaling to more than 100,000. Words and is randomly cut out of the 200 000 word original corpus that was used to acquire the aspect sentiment linguistic knowledge to define the tagset as described in Sect. 3 We kept the tagset in its descriptive format which makes it easier to experiment with different weight/score schemes at the subsequent analysis stages. Apart from aspect-sentiment conceptual tags, the corpus is annotated with metadata, such as the clinic name, review source (2GIS service), and assessment of a medical center by the review author on the scale from one to five.

The workflow of the gold annotation procedure is as follows.

1. Corpus acquisition
2. Preprocessing
   a. Spellchecking (automatically with online spellcheckers)
   b. Grammar checking (automatically with the module of the in-house tagger)
3. Tagging at the coarse concept-tags-only level (automatic with the in-house annotation platform)
4. Postediting the automatic output to the gold standard (semi-automatic with the posteditor module of the tagger.

In Fig. 4, a screenshot of the tagger interface with the coarse concept-level annotation after the lexicon look-up is shown.

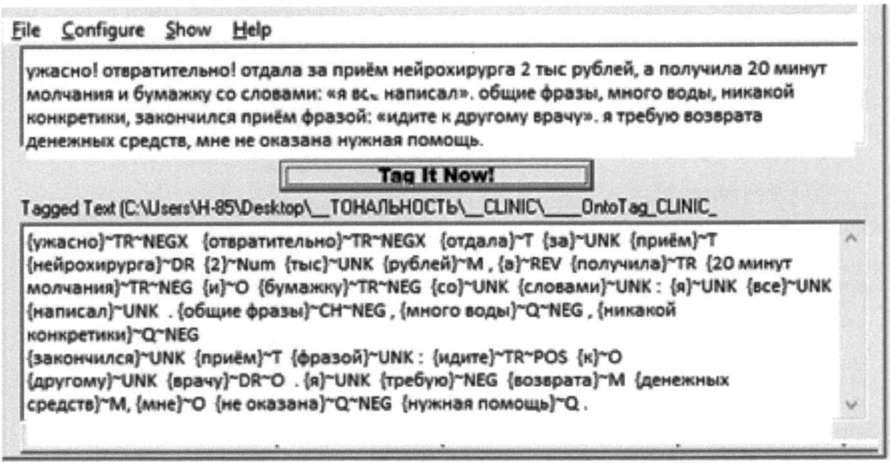

Fig. 4. A screenshot of the tagger control interface. In the bottom window, the automatic aspect sentiment annotation is shown that is further to be passed to the posteditor module.

The tagger takes a preprocessed text as input and assigns coarse or fine tags as configured. The explicit (iconic) list of lexemes' paradigms in the e-lexicon entries allows skipping morphological analysis problems (such as, for example, lemmatization) and assigns tags by a lexicon look-up, i.e., by simply matching a textual tokens against the fillers of the e-lexicon morphological zones. The lexicon look-up even for the coarse tags can lead to what we call multi-tags that appear due to the fact that some of the lexicon units are conceptually ambiguous or conceptually syncretic. At the current stage of research, tag disambiguation is done interactively through the post-editor interface. Actually, the tagger program shell is provided with another interpreter where a developer can write disambiguation rules in a simple IF-THEN-ELSE formalism to make disambiguation automatic. This is one of our future tasks.

We made the gold annotated corpus at the level of individual reviews and at the level of merged review texts, each is saved in two versions, – one with UKN and OTHER tags to be able to check on the token context, if necessary, another is cleaned and only contains tokens with aspect-sentiment relevant tags ready for calculations.

In addition, we aligned automatically annotated corpus as output by the tagger and its gold standard version after postediting. Such resource can be used in different ways, e.g., to update the annotation platform knowledge and thus make the automatic tagging more efficient or/and develop rules/metrics for automatic tag disambiguation.

8 Conclusions

In this paper, we have suggested a methodology for developing a gold standard annotated domain corpus and described actual annotation scheme and procedure that are of universal character and can be applied to other domains and languages. The research results also include programming and linguistic resources built along the suggested methodology, the main of which are, tools with flexible settings to store annotation knowledge and automate acquisition and tagging procedures, the domain ontology and a gold standard annotated Russian medical reviews corpus of 100 000 words.

The corpus can be used as gold standard for training and evaluation of aspect-based sentiment analysis systems and for creating different types of data sets to be used in different models of aspect sentiment analysis, such as rule based, machine learning or neural models. This is our future work. Apart from this, discovered linguistic specificity of the corpus, that is a not-edited general public production, may also deserve the attention of both computational linguists and sociologists.

References

1. Smetanin, S.: RuSentiTweet: a sentiment analysis dataset of general domain tweets in Russian (2022). https://www.ncbi.nlm.nih.gov/pmc/articles/PMC9454938/
2. Rogers, A., Romanov, A., Rumshisky, A., Volkova, S., Gronas, M., Gribov, A.: RuSentiment: an enriched sentiment analysis dataset for social media in Russian. In: Proceedings of the 27th International Conference on Computational Linguistics, pp. 755–763. Association for Computational Linguistics, Santa Fe, New Mexico, USA (2018)
3. Kuznetsova, E.S., Loukachevitch, N.V., Chetviorkin, I.I.: Testing rules for sentiment analysis system. computational linguistics and intellectual technologies. In: Proceedings of the International Conference Dialog-2013, vol. 2, pp. 71–80 (2013)
4. Stenetorp, P., Pyysalo, S., Topic, G., Ohta, T., Ananiadou, S., Jun'ichi Tsujii, J.: BRAT: a Web-based Tool for NLP-Assisted Text Annotation. In: Proceedings of the 13th Conference of the European Chapter of the Association for Computational Linguistics, pp.102– 107. Avignon, France (2012)
5. Rubtsova, Y.: Automatic construction and analysis of a corpus of short texts (microblog posts) for the tone classifier development and training. https://study.mokoron.com/wp-content/uploads/2014/02/rubtsova-kesw_paper-21.pdf. Date of access 10 Mar 2024
6. Bordoloi, M., Biswas, S.K.: Sentiment analysis: a survey on design framework, applications and future scopes. Artif. Intell. Rev. **56**, 12505–12560 (2023). https://doi.org/10.1007/s10462-023-10442-2
7. Loukachevitch, N.V., Chetviorkin, I.I.: Evaluating Sentiment Analysis Systems in Russian. https://aclanthology.org/W13-2403/. Date of access 20 Mar 2024
8. Kharde, V.A., Sheetal, S.: Sonawane. Sentiment Analysis of Twitter Data, A Survey of Techniques. ArXiv abs/1601.06971 (2016): n. pag

9. Swarnalatha, S., Kesavarthini, I., Poornima, S., Sripriya, N.: Med-recommender system for predictive analysis of hospitals and doctors. In: 2019 International Conference on Computational Intelligence in Data Science (ICCIDS), pp. 1–5. Chennai, India (2019). https://doi.org/10.1109/ICCIDS.2019.8862121
10. Koltsova, O., Nikolenko, S., Alexeeva, S., Nagornyy, O., Koltcov, S.: 'Detecting interethnic relations with the data from social media.' In: Alexandrov, D.A., Boukhanovsky, A.V., Chugunov, A.V., Kabanov, Y., Koltsova, O. (eds.) Digital Transformation and Global Society, pp. 16–30. Springer, Cham, Switzerland (2017)
11. Ganu, G., Elhadad, N., Marian, A.:´Beyond the stars: Improving rating predictions using review text content. In: Proceedings of WebDB, Providence, Rhode Island, USA (2009)
12. Loukachevitch, N., Blinov. P., Kotelnikov, E., Rubtsova, Y., Ivanov, V., Tutubalina, E.: SentiRuEval: testing object-oriented sentiment analysis systems in Russian. Computational Linguistics and Intellectual Technologies: Proceedings of the International Conference "Dialogue" 2015; Russian State University for the Humanities, pp. 3–13 (2015)
13. Maksimenko, O., Semina, T.: Creating a corpus for sentiment analysis. https://elibrary.ru/item.asp?id=41717736. Accessed 10 Mar 2024
14. Rouces, J., Borin, L., Tahmasebi, N.: Creating an Annotated Corpus for Aspect-Based Sentiment Analysis in Swedish. https://ceur-ws.org/Vol-2612/short18.pdf. Accessed 10 Mar 2024
15. Oralbekova, I.T.,Yergesh, B.Z.: Aspect-oriented sentiment analysis of hotel reviews on the material of the Kazakh language. https://www.researchgate.net/publication/320829528_Sentiment_analysis_on_the_hotel_reviews_in_the_Kazakh_language. Accessed 10 Mar 2024
16. Sheremetyeva, S.: Automatic extraction of linguistic resources in multiple languages. In: Proceedings of NLPCS 2012, 9th International Workshop on Natural Language Processing and Cognitive Science in conjunction with ICEIS 2012, pp. 44–52. Wroclaw, Poland (2012)
17. Sheremetyeva, S.: Universal computational formalisms and developer environment for rule-based NLP. In: Gelbukh, A. (ed.) Computational Linguistics and Intelligent Text Processing CICLing 2017. LNCS, vol. 10761, pp. 67–78. Springer, Cham (2018). https://doi.org/10.1007/978-3-319-77113-7_5

Building a Bilingual Glossary in the Domain of Computational Linguistics by Processing a Parallel Corpus

Svetlana Chistyakova and Marina Kogan(✉)

St. Petersburg Polytechnic University, Polytechnicheskaya, 29, 195251 St. Petersburg, Russia
svetlanavchistyakova@gmail.com, kogan_ms@spbstu.ru

Abstract. Existing research on bilingual glossaries highlights their significance in various specialist domains, as they provide crucial resources for text processing and communication across languages. This article specifically concentrates on creating a glossary for the field of computational linguistics, a rapidly evolving area of research that continuously expands with new texts primarily written in English. Using a statistics-based automatic term extraction algorithm on a 40.000 sentence-pair parallel corpus of texts originally written in English and translated into Russian, the glossary is constructed and analysed. The aim of the analysis is to determine terminological correspondences between the languages or the lack thereof, thus providing insight into their terminological alignment. Automatically produced bilingual glossaries can enhance the accuracy and efficiency of natural language processing tasks, such as machine translation and cross-lingual information retrieval, contribute to students' familiarising with complex concepts and terms in specialist fields like computational linguistics, and make communication and learning more effective.

Keywords: Bilingual Glossary · Computational Linguistics · Natural Language Processing (NLP) · Automatic Term Extraction · Parallel Corpus

1 Introduction

In an increasingly globalised world where English has become the lingua franca of communication, the use of bilingual glossaries has become essential in education, academic publications and many professional spheres. Students and teachers utilise bilingual glossaries to grasp complex concepts and understand terminology. Researchers rely on them to translate and comprehend academic texts and publications in different languages. In professional settings, bilingual glossaries are essential tools for individuals working in international contexts or industries where multilingual communication is required.

With the rise of English Medium Instruction (EMI) in non-English-speaking countries, there is a need for language support to aid students in comprehending academic content in English. By offering translations in their native language, bilingual glossaries enhance understanding and provide access to a wide range of information resources, supporting students' academic success and language development.

M. Bakaev et al. (Eds.): IMS 2024, CCIS 2534, pp. 25–34, 2026.
https://doi.org/10.1007/978-3-031-96177-9_3

The rapid growth of English publications in modern scientific fields prompts the pressing need to bridge the gap between comprehension of new concepts in English and discussion of modern scientific advances in one's native language. By providing translations and explanations of complex scientific terminology, bilingual glossaries enhance understanding and promote the dissemination of scientific knowledge across linguistic boundaries.

One of the rapidly changing and updating scientific fields is computational linguistics. It deals with the intersection of language and technology and relies on bilingual glossaries to support its diverse needs. In the sphere of computational linguistics, bilingual glossaries provide translations of specialised terminology and standardise concepts across multiple languages, while also contributing to natural language processing tasks.

2 Literature Review

2.1 Research on Corpus-Based Bilingual Glossaries

The importance of bilingual glossaries as essential tools in various specific fields has long been the subject of extensive research. Recent studies cover different domains such as mathematics [1], physics [2], engineering [3], medicine [4], agriculture [5], etc. These glossaries serve as valuable resources for individuals working in specific fields. As professional terminology is characterised by a higher level of complexity compared to general domain, glossaries help students and experts who may not be fluent in a particular language, or aid tourists travelling in non-English speaking countries [6]. The primary source language for such glossaries is typically English, however, there are other language pairs, for example, Portuguese/Spanish [4] or German/Portuguese [6]. While building a bilingual glossary can be a time-consuming task that requires expertise in the topic at hand, many researchers are still committed to collecting and translating terms and then compiling them into glossaries manually [1, 3, 6].

At the same time, the adoption of automatic tools for the generation of bilingual glossaries is increasingly favoured due to its efficiency and time-saving advantages. These tools are capable of automatic term extraction from extensive text corpora, thereby lessening the manual labour traditionally involved in glossary compilation. This automated process is particularly beneficial in domains characterised by dynamic terminologies.

The researchers [2] created a glossary in Physics through automatic extraction terms from a domain-specific corpus containing recent Arabic scientific articles that first had been translated into English by subject matter specialists. A basic computational algorithm was employed to extract terms and their corresponding translations from the corpus.

Some researchers utilise already existing automatic tools for term extraction. For example, Gil [5] makes use of the software AntConc, leveraging its main tools, Word List and Concordance, to extract agricultural terminology in both Spanish and English. The compilation of the glossary aims to support the internationalisation of the Spanish agricultural sector.

Another computational tool used for the automatic extraction of terms from a given corpus and their organisation into a glossary is TermSuite. It acts as a toolbox for monolingual term extraction and bilingual alignment. Daille [8] utilises TermSuite in order to process scientific terminology for various language pairs, including English-French, English-German, and English-Spanish.

Kontonatsios [9] uses the programme MetaMap and n-gram models to extract and align terms in the biomedical domain for English-French, English-Spanish, English-Greek and English-Japanese language pairs. In the target part of the parallel corpus, potential translations are identified by examining continuous sequences of up to four words.

Multi-level Termhood is proposed by Zhang and Wu [10] to extract terminology from a corpus in the domain of information technology. Multi-level termhood is used in terminology management to determine the importance or relevance of specific terms within a given domain or field. The concept involves assessing the degree of termhood for terminology candidates through corpus comparison. Research results suggest that implementing termhood constraints can enhance the effectiveness of term alignment procedures.

Cross-lingual language model is fine-tuned by [11] with a large number of e-commercial corpus consisting of different languages. The pre-trained model extracts Chinese-English and English-French language pairs by using the semantic connection between source terminology and target sentence.

2.2 Automatic Term Extraction Algorithms

The general pipeline of various term extraction algorithms involves processing a text corpus as the input and outputting a list of candidate terms that are subject to further verification. These algorithms employ rule-based, statistical, and machine learning approaches, used separately or in combinations.

The **rule-based** approach utilises predefined linguistic patterns and rules to extract terms from the text corpus based on specific criteria. According to a pattern type term extraction systems are divided into regular expression based, vocabulary based and syntax based.

Rule-based approach involves using typical constructs for term units. These patterns specify parts of speech and their syntactic relations [12]. In [13] syntax-based method as well as part-of-speech tagging is used to extract terms without a labelled corpus. Syntactic and morphological structure is stored as a sentence pattern and POS sequence of the sentence.

Rule-based approach often makes use of ontologies and dictionaries. The paper [14] describes a method for extracting important information in two steps. Initially, language patterns are used to semi-automatically identify domain terminology. Following this, natural language processing (NLP) techniques are applied based on the identified domain and sentence structural information. Extracted and lemmatised terms are filtered to reject falsely proposed lemmas, and then are ranked using linguistic and statistical indicators.

Although a rule-based system is potentially better able to cope with the unfamiliar words and word combinations than memory-based systems, it has limitations. Rule-based systems necessitate a substantial number of manually crafted rules, a process that can be labour-intensive and pose challenges in maintenance. Moreover, rule-based systems may struggle with handling ambiguity or exceptions, as they rely strictly on predefined rules, potentially resulting in errors when faced with unexpected or complex situations [15].

Another traditional approach to term extraction is **statistical** analysis, which is based on word combination frequency in a text or a collection of texts. This method is commonly used to identify n-gram terms. It makes use of statistical distribution of word combinations to identify recurring patterns and sequences that are indicative of meaningful terms. The predominant statistical metrics include entropy, TF-IDF (Term Frequency-Inverse Document Frequency) and C-value.

Entropy is commonly used in term extraction as a measure of the information content or uncertainty associated with terms within a corpus of text. Liwei [16] introduces a method for automatically extracting technical terminology from Chinese patents using information entropy techniques and DC-value. The findings demonstrate that the algorithm successfully identifies and extracts technical terms present in Chinese patent documents.

TF-IDF reflects the importance of a term in a document relative to a collection of documents. The high frequency of a specific term appearing in a small number of documents suggests that the term has a specialised meaning. Improved variations of TF-IDF, such as TF-IDF-CF or TF-IDF-ρ, continue to be recognised as prominent tools for term extraction. In [17] researchers propose an approach of keyword ranking with similarity identification, that involves identifying significant keywords in a corpus through the use of a weighted TF-IDF algorithm. This approach assigns weights to keywords based on sentences and has been shown to be effective. Its performance is assessed using precision and recall metrics across multiple datasets.

Recently, methods based on **machine learning** algorithms have been widely utilised. The machine learning approach comprises three stages: extracting sequences of words that have the potential to be terms, defining the terms and specifying their boundaries.

Kovářiková [18] describes an automatic term extraction method based on machine learning and demonstrates its several strengths, including a high success rate in identifying terms in academic texts by analysing complex relationships between individual term characteristics and providing rankings of these features. This method performed well across numerous academic disciplines in two languages (Czech and English).

The authors [19] introduce a technique for extracting terms by utilising a completely unsupervised annotator to generate training data for refining transformer models. This method retrieves terms by combining morphological signals from sub-word tokenisation with metrics for term-to-topic and intra-term similarity, calculated using sentence-encoders that are pre-trained in a general domain.

One of the extensively used solutions currently is KeyBERT, a Python package designed for keyphrase extraction utilising BERT language models. KeyBERT operates by generating BERT embeddings of the document texts. Afterwards, BERT keyphrase embeddings of word n-grams with predetermined lengths are constructed. Finally, cosine similarities between the document and keyphrase embeddings are computed to extract the keyphrases that most accurately describe the entire document [20].

3 Data and Methodology

3.1 Corpus Building and Preprocessing

For the purpose of this study, we compiled a bilingual corpus of texts in the field of computational linguistics. The texts were extracted from textbooks and their corresponding published translations produced by professional translators. Data manipulation was performed using Python 3.

Initially, the original texts in English and their corresponding translations in Russian were collected individually. The corpus was aligned using Bertalign, an automated multilingual sentence aligner capable of identifying various types of sentence correspondence, such as one-to-one, one-to-many, many-to-one, or many-to-many mappings [21]. Lastly, the aligned sentences were organised into a pandas Dataframe, resulting in a total of 44073 rows.

To enhance the efficiency of the term extraction procedures, certain sentences were excluded from the corpus. These exclusions targeted sentences that are unlikely to represent source text and its translation, such as those with significant difference in length. Additionally, sentences devoid of potential terms, that is, those featuring less than 10 characters per sentence or solely numeric content, were eliminated.

The subsequent phase involved text pre-processing, where the pipeline included lowercasing and removal of punctuation, special characters, and digits using regular expressions. Additionally, stop words were eliminated for both languages using the NLTK library [22]. Stop words are commonly used tokens that are considered to be non-informative in the context of text analysis. The NLTK library includes a list of 179 English stop words and 151 Russian stop words. Functional parts of speech like conjunctions, prepositions, and articles are often considered insignificant and were removed for both languages.

Following this, the Russian and English texts were subjected to separate preprocessing techniques. Each Russian sentence underwent tokenisation and lemmatisation through Mystem, a morphological analyser tailored for the Russian language [23]. English sentences were lemmatised using SpaCy, an NLP library designed for efficient and fast text processing tasks in many languages [24].

3.2 Term Extraction

Following the initial text processing phase, the English and Russian texts underwent preparation for term extraction. In this paper, a term is defined as a lexical unit, which is typical for a text or a set of texts [25]. We deployed the TF-IDF algorithm, which is language-agnostic and relies on a statistical approach, rendering it a suitable tool for extracting terms from both English and Russian texts, given the higher likelihood of extracting similar words. As we consider any lexically distinct unit within a specific text a term, TF-IDF is deemed an appropriate method for processing the corpus.

The Term Frequency is calculated by dividing the number of times that the term (t) appears in the document (d) by its total number of terms. For the Inverse Document Frequency the total number of documents in the collection (D) is divided by the number of documents that contain the term, the result is subjected to a logarithmic function. To obtain the TF-IDF score, the TF value is multiplied by the IDF value.

$$tf\ idf(t, d, D) = tf(t, d) \times idf(t, D) \quad (1)$$

To get a matrix of TF-IDF features we used TfidfVectorizer provided in the scikit-learn library [26]. To utilise this tool, an instance of the TfidfVectorizer class is instantiated. The raw text data (documents) is fitted and transformed using the fit_transform() method. This process converts the text data into a numerical matrix of TF-IDF features. Following this transformation, the feature names can be accessed through the get_feature_names_out() method, enabling the extraction of identified terms along with their TF-IDF scores.

We configured TfidfVectorizer with different parameters such as max_features and ngram_range to control the feature extraction process. By adjusting these parameters, we customised the algorithm to extract unigrams and bigrams. Feature names were retrieved from the TfidfVectorizer to identify terms that have been documented. The function iterated through the text data, generating TF-IDF vectors for each document. Feature indices with non-zero values were extracted to retrieve the corresponding term names, thus facilitating the calculation of keyword scores based on their TF-IDF values. To finalise the extraction process, the English and Russian terms were sorted in descending order based on their scores.

As indicated by the results, it appears that the maximum score for English terms is slightly higher compared to Russian terms. While there are some differences in the maximum and minimum, both sets of terms have a similar mean, indicating a relatively balanced distribution in the dataset. Table 1 summarises the statistical information for both English and Russian terms.

Table 1. Extracted terms features

Features	English terms	Russian terms
Count	147067	147067
Maximum score	18.1834	16.056696
Minimum score	0.009543	0.017598
Mean	0.046558	0.048283

For the further analysis we selected terms with scores exceeding 0.15, which resulted in the dataset reduction with a final composition of 4677 terms for each language. This refined dataset was utilised for further investigation and evaluation, ensuring focus on terms that exhibit higher relevance or significance within the given domain.

4 Results and Discussion

The primary objective of the glossary analysis was to ascertain the terminological correspondences between the languages or identify the lack of such correspondences. We investigated Russian terms to identify any inclusions that may not have been translated.

In order to identify the language, we used the langid library, which is based on statistical techniques and machine learning algorithms to analyse textual data and identify the language in which the text is written [27].

There are two unique categories identified by langid in the dataset. The frequency count represents that the majority of the instances (3648 out of 4677) have been identified as Russian language. However, it is noteworthy that the Russian section of the dataset contains 1029 instances (approximately 22%) that include English terms. The presence of English inclusions can be attributed to the presence of Python code in the source materials. Nevertheless, this does not account for every instance of English terms within the Russian section, prompting a more detailed examination of the terms to discern the underlying patterns.

In the next phase of the analysis, we compared Russian and English sections of the dataset to identify untranslated terms. It was evident that 710 entries were identical, indicating that they had not been translated into Russian. On further examination of the context in which these terms appeared, it became apparent that certain words had no direct translation.

Additionally, approximately 60 terms were found to be translated but retained the original English term within brackets. This indicates a hybrid approach where some terms were translated while others were kept in their original form for clarity or lack of direct translation. The analysis yielded different types of term correspondences, as showcased in Table 2 – reflecting the complexity and variety of translation challenges encountered in the dataset.

Table 2. Examples of term correspondence types

Term correspondence	English term	Russian term
Direct translation	vector	вектор
	model	модель
Translation + original	Dataset	набор данных (dataset)
	input vector	входной вектор (input vector)
No translation	sequence-to-sequence	sequence-to-sequence
	Softmax	softmax

These findings can be explained by the challenges inherent in the translation process, particularly when dealing with technical terminology. Technical terms or programming-specific concepts may not have direct equivalents in certain languages and require context-specific translations, leading to a mix of languages in the dataset. The retention of original English terms within brackets in quite a few translated terms reflects a hybrid translation approach aimed at balancing linguistic accuracy and contextual clarity.

The resulting bilingual glossary was formed taking into consideration the peculiarities of the data discovered through the analysis. While originally consisting of unigrams and bigrams, the glossary has the potential for expansion to incorporate trigrams that were extracted in the earlier stages of data processing. The cross-lingual term alignment was carried out automatically using a neural alignment tool powered by mBERT [28]. This process entailed automatic merging of the corpus word level alignment with the extracted terms using pandas library to establish accurate translations for both English and Russian sections of the dataset. The resulting glossary comprises a total of 413 lexical units including 91 bigrams and 7 trigrams.

Furthermore, the glossary underwent manual verification to identify any errors that may have occurred during the extraction process. In certain instances, the stopword list was revised to eliminate items commonly found in textbooks but not typically included in standard stopword lists (such as "chapter", "figure", etc.). Subsequent research should incorporate automated metrics to validate the efficiency of the extraction method and ensure that no terms have been overlooked during the extraction process.

5 Conclusions and Further Research

In this study, we compiled a bilingual glossary generated from a 40000 sentence-pair parallel corpus of texts written in English and translated into Russian, using statistical term extraction algorithm TF-IDF. Through the detailed examination of the dataset, it was possible to identify terminological connections between the languages.

The investigation of Russian terms detected two distinct categories within the dataset. The majority of instances were recognised as the Russian language. However, 22% of the Russian section contained English terms. The presence of English terms can be ascribed to the Python code in the source materials while also reflect the complexities inherent in the translation process, particularly in handling technical terminology. We identified entries that remained identical in the English and Russian sections, indicating that these terms lacked a direct translation. Some entries displayed a hybrid approach where terms were translated while having their English equivalent alongside.

The analysis revealed various types of term correspondences, such as direct translation, combination of translation and original term and the lack of translation. These findings illustrate the challenges involved in multilingual translation and highlight the complexity of maintaining accuracy and clarity in technical terminology across languages.

The subsequent phase of the research should involve developing a systematic and effective method of aligning terms with their translations; particularly in cases where direct translations are not available or do not perfectly match between languages. This strategic alignment process should aim to improve the precision and quality of translations while addressing the challenges associated with differences in terminologies.

The compiled bilingual glossary enriched with terminological connections between English and Russian, serves as a valuable tool for students, researchers, and professionals. It aids in improving their grasp of concepts in computational linguistics and bridging communication gaps across different languages. The integration of domain-specific knowledge bases and bilingual resources will be crucial in enhancing language learning and promoting a deeper understanding of technical terms in a multilingual educational context.

References

1. Farrugia, M., Drijvers, P., Csapodi, C., Palmér, H., Gosztonyi, K., Kónya, E.: The creation of a bilingual glossary of mathematics terms. In: Thirteenth Congress of the European Society for Research in Mathematics Education (CERME13), pp.1575–1577. Alfréd Rényi Institute of Mathematics, Budapest, Hungary and ERME (2023)
2. Awwad, H., Sawalha, M., Allawzi, A., Yagi, S.: Building translator-oriented English-Arabic physics glossary from domain corpus. Int. J. Speech Technol. **26**(1), 151–162 (2023)
3. Rohan, S., Suyono, A.: Developing an android-based bilingual e-glossary application of English for specific purposes (ESP). Engl. Lang. Teach. Educ. J. **4**(3), 225–234 (2021)
4. Cabrera, M.: Proposal for a bilingual glossary - Portuguese/Spanish - for medical care to immigrant. Belas Infiéis **5**(2), 59–72 (2016)
5. Gil, I.P.: From corpora to a semi-automatic tool: the use of model lines for the development of TorreznoTRAD. In: Gil, I.P., Ortego Antón, M.-T. (eds.) Interpreting and Translation for Agri-food Professionals in the Global Marketplace, pp. 105–118. De Gruyter (2023). https://doi.org/10.1515/9783111101729-006
6. Sadia, U., Iqbal, M., Qasim, H.: Developing bilingual glossary (English-Urdu) for tourists: a systematic approach. Int. J. Linguist. Cult. **3**(1), 185–203 (2022)
7. Alberts-Franco, C.: Corpus linguistics and bilingual terminology: the AntConc program and term extraction in German. The ESPecialist: Res. Language Specific Purposes **36**(2), 182–202 (2015)
8. Daille, B.: Building bilingual terminologies from comparable corpora: the TTCTermSuite. In: 5th Workshop on Building and Using Comparable Corpora with special topic "Language Resources for Machine Translation in Less-Resourced Languages and Domains", pp. 29–32. Istambul, Turkey (2012)
9. Kontonatsios, G.: Automatic compilation of bilingual terminologies from comparable corpora [Thesis]. The University of Manchester, Manchester, United Kingdom (2015).
10. Zhang, C., Wu, D.: Bilingual terminology extraction using multi-level termhood. Electron. Libr. **30**(2), 295–309 (2015)
11. Jia, H., Gu, S., Zhang, Y., Duan, X.: Bilingual terminology extraction from comparable e-commerce corpora. In: 2022 International Joint Conference on Neural Networks (IJCNN), pp. 01–08. IEEE (2021)
12. Shao, W., Hua, B., Song, L.: A pattern and POS auto-learning method for terminology extraction from scientific text. Data Inform. Manage. **5**(3), 329–335 (2021)
13. Das, B., Pal, S., Mondal, K., Dalui, D., Shome, K.: Automatic keyword extraction from any text document using N-gram rigid collocation. Int. J. Soft Comput. Eng. (IJSCE) **3**(2), 238–242 (2013)
14. Quirchmayr, T., Paech, B., Kohl, R., Karey, H., Kasdepke, G.: Semi-automatic rule-based domain terminology and software feature-relevant information extraction from natural language user manuals: an approach and evaluation at Roche Diagnostics GmbH. Empir. Softw. Eng. **23**(6), 3630–3683 (2018)
15. Rivas, C., et al.: Automated analysis of free-text comments and dashboard representations in patient experience surveys: a multimethod co-design study. Health Serv. Delivery Res. **7**(23), 160 (2019)
16. Liwei, Z.: Chinese technical terminology extraction based on DC-value and information entropy. Sci. Rep. **12**(1), 1–12 (2022)
17. Vetriselvi, T., Gopalan, N.P., Kumaresan, G.: Key term extraction using a sentence based weighted TF-IDF algorithm. Int. J. Educ. Manage. Eng. **9**(4), 11–18 (2019)
18. Kovářiková, D.: Machine learning in terminology extraction from Czech and English texts. Linguist. Front. **4**, 23–30 (2021)

19. Fusco, F., Staar, P., Antognini, D.: Unsupervised term extraction for highly technical domains. In: Proceedings of the 2022 Conference on Empirical Methods in Natural Language Processing: Industry Track, pp. 1–8. Abu Dhabi, UAE (2022)
20. MaartenGr/KeyBERT: https://doi.org/10.5281/zenodo.4461265. Last accessed 21 Mar 2024
21. Liu, L., Zhu, M.: Bertalign: improved word embedding-based sentence alignment for Chinese-English parallel corpora of literary texts. Digit. Scholarship Human. **38**(2), 621–634 (2023)
22. Bird, S., Klein, E., Loper, E.: Natural language processing with Python: analyzing text with the natural language toolkit. O'Reilly Media, Inc. (2009)
23. Segalovich, I.: A fast morphological algorithm with unknown word guessing induced by a dictionary for a web search engine. In: International Conference on Machine Learning; Models, Technologies and Applications 2003, pp. 273–280. Las Vegas, NV (2003)
24. Honnibal, M., Montani, I.: SpaCy 2: natural language understanding with Bloom embeddings, convolutional neural networks and incremental parsing. To appear **7**(1), 411–420 (2017)
25. Indurkhya, N., Damerau, J.: Handbook of natural language processing. 2nd edn. Chapman and Hall/CRC (2010)
26. Pedregosa, F., et al.: Scikit-learn: machine learning in Python. J. Mach. Learn. Res. **12**, 2825–2830 (2011)
27. Lui, M., Baldwin, T.: Cross-domain feature selection for language identification. In: Proceedings of 5th international joint conference on natural language processing, pp. 553–561. Chiang Mai, Thailand (2011)
28. Dou, Z., Neubig, G.: Word alignment by fine-tuning embeddings on parallel corpora. In: Proceedings of the 16th conference of the European chapter of the association for computational linguistics: main volume, pp. 2112–2128. Association for Computational Linguistics (2021)

Dataset Development for Aspect-Level Sentiment Analysis Based on Gold Standard Corpus

Olga Babina(✉) and Svetlana Sheremetyeva

South Ural State University, 76 Prospekt Lenina, Chelyabinsk 454080, Russia
{babinaoi,sheremetevaso}@susu.ru

Abstract. A key approach to carry out sentiment analysis, in particular, aspect-based sentiment analysis nowadays is using machine learning techniques that employ labeled datasets for training and tuning models to a specific task, thus making the development of relevant datasets the centerpiece of sentiment related research efforts. This paper presents a methodology for automated dataset construction, based on a gold standard annotated corpus of customer feedback on the services provided by private medical institutions. The annotation tagset comprises both tags for domain-specific concepts interpreted as opinion aspects and sentiment indicators. The proposed procedure for gold-corpus-based dataset creation includes: a) quasi-sentence segmentation of the customer review; b) token-for-token alignment of the dataset segments over the annotated corpus; c) aspect labeling of sentential units with N-dimensional binary vectors based on aspect tag extraction from the lexical units in the annotated corpus; d) sentiment labeling of the quasi-sentences based on transposing the sentiment-related tags of the corpus tokens into the values of a numerical scale. The developed dataset is a collection of tabular data that comprise quasi-sentences from customer reviews as elementary aspect-specific opinion-bearers, labeled each with a binary feature vector of aspects that allows for learning aspects as a multi-label classification problem, and positive and negative sentiment labels as floating-point numbers from the interval [0; 1], that provide for learning the opinion-bearing quasi-sentence sentiment as a regression problem.

Keywords: Dataset · Aspect-based Sentiment Analysis · Sentence Segmentation · Sentence Alignment · Multi-Label Classification · Regression · Russian

1 Introduction

Sentiment analysis has emerged as a prominent research area in recent years as it provides valuable insights into customer sentiment, public opinion, and other aspects of online communication. The task of sentiment analysis involves the automated determination of the emotional tone and sentiment expressed in a given statement. To address this problem, diverse methodological approaches have been developed, each relying on specialized

M. Bakaev et al. (Eds.): IMS 2024, CCIS 2534, pp. 35–48, 2026.
https://doi.org/10.1007/978-3-031-96177-9_4

linguistic knowledge bases. These approaches aim to capture the subjective attitudes expressed in a text, enabling the quantification and interpretation of opinions and/or emotions.

Various approaches to sentiment analysis exist, each leveraging unique strategies to extract and analyze sentiment from a text. These approaches can be broadly categorized into:

- Lexicon-based approach: Utilizes pre-compiled lexicons that assign sentiment scores to individual words or phrases. Sentiment lexicons have been developed for various languages. Among these languages, English has received the most attention, with a wide range of sentiment lexicons available. However, other languages, including Russian [1–4], have also seen the development of sentiment lexicons.
- Machine learning approach: Employs supervised or unsupervised machine learning algorithms to identify patterns and extract sentiment from text data. The approach rests on utilizing datasets that comprise linguistic units (phrases, sentences, short messages, etc.) annotated with sentiment labels. Several Russian-language datasets have been developed specifically for sentiment analysis tasks. These datasets quite frequently employ a ternary scale for labelling instances by sentiment polarity, which categorizes sentiment into three classes: positive, negative, or neutral. Some notable examples are Kinopoisk movie review dataset [5], car review dataset [6], Massive Multilingual Sentiment Corpora (Russian subset) [7], and others.
- Hybrid approach: Combines elements of both lexicon-based and machine learning approaches to enhance accuracy and robustness.

Aspect-based sentiment analysis (ABSA) is the task that involves not only determining the overall sentiment of a statement, but also pinpointing the specific aspects or features of the target entity (product, service, person, etc.) that contribute to that sentiment. Datasets specifically designed for ABSA are relatively scarce in number. Moreover, despite the growing interest in ABSA, Russian remains an under-resourced language in this field. Among the datasets in Russian, we could mention SemEval-2016 Task 5 Dataset [8], SentiRuEval-2015 Competition Track Datasets [9], TripAdvisor Hotel Review Corpus [10].

In this study, we focus on a methodology for constructing a high-quality dataset for ABSA in Russian. Our methodology leverages an existing gold standard corpus in the medical service domain that has been conceptually tagged with aspect and sentiment labels.

2 Methodology

2.1 Gold Standard Annotated Corpus

The methodology of our research was determined by the task of constructing datasets for training models for multi-aspect sentiment analysis of customer feedback on medical services. It is based on the gold standard annotated corpus as its main resource that was developed at the previous stage of our research. We here briefly describe its main features.

The gold standard corpus has been built by annotating an original collection of 1601 medical review texts broadcast by clinic patients in the Ural region. It contains reviews of 8 medical institutions totaling to more than 100,000 words. The specificity of our gold standard annotation is that the units of annotation include multicomponent phrases rather than just single words as used in most annotation and sentiment analysis projects. Such approach reduces tag ambiguity and facilitates actual aspect sentiment analysis.

The aspect-sentiment information is coded with a tagset of three conceptual meanings: sentiment proper, sentiment modifier, and aspect.

- The sentiment proper tags refer to the concepts of positive (POS), extremely positive (POSX), negative (NEG), extremely negative (NEGX). Text units of neutral sentiments are neglected.
- The sentiment modifier tags signal of strengthening (MAG), weakening (ANT) or reversing (REV) the sentiment coded by the sentiment proper tags.
- The aspect tags code the subjects of patient sentiment, such as disease treatment quality (Q), doctor qualification (CH), technical equipment (EQ), etc.

The corpus annotation unit can thus be marked-up with multiple tags depending on the amount of aspect-sentiment information it conveys.

In addition, the corpus is annotated with metadata, such as the clinic name, review source (2GIS service), and assessment of a medical center by the review author on the scale from one to five.

2.2 Dataset Construction Workflow

We propose a workflow for ABSA oriented dataset development based on the gold standard annotated corpus of customer feedback on medical services. The suggested dataset construction process involves the following steps:

Step 1: Choice of Unit of Analysis. We first select linguistic units (having considered phrases, sentences, texts) that effectively capture evaluative opinions in the medical service domain. These units, extracted from the text corpus, are to serve as instances (datapoints) for the constructed dataset and determine the level of granularity at which sentiment is analyzed and classified. This step seeks to determine the optimal level of granularity, ensuring that each self-contained and coherent linguistic unit expresses a unitary evaluative situation.

Step 2: Automatic Unit Segmentation. We automatically segment an untagged corpus of customer feedback on medical services into the chosen units.

Step 3: Corpus Alignment. We align the automatically segmented, unlabeled units of analysis with the corresponding tokens from a gold standard annotated corpus of customer reviews. The alignment allows us to transfer aspect and sentiment labels from the labeled corpus to the dataset instances.

Step 4: Aspect and Sentiment Featurization. Finally, for each instance in our dataset, we extract from the aligned gold standard corpus a list of aspects and sentiment concepts. Based on the extracted concept tags, we construct binary feature vectors of aspects and assign sentiment valence weights to each instance.

We further provide a detailed description of each step in the proposed dataset construction workflow.

Step 1: Choice of Unit of Analysis. Analysis of the medical domain corpus reveals that patients express their opinions on medical centers through elementary statements, often expressed in simple or complex sentences. These statements typically contain an indication of a single opinion aspect and an evaluative predicate. Compound sentences with asyndetically connected clauses usually convey sentiment regarding one or more aspects, all sharing the same polarity. Meanwhile, compound sentences with adversative conjunctions typically express at least two elementary opinion statements with opposing polarity. Thus, a reasonable choice of unit of analysis for an ABSA-oriented dataset seems a sentence or a clause. In the vast majority of cases, such choice results in one of three distinct cases:

- The dataset instance (sentence or clause) expresses a unitary evaluative situation, characterized by a single aspect and a single sentiment polarity.
- The dataset instance contains multiple aspects, all of which are characterized by predicates of the same polarity.
- A sentence contains a characteristic of one aspect, which is considered in comparison with another object, time, or situation, for which characteristics of opposite polarity are given.

Out of the three aforementioned cases, the third one may be most confusing, as it requires the model to be able to identify and distinguish between the different sentiment polarities to make accurate predictions. Despite its complexity, the third case occurred in only 46 out of 10,148 sentential units in the gold standard corpus, rendering it a relatively insignificant occurrence.

Thus, we propose that the optimal datapoint type for aspect-based sentiment analysis in customer feedback is a sentence and, for a compound sentence with an adversative conjunction, a clause or a sequence of subordinated or asyndetically coordinated clauses. These sentential chunks forming the text part of an instance in the dataset, we name quasi-sentences. However, the fact that an instance may render opposing sentiment polarity requires accounting for during instance featurization.

Step 2: Automatic Unit Segmentation. Modern text segmentation methods are often implemented in natural language analysis libraries such as NLTK and spaCy. We evaluated sentence segmentation algorithms, including those provided by the NLTK and spaCy's tokenization tools (for the latter library, including a dependency parsing-based algorithm, a default statistical-tagger-based segmentation, both using *ru_core_news_lg* model, and a rule-based sentencizer). Our experiments revealed that standard library methods may not always accurately determine sentence boundaries in customer reviews. This is due to both limitations in the algorithms themselves and the specific features of the language used in the text corpus. The main challenges we came across include:

- Frequent violations of spelling and punctuation norms, which may have resulted from such factors as author illiteracy, typos, automatic text correction, or the use of mobile devices for posting reviews;

- The use of Internet-specific language features, including special characters and emoticons, which may not be handled correctly by standard segmentation algorithms and pre-trained models.

To address the limitations of the sentence segmentation algorithms in handling customer feedback, we developed a domain-specific add-on to the spaCy's sentencizer for the Russian language. In particular, we enhanced the sentencizer with domain-specific rules to address linguistic challenges and improve segmentation accuracy, including:

- Punctuation Rules. We specified sequences of punctuation marks, brackets, or special characters that indicate sentence boundaries.
- Graphematic Rules. These rules account for numbered enumerations, preventing the list number separation from the subsequent text.
- Lexical Rules. We composed a short lexicon of domain-specific clipped words used to prevent erroneous sentence segmentation after periods in abbreviations.
- Antithesis Rule. The rule that, for sentences containing an adversative conjunction or other function words expressing contrariety, places the sentence boundary before the function word, resulting in clauses as units of analysis.

Application of the enhanced sentence segmentation method resulted in the automatic division of the text corpus into 10,148 quasi-sentence segments (sentences proper or clauses).

Step 3: Corpus Alignment. This step is motivated by the rationale that the conceptual data for every quasi-sentential datapoint in the developed dataset can be drawn from the corresponding textual parts of the annotated gold-standard corpus. Meanwhile, the gold standard corpus used as a source of conceptual data in this research has the following limitations:

1. The corpus consists of annotated text-level (not quasi-sentence-level) segments.
2. The annotation platform [11] used to create the annotated corpus yields the result of annotation as plain text. E.g.,

   Unannotated text: *Врач замечательная, администраторы очень приветливые.*

   Annotated text: *{Врач} ~ DR {замечательная} ~ POSX, {администраторы} ~ S {очень} ~ MAG {приветливые} ~ POS.*

   Taking these into account, drawing the datapoint-related conceptual data from the annotated texts required token-for-token alignment of the unannotated and annotated plain-text parts, which we did by traversing the dataset at this stage. Token alignment was based on calculating the ratio of graphemic identity between tokens in the annotated and unannotated corpora. This ratio was required to exceed a specified threshold, in order to account for any modifications made during the creation of the gold standard corpus, including adjustments to word boundaries and spelling corrections. As soon as the tokens are aligned, the aspect and sentiment tags can be mechanically extracted from the tagged text aligned with the corresponding quasi-sentential datapoint.

Step 4: Aspect and Sentiment Featurization. In the final stage, two types of concept tags were automatically extracted from each tagged text aligned with a dataset quasi-sentence: a) aspect tags, and b) sentiment tags. Auxiliary tags (UNK, O, Num) assigned to domain-irrelevant lexical units during annotation on the platform were excluded from consideration. As a result, aspects and sentiment are represented as features extracted and counted from tags in the tagged portion of the aligned quasi-sentences.

Aspect attributes are treated as features of the units of analysis, which together form a binary *N*-dimensional vector, where each dimension corresponds to an aspect. The binary vector's coordinate values indicate the presence or absence of the aspect tag in the tagged text corresponding to the unit of analysis. The number of tags associated with the unit of analysis was disregarded. The dimensionality of the vector space is determined by the cardinality of the set of aspect tags in the tagged corpus, resulting in *N* that equals to 19 in the current domain.

Sentiment labeling in the dataset is incorporated as follows. For each dataset unit, the total count of the sentiment proper tags (NEGX, NEG, POS, POSX) in the corresponding tagged text is computed. Given that some quasi-sentences contain statements with both positive and negative sentiment, an independent attribute is specified for each pole. Within each (positive and negative) semi-axis, a sentiment valence weight is determined based on the following rationale. The introduced sentiment tags can be arranged on an ordinal scale of sentiment valence, reflecting the degree of positive and negative attitudes towards an aspect of an object. Thus, the ordinal scale for the positive semi-axis, incorporating the modifier tags (ANT, MAG), is as follows (in the order of increasing sentiment intensity):

(Neutral) → ANT+POS → POS / ANT + POSX → MAG + POS / POSX → MAG+POSX

Treating these categories as linguistic variables, which are uniformly distributed within the range [0; 1], we derive numerical correspondences that are assigned to each tag value of the ordinal scale:

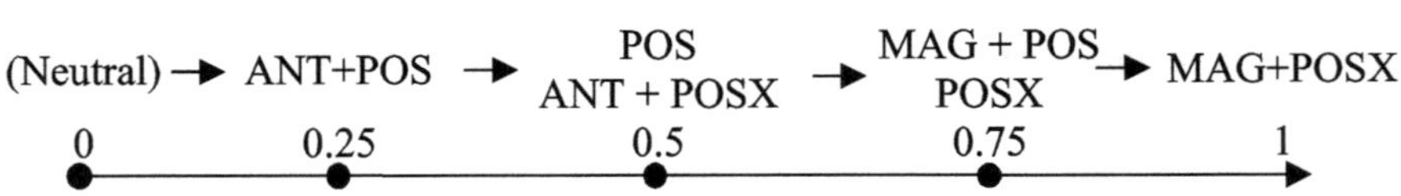

Within the ordinal scale, the sentiment proper tags are POS (corresponds to 0.5 on the numerical scale) and POSX (corresponds to 0.75), while the tags ANT and MAG function as valence modifiers by shifting the numerical values by 0.25 down and up, respectively. Meanwhile, each datapoint may contain multiple sentiment tags. Then, the generalized numerical sentiment of the unit can be calculated as a weighted sum of the sentiment tag and modifier counts normalized by the total count of the sentiment proper tags in the current datapoint.

Similarly, a numerical score can be determined for the value on the negative semi-axis.

Thus, the numerical equivalent of the feature that determines the positive and negative sentiment valence in the datapoint (quasi-sentence) can be calculated as shown in Formulas (1) and (2):

$$SV_{pos} = \frac{c(POS) \cdot 0.5 + c(POSX) \cdot 0.75 + c\left(MAG_{ptag}\right) \cdot 0.25 - c\left(ANT_{ptag}\right) \cdot 0.25}{c(POS) + c(POSX)}, \tag{1}$$

$$SV_{neg} = \frac{c(\mathrm{NEG}) \cdot 0.5 + c(\mathrm{NEGX}) \cdot 0.75 + c\left(\mathrm{MAG}_{ntag}\right) \cdot 0.25 - c\left(\mathrm{ANT}_{ntag}\right) \cdot 0.25}{c(\mathrm{NEG}) + c(\mathrm{NEGX})}, \tag{2}$$

where SV_{pos} is the numerical value of the positive sentiment valence for the datapoint; SV_{neg} is the numerical value of the negative sentiment valence for the datapoint; POSX, POS, NEG, NEGX are tags used in the annotated text aligned with the instance in the dataset (quasi-sentence); MAG_{ptag}, ANT_{ptag} are labels used to denote the modifier tags MAG and ANT, respectively, syntactically correlating with the lexical unit tagged by an item from the set *ptag*; MAG_{ntag}, ANT_{ntag} are labels used to denote the modifier tags MAG and ANT, respectively, syntactically correlating with the lexical unit tagged by an item from the set *ntag*; $ptag = \{\mathrm{POS}, \mathrm{POSX}\}$; $ntag = \{\mathrm{NEG}, \mathrm{NEGX}\}$; $c(\mathrm{Tag})$ is the Tag count in the portion of the annotated corpus aligned with the quasi-sentence in the dataset, $\mathrm{Tag} \subset \left\{\mathrm{POSX}, \mathrm{POS}, \mathrm{NEG}, \mathrm{NEGX}, \mathrm{MAG}_{ptag}, \mathrm{MAG}_{ntag}, \mathrm{ANT}_{ptag}, \mathrm{ANT}_{ntag}\right\}$.

Corpus analysis revealed the most typical cases of modifying sentiment-bearing lexical units (annotated with a sentiment proper tag) by tokens tagged with the modifiers MAG and ANT. This allowed us to formulate rules for subcategorizing the modifier tags into MAG_{ptag}, MAG_{ntag}, ANT_{ptag}, or ANT_{ntag}. The subcategorization procedure involved preliminary parsing of the quasi-sentence using a dependency parser from *spaCy* with the language model *ru_core_news_lg*. Subsequently, a rule-based search algorithm was employed to account for the modifiers when calculating the SV_{pos} and SV_{neg} (Fig. 1). According to the developed rules, the search for sentiment polarity sign prioritized the relationship of the modifier-tagged lexical unit with its parent node and, then, child nodes (in case no sentiment tag is found in the parent node). In case a sentiment tag is assigned to the lexical token, including the word representing the observed parent or child nodes, the modifier is subcategorized in accordance with the sentiment tag of a related unit.

```
Let c(MAG_ptag) = c(ANT_ptag) = c(MAG_ntag) = c(ANT_ntag)=0
For every token tagged with ANT / MAG:
 wlist = a list of words parsed as «amod» or «advmod» from the token
 For word from the found wlist:
     If word has parent and parent contains a word tagged with a tag from ptag,
     Then increment c(MAG_ptag)/c(ANT_ptag) by 1 respectively
     Else If word has child and child contains a word tagged with a tag from ptag
           Then increment c(MAG_ptag)/c(ANT_ptag) by 1 respectively
     If word had parent and parent contains a word tagged with a tag from ntag,
     Then increment c(MAG_ntag)/c(ANT_ntag) by 1 respectively
     Else If word has child and child contains a word tagged with a tag from ntag
           Then increment c(MAG_ntag)/c(ANT_ntag) by 1 respectively
```

Fig. 1. Rule-based algorithm for MAG / ANT modifier tag subcategorization based on dependency relationships

Thus, in our work, we accounted for the sentiment of only lexical tokens directly related to the lexical token annotated with the tags MAG / ANT and functioning as an adverbial or adjectival modifier in relation to the sentiment-providing unit. This approach enabled us to identify modification relations in the majority of cases within the analyzed corpus. To generalize, we posit that it is feasible to expand the set of rules, although this would necessitate further analysis.

In summary, the development of a dataset for aspect-based sentiment analysis entails, first, the identification of elementary statements within the gold standard annotated corpus and, next, the extraction of the explicit aspect categories and the calculation of the sentiment valence values (positive and negative) for each statement.

3 Results

3.1 Dataset Structure

The ABSA-oriented dataset developed as a result of applying the procedure described in Sect. 2.2 is characterized as follows. The units of analysis are quasi-sentences in Russian, extracted from customer reviews on the services at medical institutions in the Urals. The datapoints in the dataset are each described through the following attributes:

- Company: the name of a medical center with respect to which the customer feedback is provided;
- Source: the internet site, wherefrom the customer reviews were scraped;
- Text #: an arbitrary ID of the customer review, wherefrom the quasi-sentence is extracted;
- Sentence #: an integer signaling the ordinal number of the current quasi-sentence in the customer review text;
- Sentence: the text of a quasi-sentence, resulted from the sentence segmentation of customer reviews and functioning as a unit of analysis;
- Aspect Features: a set of binary features titled by twenty domain-related aspects, signaling the activation or non-activation of the corresponding aspect-denoting concept in the semantics of the current quasi-sentence;
- Positive: a feature labeling positive sentiment valence SV_{pos} as a floating-point number from the interval [0; 1];

- Negative: a feature labeling negative sentiment valence SV_{neg} as a floating-point number from the interval [0; 1];
- Total: the total count of the sentiment proper tags in a quasi-sentence.

The feature Company, Source and Text ID are inherited from the original corpus of customer reviews on medical services. Sentence numbers are dynamically generated during the sentence segmentation process. Other features are generated as described in Sect. 2 above. A fragment of the dataset is shown in Fig. 2.

3.2 Dataset Characteristics

The composed dataset comprises 10,148 datapoints representing a quasi-sentence with the respective data on the activated aspect concepts and sentiment valence of the utterance. The data provided for every quasi-sentence are complete and include no missing values.

Company	Source	Text #	Sent #	Sentence	Negative	Positive	Total	C	CH	COM	D	DOC	DR	DRUG	EQ	F	INT	L	M
ЛОТОС	2GIS	0	1	Отличный детский уролог	0.0	0.75	1	0	1	0	0	0	0	0	0	0	0	0	0
ЛОТОС	2GIS	1	2	Понравилось, что подготовительный этап можно сразу же тут и пройти,	0.0	0.5	1	0	0	0	0	0	0	0	0	0	0	0	0
ЛОТОС	2GIS	1	3	а после операции отойти от наркоза и спокойно домой поехать, если все хорошо.	0.0	0.5	2	0	0	0	1	0	0	0	0	0	0	0	0
ЛОТОС	2GIS	3	4	Скидки все отменили(	0.5	0.0	1	0	0	0	0	0	0	0	0	0	0	0	1
ЛОТОС	2GIS	3	5	отношение к клиенту стало наигранным, что не приятно.	0.5	0.0	2	0	1	0	0	0	0	0	0	0	0	0	0
ЛОТОС	2GIS	20	1	Рекомендую крутого специалиста отоларингллога К., максимально грамотный подход к работе.	0.0	0.58333	3	0	1	0	0	0	0	0	0	0	0	0	0
ЛОТОС	2GIS	39	1	Врач провела осмотр, взяла анализ, выписала препараты,	0.0	0.0	0	0	0	0	1	0	1	1	0	0	0	0	0
ЛОТОС	2GIS	39	2	но после приема препаратов стало только хуже!!!	0.75	0.0	1	0	0	0	1	0	0	1	0	0	0	0	0
ЛОТОС	2GIS	59	4	Спасибо Вам огромное❤	0.0	0.75	1	0	0	0	0	0	0	0	0	0	0	0	0
ЛОТОС	2GIS	86	17	Больше всего меня в этой ситуации злит тот факт, что когда ваши врачи задерживают приём на 20-30 минут, то это норма и даже не извиняться.	0.5625	0.0	4	0	0	0	1	0	1	0	0	0	0	0	0
ЛОТОС	2GIS	174	5	Приятен факт хорошего оборудования,	0.0	0.5	2	0	0	0	0	0	0	0	0	0	0	0	0
ЛОТОС	2GIS	174	6	но при таких доходах, как у "Лотоса" это должно быть нормой, поэтому не прибавляет баллов к оценке.	0.0	0.25	1	1	0	0	0	0	0	0	0	0	0	0	0
ЛОТОС	2GIS	208	1	Отделение химиотерапии, администратор 👍, медсестры просто 🔥🔥🔥, спасибо вам за неравнодушие!))))	0.0	0.875	3	1	0	0	0	0	0	0	0	0	0	0	0
МЕДЕОР	2GIS	675	12	Мне было совсем не страшно)))	0.0	0.5	1	0	0	0	0	0	0	0	0	0	0	0	0
МЕДЕОР	2GIS	675	13	от наркоза отошла быстро и без последствий.	0.0	0.5	2	0	0	0	1	0	0	0	0	0	0	0	0
МЕДЕОР	2GIS	830	2	Анализы в конце концов сделали,	0.0	0.0	0	0	0	0	1	0	0	0	0	0	0	0	0
МЕДЕОР	2GIS	830	3	но ещё никогда и нигде я их так долго не ждал.	0.625	0.0	2	0	0	0	0	0	0	0	0	0	0	0	0

Fig. 2. A fragment of the constructed dataset

The distribution of datapoint counts per medical center is shown in Fig. 3. The distribution by this parameter is unbalanced due to the availability of reviews for a specific medical center in the source and a stochastic variability in the review lengths.

Figure 4 demonstrates the review length variation based on *Sentence #* attribute. Text lengths primarily vary from 1 to 7 quasi-sentences, though some reviews significantly exceed this limit, reaching up to 77 quasi-sentences in length.

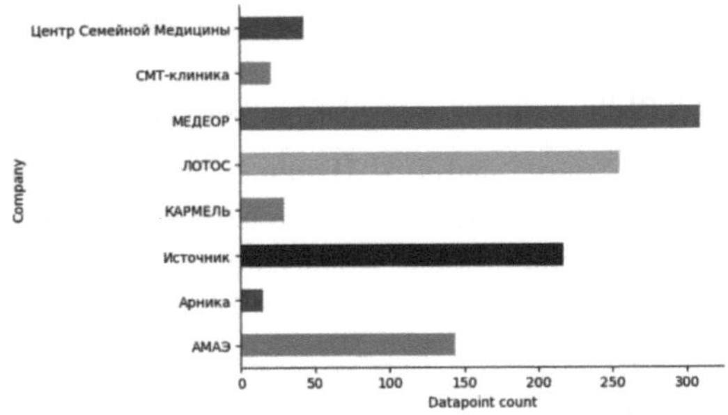

Fig. 3. Datapoint count distribution per medical centers

The total distribution of sentiment values in the positive and negative features disregarding zero values is given in Fig. 5. The proportion of positive and negative labels among dataset points is relatively uniform. The major part of values concentrates between 0.5 and 0.75, which is equivalent to positive/negative to extremely positive/negative categorical descriptions of sentiment provided by the sentiment proper tags in the gold corpus.

The aspect distribution in the constructed dataset is shown in Fig. 6. Specifically, Fig. 6a presents an overview of the most prominent concepts mentioned by customers in their reviews, including *General Impression, Clinic, Doctor, Medical Service Quality, Money Transactions.* Notably, some instances are assigned multiple aspects, while some others lack the aspect reference. As Fig. 6b shows, the majority of instances are labeled with no more than four aspects.

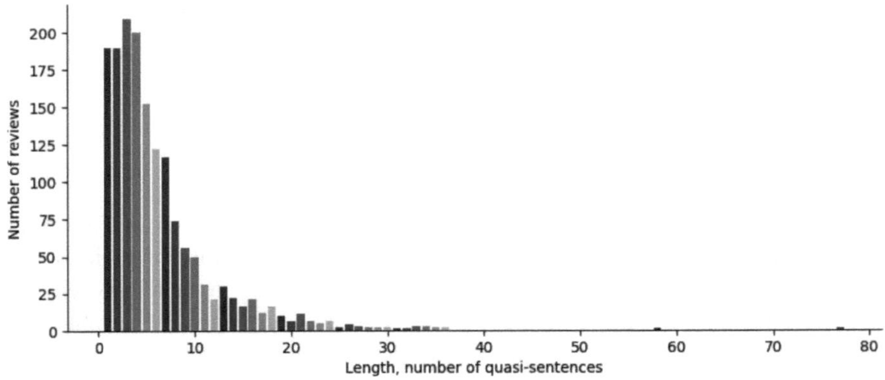

Fig. 4. Review lengths distribution in the dataset

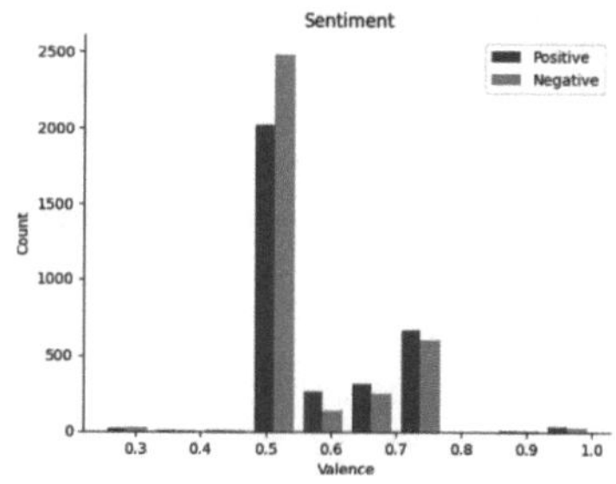

Fig. 5. Sentiment valence distribution in the dataset, zeros omitted.

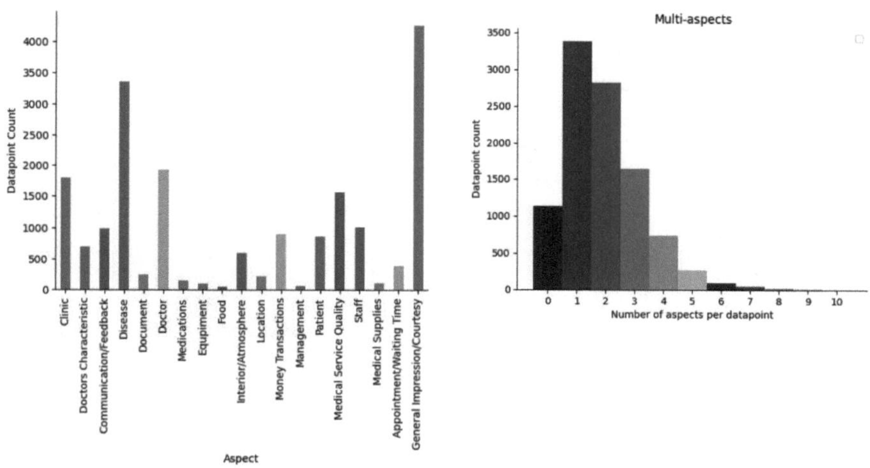

(a) (b)

Fig. 6. Aspect distribution in the dataset: (a) the distribution of datapoints labeled with each of the domain-related aspects; (b) the distribution of datapoints labeled with one or more aspects

The distribution of positive versus negative sentiment for each domain-specific aspect is shown in Fig. 7. The scatterplots reveal that the majority of instances labeled with each aspect are unequivocally referred to either positive or negative sentiment. Meanwhile, the concepts of *Clinic, Disease, Doctor, Money Transaction, General Impression* exhibit a certain degree of ambiguity, as it is not uncommon for these concepts to be activated in the instances associated with both positive and negative sentiment.

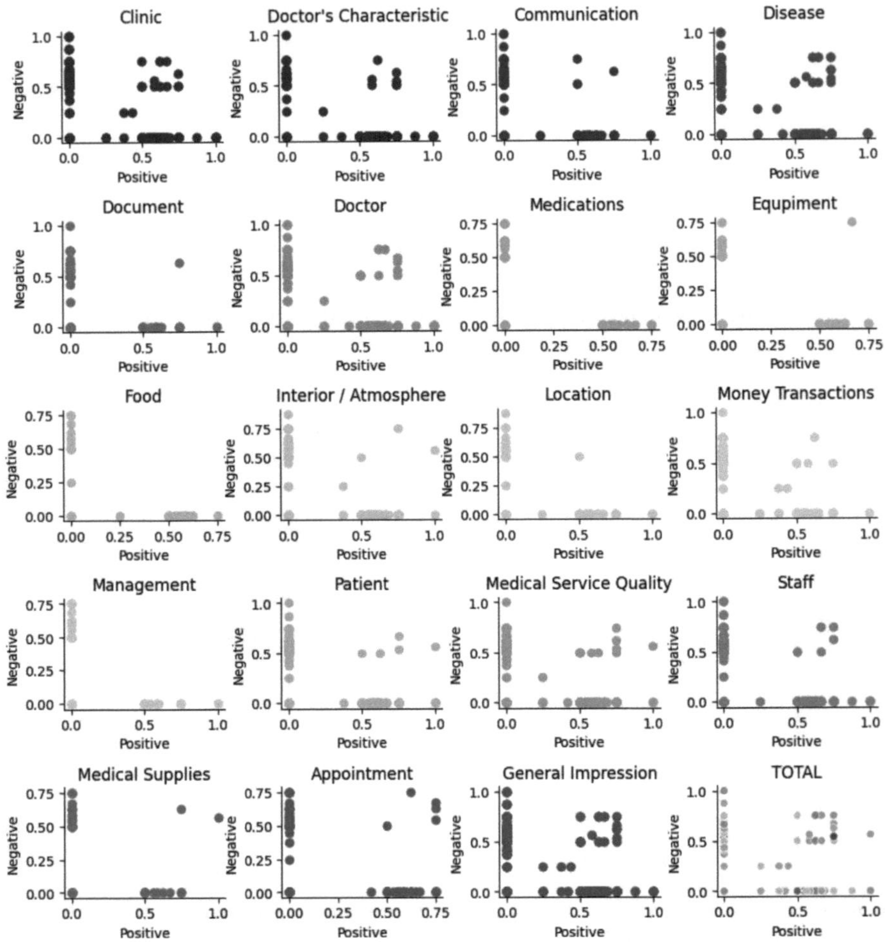

Fig. 7. Positive vs negative label distribution for domain-related aspects

4 Conclusion

The availability of a comprehensive and well-annotated dataset is crucial for advancing research in aspect-based sentiment analysis, particularly in under-resourced languages like Russian. This study presents a comprehensive methodology for constructing an ABSA-oriented dataset using a gold standard corpus. Our methodology ensures the accuracy and consistency of the extracted aspect and sentiment concepts, providing a solid foundation for future research in ABSA. The suggested dataset construction methodology contributes to the development of high-quality ABSA datasets in various domains.

The suggested methodology has been tested on developing a Russian-language dataset for the domain of customer feedback on medical services. The dataset comprises quasi-sentences as datapoints characterized each by a vector of aspect features, which allows for treating learning aspects as a multi-label classification problem, and the values of positive and negative sentiment valences, which provides for learning the opinion-bearing quasi-sentence sentiment as a regression problem. The constructed dataset may enable researchers and practitioners to:

- Develop and evaluate ABSA models specifically tailored to the medical service domain;
- Gain insights into the sentiment expressed towards different aspects of medical services in Russian;
- Compare the performance of different ABSA methods on a standardized dataset.

The resulting dataset can be used to train and evaluate machine learning models for ABSA, enabling the analysis of patient sentiment towards various aspects of medical services. This information is valuable for healthcare providers and researchers seeking to improve patient care and service delivery.

References

1. Chen, Y., Skiena S.: Building Sentiment Lexicons for All Major Languages. In: Toutanova, K., Wu H. (eds.) Proceedings of the 52nd Annual Meeting of the Association for the Computational Linguistics (Volume 2: Short Papers), pp. 383–389. Baltimore, Maryland, US, 23–25 June 2014. ACL, Baltimore, MD (2014)
2. Loukachevitch, N., Levchik, A.: Creating a General Russian Sentiment Lexicon. In: Calzolari, N., et al. (eds.) Proceedings of the Tenth International Conference on Language Resources and Evaluation (LREC'16), pp. 1171–1176. ELRA, Portorož (2016)
3. Koltsova, O., Alexeeva, S., Pashakhin, S., Koltsov, S.: PolSentiLex: Sentiment Detection in Socio-Political Discussions on Russian Social Media. In: Filchenkov, A., Kauttonen, J., Pivovarova, L. (eds.) Proceedings of the 9th Conference on Artificial Intelligence and Natural Language (AINL 2020), CCIS, vol. 1292, pp. 1–16. Springer Cham, Helsinki (2020)
4. Kulagin, D.: Publicly available sentiment dictionary for the Russian language KartaSlovSent. In: Selegey, V.P., Belikov, V.I., Boguslavsky, I.M., Dobrov, B.V., et al. (eds.) Computational Linguistics and Intellectual Technologies: Papers from the Annual International Conference "Dialogue," vol. 20, pp. 1106–1119. RSUH, Moscow (2021)
5. Blinov, P.D., Klekovkina, M., Kotelnikov, E., Pestov, O.: Research of lexical approach and machine learning methods for sentiment analysis. In: Selegey, V.P., Belikov, V.I., Boguslavsky, I.M., Dobrov, B.V. et al. (eds.) Computational Linguistics and Intellectual Technologies: Papers from the Annual International Conference "Dialogue", vol. 12(19), no. 2, pp. 51–61. RSUH, Moscow (2013)
6. Glazkova, A.V.: The evaluation of the proximity of text categories for solving electronic documents classification tasks. Tomsk State Univ. J. Control Comput. Sci. Bull. Tomsk State Univ. **2**(31), 18–25 (2015)
7. Augustyniak, Ł., Woźniak, S., Gruza, M., Gramacki, P., Rajda, K., Morzy, M., Kajdanowicz, T.: Massively Multilingual Corpus of Sentiment Datasets and Multi-faceted Sentiment Classification Benchmark. ArXiv preprint: 2306.07902. arXiv, 2023
8. Pontiki, M., Galanis, D., Papageorgiou, H., Androutsopoulos, I. et al.: SemEval-2016 Task 5: Aspect Based Sentiment Analysis. In: Bethard, S., Carpuat, M., Cer, D., Jurgens, D., Nakov, P., Zesch, T. (eds.) Proceedings of the 10th International Workshop on Semantic Evaluation (SemEval-2016), pp. 19–30. ACL, San Diego, CA (2016)
9. Loukachevitch, N. V., Blinov, P. D., Kotelnikov, E. V., Rubtsova, Yu. V., Ivanov, V.V., Tutubalina, E.: SentiRuEval: Testing Object-oriented Sentiment Analysis Systems in Russian.

In: Selegey, V.P., Belikov, V.I., Boguslavsky, I.M., Dobrov, B.V. et al. (eds.) Computational Linguistics and Intellectual Technologies: Papers from the Annual International Conference "Dialogue", vol. 14(21), no. 2, pp. 3–14. RSUH, Moscow (2015)
10. Rybakov, V., Malafeev, A.: Aspect-based sentiment analysis of russian hotel reviews. In: Aalst, W.M.P. van der, Batagelj, V., Glavaš, G., Ignatov, D.I. et al. (eds.) Proceedings of the Seventh International Conference on Analysis of Images, Social Networks and Texts (AIST 2018), CEUR WP, vol. 2268, pp. 75–84. CEUR, Moscow (2018)
11. Sheremetyeva, S.O., Babina, O.I.: A platform for knowledge assisted conceptual annotation of multilingual texts. Bull. South Ural State Univ. Series Linguist. **17**(2), 53–60 (2020). (in Russian)

Unveiling Urban Emotions: Contextual Alignment in Sentiment Analysis of Social Media Microtexts

Anna Chizhik[1,2](✉) and Katarina Cokrlic[1]

[1] Saint Petersburg State University, 7/9 Universitetskaya Emb., 199034 Saint Petersburg, Russia
chizhik@itmo.ru, katarina.cokrlic@gmail.com
[2] ITMO University, Kronverksky Prospekt 49, 197101 Saint Petersburg, Russia

Abstract. This article describes a comprehensive approach to text analysis that combines several modern natural language processing models, including spaCy, Word2Vec, BERT, and ruGPT-3. The primary goal of the development was to create a method capable of considering the contextual aspects of text, which is critical for accurate analysis of short messages on social media. The method uses multi-level analysis to achieve high accuracy in classifying texts by emotional content, taking into account the contextual significance of words and the overall emotional direction of phrases. This approach not only enhances accuracy in detecting subtle emotional cues but also adapts to the brief and often ambiguous nature of social media communication.

Keywords: Sentiment Analysis · Social Media Texts · Emotional Detection · Deep Learning Models

1 Introduction

With the development of mobile internet and, consequently, the total penetration of online communications into individuals' daily practices, social networks have become aggregators of all kinds of information, characterizing trends in individual and group moods, and, as a result, forming vectors of public opinion. By analyzing the emotional polarities of discussions on social networks, it is possible to identify common constructions of cultural shifts and vectors of emotional perceptions, which subsequently become the basis for society's perceptions. Thus, public texts from social networks can be useful, including for assessing the socio-political situation, the level of social sphere functioning, social well-being, and for analyzing the satisfaction of residents with the urban environment. Focusing on the last point, it is important to note that understanding the emotional reactions of residents to various aspects of urban life can help municipalities and urban planners make more informed decisions. For example, if the analysis shows elevated levels of dissatisfaction or stress in certain areas, this could signal the need to improve urban infrastructure, public transportation, or housing conditions in those areas.

Therefore, two relevant entities arise: "district-emotion" and its derivative – "district-emotion-social sphere". It is important to note that in the case of studying texts from

M. Bakaev et al. (Eds.): IMS 2024, CCIS 2534, pp. 49–57, 2026.
https://doi.org/10.1007/978-3-031-96177-9_5

social networks, the discussion involves a latent interaction with the individual, which implies observing the individual with their orientation towards the social group to which they belong at the moment of discussion in the social network (which distinguishes this method from traditional surveys about social well-being, where respondents are in an anonymous context and answer more from their personal positions, without the effect of direct communication with the external environment). As a result, the analysis of texts makes it possible to assess the overall emotion of the social group: either as a category describing the general emotional background of the district or linked to the social role.

Thus, the analysis of sentiments in microtexts (posts and comments on them) becomes a key tool for identifying trends present in societal moods, which is extremely important for analyzing the urban environment. In turn, the density of the urban environment, which increases social pressure and the load on infrastructure, emphasizes the importance of analyzing the sentiments of city residents as a measure to ensure sustainable and harmonious development of urban areas and reduce socio-economic disparities.

However, analyzing the sentiment of such texts is a challenging task due to their brevity, ambiguity, and contextual load. In this study, the task was set to find a method of sentiment analysis of microtexts from social networks that would consider the context of the statement, based on which a judgment about the emotion contained in the text would be made through the ratio of facts and emotional parts.

2 Related Works

Social media platforms present unique challenges for sentiment analysis, including the use of informal language, sarcasm, allusions and cultural gags.

Early works in sentiment analysis focused primarily on extracting sentiment from text using bag-of-words models that disregarded context and semantics. More recent studies, however, emphasize the importance of context in sentiment analysis. For instance, Jiang et al. proposed a model that considers situational context by incorporating external knowledge bases to enhance the accuracy of sentiment prediction in tweets [1].

Some of the most significant research using text analysis and machine learning algorithms focuses on studies involving Facebook, Twitter, and the Chinese microblogging service Sina Weibo. For example, in 2015, researchers used a machine learning algorithm to analyze textual data posted by American students on Twitter, and assessed the level of subjective well-being for each user [2]. In another study, researchers examined the emotional state of Sina Weibo users and announced that their predictive model could accurately forecast several parameters of subjective well-being [3]. Amid the COVID-19 pandemic, a research group from China conducted a study on the emotional state of the country's residents based on natural language processing and text analysis methods [4]. Their research also included a predictive analysis of social network users' activities in the public internet space (data classification and clustering). Subsequently, the posts were analyzed using sentiment analysis and fact detection. The study's results involved correlating the presence of social risks with the behaviors of individuals within social media. Notably, this research used the Word2Vec (CBoW) algorithm to create vector representations of words, and the researchers present in their article the efficiency metrics of this text vectorization method applied to the specific task of analyzing subjective well-being.

The advent of deep learning has significantly advanced the field of sentiment analysis. Models like BERT [5] have been successfully adapted to understand the nuances of language used in social media. These models are capable of capturing contextual cues that are essential for accurate sentiment interpretation. For example, group of scientists [6] demonstrated how BERT could be fine-tuned to effectively determine sentiment polarity in a context-sensitive manner, outperforming traditional models on benchmark datasets.

These models are proficient in grasping context, which enhances their ability to discern sentiments in complex scenarios. However, their capacity to accurately correlate the presence of factual information with the underlying emotional tone is not infallible. This becomes especially challenging with nuanced linguistic features like sarcasm, where the expressed sentiment may starkly contradict the literal meaning of the words. For instance, a sarcastic remark might be technically positive while intended negatively, yet these subtleties may not be consistently detected by models that prioritize contextual understanding over intricate linguistic cues.

Thus, it becomes crucial to develop an algorithm where sentiment analysis is conducted through examining the interplay between factual content within the text and its emotional components. This approach would refine the precision of sentiment detection, especially in handling intricate linguistic features such as sarcasm, where the described above models might falter.

3 Methods

The issues described above regarding the ability to grasp the context of a short text (the facts on which a user bases their comment or post) suggest that the approach to analyzing text sentiment in social media should be based on an algorithm that integrates several stages of data processing.

Our research is aimed at testing the optimality of the processing pipeline being created. In its current implementation, the algorithm consists of the following text analysis stages:

1. Text preprocessing (the input text undergoes preliminary processing according to a standard scheme, including tokenization, stop-word removal, and text normalization);
2. Identification of facts (context) and emotional components;
3. Calculation of the ratio of context to the emotional part (FR), the resulting number is used as a coefficient in the final formula for emotion assessment;
4. Emotion analysis using Word2Vec (the Word2Vec model is used to detect the emotional coloring of the text at the level of individual words, which allows for considering the semantic similarity of words to anchor words that characterize various emotional states);
5. Sentiment evaluation of the text using BERT (applied for binary classification of text sentiment as positive or negative, providing an overall impression of the text's tone);

6. Emotion evaluation using ruGPT-3 (to obtain probabilities of the text belonging to each of five emotion categories);
7. Final emotion assessment (the formula takes into account FR, W2V Score, Sentiment Score, and GPT Score, and determines the predominant emotional component of the text).

The final output of the program is a combined assessment of the text's sentiment on a five-point scale using two weighting coefficients. The combination of two neural network models in the analytical pipeline allows not only for accurate classification of the text by emotional coloring but also for considering factual information, making the analysis more context-oriented.

4 Model of Basic Emotions

Within the scope of this study, it was hypothesized that by identifying stable emotions within social groups, these could be matched with markers included in the metrics of classical measurements of social well-being. This approach could transform the category of social well-being from a state of factual assertion into a dynamic state, allowing for the analysis and, if necessary, regulation of the situation. Therefore, the category of social mood was chosen as the basis for assessing social well-being. Furthermore, to approximate classical methodology, a model of basic emotions was developed to replace the scale used in traditional surveys, with individuals assessing their emotional background in specific situations.

The developed model was based on the EQuator model of basic emotions [7], which substantiates four fundamental classes of emotional states. Adapting it to the needs of the methodology, the concept of an emotion gradient was introduced, allowing for a more precise determination of the internal potential of emotions using standard models of basic emotions accepted in psychology and cultural studies [8]. Consequently, five basic classes of emotions were identified: fear, anger, sadness, joy, and a neutral state. The scale of basic emotions was designed to consider the need to decompose each class into its constituent emotional states—for example, the class of "fear" decomposes into "apprehension," "insecurity," "anxiety," "panic," and "terror." This consideration was crucial to ensure greater accuracy in the analysis of textual data.

5 Sentiment Assessment Formula

Our approach is based on considering both the emotional component and the context of the text when determining the final emotion. The proposed formula for calculating the final emotion takes into account several key factors, allowing for a more accurate determination of the text's emotional tone.

Thus, a formula combining several components is used for the quantitative assessment of the text's emotional tone:

1) Fact-to-Emotion Ratio (FR). This parameter determines how strongly the content of the text influences its emotional tone. The higher the FR value, the greater the weight of the facts in determining the final emotion.

2) Emotion assessment using Word2Vec (W2V Score). The Word2Vec model is used to identify the emotional coloring of the text at the level of individual words. The W2V Score represents the sum of the ratings of emotional significance of the words in the text, which allows for considering emotional contexts at the word level.
3) Sentiment assessment of the text using Sentiment Score. The formula includes an assessment of the overall sentiment of the text using a sentiment classification model (currently implemented using BERT). The Sentiment Score represents a numerical evaluation reflecting the overall emotional coloring of the text, which allows adjusting the final emotion according to the overall emotional context.
4) Emotion assessment using ruGPT-3 (GPT Score). The text generation model (currently implemented using ruGPT-3) provides the ability to assess the emotional coloring of the text at a higher level of semantics. The GPT Score represents the sum of the probabilities of various emotions predicted by the model, supplementing the assessment provided by Word2Vec and Sentiment Score.

The final formula is as follows:
Final Emotion Score $= (FR \times W2V\ Score \times Sentiment\ Score) - (GPT\ Score)$.

This formula accounts for both objective and subjective aspects of the text, combining factual content with emotional and tonal coloring. It considers specific words and their emotional significance as well as the overall context and tone of the text. This comprehensive approach allows for a fuller understanding of the text's emotional component and improves the accuracy of its analysis.

6 Selected Models for Tone Assessment

During the development of the code, several libraries for working with natural language were used, as well as models necessary for assessing text sentiment.

The spaCy library was used to load the Russian language model, which subsequently enabled syntactic and morphological analysis of texts. Gensim is another important library used in the code. It is known for its implementation of algorithms for topic modeling and vector representation of text. In our case, it was used to load a pre-trained Word2Vec model for Russian and was used to obtain vector representations of words. The SciPy library is used for mathematical calculations, such as calculating the cosine distance between vectors.

Modern models based on transformer architectures, such as BERT and ruGPT-3, were also actively used in the code.

BERT (Bidirectional Encoder Representations from Transformers) is a model developed by Google. A feature of BERT is its use of bidirectional training, which allows the model to better understand the context of words in a sentence. In our code, a version of this model for Russian, blanchefort/rubert-base-cased-sentiment, specialized in analyzing the emotional coloring of texts, is used.

ruGPT-3, developed by Sberbank AI, is an adaptation of the GPT-3 model for the Russian language. GPT-3 (Generative Pre-trained Transformer 3) is used for text generation and is capable of predicting the next word based on the previous context. In the code, the ruGPT-3 model is used for classifying text by emotional coloring, outputting probabilities of various emotions.

Both models use attention mechanisms technology, allowing the model to focus on significant elements of the text. Their integration into the code is carried out through the Transformers library from Hugging Face, providing convenient access to these and other pre-trained models.

7 Data

To test the created text sentiment assessment pipeline, a dataset of public posts and comments from the social network VKontakte was collected (communities tied to specific districts were selected). The search for groups from which text data was extracted was conducted manually: each district was studied individually for social activity, then groups were collected into separate datasets, with markers assigned based on the social role of the community. Each selected group was then analyzed for publication activity and the dynamics of both verbal and non-verbal reactions of community members to these posts. This process helped to eliminate groups with low levels of social interaction among their members, reducing noise that could hinder further analysis. The final sample included 412 public groups, averaging 25 groups per district. The number of subscribers varied from 10,000 to 80,000, depending on the thematic orientation of the group; posts in the selected groups appeared with a frequency of 1–2 times per day, with comment dynamics ranging from 3 to 20 on average. Data was collected for the years 2018–2023. The average length of comments in the final sample was 525 words (with 10–15 comments per post); the average length of posts was 41 words.

The collected text data was analyzed using topic modeling (a method was developed to identify features of social roles in user comments), then posts and their comments were examined for the presence of emotional coloring (an approach was developed to assess the general emotional tone around the post). Identifying the texts' association with social roles allowed for the analysis not only of the general emotional background associated with district locations but also of the emerging interrelations between the topics discussed by users and the emotions they experienced.

Each post with all its comments was taken as a unit of analysis, as it was necessary to ascertain the emotional coloring of the conversation as a whole, rather than the relationship between particular individuals. A topic modeling algorithm was separately developed (based on LDA), and its application to the collected data enabled the detection of social sphere features. A series of experiments was conducted with the number of topics parameter; for the LDA model quality, we used relative perplexity, which takes values from the range [0, 1] (the lower, the better). It is worth noting that the success of the trained model is often assessed using the standard perplexity $P = \exp(-L/N)$. However, this depends on the dictionary size and the distribution of word frequencies in the collection. Given the specifics of our data, it was necessary to find a criterion insensitive to changes in the dictionary composition. Therefore, in the course of the experiments, the optimal parameter for our LDA model was num_topics = 15. The model identified groups of words (themes) that frequently occur together in texts. From these 15 themes, the following generalizations were extracted: ['Animals', 'Education', 'Work', 'Utilities', 'Recreation', 'District Issues', 'Transport', 'Family', 'Sports', 'City']. This allowed us to identify the social roles and spheres of interest to us. Hence, the resulting entity "social sphere - emotion - district" was formed.

The sentiment analysis was conducted on a five-point scale: fear, anger, sadness, joy, and neutral state. The algorithm for this data analysis stage is described in detail above.

8 Results

The data analysis showed that within social media conversations, urban residents often express interest in education, even in areas traditionally considered as dormitory area where the rating of this topic is not zero. Referring to the correlation matrix that reflects the overall situation, city dwellers experience intense emotions when discussing topics such as recreation, animals, education, transport/traffic, and utilities. Moreover, these discussions often contain positive connotations (Fig. 1).

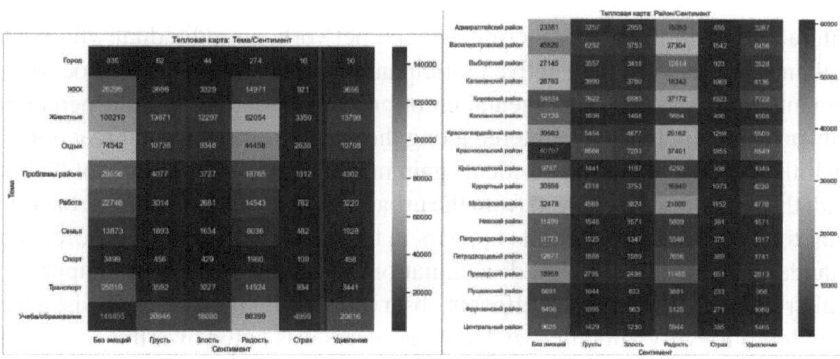

Fig. 1. Correlation matrices.

If the data is decomposed by districts and analyzed for emotional tone tied to location, several areas with a distinctly "joyful" backdrop immediately emerge. It is noteworthy that residents in these same areas tend to exhibit more pronounced other emotions (sadness, anger, surprise). However, the correlation matrix also showed that a significant number of comments on social media are of a neutral nature. Overall, this can be considered a positive trend, as it indicates that residents of the districts are in a state of satisfaction, able to conduct discussions in a respectful tone without sharp emotional outbursts.

Figure 2 shows the distribution of topics by emotions in the districts that were selected for more detailed analysis in the previous step (Kirovsky, Krasnogvardeysky, and Primorsky districts).

The charts reveal a number of patterns. It is fair to say that residents of the districts do not show interest in city-wide topics, but pay much more attention to issues related to their own district, fully confirming the null hypothesis that social well-being is linked to the location to which an individual's everyday life is tied. From the perspective of emotion distribution, social network analysis confirms survey results on the same topic, thus, it can be concluded that an individual's perception of their district correlates with the social group's perception of that district, meaning the emotional system of residents is largely oriented towards the urban environment image that arises for an individual

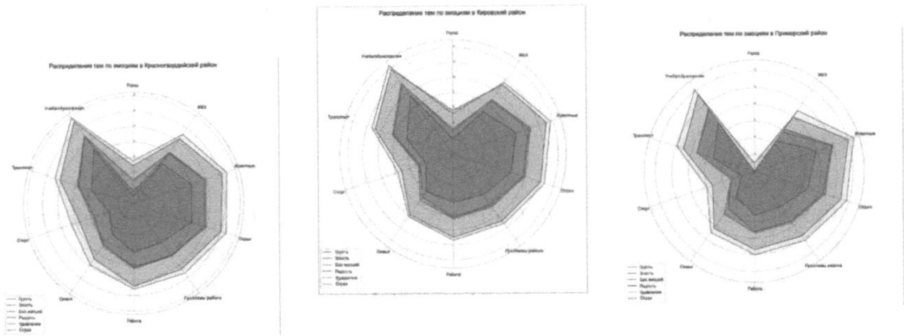

Fig. 2. Distribution of topics by emotions in three districts (Kirovsky, Krasnogvardeysky, and Primorsky districts).

when interacting with it. When entering a social network, an individual who wishes to express themselves becomes an active participant in the communicative process, and at that moment, conveys their fundamental emotion, corresponding to their perception of the urban environment they encountered along their daily route. Circular reactions are in this way linked to the experience residents gain in their district (regardless of their social role), with the connotation received from the urban environment forming the basis for the emotional tone of the discussion that appears in the social network. Therefore, contrary to the standard scheme of emotion dissemination, where individuals are suppressed by the social group, here the opposite effect is observed. Within the data analysis, a trend of increasing 'emotionality' among social network users was noted over the years, with the emotions of joy and fear showing growth starting from 2022 (while in 2021, the most characteristic were 'neutral' and 'surprise').

9 Conclusion

The proposed method demonstrated effectiveness in determining the emotional tone of short texts, which was particularly important for understanding microtexts on social networks, where the context often sets the emotional meaning of the statements.

To evaluate the quality of the sentiment analysis algorithm in short texts on social networks, the F1-score metric was used. This metric is the harmonic mean between precision and recall and allows for assessing the balance of the algorithm, taking into account both false positives and false negatives. The final F1-score value of 0.86 indicates high accuracy and completeness of classification.

Future work plans include optimizing the approach to expand its applicability and reduce computational load.

Acknowledgements. This research is supported by Russian Science Foundation and Saint Petersburg Science Foundation, grant No. 23-28-10069 «Forecasting social well-being in order to optimize the functioning of the urban digital services ecosystem in St. Petersburg»(https://rscf.ru/project/23-28-10069/).

References

1. Jiang, L., Yu, M., Zhou, M., Liu, X., Zhao, T.: Target-dependent twitter sentiment classification. Proceedings of the 49th annual meeting of the association for computational linguistics: human language technologies, pp. 151–160 (2011)
2. Volkova, S., Bachrach, Y., Armstrong, M., Sharma, V. Inferring latent user properties from texts published in social media. Proceedings of the AAAI Conference on Artificial Intelligence, V. 29. №. 1 (2015)
3. Hao, B., Li, L., Gao, R., Li, A., Zhu, T.: Sensing subjective well-being from social media. Active Media Technology: 10th International Conference, AMT 2014, Proceedings 10, pp. 324–335. Springer International Publishing (2014)
4. Li, S., Wang, Y., Xue, J., Zhao, N., Zhu, T.: The impact of COVID-19 epidemic declaration on psychological consequences: a study on active Weibo users. Int. J. Environ. Res. Public Health **17**(6), Art. 2032 (2020)
5. Devlin, J., Chang, M.W., Lee, K., Toutanova, K.: Bert: Pre-training of deep bidirectional transformers for language understanding. arXiv preprint arXiv:1810.04805 (2018)
6. Sun, M., Huang, X., Ji, H., Liu, Z., Liu, Y. (eds.).: Chinese Computational Linguistics: 18th China National Conference, CCL 2019. V. 11856, pp. 194–206. Springer Nature (2019)
7. Jack, R.E., Garrod, O.G., Schyns, P.G.: Dynamic facial expressions of emotion transmit an evolving hierarchy of signals over time. Curr. Biol. **24**(2), 187–192 (2014)
8. Ekman, P.: Basic emotions. In: Dalgleish, T., Power, M.J. (eds.).: Handbook of cognition and emotion, pp. 45–60 (1999)

RuPersWordAssociation: A New Dataset to Study Individual Association Behavior

Tatiana Litvinova[1(✉)], Viktoriya Molchanova[1], Polina Panicheva[1], Svetlana Lyubova[1], and Ivan Mamaev[1,2]

[1] Voronezh State Pedagogical University, 86 Lenina Street, Voronezh 394043, Russian Federation
centr_rus_yaz@mail.ru

[2] Baltic State Technical University "Voenmeh" Named After D.F. Ustinov, 1 Krasnoarmeyskaya Street, Saint Petersburg 190005, Russian Federation

Abstract. Word associations are among the most common paradigms for studying the human mental lexicon. While their structure and types of associations have been well studied, surprisingly little attention has been given to the individual differences in association behavior and factors affecting such behavior (emotional state and traits of respondents, type of cue words, etc.). Moreover, most research which use word association methodology rely on the assumption of homogeneity of word association behavior and available association norms. Individual association behavior is understudied. To study word association production at the level of individual, datasets are needed which contain data at the individual level, while existing association norms contain data aggregated on the level of a cue word. In this paper we present RuPersWordAssociation dataset which is, to the best of our knowledge, the largest existing (at least from publicly available) word association database with plenty of metadata (demographics, personality traits of respondents, reaction time, semantic similarity metrics) and linguistic annotation for the type of a relation between a cue word and associates (more than 22000 cue – associate pairs were annotated). We provide a detailed description of the dataset and the results of linguistic annotation and present the outcomes of the experiments which revealed individual preferences for certain types of associates. We also highlight some future directions of the application of the presented dataset to study individual mental lexicon and factors affecting individual association behavior.

Keywords: Word association · Semantics · Individual differences · Linguistic dataset · Russian language

1 Introduction

Word associations (WA) often referred to as "a language of thought" [De Deyne and Storms, 2015], have been analyzed for (at least) over a century in a wide range of disciplines, including psychology, linguistics, and speech and language therapy for different purposes, such as diagnosing psychiatric disorders, tracking developmental change, etc. (see for a bibliometric review of WA field in [Litvinova et al., 2023]). Studying WA may

M. Bakaev et al. (Eds.): IMS 2024, CCIS 2534, pp. 58–69, 2026.
https://doi.org/10.1007/978-3-031-96177-9_6

be viewed as a way to study the mind itself as WA "provides a privileged route" [De Deyne and Storms, 2015, p. 465] into the semantic structure of the lexicon.

As Fitzpatrick [Fitzpatrick, 2007, p. 321] notes, the use of the existing WA norm as the basis for comparison, which is a standard approach in WA-related research, suggests that there is a "normal", homogeneous way to respond to word association tests. However, it was shown [Fitzpatrick, 2007, 2009; Fitzpatrick et al, 2015] that the idea about homogeneity of associative responses of individuals is misleading: "not only do [native speakers] vary in the actual words they produce, they also seem to vary in the types of association they make" [Fitzpatrick, 2007, p. 327].

Publicly available WA norms do not commonly enable one to study the association meaning of a word at the individual level, since they contain aggregated data (at the level of the stimulus word or, less often, at the level of the respondents' group characteristics, mostly demographic).

Obviously, in order to study individual differences in the associative meaning of a word, WA norms of a new type are needed. In this paper, we provide a description of a new type of the dataset we have created which is designed especially for studying individual associative behavior. It contains non-aggregated (i.e., individual) responses accompanied with anonymized data about each participant (gender, age, psychological testing results); the results of linguistic annotation of cue – associate pairs over relation types (more than 22,000 cue – associate pairs were annotated manually); reaction time (RT) data collected using a special software for recording keystroke behavior; the data on the semantic similarity of the cue word and associates according to two language models. In addition to describing the dataset, we present the results of cluster analysis which showed the existence of the respondents' preferences for certain types of association responses.

As far as we know, our dataset is unique with respect to the range of data about WA it provides and numbers of annotated cue – associate pairs (we are aware of only one publicly available dataset which contains such type of annotation for English data [Chunhua et al., 2022]). Our dataset is freely available at https://github.com/Litvinova1984/word_association_dataset.

2 Word Association: Methods of Analysis

According to the literature analysis, it is possible to distinguish between two analytical approaches to processing WA data. The first approach is associated with the analysis of the level of stereotypicality of responses, i.e., with assessing the degree of proximity of responses to a certain reference dataset. The second approach involves the analysis of the cue – associate relationship. There are a few studies combining both approaches.

The choice of the methodology depends on the research question and the theoretical foundations of the study. For example, the first approach is frequently used in works related to cognitive and psychiatric disorders diagnostics with WA analysis. In recent years, a lot of attention has also been paid to the analysis of the influence of the level of creativity on the nature of associates (see, e.g., [Heinen and Johnson, 2018]). In this line of research degree of unusualness of associates is measured by calculating the semantic distance between associates and cue words expressed as cosine distance between their corresponding vectors in language models.

The study of associates via analysis of cue – associate relation types is used for identifying the differences in the "normal" WA related to age, speaking one or another language as a native/non-native one, etc. [McRae et al., 2012, Minto-García et al., 2020]. It should be noted that there is no generally accepted classification of such relations. Most are based on the Saussurian division of relations into syntagmatic (pairs of words occurring together in texts) and paradigmatic ones (members of a pair can be interchangeable in a sentence and belong to the same part of speech).

Later, in addition to these two categories, the third one was identified, i.e., associations by form (usually by sound). As a justification for distinguishing between these categories, their different nature is indicated: meaning-based responses are derived from semantic memory, position-based associations from the co-occurrence-based system, and form-based responses result from activation of phonological and orthographic knowledge.

Such a generalized classification has been used in a large number of studies, however, in the works [Fitzpatrick, 2007; Higginbotham, 2010] it was convincingly shown that it is, firstly, insufficiently detailed, and secondly, in many cases it is impossible to assign a associate to one of the categories. Fitzpatrick [Fitzpatrick, 2007] set forth a more fine-grained classification where there three categories were divided into 9 subcategories. This classification, in exact accordance or with various modifications, is used in most modern studies. However, the annotation process, as a rule, is not described in detail. The sufficiency of the separation of responses underlying the proposed classification also raises questions. E.g., in the work of Minto-García [Minto-García et al., 2020] it was shown that their classification which includes 17 types of lexical relations integrated into three groups – semantic, contextual, and morpho-phonological – better fits WA data in comparison to the traditional one which we described above.

Chunhua et al. [Chunhua et al., 2022] proposed a wide range of cue – associate relation types and attempted to formalize the annotation process by providing explanations for the associations which resulted in WAX dataset which is by now the only publicly available dataset with cue – associate relation annotation (besides the dataset we introduce in this paper).

There are a few studies proposing combining the analysis of associative data with other types of data, in particular, reaction time (RT), i.e., the duration of pauses between stimulus and response. This area of research has a long history [Wallenhorst, 1965], a number of interesting results have been obtained (e.g., that paradigmatic responses showed longer RT than syntagmatic ones, and that RT are also influenced the type of a relation between cue and associate [Minto-García et al., 2020]), however, the absence of any sustained effort to collect WA RT makes it impossible to compare WA data against the numerous other paradigms for which large-scale RT databases already exist [Singh, 2017].

Researchers are currently attempting to create large-scale databases of WA (see, for example, ongoing multilingual project Small World of Words [De Deyne et al., 2018]). However, the disadvantage of the existing databases is the absence or a small number of types of additional information - both about the respondents and WA. At the same time, "until more is known about how different variables affect WA behavior, researchers should be cautious about using independently gathered norm data as the reference point that many of these papers report strikingly little methodological detail" [Fitzpatrick et al., 2015, p. 32].

3 RuPersWordAssociation: Structure and Linguistic Annotation

3.1 Experiment Description

Stimuli selected for RuPersWordAssociation are 50 words that are important for the Russian picture of the world (for more details on cue word selection see [Litvinova and Panicheva, 2024]). The survey questionnaire contained 50 cue words, 10 of them were presented twice in random order to test the stability of the associative meaning of the word, 17 stimuli were presented both in verbal form and in the form of corresponding images.

Thus, each participant in the first stage of experiment had to produce 77 (50 verbal stimuli + 10 repeated verbal stimuli + 17 visual stimuli) associative series. 49 people took part in the first stage of experiment (of which 42 were women, the age of the participants was 17–25 years old). Our participants are students of Russian universities (Voronezh, Perm, St. Petersburg), native speakers of Russian. The information about the experiment was distributed on social networks. Those wishing to take part in the experiment received a link to the questionnaire and completed the task on their personal electronic devices.

The experiment took place in three stages: all the respondents took part in the first stage; the tasks were completed in one day. The second stage involved the participation of 10 respondents from the initial sample (selected randomly) and the implementation of the experiment on different five days, while on each day a respondent produced associates to no more than 10 stimuli from initial list, also on personal devices. The third stage involved giving responses to the same stimuli (50) orally, by the same 10 respondents as in the second stage of the experiment. It was carried out in one day, and the answers were also recorded.

During the first and second stages, file logs were also obtained making it possible to study the respondents' keyboard behavior during the production of associates.

The participants in the experiment were asked to produce five written associates to each cue word in their native language. This method of conducting association experiment is called extended word association test. Its main difference from a free experiment is that it provides access not to verbal networks, but to deep structures of knowledge (human long-term memory) and triggers the processes of natural semiosis (meaning generation) in accordance with the norms and rules of national culture (see [Litvinova and Panicheva, 2024] for more details). We limited the number of responses as research on retrieval inhibition in memory has shown that when people have to produce subsequent associate to the same cue, additional associates become hindered by a retrieval blockage [e.g., Raaijmakers and Shiffrin, 1981], and a limited number of associations per participant can minimize this influence. Diversity of stimuli also helps to reduce retrieval inhibition.

3.2 Database Metadata

Linguistic Annotation of Word Association Data. The first stage of the analysis involved three annotators—certified linguists. Before annotation, all the participants' responses were anonymized to ensure that the coder (annotator) was not subconsciously imposing a response profile on the participants' responses. This anonymized spreadsheet (not the questionnaire itself) was used to code the responses.

The annotators worked independently of each other. At the first stage of annotation process, it was proposed for the annotators to use the methodology outlined in [Chunhua et al., 2022], namely, to formulate a sentence with possible explanation for the reason of association and choose one of the most suitable types of relations from the predefined list based on the classifications proposed in recent papers [Minto-Garcia et al., 2020; Chunhua et al. 2022, etc.]. In this way, 500 associative series were annotated. However, when considering the annotation results, disagreement between annotators were observed. At the same time, for some types of relations (primarily paradigmatic ones) a significant annotator agreement was achieved as early as at this stage.

Therefore, at the second stage, speech formulas were created that simplify and clarify the process of assigning a particular associate response to the certain type. These speech formulas were created by annotators based on the results of the first stage of analysis. After that, annotator agreement reached 90.1%. In the case of disagreement, it was decided to provide two (rarely – three) possible cue – associate types (there are about 10% of such cases in our data).

Our final classification consists of 3 broad categories with following subcategories:

1. Formal-based responses (similarity of cue words and associates is based on the form): 1.1. Phonological responses (**PHON**); 1.2. Morphological responses (**MORPH**).

2. Meaning-based responses.

2.1. Language-based: 2.1.1. Syntagmatic (predicative **PRED**, attributive **CHAR**, objective **OBJ**, adverbial **ADV** responses) (syntagmatic responses, namely **CHAR** and **OBJ**, were further divided into two types – *DIR* (syntactically correct) and *IND* (cue word and associates constitute phrase but not grammatically correct); 2.1.2. Paradigmatic (synonymy **SIMIL**, hyponyms **HYP**, antonyms **ANT**) (in all cases cue word and associates are of the same part of speech).

2.2. World-knowledge based (THEMATIC): 2.2.1. **FRAME** (cue word and associates are the components of the same situation); 2.2.2. **CAUSE** (cause - effect relationships between cue word and responses); 2.2.3. **FUNC** (Functional connection between cue word and responses); 2.2.4. **MENTAL** (response contains a reference to some mental category related to a stimulus); 2.2.5. **AFFECT** (responses are attitudes to the concept denoted by cue word); 2.2.6. **SPECIFIC** (cue word and responses are contextual synonyms or responses illustrate a cue word); 2.2.7. **PRECED** (precedents, i.e., allusions to literature, art).

3. Individual responses (**INDIV**) (none of the annotators could explain or classify cue – associate pair as any type of the relationships).

A table with examples of WA for each type, appropriate speech formulas and description of relation types is available on project github page.

Data on Participants. Our dataset contains two types of metadata in relation to the respondents' characteristics, i.e., the data on their emotional state at the time of the experiment and the data on their personality traits.

Specific test options were selected following a consultation with a psychologist. Testing was carried out online, using the links provided to the participants.

One of the most influential theoretical models of human personality, "The Big Five," was used as the foundation for establishing the respondents' characteristics. This model is the most frequently used in modern works devoted to the psychological profiling of the author of a text and, more broadly, to the problem of reflecting their psychological characteristics in a text (see [Azucar et al., 2018] for review). We, however, are not aware of any work where the above model was applied to the analysis of WA.

In order to study the respondents' emotional state, Differential Emotions Scale test was used.

Testing using the Big Five questionnaire was carried out once, and testing using the Differential Emotions Scale was performed by participants each time before filling out the questionnaire.

Additional Data on Word Association. Our dataset is the first one in the Russian psycholinguistics and one of the few resources containing data on the respondents' reaction time besides associate responses per se. The respondents' keyboarding behavior was recorded using a software that the respondents had installed on their electronic devices. The software produces tsv/log files which contain complete information about how a person types a text, but at the character level. Next, using set of heuristics, we extracted the values of a respondent's reaction time, which is understood as the duration of the pause between the end of the cue word (or the previous associate) and the beginning of the first associate (or subsequent associates).

Since the transition to working with a new cue word was usually indicated by a line break symbol, the following approach was used as the main heuristic for calculating pause time: the pause times of the Shift symbol after the last letter of the cue word or response, a comma (colon), a space and the first letter of the next word were summed up. Of course, such a heuristic is not the only one possible, and in the future, it is possible to supplement the dataset with new types of the parameters related to reaction time.

For the cases where it was impossible to assign a certain value, the NA tag was used. Firstly, the users did not sometimes work with some stimuli (which is reflected in both the log file and the final dataset). Secondly, there have been cases when the log file does not contain information about associated words, but the responses to the stimuli are present in the final doc file. The NA tag was introduced, e.g., for those notations where the response tokens in the log file did not correspond to those in the final document. The users' keyboard behavior could also indicate that the user copied the previously entered associations. In this case, the NA tag was also assigned.

In the second stage of experiment, which involved 10 respondents and took place on 5 different days, which were approximately 7 to 14 days apart, 10 stimuli were assessed per day. NA tags were placed according to the same principle as described above.

The third stage of the experiment involved a change in the mode from typing responses to an oral interview when participants produced associates to the same cue word as in the first stage. The information about the exact time between pauses is not available in the current version of the dataset, but in the future, we are going to expand the dataset by transcribing spoken texts with time annotation.

The final stage of annotation of the dataset involved the processing data using the udpipe R package to obtain lemmas for cue words and associates, as well as their morphological tags from the Universal Dependencies tag set. Also, two measures of cosine similarity between cue word and response were calculated using two different types of language models – static word2vec (https://ruwikiruscorpora_upos_cbow_300_10_2021) and the contextualized RoBERTa (https://huggingface.co/symanto/sn-xlm-roberta-base-snli-mnli-anli-xnli). Lemmas for the stimuli represented by images were not assigned, and cosine distance measures were not calculated.

If the user provided an associate in the form of a lexical construction (e.g., ADJ_NOUN), all the elements of the construction were subject to lemmatization.

The summary statistics of the dataset is provided in (Table 1).

Table 1. Summary statistics of the dataset.

Stage of experiment	Number of respondents	Number of association series	Number of annotated cue – associate word pairs	Semantic similarity data	Reaction time
1	50	3773	18143	Yes	Yes
2	10	500	2500	Yes	Yes
3	10	500	2004	Yes	No

Overall, 22647 cue – associate pairs were annotated. Distribution of relation types is presented in Fig. 1S (https://github.com/Litvinova1984/word_association_dataset). Kruskal-Wallis rank sum test has shown the connection between RT and relation types ($p = 0.0001765$, Kruskal-Wallis chi-squared = 32.302, df = 9). Wilcoxon signed-rank test with Bonferroni-Holm correction shown the differences in RTs between following relation types (smaller values of RT are highlighted in bold): **MENTAL** and CHARDIR ($p = 0.016$), **MENTAL** and OBJIND ($p = 0.016$), **FRAME** and OBJIND ($p = 0.016$), **FRAME** and PRECED ($p = 0.040$), **FRAME** and SIMIL ($p = 0.020$), **MENTAL** and SIMIL ($p = 0.016$), **MENTAL** and PRECED ($p = 0.026$).

Kruskal-Wallis rank sum test revealed the connection between RT (from top-10 most frequent ones) and cosine similarity from both word2vec (Kruskal-Wallis chi-squared = 1328.6, df = 9, $p < 2.2e-16$) and RoBERTa language models (Kruskal-Wallis chi-squared = 2937.7, df = 9, $p < 2.2e-16$). Differences were found for most of the pairs except for CAUSE and FUNC, FUNC and FRAME, FRAME and CAUSE. The highest values of semantic similarity (over both models) were observed for the following relation types: SIMIL (1st), CAUSE, FUNC and FRAME (2nd), SPECIFIC (3rd), the lowest – for CHARDIR.

4 Analysis of Individual Association Behavior

4.1 Data Preparation

Using the developed dataset, we conducted a series of experiments aimed at establishing the limits of variation in the frequency of types of cue – associate relations in individual level, using a set of methods of multidimensional data analysis: the method of principal components, simultaneous clustering of features (frequencies of relation types) and participants.

We worked with the results of stage 1 of the experiment to make each participant contribution equal. We also analyzed only the responses to the verbal stimuli. We excluded the participants whose log files and typed files have some discrepancies and the respondents with only one response. The resulting dataset consists of 2640 association series. After removing the series with NA (RT or cosine values), we obtained 2577 association series with appropriate metadata. In resulting dataset, each participant (44) was presented in average with 60 association series (sd = 2.82).

First, we presented each association series as a text consisting of relation type labels, e.g. CHARDIR CHARDIR FRAME CHARDIR FRAME, while cue word, respondent ID and metadata were considered as docvars for further processing of the resulting corpus with R package quanteda [Benoit et al., 2018]. Using dfm function of this package, we obtained representation of each association series in the form of a vector of the features – frequencies of each relation type (aka bag-of-words approach).

As a result, a document-feature matrix of 2577 documents and 187 features (98.43% sparse) was obtained. Further, we removed the features based on their absolute cumulative frequency in the dataset. As a minimum threshold, we set this value to 100, which resulted in 16 features, i.e., relation types. This feature space was supplied to further analysis.

4.2 Clustering Individuals with Similar Association Preferences

First, we constructed plot describing distributions of relation types over respondents (Fig. 2S, https://github.com/Litvinova1984/word_association_dataset). As this figure clearly shows, the range of individual variation varies among relation types. To further analyze variation in dataset, we also calculated the coefficient of variation, which reflects the variability in preferences for certain types of relationships among different participants. Next, we calculated the same coefficient of variation, but this time for cue words. The result of comparing the calculated coefficients of variation in the frequency of the relation types by the stimuli and the participants is presented in Fig. 2S (https://github.com/Litvinova1984/word_association_dataset). According to Fig. 2S, variation among the word types is larger than the one among the respondents. It is well-known that some word properties (e.g., a grammatical class) impact the proportion of syntagmatic to paradigmatic responses. For example, Deese [Deese, 1962] found that nouns elicit syntagmatic responses in only around 21% of the responses; verbs and adjectives in around 50% of the responses, and adverbs in around 73%. This fact should be taken into account in the process of selection of cue words.

Further analysis (Fig. 3S-4S, https://github.com/Litvinova1984/word_association_dataset) shows that limits of individual variations vary widely across different relation types.

Next, we inspected the hidden structure of our data via principal component analysis (PCA). The frequencies of the responses of certain types in association series were used as features which were centered and scaled prior PCA.

From the numerical output (not shown here), we observe that the first two principal components explain 24.58% of the total variance, and the first three principal components explain 54.23% of the total variance.

Based on the preliminary analysis, we run a PCA with 4 components.

Correlation circle plot (Fig. 5S, https://github.com/Litvinova1984/word_association_dataset) indicates the contribution of each variable to each component, as well as the correlation between variables (indicated by a 'cluster' of variables). The largest contribution to the first component is made by the variables OBJDIR (−0.43), ADC (−0.42), CHARDIR (−0.41), PREDDIR (−0.30) (syntagmatic relations cluster) and FRAME (0.29), OBJIND (0.25), FUNC (0.24) (another cluster). The following variables have the largest contribution to the second component: CAUSE (−0.4), SIMIL (−0.36), SPECIFIC (−0.337), from one side, and PRECED (0.38), FRAME (0.35), CHARIND (0.347) from the other.

We used Ward's clustering algorithm with Euclidean distances for simultaneous clustering of the features and participants and visualized the proposed solution as heatmap (Fig. 1).

We can see that participants are clustered according to their preference of certain relation types. For examples, a cluster of participants which prefer syntagmatic relations (CHARDIR, ADC, OBJDIR, PREDIR) is clearly revealed (at the left) in contrast to the cluster of participants which prefer relation types from THEMATIC group – CAUSE, SIMIL, SPECIFIC, MENTAL (at the center) as well as relations from different subgroups (FRAME, OBJIND, CHARIND, FUNC) (to the right). Small cluster of individuals with preference to PRECED and INDIVIDUAL associations is observed.

It should be noted that statistical test did not reveal any association between cluster membership of the participants and their emotional and psychological traits. We hypothesize that individual preference for certain types of WA comes from the differences in linguistic experiences as well as in the manners in which our respondents process language (e.g., in the extent to which they make use of different types of visual and verbal information when processing language [Blajenkova and Kozhevnikov, 2009]).

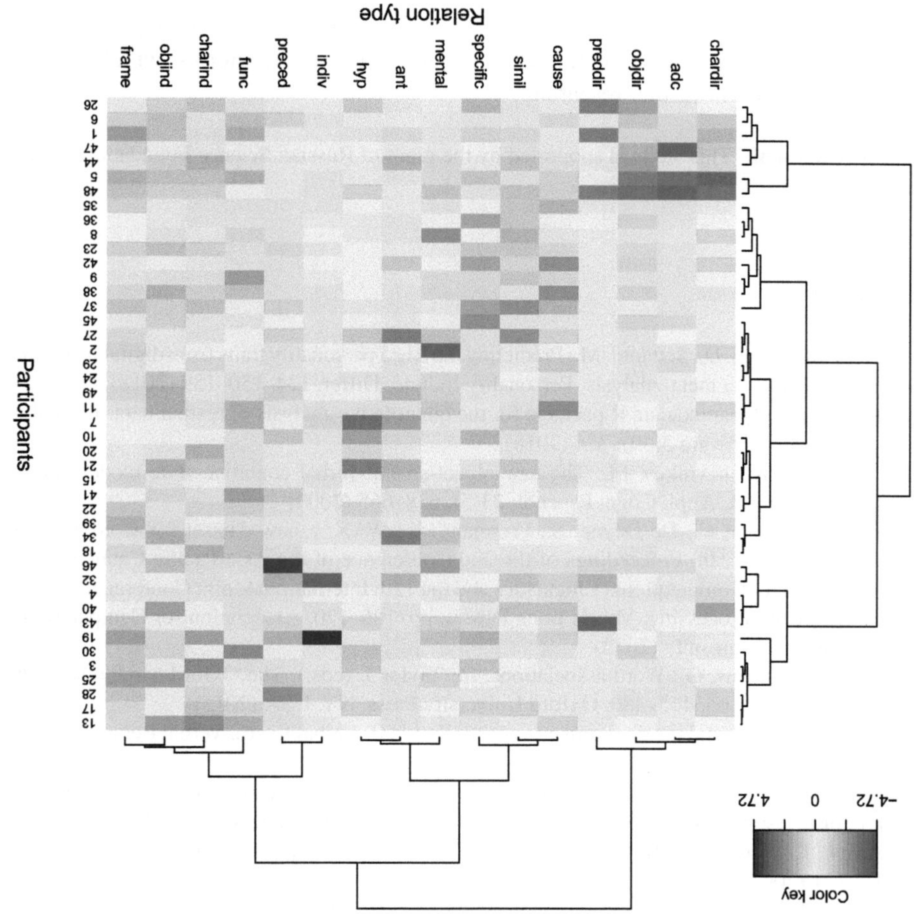

Fig. 1. Clustering features and participants

5 Conclusions

Despite the long history of using word associations to solve a variety of problems, both theoretical and practical, a lot of issues related to WA remain unresolved. In particular, the assumption of homogeneity of "normative" associative responses, most studies using WA methodology are based on, needs to be revisited. In order to address this problem, appropriate datasets are necessary containing the associates on individual level and supplied with metadata about participants characteristics, as well as behavioral correlates of responses (e.g., reaction times). The first dataset of this type presented in this paper also contains linguistic annotation on the types of the cue – associate relations according to a developed classification scheme.

Using the presented dataset, the associations have been established between the identified types of the relations, reaction times and semantic distance measures.

Based on the developed dataset, we showed the presence of individual profiles in associative behavior confirming the heterogeneity in associative norms, which must be taken into account in further research.

Acknowledgment. This study is supported by the grant of Russian Science Foundation no: 21-78-10148.

References

Azucar, D., Marengo, D., Settanni, M.: Predicting the Big 5 personality traits from digital footprints on social media: a meta-analysis. Personality Individ. Differ. **124**, 150–159 (2018)

Benoit, K., et al.: Quanteda: an R package for the quantitative analysis of textual data. Journal of Open Source Software **3**(30), 774 (2018)

Blajenkova, O., Kozhevnikov, M.: The new object-spatial-verbal cognitive style model: theory and measurement. Appl. Cogn. Psychol. **23**(5), 638–665 (2009)

Chunhua, L., Trevor, C., De Deyne, S., Frermann, L.: WAX: a new dataset for word association explanations. In: Proceedings of the 2nd Conference of the Asia-Pacific Chapter of the Association for Computational Linguistics and the 12th International Joint Conference on Natural Language Processing, Vol. 1: Long Papers, pp. 106–120. Association for Computational Linguistics, Online only (2022)

De Deyne, S., Storms, G.: Word associations. In: Taylor J. (eds.), The Oxford handbook of the word, Chapt. 26, pp. 465–480. Oxford University Press, NY, USA (2015)

Deese, J.: Form class and the determinants of association. J. Verbal Learn. Verbal Behav. **1**, 79–84 (1962)

Fitzpatrick, T., Playfoot, D., Wray, A., Wright, M.J.: Establishing the reliability of word association data for investigating individual and group differences. Appl. Linguis. **36**(1), 23–50 (2015)

Fitzpatrick, T.: Word association patterns: unpacking the assumptions. Int. J. Appl. Linguist. **17**(3), 319–331 (2007)

Fitzpatrick, T.: Word association profiles in a first and second language: Puzzles and problems. In: Fitzpatrick, T., Barfield, A. (eds.) Lexical Processing in Second Language Learners: Papers and Perspectives in Honour of Paul Meara, pp. 38–52. Multilingual Matters, Bristol (2009)

Heinen, D.J.P., Johnson, D.R.: Semantic distance: an automated measure of creativity that is novel and appropriate. Psychol. Aesthet. Creat. Arts **12**(2), 144–156 (2018)

Higginbotham, G.: Individual learner profiles from word association tests: The effect of word frequency. System **38**(3), 379–390 (2010)

Litvinova, T.A., Zavarzina, V.A., Kotlyarova, E.S., Lyubova, S.G.: Mapping the field of word association research using text mining approach. In: Proceedings of the 2023 5th International Conference on Information Technology and Computer Communications (ITCC '23), pp. 90–98. Association for Computing Machinery, NY, USA (2023)

Litvinova, T., Panicheva, P.: Individual differences in the associative meaning of a word through the lens of the language model and semantic differential. Res. Result. Theoret. Appl. Linguist. **10**(1), 61–93 (2024)

McRae, K., Khalkhali, S., Hare, M.: Semantic and associative relations in adolescents and young adults: Examining a tenuous dichotomy. In: Reyna, V.F., Chapman, S.B., Dougherty, M.R., Confrey, J. (eds.) The adolescent brain: Learning, reasoning, and decision making, pp. 39–66. American Psychological Association, Washington, DC (2012)

Minto-García, A., Arias-Trejo, N., Vargas-García, E.M.: Lexical relations in Spanish-speaking older adults. J. Psycholinguist. Res. **49**(4), 663–716 (2020)

Raaijmakers, J.G.W., Shiffrin, R.M.: Search of associative memory. Psychol. Rev. **88**, 93–134 (1981)

Singh, S.: The diagnostic utility of Kent-Rosanoff word association test in relation to response entropy. Int. J. Indian Psychol. **5**(1), 1–20 (2017)

Wallenhorst, R.: Some relations between reaction time and choice of response in word association. Psychol. Rep. **17**(2), 619–626 (1965)

Acceptability vs. Probability: Modeling Agreement Variation with ruBERT

Kseniia Studenikina(✉)

Lomonosov Moscow State University, Moscow 119991, Russia
xeanst@gmail.com

Abstract. The correlation between acceptability and probability of a sentence is an important issue both for theoretical and computational linguistics. Previous studies on this topic compared acceptability judgments and probability scores based on the unambiguous linguistic phenomena. The fact whether language model can predict possible agreement variation has been ignored. This study presents an experiment of modeling agreement variation with probability metrics. The predicate agreement with the coordinated subject in Russian was observed. We compared the acceptability judgments passed by the language speakers and the probability metrics predicted by the language model ruBERT-base without fine-tuning. We analyzed in detail which syntactic, morphological and semantic factors influence the acceptability and the probability of the sentences. The results show that the BERT language model fails to predict the agreement strategy given the variation. The subject-predicate order turns out to be the only factor which equally influences the acceptability and the probability of the sentence. Thus, the language model without fine-tuning cannot be used to parametrize predicate agreement with the coordinated subject. The sentence acceptability is based on the subtle linguistic contrasts which are not significant for the computer evaluation of its probability.

Keywords: acceptability judgments · sentence probability · language model · agreement variation · experimental syntax · Russian

1 Introduction

The ability to estimate grammatical correctness of the sentence in native language is considered a key property of the human language faculty. The grammaticality refers to the intuitive judgments based on the innate biological component – Universal Grammar. Besides the grammatical correctness, the general acceptability of the utterance is determined by the usage-based factors such as the word frequency, the sentence length, the capacity of the speaker's working memory. A common method to gather information about the utterance acceptability is called an acceptability judgment task. The acceptability judgments demonstrate to which extent the sentence seems natural to a speaker. They act as a reliable empirical data to motivate a linguistic theory and to model the human language faculty.

M. Bakaev et al. (Eds.): IMS 2024, CCIS 2534, pp. 70–84, 2026.
https://doi.org/10.1007/978-3-031-96177-9_7

Acceptability judgments are of interest for both classical binary and probabilistic theories of grammaticality. They are gradient in nature and cannot be directly accommodated in a binary formal grammar. The important question is whether the sentence acceptability can be simply reduced to its probability which is widely studied by the natural language processing.

The probability of the word sequence may be predicted by a language model. This algorithm is trained on the unlabeled text data which can be mono- or multilingual. The model analyzes which words appear together more frequently and in which order they show up. The larger and the more diverse the training set, the more complex dependencies the algorithm captures and reproduces on a new data. The first language models were purely statistical and were based on the *n*-grams frequency. To prevent a zero probability being assigned to unseen words, additional operations like smoothing were carried out. With the spread of the machine learning the language models based on the recurrent neural networks and the Transformer models have increased in popularity.

This paper presents a comparison of the acceptability judgments passed by Russian speakers and the probability metrics predicted by the language model ruBERT. The results of the syntactic experiments dealing with the predicate agreement with the coordinated subject were used. The analysis of this construction allows us to reveal the syntactic, morphological, and semantic factors which influence the choice of the probe features given more than one goal. If there is a correlation between the acceptability scores and the probability values, then these factors are also relevant for the neural models. We aim to figure out whether the language models trained on the data without the explicit grammatical information are able to acquire subtle linguistic contrasts which are important for parametrizing agreement variation.

The paper is structured as follows. The Sect. 2 reviews previous research on the acceptability and the probability of the sentences as well as on the issue of the agreement variation. The Sect. 3 presents our experiment including the data (3.1), the method (3.2) and the results (3.3). The Sect. 4 concludes.

2 Related Work

Establishing a correspondence between the acceptability and the probability of an utterance is a fundamental issue. The relation between these concepts has already been referred in the early N. Chomsky's studies [1]. He claimed that the sentences (1a) and (1b) have equally low probability since they are impossible to appear in English speech. Although both utterances are meaningless, the example (1a) is grammatically correct (in contrast to (1b)) which make (1a) more acceptable. The Chomsky's claim has been refuted by F. Pereira [2]. He suggested applying an aggregate bigram model which is useful for modeling word sequences that include unseen bigrams. As a result, the probability of (1a) is several times higher than the probability of (1b), which is shown in (2).

(1) a. Colorless green ideas sleep furiously.
b. Furiously sleep ideas green colorless.

(2) $$\frac{P(\textit{Colorless green ideas sleep furiously.})}{P(\textit{Furiously sleep ideas green colorless.})} \approx 2 \times 10^5$$ [2: 7]

More detailed research on the relation between the acceptability and the probability were presented much later [3, 4]. These studies applied an *n*-gram language model and a recurrent neural network to predict probability of English sentences. J. H. Lau, A. Clark and S. Lappin [3] selected 500 sentences from the British National Corpus and automatically translated them to four other languages and then back to English in order to generate unacceptable examples. The Pearson coefficient revealed the significant correlation between the obtained values and the human acceptability scores. Although the sentences gathered by the round-trip machine translation demonstrate diverse levels of acceptability, they do not show grammatical oppositions of the kind traditionally examined by syntacticians. That is why J. Sprouse and his colleagues [4] collected another 3 datasets for their study. The first one includes the examples from the journal "Linguistic Inquiry". The second sample consists of the sentences from D. Adger's textbook on syntax [5]. The word permutation in the example (1) resulted in 120 sentences which makes up the third set. The study shows that the language models fail to capture up to 35% of the phenomena that are accounted for in modern generative theory. The probability values demonstrate a substantial loss in coverage of phenomena that can be revealed by the acceptability judgment task.

An important drawback of these studies [3, 4] is that they did not precisely analyze the acceptability of which linguistic phenomena is predicted better by the language models and whether the same factors are relevant for the humans and the machines. The targeted syntactic evaluation was conducted using the Benchmark of Linguistic Minimal Pairs (BLiMP) [6]. The dataset covered 67 linguistic phenomena in English. An *n*-gram language model, a recurrent neural network and a Transformer model GPT-2 predicted which sentence in a minimal pair is more acceptable (3). Last model performs the best. The morphological contrasts including agreement are identified better while more subtle semantic and syntactic phenomena, e.g. negative polarity items, ellipsis and wh-movement, turn out to be more complicated for the models.

(3) a. The cats annoy Tim. (acceptable)
b. *The cats annoys Tim. (unacceptable) [6: 377]

Thus, the choice of more acceptable example for the simple cases like the subject-verb agreement is successfully resolved by the probability values. However, the language models perform poorly given the long-distance dependencies. It is important to note that the sentences with mistakes in the predicate agreement and the wh-movement differ not only in linguistic phenomenon but also in the complexity of the syntactic structure. Our central question is whether the language model may predict the choice of the subject-verb agreement strategy if the feature implication is ambiguous and the agreement variation arises.

The operations Agree and Merge are basic operation for syntactic derivation [7]. In a standard case of Agree application, the probe features are unambiguously calculated given the goal features, namely person, number and gender features. The agreement variation takes place when there are several potential controllers and there is more than one way to calculate the probe features. For example, the goal agreeing with the conjoined expressions may copy the feature of the closest conjunct or calculate it from the features of both conjuncts according to the resolution rules. With coordinated singular nouns, the attributive agreement must be singular (4) while the predicate one can be either singular or plural (5) [8].

(4) this/ *these frost and freezing fog
(5) Frost and freezing fog has/ have affected most of the country today. [8: 207]

The modeling of the agreement variation is supposed to be influenced by different factors. The most effective method to examine their influence is to rely on the data obtained from the experimental studies. It provides a researcher with negative linguistic material and allow to develop techniques for assessing the native speakers' judgments. The quantitative measurements enable to reveal the factors favoring the choice of one agreement strategy over the others. The recent years have seen a pronounced tendency to use methods of experimental syntax in research on agreement variability on the material of Slovenian [9], Serbo-Croatian [10], French [11] and German [12]. At the moment, the variable agreement in Russian is being widely investigated by the researchers from the Moscow Experimental Syntax Group[1] (MESG). They examine grammatical phenomena using experimental methods and explicitly model them within formally oriented syntactic and semantic frameworks. The methodological issues of modeling agreement variation in Russian were presented by the lead researchers of the group E. Lyutikova and A. Gerasimova [13].

The experimental studies conducted by the members of the MESG provide a reliable empirical data which can be used to analyze the correlation between the acceptability and the probability. All the experiments use the same method for the acceptability judgment task, i.e. 7-point Likert scale [14] which is the most statistically powerful one according to the research of J. Sprouse, C.T. Schütze and D. Almeida [15]. The analysis of variance of the acceptability scores allows to estimate the role of each factor as well as their interaction. Pairwise comparisons demonstrate whether the acceptability of the experimental conditions significantly differs. Similar statistical tests can be applied to the probability values. If the contrasts in acceptability are also revealed for the probability the language model should be recognized to succeed in predicting the correct agreement strategy. The next section describes the experiment of comparing the acceptability scores and the probability values based on the agreement variation in Russian.

3 Experiment

The section is structured as follows. The part 3.1. Describes the data collection procedure and the phenomena considered in the experiment. In the part 3.2, we explain the choice of the language model and the observed probability metrics. The part 3.3. Includes the results of the experiment and their discussion.

3.1 Data

The language phenomenon chosen for the automatic modeling is the predicate agreement with the coordinated subject. It enables to analyze the influence of various syntactic, morphological and semantic factors on the variation. The large amount of the acceptability

[1] https://expsynt.com/.

judgment data for this construction was obtained by the researchers of the MESG and can be used for predicting the probability values with the language models.

The predicate agreeing with the coordinated subject may calculate its features according to resolution rules or copy them from the closest conjunct [16]. Previous descriptive studies [17, 18] and prescriptive grammars [19, 20] revealed factors which influence the choice of the predicate agreement strategy with the coordinated subject. The experimental studies of MESG tested these factors in order to quantitatively estimate their effect.

The most important factor which is claimed to determine the agreement strategy is the subject-verb linear order. The direct order (SV) should mostly allow the resolution agreement. Given two conjoined singular nouns, the verb is supposed to obtain the plural number feature which is calculated as a sum of the nouns' number features (6). If the subject consists of two pronouns of different person, the predicate should commonly choose the person feature of the conjunct which is higher on the personal hierarchy: 1 > 2 > 3 [21]. Apart from that, the agreement in 3rd person feature may occurs given the 1st and the 2nd person pronouns. Both normative (2PL) and default (3PL) strategies are shown in the example (7). The reverse order (VS) is supposed to increase the possibility of the closest conjunct agreement. Thus, the singular agreement with the coordinated nouns should be acceptable for the verb in preposition (8). If the pronouns are coordinated in subject position and follow the predicate, it may copy the number and the person feature of the closest conjunct. The example (9) demonstrates the possible agreement variants for the 1st and the 2nd person pronouns, the example (10) includes the 1st person pronoun and the 3rd person proper name.

(6) Topol'	i	yasen'	**ros-li/ *ros**	v parke
poplar.M.SG	and	ash.M.SG	grew-**PL**/ grew.**SG**	in park

'A poplar and an ash grew in the park.'

(7) Ya	i	ty	**chin-im/**	**chin-yat/**	***chin-iš/**	***chin-yu**	shkaf
I.1SG	and	you.2SG	fix-**1PL**	fix-**3PL**	fix-**2SG**	fix-**1SG**	locker

'You and I are fixing the locker.'

(8) V	parke	**ros-li/**	**ros**	topol'	i	yasen'
in	park	grew-**PL**/	grew.**SG**	poplar.M.SG	and	ash.M.SG

'In the part, a poplar and an ash grew.'

(9) Shkaf	**chin-im/**	**chin-yat/**	**chin-iš/**	***chin-yu**	ty	i	ya
locker	fix-**1PL**	fix-**3PL**	fix-**2SG**	fix-**1SG**	you.2SG	and	I.1SG

'The locker, I and you are fixing it.'

(10) V	palatke	**sp-im/**	**sp-it/**	***spl-yu**	Vasya	i	ya.
in	tent	sleep.**1PL**	sleep.**3SG**	sleep.**1SG**	Vasja.3SG	and	I.1SG

'In a tent, Vasya and I are sleeping there.'

There are some factors which are postulated to decrease the acceptability of the singular agreement given the VS word order. The first one is morphological: the closest conjunct agreement should be less possible if the noun conjuncts mismatch in gender features (11). The other discussed factors concern the semantic properties of the conjuncts and the predicate. The symmetric interpretation of the predicate is claimed to block its singular agreement (12). If both conjuncts are animate nouns, the singular agreement should also be unacceptable (13).

(11) V	parke	**ros-li/**	***ros**	dub	i	bereza
in	park	grew-PL/	grew.SG	oak.M.SG	and	birch.F.SG

'In the part, a poplar and an ash grew.'

(12) Na	foto	**sliva-yutsya/**	***sliva-etsya**	lico	i	fon
on	photo	merged-PL/	merged-SG	face.SG	and	backdrop.SG

'In the photo, the face and the backdrop merged.'

(13) Na	vstrechu	**poekhal-i/**	***poekhal**	director	i	sekretar'
on	meeting	went-PL/	went-SG	chief	and	secretary

'To the meeting, the director and the secretary went.'

This study aims to reveal whether these factors equally influence the acceptability and the probability of the sentences with the predicate agreement variation. The data of 6 studies presented at the conference "Experimental Studies of Language" in 2022[2]–2023[3] is used. Table 1 demonstrates the conjunct type, the agreement features and the factors observed in these studies. The experiments of D. Vrubel [22], L. Pasko [23] and K. Studenikina [24] deal with the predicate number agreement with the coordinated nouns. D. Belova [25] and T. Davidjuk [26] study the number and the person agreement with the conjuncts including a pronoun. The experiments used 7-point Likert scale for acceptability judgments. From 75 to 126 respondents participated in each study.

Table 1. Design of the experiments which are used in the study.

Conjunct type	Agreement features	Experimental factors	Source
noun	Number	conjuncts' gender match	[22]
noun	Number	predicate symmetry, subject-verb order	[23]
noun	Number	conjuncts animacy, subject-verb order	[24]
pronouns *I*, *you*	number, person	conjuncts order, subject-verb order	[25]
pronoun *I*, noun	number, person	conjuncts order	[26]

Besides stimulus sentences, every experiment includes fillers. They demonstrated unambiguous agreement and are divided in two parts: grammatical fillers are totally correct, ungrammatical fillers have a mistake in agreement (14) or prepositional government (15). The probability values for fillers serve as a baseline. They show whether a language model succeed in acquiring non-variable agreement.

[2] http://tipl.philol.msu.ru/index.php/science/conferences/ExpLing.

[3] http://tipl.philol.msu.ru/index.php/science/conferences/ExpLing-2023.

(14) *Dima	i	Vitya	**ubiraem**		na	kuhne.
Dima	and	Vitja	clean-**2PL**		on	kitchen.

'Dima and Vitya are cleaning the kitchen.'

(15) *Kirill	i	Fedya	ush-li	**po**	kiosk.	
Kirill	and	Fedja	went-pl	for	kiosk	

'*Kirill and Fedya went for the kiosk.'

The experimental results made up a dataset of 1606 sentences (1404 stimuli, 256 fillers). Every sentence has an acceptability score which is calculated as a mean from the participants answers. The dataset includes an experiment author, a sentence text, a sentence score, a sentence type (stimulus or filler); for stimuli – subject type (two nouns, I and you, you and I, I and X, X and I), agreement strategy (singular, plural, 1st person plural, 1st person singular, 2nd person singular, 3rd person singular, 3rd person plural), linear order (SV, VS), a predicate symmetry (symmetrical, nonsymmetrical), a conjuncts animacy (animate, inanimate), a gender match (match, mismatch); for fillers – grammatical correctness (grammatical, ungrammatical). The dataset is available at the link: https://github.com/Xeanst/acceptability_probablitiy_coordination.

The next part takes a detailed look at the language model choice and metrics calculation to estimate the probability of examples from the resulting dataset.

3.2 Method

In recent years, transformer-based models have become the state-of-the-art technology for many tasks in natural language processing. Due to the attention mechanism, they detect subtle ways even distant words in a sentence influence and depend on each other. While Vanilla Transformer [27] is developed for sequence-to-sequence task, its encoder and decoder can be used separately. Unidirectional or generative models based on the transformer decoder include GPT models [28]. Their input is a sequence of previously seen words which are fed to multiple layers of "transformer blocks" in order to predict the target word. We can infer the probability of a sentence s by multiplying the estimated probabilities of each token w_i using previously seen (left) words $w_{<i}$ as context (16). Bidirectional or autoencoder models like BERT [29] are based on the transformer encoder. During its training, a random proportion of input words are masked, and the model is tasked to predict them based on non-masked words. Due to this procedure called masked language modeling, they access to both left $w_{<i}$ and right $w_{>i}$ context words when predicting the target word w_i (17).

$$(16)\ \vec{P}(s) = \prod_{i=0}^{|s|} P(w_i|w_{<i})$$
$$(17)\ \overleftrightarrow{P}(s) = \prod_{i=0}^{|s|} P(w_i|w_{<i}, w_{>i})$$

The study of J.H. Lau and his colleagues [30] examined the correlation between acceptability judgments and probability values of the transformer-based models based on English data. The results show that the bidirectional language model BERT[4] performs better that the unidirectional model GPT-2[5]. The research of acceptability and probability was also carried out in Russian. The unidirectional model ruGPT-3[6] was tested. Firstly, the probability values of ruGPT-3 were used for binary acceptability classification on RuCoLA (Russian Corpus of Linguistic Acceptability) [31]. The model performs almost random with the accuracy 55.79%. Secondly, ruGPT-3 was applied for parametrizing number variation in Russian noun phrases with the coordinated modifiers [32]. The results demonstrate that the probability values are unable to predict the preferable agreement strategy.

Thus, the unidirectional transformer-based models do not manage to adjust human acceptability judgments. Since the model analyze only the left context, a significant part of the information is lost. Specifically, the generative language models are not capable of predicting the probability of the verb form in preposition given the coordinated subject. That is why the bidirectional language model ruBERT[7] is applied in this study.

Sentence probability estimated using bidirectional context is affected by its length since longer sentences have lower probabilities. Instead of the standard language probability, the metrics PenLP (18) was calculated. It applies normalization on sentence length s and scales it with an exponent α to dampen the impact of large values ($\alpha = 0.8$).

$$(18)\ \text{PenLP} = \frac{\log P(s)}{\left(\frac{5+|s|}{5+1}\right)^{\alpha}}$$

The next part analyzes the correlation between PenLP metrics and the acceptability judgments. We will also demonstrate whether this metrics reveals the contrasts in acceptability of the agreement strategies which are relevant to the language speakers.

3.3 Results

In order to estimate the linear dependence between human acceptability judgments and ruBERT probability metrics, the Pearson correlation coefficient was calculated. The gathered dataset includes sentences with variable agreement (stimuli) as well as examples with unambiguous agreement (fillers). Estimating the correlation for these groups separately enables to define whether neural networks are capable of modeling agreement variation. The probability metrics demonstrates higher correlation with acceptability judgments for fillers ($r = 0.58$) than for stimuli ($r = 0.30$). Thus, the language model performs worse in predicting correct strategy given agreement variation.

The experimental studies of predicate agreement with the coordinated subject conducted by MESG examine various factors which may influence the number and the person feature choice. The statistical analysis of the human acceptability judgments estimates the significance of each factor. We will consider whether these factors are also relevant for the ruBERT language model by applying similar statistical analysis to

[4] https://github.com/google-research/bert.

[5] https://github.com/openai/gpt-2.

[6] https://huggingface.co/ai-forever/rugpt3medium_based_on_gpt2.

[7] https://huggingface.co/DeepPavlov/rubert-base-cased.

the probability metrics. The analysis of variance (ANOVA) is used to reveal the factor significance. The pairwise comparison estimates significant differences in acceptability and probability.

Figure 1 demonstrates the mean acceptability judgments (AJ) and the mean probability values (PenLP) for different position of subject and verb. The interaction of factors "verb number" and "subject-verb order" influences significantly the acceptability and the probability ($p < .0001$ for AJ and PenLP). The acceptability and the probability of the singular predicate increase given the VS order ($p < .0001$ for AJ, $p < .01$ for PenLP). The acceptability and the probability of the plural predicate do not depend on the linear position ($p > .05$ for AJ and PenLP). Thus, the subject-verb order determines the choice of the agreement strategy both for human and for the language model.

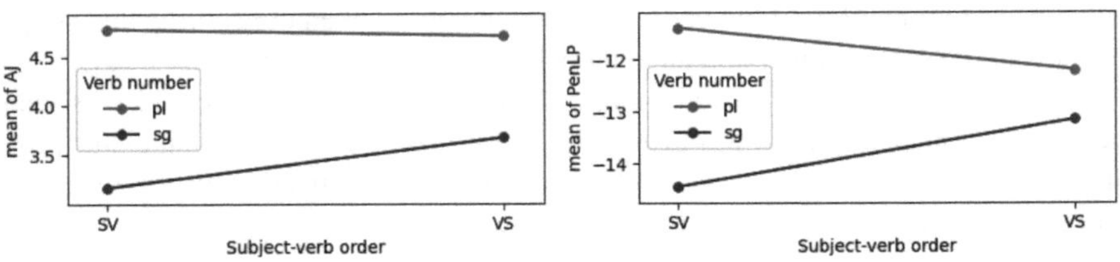

Fig. 1. Mean acceptability judgments and probability scores for different subject-verb order.

Figure 2 presents mean AJ and mean PenLP for conjuncts with gender match and gender mismatch. The interaction of the factors "verb number" and "conjuncts gender" significantly influences the acceptability ($p < .05$ for AJ) but not the probability ($p > .05$ for PenLP). The acceptability of the singular predicate decreases given the conjuncts gender mismatch ($p < .0001$ for AJ) but the probability does not change significantly ($p > .05$ for PenLP). Both the acceptability and the probability of the plural predicate do not depend on the conjuncts gender ($p > .05$ for AJ and PenLP). The results show that the gender of the conjuncts determines the agreement strategy for language speakers but not for the neural model.

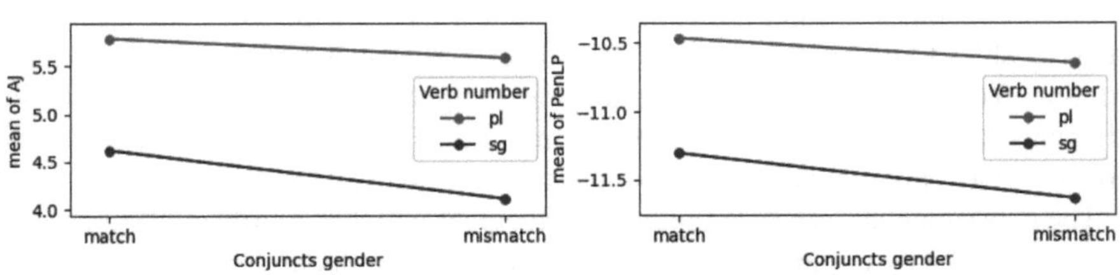

Fig. 2. Mean acceptability judgments and probability scores for conjuncts with gender match and gender mismatch.

Figure 3 demonstrates mean acceptability judgments and the mean probability values for animate and inanimate conjuncts. The interaction of the factors "verb number" and "conjuncts animacy" influences neither acceptability nor probability ($p > .05$ for AJ and PenLP). The conjuncts animacy does not change the acceptability or the probability given the singular predicate (p > .05 for AJ and PenLP) and the plural predicate (p > .05 for AJ and PenLP). Previous descriptive and corpus studies claimed that the possibility of the singular agreement decreases given the animate subject. However, this semantic factor turns out to be unsignificant both for human and for ruBERT.

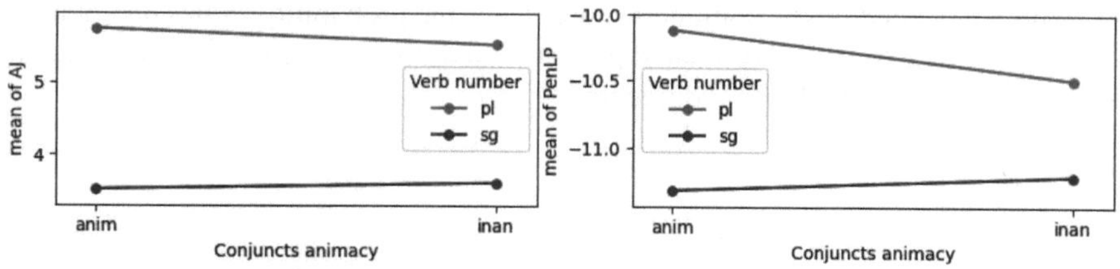

Fig. 3. Mean acceptability judgments and probability scores for animate and inanimate conjuncts.

Figure 4 presents mean AJ and mean PenLP for symmetrical and nonsymmetrical verbs. The interaction of the factors "verb number" and "verb symmetry" influences neither acceptability nor probability (p > .05 for AJ and PenLP). The verb symmetry does not change the acceptability or the probability given the singular predicate (p > .05 for AJ and PenLP) and the plural predicate (p > .05 for AJ and PenLP). The previous studies postulated the impossibility of the singular agreement given the symmetrical predicate. According to our results, this semantic factor does not determine the strategy choice for the language speakers and for the neural model.

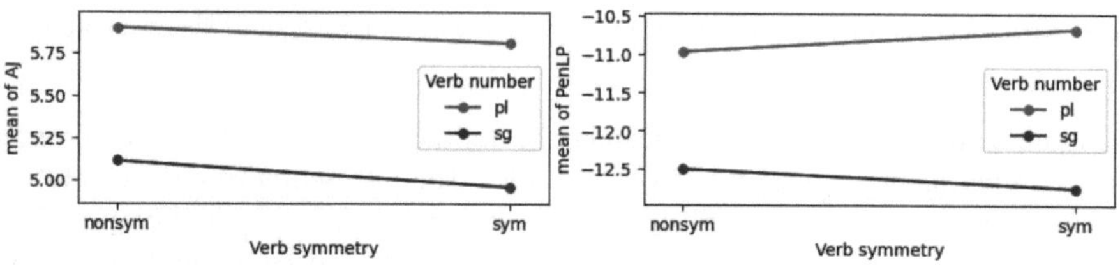

Fig. 4. Mean acceptability judgments and probability scores for symmetrical and nonsymmetrical verbs.

Figure 5 demonstrates mean acceptability judgments and the mean probability values for the coordinated 1st person pronoun *I* and 2nd person pronoun *you*. The interactions of the factors "verb agreement" and "conjuncts order" does not significantly influence the acceptability and the probability given the SV order (p > .05 for AJ and PenLP). If the verb precedes the subject (VS order), the factors interaction has a significant influence the acceptability (p < .0001 for AJ) but not the probability (p > .05 for PenLP). When the verb follows the subject (SV order), there is no significant difference in acceptability or probability between conjuncts order for 1st person plural (normative) agreement (p > .05 for AJ and PenLP), 1st person singular (closest conjunct) agreement (p > .05 for AJ and PenLP), 2nd person singular (closest conjunct) agreement (p > .05 for AJ and PenLP), 3rd person plural (default) agreement (p > .05 for AJ and PenLP). Given the VS order, the acceptability of the closest conjunct agreement increases while the probability does not change. 1st person singular predicate becomes more acceptable for the subject *I and you* ($p < .0001$ for AJ, $p > .05$ for PenLP), 2nd person singular verb turns out to be more acceptable for the subject *you and I* ($p < .0001$ for AJ, $p > .05$ for PenLP). For the verb preceding the subject, the acceptability and the probability of the normative agreement ($p > .05$ for AJ and PenLP) and the default agreement ($p > .05$ for AJ and PenLP) do not depend on the conjuncts order. Thus, the probability values do not model the strategy choice for the coordinated pronouns and do not reveal contrasts which are significant for the acceptability judgments.

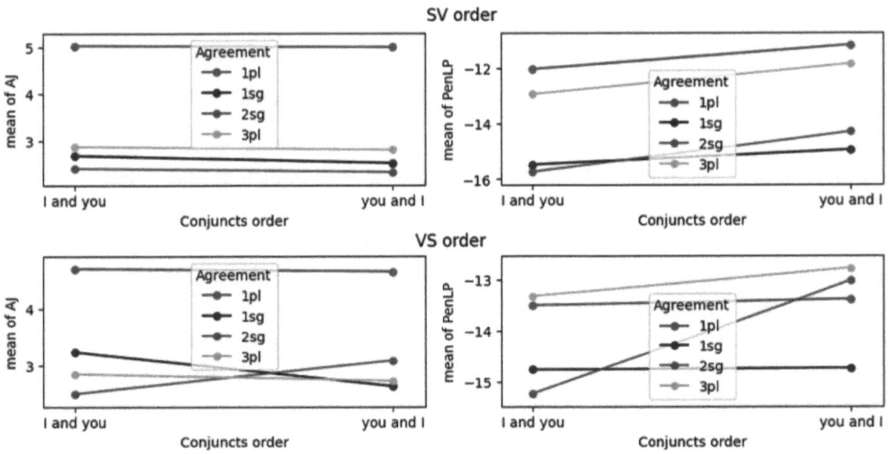

Fig. 5. Mean acceptability judgments and probability scores for the 1st and 2nd person pronouns.

Figure 6 presents mean AJ and mean PenLP for the coordinated 1st person pronoun *I* and a proper name *X* given the VS linear order. The interaction of the factors "verb agreement" and "conjuncts order" significantly influences the acceptability ($p < .0001$ for AJ) but not the probability ($p > .05$ for PenLP). The 1st person plural (normative) agreement and the 1st person singular (closest conjunct) agreement are more acceptable for the subject *I and X* than for the subject *X and I* (1st PL: $p < .001$ for AJ, 1st SG: $p < .0001$ for AJ). The 3rd person plural (default) agreement and the 3rd person singular (closest conjunct) agreement are more acceptable for the subject *X and I* than for the subject *I and X* (3rd PL: $p < .01$ for AJ, 3rd SG: $p < .0001$ for AJ). The probability of all the agreement strategy does not depend on the conjuncts order (1st PL, 1st SG, 3rd SG, 3rd PL: $p > .05$ for PenLP). The results show that the conjuncts order determines the agreement strategy for language speakers but not for the neural model.

According to our experiment, the subject-verb position is the only factor which equally influences the acceptability and the probability of the predicate agreement strategy when the feature calculation is ambiguous. The acceptability is also determined by the gender feature (mis)match for noun conjuncts and by the conjuncts order for subject including a pronoun. However, the probability of the sentences with different agreement

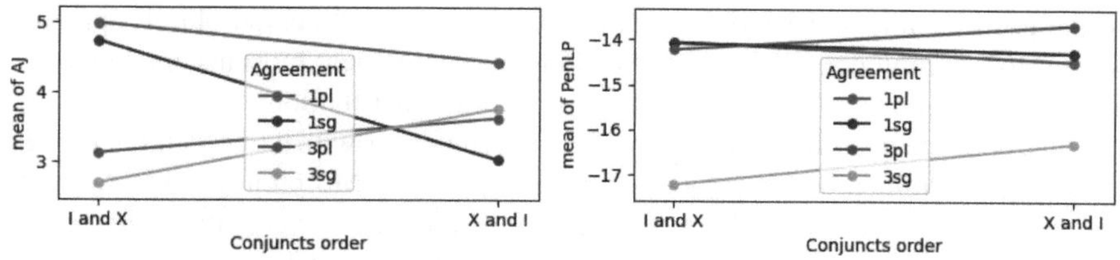

Fig. 6. Mean acceptability judgments and probability scores for the subject *I and X* given VS order.

strategies does not depend on these factors. Contrary to the previous research, the semantic characteristics of the conjuncts (animacy) and the predicate (symmetry) influences neither acceptability, nor probability of the sentences.

4 Conclusion

In this paper, we have analyzed the correlation between the acceptability and the probability of the sentences based on the agreement variation in Russian. Previous studies did not observe what exactly are the factors influencing the acceptability judgments passed by language speakers and the probability values predicted by neural models. In addition, unidirectional language models GPT were mostly applied in previous research. Since they analyze text from left to right, the left context is considered but the right context is ignored. We compared in detail which syntactic, morphological and semantic factors determine the choice of the predicate agreement strategy given the coordinated subject. The linguistic competence of the bidirectional language model ruBERT-base was tested. The metrics PenLP was calculated since it normalizes the language probability by the sentence length.

The language model was expected to predict the highest probability to the agreement strategy which is the most acceptable for human. However, this assumption has not been confirmed. The probability metrics more accurately reflect differences in the acceptability for the sentences with unambiguous agreement. The correlation between the acceptability and the probability is lower for the examples with the agreement variation.

The probability values most accurately capture the acceptability contrasts for the different linear orders of subject and verb (direct order SV / reverse order VS). The singular predicate agreement turns out to be more acceptable and more probable given the VS order while the acceptability and the probability of the plural predicate agreement does not depend on the word order. The acceptability of the singular agreement decreases if the conjuncts mismatch in gender features, but the probability is not determined by this factor. The semantic characteristics of the conjuncts (animate/ inanimate) and the predicate (symmetric/ nonsymmetric) influence neither acceptability nor probability of the sentences. For the coordinated 1st and 2nd person pronouns and SV order, the normative (1st person plural) agreement in the most acceptable while the most probable strategy is the default one (3rd person plural). For the coordinated 1st and 2nd person pronouns and VS order, the acceptability of the closest conjunct agreement (1st or 2nd person singular) increases but the probability does not change. If the subject consists of the pronoun *I* and the proper name, the VS order makes the normative (1st person plural) agreement and the closest conjunct (1st or 3rd person singular) agreement most acceptable, but the language model does not predict the same probability distribution.

Thus, both acceptability and probability of the sentences with the agreement variation are mostly determined by the subject-verb linear position. Morphological factors influence the acceptability but not the probability of the utterances. Semantic characteristics of the subject and the verb do not cause differences in the acceptability or the probability. We can conclude that the bidirectional model ruBERT-base trained on a big amount of the unlabeled texts does not acquire a number of important grammatical aspects. It cannot be applied to model the variable predicate agreement with the coordinated subject in Russian. The concept "probability" is only partly related to the concept "acceptability". The acceptability judgments demonstrate subtle contrasts which are important for the choice of the agreement strategy. However, these differences are not reflected by the probability values predicted by the language model.

Acknowledgments. We thank Moscow Experimental Syntax Group for providing the results of the syntactic experiments. This work was supported by Non-commercial Foundation for Support of Science and Education «INTELLECT».

References

1. Chomsky, N.: Three models for the description of language. IRE Trans. Info. Theory **2**(3), 113–124 (1956)
2. Pereira, F.: Formal grammar and information theory: together again? Philosophical Transactions of the Royal Society of London. Series A: Mathematical, Physical and Engineering Sciences **358**(1769), 1239–1253 (2000)
3. Lau, J.H., Clark, A., Lappin, S.: Grammaticality, acceptability, and probability: a probabilistic view of linguistic knowledge. Cogn. Sci. **41**(5), 1202–1241 (2017)
4. Sprouse, J., Yankama, B., Indurkhya, S., Fong, S., Berwick, R.C.: Colorless green ideas do sleep furiously: gradient acceptability and the nature of the grammar. The Linguistic Review **35**(3), 575–599 (2018)
5. Adger, D.: Core syntax: A minimalist approach. Oxford University Press, Oxford (2003)
6. Warstadt, A., et al.: BLiMP: The benchmark of linguistic minimal pairs for English. Trans. Ass. Computat. Linguist. **8**, 377–392 (2020)
7. Chomsky, N.: The Minimalist Program. MA, MIT Press, Cambridge (1995)
8. Corbett, G.G.: The agreement hierarchy. J. Linguist. **15**(2), 203–224 (1979)
9. Marušič, F., Nevins, A.I., Badecker, W.: The grammars of conjunction agreement in Slovenian. Syntax **18**(1), 39–77 (2015)
10. Arsenijević, B., Mitić, I.: Effect of animacy and agentivity on the processing of agreement in Serbo-Croatian. In: Živančević-Sekeruš, I., Halupka-Rešetar, S., Martínez-Ferreiro S. (eds.) Studies in languages and mind. Selected papers from the 3rd Workshop in Psycholinguistics, Neurolinguistic and Clinical Linguistic Research, pp. 41–77. Novi Sad, Faculty of Philosophy (2016)
11. An, A., Abeillé, A.: Number agreement in French binomials. Empirical Issues in Syntax and Semantics **12**, 31–60 (2019)
12. Himmelreich, A., Hartmann, K.: Agreement with disjoined subjects in German. Glossa: A Journal of General Linguistics **8**(1), 1–44 (2023)

13. Lyutikova, E.A., Gerasimova, A.A.: Issledovanie variativnogo soglasovaniya v russkom yazyke: problemy i metody [Studying agreement variation in Russian: Problems and methodology]. Rhema **2**, 9–27 (2023)
14. Likert, R.: A technique for the measurement of attitudes. Archives of Psychology **22**(140), 5–55 (1932)
15. Sprouse, J., Schütze, C.T., Almeida, D.: A comparison of informal and formal acceptability judgments using a random sample from Linguistic Inquiry 2001–2010. Lingua **134**, 219–248 (2013)
16. Corbett, G.G.: Resolution rules: Agreement in person, number, and gender. In: Gazdar, G., Klein, E., Pullam, G.K. (eds.) Order, Concord and Constituency, pp. 175–205. Boston, De Gruyter Mouton, Berlin (1983)
17. Pekelis, OE.: "Chastichnoe soglasovanie" v konstrukcii s povtoryayushchimsya soyuzom: korpusnoe issledovanie osnovnyh zakonomernostej ["Partial agreement" in a construction with a repeating conjunction: A corpus study of the main patterns]. Voprosy Jazykoznanija **4**, 55–86 (2013)
18. Sannikov, V.Z.: Russkij sintaksis v semantiko-pragmaticheskom prostranstve [Russian syntax in the view of semantics and pragmatics]. Yazyki slavyanskih kul'tur, Moscow (2008)
19. Grammatika russkogo yazyka. In: Shvedova, N.Yu. (ed.) Grammar of the Russian language. Moscow, Nauka (1980)
20. Rozental, D.E., Dzhandzhakova, E.V., Kabanova, N.P.: Spravochnik po pravopisaniyu, proiznosheniyu, literaturnomu redaktirovaniyu [A guide to spelling, pronunciation, literary editing]. CheRo, Moscow (1999)
21. Zwicky, A.: Hierarchies of Person. Chicago Linguistics Society **13**, 714–733 (1977)
22. Vrubel, D.D.: Sinkretichnoe soglasovanie po rodu v konstrukciyah s povtoryayushchimsya soyuzom i [Syncretic gender agreement with coordinate constructions with correlative conjunction i…i]. The student conference "Experimental studies of language". Lomonosov Moscow State University, Moscow (2022)
23. Pasko, L.I.: Predikativnoe soglasovanie s sochinennym podlezhashchim i simmetrichnost' predikata [Predicate agreement with coordinated subject and symmetry of the predicate]. The student conference "Experimental studies of language". Lomonosov Moscow State University, Moscow (2022)
24. Studenikina, K.A.: Vliyanie odushevlennosti kon"yunktov i linejnoj pozicii skazuemogo na vybor strategii predikativnogo soglasovaniya [The role of the conjuncts animacy and the predicate linear position on the predicate agreement]. The student conference "Experimental studies of language". Lomonosov Moscow State University, Moscow (2023)
25. Belova, D.D.: Predikativnoe soglasovanie s podlezhashchim, vyrazhennym mestoimennymi kon"yunktami [Predicate agreement in person and number with pronominal coordinated subjects]. The student conference "Experimental studies of language". Lomonosov Moscow State University, Moscow (2022)
26. Davidyuk, T.I.: Vliyanie argumentnoj struktury predikata na lichno-chislovoe soglasovanie s sochinyonnym podlezhashchim [The influence of the predicate argument structure on the person-number agreement with the coordinated subject]. The student conference "Experimental studies of language". Lomonosov Moscow State University, Moscow (2022)
27. Vaswani, A., et al.: Attention is all you need. Adv. Neural. Inf. Process. Syst. **30**, 5998–6008 (2017)
28. Radford, A., Narasimhan, K., Salimans, T., Sutskever, I.: Improving language understanding by generative pre-training. Technical Report, OpenAI (2018)
29. Devlin, J., Chang, M.W., Lee, K., Toutanova, K. BERT: Pre-training of Deep Bidirectional Transformers for Language Understanding. Proceedings of the 2019 Conference of the North American Chapter of the Association for Computational Linguistics: Human Language Technologies 1, 4181–4186 (2019)

30. Lau, J.H., Armendariz, C., Lappin, S., Purver, M., Shu, C.: How furiously can colorless green ideas sleep? Sentence acceptability in context. Trans. Ass. Computat. Linguist. **8**, 296–310 (2020)
31. Mikhailov, V., et al.: RuCoLA: Russian Corpus of Linguistic Acceptability. Proceedings of the 2022 Conference on Empirical Methods in Natural Language Processing, pp. 5207–5227. Abu Dhabi, United Arab Emirates, Association for Computational Linguistics (2022)
32. Studenikina, K.A.: Parametrizing number variation in Russian noun phrases with experimental studies and language modeling. Research Result. Theoretical and Applied Linguistics **9**(1), 192–205 (2023)

Out-of-Dictionary Meanings Detecting Using Word-Sense Disambiguation Algorithms

Darya Borodina[1] and Dmitry Morozov[2(✉)]

[1] Saint Petersburg State University, 7-9 Universitetskaya Embankment, St Petersburg 199034, Russia

[2] Novosibirsk State University, 1 Pirogova Street, Novosibirsk 630090, Russia

morozowdm@gmail.com

Abstract. Automatic semantic shift detection can be used in a number of applied problems in linguistics, from compiling explanatory dictionaries to analyzing historical documents. In this paper, we consider the related problem of word-sense disambiguation (WSD) and the feasibility of adapting algorithms based on explanatory dictionaries to detect out-of-dictionary meanings. We selected 50 reference words, for which we collected a dataset of context-gloss pairs based on the National Media subcorpus of the Russian National Corpus, news feed of the Vkontakte social network, and the Big Explanatory Dictionary of the Russian Language. We adapted four algorithms originally developed for the WSD problem. The best quality (F1-score = 0.96) was achieved through the GlossBERT algorithm. We also assessed the generalization ability of this algorithm applying a train-test split by reference words. In this case, F1-score dropped significantly to a value of 0.71.

Keywords: Semantic Shift Detection · Word-Sense Disambiguation · Natural Language Processing

1 Introduction

Every language develops and changes over time, reflecting the corresponding changes in the world around us. All language levels are prone to changes, but the lexical system changes the most as it is the most mobile and unstable language level [2]. In particular, over the course of language history some words can change their meanings. Such changes are called semantic shifts, and they are a complex linguistic phenomenon, which has various causes and is influenced by many different factors. While research on semantic shifts in historical and cognitive linguistics has been conducted for quite a long time, computational approaches to this problem have advanced considerably in the last two decades. An automatic detection of semantic shifts is an important task in the field of computational linguistics and automatic text analysis. The problem is solved not only for its own sake, but it also finds wide applications in other research fields and can significantly contribute to the solution of various tasks of natural language processing. For example, automatic lexical-semantic change analysis can significantly contribute to

M. Bakaev et al. (Eds.): IMS 2024, CCIS 2534, pp. 85–104, 2026.
https://doi.org/10.1007/978-3-031-96177-9_8

the development of lexicography. Since adding new meanings to explanatory dictionaries is an extremely complex and time consuming process, at the moment, many dictionaries do not contain all the current meanings of words. Finding new word meanings using computational methods could also provide a more formal methodology, which relies less on the dictionary-writers' subjective judgments. At the same time, the quality of automatic generation of interpretations is still far from ideal, and such algorithms cannot be used without proofreading by experts [1, 23]. However, hybrid methods can also be considered. In particular, language model could suggest a list of candidate words that presumably have undergone a semantic shift, and then this list should be checked and adjusted by experts [27]. The approach in which the algorithm finds contexts with supposedly new meanings of the word also seems promising. In this case, the speed of updating the dictionary with new meanings can be much higher, because the compilers of the dictionary do not need to look at those contexts where the word is used in one of the previously recorded meanings, which obviously constitute the majority. Both of these approaches rely on automatic search for semantic shifts.

Many algorithms have been proposed to find semantic shifts. In some cases, the task of detecting shifts in diachronic corpora is considered; in others, examples of the use of a word and its dictionary meanings are compared. Therefore, the semantic shift detection is closely related to the word-sense disambiguation (WSD). In WSD, for a given context and each of the known meanings of a word, consistency is assessed, then the meanings are ranked, and the most appropriate one is selected. However, given the low consistency of all known meanings of a word with the context, one can assume the word is used in a non-dictionary meaning. In this work, we seek to answer the following research question: how effective are WSD algorithms based on explanatory dictionaries in identifying out-of-domain word senses, i.e. in detecting semantic shifts?

2 Related Work

Almost all papers on automatic search and description of semantic shifts rely on the distributional hypothesis: the meaning of words depends on their contexts and vice versa [9]. Among these approaches, two groups can be distinguished: in the first group, the authors try to directly establish the fact of the shift, while in the second one, the subject of research is the direction of the shift and the attempt to describe the new meaning of the word. Works of the second type include, for example, those applying topic modeling [20] and clustering of contexts with subsequent generation of a description for the cluster [25, 33]. There are also works that rely on the generation of glosses using Transformer-based neural approaches [10, 11].

For our research, the first type is more interesting. Among them, we can highlight both works that employ static vectors and those that use contextualized representations. For instance, Kaufmann et al. have used count-based vectors to calculate the semantic density of word sense: the increasing density between two time periods testifies to narrowing the word sense [31]. Kim et al. [13] used Word2Vec architecture [24] and trained word embedding model for each diachronic subcorpus of Google Book Ngrams English fiction, vectors were compared with cosine similarity measure. The vector representation can also be augmented with syntactic information [15]. Methods based on contextualized representations have been implemented by Bamler et al. [3], Rosenfeld et al. [29] and Dubossarsky et al. [8]. Such approaches look promising: for example, Dubossarsky et al. achieved a value of 0.74 in terms of the F1 metric in the binary classification problem.

In recent years, approaches to the problem have been largely developed within the framework of various competitions. In particular, the problem was solved as a part of SemEval (2020) [32], EVALITA (2020) [5] and RuShiftEval (2021) [18] competitions. The participants of SemEval were supposed to solve the problem for multiple languages, while those of EVALITA and RuShiftEval had only Italian and Russian data, respectively. The organizers of the two first competitions provided participants with only two diachronic corpora, and at the RuShiftEval three of them were proposed. Everyone was provided with a list of target words, including stable ones and those that have undergone semantic change. The general task of semantic shift detection can be divided into two related subtasks: binary classification (to identify if a word has undergone a semantic change between the diachronic corpora) and ranking (to rank target words according to the degree of their semantic shifts). As a part of SemEval competition, both subtasks have been solved while the participants of EVALITA were given only the binary classification subtask, and those of RuShiftEval—only the ranking one. No training data was provided at SemEval and EVALITA competitions; therefore, only unsupervised methods could be used to solve the problem, but the participants of RuShiftEval could implement supervised models using marked-up data. To assess the quality of the proposed models, the results were compared to the gold standard obtained manually.

The competitions allowed to study the subject area much better. At the same time, the results obtained do not always completely coincide. Thus, in the SemEval and EVALITA competitions, all best performing systems used static-type embedding models, while systems with contextualized vectors did not show such a high quality. The opposite is observed when analyzing the results of RuShiftEval: contextualized embeddings have shown much better performance than static ones. Fine-tuning models on marked-up data proved to be effective. It was also shown that a priori linguistic knowledge improves a model's quality. For instance, glosses from WordNet thesaurus were used by Rachinsky et al. [28]. Ryzhova et al. took into account changes in the morphological profile of the word [30]. Perhaps the main result obtained can be called the high quality achieved: for example, the best models presented within EVALITA reach 0.944 according to the Accuracy metric.

3 Data and Methods

3.1 Data

Unfortunately, we were unable to find datasets suitable for the purposes of our experiment. Therefore, we decided to create such a dataset ourselves during a linguistic experiment. First, we selected two groups of 25 words each, mentioned in the Big Explanatory Dictionary of the Russian Language (BEDRL) [19]. The first group included words for which presumably one of the actual meanings is not mentioned in the BEDRL. We identified these words by comparing interpretations from BEDRL and alternative dictionaries and encyclopedias with a higher update rate (Wiktionary[1], Wikipedia[2], Kartaslov.ru[3], Dictionary of the Internet.ru language [14]). Words of this kind include, for example, *двушка* 'dvushka' (according to the BEDRL, a coin with a denomination of two kopecks, but Wiktionary also records another common meaning—a two-room apartment). The second group included words for which we were unable to find alternative interpretations not mentioned in the BEDRL. Words of the second kind include, for example, *пальто* 'coat' (according to the dictionary, a type of long-cut outerwear, usually below the knees, worn over a dress, suit, etc.). A complete list of words is provided in Appendix A.

For each of the collected words, we selected 100 contexts, using two sources: the RNC National Media subcorpus and the news feed of the VKontakte social network (equally divided). In the case of VKontakte, we employed the API and retrieved the last 50 uses of the word at the time of collection in publicly available posts. In the case of RNC, we selected one example per text from the most recently published texts. This approach allowed us to include the most relevant examples of word usage in the dataset. In addition, posts on social networks are close to colloquial speech, where new meanings of words are most often born. We limited the context to one sentence; the average length of contexts was 16 words.

Next, we used a telegram bot to mark up the data. Each question included the dictionary gloss of the target word in the form «WORD—1. Meaning 1. 2. Meaning 2.» and its context from RNC or from the VKontakte social network. We invited more than 100 native speakers at the age from 18 to 60 years old with different education and profession as respondents. Each annotator sequentially answered questions about context-gloss pairs mixed randomly. People were asked to compare a set of dictionary interpretations of a target word with its context and to decide whether the meaning of the word in the context coincides with at least one dictionary interpretation or not. If so, word meaning in the context is considered to coincide with the interpretation as a whole. During the data markup the respondents were asked to choose one of the four options characterizing the correspondence of word meaning in context to its dictionary interpretations: "exactly yes", "probably yes", "probably no", "exactly no". The resulting label for each context-gloss pair was determined by simple majority given that the first two options were considered as Class 1 and the last two—as Class 0. If Class 0 and Class 1 were equally represented for a context-gloss pair, class with a larger number of "confident" answers (i.e. "exactly yes/no") was chosen. In total, 119 people participated in the data markup, each respondent assessed on average 133 gloss-context pairs. A total of 15,828 marks were collected for 5,000 contexts. We excluded from consideration contexts that received fewer than three responses. Since the resulting sample turned out to be unbalanced (71% of Class 1 and 29% of Class 0), we limited the sample to 3000 contexts, including all contexts of Class 0 with the exception of a few particularly dispersed cases and supplementing with contexts of Class 1. The final dataset included 1400 contexts of Class 0 and 1600 Class 1 contexts. Our marked-up dataset is now publicly available [7].

[1] https://ru.wiktionary.org/.
[2] https://ru.wikipedia.org/.
[3] https://kartaslov.ru/.

3.2 Algorithms

We adapted to our problem four algorithms originally developed for solving polysemy: the Lesk algorithm [21], the extended Lesk algorithm [4], an algorithm based on cosine similarity comparison [6], and the GlossBERT algorithm based on a pre-trained BERT model [11]. In the original works, these algorithms were used to search for the gloss from a list of known ones that most closely matches the given context of use of the word. In our case, the task was a binary classification problem: using a pair (context of use of the word, word gloss) to determine whether at least one BEDRL meaning is appropriate. To assess the quality of classification, the Precision, Recall and F1 metrics were used.

Lesk algorithm [21] relies on counting the word-by-word intersection of target gloss and *context extended gloss* i.e. glosses of all words in context sentence: the greater the intersection, the more likely it is that the word is used in the corresponding meaning. We examined five variations of this algorithm, differing in the set of parts of speech that were included in the calculation. The Lesk-1 model take into account all words, the Lesk-2 model do nouns, adjectives, verbs and adverbs, the Lesk-3 model do only nouns, the Lesk-4 model do nouns and verbs, and finally the Lesk-5 model do nouns, adjectives and verbs. Thus, the algorithm consists of the following steps. First, target gloss and context sentence are tokenized and lemmatized (different part of speech sets are taken into account depending on the model version). Next, dictionary interpretations for each word in the context are obtained and combined with each other. Only words of particular parts of speech are taken into account and word repetitions are ignored as well as the interpretation of the target word itself is not taken into consideration. The resulting set of words is considered as *context extended gloss*. Finally, the word-by-word intersection of target and context extended gloss is calculated. If more than one meaning is presented in the dictionary, the intersection is calculated for each interpretation independently.

For example, given the gloss of the target word *кенгуру* 'kangaroo': *"сумчатое австралийское млекопитающее с длинными задними и короткими передними ногами, передвигающееся прыжками"*[4] and its context *"Кофта с карманом «кенгуру», рукав спущен."*[5] the stages of the Lesk-3 model functioning are represented in the Table 1. This model takes into consideration only nouns when calculating the intersection size. The intersection of context and gloss is empty, which is in this case a correct answer: the meaning of the target word in context does not correspond to its dictionary interpretation.

[4] A marsupial Australian mammal with long hind legs and short forelegs, moving by leaps.

[5] Jacket with kangaroo pocket, sleeve down.

Table 1. Stages of the Lesk-3 algorithm for *кенгуру* 'kangaroo' in the sentence *"Кофта с карманом «кенгуру», рукав спущен" ["Jacket with kangaroo pocket, sleeve down"].*

Target word	*кенгуру* 'kangaroo'
Dictionary interpretation preprocessed	*передняя* 'hall', *млекопитающее* 'mammal', *прыжок* 'jump', *нога* 'leg'
Context sentence preprocessed	*кофта* 'sweater', *рукав* 'sleeve', *карман* 'pocket'
Set of interpretations for each word in context sentence	*кофта* 'sweater': *одежда* 'clothes', *юбка* 'skirt', *брюки* 'trousers' *рукав* 'sleave': *жидкость* 'liquid', *русло* 'riverbed', *материал* 'material', *локоть* 'elbow', *кишка* 'gut', *газ* 'gas', *ответвление* 'branch', *главное* 'main', *одежда* 'clothes', *труба* 'pipe', *река* 'river', *отвод* 'removal', *кисть* 'hand' *карман* 'pocket': *внимание* 'attention', *положение* 'position', *судно* 'ship', *выстрел* 'gunshot', *неосторожность* 'carelessness', *число* 'number', *вместилище* 'container', *производство* 'production', *река* 'river', *действие* 'action', *борт* 'side', *вязание* 'knitting', *упругость* 'elasticity', *организация* 'organization', *привязь* 'leash', *оружие* 'weapon', *область* 'area', *вязка* 'knitting', *крючок* 'hook', *спица* 'knitting needle', *течение* 'river flow', *вес* 'weight', *проступок* 'misconduct', *газ* 'gas', *край* 'edge', *петля* 'loop', *наказание* 'punishment'
Intersection of the target gloss and the context extended gloss	—

For each of the models, a search was carried out for the optimal threshold value of the intersection size. Words with more than one interpretation are considered to be used in the dictionary meaning if the intersection size of context and at least one dictionary interpretation exceeds the threshold value.

The extended Lesk algorithm [4] is designed to eliminate one of the main shortcomings of the original algorithm: the interpretations of only those words that are directly present in the context sentence are taken into account that is why it is very unlikely to detect intersecting words in short sentences which is particularly true for contexts from social networks. Moreover, the Lesk algorithm does not consider the semantics of words, which is why synonyms, for example, are not taken into account in the intersection. In the extended algorithm, contexts are supplemented with words that have semantic relationships with words from the source text. To search for such words, a prepared thesaurus is used, in our case, RuWordNet [22].

After expanding the context with semantically related words, dictionary interpretations for each word of this extended context are obtained and a set of these interpretations is considered as context extended gloss which is then intersected with a target gloss. Table 2 shows in more detail the steps of the ExtLesk-2b model for the target word *отстой* 'to suck' and the context sentence "*Премия Дарвина—это отстой.*"[6]. Here the context is extended with hyponyms, hypernyms, meronyms and holonyms and only nouns, verbs and adjectives are taken into account when calculating the intersection size. Again, in this context-gloss pair the word meaning in context is different from that listed in the dictionary and the intersection is empty which is a correct answer of the model.

Table 2. Stages of the ExtLesk-2b model functioning for the target word *отстой* 'otstoy' in the sentence *"Премия Дарвина—это отстой." ["The Darwin Prize sucks"].*

Target word	*отстой* 'to suck'
Dictionary interpretation preprocessed	*частица* 'corpuscle', *дно* 'bottom', *осесть* 'settle down', *жидкость* 'liquid', *сосуд* 'vessel', *вещество* 'substance'
Context sentence preprocessed	*Дарвин* 'Darwin', *премия* 'prize'
Sematically related words for each word in context sentence	*Дарвин*: - *премия 'bonus'*: *вознаграждение* 'award', *грамота* 'diploma', *бонус* 'bonus', *стипендия* 'scholarship', *победитель* 'winner', *стимулирование* 'stimulation', *материальный* 'material', *знак* 'sign', *нобелевский* 'Nobel', *именной* 'personal', *наградной* 'award-winning', *награда* 'award', *почётный* 'honorary', *медаль* 'medal', *государственный* 'state', *премия* 'award', *приз* 'prize', *вымпел* 'pennant', *кинопремия* 'film award'
Set of interpretations for each word in extended context	*победитель* 'winner': *одержать* 'to win', *средство* 'tool', *достижение* 'achievement', *победа* 'victory', *победить* 'to win' *вознаграждение* 'award': *являться* 'to be', *награда* 'award', *плата* 'pay' ...
Intersection of the target gloss and the context extended gloss	—

Table 3 lists the diverse variants of the model we tested, taking into account various types of semantic relations and the part-speech affiliation of the words analyzed. Similar

[6] "The Darwin Prize sucks".

to the first family of models, for each of the models a search was carried out for the optimal threshold value of the intersection size.

Table 3. Variants of the extended Lesk algorithm.

Algorithm	Utilized semantic relations	Utilized parts of speech
ExtLesk-1a	hyponyms / hypernyms, synonyms, antonyms, domains / their attributes, meronyms / holonyms, classes / their instances, premises / possible conclusions from them, causes / effects	all
ExtLesk-1b		nouns, adjectives, verbs
ExtLesk-2a	hyponyms / hypernyms, meronyms / holonyms	all
ExtLesk-2b		nouns, adjectives, verbs
ExtLesk-3a	hyponyms / hypernyms, domains / their attributes, meronyms / holonyms, synonyms	all
ExtLesk-3b		nouns, adjectives, verbs

The algorithm CosSim [6] is based on comparing context and gloss embeddings using cosine similarity. Similar to the ExtLesk-models, context sentences are expanded with semantically related words from RuWordNet thesaurus. Embeddings of individual words are calculated through a static model (in our case, ruwikiruscorpora_upos_cbow_300_10_2021 [17]), and then context and gloss embeddings are computed as the weighted sum of vectors of individual words. The weights are inverse document frequency (IDF), context sentences are considered as documents.

Finally, the GlossBERT algorithm [12] is based on additional training of a pretrained BERT model on the task of binary classification of gloss-context pairs with target labels: 1 if context corresponds to the dictionary interpretation and 0 otherwise. The authors examined several strategies for forming pairs (with and without highlighting the search word in a gloss and context). In our case, the searched word was highlighted in the gloss (each gloss had the form "WORD—1. Meaning 1. 2. Meaning 2."), but not in the context. If a target word had more than one meaning listed in the dictionary, all of them were presented to the model as a whole. We used rubert-base-cased [16] as a pretrained model.

4 Results and Discussion

For Lesk and ExtLesk algorithms, we analyzed different possible values of the classification threshold. It turned out that in all cases the optimal solution according to F1-score is to consider the context to coincide with the gloss if they intersect at least in one word. Figures 1 and 2 show the value of the F1-score at different threshold values for Lesk and ExtLesk algorithms, respectively.

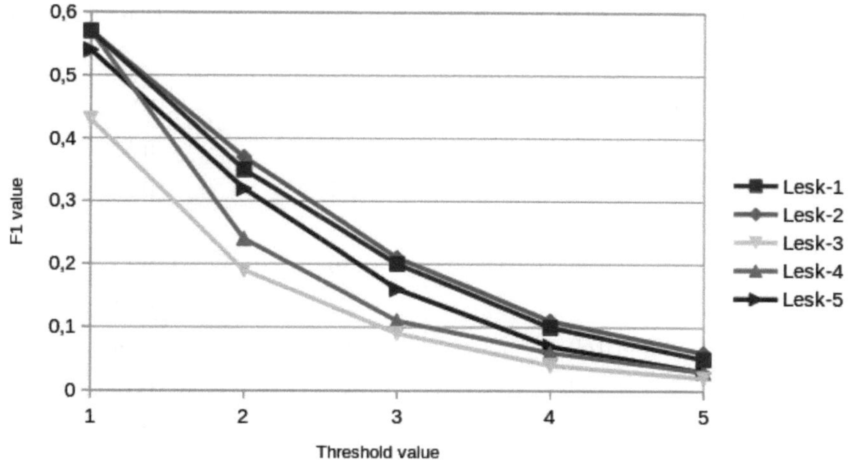

Fig. 1. F1-score of Lesk variants at different threshold values.

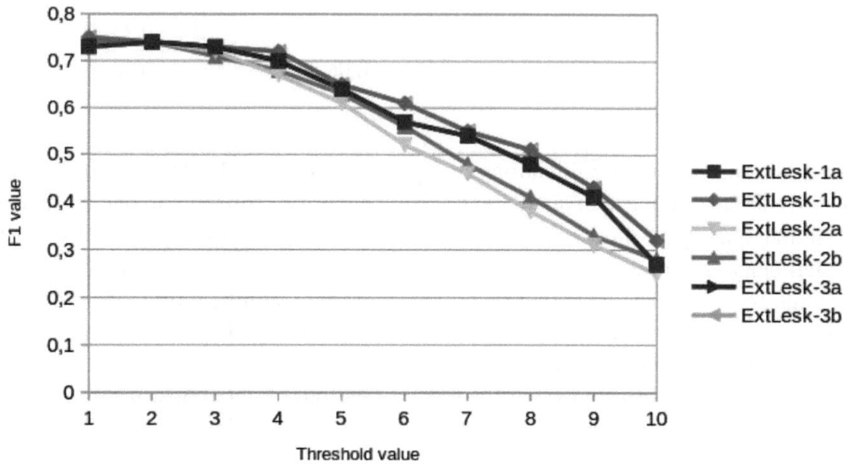

Fig. 2. F1-score of ExtLesk variants at different threshold values.

The results obtained are presented in Table 4. The results clearly indicate that the GlossBERT algorithm is qualitatively superior to other approaches. Despite the high recall values of the ExtLesk and CosSim algorithms, the results obtained using them show significantly lower precision.

Table 4. Precision, Recall, and F1-score for binary classification problem. Class 1 corresponds to the absence of semantic shift.

Algorithm	Precision	Recall	F1
Lesk-1	0.69	0.48	0.57
Lesk-2	0.68	0.49	0.57
Lesk-3	0.71	0.31	0.43
Lesk-4	0.69	0.39	0.57
Lesk-5	0.73	0.42	0.54
ExtLesk-1a	0.60	0.96	0.74
ExtLesk-1b	0.60	1.00	0.75
ExtLesk-2a	0.61	0.93	0.74
ExtLesk-2b	0.60	0.99	0.74
ExtLesk-3a	0.60	0.96	0.74
ExtLesk-3b	0.60	1.00	0.75
CosSim	0.58	0.98	0.73
GlossBERT	0.96	0.96	0.96

In addition, various modifications of Lesk and extended Lesk algorithms did not bring a significant increase in quality and, on the contrary, reduced it in one of the cases. The similar quality of the Lesk-family models can be possibly explained by the fact that dictionary interpretations contain much fewer verbs and adverbs than adjectives and nouns so both verbs and adverbs do not contribute significantly when calculating the context-gloss intersection. Consequently, the accounting of different parts of speech has almost no effect on the classification quality. As for the ExtLesk-family algorithms, the modifications differing in sets of semantic relations show almost the same quality probably because many semantic relations from the RuWordNet thesaurus, such as, for example, "classes/their instances" or "premises/conclusions", are rather rare and do not contribute effectively to the context expanding.

By analyzing the false positive answers of the GlossBERT model (i.e. the cases where, according the model, the context corresponds to the gloss, but in fact it does not), several types of errors can be listed. Firstly, there are pairs with rather short context sentences such as, for example, *"Но читала на форуме садоводов."*[7], so the small context length is the common limitation both for base approaches and for the more complex ones. Secondly, some ambiguous cases can be identified: there are context sentences where target words are used in a metaphoric sense which is very close to that listed in the dictionary and it is difficult to definitely decide whether it is a new meaning or the same one. When creating the dataset such target words were considered as stable ones. Such examples include the target word *синица* 'parus (bird)' in phrases

[7] "But I read it on the gardeners' forum".

like *"Лучше синица в руках, чем журавль в небе"*[8] or the word *партитура* 'score' in phrases like *"световая партитура"*[9]. Such contexts can be ambivalent not only for the model, but also for the human annotators.

As for the false negative answers of the GlossBERT model (i.e. according to the model the context does not coincide with the gloss, but in fact it does), it is worth mentioning that the most false negative responses were received for the target word *конгениальный* 'congenial'. Moreover, for most target words in false negative section samples of positive and negative classes are more or less equally represented: *гавань* 'harbor' (48 and 52 samples of Class 1 and Class 0 respectively), *кенгуру* 'kangaroo' (63 and 47 samples), *почта* 'post office' (64 and 46 samples). It is true for the target word *конгениальный* 'congenial' as well (56 and 44 samples of Class 1 and Class 0 respectively). Unfortunately, we were unable to identify some clearer patterns of false negative misclassification.

The achieved quality of the GlossBERT algorithm suggests that it can be used to mark up words that are not included in the training set. To assess the generalization ability of the GlossBERT algorithm, we compared two models with different train-test sampling strategies. In the first case (GlossBERT-1), gloss-context pairs were divided randomly; in the second one (GlossBERT-2), we divided the pairs so that the training and test samples did not intersect in the context/meaning base words. We have built the test set in such a way that it includes approximately equally positive and negative classes. We have chosen 10 target words five of which are presumably stable (i.e. words with all meanings listed in BEDRL, for instance the word *прилагательное* 'adjective') and for the remaining five words one of the actual meanings is not mentioned in the BEDRL (for instance the word *читалка* 'reading room'). In total, the test set included 1000 context-gloss pairs. The results of this experiment are shown in Table 5. It can be seen that in the case of GlossBERT-2, despite the remaining high recall, the precision value decreased. The largest number of false positive answers was received for the target word *читалка* 'reading room' (71 context-gloss pairs were classified as positives i.e. according to the model the context corresponds to the gloss while in fact the word is used in the out-of-dictionary meaning). There are also quite a lot of false positive labels received by the words *буханка* 'loaf' and *синица* 'parus (bird)' (30 and 28 respectively). The word синица in misclassified contexts is used in metaphoric sense (phrases like *"синица в руках или журавль в небе"*[10]) and in these cases the model's errors are consistent with those of GlossBERT-1 algorithm, which is not true for the words *читалка* and *буханка*: their contexts clearly belong to the Class 0. Finally, the classification quality has decreased significantly for the target word *конгениальный* 'congenial': now it is present not only in the false negative section, as it was for the GlossBERT-1 model, but is also numerous in the false positive one.

[8] Literal translation: a parus in hand is better than a scane in the sky. English equivalent of the phrase: better a fowl in hand than two flying.

[9] The light score.

[10] Literal translation: a parus in hand is better than a scane in the sky. English equivalent of the phrase: better a fowl in hand than two flying.

Table 5. Precision, Recall, and F1-score for GlossBERT algorithm depending on the strategy of dividing the sample into training and test.

Algorithm	Precision	Recall	F1
GlossBERT-1	0.96	0.96	0.96
GlossBERT-2	0.56	0.96	0.71

5 Conclusion

During the historical development of a language some words change their meanings. These changes are called semantic shifts and reflect the corresponding changes in the world around us. Automatic semantic shift detection is a relevant problem in the natural language processing and computational linguistics research area, contributing to solving other problems of automatic text analysis. In particular, semantic change detection is put into practice in computational lexicography: as it is difficult and time-consuming to fix new word senses in explanatory dictionaries, many of them do not contain all relevant word meanings. Automatic detection of new senses could keep explanatory dictionaries up to date.

In our research, we implemented four different algorithms of automatic detection of semantic shifts, which were initially developed for word sense disambiguation task. Among those used were both algorithms based on calculating the word-by-word intersection of gloss and context, and those based on a vectorized representation of the text. We created a dataset containing pairs "gloss-context" annotated by native speakers with a target label (1 if the context corresponds to the gloss, and 0 otherwise). Contexts were collected from the Russian National Corpus National Media subcorpus and the news feed of the Vkontakte social network. The GlossBERT algorithm considerably outperformed all other approaches and showed the values of precision, recall and F1-score of 0.96, 0.96, and 0.96, respectively. Despite this, generalization ability of this algorithm turned out to be insufficient: when tested on a sample that did not intersect with the training one on reference words, the value of precision and F1-score significantly decreased to 0.56 and 0.71, respectively. Futher research may focus on improving the quality of the model by increasing the number of training examples and variety of training data. Automatic generation of glosses is another potential area of further research.

Appendix A

List of Possibly Shifted Words Used in the Experiment

Source of alternative meaning is indicated in square brackets after gloss

1. токсичный
   - Gloss from BEDRL: Capable of causing poisoning.
   - Alternative meaning: Creating an unhealthy environment around oneself (about a person). [Wiktionary]

2. пендель
   - Gloss from BEDRL: Kick to the buttocks.
   - Alternative meaning: Strong motivating influence. [Wiktionary]
3. читалка
   - Gloss from BEDRL: A specially equipped room at a library, club, etc. for reading and/or studying with books.
   - Alternative meaning: E-book. [kartaslov.ru]
4. баян
   - Gloss from BEDRL: A large harmonica with a complex fret system.
   - Alternative meaning: figurative, slang. An already mentioned old joke or already repeatedly reported information that is not interesting for any of the recipients. [Wiktionary]
5. буханка
   - Gloss from BEDRL: Whole pan bread (usually black).
   - Alternative meaning: UAZ minibus. [Wiktionary]
6. нелицеприятный
   - Gloss from BEDRL: Impartial, fair.
   - Alternative meaning: Unpleasant, rude, harsh, offensive. [Wiktionary]
7. конгениальный
   - Gloss from BEDRL: Very close, matching in spirit, way of thinking, talent.
   - Alternative meaning: Brilliant, very brilliant. [https://mel.fm/gramotnost/chto-eto-znachit/9143268-congenial]
8. паутина
   - Gloss from BEDRL: 1. A network of thin threads obtained from the sticky juice secreted by the spider. A separate thread of such a network. 2. Something that in appearance resembles such a network.
   - Alternative meaning: Internet. [Wikipedia]
9. почта
   - Gloss from BEDRL: 1. A communications institution in charge of sending letters, periodicals, parcels, money, etc.; building, premises where this institution is located. 2. Delivery of something by means of such institutions. 3. What is delivered by this institution (letters, parcels, etc.).
   - Alternative meaning: Email. [Wiktionary]
10. форум
    - Gloss from BEDRL: 1. Wide representative assembly. 2. In ancient Rome: the square where the public life of the city took place.

- Alternative meaning: Same as web forum; a class of web applications for organizing communication between site visitors, as well as a part of the site that uses such an application, intended for public discussion of any issues. [Wiktionary]

11. пост
    - Gloss from BEDRL: 1. A place, point (usually equipped with technical devices) from where you can observe someone or something. or to protect someone or something. 2. A person or group of persons stationed at a certain place to protect something, to monitor something. 3. Responsible position.
    - Alternative meaning: Publication or news on the Internet, on a blog. [Wikipedia]
12. корона
    - Gloss from BEDRL: 1. A golden crown with precious jewelry as a symbol of the power of the monarch. 2.The power of the monarch. State, government in monarchical countries. 3. A light halo around the Sun, visible during a solar eclipse.
    - Alternative meaning: Coronavirus, covid. [Wiktionary]
13. кенгуру
    - Gloss from BEDRL: An marsupial Australian mammal with long hind legs and short front legs that moves by hopping.
    - Alternative meaning: Kangaroo pocket. [Wiktionary]
14. презентация
    - Gloss from BEDRL: 1. Presentation of a bill of exchange to the person obligated to make the payment. 2. Public presentation of smth. New, recently appeared, created.
    - Alternative meaning: A special document with multimedia content, the display of which is controlled by the user.[Wiktionary]
15. двушка
    - Gloss from BEDRL: Coin with a nominal value of two kopecks.
    - Alternative meaning: Two-room apartment. [Wiktionary]
16. планшет
    - Gloss from BEDRL: 1. A board with drawing paper pasted on it for drawing a site plan for geodetic surveying. 2. Plan obtained during geodetic survey of the area. 3. Flat bag with a transparent top side for carrying cards.
    - Alternative meaning: 1. Same as a graphics tablet - an input device that allows you to transfer hand-drawn graphic images (drawings, blueprints, handwritten text) to a computer. 2. Same as tablet computer - a type of computer, usually without a keyboard, with touch input. [Wiktionary]
17. конкретный
    - Gloss from BEDRL: Really existing, objectively defined (opposite: abstract).
    - Alternative meaning: High quality, good. [Wiktionary]

18. отстой
    - Gloss from BEDRL: Particles, substance or liquid that have settled to the bottom of a container.
    - Alternative meaning: Something bad, low quality. [Wiktionary]
19. реальный
    - Gloss from BEDRL: 1. Actually existing, real, not imaginary. 2. Possible to implement, feasible. 3. Based on understanding and taking into account the true conditions of reality, soberly practical.
    - Alternative meaning: High quality, applaudable. [26]
20. диванный
    - Gloss from BEDRL: Related in meaning to the noun, sofa is a type of (usually upholstered) furniture with a long back and arms (or pillows and bolsters), intended for sitting and lying.
    - Alternative meaning: Having no practical experience in any field, but talking about it, guided by his own amateurish ideas (sitting at home, "on the couch"). [Wiktionary]
21. газель
    - Gloss from BEDRL: 1. A small ungulate of the antelope group, distinguished by its slenderness and running speed. 2. About a slender, graceful girl (usually in poems about the East).
    - Alternative meaning: The GAZ brand, a car under this brand. [Wiktionary]
22. жесть
    - Gloss from BEDRL: Thin sheet steel, usually coated with tin.
    - Alternative meaning: A very strong assessment of an impressive or frightening event, object, phenomenon, etc., as well as such an event itself [14].
23. ламповый
    - Gloss from BEDRL: Adjective of lamp.
    - Alternative meaning: Real, authentic and sincere [14].
24. комментарий
    - Gloss from BEDRL: 1. Interpretation, explanation of something. Text by notes. 2. Reasoning, explanatory or critical remarks about something.
    - Alternative meaning: A message that follows the main text (an article or entry on a blog or social network) and is meaningfully directly or indirectly related to it [14].
25. пирожок
    - Gloss from BEDRL: A small pie with filling inside, usually oval shaped.
    - Alternative meaning: A quatrain without capital letters, punctuation or rhyme, written in iambic tetrameter with alternating feminine and masculine endings (9–8-9–8 syllables) [14].

List of Stable Words Used in the Experiment

1. герб
   - Gloss from BEDRL: A distinctive sign, emblem of a state, city, class, clan, etc., depicted on banners, coins, seals, etc.
2. ватман
   - Gloss from BEDRL: Thick, high-grade paper with a rough surface for drawing and watercolor painting.
3. автомобиль
   - Gloss from BEDRL: A self-propelled vehicle with an internal combustion engine for transporting passengers and goods on trackless roads.
4. выпускник
   - Gloss from BEDRL: A student in his final year of study (at school, college, university, etc.); one who graduated from a given educational institution.
5. инженер
   - Gloss from BEDRL: Specialist with higher technical education.
6. синица
   - Gloss from BEDRL: A small songbird of the passerine order.
7. отвёртка
   - Gloss from BEDRL: A tool for tightening and unscrewing screws and bolts.
8. суббота
   - Gloss from BEDRL: The sixth day of the week preceding Sunday.
9. прилагательное
   - Gloss from BEDRL: A part of speech that denotes the quality, property or belonging of an object and varies by case, number and in the singular by gender.
10. суффикс
    - Gloss from BEDRL: The part located between the root and the ending.
11. байдарка
    - Gloss from BEDRL: A light, narrow sports boat without rowlocks with a closed bow and stern, steered by a two-bladed oar.
12. медаль
    - Gloss from BEDRL: An insignia (with a dignity lower than the order) in the form of a metal circle with something. With a relief image and inscription, issued for outstanding military and civil merits.

13. трамвай
    - Gloss from BEDRL: Urban ground electric railway; a train for such a road or a carriage.
14. пальто
    - Gloss from BEDRL: A type of long-cut outerwear, usually below the knees, worn over a dress, suit, etc.
15. открытка
    - Gloss from BEDRL: Postcard for an open (without envelope) letter; a card of this format with an artistic image.
16. флейта
    - Gloss from BEDRL: A high-pitched woodwind musical instrument in the form of a cylindrical or slightly conical tube with holes and valves.
17. особенность
    - Gloss from BEDRL: A characteristic, distinctive property, quality, sign of someone or something.
18. полуостров
    - Gloss from BEDRL: A part of land washed on three sides by water, and on the fourth side adjacent to the mainland or island.
19. партитура
    - Gloss from BEDRL: A musical notation of a polyphonic musical work, in which the parts of all voices are given one above the other in a certain order.
20. гавань
    - Gloss from BEDRL: A natural or artificial coastal part of a body of water protected from wind and waves, serving as a place for parking, mooring and repair of ships.
21. компьютер
    - Gloss from BEDRL: Electronic computer.
22. водохранилище
    - Gloss from BEDRL: An artificial reservoir for accumulating and storing water, created by blocking a river, stream, etc. with a dam.
23. фотоаппарат
    - Gloss from BEDRL: Camera.
24. ночь
    - Gloss from BEDRL: Part of the day from sunset to sunrise, from evening to morning.

25. акула

    - Gloss from BEDRL: A large predatory marine fish with a spindle-shaped body and a large mouth (it lives in tropical seas, in Russia it is found in the Black, Barents, Baltic and Far Eastern seas; it is a commercial object).

References

1. August, T., Reinecke, K., Smith, N.A.: Generating scientific definitions with controllable complexity. In: Proceedings of the 60th Annual Meeting of the Association for Computational Linguistics (Volume 1: Long Papers), pp. 8298–8317 (2022). https://doi.org/10.18653/v1/2022.acl-long.569
2. Bakhaeva, L.M., D, M.T.: Outdated vocabulary as a conservation factor of national culture [Ustarevshaya lexica kak factor sochranenia national'noi kulturi]. Humanities and Social Sciences [Gumanitarnie i sotsialnie nauki] (2022)
3. Bamler, R., Mandt, S.: Dynamic word embeddings. ICML 2017 (2017)
4. Banerjee, S., Pedersen, T.: Extended gloss overlaps as a measure of semantic relatedness. IJCAI-2003 (2003)
5. Basile, P., Caputo, A., Caselli, T., Cassotti, P., Varvara, R.: Diacr-ita @ evalita2020: Overview of the evalita2020 diachronic lexical semantics (diacr-ita) task. In: Basile, V., Croce, D., Di Maro, M., Passaro, L. (eds.) Proceedings of the Seventh Evaluation Campaign of Natural Language Processing and Speech Tools for Italian. Final Workshop (EVALITA 2020). CEUR Workshop Proceedings (CEUR-WS.org) (2020)
6. Basile, P., Caputo, A., Semeraro, G.: An enhanced Lesk word sense disambiguation algorithm through a distributional semantic model. In: Tsujii, J., Hajic, J. (eds.) Proceedings of COLING 2014, the 25th International Conference on Computational Linguistics: Technical Papers, pp. 1591–1600. Dublin City University and Association for Computational Linguistics. Dublin, Ireland (2014), https://aclanthology.org/C14-1151
7. Borodina, D., Morozov, D.: Gloss-Context Consistency. Mendeley Data V1 (2024). https://doi.org/10.17632/rngjnnvxjm.1
8. Dubossarsky, H., Hengchen, S., Tahmasebi, N., Schlechtweg, D.: Time-out: Temporal referencing for robust modeling of lexical semantic change. In: Korhonen, A., Traum, D., M'arquez, L. (eds.) Proceedings of the 57th Annual Meeting of the Association for Computational Linguistics, pp. 457–470. Association for Computational Linguistics, Florence, Italy (2019). https://doi.org/10.18653/v1/P19-1044, https://aclanthology.org/P19-1044
9. Firth, J.: A synopsis of linguistic theory, 1930–1955. In: Studies in Linguistic Analysis. Philological Society, Oxford (1957)
10. Giulianelli, M., Del Tredici, M., Fern´andez, R.: Analysing lexical semantic change with contextualised word representations. In: Jurafsky, D., Chai, J., Schluter, N., Tetreault, J. (eds.) Proceedings of the 58th Annual Meeting of the Association for Computational Linguistics, pp. 3960–3973. Association for Computational Linguistics, Online (2020). https://doi.org/10.18653/v1/2020.acl-main.365, https://aclanthology.org/2020.acl-main.365
11. Hu, R., Li, S., Liang, S.: Diachronic sense modeling with deep contextualized word embeddings: An ecological view. In: Korhonen, A., Traum, D., M'arquez, L. (eds.) Proceedings of the 57th Annual Meeting of the Association for Computational Linguistics. pp. 3899–3908. Association for Computational Linguistics, Florence, Italy (2019). https://doi.org/10.18653/v1/P19-1379, https://aclanthology.org/P19-1379

12. Huang, L., Sun, C., Qiu, X., Huang, X.: GlossBERT: BERT for word sense disambiguation with gloss knowledge. In: Inui, K., Jiang, J., Ng, V., Wan, X. (eds.) Proceedings of the 2019 Conference on Empirical Methods in Natural Language Processing and the 9th International Joint Conference on Natural Language Processing (EMNLP-IJCNLP), pp. 3509–3514. Association for Computational Linguistics, Hong Kong, China (2019). https://doi.org/10.18653/v1/D19-1355, https://aclanthology.org/D19-1355
13. Kim, Y., Chiu, Y.I., Hanaki, K., Hegde, D., Petrov, S.: Temporal analysis of language through neural language models. In: Danescu-Niculescu-Mizil, C., Eisenstein, J., McKeown, K., Smith, N.A. (eds.) Proceedings of the ACL 2014 Workshop on Language Technologies and Computational Social Science, pp. 61–65. Association for Computational Linguistics, Baltimore, MD, USA (2014). https://doi.org/10.3115/v1/W14-2517, https://aclanthology.org/W14-2517
14. Krongauz, M., Litvin, E., Merzliakova, V.: Dictionary of the Internet .ru language [Slovar' yazika interneta .ru]. AST-Press (2016)
15. Kulkarni, V., Al-Rfou, R., Perozzi, B., Skiena, S.: Statistically significant detection of linguistic change. In: Proceedings of the 24th International Conference on World Wide Web, p. 625–635. WWW '15, International World Wide Web Conferences Steering Committee, Republic and Canton of Geneva, CHE (2015). https://doi.org/10.1145/2736277.2741627, https://doi.org/10.1145/2736277.2741627
16. Kuratov, Y., Arkhipov, M.: Adaptation of deep bidirectional multilingual transformers for russian language. In: Computational Linguistics and Intellectual Technologies: Proceedings of the International Conference "Dialogue 2019" (2019)
17. Kutuzov, A., Kuzmenko, E.: WebVectors: A Toolkit for Building Web Interfaces for Vector Semantic Models, pp. 155–161. Springer International Publishing, Cham (2017). https://doi.org/10.1007/978-3-319-52920-2_15, https://doi.org/10.1007/978-3-319-52920-2_15
18. Kutuzov, A., Pivovarova, L.: Rushifteval: A shared task on semantic shift detection for russian. In: Computational linguistics and intellectual technologies:. No. 20 in Komp'^uterna^a lingvistika i intellektual'nye tehnologii - Computational Linguistics and Intellectual Technologies, Redkollegija sbornika, Russian Federation (2021). https://doi.org/10.28995/2075-7182-2021-20-533-545, http://www.dialog-21.ru/en/
19. Kuznetsov., S.A. (ed.): The Big Explanatory Dictionary of Russian language. Norint Publ., St. Petersburg (2000)
20. Lau, J.H., Cook, P., McCarthy, D., Newman, D., Baldwin, T.: Word sense induction for novel sense detection. In: Daelemans, W. (ed.) Proceedings of the 13th Conference of the European Chapter of the Association for Computational Linguistics, pp. 591–601. Association for Computational Linguistics, Avignon, France (2012). https://aclanthology.org/E12-1060
21. Lesk, M.: Automatic sense disambiguation using machine readable dictionaries: how to tell a pine cone from an ice cream cone. In: Proceedings of the 5th Annual International Conference on Systems Documentation, p. 24–26. Association for Computing Machinery, New York, NY, USA (1986). https://doi.org/10.1145/318723.318728
22. Loukachevitch, N., Lashevich, G.: Multiword expressions in russian thesauri ruthes and ruwordnet. In: 2016 IEEE Artificial Intelligence and Natural Language Conference (AINL), pp. 1–6 (2016)
23. Malkin, N., Lanka, S., Goel, P., Rao, S., Jojic, N.: GPT perdetry test: Generating new meanings for new words. In: Proceedings of the 2021 Conference of the North American Chapter of the Association for Computational Linguistics: Human Language Technologies, pp. 5542–5553 (2021)
24. Mikolov, T., Chen, K., Corrado, G.S., Dean, J.: Efficient estimation of word representations in vector space. In: International Conference on Learning Representations (2013). https://api.semanticscholar.org/CorpusID:5959482

25. Mitra, S., et al.: An automatic approach to identify word sense changes in text media across timescales. Natural Language Engineering, pp. 1–26 (2015). https://doi.org/10.1017/S135132491500011X
26. Novikov, V.: Dictionary of fashionable words: the linguistic picture of modernity [Slovar' modnich slov: yazikovaya kartina sovremennosti]. Dictionaries of the XXI century [Slovari XX veka] (2015)
27. Petersson, S., Sk¨oldberg, E.: Semantic change in swedish – from a lexicographic perspective. In: Computational approaches to semantic change. Language Science Press (2021)
28. Rachinskiy, M., Arefyev, N.: Zero-shot cross-lingual transfer of a gloss language model for semantic change detection. In: Computational linguistics and intellectual technologies:. No. 20 in Komp'yuternaya lingvistika i intellektual'nye tehnologii - Computational Linguistics and Intellectual Technologies. Redkollegija sbornika (2021). https://api.semanticscholar.org/CorpusID:240068031
29. Rosenfeld, A., Erk, K.: Deep neural models of semantic shift. In: Walker, M., Ji, H., Stent, A. (eds.) Proceedings of the 2018 Conference of the North American Chapter of the Association for Computational Linguistics: Human Language Technologies, Volume 1 (Long Papers), pp. 474–484. Association for Computational Linguistics, New Orleans, Louisiana (2018). https://doi.org/10.18653/v1/N18-1044, https://aclanthology.org/N18-1044
30. Ryzhova, A., Ryzhova, D., Sochenkov, I.: Detection of semantic changes in russian nouns with distributional models and grammatical features. In: Computational linguistics and intellectual technologies. No. 20 in Komp'yuternaya lingvistika i intellektual'nye tehnologii - Computational Linguistics and Intellectual Technologies, Redkollegija sbornika, pp. 597–606 (2021). https://doi.org/10.28995/2075-7182-2021-20-597-606
31. Sagi, E., Kaufmann, S., Clark, B.: Semantic density analysis: Comparing word meaning across time and phonetic space. In: Basili, R., Pennacchiotti, M. (eds.) Proceedings of the Workshop on Geometrical Models of Natural Language Semantics, pp. 104–111. Association for Computational Linguistics, Athens, Greece (2009). https://aclanthology.org/W09-0214
32. Schlechtweg, D., McGillivray, B., Hengchen, S., Dubossarsky, H., Tahmasebi, N.: SemEval-2020 task 1: Unsupervised lexical semantic change detection. In: Herbelot, A., Zhu, X., Palmer, A., Schneider, N., May, J., Shutova, E. (eds.) Proceedings of the Fourteenth Workshop on Semantic Evaluation, pp. 1–23. International Committee for Computational Linguistics, Barcelona (online) (2020). https://doi.org/10.18653/v1/2020.semeval-1.1, https://aclanthology.org/2020.semeval-1.1
33. Wijaya, D.T., Yeniterzi, R.: Understanding semantic change of words over centuries. In: Proceedings of the 2011 International Workshop on DETecting and Exploiting Cultural DiversiTy on the Social Web, pp. 35–40. Association for Computing Machinery, New York, NY, USA (2011). https://doi.org/10.1145/2064448.2064475, https://doi.org/10.1145/2064448.2064475

Text Preprocessing for Keyword and Key Phrase Extraction

Alexandra Troshina(✉)

St Petersburg State University, St. Petersburg, Russia
troshina26@mail.ru

Abstract. This article explores various text preprocessing techniques for the extraction of keywords and key phrases. It delves into methods such as text lemmatization, stop-word removal, and number removal, comparing their efficacy with unprocessed text in keyword extraction. Evaluation is based on the ability of keyword sets to retrieve relevant news articles from search engine queries. The study employs multiple keyword extraction tools for comprehensive analysis.

Keywords: Keyword Extraction · Text Preprocessing · Lemmatization · Stop-Word Removal · Search Engine

1 Introduction

Automatic keyword and key phrase extraction is a foundational task within computational linguistics. Its advantages over manual extraction are paramount, particularly its capability to handle extensive text volumes and provide real-time results. The need for preprocessing texts is especially important in the context of news, which is the primary focus of this article. Information retrieval is crucial in modern society, yet the vastness of digital data poses challenges in efficiently navigating and locating pertinent information. Automated keyword extraction is indispensable in the news domain for several reasons: the sheer volume of news content necessitates automated processes, as manual extraction cannot feasibly handle such scale. Additionally, the time-sensitive nature of news demands rapid processing, with keyword extraction aiding in discerning important topics and events relevant to users in real-time. Nowadays various techniques exist for defining keywords and key phrases in text, encompassing both supervised and unsupervised methods, including statistical methods such as YAKE! and KP-Miner, graph-based methods like TopicRank and TextRank, as well as LLM-based tools such as KEA and KeyBERT, alongside fine-tuning LLM [1, 4]. While selecting the optimal key extraction tool presents one challenge, another issue is the necessity for preprocessing the texts.

This study aims to determine the necessity and extent of preprocessing texts for effective keyword extraction in information retrieval tasks.

The paper is structured as follows: in the first section, we introduce the topic. The second section is dedicated to an overview of related work. In the third, fourth, and fifth sections, we discuss the principles of creating the dataset, using keyword lists as queries, and our evaluation methodology, respectively. The sixth section presents the results of

M. Bakaev et al. (Eds.): IMS 2024, CCIS 2534, pp. 105–112, 2026.
https://doi.org/10.1007/978-3-031-96177-9_9

our experiments and statistical tests. Finally, in the seventh section, we draw conclusions based on the data obtained.

2 Related Work

The majority of previous studies show that text preprocessing, including tokenization, normalization, lemmatization, stemming, and stop-word removal, has a significant impact on the quality and accuracy of keyword extraction. Comprehensive preprocessing helps improve results by reducing noise and enhancing the relevance of extracted keywords.

In the study [3] the impact of various preprocessing steps, such as lemmatization, stemming, and stop-word removal, on the keyword extraction process is examined. The author concludes that lemmatization and stemming improve the accuracy of keyword extraction, while stop-word removal helps reduce data volume and enhance keyword relevance.

The paper [5] explores the use of preprocessing methods such as tokenization, normalization, and stop-word removal in the context of the RAKE (Rapid Automatic Keyword Extraction) method. The authors evaluate the impact of each preprocessing step on the quality of keyword extraction. They find that preprocessing, including tokenization and stop-word removal, significantly improves the accuracy of keyword extraction using the RAKE method. Text normalization helps reduce data variability and improve results.

3 Creating the Dataset

We gathered 64 news articles from the Fontanka.ru news agency, all dated March 8th, 2024. The date was chosen at random. The articles comprise the total output for this date, with the exception of those in the sections Doctor Piter, Afisha+, Construction, and Lifestyle, as these represent genres other than news articles, which were the focus of the present investigation. We removed mentions of the Fontanka news agency from the texts to ensure that it would not appear in the keyword sets and distort the search results. Then these texts underwent preprocessing using six different methods, while the seventh variant remained unaltered:

1. Lowercase + lemmatization
2. Lowercase + lemmatization + stop-word removal
3. Lowercase + lemmatization + stop-word removal + number removal
4. Lowercase + stop-word removal + number removal
5. Lowercase + stop-word removal
6. Lowercase only
7. No changes applied

As an example of the output, we present two versions of the same news article. The first version shows the “no changes applied” variant, and the second is the “lowercase + lemmatization + stop-word removal” variant:

1. 'Посольства Швеции, Чехии и Южной Кореи, а также правительство Канады предупредили своих граждан о возможных терактах в Москве, ссылаясь на сообщения посольства США, 8 марта пишет «». Они сообщили об «ухудшении ситуации с безопасностью в стране» и призвали избегать мест массового скопления людей. Так, чешское посольство обеспокоено появившимися сообщениями «о возможных нападениях экстремистских группировок в крупных российских городах», говорится на его официальном сайте. Ранее с похожими предупреждениями выступили МИД Латвии, Германии и Великобритании. Они, как писали СМИ, призвали избегать поездок в Россию и ближайшие 48 часов остерегаться массовых мероприятий.'
2. 'посольство швеции, чехия южный кореи, правительство канада предупредить гражданин возможный теракт москве, ссылаться сообщение посольство сша, март писать «». сообщить «ухудшение ситуация безопасность стране» призвать избегать место массовый скопление людей. так, чешский посольство обеспокоить появиться сообщение «о возможный нападение экстремистский группировка крупный российский городах», говориться официальный сайте. ранее похожий предупреждение выступить мид латвии, германия великобритании. они, писать сми, призвать избегать поездка россия близкий 48 час остерегаться массовый мероприятий.'

Following preprocessing, we employed two distinct keyword extraction tools to extract keywords and key phrases. For our research, we selected two different methods: RuTermExtract [7] and TopicRank [2].

RuTermExtract is a method and tool for automatic extraction of key terms from Russian-language texts. RuTermExtract combines linguistic and statistical methods. The linguistic aspect involves morphological and syntactic analysis to identify word forms and structural elements of the text and considers grammatical features of the Russian language, such as cases, genders, and numbers. Based on the results of linguistic analysis, candidates for key terms are identified. These candidates can be either individual words or phrases. Subsequently, statistical measures, such as TF-IDF (term frequency-inverse document frequency), are used to evaluate the importance of each candidate. This helps to filter out less significant terms. Key terms are ranked by importance, and the top n most relevant terms are selected to represent the content of the text. RuTermExtract is optimized for processing Russian-language texts and is often used as one of the most effective tools, which is based on morphological tagging and statistical methods [6].

TopicRank is a key phrase extraction method based on topic segmentation and ranking. Proposed by Bougouin et al. [2], it combines a graph-based approach with topic analysis of the text. The text is divided into segments, each representing a potential topic. This step allows for the consideration of the semantic cohesion of words and phrases within topics. Based on the identified topics, a weighted undirected graph is constructed, where nodes are key phrase candidates and edges represent their co-occurrences within the same topic segment. The PageRank algorithm is used to rank the nodes in the graph. Each key phrase is assigned a weight reflecting its importance in the context of the text's topics. The key phrases with the highest rank values are selected as the final set of key phrases. The main advantage of TopicRank lies in its consideration of the text topical structure, which allows for more accurate extraction of key phrases that reflect the main themes of the document.

4 Using Keywords as Search Queries

After creating seven distinct sets of keyword groups for each of the two selected algorithms, we input them into the Google search engine and requested 10 results for each. As an example of the queries, we present four versions of the keyword sets derived from the same article:

1. RuTermExtract algorithm, the "no changes applied" variant: ['сообщение посольства сша', 'массовое скопление людей', 'крупные российские города', 'ближайшие 48 часов', 'южная корея'];
2. RuTermExtract algorithm, the "lowercase + lemmatization + stop-word removal" variant: ['сообщение', 'массовый скопление людей', 'крупный российский города', 'близкий 48 час', 'южный корея'];
3. TopicRank algorithm, the "no changes applied" variant: ['сообщение посольство сша', 'посольство швеции', 'мид латвии', 'похожий предупреждение', 'правительство канада'];
4. TopicRank algorithm, the "lowercase + lemmatization + stop-word removal" variant: ['мид латвии', 'россию', 'ближайшие', 'германии', 'возможных терактах'].

As we can see, all the sets differ depending on the algorithm selected and the degree of preprocessing applied.

To automate this process, we started a Custom Search Engine. The Google Custom Search Engine (CSE) allows for the creation and customization of search engines that can be seamlessly integrated into websites or applications. The following code represents a URL request to the Google Custom Search API, specifically designed for news search. The parameter *tbm* = *nws* indicates a focus on news content within the API: url = https://www.googleapis.com/customsearch/v1?q={query}&cx={self.cx}&key = {self.api_key}&start = {start_index}&tbm = nws.

It is important to note that the search results in Google Custom Search Engine and regular Google search may vary due to differences in indexing frequency and personalization. Difference in indexing frequency means that Google's primary search index undergoes continuous updates, ensuring the inclusion of the most recent and relevant content in search results. With Google Custom Search Engine, the indexing frequency may vary based on settings and configuration, impacting the freshness and relevance of search outcomes. Personalization of result infers that customer's search through the Google web interface can be personalized based on their search history, location, and other parameters, while queries through the Google Custom Search API may be more standardized. An observation of this disparity was evident when comparing search results for local St Petersburg news, particularly regarding minor local events. Google's main search displayed significantly more relevant results, leveraging location data, whereas Google Custom Search Engine yielded less satisfactory results. However, the variation in results across most queries was minimal.

5 Evaluation Method

For evaluation purposes, we measured effectiveness by counting the occurrences of news covering the same event in search results. To automate this process, we compared the publication dates of the original news text from which keywords were extracted with the dates of news articles in the search results.

Ideally the news covering the same event had to refer to the same date as the original news from which we extracted the key phrases. We understand that the same event may be the topic of the news 1 or 2 days mostly, so we considered all the news that were published exactly on the date of the original news, 1 day before the original news and 1 day after. If our search results date coincided with our date set, we stated that the search succeeded ("successful search results" in the Table 1 below). If it was some other date – our search failed ("false search results" in the Table 1 below).

The problem with this technique was that it is not always possible to establish the publication date automatically. We implemented several varying methods; however, we couldn't always establish the dates. After undertaking a manual investigation we saw that practically all the news, where it was impossible to establish the date, were indeed irrelevant to our search (only 1 news out of 50 was indeed covering the same event as the seed news; it was the digest site of the week news), so it was possible to count these results as failed search. However, we decided to show them as a separate figure in this paper. Thus, we got 5 tables with 3 columns each showing the distribution of the 10 results for each keyword query: number of successful search results, number of false results and number of unclear search results.

6 Statistical Tests on the Datasets

The results of the Shapiro-Wilk test indicated that our data did not exhibit normal distribution. Therefore, we chose to utilize a nonparametric test such as the Kruskal-Wallis test, which is appropriate for this type of non-normally distributed data.

When we tested the data, obtained with the help of the keywords extracted by TopicRank, the test showed the statistical difference in our data:

Kruskal-Wallis Results – The number of successful search results:

Statistic: 29.77789106465549, p-value: 4.332016808557898e-05.

The null hypothesis posits that the degree of preprocessing does not affect the effectiveness of keyword extraction. However, our results indicate a clear impact, rejecting the null hypothesis.

On looking at the figures in the table below, which represent the total number of successful and unsuccessful search results, we can see the big difference between the numbers representing preprocessing with lemmatization and without it, with lemmatization deteriorating the results by 2 times.

The data obtained while working with keywords extracted by the RuTermExtract algorithm were also subjected to analysis using the Kruskal-Wallis statistical test, which did not reveal a statistically significant difference between the obtained results:

Kruskal-Wallis Results – The number of successful search results:

Statistic: 3.8839013163629033, p-value: 0.69238418823597.

Indeed, upon examining the data table, it is evident that the overall number of successful results obtained differs insignificantly. This may be attributed to the fact that

Table 1. Table representing the total numbers of the search results.

Pre-processing type	Number of successful search results	Number of false search results	Number of unclear search results
RuTermExtract			
Lowercase + lemmatization	104	238	288
Lowercase + lemmatization + stop-word removal	109	252	259
Lowercase + lemmatization + stop-word removal + number removal	116	243	260
Lowercase + stop-word removal + number removal	94	211	285
Lowercase + stop-word removal	125	212	263
Lowercase only No changes applied	137 124	208 247	255 249
TopicRank			
Lowercase + lemmatization	86	264	280
Lowercase + lemmatization + stop-word removal	86	239	305
Lowercase + lemmatization + stop-word removal + number removal	75	226	309
Lowercase + stop-word removal + number removal	142	255	253
Lowercase + stop-word removal	144	219	257
Lowercase only	130	243	247
No changes applied	124	247	249

the algorithm itself incorporates a mechanism for lemmatization. However, it is still noticeable that lemmatization slightly deteriorates the results.

Additionally, it appears that removing digits has a small positive effect. In 3 out of 4 datasets, the removal of digits resulted in a slight increase in successful search results.

7 Conclusion

Overall, we can state that preprocessing is undeniably an important step to consider when implementing automatic keyword extraction. However, unlike numerous prior studies that emphasize the importance of lemmatization, our findings indicate that its application during preprocessing can actually deteriorate search results. This outcome diverges significantly from the established understanding in the field of natural language processing, where lemmatization is typically seen as a beneficial step that enhances the normalization of text and facilitates more accurate keyword extraction.

The observed negative impact of lemmatization in our case may be attributed to several factors. First, the characteristics of the Russian language, including its complex morphology and rich inflectional system, may play a role in this phenomenon. The process of lemmatization in Russian can be more intricate compared to other languages, potentially introducing errors or ambiguities that were not present in the original text. These errors can propagate through the search process, leading to decreased relevance and accuracy of the retrieved results.

Moreover, our study focused on news articles, where the exact wording and phrasing are often critical for accurately conveying the specific events and details being reported. The nuanced differences between inflected forms of words can be vital for the search engine to understand and match the user's query with the most relevant documents. By lemmatizing the text, we may lose some of these critical distinctions, resulting in a diminished search performance.

The significance of other steps in the preprocessing stage varies depending on the algorithm chosen. The removal of stop-words and numbers improved the efficiency of search when applying the TopicRank algorithm, making the version with stop-word and number removal, but without lemmatization, the most effective. However, removing stop-words and numbers deteriorated the results of RuTermExtract compared to the text with no changes. The best version for RuTermExtract proved to be the application of lowercase only.

In conclusion, careful consideration of preprocessing procedures is essential, taking into account the specific algorithm used for keyword extraction. The effectiveness of these preprocessing steps can significantly impact the performance of the search results, emphasizing the need for individualized preprocessing strategies for each algorithm.

References

1. Alami Merrouni, Z., Frikh, B., Ouhbi, B.: Automatic keyphrase extraction: a survey and trends. J. Intell. Inf. Syst. **54**(2), 391–424 (2020)
2. Bougouin, A., Boudin, F., Daille, B.: TOPICRANK: graph-based topic ranking for keyphrase extraction. In: Proceedings of the International Joint Conference on Natural Language Processing (IJCNLP), pp. 543–551 (2013)

3. Hulth, A.: Improved automatic keyword extraction given more linguistic knowledge. In: Proceedings of the 2003 Conference on Empirical Methods in Natural Language Processing (EMNLP), pp. 216–223 (2003)
4. Glazkova, A.V., Morozov, D.A., Vorobeva, M.S., Stupnikov, A.A.: Keyphrase generation for Russian-language scientific texts using mT5. Model. Anal. Inf. Syst. **30**(4), 418–428 (2023)
5. Rose, S., Engel, D., Cramer, N., Cowley, W.: Automatic keyword extraction from individual documents. In: Text Mining: Applications and Theory, pp. 1–20 (2010)
6. RuTermExtract. https://github.com/igorshevchenko/Ruterextract. Last accessed 30 March 2024

Fear and Loathing in Russian Literature: A Case of Emotion Annotation of Short Stories of the 20th Century

Anna Moskvina and Margarita Kirina(✉)

National Research University Higher School of Economics,
123 Griboyedova Embankment, St. Petersburg 190068, Russia
mkirina@hse.ru

Abstract. The paper presents an investigation of the emotional aspect of the Russian short story of the 20th century. Our study is two-fold: firstly, we delve into emotional representation at the lexical level, building upon previous work on utilizing vector models to quantify emotional content. Following this line of research, we introduce an annotated corpus where words are tagged as expressing specific emotions as recognized by readers. Previously automatically derived lexical distributions are evaluated against the annotated data, comparing lexical diversity, frequencies and part-of-speech distributions. Secondly, we explore the perceptual aspect of emotions by conducting an experiment where readers assess their emotional experience while reading using valence and arousal scales. As a result, an exploratory analysis was conducted, revealing certain tendencies in readers' affective perception of texts. Current study attempts to bring together the lexical expression of emotions in fiction texts and the subjective experience of emotional affect during reading.

Keywords: Sentiment Analysis · Distributional Semantics · Corpus of Russian Short Stories · Russian literature · Emotional Lexicon

1 Introduction

The task of processing the emotional component of data, including both text and speech, stands as a pivotal area within contemporary natural language processing (NLP). It encompasses fields such as sentiment analysis, opinion mining, emotion detection and classification. Typically, the automatic analysis of emotions involves classifying text fragments, ranging from news articles to messages, posts, and comments, by mapping them to expressed or induced emotion labels based on psychological models [1]. Assessing the emotional component of data has found a diverse array of applications, from simulating behavior in dialogue systems to identifying potentially dangerous users or even supporting clinical research [1–3]. In the context of analyzing emotions in literary texts, despite the more scholarly objectives of such studies, these methodologies have also been extensively applied [4–6]. One important direction is building and refining the resources such as annotated corpora and sentiment lexicons [7].

M. Bakaev et al. (Eds.): IMS 2024, CCIS 2534, pp. 113–129, 2026.
https://doi.org/10.1007/978-3-031-96177-9_10

This paper introduces an emotionally annotated sub-corpus of the Corpus of Russian short stories, comprising 220 texts evenly distributed across the 20th century. It features two types of annotations: lexical, based on a categorical approach to emotion description, and the one that will be referred to as affective, relying on a dimensional approach and using text segments as units. Emotional vocabularies were derived from the first type of annotation, associated with 11 emotional categories. The affective annotation, mapping each text segment with readers' perception scores provides valuable data for machine learning. The combination of the two approaches offers insights into the relationship between lexical levels and perception. In addition to the methodology and annotator guidelines, the paper also presents an analysis of emotional rating distributions and compares them with the results of automatically computed scores, thereby contributing to a deeper understanding of emotion expression in literary texts.

2 Annotating Emotions

2.1 Approaches

Despite the absence of a universally accepted definition of emotion and methods for its measurement, two primary approaches are acknowledged for defining or describing emotional content [1, 8, 9]. The categorical method entails compiling a list of emotions, which can be basic or extend to complex and hierarchical structures. Alternatively, the dimensional approach represents emotions through values on several scales reflecting emotion components. The VAD model (valence, arousal, dominance), also referred to in terms of evaluation, activation, and power, is the most prominent framework. Valence rates the emotion on a positive-negative spectrum, arousal quantifies its intensity, and dominance assesses the locus of control, internal or external. Though originating from psychological studies, both methodologies have been integrated into computational data analysis tasks.

2.2 Annotated Datasets

Like many domains in computational linguistics, automatic emotion detection and categorization starts with data annotation, laying the groundwork for all subsequent analysis and modeling. Annotated corpora serve as datasets for training and testing machine learning models, provide a standardized benchmark, and represent data for investigation on their own. The two main approaches to describing emotions (categorical and dimensional) are represented in different markup guidelines used for annotating text data. The most popular appears to be the categorical model, i.e. using a set of predefined emotional labels.

Existing emotion-annotated datasets for the Russian language predominantly utilize a categorical approach for emotional analysis, where each sentence or short text—often derived from social media platforms like posts or tweets—is labeled with a specific emotional tag. They are used to train models to detect emotions in texts and perform multi-label categorization of emotional content. One of the biggest available datasets is the Corpus for Emotions Detecting in Russian-language text (CEDR) [10] that comprises

9,410 comments from various social sources, annotated for five emotion categories: joy, sadness, surprise, fear, and anger. Another resource, the RuIzardEmotions: A Dataset of Fine-Grained Emotions[1], consists of translated Reddit posts, applying 10 labels based on Izard's model of emotions. The well-known RuSentiment dataset [11] focuses on default sentiment values, providing positive or negative labels for texts, but also includes tags for speech acts, and provides insightful guidelines explaining that sentiment may dwell both in the speaker's mood and their attitude towards a topic, how does mixed sentiment work, how to interpret smiley punctuation and hashtags and so on.

In their survey, Bostan and Klinger [1] comprised 14 annotated resources for English that varied in the source (e.g. social media, news), annotation procedure (e. g. crowd-sourcing, expert-based, self-reporting), and the emotion model used for annotation (9 of 14 resources were annotated with the six basic emotions). They also built a unified dataset, comprising all of the resources. In [12] English news headlines were annotated with both associated emotions and the reader's perception. In their work, Kim and Klinger [13] present an annotated corpus of literature featuring a complex markup designed to model emotional interactions between characters. Another noteworthy contribution is described in [14], where the authors introduce EmoTales, a fictional dataset of tales annotated with emotions. This dataset utilizes a nuanced approach, combining fine-grained categorical emotional models with dimensional annotation. Additionally, the paper offers extensive post-processing analysis, providing significant insights into the domain.

2.3 Lexical Resources

In addition to annotated datasets, there are also lexical resources that provide lists of words and their associated emotions or sentiment values. They too can serve as a tool for enhancing emotion detection algorithms. Sometimes existing dictionaries of evaluative lexicon or similar ones are translated to the target language [3]. Regarding the task of compiling dictionaries, it is worth noting that ready-made dictionaries can be manually expanded taking into account the specifics of the subject area. The use of crowdsourcing platforms is becoming increasingly popular for data collection. One of the well-known similar projects is LINIS Crowd, where anyone interested can participate in creating the PolSentiLex sentiment dictionary for the Russian language [15]. A common approach is when each word in the dictionary is associated with a numeric sentiment rating. For example, in the AFINN [16] dictionary «aggressive» has the score of -2, «advances» of 1. Words from the dictionary are matched with words from the analyzed text, and then the assigned ratings are summed at the sentence level and further at the level of a certain text fragment. Sentiment may be either assigned to text as a whole, but depending on the task and the data being analyzed, the researcher may be interested in determining the rating for a particularly grained text segment (for example, a paragraph). Sometimes sentiment ratings are assigned not only to individual words but also to n-sequences of words. In [17], an interesting approach to creating such a lexicon is discussed – SCL-OPP, which primarily considers the sentiment of phrases consisting of polar-opposite words (e.g. freaking love that has 0.922 score, truly missed –0.422).

[1] https://huggingface.co/datasets/Djacon/ru-izard-emotions.

The NRC VAD Lexicon [9] and Affective Norms for English Words (ANEW) by Bradley and Lang [18] exemplify resources employing the VAD scale, rating words across pleasure (happy vs. unhappy), arousal (excited vs. calm), and dominance (controlled vs. in control). While ANEW utilizes the Self-Assessment Manikin (SAM) for its assessments, the NRC VAD Lexicon adopts a Best–Worst Scaling method, which its creators argue offers a more precise evaluation of emotions.

3 Selecting Subcorpus and Preprocessing

For annotation, we selected the subcorpus from the Russian Short Story Corpus [19]. This sample comprises 220 Russian short stories spanning from 1901 to 2000, providing a comprehensive sample for the analysis of the evolution of language and narrative styles across the century, with a total of 487,170 tokens. For each year within this period, 2 to 4 stories were selected, leading to an average story length of approximately 5,300 tokens. The dataset was distributed among annotators, with each annotator handling an average of around 44,300 tokens. Before the annotation process, the texts of the stories were divided into fragments in such a way that each fragment represented a small excerpt of text, comprising several sentences, to ensure it was conveniently displayed in the annotation interface. These fragments also served as units for affective annotation, meaning each fragment would be assigned with emotional ratings as a whole. Efforts were made to preserve the narrative's semantic integrity as much as possible—maintaining the original paragraph division, keeping dialogues together, and so on.

All the stories in the corpus were processed with the tool for analyzing emotions in literary texts developed in previous work[2], and the resulting emotional scores and weighted word lists were compared against the results of manual annotation. The program is based on a vector space model. For each word in a given text, a degree of semantic association was calculated based on the cosine distance using the model fastText Skipgram (trained on Russian National Corpus)[3]. A list of labels—nouns denoting the corresponding emotions, such as *happiness* ("schastye"), *contentment* ("udovolstvie"), *surprise* ("udivleniye"), *anger* ("zlost'"), *sadness* ("grust'"), *fear* ("strakh"), *disgust* ("otvrashcheniye"), and *shame* ("styd") were used as a lexical representation of a corresponding emotion. Words whose proximity to the label exceeded the threshold value are considered semantic associates. The following formula was used to calculate the emotional score for the whole story:

$$E_{score} = \sum_{i=1}^{n} \sqrt{w_{i_{score}}} \cdot w_{i_{freq}}$$

Here, n is the number of emotional words in the story based on the defined threshold, w_{score} is the score calculated as cosine similarity and w_{freq} is how many times this word has occurred in the text. E_{score} is calculated per each emotion and is normalized by the length of the texts in tokens. Each story thus receives a vector type list of values

[2] http://vectors.nlpl.eu/repository/20/181.zip.

[3] http://vectors.nlpl.eu/repository/20/181.zip.

characterizing its emotional content. Details of the program's design and some experiments are presented in [20]. Current study is not focused on the final text-level emotional scores, but employs the vocabularies and frequencies of emotional words obtained in the process.

4 Annotation Process

For the annotation task, 22 philology students were enlisted as expert annotators. Each annotation type was conducted by two independent annotators, and the stories allocated for lexical and affective annotations were varied for each expert pair. This meant that if an annotator worked on a story for one type of annotation, they would not encounter the same story for the other type but would receive a different one instead. Due to the limited number of annotators, inter-annotator agreement was not calculated at this research phase. Nonetheless, in future work the presence of dual annotations per text can be factored into the analysis, either by averaging them, selecting intersections or employing more complex strategy. Moreover, having two annotations offers the possibility to identify and rely on the more accurate annotator, potentially excluding the less consistent one from the analysis.

4.1 Lexical Annotation with Emotional Categories

The first type of emotional annotation stemmed from previous research and entailed annotating the separate words that contribute to the emotiveness of a given text based on a categorical model of eleven emotion tags. The idea behind this was to find out what lexical units contribute to the emotions either experienced by characters or representing the mood of the narrative. The guidelines for the annotators provided the following conditions for marking words with a particular tag: 1) they express a specific emotion (e.g., "shame", "joyful", "disgusting", "delight"), 2) they have a clear positive or negative meaning either literally or in context (e.g., «wonderful», «mean», «cold»—if about a person), 3) they carry a strong emotional connotation affecting the text's mood and reader's perception (e.g., "shake" from fear, "sigh" from sadness). Emotional tags represented 11 categories and were as follows: e_fear for fear-related emotions, e_sad for sadness, e_anger for anger, e_disgust for disgust, including contempt, e_shame for shame and embarrassment, e_happy for happiness, e_pleasure for physical pleasure, e_amuse for amusement, e_surp for surprise, e_pride for pride in achievement, and e_relief for relief. Although most of them are self-explanatory, some additional comments were given to the annotators. The other two tags s_pos and s_neg were introduced for words that denote a positive or negative tone without pinpointing a specific emotion, for the occasions when it was hard to identify a particular emotion. Tags can overlap, allowing a word associated with multiple emotions in a particular context to be assigned more than one tag.

The annotation process was conducted on the Doccano platform [21], utilizing the sequence labeling annotation type. Annotators were presented with individual paragraphs, enabling them to select any word and assign an emotional tag from a predefined list. Paragraphs were displayed sequentially, allowing for the reading of each story in its entirety. Annotators had the flexibility to revisit previous paragraphs and revise their annotations as needed. Figure 1 demonstrates the interface for annotators.

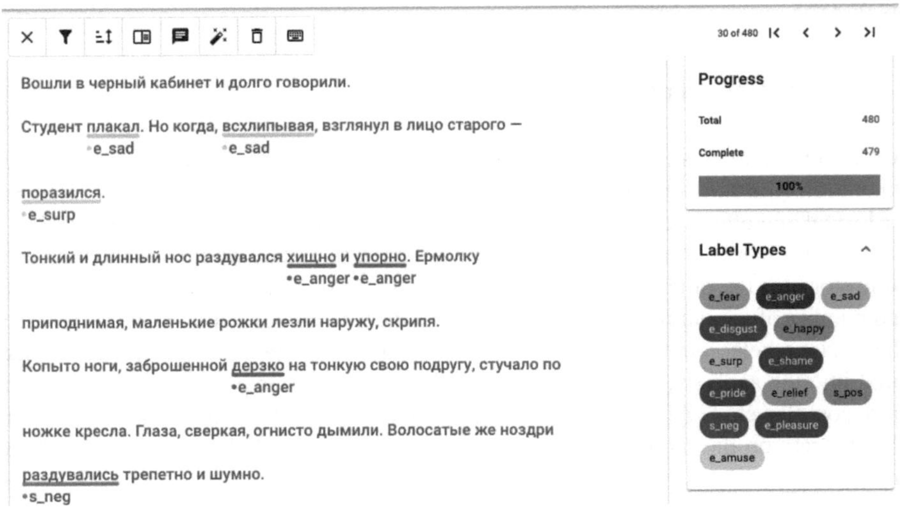

Fig. 1. Annotator interface for lexical annotation

The source results of the annotation are compiled in the JSONL format, ensuring structured and accessible data for analysis. The output format employs positional tagging to demarcate specific text spans associated with emotional expressions, identified by start and end indices along with an emotional tag.

A total of 70,424 lexical units have been identified by annotators, of which the most frequent turned out to be sentiment tags—24925 (35%) for negative and 20653 (29%) for positive. Among the emotions, the top tags were *e_sad* with 5058 (20% of emotions), *e_fear* with 4471 (18%), *e_happy* with 3485 (14%), *e_anger* with 3385 (14%). The least popular tags turned out to be *e_pride* with 834 (3%) and *e_relief* with 518 (2%). 3,713 (about 5%) out of selected sequences are compound constructions of several words. There were no technical restrictions on selecting multiword sequences, although the guidelines constantly referred to single-word items. This allowed for preserving our focus on the lexical units but keeping some multiword expressions that cannot be meaningfully decomposed. The example of ambiguous multiword expression that received different emotional tags is "Gospodu pomiluj" ("Lord have mercy"), which was tagged with both *e_fear* and *e_relief* tags.

4.2 Affective Annotation with Dimensions

For the second annotation type on the same sub-corpus, the focus shifted to assessing the reader's perception and the affective impact of the fictional text. Two dimensions were utilized: valence, indicating the emotion's position on a positive-negative scale, and arousal, reflecting the emotion's intensity, both physiologically and otherwise. For example, the exclamation "I have never been so happy!" would score high in both positive valence and arousal, representing intense positive feelings. Conversely, the term "anxiety" might be assigned a high arousal score for its strong emotional impact and a low/negative valence due to its negative nature. The text fragments were presented to annotators in Excel spreadsheets, again allowing for the reading of the story from start to finish. For each fragment, two scores were expected to be filled in. The results were compiled into a single CSV file to facilitate the integration of the two types of annotations.

This markup strategy extends beyond the lexicon associated with emotions. We build our approach on the following key principles. Firstly, dimensions of valence and arousal apply not only to words directly related to emotions but also to all lexical items (for example, the word «wound» would presumably have low values on both scales). Secondly, paragraphs serve as the units of analysis. It is assumed that a text segment, as a whole, leaves the reader with a certain feeling that can be assessed on the valence and arousal scales. Finally, if the feelings are sufficiently strong but the emotional tone is unclear or mixed, a valence can be evaluated as 0 (if there's no predominant emotion), but a high arousal value should be chosen. The value ranges are as follows: valence from −3 (intensely negative) to 3 (intensely positive emotion), arousal from 1 (minimal emotional expression, very calm) to 5 (the text caused a very strong emotional response).

Table 1 demonstrates an example from the guidelines. The following fragment elicits quite strong emotions, hence an arousal value of 3 or 4 would be appropriate. Meanwhile, the sentiment is clearly negative, marked by disappointment and shame, warranting a valence of −3 or −2.

Table 1. Affective annotation sample

Segment_id	Text	Text (translation)	Valence	Arousal
S026_59	Эти письма были кладом, сокровищем—и он легкомысленно выпустил их из рук. Хорошо, что Икс, не знает! Он смеялся бы над ним! И был бы прав. Был бы трижды прав	These letters were a treasure, and he carelessly let them slip through his fingers. Good that X doesn't know! He would laugh at him! And he would be right. Thrice right	−2	4

It was expected that many fragments may not be particularly emotionally impactful to the reader. The most neutral ratings are 0 on the valence scale and 1 on the arousal scale (not 0). However, if the text is rather pleasant or creates a nice atmosphere (a walk, family dinner), then a valence of 1 was recommended to be assigned. The annotators were explicitly asked to take their time and calmly read and assess each paragraph.

The distribution of valence values reveals a tendency towards neutrality: the most common value is slightly negative (−1), observed 2,581 times, accounting for 24% of the dataset. This is followed by a neutral score (0) with 2,151 occurrences (20%), and slightly positive (1) with 1,978 instances (18%). The fourth and fifth positions are occupied by −2 and 2, respectively. The least frequent scores are −3, with 1,027 instances (9%), and 3, the least common, with only 432 occurrences, representing 4% of the data. The distribution of arousal values demonstrates a gradation towards lower intensities. The most frequently observed value is 1, recorded 3,147 times and constituting 29% of the dataset. This is closely followed by an arousal level of 2, with 2,915 occurrences (27%), and then level 3, which occurred 2,400 times (22%). Higher intensities are less common, with value 4 assigned to 1,460 segments (13%) and the highest intensity, level 5, the least frequent at 982 occurrences, making up 9% of the data. This pattern suggests that emotions of lower intensity are more prevalent in the analyzed stories. Here, all provided values are based on the total count of assigned scores without applying any strategy to integrate both annotators.

5 Comparison of Automatic and Expert Labeling

We conducted two versions of lexical annotation: automatic and expert. The automatic detection of emotional words used a distributive semantics approach as described in Sect. 3, with score thresholds for cosine-similarity based score set at 0.4 and 0.5. We retained results from the 0.4 threshold as a basis for frequency dictionaries to capture a broader range of lexical choices, also taking into account the score value's significance in determining the proximity of a word to the designated prototypical word for each emotion. Thus, we computed the mean ranks for automatically labeled words by averaging their positions in a dictionary sorted by frequency at first and then sorted by score. Then, the frequency lists of manually labeled lexis were obtained. For now, we have not applied any annotation strategy to resolve differences in annotations and each tag was counted as one occurrence of the emotion. If two annotators tagged the same word with the same tag its frequency was incremented by two. This may seem controversial but we do not compare the exact frequencies now but rather focus on the approximating the level of emotion as recognized by reader. The technique of manual annotation was described in detail in Sect. 4. At last, the comparative frequency lists of words associated with each emotion through both expert annotation and automatic methods were generated.

The comparison of the results of emotional lexis labeling obtained automatically and manually was twofold. Firstly, we examined how the amount of lemmatized emotional lexis types differs depending on the way of its identification.

Fig. 2. Number of lemma types per emotion: automatic annotation (left) vs. expert annotation (right)

As can be seen from Fig. 2, both distributions show that certain emotions like *sadness*, *fear*, and *anger* are highly represented with both automatic and manual labeling, suggesting a convergence in identifying these emotions. However, there are notable differences. For instance, *anger* is the most frequent category in the automatic annotation but ranks third in the manual annotation; while *sadness* tops the manual annotation but is second in the automatic. *Fear* and *disgust* are also prominent in both but with different rankings. It's interesting to note that *happiness*, *relief*, *pleasure*, and *shame* have more counts in the manual annotation, potentially indicating these emotions might be more nuanced and less obviously lexicalized.

Next, we delved into investigation of the patterns concerning the lexical groups per each emotional category. The upper zone of the comparative frequency list can be found in Appendix A. It can be noted that some common terms identified by both methods, like "*vesyolyj*" (*cheerful*) for amusement, "*boyat'sya*" (*to fear*) for fear, and "*udivit'sya*" (*to be surprised*) for surprise. This implies that certain words are strongly and consistently associated with their respective emotions across different annotation methods. The data showcases the complexity of emotional expressions and their contextual dependencies. Another interesting observation concerns some words that appear across different emotional categories, e.g. "*uzhas*" (*terror*), "*strah*" (*fear*), "*udovol'stvie*" (*contentment*), "*schast'e*" (*happiness*), "*naslazhdenie*" (*pleasure*), "*zloba* (*anger*)", etc. This indicates that certain words are used in a variety of ways and carry different meanings depending on the context in which they are used. This may suggest a diverse range of semantic components at play in different artistic and communicative situations, for example, when depicting the feelings of characters, speech interactions, etc. Moreover, figurative contexts also may broaden the semantic flexibility of such words. It is probable that not only the specifics of automatic annotation procedure mentioned before, but also this figurative transmission of contextual words meaning has led to a wider range of lexis determined manually.

As it can be seen from table above[4] the upper zone of frequency dictionaries per emotion in a number of cases significantly overlaps (in bold). Interestingly, the label-word (underlined in bold) itself, for automatically obtained lists, is often not very frequent for a corresponding emotion (see "*zloba*" for anger, "*grust'*" for sadness). It may also point towards implicit ways of emotion depiction in a line of contexts.

Next, a part-of-speech analysis allowed us to determine that the emotive lexis is mainly expressed via verbs, nouns, adjectives, and adverbs. Though this observation is not entirely novel—the existing dictionaries of emotive lexis also confirm this part-of-speech preferences, it is noticeable that human annotators unlike the model tend to label verbs (4205 expert annotated lexical types vs. 1532 machine annotated lexical types), adjectives (1891 vs. 736), and adverbs (742 vs. 191) more often[5]. The nouns, however, are relatively similar in the number of types among both samples (2364 vs. 2450).

To elaborate on the intersection between the lexical types in the samples, we calculated the amount of common lexis opposed to the total number of unique lexical types. The results presented in Table 3 indicate the largest overlap in the depiction of such emotions as anger, surprise, and amusement. Though it has already been stated based on the frequency dictionaries for surprise and amusement above, the results for anger are

[4] Here, for demonstrative purposes, only two emotions were taken—the most lexically diverse according to the total number of lexical types, both manually and automatically.

[5] Note that results have no statistical significance (t-test = 1.23, p-value > 0.1).

Table 2. Frequency lists of emotional lexis: expert annotation (e_lemma) vs. automatic annotation (a_lemma) (top-10 words per emotion) (fragment)

e_lemma	freq	a_lemma	mean_rank	freq	score
anger					
zloj	74	zloba	18	27	0,81
serdito	48	dosada	18	28	0,68
krichat'	40	nenavist'	21,5	26	0,65
zakrichat'	36	obida	22	38	0,61
kriknut'	35	zhalost'	25,5	29	0,61
rugat'sya	34	toska	39	67	0,54
razdrazhenie	33	gorech'	39	24	0,57
rasserdit'sya	32	**zlost'**	39,5	14	1,00
zlo	30	otchayanie	44	44	0,54
rugat'	28	yarost'	44,5	13	0,70
sadness					
plakat'	176	**grustnyj**	7,5	83	0,72
sleza	157	**toska**	8	67	0,73
grustnyj	134	radost'	22,5	125	0,53
zaplakat'	88	zhalost'	22,5	29	0,62
toska	82	gorech'	25	24	0,72
vzdohnut'	82	**grust'**	25	23	1,00
zhalko	63	**pechal'nyj**	26,5	44	0,54
pechal'nyj	44	dosada	28,5	28	0,57
otchayanie	43	nezhnost'	28,5	22	0,65
grust'	38	otchayanie	33	44	0,53

quite intriguing since there was no obvious overlap noticed when comparing the upper zones of the frequency lists (see Table 2). With regards to the part-of-speech distribution, it is found that the common lexical types among emotions are mainly nouns (255), then verbs (161), adjectives (122), and adverbs (54). Some other parts of speech, as well as in the cases above, are also present but in rather small numbers.

Table 3. Number of common emotional lexis per category

Emotion	Total unique types	Number of common lexis	%	Total unique types	Number of common lexis	%
	threshold 0.4			threshold 0.5		
anger	2598	262	10,08	1478	57	3,86
surprise	714	72	10,08	475	34	7,16
amusement	943	93	9,86	518	26	5,02
sadness	2057	174	8,46	1655	51	3,08
shame	801	65	8,11	567	18	3,17
pleasure	755	51	6,75	596	22	3,69
pride	719	46	6,40	465	17	3,66
fear	1862	114	6,12	1628	21	1,29
disgust	1552	82	5,28	1115	24	2,15
relief	297	14	4,71	240	5	2,08
happiness	1091	26	2,38	1022	9	0,88

It seems that the lesser the lexical intersection of emotions, the more its complexity in terms of perception. For instance, V. I. Kryzhanovskaya's "Na Moskve" (1906) is characterized by the following distribution of emotional lexis labeled manually (e_count) and automatically (a_count) (see Fig. 3, note that percentage derives from comparing the number of emotional lexis per category with the total number of words in the story). The most prominent category is *fear* based on manual annotation; however, in terms of automatic identification of lexis the *disgust* seems to be more present. This is consistent with previous experiments dedicated to comparison of reader's perception and linguistic characteristics of text on the lexical level [22]. It was discussed that *anger* and *disgust* seem to be interchangeable when it comes to assigning one of these categories to a text as a whole [ibid.].

Referring to the text, one can find examples pointing to the observed "substitution" of emotional categories of fear and anger found in the lexical annotation results: *Komu zhe golovu* ***rubit'****-to budut? Kogo zhdet* ***lyutaya kazn'****? Kto tot* ***strashnyj zlodej****, kotorogo hotyat* ***pytat' i kaznit'*** *tyomnoj noch'yu?*. (*Whose head will they cut off? Who will face the cruel execution? Who is the terrible villain who they want to torture and execute on a dark night?*). The lexis found here does not directly (and in terms of vector space representation as well) point to a certain emotional label, but rather leans towards the reader's perception, the story's "atmosphere" and the plot matters. This observation also contributes to the suggestion of the situational and, therefore, implicit, emotions depiction in literary texts.

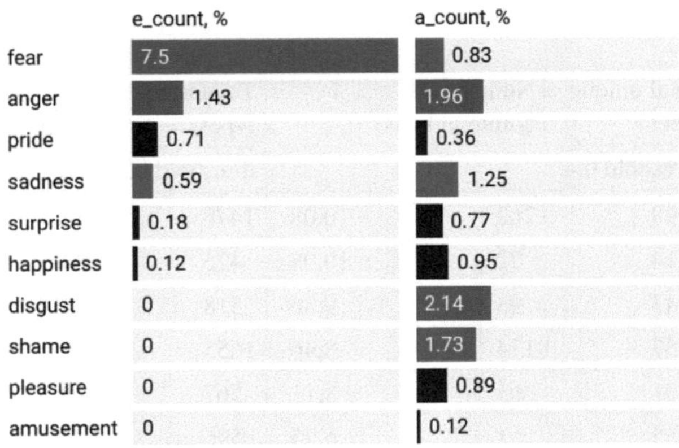

Fig. 3. Proportion of emotional lexis: expert annotation (e_count) vs. automatic annotation (a_count)

6 Conclusion

Two types of emotional annotation were performed on the balanced sample of Russian short stories. The methodology was discussed and resulting data was processed and analyzed. A preliminary comparison of lexis distributions obtained automatically and manually allowed us to point out certain similarities in emotional content assessment, as well as the peculiarities of each approach.

Future work will involve conducting a deeper analysis of the obtained annotations to create an emotional portrait of the century and identify trends in the emotional and affective components of the Russian short story. It will be particularly interesting to examine the distribution of arousal intensity throughout the narrative and to investigate the presence or absence of so-called emotional arcs. Additionally, it seems promising to integrate identified lexical markers with dimensional scores. Lexical markers and affective ratings could also be utilized in training models capable of predicting emotions.

Acknowledgements. The paper was prepared within the framework of the Basic Research Program at HSE University in 2024 (project "Text as big data: methods and models for working with large textual data").

Appendix A

Upper zone of frequency lists of emotional lexis:expert annotation (e_lemma) vs. automatic annotation (a_lemma)

e_lemma	freq	a_lemma	mean_rank	freq	score
amusement					
vesyolyj	98	radost'	6	125	0,60

(*continued*)

(*continued*)

e_lemma	freq	a_lemma	mean_rank	freq	score
smeyat'sya	98	smekh	9,5	85	0,59
smekh	47	veselie	16,5	18	0,73
zasmeyat'sya	43	radostnyj	22	59	0,54
smeshnoj	34	prazdnichnyj	26,5	17	0,56
ulybnut'sya	26	hohot	27,5	16	0,56
usmekhnut'sya	22	veselo	33,5	54	0,51
rassmeyat'sya	21	prazdnik	38,5	55	0,50
ulybat'sya	16	vostorg	50	40	0,49
prazdnik	16	veselit'sya	50	6	0,65
anger					
zloj	74	zloba	18	27	0,81
serdito	48	dosada	18	28	0,68
krichat'	40	nenavist'	21,5	26	0,65
zakrichat'	36	obida	22	38	0,61
kriknut'	35	zhalost'	25,5	29	0,61
rugat'sya	34	toska	39	67	0,54
razdrazhenie	33	gorech'	39	24	0,57
rasserdit'sya	32	zlost'	39,5	14	1,00
zlo	30	otchayanie	44	44	0,54
rugat'	28	yarost'	44,5	13	0,70
disgust					
gryaznyj	24	uzhas	9,5	86	0,58
protivno	21	strah	13	92	0,55
gryaz'	20	nenavist'	18	26	0,66
brezglivyj	19	zhalost'	21,5	29	0,56
prezrenie	15	otchayanie	25,5	44	0,53
nepriyatnyj	15	zloba	28	27	0,54
prezritel'no	14	dosada	31	28	0,53
protivnyj	14	naslazhdenie	33,5	20	0,54
otvrashchenie	12	brezglivyj	36,5	13	0,62
otvratitel'no	11	prezrenie	37,5	11	0,70
fear					
boyat'sya	223	strah	3,5	92	1,00
strashnyj	180	uzhas	5	86	0,70
strah	148	toska	8,5	67	0,58

(*continued*)

(*continued*)

e_lemma	freq	a_lemma	mean_rank	freq	score
uzhas	81	otchayanie	12,5	44	0,56
trevozhnyj	72	boyat'sya	16,5	193	0,51
ispugat'sya	66	zhalost'	17	29	0,57
volnenie	60	trevoga	19	31	0,56
ispuganno	53	ispug	24	17	0,68
trevoga	44	styd	26	17	0,60
vzdrognut'	43	nenavist'	28	26	0,52
happiness					
radost'	172	schastie	3,5	107	0,81
vesyolyj	149	radost'	4	125	0,63
schastlivyj	136	schastlivyj	5,5	93	0,62
schastie	110	lyubov'	14	178	0,49
ulybnut'sya	103	beda	16	51	0,49
ulybka	94	neschastie	17	24	0,56
smeyat'sya	87	udacha	17	9	0,61
ulybat'sya	84	gore	18	41	0,49
radostno	79	udovol'stvie	19,5	58	0,47
rad	66	slava	19,5	52	0,47
pleasure					
udovol'stvie	65	udovol'stvie	5	58	0,77
lyubit'	49	radost'	8	125	0,57
priyatnyj	35	naslazhdenie	10,5	20	1,00
lyubov'	26	schastie	11	107	0,55
naslazhdenie	23	sladost'	21,5	9	0,62
tyoplyj	17	sladostnyj	24	11	0,55
dovol'nyj	16	blazhenstvo	25,5	8	0,61
nezhnyj	14	oshchushchenie	25,5	57	0,51
smeyat'sya	12	vostorg	26	40	0,51
pocelovat'	10	stradanie	27,5	18	0,52
pride					
gordost'	48	gordost'	6	32	1,00
gordit'sya	21	nenavist'	15,5	26	0,56
geroj	17	gordyj	16	18	0,57
gordo	12	obida	18	38	0,52
gordyj	12	gordo	20,5	14	0,61

(*continued*)

(*continued*)

e_lemma	freq	a_lemma	mean_rank	freq	score
torzhestvenno	11	gordit'sya	22	16	0,55
pobeda	10	zavist'	22,5	14	0,57
molodec	9	zloba	23	27	0,51
torzhestvennyj	8	dostoinstvo	26	15	0,53
pobedit'	8	prezrenie	28	11	0,55
relief					
uspokoit'sya	27	oblegchenie	5,5	15	1,00
oblegchenie	24	oblegchyonno	7,5	9	0,67
nakonec	19	udovol'stvie	9	58	0,48
uspokoit'	17	radost'	9	125	0,48
oblegchyonno	17	oblegchit'	12	6	0,64
vzdohnut'	16	udovletvorenie	14	7	0,50
spokojnyj	12	ogorchenie	14,5	5	0,54
spokojno	11	zatrudnenie	16,5	5	0,49
spokojstvie	8	naslazhdenie	16,5	20	0,45
uspokaivat'sya	8	stesnenie	18,5	4	0,51
sadness					
plakat'	176	grustnyj	7,5	83	0,72
sleza	157	toska	8	67	0,73
grustnyj	134	radost'	22,5	125	0,53
zaplakat'	88	zhalost'	22,5	29	0,62
toska	82	gorech'	25	24	0,72
vzdohnut'	82	grust'	25	23	1,00
zhalko	63	pechal'nyj	26,5	44	0,54
pechal'nyj	44	dosada	28,5	28	0,57
otchayanie	43	nezhnost'	28,5	22	0,65
grust'	38	otchayanie	33	44	0,53
shame					
stydno	67	strah	6	92	0,60
nelovkij	53	stydno	15,5	38	0,56
vinovatyj	53	obida	16,5	29	0,59
smushchenno	26	gordost'	19	38	0,54
styd	26	zhalost'	19	100	0,50
nelovkost'	20	dosada	20	146	0,49
smushchyonnyj	18	gorech'	24	17	1,00

(*continued*)

(*continued*)

e_lemma	freq	a_lemma	mean_rank	freq	score
stesnyat'sya	16	styd	24,5	28	0,54
vina	15	nelovkost'	26	67	0,49
smutit'sya	12	zlost'	27	32	0,51
surprise					
udivit'sya	85	udivlenie	7	49	1,00
udivlenie	76	udivlenno	14	30	0,74
neozhidanno	70	nedoumenie	17	25	0,73
vdrug	66	udivit'sya	19	59	0,56
udivitel'nyj	53	lyubopytstvo	20,5	38	0,58
udivlenno	47	vostorg	21,5	40	0,57
neozhidannyj	38	izumlenie	23	15	0,89
udivlyat'sya	33	udivlyat'sya	25,5	27	0,58
udivit'	30	uzhas	27	86	0,51
porazit'	27	ispug	27,5	17	0,60

References

1. Bostan, L.A.M., Klinger, R.: An analysis of annotated corpora for emotion classification in text. In: Proceedings of the 27th international conference on computational linguistics. pp. 2104–2119 (2018).
2. Birjali, M., Kasri, M., Beni-Hssane, A.: A comprehensive survey on sentiment analysis: approaches, challenges and trends. Knowl. Based Syst. **226**, 107134 (2021)
3. Lukashevich N.V.: Avtomaticheskij analiz tonal'nosti tekstov: problemy i metody [Automatic sentiment analysis: problems and methods]. *Intellektual'nye sistemy. Teoriya i prilozheniya.* **26** (1), 50–61 (2022)
4. Kim, E., Klinger, R.: A survey on sentiment and emotion analysis for computational literary studies. arXiv preprint arXiv:1808.03137 (2018)
5. Jacobs, A.M., Herrmann, B., Lauer, G., Lüdtke, J., Schroeder, S.: Sentiment analysis of children and youth literature: is there a pollyanna effect? Front. Psychol. **11**, 574746 (2020)
6. Mohammad, S.M.: From once upon a time to happily ever after: tracking emotions in mail and books. Decis. Support. Syst. **53**(4), 730–741 (2012)
7. Joshi, A., Bhattacharyya, P., Ahire, S.: Sentiment resources: lexicons and datasets. In: A Practical Guide to Sentiment Analysis, pp. 85–106. Springer International Publishing, Cham (2017). https://doi.org/10.1007/978-3-319-55394-8_5
8. Westbury, C., Keith, J., Briesemeister, B.B., Hofmann, M.J., Jacobs, A.M.: Avoid violence, rioting, and outrage; approach celebration, delight, and strength: Using large text corpora to compute valence, arousal, and the basic emotions. Q. J. Exp. Psychol. **68**(8), 1599–1622 (2015)
9. Mohammad, S.: Obtaining reliable human ratings of valence, arousal, and dominance for 20,000 english words. In: Proceedings of the 56th Annual Meeting of the Association for Computational Linguistics (Volume 1: Long Papers), pp. 174–184 (2018, July)

10. Sboev, A., Naumov, A., Rybka, R.: Data-driven model for emotion detection in Russian texts. Procedia Comput. Sci. **190**, 637–642 (2021). https://doi.org/10.1016/j.procs.2021.06.075
11. Rogers, A., Romanov, A., Rumshisky, A., Volkova, S., Gronas, M. and Gribov, A.: RuSentiment: an enriched sentiment analysis dataset for social media in Russian. In: Proceedings of COLING 2018, pp. 755–763 (2018)
12. Bostan, L., Kim, E., Klinger, R.: Goodnewseveryone: a corpus of news headlines annotated with emotions, semantic roles, and reader perception. arXiv preprint arXiv:1912.03184 (2019)
13. Kim, E., Klinger, R.: Who feels what and why? annotation of a literature corpus with semantic roles of emotions. In: Proceedings of the 27th International Conference on Computational Linguistics. pp. 1345–1359 (2018)
14. Francisco, V., Hervás, R., Peinado, F., Gervás, P.: EmoTales: creating a corpus of folk tales with emotional annotations. Lang. Resources Eval. **46**(3), 341–381 (2012). https://doi.org/10.1007/s10579-011-9140-5
15. Koltsova, O., Alexeeva, S., Pashakhin, S., Koltsov, S.: PolSentiLex: sentiment detection in socio-political discussions on Russian social media. In: Artificial Intelligence and Natural Language, pp. 1–16. Springer International Publishing, Cham (2020). https://doi.org/10.1007/978-3-030-59082-6_1
16. Nielsen, F.Å.: A new ANEW: evaluation of a word list for sentiment analysis in microblogs. arXiv preprint arXiv:1103.2903 (2011)
17. Kiritchenko, S., Mohammad, S.M.: Examining gender and race bias in two hundred sentiment analysis systems. arXiv preprint arXiv:1805.04508 (2018)
18. Bradley, M.M., Lang, P.J.: Affective norms for English words (ANEW): instruction manual and affective ratings. Technical Report C-1, the Center for Research in Psychophysiology, University of Florida. Vol. 30, No. 1 (pp. 25–36) (1999)
19. Martynenko, G.Ya., Sherstinova, T.Yu., Popova, T.I., Melnik, A.G., Zamirajlova, E.V.: O printsipakh sozdaniya korpusa russkogo rasskaza pervoy treti XX veka. In Proc. of the XV Int. Conf. on Computer and Cognitive Linguistics 'TEL 2018'. Kazan, pp. 180–197 (2018)
20. Moskvina, A., Kirina, M.: Where is happily ever after? A study of emotions and locations in Russian short stories of 1900–1930. In: Digital Geography: Proceedings of the International Conference on Internet and Modern Society (IMS 2023), pp. 123–135. Springer Nature Switzerland, Cham (2024). https://doi.org/10.1007/978-3-031-67762-5_10
21. Nakayama, H., Kubo, T., Kamura, J., Taniguchi, Y., Liang, X.: doccano: text annotation tool for human. (2018). https://github.com/doccano/doccano.
22. Moskvina A.D, Kirina M.A.: Lexical distribution of emotions in Russian short stories of the beginning of the 20th century. In: Corpus Linguistics - 2023 (in print)

Prepositional Phrase Classification in Russian with Transformer Models

Andrei Belyi, Daria Boitsova[(✉)], and Ekaterina Botvineva

Saint Petersburg State University, St. Petersburg, Russian Federation
{st078167,st087202,st085755}@student.spbu.ru

Abstract. In this paper we discuss the task of prepositional phrase classification in the Russian annotated corpus of prepositional phrases. As previous research has shown, differentiation of highly confused classes, namely THEME and OBJECT classes, remains a problem waiting for the computational solution. Since simple classifier architecture demonstrates significant performance on these classes, we propose a tree-based classifier architecture to improve performance on the whole and these classes specifically. This architecture consists of a main classifier validating its decisions concerning troublesome classes with another supporting classifier, trained to differentiate between the classes causing performance dropdown. We experiment with various types of classifiers inside of our architecture and various embedding models for the Russian language, which we use for encoding the dataset. The best result that we managed to achieve is an overall F1-score of 0.76 on the validation set using the classifier trained with DeepPavlov/rubert-base-cased model and SVM (Support Vector Machines) classifiers.

Keywords: prepositional phrases · text classification · phrase embeddings · transformers · word sense disambiguation

1 Introduction

In the realm of natural language processing, the accurate semantic classification of prepositional phrases (PP) stands as a significant challenge, particularly in languages like Russian where polysemy is prevalent. Within the framework of our project, we treat separate meanings of PPs as *syntaxemes*.

The goal of our work is to improve an effective classifier for Russian prepositional phrases, addressing the issue of extreme class confusion pointed out in previous work by V. Gudkov [9]. To tackle this challenge, we propose a novel tree-based classifier architecture tailored to enhance performance across all classes, with a particular focus on resolving the confusion between THEME and OBJECT syntaxemes. This architecture comprises a primary classifier augmented by a secondary supporting classifier, strategically trained to mitigate performance downturns associated with troublesome classes. By leveraging this architecture, we aim to not only improve overall classification accuracy but also specifically target the problematic classes that have eluded satisfactory resolution in previous studies.

M. Bakaev et al. (Eds.): IMS 2024, CCIS 2534, pp. 130–139, 2026.
https://doi.org/10.1007/978-3-031-96177-9_11

2 Related Work

Preposition classification is the subject of many studies. Most of them concern primary prepositions. These studies can be divided into two categories: ontological description of prepositions and classification of prepositional phrases with state-of-the-art architectures.

It is worth mentioning the work of I. Azarova and V. Zakharov [1] which is dedicated to the creation of corpus-driven semantic-ontological descriptions of Russian prepositional constructions. They describe the underlying framework for organising semantic categories of temporal and locative syntaxemes, derived using an advanced method for the analysis of the frequency of prepositional constructions. They propose two rubrics: 1) localization, which consists of 4 syntaxemes, namely, a) locative, b) directive, c) departed, and d) transitive; and 2) temporative, which has 3 syntaxemes, a) temporal, b) aspective, and c) taxis. All the syntaxemes also include subsyntaxemes like locative_1, transitive_2, intervallum, antecedent, etc. Semantic rubrics are made to describe the meaning of prepositional constructions. Azarova and Zakharov chose the most frequent ones. It is important to emphasise that within their ontology, there are not only hierarchical connections between syntaxemes and subsyntaxemes but also lateral connections between units belonging to different semantic categories [1]. Another ontological description of Russian prepositions can be found in the article Azarova I. et al. [2]. In the paper, the authors explore the structure of synonymic and quasi-synonymic semantic relationships among primary and secondary prepositions in Russian. The results of their methodology illustrate the semantics of the locative rubric. As the locative rubric is the most frequent one, I. Azarova and V. Zakharov examine it in the paper on prefixal modification of prepositional syntaxemes [3]. They rely on G.A. Zolotova's [4] classification and expand on the syntaxemes from her dictionary, organising it into a three-level ontology that specifies how syntaxemes are realised. M. Khokhlova and V. Rubiner examine the frequency and length of prepositional phrases in the model "preposition + noun phrase" within texts related to legal topics. Their analysis focuses on four types of prepositional phrases: "preposition + noun", "preposition + pronoun/pronominal adjective + noun", "preposition + pronoun/pronominal adjective + noun", and "preposition + adjective + noun". The study is grounded in quantitative grammar.

Since prepositions exhibit extensive polysemy, encompassing a diverse range of meanings that encode substantial semantic information [6], it is important but hard to classify them correctly. One of the approaches that showed decent results is presented in the paper by S. Pawar, A. Mittal et.al [7]. They proposed to implement BERT for getting a contextual representation of a preposition and a multilayer perceptron (MLP) to predict the preposition's sense. They used the SemEval-2007 Task 6 dataset [13], with 34 prepositions and 332 senses. Their system shows a result of 86.95% accuracy.

In another research on preposition sense disambiguation using the SemEval dataset H. Gong, J. Mu et al. [6] compared two methods: unsupervised learning of the senses, conducted by k-means clustering, and supervised learning, for which they used standard support vector machines (SVM), multilayer perceptron (MLP) and weighted k-nearest neighbour (k-NN) classifiers. The word embeddings were trained with the Word2Vec CBOW model [11].

Since there is not much work done on the sense disambiguation of Russian prepositions, it is worth mentioning two important papers, both written by V. Zakharov, V. Gudkov, et al.

The first one proposes a corpus of Russian prepositional phrases which was generated using a SynTagRus pretrained UDPipe model [8] to extract prepositions and the OpenCorpora morphological annotation with the help of PyMorphy2 which was added to facilitate the subsequent part of the annotation [9]. Supervised classification was performed on vectors obtained via FastText [12]. They achieved a 0.65 F1-score for the whole set of semantic categories. However, only 4 categories were effectively recognized due to their high frequency, those categories being DESTINATION, QUANTITY, LOCATION and TEMPUS, where individual F1-score is between 0.70 and 0.81.

The second work presents an analysis of Russian secondary prepositions, focusing on multiword prepositions (MWPs) [10]. The main difficulty they faced was the fact that secondary prepositions are not well-studied and described. They proposed a methodology that helps to determine the status of MWPs with the usage of a set of units expressing causal relations.

3 Data

The experiment was carried out on the subset of the annotated Russian corpus of prepositional phrases, designed specifically for this task by V. Gudkov [9]. As of now, the corpus has no analogues.

The original dataset consists of both simple and complex prepositions with their headword and corresponding noun phrases. The list of prepositions to extract was collected on the basis of well-known dictionaries and corpora, the list of which can be found in the original work. The homonyms and idioms were filtered out and normalization was applied to avoid some variable forms being treated differently (the authors cite the variants of о/об/обо).

The phrases containing the prepositions in the list were extracted from the Taiga news subcorpus, and manual annotation was applied to a randomly chosen subset of 10,000 extracted prepositional phrases. The manual annotation guidelines were based on the generalized version of Zolotova-Mikhailova's classification with the resulting tagset containing 15 labels. Further we list those labels in order of decreasing frequency with examples from the original work:

1. LOCATION: лежит между горами (lies between mountaints);
2. THEME: думал о сыне (was thinking of his son);
3. TEMPUS: откроют к ноябрю (will open by November);
4. OBJECT: ударить об стол (hit against the table);
5. DIRECTION: плыть против течения (swim against the tide);
6. QUALITY: слишком стар для службы (too old for service);
7. SOURCE: услышала от подруга (heard from a friend);
8. DESTINATION: комната для курения (room for smoking);
9. QUANTITY: состоять из 3 частей (consist of 3 parts);
10. COMMITMENT: Татьяна с Ольгой (Tatiana with Olga);
11. CAUSE: краснеть при мысли (blush at the thought);

12. POTENTIAL: застраховать от забот (secure from worries);
13. SITUATION: богослужение под дождём (worship in the rain);
14. TRANSGRESSION: превращение из куколки (metamorphosis from chrysalis);
15. INSTRUMENT: протрите сквозь сито (push through a sieve).

Original work also points out the issue of class imbalance in the dataset, noting especially POTENTIAL, SITUATION, TRANSGRESSION and INSTRUMENT classes as severely underrepresented. Several categories are mentioned to be semantically close and as such they are shown to be fused together by the classifier, the most prominent example of which is OBJECT and TOPIC classes.

In this paper we worked with the subset of the original dataset: we removed the prepositional phrases with derived prepositions and we excluded 5 of the least represented classes (that is, CAUSE, POTENTIAL, SITUATION, TRANSGRESSION, INSTRUMENT). That decision was motivated by our desire to focus on the issue of class confusion and distance ourselves from the issue of underrepresentation. The size of the dataset after our transformations is 8240 prepositional phrases. Figure 1 shows frequency distribution among the labels in our experimental dataset.

The frequency characteristics of the correlation between prepositions and their meanings in our corpus are described in detail in the article [20].

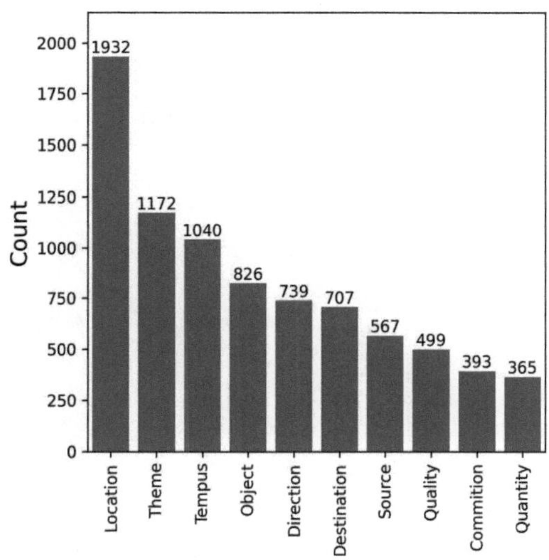

Fig. 1. Frequency by label in the experimental dataset.

Figure 2 demonstrates two-dimensional representation of PP vector space, produced by t-SNE in scikit-learn. Data representation reveals diffuse class structure. Figure 3 focuses on the two highly confused classes of OBJECT and THEME syntaxemes and proves their weak juxtaposition.

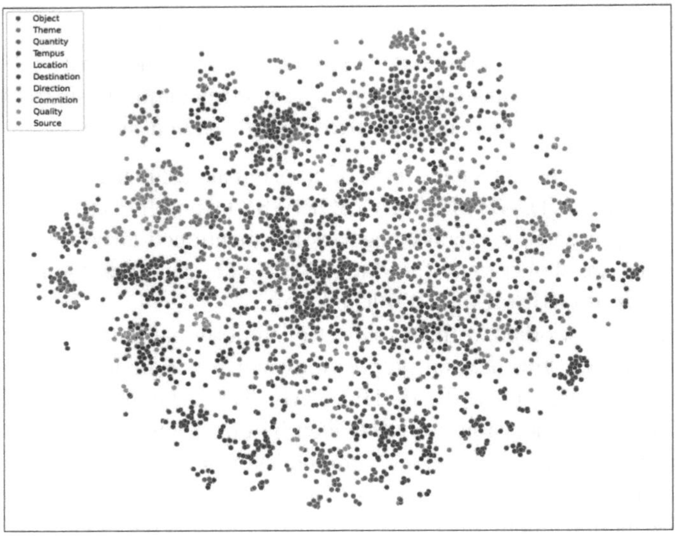

Fig. 2. Visualization of PP vector space (DeepPavlov/rubert-base-cased model).

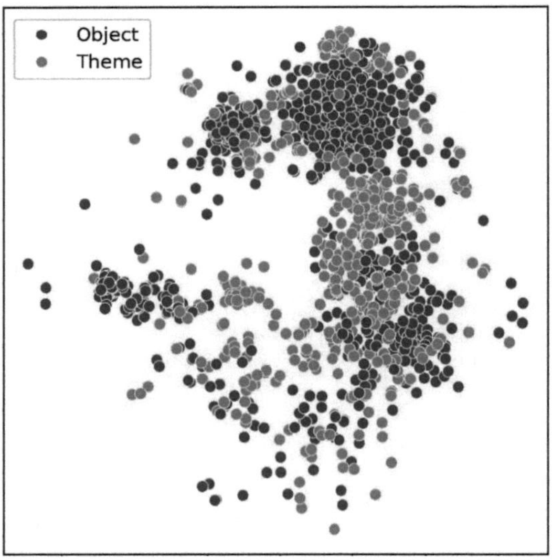

Fig. 3. Visualization of OBJECT and THEME prepositional phrases' embeddings (DeepPavlov/rubert-base-cased model).

4 Experimental Setup

The goal of our work is to improve an effective classifier for Russian prepositional phrases, addressing the issue of extreme class confusion pointed out in previous work by V. Gudkov [9]. The issue we are specifically aiming to resolve is the confusion between THEME and OBJECT preposition classes, which proved to be the most difficult for all classifiers in the initial implementation. These classes are also among the best represented in the dataset and so we believe them to produce the most robust results.

We obtained vector representation for sentences in the corpus using various pre-trained BERT language models for the Russian language. The list of the models used is as follows:

- sentence-transformers/LaBSE [19];
- cointegrated/LaBSE_en_ru – a truncated version of LaBSE that only has English and Russian tokens in vocabulary [17];
- ai-forever/ruRoberta-large [16];
- RussianNLP/ruRoBERTa-large-rucola – finetuned for Russian Corpus of Linguistic Acceptability (RuCoLA) [18];
- DeepPavlov/rubert-base-cased – a version of RuBERT initialized through multilingual version of BERT-base [14];
- ai-forever/sbert_large_mt_nlu_ru – BERT model for sentence embeddings in Russian language [15].

DeepPavlov/rubert-base-cased model was converted to SBERT with help of Sentence-Transformers library [21], which allows to create sentence-level vector representations based on BERT models with additional mean pooling layer.

After obtaining sentence embeddings we classified them using scikit-learn implementations of several multiclass classifiers, namely:

- support vector machine classifier (SVM);
- support vector machine classifier with stochastic gradient descent (SGD) training (SVM-SGD);
- logistic regression classifier (LR);
- logistic regression classifier with SGD training (LR-SGD);
- multilayer perceptron classifier (MPL);
- perceptron classifier with SGD training (MLP-SGD).

The initial implementation included simple single-classifier architecture, but during initial testing, we realised that this architecture failed to address the issue of class confusion that we had put in front of us. The most notable examples of this confusion are THEME and OBJECT classes, receiving F1-scores of 0.39 and 0.51 respectively. To improve performance on those classes we propose a tree-structured classifier consisting of two separate sequential classifiers.

Thus, our model consists of a main multi-class classifier, assigning initial labels, and support binary classifier, trained specifically on instances of confused classes. After encountering an instance of one of the confused classes, the main classifier sends the problematic instance to the specialised classifier whose decision is considered final. In this task, we used only one support classifier for the most confused classes of Topic and Object. Theoretically, this model can be furthered for various binary classifiers, but this setup remains out of the scope of our experiment. It could be as well experimented with different types of classifiers inside of this architecture, but in our setup, we use identical classifying algorithms in every implementation. Figure 4 represents the described architecture and (Fig. 5) demonstrates the workflow.

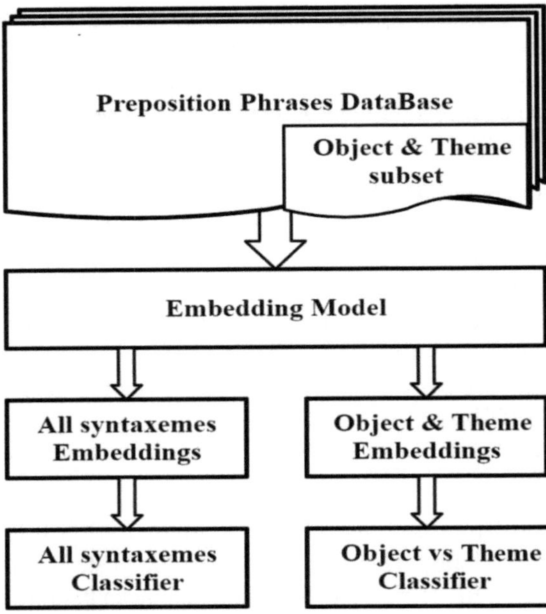

Fig. 4. Tree-classifier architecture.

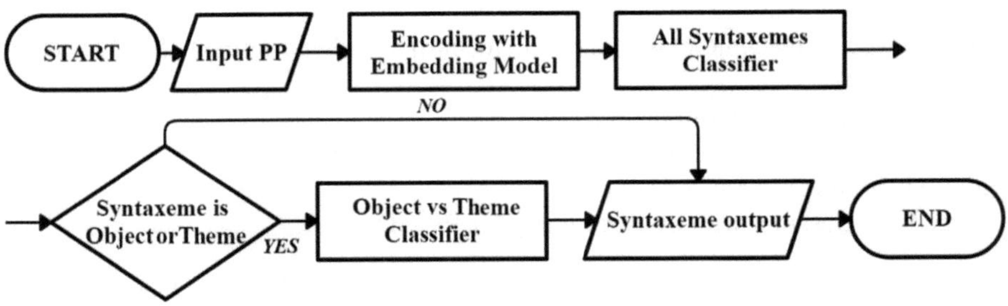

Fig. 5. Flow diagram of tree-classifier architecture.

The results of classification were evaluated through conventional means of measuring classification performance, the most important measure for us being F1-score as an overall representation of performance. To account for the class imbalance, we used weighted F1-score, which averages the scores for all the labels by weighting them by the amount of the label support.

To ensure robustness of the evaluation, we used the k-folding method StratifiedKFold from scikit-learn library with 10 folds. The method ensures that the folds maintain the distribution of classes from the original dataset. Standard deviation between F1-scores obtained on each of the folds does not exceed 0.002.

5 Experimental Results

Table 1 compares the results of baseline (single) and final (tree-based) classifiers. As is shown, both the choice of classifier and the choice of base model affect the algorithm performance.

In general, all of the classifiers with SGD training received slightly lower scores than the basic implementations of the same classifiers. This difference becomes more significant when we consider LaBSE model, where F1-score drops from 0.75 for simple SVM classifier to 0.53 for SVM classifier with SGD with the same pattern for all the other classifier types.

Out of three classifier types used for testing, the SVM classifier proves to be superior in most cases, trailing behind only with ai-forever/ruRoberta-large and ai-forever/sbert_large_mt_nlu_ru models. The perceptron classifier showed worse average performance out of all three classifiers. It can be explained by its tendency to focus on non-significant features of the dataset and collinearity problems. However, it should be noted that average performance of all those classifiers is extremely close with F1-scores of 0.71 for perceptron, 0.72 for logistic regression, and 0.73 for SVM, so another classifier may prove to be best with further architecture and vector representation experiments.

The best-performing model after averaging the scores for all the classifiers is ai-forever/ruRoberta-large, where the dropdown on the SGD-trained classifiers is less pronounced. However, the single best result was obtained on another model: SVM classifier

Table 1. Classification results (F1-score).

Model	SVM		MLP		LR	
	baseline	final	baseline	final	baseline	final
LaBSE	0,71	0,75	0,65	0,68	0,70	0,72
LaBSE_en_ru	0,71	0,75	0,68	0,71	0,68	0,72
ruRoberta-large	0,72	0,73	0,70	0,75	0,71	0,75
ruRoBERTa-large-rucola	0,71	0,72	0,66	0,71	0,70	0,70
rubert-base-cased	0,75	0,76	0,67	0,71	0,70	0,70
sbert_large_mt_nlu_ru	0,65	0,68	0,64	0,68	0,66	0,70
Model	SVM-SGD		MLP-SGD		LR-SGD	
	baseline	final	baseline	final	baseline	final
LaBSE	0,50	0,53	0,47	0,48	0,53	0,57
LaBSE_en_ru	0,65	0,68	0,66	0,68	0,66	0,70
ruRoberta-large	0,70	0,74	0,69	0,72	0,72	0,75
ruRoBERTa-large-rucola	0,70	0,71	0,63	0,64	0,69	0,70
rubert-base-cased	0,70	0,70	0,62	0,64	0,69	0,70
sbert_large_mt_nlu_ru	0,65	0,68	0,65	0,68	0,65	0,68

with DeepPavlov/rubert-base-cased model achieves F1-score of 0.76. This score is higher than the F1-score of Gudkov et al. [12] of 0.65 for all labels.

To assess the impact of our architecture choices, all of the results were compared with baseline – the result of single-classifier implementation with a given model and classifier. Despite support classifiers' average performance (0.6 on average), adding a support classifier consistently improves general performance on all classifier-model variations except for three implementations where the results stay the same: logistic regression and SVM with SGD on DeepPavlov/rubert-base-cased and logistic regression on RussianNLP/ruRoBERTa-large-rucola. The changes may seem small, but it's worth noting that the improvement over all classes is attained through improvement over the most confused THEME and OBJECT classes. The improvement over these two classes changes the F1-score from 0.4 to 0.6 in the best-case scenario, improving overall performance accordingly. The achieved results give hope in regards to applying the pro posed architecture to a bigger number of classes for further performance improvement, but these experiments remain out of the scope of current work.

6 Conclusion

In this paper we discussed the issue of automatic classification of Russian prepositional phrases. Different systems of ontological descriptions of the preposition phrases were proposed in previous years, their authors indicating the issue of high polysemy among the prepositions. Building upon the previous work concerning Russian language, we carry out experiments to improve the quality of automatic classification, and to achieve this goal we use embeddings obtained from pre-trained BERT models for Russian language as opposed to FastText embeddings of the previous work and apply a tree-structured classifier architecture to resolve class confusion between THEME and OBJECT classes. The experiments have shown that the best F1-score of 0.76 is obtained with the SVM classifier and RuBERT-base-cased model. The overall improvement due to our architecture is subtle but consistent on all implementations. This suggests that the proposed type of architecture can be extended for less distinct classes with further performance improvement, but this remains a topic for future studies.

References

1. Zakharov, V., Azarova, I.: Grammatical parallelism of Russian prepositional localization and temporal constructions. In: Text, Speech, and Dialogue: 23rd International Conference, TSD 2020, Brno, Czech Republic, September 8–11, 2020, Proceedings, pp.122–134.Springer-Verlag. (2020)
2. Azarova, I., Khokhlova, M., Zakharov, V., Petkevič, V.: Ontological description of Russian prepositions. In: Proceedings of the III International Conference on Language Engineering and Applied Linguistics, Saint Petersburg, Russia, November 27, 2019, pp 245–257 (2019)
3. Azarova, I.V., Zakharov, V.P.: Prefixal modification of prepositional case localisation syntaxemes in Russian. Struct. Appl. Linguist. in print
4. Zolotova, G.A.: Syntactic dictionary: Repertory of elementary units of Russian Syntax. Nauka, Moscow (1988)

5. Khokhlova, M.V., Rubiner, V.I.: On quantitative analysis of Russian prepositional constructions based on legislative texts. In: Proceedings of the International Conference Corpus Linguistics-2019, Saint Petersburg, Russia, pp 149–154 (2019)
6. Gong, H., Mu, J., Bhat, S., Viswanath, P.: Preposition sense disambiguation and representation. In: Proceedings of the 2018 Conference on Empirical Methods in Natural Language Processing, EMNLP, Brussels, Belgium, pp. 1510–1521 (2018)
7. Pawar, S., Thombre, S., Mittal, A., Ponkiya, G., Bhattacharyya, P.: Tapping BERT for Preposition Sense Disambiguation. ArXiv preprint (2021)
8. Straka, M., Straková, J.: Tokenizing, POS tagging, lemmatizing and parsing UD 2.0 with UDPipe. In: Proceedings of the CoNLL 2017 Shared Task: Multilingual Parsing from Raw Text to Universal Dependencies, Vancouver, Canada, pp. 88–99 (2017)
9. Gudkov, V., Golovina, A., Mitrofanova, O., Zakharov, V.: Russian prepositional phrase semantic labelling with word embedding-based classifier. In: Ronzhin, A., Noskova, T., Karpov, A. (eds.) R. Piotrowski's Readings in Language Engineering and Applied Linguistics. PRLEAL-2019, CEUR Workshop Proceedings, vol. 2552, pp. 272–284 (2019)
10. Zakharov, V., Golovina, A., Alexeeva, E., Gudkov, V.: Russian secondary prepositions: methodology of analysis. In: CEUR Workshop Proceedings, vol. 2780, pp. 187–201 (2020)
11. Mikolov, T., Chen, K., Corrado, G.S., Dean, J.: Efficient estimation of word representations in vector space. In: International Conference on Learning Representations (2013)
12. Bojanowski, P., Grave, E., Joulin, A., Mikolov, T.: Enriching word vectors with subword information. Trans. Assoc. Comput. Linguist. **5**, 135–146 (2016)
13. Litkowski, K.C., Hargraves, O.: SemEval-2007 task 06: word-sense disambiguation of prepositions. In: Proceedings of the Fourth International Workshop on Semantic Evaluations (SemEval-2007), Prague, Czech Republic, pp. 24–29 (2007)
14. Kuratov, Y., Arkhipov, M.: Adaptation of deep bidirectional multilingual trans formers for Russian language. (2019)
15. ai-forever/sbert_large_mt_nlu_ru | HuggingFace. https://huggingface.co/ai-forever/sbert_large_mt_nlu_ru. Last accessed 24 April 2024
16. Zmitrovich, D., et al.: A family of pretrained transformer language models for Russian. (2023)
17. LaBSE-en-ru | HuggingFace. https://huggingface.co/cointegrated/LaBSE-en-ru. Last accessed 24 April 2024
18. Mikhailov, V., Shamardina, T., Ryabinin, M., Pestova, A., Smurov, I., Artemova, E.: RuCoLA: Russian corpus of linguistic acceptability. In: Proceedings of the 2022 Conference on Empirical Methods in Natural Language Pro-cessing. Abu Dhabi, United Arab Emirates, pp. 5207–5227 (2023)
19. Feng, F., Yang, Y., Cer, D.M., Arivazhagan, N., Wang, W.: Language-agnostic BERT sentence embedding. In: Annual Meeting of the Association for Computational Linguistics (2020)
20. Rodina A., Goncharova, A., Vybornaya, V.: Frequency characteristics of prepositions and their meanings in the database of prepositional constructions. (2024), preprint
21. SentenceTransformers. https://www.sbert.net/docs/training/overview.html. Last accessed 24 April 2024

Abstractive Summarization of Russian Medical Texts with Automatic Markup of Multiword Named Entities

Daria Boitsova(✉)

Saint-Petersburg State University, Saint-Petersburg, Russia
st078167@student.spbu.ru

Abstract. Text summarization is a type of semantic compression that involves constructing a reduced version of a text while preserving the most important components of its content. Named entity recognition is a task that helps to extract terms denoting persons, organizations, locations, notions specific for the field of knowledge in question. This paper examines the effect of multi-word named entity markup on the quality and semantic accuracy of Russian medical text abstractive summarization. Pretrained transformers T5 and GPT3 were used to test the hypothesis, and the results were evaluated using metrics BERTScore, BLEU, ROUGE-1, ROUGE-2 and ROUGE-L. The experiments were carried out for two datasets: a corpus of medical articles from the Russian Medical Journal and a dictionary of multi-word medical terms. We evaluated results of summarization obtained in two modes: with and without NER. The findings suggest that the markup has no significant impact on the results, with the summarization output showing better performance without markup. In addition, an application for summarizing medical texts in Russian, English and German was developed in the course of this work.

Keywords: Abstractive summarization · Named Entity Recognition · BioNLP · ruT5 · ruGPT3

1 Introduction

Communication in modern society involves the exchange of information in large amounts. With the growth of knowledge about the world and ourselves, the size of processed data is rapidly increasing. Nowadays, the information explosion is affecting almost all fields of intellectual activity, including health care. Such sciences as bioinformatics and clinical informatics are engaged in this area through data processing. Since medical documentation is processed in a textual format, methods and tools of computational linguistics (in particular, BioNLP) find their application here: information extraction from medical records, analysis of dialogues between a doctor and a patient, retrieval of terminology from medical texts, work with databases of diseases and their symptoms, medicines, machine translation, etc.

Medicine is a vast field of knowledge represented by different types of information sources: specialized literature (scientific publications, medical reference books, etc.)

M. Bakaev et al. (Eds.): IMS 2024, CCIS 2534, pp. 140–151, 2026.
https://doi.org/10.1007/978-3-031-96177-9_12

and texts for patients (doctors' blogs, popular articles, etc.). During correspondence between a physician and a patient it is necessary to choose the appropriate means of communication to ensure understanding without any loss or distortion of information. At the same time, many medical documents are difficult for non-specialists in their full form, so it would often be more useful for a patient to use an abridged version (abstract or synopsis). Consequently, the task of automatic summarization of medical records is becoming increasingly important.

Summarization refers to the procedures of semantic compression and involves the construction of an abridged version of the text while preserving the most important components of its content. There are two types of summarization: the extractive approach, which is a method that forms a summary out of pieces taken from the original text, and the abstractive approach, which generates a new text, generalizing the main idea of the original text. The latter is being considered in this paper.

It is also necessary to consider that medical texts are full of different types of domain-specific named entities: names of diagnoses, symptoms, medicines, medical procedures, etc. Named entity recognition is the task of extracting lexemes or constructions from the text that denote names of people, names of organizations, geographical names, units of measurement, etc. The loss of such terms from the text can be harmful to the semantic meaning of the summarized text, especially with multi-word terms.

So far, there are no scientific and applied research works in the field of computational linguistics that offer a solution to this problem. This paper examines the impact of multi-word entity markup on the quality of summarization.

Thus, the relevance of the research lies in the need to develop hybrid algorithms for the summarization of medical texts which take account named entities, and in the development of specialized corpora for the training and fine-tuning of neural network models for the needs of BioNLP. The aim of the current research is to develop an effective algorithm that summarizes medical texts in Russian and evaluates the degree of influence of named entity markup on the quality of summarization results.

To achieve this goal, the following tasks were formulated:

1. study of existing resources in the field of BioNLP;
2. formation of a corpus of medical texts for conducting experiments on summarization taking into account the markup of named entities;
3. study of the named entity extraction approaches, creation of a markup scheme of named entities to be used for the experimental corpus of medical texts;
4. preprocessing of the experimental corpus of medical texts and extraction of named entities;
5. study of existing text summarization algorithms and their adjustment to BioNLP tasks;
6. tuning of summarization models for carrying out experiments on summarization of medical texts with and without named entities;
7. evaluation of experimental results.

The paper is organized as follows: Sect. 2 presents related work. Section 3 introduces used datasets and evaluation metrics. The methodology is showed in Sect. 4. The results are discussed in Sect. 5. Finally, Sect. 6 represents conclusions and future work.

2 Related Work

In NLP, computational semantics has developed methods for semantic compression of texts, allowing for a concise yet clear representation of their content. This process includes lexicosemantic and morphosyntactic simplification of the original data (Kovalev, 2023).

Semantic compression can be performed at the word level, e.g., key phrase extraction, and at the sentence level, such as the generation of headings and annotation. Nowadays, due to the problem of information overload, we can observe a growing interest in the development of automatic abstracting and annotation programs (Batura, 2019).

Text summarization refers to the process of extracting the most important information from a document (Batura 2019). This process is used to highlight the most significant features, which are then summarized into a reduced version of the original document. The summarized text can be in the form of a paragraph, a sentence or even a few words (Marek 2021).

There are currently two types of text summarization: extractive and abstractive. Some researchers also distinguish a hybrid approach, which is a combination of extraction and abstraction (Batura, 2019). The extractive approach uses the simplest and most straightforward way of implementing summarization. First, the algorithm evaluates the relevance of sentences in the source text, then selects N number with the highest ranking, i.e. the most informative ones, and then makes a summary from them (Marek, 2021). The advantage of this method is that despite the simplicity of this approach, it always outputs syntactically correct sentences. On the other hand, extractive summarization algorithms are limited by the fact that they only use sentences from the source text to produce summaries, hence they cannot produce more elaborate summaries. The abstractive approach is a newer and more complicated type of summarization. This method generates summaries from sentences that are not part of the source text. The tasks of the algorithm include understanding the input text, finding the most relevant paragraphs and generating syntactically correct sentences. Morphology, syntax and semantics are taken into account to form a logically and meaningfully connected text (Batura 2019). One of the main disadvantages of abstract summarization is the hallucination of models, as they can generate unreliable information by distorting entities.

Some researchers emphasize five approaches to automatic summarization: statistical, coherent, algebraic, graph and machine learning based methods (Bharti 2017). The first approach is mostly used for keyword extraction in documents, for which the following document features are used: term frequency (TF), word frequency - inverse document frequency (TF-IDF), etc. The second approach is related to extracting the consistency relations of elements in the text. The third one is carried out using eigenvectors and matrices. There are many summarization algorithms based on the algebraic approach, e.g. singular value decomposition (SVD), latent semantic analysis (LSA), non-negative matrix factorization (NMF). In the fourth, graph-based approach, text fragments are represented as vertices of a graph and semantic relations between vertices by edges. In the last approach, the algorithm is trained on a labelled dataset, producing as output a function that approximates the relationship between text units.

Today, deep learning models are widely used for automatic summarization tasks, with the most popular one being the model based on Transformer type architecture, which uses a self-awareness mechanism that works by establishing the degree of importance or relationship between a given word and its entire environment. BERT (Devlin 2019), BART (Lewis, 2019), T5 (Raffel, 2019), GPT (Browm, 2020) are the main models for automatic text summarization. BERT (Bidirectional Encoder Representations from Transformers) encoder type model used for extractive abstracting. The RuBERT model was pre-trained for Russian. BART (Bidirectional and Auto-Regressive Transformer) model of seq2seq type, as it includes both encoder and decoder. This model is autoregressive, i.e. the selection of the current word depends on the one selected by the previous one. It is used for abstract summarization. T5 (Text-to-Text Transfer Transformer) is another abstract summarization model consisting of encoder and decoder, containing 12 transformation blocks. GPT (Generative Pre-trained Transformer) is a decoder type model that can take a small amount of data as input and generate a large number of words related to the original data after a pre-training step.

Although modern methods of automatic text summarization are constantly improving, they still encounter problems such as hallucinations and the replacement of named entities with vague synonyms or even them entirely. Scientific texts are most vulnerable to these problems. The substitution or omission of a term can completely distort the meaning of a summary. To address the above shortcomings, a named entity recognition model is added to the summarization model by first implementing the NER (Named Entity Recognition) model and then performing summarization.

For example, such an algorithm was presented in (Berezin, 2022), where they used RoBERTa to recognize named entities, which were then masked in the text and reconstructed with the trained BART model. The BART model was fine-tuned on the summarization task. Their experiment showed that with the Masked Named Entity Language Model (MNELM), it is possible for the BART to achieve higher precision and recall of named entity inclusion.

In (Alshibly, 2023) and (Marek, 2021) summarization was performed with the named entities marked up first with Spacy library. Both experiments were performed on news articles: on an English language corpus in the former and on a Czech language dataset in the latter. Both papers showed positive results.

Furthermore, some researchers, as shown in (Senthamizh, 2022), use document clustering for named entity recognition and keyword extraction (Bharti, 2017). This also showed promising results.

Named entities are words or word combinations that distinguish certain objects or phenomena in a number of similar objects or phenomena. Recognizing named entities in scientific discourse is an interesting yet challenging task, as it can involve ambiguous lexemes in a text. Some text elements have multiple meanings or can be interpreted in more than one way, thus leading to ambiguity.

There exist many approaches to solving the problem of named entity disambiguation, such as hidden Markov chains, support vector method, maximum entropy method etc. However, the most popular are machine learning supervised learning methods, where the model is first trained on an already labelled corpus, which is usually created manually. Transformer type models, especially of the BERT class, are gaining popularity. For example, for the NER task there is a RuBioRoBERTa model that has been pre-trained on the Russian-language medical literature (Yalunin, 2022). Frameworks such as Stanza, developed by the Stanford NLP Group, provide pre-trained models for multiple languages and offer accurate NER capabilities. Similarly, Natasha, a Russian NLP library, focuses on processing Russian text and excels in identifying named entities specific to the language, utilizing both rule-based approaches and machine learning techniques.

3 Datasets and Evaluation Metrics

3.1 Dataset

Medical data is hard to access due to the confidentiality of medical information. Datasets in English are easy to find. One of the most popular databases is PubMed which is a collection of references on biomedical topics. Unfortunately, there are fewer open corpora for the Russian language. The RuDREC corpus (the Russian Drug Reaction Corpus (Tutubalina, 2020)) was developed particularly for the task of labelling named entities. It is a Russian corpus of reviews on pharmaceuticals designed to identify named entities related to the health and efficacy of pharmaceuticals. The marked part contains 500 reviews and 68036 tokens. There is also the RuCCoN corpus (Nesterov, 2022), a dataset with extracted entities. One of the recently developed recourses is NEREL-BIO (Loukachevitch, 2022) which includes the annotated schema and corpus of annotations in English and Russian from PubMed, in which entities are tagged. RuMedPrimeData [24] a corpus of patient outpatient visits that was collected at the Siberian State Medical University. The corpus contains symptoms, history, date of admission, ID of visit and patient, and disease code.

In this work, two datasets were used: a corpus of papers from the Russian Medical Journal [25] and a dataset of multi-word biomedical terms. These datasets were collected specifically for these experiments. The first one contains 123 texts with their annotations and titles. Texts contain a total of 316299 tokens and annotations consist of 27057 tokens. Although the main topic of the corpus is COVID-19, papers still match to other different subtopics, e.g. infectious diseases, psychiatry, obstetrics, vaccination, pediatrics, dietetics, gastroenterology, etc. An example of the data is presented in Table 1.

Table 1. Data example.

	Unnamed: 0	header	annotation	text
80	80	Особенности ведения пациентов с нейродегенерат...	\n\nДанных за то, что нейродегенеративные забо...	\n\n\n\n Введение \n\r\n\t Нейродегенеративные...
56	56	Серия случаев вторичной тромботической микроан...	\n\r\n\t Тромботическая микроангиопатия (ТМА) ...	\n\n\n\n Введение \n\r\n\t За 2020 г. в отделе...
63	63	Целесообразность комплексного подхода к лечени...	\n\r\n\t Пандемия новой коронавирусной инфекци...	\n Введение \n\r\n\t Проблема патологии гепато...
50	50	Роль тревожных расстройств у пациентов с серде...	\n\nБолезни системы кровообращения (БСК) — одн...	\n Введение \n\r\n\t Болезни системы кровообра...
69	69	Причины прогрессирования глаукомы во время пан...	\n\nНовая коронавирусная инфекция может стать ...	\n Введение \n\r\n\t Всемирная организация здр...

The medical dictionary consists of 242 multi-word entities. They were collected from various medical dictionaries, the main source was Metathesaurus [23], which contains information from the Russian State Central Scientific Medical Library. The dictionary is lemmatized and is in the following format: {'token1 token2': 'token1_token2'}.

3.2 Rouge

To evaluate the performance of the models were implemented 4 metrics: ROUGE-1, ROUGE-2, ROUGE-L (Lin, 2004), BERTScore (Zhang, 2020), BLEU (Papineni, 2002). To compute the ROUGE-L and ROUGE-N metric the rouge library was applied, for BLEU and BERTScore – the NLTK library.

ROUGE stands for Recall-Oriented Understudy for Gisting Evaluation. It is a set of metrics used for evaluating automatic summarization and machine translation models in natural language processing. ROUGE is designed to assess the output based on the reference summaries (annotations). It focuses on 2 key factors: Precision and Recall.

ROUGE-1 evaluates the overlap of unigrams between the generated summary and the reference summary, ROUGE-2 measures the overlap of bigrams, while ROUGE-L evaluates the longest common subsequence between the generated summary and the reference summary.

3.3 BERTScore

BERTScore is an automatic evaluation metric that calculates similarity scores between each token in the generated sentence and each token in the reference sentence. It is considered a more reliable metric, as it shows a strong correlation with human judgment.

3.4 Bleu

BLEU stands for BiLingual Evaluation Understudy. Initially, it was developed for machine translation evaluation but it can be also used to evaluate text summarization results. Scores are calculated by comparing sentences of the generated text with a set of reference sentences.

4 Experiments

The experimental procedure includes the following stages: Fig. 1 illustrates the structure of the experiment.

4.1 Preprocessing

In natural language processing, data preprocessing plays a major role. The proposed algorithm for preprocessing is the following: at first, sentences are being tokenized and then put to lemmatization. It was decided to use NLTK library for sentence tokenization and Pymorphy2 for the lemmatization.

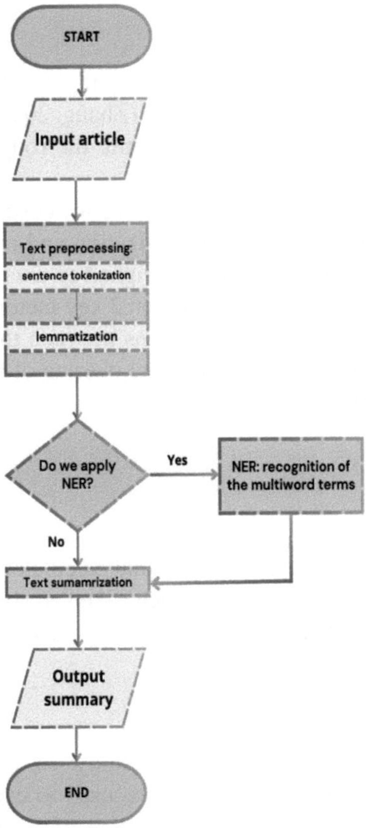

Fig. 1. Experiment's procedure.

4.2 Ner

Since this paper presents the comparison of summarization task performed with and without Named Entity Recognition, it is possible to go both ways. Even though that there exists state-of-art approaches for NER using pre-trained transformer models like RuBioRoBERTa (Yalunin, 2022), RuDR-BERT (Tutubalina, 2020), etc., for this task was decided to develop a simple algorithm. It goes through the lemmatized sentences and searches them for entities from the dictionary. When the algorithm found the required entities, it replaces them with those in the dictionary, so for example, if a sentence contains the phrase "короновирусный инфекция", the programme replaced it with the one in the dictionary, i.e. "короновирусные_инфекция". This markup was to help ensure that multi-word entities were not split during summarization and were passed to the generated text as complete entities.

4.3 Summarization

For the summarization task, an abstractive method was chosen. Two models were taken: T5 and GPT3. T5, or text-to-text transfer transformer, has a transformer architecture. It processes input texts with an encoder and then generates new texts with decoders. GPT3, or Generative Pre-trained Transformer, is a language model that has been trained on a vast amount of different data, can solve any text generation problem.

The models used in this paper were rut5_base_sum_gazeta and rugpt3medium_sum_gazeta. These models were pre-trained on the Gazeta dataset (Gusev, 202), which was developed specifically for the summarization task. This dataset consists of pairs of source texts of news in Russian and their summarized version.

4.4 Application for the Summarization of Medical Texts

In the current work, an application was developed using the Streamlit framework for creating interactive web apps. This application allows the user to select the summarization model for Russian, English and German, along with the number of sentences produced in the output summary..

The application contains the following models:

- IlyaGusev/rugpt3medium_sum_gazeta
- Shahm/t5-small-german
- Falconsai/medical_summarization
- sacreemure/med_t5_summ_ru

The latter model is a fine-tuned model for summarization of Russian biomedical articles that was fine-tuned on 3 epochs and a corpus of medical articles from the RMJ website.

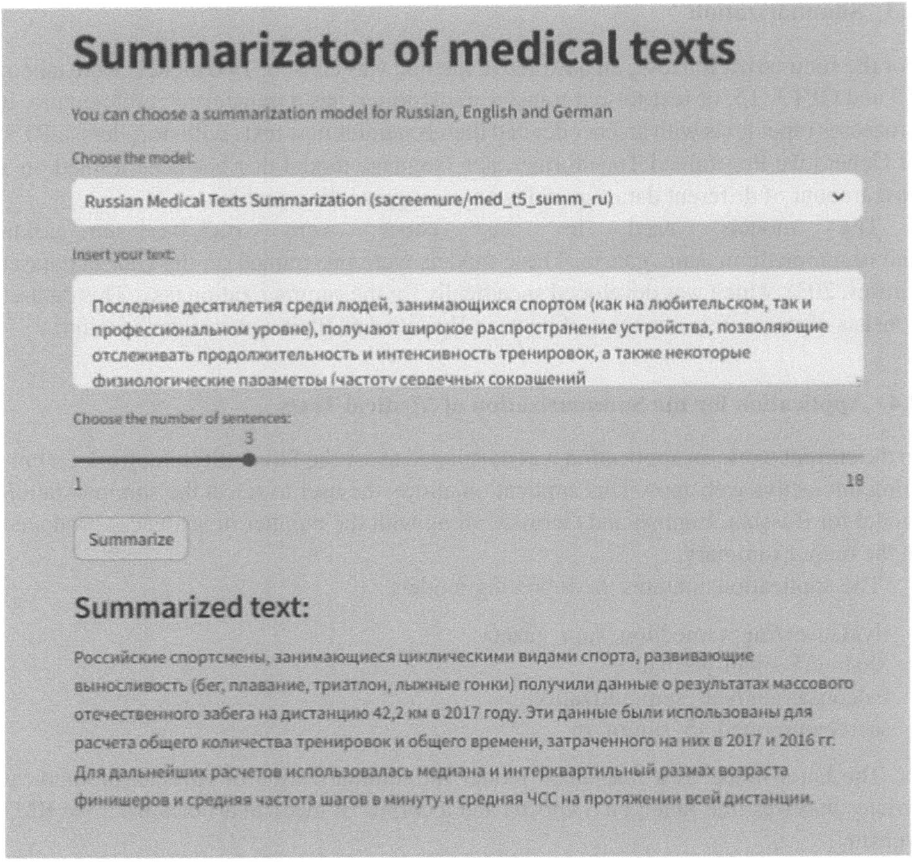

Fig. 2. Web app for summarization of medical texts.

5 Results

In course of experiments, we were able to study if named entities markup influences the results of summarization models or not. As the Table 2 shows, the best results were achieved with ruGPT3 model without markup of named entities. The second best is ruT5 which was also used without NER.

It is seen on the Fig. 2 that the highest scores were presented with BERTScore. It is possible to see that the results of this metric are pretty close as it relies on the semantic proximity of the produced summary and the original medical text. The lowest results were given by BLEU Fig. 3.

An expert evaluation on three criteria: readability, meaningfulness and whether the text is an annotation was also conducted to conduct a comparative analysis of the fine-tuned T5 model for summarising medical texts and the GPT3 model. The results showed that the ilyagusev/rugpt3medium_sum_gazeta model summarises better than the pre-trained sacreemure/med_t5_summ_ru.

Table 2. Summarization models' comparison.

Model	ROUGE-1	ROUGE-2	ROUGE-L	BERTScore	BLEU
rugpt3medium_sum_gazeta with NER	0.052	0.0065	0.049	0.61	0.00036
rut5_base_sum_gazeta with NER	0.085	0.018	0.081	0.64	0.0016
rugpt3medium_sum_gazeta	**0.2**	**0.082**	**0.19**	**0.7**	**0.051**
rut5_base_sum_gazeta	0.1	0.032	0.097	0.65	0.0031

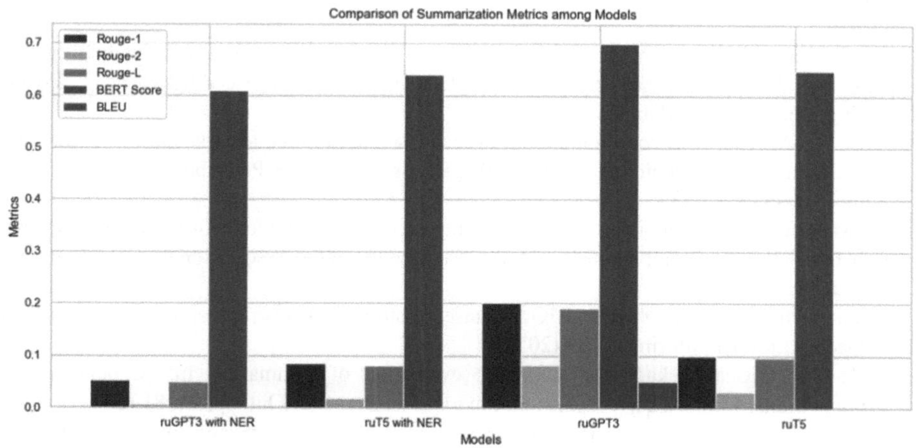

Fig. 3. Comparison of Summarization Metrics.

6 Conclusion and Future Work

Summarisation holds a significant relevance in the biomedical field. It allows texts to be shortened, thereby improving their comprehension by users. These texts contain a large number of special terms, so-called named entities, which if lost, the generated texts will not make sense. Unfortunately, nothing has been done in the field of summarisation of medical texts in Russian, so in our paper we consider summarisation with and without entity extraction. The results show that entities do not affect the performance of abstractive models and even worsen metric estimates. It is essential to mention that the models were not fine-tuned for medical texts.

In the future, the plan is to:

1. Pre-train the summarization models on our corpus;
2. Use not only abstractive summarization but also extractive;
3. Devote more attention to named entity recognition, using other algorithms for their extraction.

References

Alshibly, I.: Text summarization of News Articles based on named entity recognition using Spacy library (2023)

.Batura T.., Bakieva M. Методы и системы автоматического реферирования текстов // Новосибирск: ИПЦ НГУ. (2019)

Bharti, S.K.: Automatic Keyword Extraction for Text Summarization: A Survey (2017)

Berezin, S., Batura, T.: Named entity inclusion in abstractive text summarization. In: Cohan, A., et al. (eds.) Proceedings of the Third Workshop on Scholarly Document Processing, pp. 158–162. Gyeongju (2022)

Brown, T.B., et al.: Language Models are Few-Shot Learners. ArXiv abs/2005.14165 (2020)

Devlin, J., et al.: BERT: Pre-training of Deep Bidirectional Transformers for Language Understanding. In: North American Chapter of the Association for Computational Linguistics (2019)

Gusev, I.: Dataset for Automatic Summarization of Russian News. In: Artificial Intelligence and Natural Language: 9th Conference, AINL 2020, Helsinki, Proceedings 9, pp. 122–134. Springer International Publishing (2020)

Kovalev, R.: Автоматическое упрощение русскоязычных юридических текстов на основе извлечения фактической информации. Bachelor's thesis, Saint-Petersburg State University, Saint Petersburg (2023)

Lewis, M., et al.: BART: denoising sequence-to-sequence pre-training for natural language generation, translation, and comprehension. In: Annual Meeting of the Association for Computational Linguistics (2019)

Loukachevitch, N.V., et al. :NEREL-BIO: a dataset of biomedical abstracts annotated with nested named entities. Bioinformatics **39** (2022)

Lin, C.: ROUGE: a package for automatic evaluation of summaries. In: Association for Computational Linguistics, Vol. Text Summarization Branches Out, pp. 74–81 (2004)

Marek, P., Müller, Š: Text summarization of czech news articles using named entities. The Prague Bull. Math. Linguist. **116**, 5–25 (2021)

Műller, Š.: Text Summarization Using Named Entity Recognition. Bachelor's thesis, Czech Technical University, Prague (2020)

Nesterov, A, Zubkova, G., Miftahutdinov, Z., et al.: RuCCoN: clinical concept normalization in Russian. In: Findings of the Association for Computational Linguistics: ACL 2022, pp. 239–245. Dublin, Ireland (2022)

Papineni, K., Roukos, S., Ward, T., Zhu, W.: BLEU: a method for automatic evaluation of machine translation. In: Proceedings of the 40th Annual Meeting of the Association for Computational Linguistics (2002)

Payal, M., Kumar, Dr. T. A., Kumar, K.S.: Integrating natural language processing (NLP) and machine learning techniques for healthcare industries. Int. J. Innov. Res. Comput. Commun. Eng. **10**(5), 3030–3036 (2022)

Polyakova, I., Pogoreltsev, S.: Extractive russian text summarization as greedy sentence sequence continuation search with probabilities from pretrained language models. In: Golenkov, V., et al. (eds.) Open Semantic Technologies for Intelligent Systems, pp. 303–308. Minsk (2021)

Raffel, C., et al.: Exploring the limits of transfer learning with a unified text-to-text transformer. J. Mach. Learn. Res. **21**,140:1–140:67 (2019):

Senthamizh, S.R, Arutchelvan, K.: Automatic text summarization using document clustering named entity recognition. Int. J. Adv. Comput. Sci. Appl. **13**(9), (2022)

Tutubalina, E., et al: The russian drug reaction corpus and neural models for drug reactions and effectiveness detection in user reviews. Bioinformatics. Oxford, England. (2020)

Yalunin, A., et al.: RuBioRoBERTa: a pre-trained biomedical language model for Russian language biomedical text mining. *ArXiv* abs/2204.03951 (2022)

Zhang, T., Kishore, V., Wu, F., Weinberger K. Q., Artzi, Y.: BERTScore: Evaluating Text Generation with BERT. In: Proceedings of the International Conference on Learning Representations (2020)

Metathesaurus. https://www.nlm.nih.gov/research/umls/sourcereleasedocs/current/MSHRUS/index.html

RuMedPrimeData. h ttps://zenodo/5765873#.YbBlXT9Bzmw

Russian Medical Journal. https://www.rmj.ru/

Argument Mining in Scientific Communication: Comparative Study

Irina Akhmadeeva(✉), Elena Sidorova, and Daria Ilina

A. P. Ershov Institute of Informatics Systems, Siberian Branch, Russian Academy of Sciences, Academician Lavrentyev Avenue, Novosibirsk 630090, Russian Federation
i.r.akhmadeeva@iis.nsk.su

Abstract. The paper presents the results of a study of argumentative relations based on marked-up corpora of texts of scientific communication. The authors investigated individual genre categories to assess the influence of genre features on the quality of argumentation extraction. The length of analyzed texts is at least several paragraphs, which allows quantitative and qualitative estimation of long-range relations. Long-range relations are considered to be argumentative relations between statements that are located at a distance of more than one sentence. The authors carried out a statistical comparative analysis of the relative position and distance between the components of arguments in sub-corpora that contain texts of 5 scientific and popular science subgenres. The experimental study considered the task of argument relation prediction, including long-range relations. The complexity of this task is due to several problems: issues of determining the boundaries of statements – candidates for the roles of premises or conclusions of arguments; uncertainty about the mechanism for the prediction of relations between segments that are located at long distances, and lack of agreement between experts when marking long-range relations. The paper proposes a neural network approach based on the Longformer model, which allows taking into account a fairly wide context of statements. Three models that take into account different context lengths are considered. The best results (0.72 f1-measure) were achieved on the Longformer-large model, which takes into account the context of paragraph-sized statements.

Keywords: Argument Mining · Long-Range Argumentative Relations · Longformer Model · Scientific Communication · Argument Relation Prediction

1 Introduction

Argumentation appears in speech when the participants of communication discuss a thesis supported or disproved with some arguments. One can use not only logical reasoning (cause to effect inference, negative proof, whole to part inference etc.), but references to experts, moral aspects of situation, participants and their beliefs as well [1]. Computational methods, such as information mining and opinion mining, identify statements expressed in texts, but ignore the underlying reasons. Argument analysis overcomes this by automatically reconstructing justifications and refutations in texts.

M. Bakaev et al. (Eds.): IMS 2024, CCIS 2534, pp. 152–166, 2026.
https://doi.org/10.1007/978-3-031-96177-9_13

Argument Mining (AM) is an actively developing area of natural language processing (NLP). Argumentation analysis has many applications: in the law [2–4], in the analysis of news reports [5] and debates [6], in applied research [7], for detecting errors [8] and assessing the persuasiveness of text [9]. Modeling of argumentation is a separate area of research [10, 11], in our research we base on D. Walton's schemes [12] and their formalization in the Argument Interchange Format (AIF) [13]. The widespread use of the task-independent ontology AIF, which includes a description of about 60 argumentation schemes, allows us to talk about the global concept of Argument Web [14], combining resources and software for various AM tasks [15].

The goal of AM is to automatically identify the components of argumentation in a text: premises, conclusions, and argumentative relationships. The following set of subtasks is usually considered as a pipeline:

1. detection of argumentation or identification of argumentative text fragments (Argument Detection);
2. classification of identified text fragments in accordance with their role in the structure of the argument (Argument Component Classification);
3. establishing argumentative relationships between text fragments (Argument Relation Prediction);
4. classification of argumentative relationships in accordance with a given argumentation model (for example, D. Walton's schemes).

Among these tasks, Argument Relation Prediction is a key one, since it allows to build networks or graphs of related statements for texts, including large texts. However, in most studies, the task is considered either in the context of a given thesis, or for statements located nearby in the text. That does not allow linking text fragments that are located at a distance greater than a sentence or text paragraph.

This paper conducts a study of argumentative relations in scientific communication. The length of analyzed texts is at least several paragraphs, which allows quantitative and qualitative estimation of long-range relations. The paper also proposes an approach to the argument relation prediction based on the Longformer type of neural network models, and provides a comparative study of the quality of the extraction from texts of different subgenres of scientific communication.

2 Related Works

The use of deep learning (DL) methods for NLP has revolutionized many tasks in this field. It has opened up opportunities for further development of the fundamentals and solved much more ambitious problems, including tasks of argumentation analysis [16, 17]. However, the results of DL models in argument relation prediction often remain comparable to those of classic methods, such as support vector machine. Work [18] shows that, despite the significant superiority of the BERT model in the task of classifying argumentative statements, it is less effective when solving the problem of argument relation prediction.

Paper [19] considers the problem of finding relationships between components of arguments in essays written in English by non-native speakers. The authors determined connections between sentences and on their basis formed a tree-like structure of argumentation in the text using the sequential application of the BERT language model and the BiLSTM neural network.

[20] shows that argument relations are associated with various statistics, such as discourse markers. In [4], an approach to classifying argument components at the level of word tokens is proposed. Token-level classification not only improved sentence classification results compared to state-of-the-art sentence classification models such as Longformer, BERT, and Legal-BERT, but also showed that certain tokens, which are indicators of argumentation, have the most significant impact on the results. Using argumentation indicators to predict argument relations in Russian-language texts leads to better results for statements related by short context [21]. However, for the task of identifying components of an argument located at a distance greater than the sentence, the presence of indicators near the components actually only shows that the statement belongs to the argument.

The problem of argument relation prediction over long distances is similar to the problem of Event Argument Extraction (EAE) – detection of relations between events [22, 23]. Document-level EAE requires identification of long-range dependencies, which often span across multiple sentences. Various approaches are used to solve this problem: a) document-based question-answering method, such as DocMRC [24]; b) global encoding methods, such as Dynamic Global Memory [25]; c) generative methods, which proposes a sequence-to-sequence model, such as BART-Gen [22]; d) methods using extra supervisions, for example, TSAR [26], which utilizes abstract meaning representation (AMR) resources; e) logic methods, such as Chain Reasoning Paradigm [27] which integrates fuzzy logic into the optimization process, and so on.

For our purposes, we use a Document-Level Argument Relation Prediction approach, which uses a Longformer model to build embeddings of statements and their context and fine-tuning to specialize the model for the task of predicting the presence of a directed argument relation (support or attack).

3 Modelling Argument Relations

Our work uses a neo-rhetoric theory of argumentation, in which methods of proving a thesis are assessed not in the categories of truth and logical correctness, but in terms of persuasiveness and relevance. Not only the content of the thesis and evidence are important, but also the addressee of the argument. The consistency of the argument is assessed by the criterion of audience agreement with the author's point of view, and not by strict compliance with logical rules [28].

One of the main concepts of the theory of argumentation is the argumentation scheme [10]. It is defined as a model by which "a transfer of acceptance from the explicit premise to the standpoint must be aimed for", "conventionalized ways of displaying a relation between that which is stated in the explicit premise and that which is stated in the standpoint" [29]. The work uses D. Walton's argument model: an argument consists of a standpoint being proven (conclusion) and one or more premises. Here is an example of an argumentation scheme "Argument from Negative Consequences":

BadConsequence_Premise: If *A* is brought about, bad consequences will plausibly occur.

Conclusion: A should not be brought about.

Some schemes are accompanied by "critical questions", aimed at confirming the validity of the premises and deducing the thesis from them and representing possible questions from the opponent. So, to the Argument from Negative Consequences scheme one question is attached: There are consequences of the opposite value that ought to be taken into account [12].

The ontology AIF based on the set of D. Walton's argumentation schemes contains two types of argumentation schemes: supporting (Inferences), that prove a standpoint, and attacking (Conflicts), that refute a supporting argument. Most attack schemes are exceptions based on critical questions and apply to certain supporting schemes. E.g., the Opposite Consequences Conflict scheme is based on the critical question to Argument from Negative Consequences.

3.1 Corpora with Argument Annotations

We adhere to the hypothesis studying the argument relations should include texts of different genres. This hypothesis is based on the following considerations:

- In different spheres of communication and genres, the pragmatic task of convincing the addressee in the validity of a standpoint may be relevant or not. E. g., in debates it is the main task, but it may not appear at all in a news report.
- Depending on the purpose of communication, the audience, the relationship of the communicants, the topic and other genre characteristics, the repertoire of argumentation schemes can vary significantly.

The material of the study includes 5 corpora of texts on scientific topics: science news, analytical popular science articles (from the website habr.com), short academic papers, full-length academic papers with the reviewer's comments, and reviews on articles.

The corpora were annotated on the ArgNetBank Studio platform [30]. The annotators have modeled argumentative structure of the texts according to the AIF standard [13] by constructing a directed coherent graph (see Fig. 1) with informational nodes, which correspond to statements, and argumentation nodes. The set of all argument relations in the graph is described by the internal connections of the arguments in accordance with the reasoning schemes that they express. Supporting argument relations (green oval blocks) and attacking (conflicting) ones (red oval blocks) are distinguished.

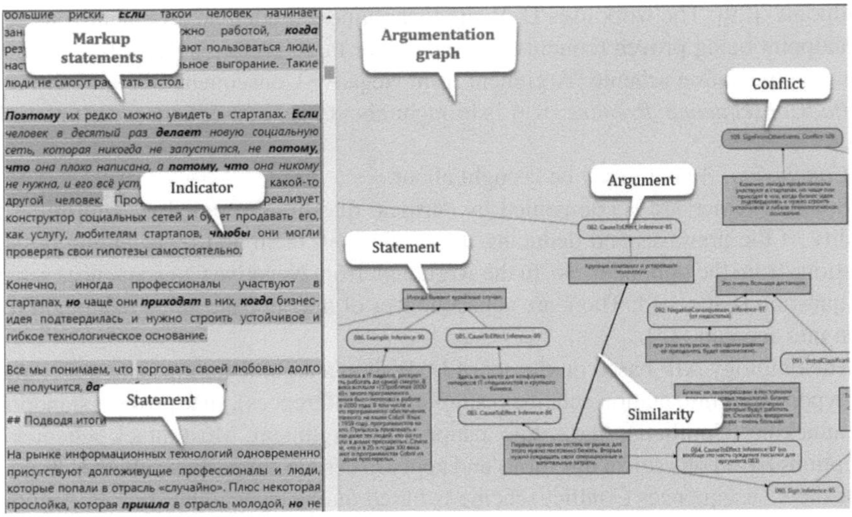

Fig. 1. Argumentation markup. Rectangular blocks represent statements; oval blocks – connections between statements (color figure online).

The whole corpus (with 5 sub-corpora) has the following features.

- The corpus consists of several sub-corpora in accordance with the specified genre categories.
- The corpus as a whole and its sub-corpora are thematically neutral. However, in general, IT topic predominates due to the specificity of the sources of material.
- The boundaries between genres are transparent: each of them has its own genre goal, features of content representation and textual features. Science news are short texts about discoveries in research. Analytical popular science articles usually contain long explanations within complex argumentative structure. Short academic papers provide concise description of the study and include one main thesis at the end of the text. Full-length academic papers are more detailed; they may not have a main thesis at all; and they are accompanied by a reviewer's comments. Reviews on articles are very short, and the entire text justifies the decision whether an article can be published. For more details see [31].
- The number of attacking arguments in the corpus is small compared to supporting arguments. This is due to the peculiarity of the analyzed genres: in monologue texts, which make up most of the corpus, the expression of counterarguments is not frequent. In this regard, we have not yet considered the task of dividing argumentation into supporting and refuting.

Currently, the marked corpus contains 150 texts; annotated comments were not taken into account in this study. In total, 217 different annotations were created and 11.4 thousand arguments were marked.

3.2 Quantitative Analysis of the Degree of the Distance Between the Components of the Argument

To search for argument relations in large texts, it is necessary to develop a mechanism for preliminary construction of hypotheses, i.e. determine how the input text will be divided into statements, and which pairs of statements will be checked by our model for argument relations.

The work [32] considered pairs of statements obtained with a sliding window technique. Two consecutive segments (sentences and/or clauses) were taken as a window and the entire text was viewed using such a window. From the segments falling each time into window, pairs were put to the training dataset. Each pair was checked whether they were statements of the same argument and, if yes, what roles they played in the structure of this argument. On the basis of this information, a decision was made about the presence and direction of the argument relation. We will call the argument relations predicted in this way "short-range relations". The statistics on the occurrence of short-range and long-range relations in the text corpus is as follows (see Fig. 2).

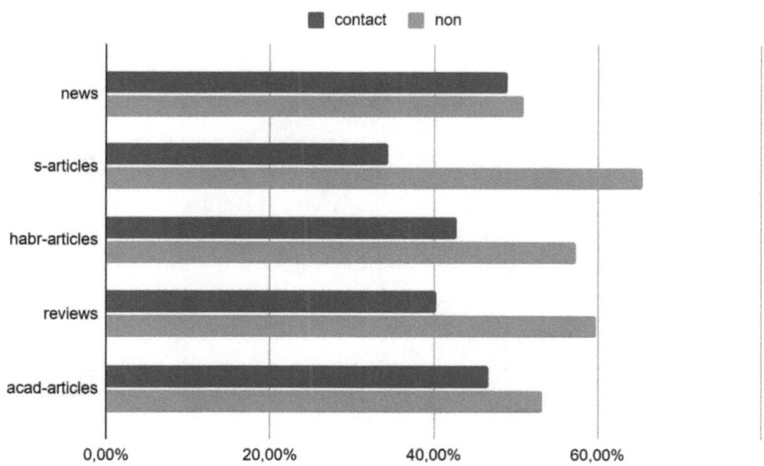

Fig. 2. Horizontal bar chart displays the percentage distribution between short-range 'contact' (blue) and long-range 'non' (red) relations for each of five sub-corpora: 'news', 's-articles', 'habr-articles', 'reviews', and 'acad-articles'. Each sub-corpus has two bars, one blue and one red, representing the two relation types. The x-axis ranges from 0% to 80%. The chart highlights differences in the proportion of 'contact' and 'non' relations across the sub-corpora.

The diagram shows that the ratio of short-range and long-range relations throughout the entire corpus is approximately 40% to 60%. This ratio varies slightly depending on the genre: for example, in science news the number of short-range relations is bigger, but there are still fewer of them than long-range ones. It can also be noted that the number of relations with intersecting and nested statements is less than 1%.

The sliding window technique is not suitable for constructing hypotheses of long-range relations. Therefore, we explored various options for the position of statements related to one argument (premise and conclusion) relative to each other. The following options were considered:

- one clause: the premise and conclusion are in one clause or in a simple sentence;
- one sentence: the premise and conclusion are in different clauses of the same sentence;
- contact sentences: the premise and conclusion are in different adjacent sentences;
- one paragraph: the premise and conclusion are in different non-contact sentences of the same paragraph;
- consecutive paragraphs: the premise and conclusion are next to each other, but in adjacent paragraphs (in the last sentence of the previous paragraph and the first sentence of the next paragraph);
- adjacent paragraphs: the premise and conclusion are in non-consecutive sentences of adjacent paragraphs;
- unrelated sentences: the premise and conclusion are in sentences, the distance between which is more than one paragraph;
- other cases: the premise or conclusion includes several sentences or paragraphs.

The following diagram (see Fig. 3) demonstrates the ratios of segments of the corpus that include the entire argument (i.e., both the premise and the conclusion).

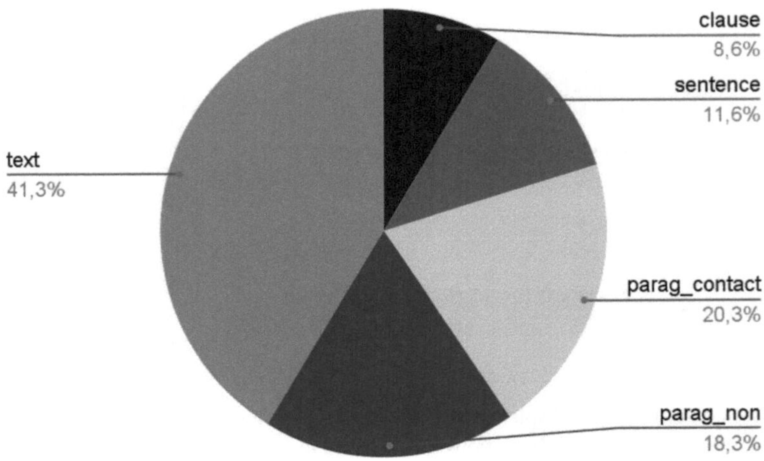

Fig. 3. Diagram of ratio of segments that include arguments.

This information allows estimating how far the components of an argument can be located in the text. Segments of the types “clause”, “sentence”, “parag_contact” (contact premise and conclusion within a paragraph) correspond to short-range relations, “text” and “parag_non” (premise and conclusion within a paragraph, but not contact) – long-range relations. It should also be noted that cases where an argument is located in one clause (8.6%) are also difficult to recognize, since the mechanism for identifying the boundaries of such statements is unclear.

Figure 4 shows the ratio of the distances between argument components in the texts of different genres.

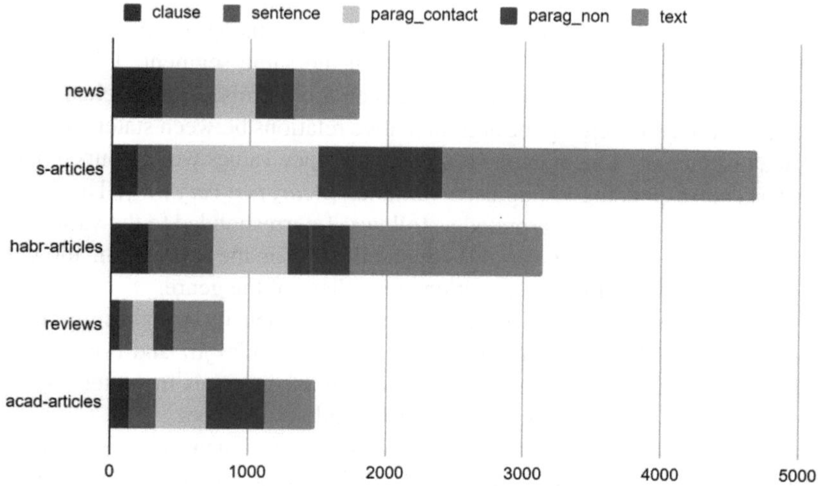

Fig. 4. Diagram of ratios of segments that include arguments for different genres.

In this diagram, the ratios are shown in absolute values. A significantly larger number of arguments for scientific articles is due to the fact that this sub-corpus has double markup and each markup is considered independently.

At the next step, we measured the distances between the components of arguments in sentences and paragraphs (see Fig. 5) to test a hypothesis about the high density of argument components: the more the distance between premises and conclusions, the less the number of the pairs. There may be outliers associated with relations with the main theses, which is usually located at the beginning or end of the text.

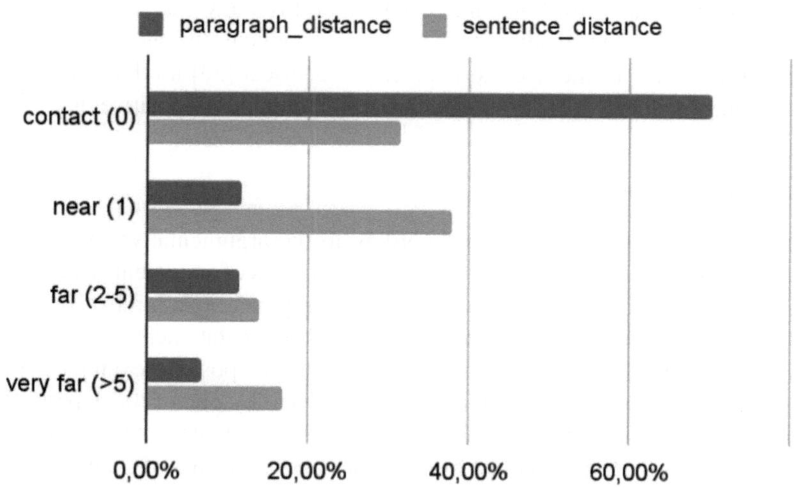

Fig. 5. Diagram of general ratio of segments that include arguments.

Distances were measured in segments (sentences or paragraphs), where 0 means that the premise and conclusion were located in the same segment, 1 – in adjacent segments, >1 – the number of segments between the premise and conclusion. Long-range relations are considered to be argumentative relations between statements that are located at a distance of more than one sentence. Distance values were grouped based on fuzzy criteria corresponding to linguistic variables $\{near, far, very\,far\}$. The numerical values of the distances were interpreted as follows: 1 corresponded to the variable *near*, 2–5 – *far*, >5 – *very far*. These variables do not depend on the text length, allowing for the consideration of long-range connections regardless of the genre.

The results of the analysis showed that, in general, the density hypothesis for relations is confirmed – only 18.1% of relations correspond to variables *far* and *very far* relative to the distance in paragraphs. However, an analysis of distances in sentences showed that long-range relations can be formed at fairly random distances.

Thus, various distances of statements related to one argument (premise and conclusion) relative to each other were considered. This made it possible to develop several mechanisms for generating hypotheses for argument relation prediction and constructing datasets that take into account long-range relations – about 60% of all relations. However, it has not yet been possible to solve the problem of non-standard segmentation – these are statements that are not a clause or a sentence.

Currently, the overall estimate of the number of argument relations marked by annotators and included in our dataset is 52.9%.

4 Argumentative Relations Extraction

To apply machine learning to the problem of argument relation prediction, it is necessary to create datasets containing positive and negative examples of pairs of statements based on the existing text markups. Since the emphasis in this study was on extracting long-range relations, we limited ourselves to considering statements that are a single sentence. This limitation is due to the need to balance the datasets [33] so that the number of negative examples does not differ too much from the number of positive ones.

4.1 Data Preparation

The training dataset was constructed according to the argumentative markups of the texts and contains positive and negative examples of pairs of statements (premise, conclusion). A pair is a positive example if there is an argument relation between premise and conclusion, and a negative example otherwise. Pairs of statements that two or more experts considered to be argumentative were selected as positive examples. Pairs of statements that were considered argumentatively related by one of the experts and not by the other were considered ambiguous and did not participate in the construction of the dataset. In texts that were marked by only one expert, all pairs of statements labeled by him were considered positive. Negative examples were selected as follows: for each positive pair of statements, a pair was generated in which the statements were in the same paragraphs (or in neighboring paragraphs, in the absence of suitable statements) and between which there was no path from premise to conclusion in the argumentation graph. E. g., the pair of statements (s3, s2) in Fig. 6 is a positive example and the pair (s4, s1) is a negative example. In this way, 4788 positive examples and 4694 negative examples were obtained.

To investigate the impact of context on the quality of argument relation prediction, three variants of the dataset were constructed:

- no-context: only the statements themselves;
- paragraph-context: statements and the paragraphs that contain those statements;
- full_text-context: statements and the entire encompassing text.

4.2 Model Description

Since the context of statements (paragraph or whole text) can be longer than 512 tokens, classical BERT models cannot be used to build vector representations of contexts and tokens that are part of the statements. Therefore, for all three variants of the dataset we used the pre-trained models with Longformer [34] architecture: kazzand/ru-longformer-tiny-16384 (tiny) and kazzand/ru-longformer-large-4096 (large). The length of analytical popular science articles (from the website habr.com) and full-length academic papers often exceeds 4096 tokens, so it is impossible to use the longformer-large model to obtain a vector representation of the whole text. For these corpora, only the longformer-tiny model was used on the dataset variant including the whole text as a context.

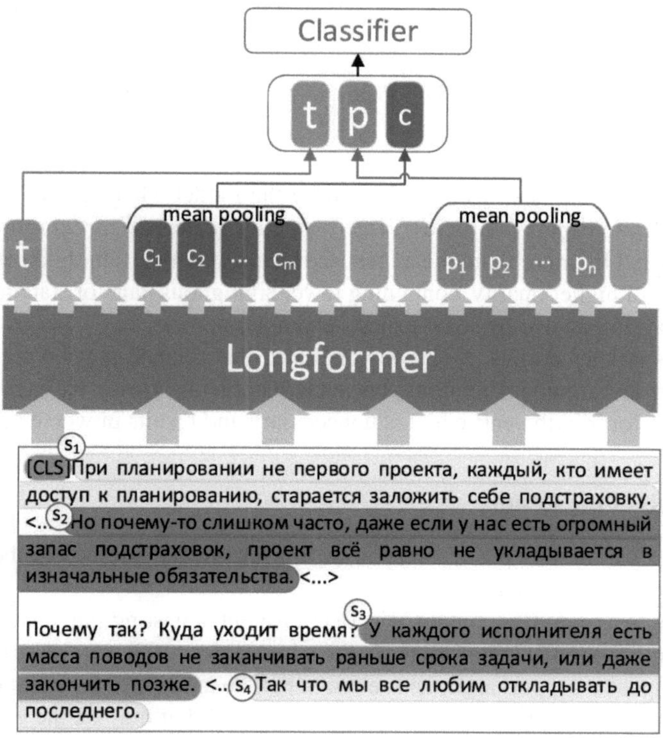

Fig. 6. Model architecture.

Figure 6 illustrates the architecture of the model designed for predicting the argument relation between a pair of statements given the context of their occurrence. The vector representations of statements are constructed by averaging the embeddings of corresponding tokens, while the vector representation of context is the [CLS] token embedding. The concatenation of these three vectors (p – premise embedding, c – conclusion embedding, and t – context embedding) is fed into the fully connected layer for classification into two classes: the presence or absence of an argument relation.

Table 1. Experimental results for predicting the presence of an argumentative relation.

Corpus	Model	no-context			paragraph			full text		
		p	r	f1	p	r	f1	p	r	f1
s-articles	tiny	51.03	61.49	55.77	61.2	69.57	65.12	50.28	55.28	52.66
	large	51.4	68.32	58.67	65.31	79.5	**71.71**	52.89	79.5	63.52
habr-articles	tiny	50.21	57.88	53.78	52.36	76.6	62.2	54.55	13.3	21.39
	large	50.12	100	66.78	50.97	84.24	63.5	–	–	–
news	tiny	63.16	54.55	58.54	50	50	50	50	95.45	65.63
	large	52.17	54.55	53.33	66.67	54.55	60	47.05	36.36	41.03
reviews	tiny	47.37	60	52.94	43.59	56.67	49.28	51.02	83.33	63.29
	large	51.4	68.32	55.88	51.85	46.67	49.12	50	80	61.54
acad-articles	tiny	56.43	40.31	47.02	58.71	79.08	67.39	52.46	16.33	24.9
	large	53.47	27.55	36.36	61.4	35.71	45.16	–	–	–

Table 1 shows the best results achieved by the model when applied to the corpus of short academic papers (s-articles). The distinctive feature of this corpus is that each text is annotated by more than one expert. Consequently, the training dataset based on this corpus is of higher quality, containing fewer ambiguous pairs of statements that are considered argumentative by some experts and not by others.

For the s-articles corpus, it can be concluded that context plays a significant role in predicting the argument relations between statements. However, excessively long context in the form of the entire text is unnecessary and results in worse quality.

4.3 Analysis of the Results

An expert analysis of false positive responses from the model that showed the best results was carried out on a test sample.

False positive responses contain pairs of equivalent or nesting statements (13%); pair that can compose conflict argumentation (8%). In addition, 10% were pairs of statements that can compose a support argument relation, but the annotators have not done that.

A number of language factors have been identified that may be the causes of false positive responses from models:

- lexical repetitions (including the use of cognate words) in candidates for the roles of premises and conclusions (except for cases when the most frequent words for the text are repeated) – 30% of false positive responses;
- repetitions of words and phrases that are frequent in the text – 52%;
- presence of synonyms in candidate statements – 20%;
- presence of an anaphoric pronoun in the candidate-conclusion that agrees with the noun or phrase in the candidate-premise – 7%;
- proximity of statements: e. g., the candidate-premise is the last sentence of a previous paragraph, and the candidate-conclusion is the first sentence of the next – 7%.

In addition, in long texts, the position of the candidates-conclusions could play a role: only 32% of them are not included in the so-called "strong positions" of the text – they are not the first and last sentences of paragraphs and are not included in the first and last paragraphs. This indicator was not applied for science news and reviews, since in texts of these genres, the length of a paragraph rarely exceeds two sentences.

The analysis shows the prospects of introducing methods of preliminary linguistic analysis of text, in particular, establishing equivalence relations between text fragments, resolving anaphora, removing stop words, taking into account direct or indirect speech, as well as introducing features related to the formal structure of the text.

5 Conclusion

The paper presents the results of the study of argument relations on the material of annotated corpora of texts of scientific communication. We conducted the analysis across different genres to account for different quality of annotations between genres and to evaluate the impact of genre-specific features on the quality of argument mining. We involved statistical, experimental, and linguistic analyses of the material.

In the experimental study, we examined the task of argument relation prediction, including long-range ones. The complexity of this task arises from: a) difficulties in identifying the boundaries of statements that could serve as premises or conclusions of arguments, b) the unclear mechanism for constructing hypotheses between distant segments, and c) the lack of agreement among experts, resulting in datasets of suboptimal quality. The results obtained from the neural network approach demonstrate consistent performance only on the corpus of short scientific articles, characterized by multiple expert annotations per text, from which only arguments matching in different markups were selected for the datasets. The best performance (f1-measure = 0.72) was achieved by the longformer-large model, which takes into account the statement's context with the size of a paragraph.

Further development of the approach involves (a) improving the quality of the datasets, (b) exploring neural network approaches for predicting statement boundaries, and (c) exploring methods for establishing equivalent relations between statements.

Acknowledgments. The study was supported by the Russian Science Foundation grant No. 23-11-00261, https://rscf.ru/project/23-11-00261/.

References

1. Toulmin, S.: The Uses of Argument. Cambridge University Press, Cambridge (1958)
2. Rotolo, A., Sartor, G.: Argumentation and Explanation in the Law. Front. Artif. Intell. (2023). https://doi.org/10.3389/frai.2023.1130559
3. Moens, M.-F., Boiy, E., Mochales Palau, R., Reed, Ch.: Automatic detection of arguments in legal texts. In: Proceedings of the 11th International Conference on Artificial Intelligence and Law (ICAIL '07), pp. 225–230. Association for Computing Machinery, New York (2007), https://doi.org/10.1145/1276318.1276362
4. Xu, H., Ashley, K.: Multi-granularity argument mining in legal texts. In: Francesconi, E., Borges, G., Sorge, C. (eds.) Legal Knowledge and Information Systems: JURIX 2022: The Thirty-fifth Annual Conference, Saarbrücken, Germany, 14–16 December 2022. IOS Press (2022). https://doi.org/10.3233/FAIA220477
5. Musi, E., Carni, E., Reed, Ch., Yates, S., O'Halloran, K.: Developing misinformation immunity: how to reason-check fallacious news in a human–computer interaction environment. Soc. Media + Soc. (2023). https://doi.org/10.1177/20563051221150407
6. Lawrence, J., Snaith, M., Konat, B., Budzynska, K., Reed, C.: Debating technology for dialogical argument: sensemaking, engagement, and analytics. ACM Trans. Internet Technol. **17**(3), 1–23 (2017). https://doi.org/10.1145/3007210
7. Lawrence, J., Pereira-Fariña, M., Visser, J.: Argument mining and analytics in archaeology. In: Gonzalez-Perez, C., Martin-Rodilla, P., Pereira-Fariña, M. (eds.) Discourse and Argumentation in Archaeology: Conceptual and Computational Approaches, pp. 263–290. Springer International Publishing, Cham (2023). https://doi.org/10.1007/978-3-031-37156-1_12
8. Ruiz-Dolz, R., Lawrence, J.: Detecting argumentative fallacies in the wild: problems and limitations of large language models. In: Proceedings of the 10th Workshop on Argument Mining Association for Computational Linguistics, pp. 1–10 (2023). https://aclanthology.org/2023.argmining-1.1.pdf. Last accessed 25 Mar 2024
9. Zagorulko, Y., Garanina, N., Sery, A., Domanov, O.: Ontology-based approach to organizing the support for the analysis of argumentation in popular science discourse. In: Sergei, O.K., Aleksandr, I.P. (eds.) Artificial Intelligence: 17th Russian Conference, RCAI 2019, Ulyanovsk, Russia, October 21–25, 2019, Proceedings, pp. 348–362. Springer International Publishing, Cham (2019). https://doi.org/10.1007/978-3-030-30763-9_29
10. Macagno, F.: Argumentation schemes in AI: a literature review. Introduction to the special issue. Argument Comput. **12**(3), 287–302 (2021). https://doi.org/10.3233/AAC-210020
11. Kononenko, I., Sery, A., Shestakov, V., Sidorova, E., Zagorulko, Y.: An approach to classifying walton's argumentation schemes. In: 2023 IEEE XVI International Scientific and Technical Conference Actual Problems of Electronic Instrument Engineering (APEIE), pp. 1540–1545. Novosibirsk (2023), https://doi.org/10.1109/APEIE59731.2023.10347573
12. Walton, D., Reed, C., Macagno, F.: Argumentation Schemes. Cambridge University Press, New York (2008)
13. Rahwan, I., Banihashemi, B., Reed, C., Walton, D., Abdallah, S.: Representing and classifying arguments on the semantic web. Knowl. Eng. Rev. **26**(4), 487–511 (2011)
14. Reed, C., et al.: The argument web: an online ecosystem of tools, systems and services for argumentation. Philos. Technol. **30**(2), 137–160 (2017). https://doi.org/10.1007/s13347-017-0260-8
15. Lawrence, J., Visser, J., Reed, C.: Translational argument technology: engineering a step change in the argument web. J. of Web Semant. **77**, 100786 (2023). https://doi.org/10.1016/j.websem.2023.100786
16. Stede, M., Schneider, J., Hirst, G.: Argumentation Mining. Morgan & Claypool, San Rafael (2019)

17. Lawrence, J., Reed, C.: Argument mining: a survey. Comput. Linguist. **45**(4), 765–818 (2019). https://doi.org/10.1162/coli_a_00364
18. Chen, T.: BERT Argues: How Attention Informs Argument Mining. Honors Theses. 1589 (2021), https://scholarship.richmond.edu/honors-theses/1589, last accessed 2023/03/25
19. Putra, J. W. G., Teufel, S., Tokunaga, T.: Multi-task and multi-corpora training strategies to enhance argumentative sentence linking performance. In: Proceedings of the 8th Workshop on Argument Mining, pp. 12–23. Association for Computational Linguistics, Punta Cana (2021)
20. Opitz, J., Frank, A.: Dissecting content and context in argumentative relation analysis. In: Stein, B., Wachsmuth, H. (eds.) Proceedings of the 6th Workshop on Argument Mining, pp. 25–34. Association for Computational Linguistics, Florence (2019). https://doi.org/10.18653/v1/W19-4503
21. Sidorova, E.A., et al.: An integrated approach to the analysis of argumentative relationships in scientific communication texts. Ontol. Des. **13**(4), 562–579 (2023). https://doi.org/10.18287/2223-9537-2023-13-4-562-579. [In Russian]
22. Sha, L., Heng, J., Jiawei, H.: Document-level event argument extraction by conditional generation. In: Toutanova, K., Rumshisky, A., Zettlemoyer, L., et al. (eds.) Proceedings of the 2021 Conference of the North American Chapter of the Association for Computational Linguistics: Human Language Technologies, pp. 894–908. Association for Computational Linguistics (2021). https://doi.org/10.18653/v1/2021.naacl-main.69
23. Zhang, X.F., Blum, C., Choji, T., Shah, S., Vempala, A.: ULTRA: Unleash LLMs' Potential for Event Argument Extraction through Hierarchical Modeling and Pair-wise Self-Refinement. arXiv preprint (2025). https://doi.org/10.48550/arXiv.2401.13218
24. Jian, L., Chen, Y., Xu, J.: Machine reading comprehension as data augmentation: a case study on implicit event argument extraction. In: Moens, M.-F., Huang, X., Specia, L., Wen-tau Yih, S. (eds.) Proceedings of the 2021 Conference on Empirical Methods in Natural Language Processing, pp. 2716–2725, Association for Computational Linguistics, Online and Punta Cana, Dominican Republic (2021), https://doi.org/10.18653/v1/2021.emnlp-main.214
25. Du, X., Li, S., Ji:, H. Dynamic Global Memory for Document-Level Argument Extraction. In: Muresan, S., Nakov, P., Villavicencio, A. (eds.) Proceedings of the 60th Annual Meeting of the Association for Computational Linguistics, vol. 1, pp. 5264–5275, Association for Computational Linguistics, Dublin, Ireland (2022), https://doi.org/10.18653/v1/2022.acl-long.361
26. Xu, R., Wang, P., Liu, T., Zeng, S., Chang, B., Sui, Z.: A two-stream AMR-enhanced model for document-level event argument extraction. In: Proceedings of the 2022 Conference of the North American Chapter of the Association for Computational Linguistics: Human Language Technologies, pp. 5025–5036. Association for Computational Linguistics, Seattle, United States (2022), https://doi.org/10.18653/v1/2022.naacl-main.370
27. Liu, J., Liang, C., Xu, J., Liu, H., Zhao, Z.: Document-level event argument extraction with a chain reasoning paradigm. In: Proceedings of the 61st Annual Meeting of the Association for Computational Linguistics, vol. 1, pp. 9570–9583. Association for Computational Linguistics, Toronto, Canada (2023)
28. Perelman, C., Olbrechts-Tyteca, L.: The New Rhetoric: A Treatise on Argumentation. University of Notre Dame Press, London (1971)
29. van Eemeren, F.H.: The state of the art in argumentation theory. In: van Eemeren, F.H. (ed.) Crucial Concepts in Argumentation Theory, pp. 11–26. Amsterdam University Press, Amsterdam (2001)
30. Sidorova, E.A., Akhmadeeva, I.R., Zagorulko, Yu.A., Sery, A.S., Shestakov, V.K.: Research platform for the study of argumentation in popular science discourse. Ontol. Des. **10**(4), 489–502 (2020). https://doi.org/10.18287/2223-9537-2020-10-4-489-502. (In Russian)

31. Timofeeva, M.K., Ilina, D.V., Kononenko, I.S.: Argumentative annotation of the scientific internet-communication corpus: genre analysis and study of typical reasoning models based on the ArgNetBank studio platform. NSU Vestnik. Series: Linguist. Intercult. Commun. **22**(1), 27–49 (2024). https://doi.org/10.25205/1818-7935-2024-22-1-27-49
32. Sidorova, E., Akhmadeeva, I., Kononenko, I., Chagina, P.: The role of indicators in argumentative relation prediction. computational linguistics and intellectual technologies. In: Proceedings of the International Conference "Dialogue 2023", pp. 477–485 (2023), https://doi.org/10.28995/2075-7182-2023-22-477-485
33. Salomatina, N., Sidorova, E., Pimenov, I.: Applying machine learning methods to identify argumentative connections in scientific communication texts. Ontol. Des. **14**(1), 82–93 (2024). https://doi.org/10.18287/2223-9537-2024-14-1-82-93. (in Russian)
34. Beltagy, I., Peters, M., Cohan, A.: Longformer: The Long-Document Transformer (2020). ArXiv preprint 2004.05150

Paragraph Classification and Text Analysis for Automated Document Formatting: Developing and Refining Approaches

Nail Nasyrov(✉), Dmitry Fedorov, Aleksei Bezgin, Nikita Mazein, Kseniia Tikhonova, and Nataliya Gorlushkina

ITMO University, Kronverksky Pr. 49, Bldg. A, St. Petersburg 197101, Russia
pasdel@itmo.ru

Abstract. The primary task in automated formatting of document elements is identifying their classes. An algorithm for classifying elements within a text document was based on Gradient Boosting on decision trees implemented in CatBoost. To enhance classification quality the following approaches have been considered: data preprocessing and feature engineering tailored to the dataset's specifics, training alternative models applicable to this task such as Logistic Regression, K-Nearest Neighbors classifier, Random Forest Classifier, as well as optimizing the hyperparameters of CatBoost and of the above models.

A hypothesis regarding the sequential structure of the object space for determining an object's class based on its context is explored. This involves training an LSTM model on selected features specifically tailored for the purpose. The identification of paragraph features for these models involves graphemic, semantic, and syntactic computer analysis. The study analyzes the combination of these approaches and its outcomes. The findings can be applied to classify elements formatted according to various text document standards for subsequent automated verification of compliance with assumed requirements.

Keywords: Text Analysis · Standard Control · CatBoost · LSTM · Multiclass Classification · Hyperparameter Tuning

1 Introduction

Meeting the requirements for document layout is essential both for graduate qualification papers [1] and for articles to be published in peer-reviewed journals. Each country has its own set of regulatory standards and methods. In the USA, several document layout styles are used for research papers, including APA, MLA, and Chicago/Turabian [2]. GOST 7.32–2017 is the official layout standard used in Russia, Kyrgyzstan, Kazakhstan, Armenia, and Azerbaijan for presenting reports on academic work and graduate qualification papers [3].

In addition, it is common for educational institutions to have their internal standards and requirements for the academic paper layout, which specify the structure of the document, its length, and other parameters [4, 5]. Adhering to these standards is vital

M. Bakaev et al. (Eds.): IMS 2024, CCIS 2534, pp. 167–182, 2026.
https://doi.org/10.1007/978-3-031-96177-9_14

for the successful presentation of a thesis, as well as for its grading. The importance of following these standards is emphasized by the scientific community as part of a researcher's academic competence [6]. Publishing houses, including the international company Springer, have their specific requirements for accepting papers for publication [7]. We can also check the formal requirements to identify any errors or inconsistencies in the layout to avoid facing similar issues [8].

This paper refers to standard control as the process of verifying document formatting and compliance with requirements. Importantly, expert standard control can be time consuming and costly [9]. On the other hand, depending on the qualification of the person performing the standard control, some errors in the formatting may be overlooked.

Information systems have long been used to optimize the process of checking graduate qualification papers, for example, for anti-plagiarism checks and overall quality of writing [10].

The analysis of solutions for automated standards control has revealed the existing software to check the compliance of the layout of elements with the requirements [11, 12]. An element is defined as a fundamental structural component that represents the content of a specific type. Elements can be grouped into several classes including common paragraphs, headings, list elements, tables, table captions, images.

The information about tables, images, formulas, and vector elements in.docx files can be retrieved directly from the document. Detecting the class of an element is crucial for further automated standardization. Once the class is detected, its formatting is checked. Information about paragraphs, images, tables, and other elements can be extracted from pdf [13], odt, or docx files [14].

The analyzed automated standard control software demonstrates the use of deterministic algorithms to verify the layout of some elements. This technique proves to be highly effective when the paragraph class is predetermined, for example, the common paragraph, title, or image caption. Consequently, the effectiveness of an automated standards control system depends heavily on the precise definition of the paragraph class within a text document.

To overcome the limitations of manual checking by experts, an online service for checking the formatting automatically has been developed [15], which is based on the classification of the text document elements. The authors demonstrate high-quality classification of paragraph types using one of the state-of-the-art algorithms – CatBoost [16]. The recent study also explores the potential of addressing the task of paragraph type classification using the same algorithm. However, we propose a more detailed approach to dataset handling, a higher quality division into training and testing sets taking into account stratification by the target variable, a more diverse training set, a deeper interpretation of the algorithm characteristics, and calculation of metrics stratified by unique classes, which provides a more precise assessment of the algorithm performance. We applied the feature extraction method as described in article [15], and trained CatBoost with the parameters from the same paper as the baseline model. On our dataset, the model achieved a Macro F1 Score of 0.90.

The study aims to develop a method to optimize the classification of a text element extracted from a document. To meet the above aim, the following objectives were formulated:

- Dataset analysis, feature extraction, elimination of dataset shortcomings,
- Selection of relevant machine learning models, and optimization of their hyperparameters to implement element classification,
- Assessment of the prospects and feasibility of using LSTM for predicting the next paragraph type by context,
- Quality evaluation of each of the selected models on each set of modified data resulting from Data Preprocessing and Feature Engineering,
- Comparative analysis of the obtained results and development of methodology for optimizing text feature classification.

Selecting the best solution is a comprehensive task combining machine learning and data processing methods that provide the best balance between model training time and prediction quality.

In the sections below the paper discusses the suggested combination of methods in more detail in the perspective of the challenge described and the results obtained.

Although these methods are primarily intended for data preprocessing of textual information in docx file format, they can also be applied to other file formats.

2 Data Preprocessing and Feature Engineering

The paragraph is a crucial element in text documents. It is the basis for formatting text elements. Each paragraph has a finite number of attributes that can be extracted from a docx file.

The present research uses a dataset that includes attributes for indentation line, interline spacing, alignment, element style defined by the text editor, the type of lettering, and other text elements. These parameters are determined automatically by an application specifically developed for the purpose. The list of parameters was based on the requirements for the layout of text elements outlined in GOST 7.32-2017.

The initial dataset consists of 1919 lines, each representing 20 paragraph characteristics and the CurElementMark label, which is assigned to one of the 8 possible classes. This label was determined manually by experts through analyzing texts written by students. A detailed description of the identified classes is given below in Table 1.

Table 1. Description of the classes identified during the analysis.

b1	First level header	b2	Second level header
b3	Third level header	c1	Common paragraph
c2	Paragraph before the list	d2	The element of a plain listing
f1	Table caption	h1	Picture caption as a separate paragraph

The dataset represents a set of values characterizing each paragraph – FullBold, FullItalic, Alignment, KeepLinesTogether, KeepWithNext, LeftIndentation, LineSpacing, NoSpaceBetweenParagraphsOfSameStyle, OutlineLevel, PageBreakBefore, RightIndentation, SpaceAfter, SpaceBefore, SpecialIndentation. The dataset also contains some features whose values cannot be directly retrieved from the docx document, for example, paragraph parameters.

Detailed dataset statistics of the features is presented in Tables 2 and 3.

Table 2. Detailed dataset statistics of numerical features.

Feature	Description	Min	Max	Median	Standard deviation
SymbolCount	Number of characters in a paragraph	5	1852	136	241.368
WordsCount	Number of words in a paragraph	1	266	16	30.555
SpecialSymbolsCount	Number of punctuation marks	0	50	3	6.076

Table 3. Detailed dataset statistics of categorical features.

Feature	Description	Null values	Most common value
Lowercase	All letter characters are written in lowercase	-	False
Uppercase	All letter characters are written in uppercase	-	False
LastSymbolPd	The last character of the string	428	"."
FirstKeyWord	The first word of the paragraph	1361	listLevel1

The following section demonstrates that the empirically added features "FirstKeyWord" and "LastSymbolPd" are essential for classifying elements within a DOCX document. These features are described in detail below.

- "LastSymbolPd" refers to the last character of a line, chosen from the set {".", ",", ";", null}. According to GOST 7.32–2017, certain paragraphs have specific requirements for their ending characters, necessitating the analysis of these values within the dataset.
- "FirstKeyWord" is defined as the sequence of characters preceding the first space, provided it is meaningful. The values of "FirstKeyWord" are identified for such elements as lists (both numbered and bulleted), heading numbers, table captions, and image captions. For instance, if a paragraph begins with "Fig.", "Figure", or "Fig.*N*", the "FirstKeyWord" value will be "Figure". This is programmatically determined during the parsing of the DOCX file.

2.1 Expanding the Dataset with Additional Attributes

Our graphemic and semantic analysis of text data revealed a significant impact of certain features, such as the first word of the paragraph and the last character, on the class of the paragraph considered. This approach is non-trivial and deserves further consideration.

Based on a thorough analysis of the requirements outlined in the GOST 7.32–2017 standard and on a comprehensive review of over 10 000 paragraphs from student graduate papers, specific rules have been established for certain paragraph classes. For example, if the initial word is "figure-drawing" without a space, then the FirstKeyWord feature for the current paragraph is designated as "Figure". A similar approach is used to identify the initial words for a paragraph of the "table caption" type ("TableCaption") or a list ("List").

The last characters of paragraphs have been shown to follow a pattern. This is demonstrated by the LastSymbolPd feature. Elements of the "common paragraph" class tend to end with ".", while elements of the "list" class are more likely to end with ".", ",", ";". Elements of the "first level heading", "second level heading", and image captions should not end with a punctuation mark. As will be shown below, these characteristics play an important role in classifying text elements.

In addition, during data analysis, the number of characters, special characters (like ".", ";", "," and "-") and words in a paragraph were found to identify the current element class. As a result, the dataset was updated to include attributes for SymbolCount, WordsCount and SpecialSymbolsCount.

2.2 Class Imbalance

As demonstrated in Fig. 1, there is a disproportionate distribution of class frequencies between majority classes (c1, c2, d2) and minority classes (b1, b2, b3, f1, h1) in the data.

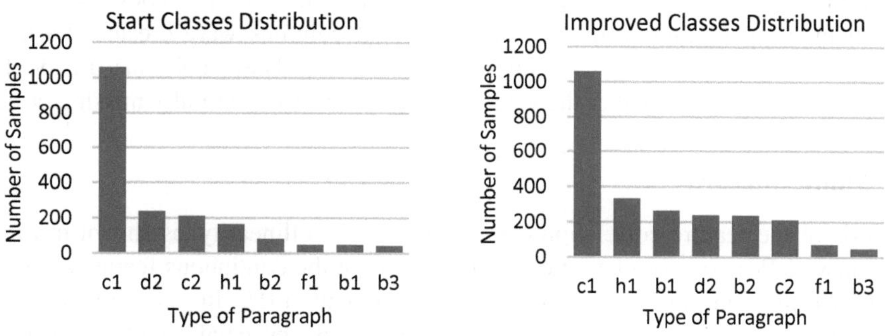

Fig. 1. Frequency distribution between majority and minority classes before and after removing the imbalance.

To mitigate the class imbalance, the distribution between element classes had to be adjusted. As the dataset reflects real-life cases, using oversampling methods (e.g., Random Oversampling) did not seem feasible. To address the imbalance, we collected new documents formatted in accordance with GOST 7.32–2017, and extracted features using the previously employed parsing tool, resulting in a new dataset comprising 6133 objects. Subsequently, using our previously trained baseline CatBoost model, we classified the new dataset, obtaining class labels and probabilities indicating the likelihood of the object being assigned to a specific class, alternatively referred to as the confidence of the model on a particular object. For each minority class, we set the threshold at 0.9 confidence and devised specific heuristics applicable to particular classes. For instance, we adjusted weights for the classes where the model exhibited the lowest confidence, aiming to achieve a higher confidence for the objects with a specific feature equated to a value unique to the respective class [17]. The described actions labeled 572 text elements belonging to minority classes. These labeled objects, along with their corresponding contexts, from which features were extracted, were reviewed by an expert. Following this review, 523 correctly classified objects remained in the new dataset, resulting in a labeling accuracy of 91.4% on the new data. The total number of rows in the final dataset after concatenation amounted to 2442.

2.3 Missing Values

Machine learning algorithms typically exhibit sensitivity to missing values. However, for certain features of the dataset, such as LastSymbolPd, a missing value indicates that the paragraph does not end with a punctuation mark. This situation is acceptable according to GOST 7.32–2017 for certain classes of text elements, such as headings, image captions, and table captions.

To determine the correct action for handling missing values it is necessary to consider the analyzed content. In our case, besides the already mentioned LastSymbolPd, some missing values were also partially present in the feature FirstKeyWord. The optimal solution to this problem, in terms of algorithm performance quality, was found to be filling empty values with the mode.

Additionally, since a missing value in these columns also conveys information about the paragraph structure, two additional columns were created, LastSymbolPd_missed and FirstKeyWord_missed, respectively. These columns are boolean vectors demonstrating whether the value in the given row was initially missing or not.

2.4 Multicollinearity

Analysis of the feature correlation has revealed multicollinearity, as shown in Fig. 2. The pairwise Pearson correlation coefficient between the continuous features SymbolCount, WordsCount, and SpecialSymbolsCount is within 0.9. In general, such correlations between features can result in unreliable results, especially with the distance-metric models. To ensure the completeness and interpretability of the data, we decided to address the potential problem according to the individual characteristics for each of the algorithms, rather than eliminate continuous attributes.

Single experiment is a combination of preprocessing steps to build a dataset that is used for model training. The number of experiments X is calculated as the number of combinations without repetitions of preprocessing steps multiplied by the number of chosen model types:

$$X = M \cdot \sum_{k=1}^{4} \frac{n!}{k! \cdot (n-k)!} \quad (1)$$

where "n" is the number of data preprocessing and feature engineering methods, "M" is the number of models used for element classification.

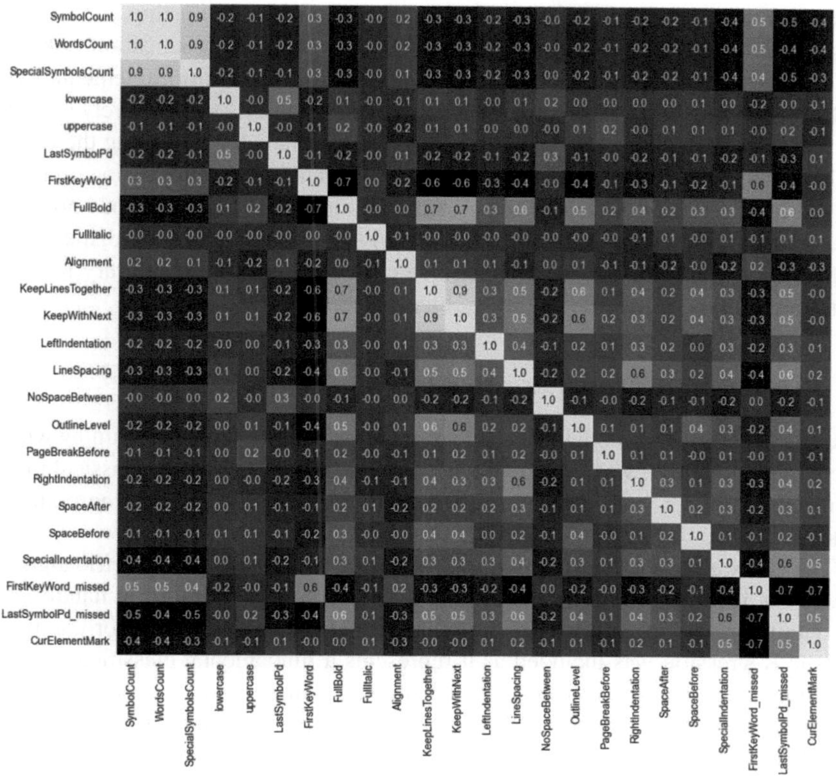

Fig. 2. Pairwise Pearson correlation feature analysis

A total of 60 experiments have been conducted overall.

$$X = 4 \cdot \sum\nolimits_{k=1}^{4} \frac{4!}{k! \cdot (4-k)!} = 60 \quad (2)$$

The results presented further showcase the optimal performance achieved by each method.

3 Reasoning Behind the Choice of Models

This section describes the models selected for training and using within the experiment and provides the rationale underlying their selection.

3.1 Gradient Boosting

Despite the rapid development of neural network algorithms for text processing, classical machine learning methods that are trained on descriptive features extracted from data should not be underestimated.

One of the most effective classical algorithms is Gradient Boosting, which remains a high-quality and reliable tool for addressing regression and classification tasks [18].

The key feature that makes Gradient Boosting in the CatBoost implementation particularly attractive within this research perspective is its ability to effectively handle categorical features without any prior encoding. The rationale for preferring the CatBoost implementation of Gradient Boosting has been detailed in the Introduction section.

The high correlation among some of the features in the dataset does not prevent us from using of this approach since the underlying algorithm is not a distance metric method but is based on binary decision tree classifiers, which, in contrary to distance metric algorithms, is not affected by multicollinearity [19].

3.2 Classical Machine Learning Models

Efficacy of CatBoost, a model that can require more than two hours for training with specific hyperparameters, was evaluated together with that of alternative classical machine learning algorithms such as K-Nearest Neighbors (KNN), Logistic Regression, and Random Forest.

The KNN algorithm was chosen as it is one of the most popular metric algorithms that do not make assumptions about data distribution. Its flexibility in handling various data types and its intuitive nature make it a valuable benchmark for comparison. Logistic Regression was included as it represents a fundamental classification model, providing a baseline for performance evaluation. Random Forest was selected because it is considered one of the most effective classical machine learning algorithms ranking second only after Gradient Boosting, offering a robust balance between accuracy and computational efficiency.

Employing these alternatives has the potential to reduce training time without significantly compromising classification quality.

3.3 Long Short-Term Memory (LSTM)

When classifying the type of an incoming paragraph, it can be useful to consider its positions in a document besides its own features. Syntactic analysis was applied to address this fundamental problem of computational linguistics. The corresponding task was to attempt to discover the most typical n-grams, representing the most frequently occurring continuous sequences.

Interpreting a document structure through a correctly formatted sequence of paragraphs according to regulatory acts provides researchers with an opportunity to regard an incoming file as a time series of paragraph types. This approach suggests the potential application of recurrent neural networks, particularly the Long Short-Term Memory (LSTM) architecture. It has demonstrated its efficacy in similar tasks [20], allowing for effective labeling of an entire document based on marked input of significantly shorter length. Moreover, LSTM has previously demonstrated performance comparable to that of CatBoost in similar tasks, further validating its suitability for this application [21].

4 Experimental Procedure

Each stage of the experiment included five steps: formulating hypotheses about the data, making changes to the data, tuning hyperparameters, training models based on the updated data, and evaluating the results. Hypotheses about the data and the algorithm for testing hypotheses have been described above in the Data Preprocessing and Feature Engineering section.

To optimize hyperparameters during training, we employed the Optuna framework [22]. Hyperparameter ranges were determined based on heuristics specific to each model, and tuning was conducted using the training set. ROC-AUC Score was determined to be the metric on which optimization is performed. The primary quality metric is the F1-score, stratified by classes and across different aggregations: micro, macro, and weighted. A comparative analysis of metrics is presented in the Results section.

4.1 Logistic Regression

Despite its simplicity, the Logistic Regression algorithm remains competitive for both academic and practical tasks. Its high degree of interpretability, easy tuning and training also contribute to its relevance for this study.

Logistic Regression relies on the concept of the distance in the feature space to separate it into subspaces corresponding to different classes. Therefore, prior to training, continuous features have to be standardized and categorical features encoded using the one-hot encoding algorithm. To address the issue of feature correlation, a mandatory non-zero parameter for l2 regularization was introduced [23].

4.2 K-Nearest Neighbors Classifier

The advantages of the K-Nearest Neighbors (KNN) method are similar to those of Logistic Regression. However, it has a more sophisticated methodology for training and prediction, which involves multiple hyperparameters, allowing for additional tuning opportunities with the Optuna framework.

Since the algorithm does not operate on string data types and represents a family of metric models, data preprocessing similar to Logistic Regression was performed. However, with KNN, only WordsCount, the feature with the highest variance, was retained out of the three strongly pairwise uncorrelated features SymbolCount, WordsCount, and SpecialSymbolsCount.

4.3 Random Forest

The Random Forest algorithm is a bagging technique based on binary decision trees, which follows the wisdom of the crowd principle to make the final decision about classification for a particular object. Independent learning based algorithms accelerates compared to Gradient Boosting, remaining competitive in quality [24].

Similarly to Gradient Boosting, all three continuous features – SymbolCount, WordsCount, SpecialSymbolsCount – were retained during training.

4.4 CatBoost

As stated above, we trained the CatBoost model on the original dataset consisting of 1919 rows, employing the model parameters outlined in the article [15]. This model served as our baseline, achieving a Macro F1 Score of 0.90 on the original dataset. Subsequently, we utilized this algorithm to label new data to increase the number of samples for minority classes. For hyperparameter tuning and training the final model with the highest performance, we used an expanded dataset with 2442 samples. For the best model Shapley values were calculated, which are described in the Results section.

4.5 LSTM

Training the LSTM model requires a meticulously built dataset. At the first step, we segmented sequences of paragraphs for each document, resulting in 134 long chains. Subsequently, we determined the minimum length of the context chain, based on which the model would be trained to predict the class of the following paragraph. We chose a minimum length of four, as the minimum context should consist of three elements plus one target.

Having established this parameter, within each of the long chains we sliced N minus four training examples, where N represents the number of elements in the chain. We also developed a custom data loader that added paddings to the batch objects to equalize the length of all chains in the batch to the maximum within the batch. We employed pre-padding in our custom data loader because it has been shown to improve model accuracy on the same data compared to post-padding [25]. This approach ensures uniform length for all chains within a batch, optimizing training performance. As a result, we generated 793 chains, subsequently divided into train and test subsets with an 80:20 ratio stratified by the target variable.

For the model architecture, we utilized an LSTM block with three layers, which takes vectors from a custom embedding layer as input. Subsequently, the vector representation obtained after passing the sequence through the network is fed into two fully connected layers with batch normalization between them, resulting in a vector of 8 logits. By selecting the index with the highest confidence, we obtain the prediction of the following class based on the current context.

During training, we employ cross-entropy as the loss function and the Adaptive Moment Estimation algorithm with regularization for optimizing the model weights.

During the experiments we were searching both for the optimal model architecture and its parameters and for the appropriate optimizer parameters. While we achieved an accuracy of 0.73 on the test set, upon examining metrics by class, the model appeared to predict only 3 out of 8 classes with non-zero accuracy, which is an unacceptable outcome.

Analysis of N-grams in the original dataset revealed that elements from similar types of paragraphs are frequently repeated. Setting a requirement for at least two unique classes in a sequence, a pattern of the length of 13 was identified, occurring only twice in the dataset. Longer patterns were not revealed. In the context of the documents where the number of paragraphs can reach several hundred, the absence of longer patterns suggests a lack of strict contextual coherence among paragraphs in general.

5 Results

Hyperparameters used in final models during training are shown in Table 4.

Table 4. Final hyperparameters of the models

Model	Hyperparameters
KNN Classifier	n_neighbors = 10
Logistic Regression	penalty = "l2" C = 0.831
Random Forest Classifier	n_estimators: 101 criterion: entropy min_samples_split: 3 min_samples_leaf: 2
CatBoost	iterations: 950 learning_rate: 0.034 l2_leaf_reg: 6.825e-05 random_strength: 0.004 colsample_bylevel: 0.057 depth: 8 boosting_type: Ordered bootstrap_type: Bayesian bagging_temperature: 5.428 auto_class_weights = "SqrtBalanced" loss_function = "MultiClass"

Table 5 presents the F1-scores for each algorithm described, along with the corresponding hyperparameters, across all unique classes.

Table 5. F1-scores for each model by classes

	KNN Classifier	Logistic Regression	Random Forest Classifier	CatBoost
b1	0.96	**1.00**	0.99	**1.00**
b2	0.89	0.99	0.99	**1.00**
b3	0.29	0.78	0.82	**0.89**
c1	0.98	0.98	0.98	**0.98**
c2	0.95	**0.98**	0.97	0.95
d2	0.95	0.98	0.98	**0.98**
f1	0.92	**1.00**	**1.00**	**1.00**
h1	0.98	**1.00**	**1.00**	**1.00**

Table 6 presents F1-scores averaged across three main methodologies.

Table 6. Averaged F1-scores for each model

	KNN Classifier	Logistic Regression	Random Forest Classifier	CatBoost
F1-micro	0.95	0.98	0.98	**0.98**
F1-macro	0.86	0.96	0.97	**0.98**
F1-weighted	0.95	0.98	0.98	**0.98**

The training time for the KNN Classifier, Logistic Regression, and Random Forest Classifier was 0.20, 0.56, and 0.53 s, respectively. CatBoost exhibited the longest training time, taking 97.59 s. The significant disparity is attributed to the complexity of gradient boosting, which is more computationally intensive compared to the other algorithms. Additionally, the extended training time is affected by our model using the "boosting_type" parameter set to "Ordered", which further increases the training time [16].

The data presented suggests that the trained classical machine learning algorithms combined with the selected data preprocessing methodologies on average demonstrate very high quality in paragraph classification. The best performing algorithm in terms of the number of classes with the highest F1-score and the best averaging remains Gradient Boosting in CatBoost implementation.

For a more profound investigation into the error attributes of the optimal algorithm, a confusion matrix was generated and is presented in Fig. 3.

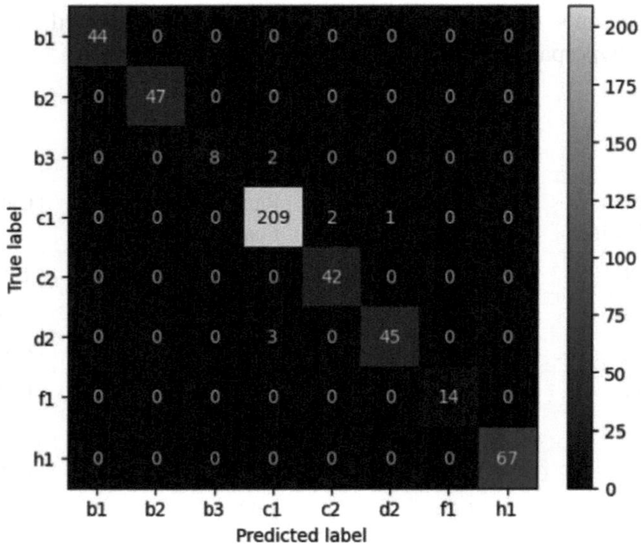

Fig. 3. Confusion matrix from CatBoost predictions

The analysis of the confusion matrix has shown that the misclassification error pertaining to classes c1, c2, and d2 can be attributed to specific instances where the classifier has incorrectly categorized the objects from the c1 class as c2 or d2. This was due to deviations from standard formatting conventions for regular paragraphs, for example, a missing value (no punctuation) at its end. In three instances, the classifier confused d2 with c1 because of the aforementioned errors and of the absence of the typing (listLevel1) inherent to the d2 class in the paragraphs.

These deviations are common when working with real-world data. Therefore, a potential solution to mitigate this issue would be the acquisition of a larger number of samples from the above classes, as well as from b3, which is underrepresented in the dataset and could benefit from an increased sample size to further improve the classifier performance.

For the best trained algorithm additional interpretation has been conducted for the contribution of each feature to the decision-making process regarding the class of each text element. Calculations were performed using the SHAP library [26], which provides interpreting machine learning models based on Shapley values, a concept from game theory [27].

A visualization of averaged absolute Shapley values for the trained boosting model is presented in Fig. 4.

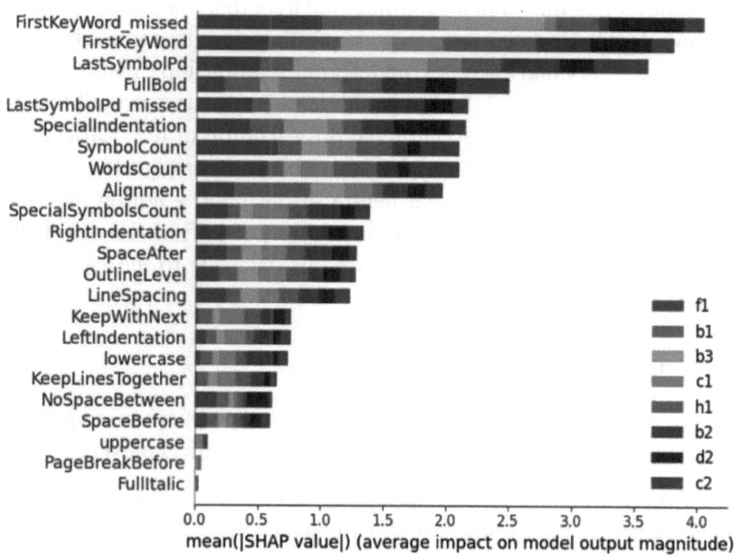

Fig. 4. SHAP values extracted from best performing CatBoost classifier by classes.

The greatest contribution is made by the features related to the first and last specific elements: key words and symbols, as well as identifiers indicating whether this value was missing in the original dataset. In our case, uppercase, PageBreakScore, and Fullitalic indicators on average make almost no contribution to the predictions of the model.

During hyperparameter tuning we also extracted the Optuna hyperparameter scores to show which of them contributed the most to the model's performance boost, this result is shown in Fig. 5.

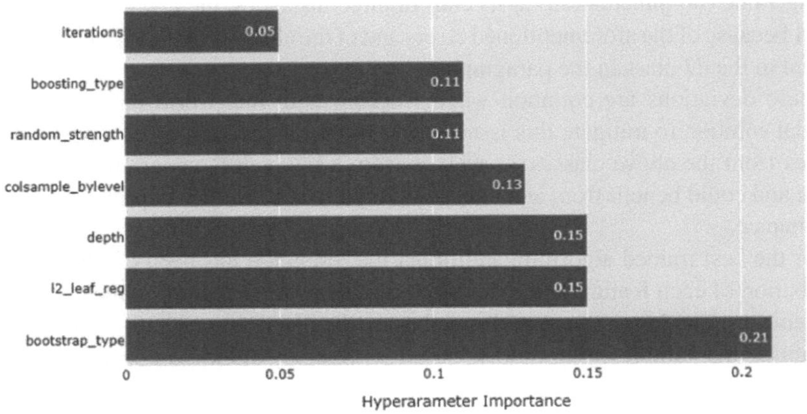

Fig. 5. Hyperparameter importances for best performing CatBoost classifier.

The figure shows that the three most influential hyperparameters are bootstrap_type, l2_leaf_reg, and depth. Bayesian bootstrap being the most important hyperparameter implies potential outliers and complex underlying relationships within our data [28]. The subsequent importance of l2_leaf_reg and depth suggests susceptibility to overfitting in our CatBoost model. Additionally, the prioritization of the "Ordered" value for the boosting_type hyperparameter, which ranks 4th by importance for our model, may indicate the co-dependent or contextual nature of our data, a notion investigated and supported for specific classes through the utilization of LSTM. However, the LSTM model itself was not proved to be efficient on our data due to the lack of contextual dependencies in most classes.

6 Conclusion

In accordance with the outlined objectives within the scope of optimizing the classification of text document elements, the following outcomes were achieved:

- following a linguistic analysis, the dataset was refined by incorporating paragraph features of text elements, mitigating the class imbalance inherent in scientific documents, and appending statistical features for each text element,
- 60 experiments were conducted to investigate the hypothesis regarding the impact of dataset parameters, as described in the Data Analysis section; these experiments yielded insights into the accuracy and effectiveness of employing the models discussed, considering successive dataset transformations,
- the hypothesis regarding contextual dependencies in data investigated through LSTM, was invalidated for all classes except three; performance indicators of LSTM did not warrant its utilization as a supplementary or alternative tool in predicting the following paragraph type based on context,

- findings indicated that CatBoost, utilizing Gradient Boosting on decision trees, yielded the most favorable outcome compared to alternative machine learning algorithms such as Random Forest Classifier, K-Nearest Neighbors classifier, and Logistic Regression,
- analysis revealed that refining CatBoost hyperparameters with the modified dataset substantially enhanced the accuracy of text document feature classification, boosting the Macro F1 Score from 0.90 for the baseline model to 0.98 for the final model.

The described methodology, based on the analysis of standard requirements, text document layout regulations, selection of machine learning algorithms, and optimization of hyperparameters, can be used to classify elements of text documents of various formats. The results obtained can be used both in the existing automated standardization tools and in new services under development.

References

1. Kozyreva, A., Nazarenko, U., Berezhkov, A., Nasyrov, N.: Analysis of the text of the FQP for automated standard control of documents. J. Phys: Conf. Ser. **2131**(2), 022102 (2021)
2. Pechinkina, O., Vepreva, T.: Information literacy in learning academic writing. Int. J. Media Inform. Literacy **8**(1), 168–177 (2023)
3. GOST 7.32-2017. System of standards on information, librarianship and publishing. The research report. Structure and rules of presentation. https://docs.cntd.ru/document/1200157208. Last accessed 7 Apr 2024
4. ITMO University, SFE documents. https://student.itmo.ru/en/gia_docs. Last accessed 7 Apr 2024
5. Middle Georgia State University, Formatting MLA Style Research. https://www.mga.edu/student-success-center/docs/Formatting_MLA_Style_Research_Paper.pdf. Last accessed 7 Apr 2024
6. Ageenko, N.V., Menshenina, S.G., Dobrova, V.V., Labzina, P.G.: Practical aspects of academic literacy development in higher education institution. Higher Educ. **30**(7), 117–127 (2021)
7. Springer, Preparation: https://www.springer.com/gp/authors-editors/journal-author/journal-author-helpdesk/preparation/1276. Last accessed 7 Apr 2024
8. Yurin, D.S., Shipunova, E.V., Deniskina, A.R.: Detection of mistakes and nonconformities in design documentation by checking formal requirements. Izvestiya TulGU **5**, 169–174 (2023). (in Russian)
9. Voronkova, P.N., Francuzova, Y.V.: Quality assurance of engineering documentation in a way of automated compliance assessment. Izvestiya TulGU **8**(pt. 1), 195–198 (2017)
10. Skakovskaya, L.N., Medvedeva, O.N., Midorenko, D.A., Zhdanova, O.V., Suponev, N.P.: Information systems for evaluation the quality of graduation qualification theses. High. Educ. Russia (5), 110–114 (2015). (in Russian)
11. Starichenko, B.E., Ustinov, M.A.: Program of automation verification of text documents formatting. Pedagogical Educ. Russia **8**, 163–168 (2018)
12. Noddletools, Product Overview. https://www.noodletools.com/overview. Last accessed 7 Apr 2024
13. Martsinkevich, V., Berezhkov, A., Tereshchenko, V., Gorlushkina, N., Tretjakova V.: Algorithms for extracting lines, paragraphs with their properties in PDF documents. ES3 Web of Conf. **389**(08024) (2023)

14. Martsinkevich, V.I., Larionova, G.S., Tereshchenko, V.V., Sitnikova, K.A., Gorlushkina, N.N.: Analysis of the possibilities of parsing electronic text documents for the automation of standard control. Ekonomika. Pravo. Innovacii, (3), 47–57. (2022). (in Russian)
15. Nasyrov, N.F., Komarov, M.S., Tartynskikh, P.S., Gorlushkina, N.N.: Automated formatting verification technique of paperwork based on the gradient boosting on decision trees. Procedia Comput. Sci. **178**, 365–374 (2020)
16. Prokhorenkova, L., Gusev, G., Vorobev, A., Dorogush, A. V., Gulin, A.: CatBoost: unbiased boosting with categorical features. In: Advances in Neural Information Processing Systems, vol. 31 (2018)
17. Google for Developers, Imbalanced Data. https://developers.google.com/machine-learning/data-prep/construct/sampling-splitting/imbalanced-data. Last accessed 7 Apr 2024
18. Ibrahim, A.A., Ridwan, R.L., Muhammed, M.M., Abdulaziz, R.O., Saheed, G.A.: Comparison of the CatBoost classifier with other machine learning methods. Int. J. Adv. Comput. Sci. Appl. **11**(11) (2020)
19. Chowdhury, S., Lin, Y., Liaw, B.Y., Kerby, L.: Evaluation of tree based regression over multiple linear regression for non-normally distributed data in battery performance. Int. Conf. Intell. Data Sci. Technol. Appl. **2022**, 17–25 (2022)
20. Vaněk, J., Michálek, J., Zelinka, J., Psutka, J.: A comparison of adaptation techniques and recurrent neural network architectures. In: Dutoit, T., Martín-Vide, C., Pironkov, G. (eds.) SLSP 2018. LNCS (LNAI), vol. 11171, pp. 79–90. Springer, Cham (2018). https://doi.org/10.1007/978-3-030-00810-9_8
21. Galanti, R., et al.: An explainable decision support system for predictive process analytics. Eng. Appl. Artif. Intell. **120**, 105904 (2023)
22. Optuna Homepage. https://optuna.org/. Last accessed 7 Apr 2024
23. Bidzhoyan, D.S., Bogdanova, T.K., Neklyudov, D.Y.: Evaluation of the bank's reliability as an investment object. π-Economy **11**(4), 70–84 (2018)
24. de Sousa, M.N., Sant'Ana, R., Fernandes, R.P., Duarte, J.C., Aploinário, J.A., Thomä, R.S.: Comparison of Random Forest and Gradient Boosting Fingerprints to Enhance an Outdoor Radio-frequency Localization System (2020)
25. Dwarampudi, M., Reddy, N. V.: Effects of padding on LSTMs and CNNs (2019). arXiv preprint arXiv:1903.07288
26. Shap Homepage. https://shap.readthedocs.io/en/latest/index.html. Last accessed 7 Apr 2024
27. Bhattacherjee, B., Bose, C., Chakraborty, A., Sengupta, R.: Boosted top tagging and its interpretation using Shapley values (2022). arXiv preprint arXiv:2212.11606
28. Rubin, D.B.: The Bayesian bootstrap. Annals Stat. 130–134 (1981)

Interactive Systems & Information Society Technologies: Interactive Systems, Software and Artificial Intelligence Technologies

Software User Activity Model for Event Pattern Recognition

Tatiana Shulga[1(✉)], Aleksandr Sytnik[1], and Nikita Danilov[2]

[1] Yuri Gagarin State Technical University of Saratov, 77 Politechnicheskaya Street, Saratov 410054, Russia
taiss@yandex.ru

[2] EPAM, Av. Imperio Argentina, 19-21, 2º Planta, 29004 Málaga, Spain

Abstract. The paper describes the approaches used in the usability assessment of user interfaces based on the idea of searching patterns in user behavior. The existing research in this domain is described. It is shown that the task of recognizing patterns of user behavior can be represented as a task of searching for sequential patterns of Data Mining. We propose a user activity model for the recognition of event patterns. By event, we mean a fact recorded at a certain time during the interaction of a certain user on a certain device with the software user interface. This model can be used in the analysis of the usability of user interfaces and can be used to solve problems of increasing the efficiency of user interaction with information systems. Also, we propose an algorithm for the recognition of repetitive event patterns, which uses the methods of Data Mining (association rules and sequential patterns). Testing of this algorithm showed that it allows experts to detect previously unknown patterns of user interaction with information systems at a lower time cost.

Keywords: usability · user interface · repetitive event patterns · user activity data · sequential patterns

1 Introduction

The analysis of the process of user interaction with the information system is necessary for solving many urgent issues both in the domain of auditing user actions [1–3] and in the domain of developing information and robotic systems [4]. For example, one of the standard phases in the development of modern information systems is usability testing (ISO 9241–11: 2018 [5]), which usually consists of two stages [6]. The first stage is to collect data on the actions performed by users through interaction with the graphical interface of the system (mouse cursor movement, mouse keystrokes, keyboard keystrokes, etc.), and the characteristics of actions (cursor coordinates, frequency of pressing, keys used, etc.). Such data is denoted by the well-established term "user activity" [7–10]. The second stage is the analysis of this data by an expert to identify problems associated with usability, which is a time-consuming task.

M. Bakaev et al. (Eds.): IMS 2024, CCIS 2534, pp. 185–194, 2026.
https://doi.org/10.1007/978-3-031-96177-9_15

To implement the first stage, data collection, various methods and tools are used, for example, we have proposed software for collecting user activity data based on an ontological model [11]. This article focuses on the second stage, the analysis of the collected data. To solve the problems of increasing the efficiency of user interaction with information systems, many researchers propose to analyze user activity patterns, i.e. repetitive sequences of actions. However, the existing methods of analysis are focused on finding only patterns predetermined by researchers. These methods do not use existing association rule mining and pattern recognition mining to find new (previously unknown) patterns. We propose an algorithm for searching for repetitive event patterns of user activity, which uses the methods of data mining (association rules and sequential patterns) and allows experts to detect previously unknown patterns of user interaction with information systems at a lower time cost.

2 Overview of Existing Approaches

The process of user interaction with software can be schematically represented as follows. The software user formulates a plan in his head and performs it as a sequence of actions [12] to achieve the goal. After that, he examines the state of the interface and evaluates the result, determining what actions it needs to perform further in accordance with the previously set goal.

Difficulties in the interaction between user and software interface may arise due to the complexity of the action plan formulation (decision on further action, articulation translation) or lack of understanding of the system response (the relationship of changes in the interface with the actions performed, observation translation) [12]. These issues affect user behavior. For example, there is a pause in the process of interaction to select further actions. Or, the user tries different actions in a row, returning after receiving an incorrect result. The presence of such sequences of actions (event patterns) can be associated with usability problems of the user interface.

User activity data contains a lot of information about the process of user interaction with the software interface [13]. Quite a long time ago, researchers realized that it is possible to automatically analyze the collected data to find similar patterns of events that signal problems of usability [12]. Automatic analysis saves time and money, because experts focus on specific areas where such patterns have been identified, instead of analyzing all the data.

An indicator of usability problems is the presence of frequently repeated identical sequences of actions (repetitive pattern) [12]. That can mean that the user is trying to reach the goal and fails each time. However, it's noted that repetitive patterns can also be formed due to repetitive tasks, which can be normal correct behavior. Therefore, we need to understand the specifics of the software.

Some researchers suggest tracking such metrics (as indicators of possible usability problems) [14]:

- the number of online help calls;
- the number of undo actions;
- the number of error messages or warnings encountered;
- the number of actions without the expected effect;

- frequent opening-closing of drop-down lists;
- pressing the same button more than once.

Other methods are based on the detection of information search problems by the user while browsing the website [15]. For example, a pattern associated with the user's mouse movement is highlighted. It's known that users use the mouse cursor not only to click links or buttons. In the process of visual search on a page, the user typically moves the cursor after the items. Since elements are often located horizontally or vertically, the user moves the mouse cursor horizontally or vertically, respectively. Therefore, it is possible to detect the vertical/horizontal mouse cursor movement event pattern. This is an indicator that in this case, the user has spent a lot of time searching for the item.

Stable scrolling events on the page, with almost the same pauses, indicate that the user is reading the content. However, a series of quick up-and-down scrolling actions may mean that the user is forced to scan the entire contents of the page trying to find the right block of information on the page [15].

Sandrine Balbo identified similar patterns of events in more detail and developed the software WAUTER (Web Automatic Usability Testing EnviRonment) [16]. She proposed a task-oriented model for evaluating the usability of the software system. User actions are compared to an ideal task model to detect any inconsistencies between them. In this case, the following patterns are highlighted.

- Action Cancellation. Cancel the action as soon as it is executed. For example, a user returns to the previous web page immediately after navigating to it. A possible reason is that the user did not plan to visit this web page and moved by accident, due to navigation problems.
- Action Re-occurrence. Frequent repetitions of simple actions, such as mouse clicks or keystrokes, may indicate insufficient responsiveness of the interface, which leads the user to think that the system does not recognize its action.
- Direction Shift. Change direction when the user stops the current task and starts another. For example, a user can stop searching for an item in a list and instead go to the search in a text box. A possible cause is difficulty in limiting further action.
- Irritant Actions. Unrelated actions in the process of the task also signal usability problems.

Some researchers identify patterns associated with viewing the website and transitions between web pages (browsing) [17]. The user's move paths are compared to some set of expected and well-known paths. Different ways belong to the category of unexpected (unexpected browsing) and can signal the problems of usability.

A pattern associated with transitions between web pages can also be a situation where the user quickly moves from page to page without staying on each [15].

3 Recognition of Event Patterns

These methods of user behavior patterns search have much in common with the task of searching sequential patterns of Data Mining [18]. In most cases, all patterns are sequential and only events kinds vary. However, user activity data is almost always not a set of short transactions, but a large set of actions, which in most cases cannot be correctly divided into subsets [16].

As noted above, one of the possible reasons for the occurrence of regularly repeated patterns in user activity data is the presence of errors or difficulties in interaction with the interface. In this case, there may be a decrease in both the efficiency and effectiveness of users. Therefore, reducing the number of such patterns reduces the risk of errors.

Another possible reason for having repetitive patterns in user activity data is the need to perform the same recurring action chains to complete the tasks. Naturally, automation interim action reduces resource costs. Therefore, the less the user performs the same type of chain of actions, the less risk of error and fewer resource costs, and therefore, the more effective the interaction.

Let's introduce a few basic concepts necessary to adapt the theory of sequential pattern mining to the field of usability evaluation.

Event – a fact recorded at a certain time during the interaction of a certain user on a certain device with the software user interface [14]. An event has a non-empty unique set of attributes: registration time, event type (for example, mouse click, command execution), and special attributes that depend on the event type. For example, a mouse click event can contain the name of the key (left, right), the type of click (single, double), the coordinates of the mouse cursor position, etc. Command execution event (command event) can contain: button name, command name, end execution method (mouse click, hotkey, "Enter" key).

Session – a fixed period during which the user interacted with the software system. Within the session, all events are accumulated and stored in chronological order. It is important to note that each event is unique and can only be included in one session.

4 User Activity Model for Recognition of Event Patterns

Let us present a user activity model designed to search for sequential patterns, which will allow us to use the data mining methods (association rules and sequential patterns).

Denote E – set of all events ordered by the time of registration: $E = \{e_1 \ldots e_n\}$, where n is the number of events.

It should be noted that each event has a non-empty unique set of attributes, and, therefore, is unique.

Denote C_E – the set of all defined event classes: $C_E = \{c_1 \ldots c_k\}$, where k is the number of event classes.

To classify events, a subset-valued classifying function f is introduced, which can be written as $f(e) \subset C_E : f(e) = \langle c_E \in C_E \rangle$.

The classification rules and the set of classes must of course be determined by an expert. Note that, depending on the objectives of the study, some of the events can be ignored. For example, an expert may be interested only in team events, i.e. associated with invoking a command. In this case, we will say that events have been filtered.

In what follows, we will understand an event as an event after the classification, i.e. event class. Accordingly, by session, we mean the session after classification and filtering, because searching for regular sequential patterns is not possible before these steps due to the uniqueness of each event.

Denote S' – the set of all fixed sessions, after classification and filtering: $S' = \{s'_1 \ldots s'_m\}$.

The session after classification is the placement of elements of the set C_E with repetitions: $s'_i = \langle c_{i1} \ldots c_{ij} \rangle$, where $\{c_{ij}\}, i = \overline{1, m}, j = \overline{1, l'_i}$ – separate event of the i-th session, l'_i – cardinality of the placement s'_i.

Let's denote n' – the total number of events in sessions after classification and filtering:

$$n' = \sum_{i=1}^{m} l'_i,$$

where m – cardinality of the set S', l'_i – cardinality of the placement s'_i.

For example, let's say we have a session:

$$\text{s} = \langle \text{click1}, \text{commandA}, \text{click2}, \text{move1}, \text{commandA}, \text{commandB} \rangle$$

Let us define the classifying function

$$f = \begin{cases} 1, \ \textit{if command A} \\ 2, \ \textit{if command A} \\ \emptyset, \ \textit{in other cases} \end{cases}$$

Applying the classifying function, we get the session: $s' = 1, 1, 2$.

Sequential pattern theory implies that there are many candidates for which the level of support is being tested. First, let's define the concepts of pattern and pattern support for a single session.

Let P be the set of candidates for sequential patterns:$P = \{p_1 \ldots p_r\}$.

The pattern is the placement of elements of the set C_E with repetitions

$$p_i = \langle c_{i1} \ldots c_{ij} \rangle,$$

where $\{c_{ij}\}, i = \overline{1, r}, j = \overline{1, q_i}, c_{ij} \in C_E$ – separate event of the i-th pattern, r – cardinality of the set P, q_i – cardinality of the placement p_i, that is, the number of events in the pattern.

We will consider the length of the pattern or session as the number of events in the specified location. We will assume that the pattern p is included in the session s' if all elements of p are contained in s', and the order of the elements in the subset of s' corresponds to the order of the elements of p.

Let $\mu_p^{s'}$ denote the number of occurrences of pattern p in session s', calculated as the number of non-overlapping ordered occurrences. For example, let there be a session $1, 2, 1, 2, 1, 2, 3, 1, 2, 1$ and a pattern $1, 2, 1$. The number of occurrences of μ will be equal to 2 because the 3rd session element (1) has already been counted.

A pattern p is said to be session-maintained s', and therefore user-maintained if the number of occurrences of $\mu_p^{s'}$ is greater than zero.

Let $\lambda_p^{s'}$ be the support of pattern p by session s', calculated as

$$\lambda_p^{s'} = \frac{\mu_p^{s'} * q}{l}, \lambda_p^{s'} \in [0; 1],$$

where $\mu_p^{s'}$ – the number of occurrences of pattern p in the session s', q – pattern length p, l – session length s'.

Therefore, for a single session, we can describe the support value as a proportion of the content of the pattern in the session. This is necessary to compare different patterns in terms of the degree of influence on the process of user interaction with the information system, which cannot be done based on only the value of the number of occurrences.

For example, let there be a session: $\langle 2, 1, 2, 1, 3, 2, 1, 2, 1, 3 \rangle$.

Calculate the values of μ and λ for the following patterns:

$p_1 = 2, 1, \mu = 4, \lambda = 0.8.$
$p_2 = 2, 1, 2, 1, \mu = 2, \lambda = 0.8.$
$p_3 = 2, 1, 2, 1, 3, \mu = 2, \lambda = 1.$
$p_4 = 3, 2, 1, 2, 1, \mu = 1, \lambda = 0.5.$

Support of pattern p_1 is the same as support of pattern p_2 and is equal to 0.8. However, support of pattern p_3 is equal to 1 (it completely constitutes the session), which means it is a more likely candidate for the close attention of an expert.

Let us analyze how the values of μ and λ change with an increase in the number of regular sequences of events. To do this, repeat the set of events in the session:

2, 1, 2, 1, 3, 2, 1, 2, 1, 3, 2, 1, 2, 1, 3, 2, 1, 2, 1, 3

Calculate the values of μ and λ for the following patterns:

$p_1 = 2, 1, \mu = 8, \lambda = 0.8$
$p_2 = 2, 1, 2, 1, \mu = 4, \lambda = 0.8$
$p_3 = 2, 1, 2, 1, 3, \mu = 4, \lambda = 1$
$p_4 = 3, 2, 1, 2, 1, \mu = 3, \lambda = 0.75$

Support of patterns p_1, p_2, and p_3 have remained the same despite the increase in the number of occurrences. The number of occurrences of p_4 has increased by 3 times, but the support has increased by only 0.25. The pattern p_3 still makes up the entire session, in fact, completely defining the user's interaction with the user interface, and therefore remains the most likely candidate for detailed analysis by an expert.

Considering that there can be any number of sessions, it is necessary to aggregate the support value while preserving their semantics, namely preserving the proportion of the pattern content in sessions. Therefore, the total support of pattern p by multiple sessions is calculated as a weighted arithmetic average.

Let $\lambda_p^{S'}$ be the support of the pattern p by the set of sessions S'', calculated as

$$\lambda_p^{S'} = \sum\nolimits_{i=1}^{m} \left(\frac{\mu_p^{s_i'} * q}{l_i} * \frac{l_i}{n'} \right) = \sum\nolimits_{i=1}^{m} \frac{\mu_p^{s_i'} * q}{n'}, \lambda_p^{S'} \in [0; 1],$$

where S' is the set of sessions after classification and filtering, m is the cardinality of the set S', $\mu_p^{s_i'}$ is the number of occurrences of pattern p in session s_i', q is the length of pattern p, l is the length of session s_i', n' – total number of events in sessions after classification and filtering.

When analyzing the process of user interaction with an information system, it makes sense to limit the maximum length of the required pattern. Short-term human memory has certain limitations, and for the average user, remembering and reproducing more than 7–9 elements is a difficult task [20]. With a high degree of probability, sequential patterns of greater length will contain events related to completely different tasks (subtasks) solved by the user.

Thus, taking into account the above, we formulate a user activity model designed to search for sequential patterns:

$$M = \{E, S, C_E, f, q_{max}, S', P, \Lambda\},$$

where:

$\boldsymbol{E} = \{e_i\}, i = \overline{1, n}$ – set of events with attributes;
$\boldsymbol{S} = \{s_i\}, i = \overline{1, m}$ – set of sessions before classification;
$\boldsymbol{C_E} = \{c_i\}, i = \overline{1, k}$ – set of event classes множество классов событий;
$\boldsymbol{f(e_i)} = e_i : E \to C_E$ – subset-valued event classification function;
$\boldsymbol{q_{max}} \in \mathbb{N}$– maximum pattern length determined by an expert;
$\boldsymbol{S'} = \{s_{i'}\}, i = \overline{1, m}$ – set of sessions after classification;
$\boldsymbol{P} = \{p_i\}, i = \overline{1, r}$ – set of sequential patterns;
$\boldsymbol{\Lambda} = \left\{\lambda_{p_i}^{S'} \in \mathbb{R} | p_i \in P, \lambda_{p_i}^{S'} \in [0; 1]\right\}, i = \overline{1, r}$ – set of values of support for sequential patterns.

This model can be used in the analysis of the usability of user interfaces and can be used to solve problems of increasing the efficiency of user interaction with information systems.

Data Mining has a well-developed theory of searching for associative rules and sequential patterns. The adaptation and application of existing methods (such as AprioriAll [19], AprioriSome, DynamicSome, etc.) will significantly optimize the calculation of support values for generated pattern candidates. We propose an algorithm for the recognition of repetitive event patterns based on the model described above and using the Apriori method to find sequential patterns.

Input data: A set of events with a set of attributes, a set of sessions before classification, a set of event classes, a subset-valued event classification function, and a value of the maximum length of the pattern.

Output data: A set of consecutive patterns and their support values – real numbers from the segment [0, 1].

Step 1. Get input.
Step 2. Determine the set of classes and the classification function.
Step 3. Classify events in sessions.
Step 4. Form a set of repetitive event patterns as a set of all combinations of classes with repetitions of length from 1 to a given maximum length.
Step 5. Calculate pattern support values using the Apriori algorithm with min_supp > 0.
Step 6. Give the set of patterns and support values to the output.

The resulting support values allow ranking patterns by priority for detailed analysis. Thus, the expert can concentrate on the most significant patterns for the process of users working with the information system, which reduces his time costs. The set of patterns, however, will depend on the goals of the analysis being carried out.

Further, the expert can put forward hypotheses about the necessary changes in the user interface to improve the efficiency of user interaction with the information system. When making decisions, an expert needs to take into account many different factors: the features of the graphical interface, the psychological factors of using the information system, and the characteristics of users.

Changing the user interface will entail changing the event sets, sessions, and sequence patterns, as the sequence of actions required to achieve users' goals will change.

Thus, it can be argued that the expert's task is to move from the current user activity model to a new one, with a different composition of sessions and patterns, and, consequently, different pattern support values, and user time consumption.

After making changes to the graphical user interface, it is possible to recollect and analyze user activity data, which can confirm or refute the hypothesis put forward earlier.

5 Approbation of the Developed Algorithm

Approbation of the developed algorithm was carried out on application software, the purpose of which is the execution and sale of insurance contracts. Two experts independently reviewed collected user activity data across 27 regions to identify usability issues. By region, we mean the area of the user interface, for example, the entire window, or a separate part of it. The region is associated with the session.

Expert #1 used heat maps and analysis of transitions between windows or regions. Expert #2 used the developed algorithm to identify patterns. The indicators and results are presented in the table.

Region	Indicators of expert # 1, WITHOUT using the developed algorithm for recognition of repetitive event patterns		Indicators of expert # 2, using the developed algorithm for recognition of repetitive event patterns	
	Number of problems detected	Relative time spent	Number of problems detected	Relative time spent
№1	6	1	7	0,8
№2	4	1	5	0,7
№3	3	1	3	0,9
№4	2	1	1	0,5
№5	3	1	4	0,7
…	…	…	…	…
№27	5	1	4	0,7
Total	81	1	94 16% more	0.65

It can be noted that Expert#2, who used the developed algorithm for recognition of repetitive event patterns, found more problems at a lower time cost, compared to Expert#2, who used classical heat maps and analysis of transitions between windows or regions.

6 Conclusion

The review shows that there is an extensive layer of research in the field of analysis of patterns of user behavior. This subject has great potential, because of the obvious savings of resources and time in the automatic analysis of data user activity to detect aspects of the software interface that require detailed research.

The task of repetitive event patterns search in user activity data has much in common with the task of sequential patterns search from the data mining domain. Therefore, it is possible to adapt and apply the existing theory, which will allow using the previously created developments in the new field.

Using the concepts of session, repetitive event pattern, and pattern support (from Data Mining theory), we proposed a mathematical model to describe user activity. This model can be used in the analysis of the usability of user interfaces and can be used to solve problems of increasing the efficiency of user interaction with information systems.

Based on the proposed model and the well-known Apriori method to find sequential patterns, we developed an algorithm for the recognition of repetitive event patterns. Testing of this algorithm showed that it allows experts to detect previously unknown patterns of user interaction with information systems at a lower time cost.

References

1. Zhang, Y., Li, Y., Ji, W.: A Trajectory-Based User Movement Pattern Similarity Measure for User Identification. IEEE Trans. Netw. Sci. Eng. **10**, 1–12 (2023). https://doi.org/10.1109/TNSE.2023.3274516
2. Rendle, S., Zhang, L.: On reducing user interaction data for personalization. ACM Trans. Recommender Syst. (2023). https://doi.org/10.1145/3600097
3. Malik, A., Serbetci, B., Elia, P.: Coded caching in networks with heterogeneous user activity. IEEE/ACM Trans. Netw. **31**(6), 2886–2901 (2023). https://doi.org/10.1109/TNET.2023.3270567
4. Raggioli, L., D'Asaro, F., Rossi, S.: Deep reinforcement learning for robotic approaching behavior influenced by user activity and disengagement. Int. J. Soc. Robot. (2023). https://doi.org/10.1007/s12369-023-01044-7
5. ISO 9241-11:2018. Ergonomics of human-system interaction — Part 11: Usability: Definitions and concepts. https://www.iso.org/standard/63500.html. Last accessed 3 Nov 2023
6. Pavlicek, J., Pavlickova, P. :Usability Testing Methods and Usability Laboratory Management (2023). https://doi.org/10.5772/intechopen.109140
7. Cuomo, D.L., Bowen, C.D.: Stages of user activity model as a basis for user-system interface evaluations. Proc. Human Factors Soc. **2**, 1254–1258 (1992)
8. Yang, D., Zhang, D., Zheng, V.W., Yu, Z.: Modeling user activity preference by leveraging user spatial temporal characteristics in LBSNs. IEEE Trans. Syst., Man, and Cybern: Syst. **45**(1), 129–142 (2015)

9. Woerndl, W., Manhardt, A., Schulze, F., Prinz, V.: Logging user activities and sensor data on mobile devices. In: Atzmueller, M., Hotho, A., Strohmaier, M., Chin, A. (eds.) MSM/MUSE -2010. LNCS (LNAI), vol. 6904, pp. 1–19. Springer, Heidelberg (2011). https://doi.org/10.1007/978-3-642-23599-3_1
10. Mileff, P.: Role of user activity monitoring in RPA processes. Producti. Syst. Inform. Eng. 11, 27–42. (2023). https://doi.org/10.32968/psaie.2023.1.3
11. Shulga, T., Sytnik, A., Danilov, N., Palashevskii, D.: Ontology-based model of user activity data for cyber-physical systems. In: Kravets, A., Bolshakov, A., Shcherbakov, M. (eds.) Cyber-Physical Systems: Advances in Design & Modelling. Studies in Systems, Decision and Control, vol. 259, pp. 205–216. Springer, Cham (2020)
12. Siochi, A.C., Ehrich, R.W.: Computer analysis of user interfaces based on repetition in transcripts of user sessions. ACM Trans. Inform. Syst. **9**(4), 309–335 (1991)
13. Danilov, N., Shulga, T., Frolova, N., Melnikova, N., Vagarina, N., Pchelintseva, E.: Software usability evaluation based on the user pinpoint activity heat map. Adv. Intell. Syst. Comput. **465**, 217–225 (2016)
14. Swallow J., Hameluck D., Carey T.: User Interface Instrumentation for Usability Analysis: A Case Study, CASCON'97, Toronto, Ontario, November, Case Study (1997)
15. Shah, I.: Event patterns as indicators of usability problems in Journal of King Saud University. Comput. Inform. Sci. **20**, 31–43 (2008)
16. Balbo S., Goschnick S., Tong D., Paris C.: Leading usability evaluations to WAUTER. In: Proceedings of the 11th Australian World Wide Web Conference (AusWeb), Gold Coast, Australia, Southern Cross University, pp. 279–290 (2005)
17. Ting I., Kimble C., Kudenco D.: UBB mining: finding unexpected browsing behaviour in clickstream data to improve a web site's design. In: Proceedings of IEEE/WIC/ACM International Conference on Web Intelligence (WI2005), France, pp. 179–185 (2005)
18. Mabroukeh, N.R., Ezeife, C.I.: A taxonomy of sequential pattern mining algorithms. ACM Comput. Surv. **43**(1), article no. 3 (2010)
19. Aloysius, G., Binu, D.: An approach to products placement in supermarkets using PrefixSpan algorithm. J. King Saud Univ.-Comput. Inform. Sci. **25**(1), 77–87 (2013)
20. Miller, G.A.: The magical number seven, plus or minus two: some limits on our capacity for processing information. Quarterly (63), 81–97 (1956).

UnnMindFlex: Harnessing Aerobic Exercise for Personalized Cognitive Growth

Samuel Olawuwo[1,2], Valeriia Viakhireva[1], Chalachew Kassaw[1,3], and Valeriia Demareva[1(✉)]

[1] Lobachevsky State University, Nizhny Novgorod, Russia
valeriia.demareva@fsn.unn.ru
[2] University of Jos, Jos, Nigeria
[3] Dilla University, Dilla, Ethiopia

Abstract. In today's challenging world, cognitive fitness is critical to academic success and overall well-being, especially among academically challenged college students. Cognitive skills such as memory, attention, and problem-solving are necessary to achieve development and academic excellence in students. The paper aims at presenting pioneering research on the development of a prototype mobile application tailored for individualized cognitive growth through aerobic exercise. A prototype of a mobile application UnnMindFlex integrates the principles of exercise, cognitive psychology, and technology to deliver tailored interventions. The application provides users with personalized exercise programs, real-time heart rate variability (HRV) monitoring, and cognitive assessment tools. UnnMindFlex aims to improve cognitive performance and promote neuroplasticity using the benefits of aerobic exercise. This study presents the theoretical foundations, design principles, and implementation strategies of UnnMindFlex.

Keywords: Cognitive Growth · Mobile Application · Prototype · Aerobic Exercise · Heart Rate Variability

1 Introduction

In today's fast-paced high-stress world, the pursuit of cognitive enhancement has become more pertinent, especially for university students who must maintain optimal mental function while meeting academic challenges. The importance of cognitive fitness in achieving academic excellence and well-rounded personal development among students is becoming increasingly apparent to people. Cognitive skills such as memory, attention, and problem-solving abilities significantly impact academic performance, career success and well-being [1]. In [2, 3] it is suggested that aerobic exercise may be a useful tactic for enhancing cognitive functioning. Aerobic exercise promotes the growth of new neurons in brain regions implicated in memory and learning in addition to strengthening existing ones [4]. Furthermore, it has been shown that aerobic exercise improves heart rate variability (HRV) - a gauge of autonomic nervous system performance connected to thought processes and emotional regulation [5]. Taking these points into account, we

M. Bakaev et al. (Eds.): IMS 2024, CCIS 2534, pp. 195–203, 2026.
https://doi.org/10.1007/978-3-031-96177-9_16

introduce UnnMindFlex - a prototype of a mobile application that uses aerobic exercise to support tailored cognitive growth. UnnMindFlex aims to empower students to optimize their cognitive abilities, enhance their academic achievement, and form a lifelong commitment to cognitive health and well-being.

The novelty of UnnMindFlex lies in its integration of personalized exercise programs, real-time heart rate variability (HRV) monitoring, and cognitive assessment tools, offering a comprehensive and individualized approach to mental wellness and cognitive fitness within a single platform.

2 Related Works

Numerous studies have shown that aerobic exercise improves cognitive functioning at all stages of life. Research has demonstrated that aerobic exercise, which is defined as prolonged physical activity that raises heart rate and oxygen consumption, has a positive impact on several cognitive domains including processing speed, executive functions, attention, and memory [2, 6]. Aerobic exercise regularly has been linked to improvements in cognitive functioning according to many studies. The results of a longitudinal study [2] demonstrated that compared to sedentary controls, older adults who were engaged in a 1-year aerobic exercise program had significantly higher hippocampus volumes, leading to improvements in memory function. Similar to this a meta-analysis in [6] revealed that aerobic exercise interventions produced benefits on cognition possibly due to an improvement in synaptic activity, blood flow and brain irrigation, and an improvement in neuronal plasticity.

Younger populations such as children and college students can also benefit from aerobic exercises' cognitive advantages as well as older adults. In a meta-analysis with compiled data from 29 studies it was found that acute aerobic exercise sessions considerably enhanced cognitive functioning in tasks pertaining to memory, processing speed, and attention in all age groups [1]. In a randomized controlled trial, it was shown that in comparison to a control group preadolescent children's academic achievement was enhanced by a 10-weeks exercise intervention [3]. Neurobiological, physiological, and psychological variables are some of the many underlying mechanisms through which aerobic exercise affects cognitive performance. By increasing the synthesis of neurotrophic factors like brain-derived neurotrophic factor (BDNF), which supports the growth and survival of neurons involved in learning and memory processes, aerobic exercise enhances neuroplasticity [4]. Aerobic exercise also improves cerebral blood flow, reduces inflammation, and increases synaptic connectivity—all of which are linked to better cognitive functioning [7, 8]. Across all age groups the idea that aerobic exercise improves cognitive functioning is continuously supported by evidence from research publications. These results highlight how crucial it is to include frequent aerobic exercise in lifestyle interventions meant to enhance mental health and overall wellbeing.

Heart rate variability (HRV) is a prominent metric of cardiovascular health and autonomic nervous system (ANS) function. As such, the relationship between HRV and aerobic exercise has received much attention lately [5]. The dynamic interplay between the sympathetic and parasympathetic branches of the ANS is reflected in the variation in the time intervals between successive heartbeats or HRV [9].

According to [10], aerobic exercise has been repeatedly linked to changes in HRV patterns which are suggestive of improved cardiac autonomic regulation and vagal tone. Longitudinal studies have shown that consistent engagement in aerobic exercise training raises HRV parameters including total power, which indicates overall HRV, and high-frequency (HF) power, which indicates parasympathetic activity [11]. These results imply that aerobic exercise improves cardiovascular regulation and promotes a shift towards greater parasympathetic dominance by improving ANS function. There are several different mechanisms at play in the association between HRV and aerobic exercise including both acute and long-term adaptations. Acute aerobic exercise causes a brief shift in heart rate during and right after exercise because it activates the baroreflex and raises cardiac output [5]. Persistent improvements in HRV parameters are brought about by structural and functional changes that chronic aerobic exercise brings about in the heart and autonomic nervous system [10].

Furthermore, it appears that there is a dose-dependent relationship between aerobic exercise and HRV with higher exercise volumes and intensities being linked to larger increases in HRV [5]. Individual variations in response to aerobic exercise training should be considered, though the degree of HRV adaptations may vary depending on a person's age, degree of fitness and genetic makeup [10]. According to the literature there is a strong correlation between HRV and aerobic exercise and HRV parameters and cardiac autonomic modulation improve with consistent aerobic exercise training. As a modifiable lifestyle factor that promotes cardiovascular health and autonomic balance, these findings highlight the significance of aerobic exercise.

An emerging field that aims to maximize cognitive function and performance is the development of systems or platforms for cognitive enhancement. These systems cover a wide variety of techniques such as wearable technology digital apps and web-based platforms all of which are intended to target cognitive domains and enable individualized interventions [12]. Digital brain training applications which provide interactive exercises and games intended to test cognitive abilities like memory attention and problem-solving skills are one well-known type of cognitive enhancement platforms. Consumers looking for engaging and adaptable training programs to enhance cognitive function have become more interested in commercial platforms like Lumosity CogniFit and Peak [13]. These platforms frequently use the insights from neuroplasticity research and cognitive psychology to create training exercises that support skill retention over time. Emerging as potentially effective instruments for improving cognitive function wearable technology provides in-the-moment tracking and analysis of behavioral and physiological parameters associated with cognitive function. Users can monitor factors like stress levels, physical activity levels and sleep quality with devices like smartwatches, fitness trackers and EEG headbands. These factors can have an impact on cognitive function [14]. Wearable technology enables users to make well-informed lifestyle decisions that promote cognitive health and wellbeing by combining data from several sensors and offering personalized insights.

Moreover, digital health interventions and online platforms have been created to provide a wider audience with evidence-based methods for improving cognitive function. These platforms frequently combine aspects of lifestyle interventions mindfulness-based practices and cognitive-behavioral therapy (CBT) to address aspects of stress management, sleep hygiene, and nutrition that affect cognitive function [15]. Online platforms can reach people from a wide range of demographic backgrounds and geographic locations by offering scalable and easily accessible interventions. This decentralizes access to cognitive enhancement resources and makes them more widely available. Various methods for enhancing cognitive function and well-being are available through the platforms and systems currently in use for cognitive enhancement. With these technologies' help, people will be able to maximize their cognitive capacities and lead longer healthier lives. These technologies range from wearables and online platforms to digital brain training apps.

There is still a number of gaps in the current body of knowledge even with technological advancements and the proliferation of cognitive enhancement platforms. One important gap is the lack of individualized methods for cognitive enhancement and the inadequate knowledge of individual variability in cognitive response to interventions [16]. Even though current platforms provide standardized training courses or interventions they frequently ignore the various cognitive profiles and needs of users which leads to less-than-ideal results for some people [17]. The incorporation of various contextual and lifestyle factors into cognitive enhancement interventions represents another gap. Certain platforms concentrate exclusively on cognitive training activities or exercises thereby disregarding other controllable elements that have been linked to altered cognitive function [15]. Optimizing cognitive health and performance requires a comprehensive strategy that considers the interactions between cognitive, physiological, and environmental factors. In addition, the development and assessment of cognitive enhancement platforms require increased openness and scientific soundness. Many currently in use interventions rely on marketing claims or anecdotal testimonials rather than empirical evidence to support their safety and efficacy [13].

Furthermore, a lack of sample sizes, short follow-up periods, and methodological flaws characterize most research on cognitive enhancement technologies, which limits the findings generalizability and dependability [12]. The creation of customized platforms or systems for cognitive enhancement that consider individual variations in lifestyle choices, cognitive function, and environmental contexts is needed to close these gaps [17]. Researchers and developers can maximize the effectiveness and engagement of cognitive enhancement efforts by creating customized interventions that dynamically adapt to users' needs and preferences by utilizing advancements in digital health technologies artificial intelligence and personalized medicine [16]. The gaps in our current understanding highlight how critical it is to move toward individualized cognitive enhancement systems that are responsive to context and individual variability in their approach and also empirically supported.

Further on we would like to present a prototype of UnnMindFlex, an application designed to provide simple access to cognitive skills enhancement. Gathering the abovementioned experience and challenges to creating a complex system for cognitive enhancement, we worked out several crucial principles, which formed a basis for our work. First and foremost, the proposed system should be automatic to avoid human-factor errors. Second, it should be based on fundamental scientific data. Third, it should be sensitive to human physical and mental state as many people may not be aware if they have health issues. Forth, it should be scalable, accessible, and easy to use and to track progress.

3 Description of UnnMindFlex Prototype

Taking previously mentioned principles into account, we suggest a prototype for mobile application (screens were created in Figma - a browser-based web design tool), because mobile platforms provide accessibility, scalability, and simple access to wireless connections (ex. Bluetooth protocol). To grant safety the app is based on biological feedback and considers real-time data, derived from HRV. To analyze properly the user's fitness level, the system requires a wearable heart rate sensor connection (e.g. Polar H10) - Fig. 1 (A). Depending on user's objectives and his\her physical state, the app will suggest a cognitive training program of a certain type and intensity.

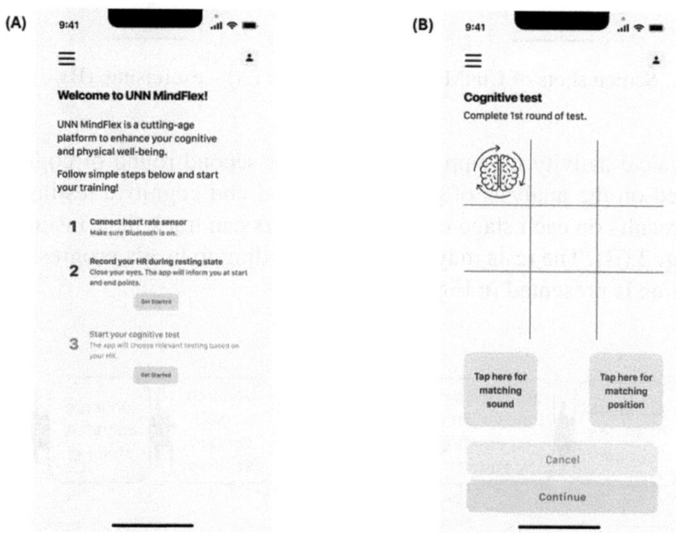

Fig. 1. Screen shots of UnnMindFlex prototype: (A) – welcome screen, (B) – cognitive test.

UnnMindFlex includes cognitive testing tasks to evaluate users' cognitive performance in several domains including memory, attention, and others. For example, it can suggest undergoing a mixed n-back testing, as seen on Fig. 1 (B) to assess properly current state of cognitive skills. For attention, we can use go/no-go test, visual reaction test, and others. The choice of cognitive tests in UnnMindFrex was based on established principles of cognitive neuroscience and psychological research. We prioritized tests with demonstrated validity and reliability in measuring cognitive abilities such as memory, attention, executive functions, processing speed, and problem-solving skills.

To enhance chosen cognitive domains the app will suggest a sufficient workout aerobic session - Fig. 2 (A). HRV is kept under control during exercising to monitor user's state and avoid excessive physical load.

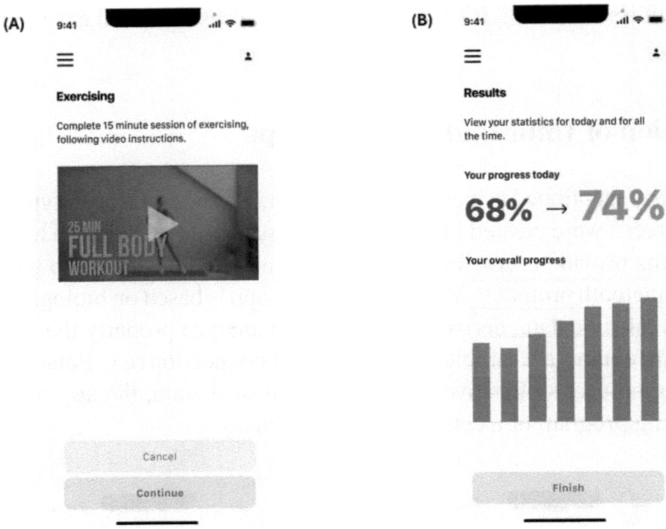

Fig. 2. Screen shots of UnnMindFlex prototype: (A) – exercising, (B) – results.

After physical activity the app will suggest the second round of cognitive testing, which is based on the analysis of previous physical and cognitive testing results. The app collects results on each stage of testing, so users can track their instant and overall progress - Fig. 2 (B). The tests may also vary according to user's progress.

The pipeline is presented in Fig. 3.

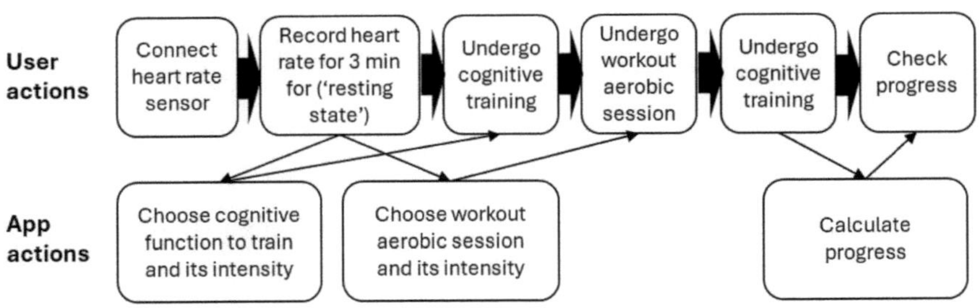

Fig. 3. General pipeline of UnnMindFlex app.

The demonstrated pipeline emphasizes how all the stages work together seamlessly to create a system that is both comprehensive and individualized for cognitive development through aerobic exercise.

Thus, the developed prototype application for individualized cognitive growth addresses many gaps identified in the Related Works section. Firstly, the application is based on an individualized approach – cognitive training and aerobic exercise regimens are tailored to the user's current body state. The user's current state is assessed during the Resting state stage. This helps to address the previously noted problem of the lack of individualized methods for cognitive enhancement [16]. Secondly, the application aims to consider certain controllable elements that have been associated with altered cognitive function [15], and at present, we have included the factor of physical activity. This allows us to account for the close interactions between different factors - cognitive, physiological, and environmental ones. By closing the gap associated with insufficient scientific evidence for proposed solutions for cognitive growth [13], we conduct laboratory experiments to clarify the impact of aerobic exercises on cognitive functions in experimental and control groups. Preliminary results demonstrate that working memory performance increases after a 15-min aerobic exercise compared to a control group without an exercise session in a randomized controlled trial.

The developed prototype application satisfies the formulated principles. UnnMindFlex is automatic, and pre-programmed stages help to avoid human-factor errors. Although fundamental scientific evidence is still being established, preliminary results show that cognitive performance improves after aerobic exercise. UnnMindFlex considers the customer's body state while choosing cognitive and aerobic training. Lastly, the prototype application provides tracking of progress and is scalable and easy for further development.

Implementation strategies for UnnMindFlex can include the following:

- Conducting user research, gathering feedback, and iteratively refining the application based on user input.
- Collecting big data on cognitive function, physical activity levels, and other relevant metrics to update personalized recommendations using AI. AI data analysis will be implemented through advanced machine learning algorithms trained on collected data.
- Ensuring that UnnMindFlex is accessible to a wide range of users, including those with disabilities or special needs.
- Implementing robust security measures to protect user data and privacy.
- Collecting feedback from users, conducting regular performance reviews, and updating the application with new features and optimizations as needed.
- Forging partnerships with healthcare providers, fitness professionals, and academic institutions to validate the effectiveness of UnnMindFlex and leverage expertise in cognitive science, exercise physiology, and technology development.

4 Conclusions

The UnnMindFlex prototype offers a promising solution to the increasing demand for cognitive enhancement, particularly among university students facing academic pressures. By leveraging aerobic exercise's benefits on cognitive function, UnnMindFlex aims to empower users to optimize their cognitive abilities for academic success and lifelong cognitive well-being.

The application incorporates key principles such as automation, evidence-based design, consideration of the user's physical and mental state, scalability, and accessibility. Tailoring cognitive training and aerobic exercise regimens to individual needs fills the gap in current methods for cognitive enhancement. Preliminary results indicate improved cognitive performance post-aerobic exercise sessions, underscoring UnnMindFlex's potential effectiveness.

To implement UNNMindFlex effectively, strategies include user-centric design, data-driven personalization, ensuring accessibility and security, continuous improvement through user feedback, and collaboration with cognitive science and technology experts. These strategies aim to refine UNNMindFlex into a comprehensive tool for cognitive growth, benefiting users across various demographics.

References

1. Chang, Y.K., Labban, J.D., Gapin, J.I., Etnier, J.L.: The effects of acute exercise on cognitive performance: a meta-analysis. Brain Res. **1453**, 87–101 (2012). https://doi.org/10.1016/j.brainres.2012.02.068
2. Babaei, P., Azari, H.B.: Exercise training improves memory performance in older adults: a narrative review of evidence and possible mechanisms. Front. Hum. Neurosci. **15**, 771553 (2022). https://doi.org/10.3389/fnhum.2021.771553
3. Takehara, K., et al.: Exercise intervention for academic achievement among children: a randomized controlled trial. Pediatrics **148**(5), e2021052808 (2021). https://doi.org/10.1542/peds.2021-052808
4. Voss, M.W., Vivar, C., Kramer, A.F., van Praag, H.: Bridging animal and human models of exercise-induced brain plasticity. Trends Cogn. Sci. **17**(10), 525–544 (2013). https://doi.org/10.1016/j.tics.2013.08.001
5. Borresen, J., Lambert, M.I.: Autonomic control of heart rate during and after exercise: measurements and implications for monitoring training status. Sports Med. **38**(8), 633–646 (2008). https://doi.org/10.2165/00007256-200838080-00002
6. Ferrer-Uris, B., Ramos, M.A., Busquets, A., Angulo-Barroso, R.: Can exercise shape your brain? A review of aerobic exercise effects on cognitive function and neuro-physiological underpinning mechanisms. AIMS Neuroscience **9**(2), 150–174 (2022). https://doi.org/10.3934/Neuroscience.2022009
7. Hötting, K., Röder, B.: Beneficial effects of physical exercise on neuroplasticity and cognition. Neuroscience and Biobehavioral Reviews **37**(9 Pt B), 2243–2257 (2013). https://doi.org/10.1016/j.neubiorev.2013.04.005
8. Stillman, C.M., Cohen, J., Lehman, M.E., Erickson, K.I.: Mediators of physical activity on neurocognitive function: a review at multiple levels of analysis. Front. Hum. Neurosci. **10**, 626 (2016). https://doi.org/10.3389/fnhum.2016.00626
9. Task Force of the European Society of Cardiology and the North American Society of Pacing and Electrophysiology. Heart rate variability: standards of measurement, physiological interpretation, and clinical use. Circulation **93**(5), 1043–1065 (1996)
10. Michael, S., Graham, K.S., Davis, G.M.: Cardiac autonomic responses during exercise and post-exercise recovery using heart rate variability and systolic time intervals - a review. Front. Physiol. **8**, 301 (2017). https://doi.org/10.3389/fphys.2017.00301
11. Stanley, J., Peake, J.M., Buchheit, M.: Cardiac parasympathetic reactivation following exercise: implications for training prescription. Sports Med. **43**(12), 1259–1277 (2013). https://doi.org/10.1007/s40279-013-0083-4
12. Lumsden, J., Edwards, E.A., Lawrence, N.S., Coyle, D., Munafò, M.R.: Gamification of cognitive assessment and cognitive training: a systematic review of applications and efficacy. JMIR Serious Games **4**(2), e11 (2016). https://doi.org/10.2196/games.5888
13. Simons, D.J., et al.: Do 'brain-training' programs work? Psychological Science in the Public Interest **17**(3), 103–186 (2016). https://doi.org/10.1177/1529100616661983

14. Welsh, M.R., et al.: The use of heart rate variability in esports: a systematic review. Psychol. Sport Exerc. **69**, 102495 (2023). https://doi.org/10.1016/j.psychsport.2023.102495
15. Li, Y., Yang, N., Zhang, Y., Xu, W.: The relationship among trait mindfulness, attention, and working memory in junior school students under different stressful situations. Front. Psychol. **12**, 558690 (2021). https://doi.org/10.3389/fpsyg.2021.558690
16. Anguera, J.A., et al.: Video game training enhances cognitive control in older adults. Nature **501**(7465), 97–101 (2013). https://doi.org/10.1038/nature1248
17. Owen, A.M., et al.: Putting brain training to the test. Nature **465**(7299), 775–778 (2019). https://doi.org/10.1038/nature09042

Research of Network Rationality: Justification of the Idea for the Computer Modeling Project of Rational-Value Communication

Konstantin Kondratenko(✉)

SPb University, St. Petersburg, Russia
k.kondratenko@spbu.ru

Abstract. The article is devoted to the study of communication of rational-value systems, a concept proposed by the author to explain and unite the physical and technical worlds, individual and social levels of consciousness, political decision-making and their implementation, etc. The concept of rational-value systems is based on several scientific approaches: structural-functionalist, cybernetic, behavioral, etc. The article analyzes the possibility of modeling rational communication and examines the types of rational-value communication. The author proposed the following characteristics of communication of this kind: the strength and distance of the semantic connection, the strategy of behavior and options for moves, the level of communication tension as a result of uncertainty, the chances and risks of combining two or more communicants, etc. As a result, the article presents an example of a data window of a rational interaction network - value systems.

Keywords: Rational Systems · Rational-Value Systems · Rational-Value Communication · Theory of Rational Systems · Network Rationality

1 Introduction

Rational-value systems (RVS) [1] - one of the types of rational systems that have two main elements responsible for rational abilities (data analysis, decision-making, search for connections and patterns, etc.) and value picture of the world. A rational system is an abstraction designed to unite the physical and technical worlds, individual and social levels of consciousness, political decision-making and their execution, etc. (about other types of rational systems: [2–5]).

The RVS concept is based on a complex of scientific approaches. Thus, in particular, the dominance of the semantic center of the individual over other structures is justified by the creator of the semantic theory of thinking O.K. Tikhomirov [6, 7], and the origins of the study of the semantic sphere can be found in the works of the classics of Russian psychology - L.S. Vygotsky, A.N. Leontyev, S.L. Rubinshtein and others [8]. D.A. Leontiev introduces the concept of a "dynamic semantic system", which describes the hierarchy of a person's value systems, beliefs and personal meanings [9]. In addition, in domestic psychology the concept of "value-semantic sphere" has been developed [10], while the concept of "value-semantic communication" is used mainly in practical

M. Bakaev et al. (Eds.): IMS 2024, CCIS 2534, pp. 204–215, 2026.
https://doi.org/10.1007/978-3-031-96177-9_17

psychology and pedagogy [11, 12]. Close to the concept of RVS is D. Kahneman's theory of two-system thinking [13], which describes thinking as a process of interaction between the intuitive, affective and fast System 1 and the slow, analytical and rational System 2.

The author of the article believes that the abstraction of the RVS can be expanded to a group of interests, an organization and a conditional social whole, subject to the main criterion - the presence of a rational and semantic block. Moreover, the article [1] raises the problem of the possibility of using abstraction to describe technical systems. The main difficulties of extending the abstraction to the world of artificial intelligence are establishing the semantic component as dominant (as well as modeling the semantic block), as well as passing the Turing test.

The RVS concept also has a political meaning: the architecture of individual RVSs is projected onto the collective and political architecture. Developed forms of political structure are possible only with the development and relative independence of the rational block from the semantic one, including for imposing the will of the intellectual minority on the non-intellectual majority. The value block, being a set of beliefs and value systems (in this case, the author, following the tradition of V. Frankl, does not distinguish between values and meanings [14]), with sufficient development, defines itself as a fairly tough and authoritarian ruler, trying to subordinate all other components of the RVS, and only rational the block is able to balance the system. The architecture of the RVS, described earlier, generally coincides with the ideas of K. Deutsch [15].

The RVS concept, therefore, tries to explain, based on the theories of social and human sciences, the behavior of man and society in the digital space, to unite man, society, government and technology. This article deals with RVS communication, methods of its interpretation and computer modeling. The author raises the problem of transforming network analysis for problems of describing the interaction of RVSs, and offers a solution to it. The article ends with a detailed description of the idea of the computer modeling project for RV-communications.

2 Study of Modeling Rational-Value Communication Principles and Foundations

2.1 V-Communication

There are many networks of rational-value communication: they include not only the three types mentioned, but also types of these types, for example, a value network from the position of RVS_1, from the position of RVS_2, the average of these positions and the real network of value communication at the moment. Perhaps these species are divided into subspecies. In reality, this means that the point of view of the same process introduces its own characteristics into the modeling; in a sense, the actual process is the crust of the pie, with layers of meaning on top of it. However, as we multiply networks, we move further and further away from the possibility of designing RV-communications.

Let's say that each type includes a real network and an ideal one – a network of expectations, interests and assessments. But which of these "layers" is more significant? From the point of view of the *modeling block* [1], the situation is as follows: if real communication does not introduce significantly new things into the experience of acquiring, caring and losing values, then it is less important, but if it introduces the modeling block into the area of uncertainty [16, 17], then experience will no longer play a significant role and, therefore, the real communication network will be more significant.

Suppose that RVS_1 evaluates value communication as typical, i.e., for example, evaluates the significance of a particular interaction as 0.3 (or the "typicality" of the situation as 0.7), while RVS_2 evaluates interaction with RVS_1 as 0. 8, i.e. The "typicality" of the situation is assessed as 0.2. In addition, the desired state (distance) of RV-communication for "typical" situations will be to a greater extent "programmed" by previous experience, while the greater significance of real communication blurs the RV's understanding of the desired state. If you set the threshold value at 0.5 (i.e. if the significance of real communication is assessed in the range from 0.0 to 0.49), then such a division will not cause difficulty: for RVS_1 you can fix the strict desired distance as 1, while time for RVS_2 is less than the current one. However, this is too serious a simplification, especially in view of the plurality of points of view of the RVS. RVS_2, due to the high importance of real communication, it is difficult to establish not only the desired, but also the real distance, not to mention the high probability of behavioral errors inherent in a situation of uncertainty.

The example of a high spread of values between assessments of the significance of RV-communication and its "typicality" simplifies the situation with modeling value communication using a modeling block. Let's consider the example already mentioned above, in which $V_{RVS1} = 0.3$, $V_{RVS2} = 0.8$, $R_{RVS1} = 3$ and $R_{RVS2} = 2$, where V is the assessment of the significance of RV-communication between RVS_1 and RVS_2 and R is the estimate of the "typical" distance between RVS_1 and RVS_2. Let us also assume that $R_{V\ RVS1} < R_{RVS1}$ and $R_{VRVS2} < R_{RVS2}$, where R_V is the desired distance between RVS_1 and RVS_2. Let's determine the basic value of the distance. The assessment of the "typicality" of the RVS_2 situation can be neglected due to uncertainty. The only specific value in this case is RPЦC1. Experience suggests that the distance between systems will probably remain three, however, the desire of systems to reduce this distance will give a value of two in the future. So, R $(RVS_1, RVS_2) = 3$, but F_R $(RVS_1, RVS_2) =$ 3(2), where F_R is the *strength of the value connection* between RVS_1 and RVS_2. If the value object is a "silent" elementary system, then the calculation of the distance and strength of the semantic connection is made on the basis of the RVS data (on the graph, the difference will be in the unidirectionality of the edge). The case in which estimates of the significance of a connection will be higher than its "typicality" does not cancel the logic of the calculation, but adds a category of probability to the final result; On the graph, the probability can be indicated by a dotted line to indicate the instability of this relationship.

2.2 R-Communication

Satisfying rational interest in RV-communication is a kind of *game* [18] in which the parties unite to play against someone else, or play against each other, defending their own interests. Behind the RVS is the personal experience of subjectively determined victories and defeats, which is translated, among other things, into specific RV-communication (the RVS in a particular case will strive for victory and not allow defeat). Based on what the RVS calls victory or defeat in RC-communication in general and in specific communication in particular, one can judge the features of the interaction of the RVS with value objects, i.e. about a rational picture of the world of values of a particular system.

From the position of the modeling block in RV-communication, four activated components can be distinguished: someone else's completed experience, someone else's incomplete experience, one's own completed experience and one's own incomplete experience. Incomplete experience is free fields in the table of "victories" and "defeats" of various systems; "victories" and "defeats" are the values-means that the RVS managed to "capture" in the course of the RCS communication. In order not to dive deeply into this issue, let's name random (we'll leave aside how important they are) value-means: power and control, trust, respect, comfort of communication. If the RVS defines the "capture" of the majority of them as a "victory," then it ascribes to itself the "victory" over another RVS in the course of RV-communication. It logically follows from this that the other side may have a different opinion regarding "victories" and "defeats", however, if the points of view agree on everything, then these relations can be defined as consensus, in most or half of the criteria - as compromise, if there is less in common, than different - as competitive, and in the absence of common points of view - as meaningless.

Let us assume that the assessments of the significance of the criteria, as well as the "wins" and "defeats" of RVS_1 and RVS_2 look like this (Table 1):

Table 1. Example of RV-communication indicators.

	RVS_1 assessment			*RVS_2 assessment*		
Criteria	**Crit. sign.**	**"RVS_1"**	**"RVS_2"**	**"RVS_1"**	**"RVS_2"**	**Crit. sign.**
Power / control	1	1	0	1	1	0,5
Trust	0,75	0	1	x	x	1
Respect	0,5	1	1	1	0	0,25
Comfort	0,25	x	x	-1	1	0,75

"X" means incomplete experience. The significance of the criteria ranges from the most (1) to the least (0.25) significant, and these estimates in this case do not coincide. The value "1" is assigned to "victory," "0" to neutrality, and "-1" to "defeat." The obvious metric to take away from these scores is game readiness. The sum of criteria significance indicators for RVS_1 is 1.5 out of 2.5 possible, or 60%, while the same indicator for RVS_2 is 1.75, or 85.7%. So, $K_{gRVS1} = 0.6$ and $K_{gRVS1} = 0.857$, where K_g is the *game readiness coefficient*.

The second indicator that is significant is the *level of tension resulting from uncertainty* [19, 20]. If we take as an axiom the fact that rational systems avoid uncertainty, trying to turn it into certainty, then this level is not difficult to determine: RVS_1 estimates uncertainty at around 0.25, which in the total sum of estimates of 2.5 is equal to 10%, or $U_{RVS1} = 0.1$. The intensity level of RVS_2 is higher – 40%, or $U_{RVS2} = 0.4$. It is also worth paying attention to the fact that for RVS_1 the fourth criterion, assessed indefinitely, is not important for the formation of interest and, therefore, can be neglected, but for RVS_2 this is hardly possible. In other words, in such interaction one can observe a conflict between universalism and particularism: if RVS_1 shows a willingness to play according to criteria 1 and 3 with firm intentions based on established beliefs, then for RVS_2 the situation looks completely different. According to the fourth criterion, RVS_2 assesses the situation as typical, but according to the second - not, and this criterion is of paramount importance.

The third element of the game is *strategy*. The parties have six strategies available, presented in Table 2.

Table 2. Range of rational communication strategies

Experience criterion Rule source criterion	Playing on completed experience	Playing on uncompleted experience
"My own" game	(1) strategy "Own experience"	(2) "Situation" strategy
"Alien" game	(3) "Norm" strategy	(4) "Observer" strategy
Cooperative play	(5) strategy "Common traditions"	(6) "Contract" strategy

There can be three sources of game rules - the system itself, other systems and the rational interaction of two or more systems, while the rules are taken either in ready-made form, and in this case the system appeals to its own experience, accepted norms or established traditions, or decides to act according to the situation, observe similar cases or negotiate with another system.

To determine the significance of each strategy in the behavior of two RVSs, we will use T. Saaty's method [21], comparing assessments of our behavior and the behavior of the other system. Let's assume these estimates will look like this (Tables 3 and 4):

Table 3. RVS_1 and RVS_2 assessments of the RVS_1 strategy

RVS_1	1	2	3	4	5	6
1	1	5	3	3	5	1
2	1/5	1	1	7	3	1/3
3	1/3	1	1	3	3	1/7
4	1/3	1/7	1/3	1	1	1/9
5	1/5	1/3	1/3	1	1	1/5
6	1	3	7	9	5	1

'RVS_1'	1	2	3	4	5	6
1	1	3	1/5	3	7	1
2	1/3	1	1/3	3	1	1/3
3	5	3	1	5	3	3
4	1/3	1/3	1/5	1	1/3	1/5
5	1/7	1	1/3	3	1	1/3
6	1	3	1/3	5	3	1

Table 4. RVS_2 and RVS_1 assessments of the RVS_2 strategy

RVS₂	1	2	3	4	5	6
1	1	1/3	3	5	5	1/3
2	3	1	5	7	5	1/3
3	1/3	1/5	1	1/3	1/5	1/7
4	1/5	1/7	3	1	1/3	1/9
5	1/5	1/5	5	3	1	1/5
6	3	3	7	9	5	1

'RVS₂'	1	2	3	4	5	6
1	1	1/5	1/3	5	1/7	3
2	5	1	5	7	3	5
3	3	1/5	1	3	1/3	1/3
4	1/5	1/7	1/3	1	1/5	1/5
5	7	1/3	3	5	1	5
6	1/3	1/5	3	5	1/5	1

Priority vector RVS_1 {0.2979; 0.1277; 0.1048; 0.0419; 0.0489; 0.3784} (λ_{max} = 6.5186; CI = 0.1037; CR = 0.0836) is more consistent than the vector "RVS_1" {0.1983; 0.0901; 0.3851; 0.0439; 0.0782; 0.2041} (λ_{max} = 6.637; CI = 0.1274; CR = 0.1027). If we assume that RVS_2, at least with its assessment, makes adjustments to the strategy of RVS_1, then it is better to calculate the general vector of estimates, in this case equal to {0.2481; 0.1089; 0.245; 0.0429; 0.0636; 0.2913}, i.e. strategies 1, 3 and 6 are likely to dominate the behavior of RVS_1, determining its behavior in 78% of cases (leading strategy 6 - in 29%). In turn, the priority vector RVS_2 {0.1594; 0.2648; 0.0328; 0.0429; 0.0786; 0.4212} (λ_{max} = 6.722; CI = 0.1444; CR = 0.1164) indicates a tendency to evaluate one's own commitment to strategies 2 and 6, but RVS_1 has a different opinion: the priority vector "RVS_2" obtained on the basis of its assessments {0.0524; 0.4232; 0.0871; 0.0306; 0.2695; 0.1368} (λ_{max} = 6.8752; CI = 0.175; CR = 0.1411) indicates the tendency of the behavior of RVS_2 from the position of RVS_1 to strategies 2 and 5. "Average" vector {0.1059; 0.344; 0.0599; 0.0368; 0.174; 0.279} indicates the leadership of strategies 2 and 6 (62.3%), "silver" is won by strategies 1 and 5 (28%), "bronze" by strategies 3 and 4 (9.6%).

Finally, the fourth component of the game is the *moves* themselves. The outcome of the game can have nine possible results, presented in Table 5:

Table 5. Example of RVS_1 and RVS_2 expectations and behavior ratings.

		RVS₂		
		lose	draw	win
RVS₁	lose	$RVS_1 = -1$	$RVS_1 = -1$	$RVS_1 = 1$
		$RVS_2 = -1$	$RVS_2 = 0$	$RVS_2 = 1$
	draw	$RVS_1 = 0$	$RVS_1 = 0$	$RVS_1 = 0$
		$RVS_2 = -1$	$RVS_2 = 0$	$RVS_2 = 1$
	win	$RVS_1 = 1$	$RVS_1 = 1$	$RVS_1 = 1$
		$RVS_2 = -1$	$RVS_2 = 0$	$RVS_2 = 1$

The results on the field are arranged according to the "game square" principle: in the upper left corner, the lose-lose strategy is counter to the win-win strategy in the lower right corner and counter to the "zero-sum" games located in other corners of the square. The strategies located in the corners of the square are *dominant* strategies, and the draw in the center represents the Nash equilibrium. The parties can make moves, gradually or abruptly increasing or decreasing their winnings.

The game according to the "power and control" criterion begins with the move of RVS_1, which imposes a win-draw outcome. RVS_2 responds with a win-win proposal. If RVS_1 decides to play a sequential game, then it will have three options in its hands: aggravate the non-cooperative game and occupy the win-lose field, agree to a cooperative win-win game, or take a "dead spot" position. For the first option of the move, RVS_2 can agree to the initial conditions of RVS_1, thus making an imposed compromise, play to increase the draw-win result or take a draw-draw position, for the second option the answer will be to complete the game, for the third - to play to increase the result one of the parties, etc. The game based on the "trust" criterion has not yet begun: we know the expected move of RVS_1, but we do not know the move of the initiator of the game RVS_2, but even in this case we can calculate the options for moves.

Previously, it was proposed to depict the quality of cooperation using a square located in the center of the arc, but the research conducted above suggests a different meaning of this symbol: the scattering of systems' strategies can be depicted with a square. The smallest square will indicate consensus, the medium size will indicate the location of strategies within one dominant strategy, the large size will indicate the maximum dispersion of strategies. Since there can be four types of medium-sized squares, they can be designated in different ways, for example, with vertical stripes inside the square, indicating the serial number of the dominant strategy (I – lose-lose, II – lose-win, III – win-lose, IV – win-win).

2.3 B-Communication

The projection of behavioral communication onto the modeling block represents the *expected results.* Indeed, the goals of the impact of one RVS on another are short-term or long-term goals, which ultimately come down to the RVS itself, the other RVS, both systems, or, if we take all three results together, to what is expected based on past experience and the experience of interaction between the two systems attitude. The modeling block received this name for its ability to simulate the result of the future, i.e. analyze the real relationships of systems and produce a realistic perspective projection of these relationships. In addition, the systems themselves somehow relate to real and future relationships, i.e. form *attitudes towards relationships.* If we place different emphasis on this triad (or tetrad) of relationships, then we can distinguish four accents of varying degrees of significance: emphasis on real relationships (maximum significance), emphasis on attitude to real relationships (low significance), emphasis on attitude to the projection of relationships (medium significance), emphasis on attitudes towards relationships of the past (medium significance). Significance is characterized by the power of influence on behavioral communication, and this power can be both destructive and creative. On the other hand, behavior itself can be based on itself (low significance), on a semantic or rational block (medium significance) and on a semantic and rational block at the same time (high significance). If we place the priority of relationships on the *OY* scale and behavior characteristics on the *OX* scale, we get the following diagram (Fig. 1):

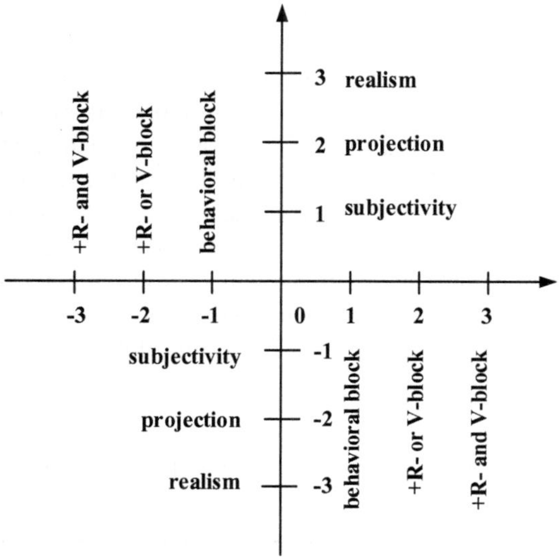

Fig. 1. Indicator scale of behavioral communication importance.

We will introduce a third RVS_3 for independent examination and assessment of the systems interaction. It is impossible to penetrate the R- and V-blocks, they are two things-in-themselves in one system, but behavior can be subjected to independent observation. Suppose that RVS_3 evaluates the behavioral characteristics of RVS_1 as "behavioral realism" with coordinates (1; 3) and the characteristics of RVS_2 as "rational-value subjectivity" with coordinates (3; 1). Their cooperation can give the maximum result (3; 3), but it can also deviate in one direction or another. So, firstly, an independent observer can evaluate the behavioral characteristics of the systems (B_{RVS1} = 1; 3 and B_{RVS2} = 3; 1) and the maximum result of behavioral interaction (B_{max} = 3; 3). In this case, we are talking rather about trends, i.e. the inclinations of the RVS to one or another type of behavior, however, it is the inclinations that define the coordinate grid. If one or another RVS goes beyond the "common" square, then this will inevitably result in a transformation or rupture of interaction. The square, thus, symbolizes the value space of behavioral consensus (behavior itself may well be competitive in some issues and cooperative in others related to the consensus space). The consensus space may be larger or smaller than the one given in the example, but the larger it is, the less opportunity there is to accurately predict its development, and vice versa, a small space provides more opportunities. So, secondly, a third party can assess the scale of the consensus space (S_{cons} = 2) and, therefore, the ability of systems to act as a whole.

Finally, thirdly, RVS_3 can assess the intentions of the parties to act as a single entity [22]. To do this, it is also necessary to introduce a basis for integration - a fourth system, against which the parties are ready or not ready to play a joint game. Traditionally, network theory depicts such relationships as positive or negative attitudes, and the positive ones often form clusters. However, the network of attitudes is not able to answer the question that is being asked at the moment, namely how similar the behavior of RVS_1 is to the behavior of RVS_2. If an independent observer cannot distinguish the elements of behavior of RVS_1 from the elements of behavior of RVS_2 in the absence of the opportunity to directly observe at least one system, then in this case we can say that the systems were able to act as a single whole. There are a large number of behavior elements, and the table can be expanded to impressive size, but it is more important to clarify the principle here. From the author's subjective point of view, the main elements of behavior include motives, the actions themselves and goals. The motives of RVS_1 can be similar to the motives of RVS_2 and vice versa, just as the actions and goals of one system can be similar to the actions and goals of another. At the same time, we are not talking about similarity in the case of comparing different elements to each other: we can assert, for example, that the actions of RVS_1 correspond to the motives of RVS_2 and the motives of RVS_2 correspond to the actions of RVS_1. The results of this correlation are presented in Table 6.

Table 6. Table of correspondence and similarity of RVS_1' and RVS_2's elements behavioral structures

		RVS_2		
		motives	**actions**	**goals**
	motives	0,2; 0,4	0,7; 0,9	0,8; 0,7
RVS_1	**actions**	0,6; 0,8	0,6; 0,5	0,7; 0,8
	goals	0,9; 0,7	0,8; 0,7	1,0; 1,0

In Table 6 presents the results of correlating some elements to others. The white diagonal describes the similarity of the behavioral elements of one system to other elements, the gray cells indicate correspondence. It is worth explaining where these values come from. These data cannot be provided by the systems themselves due to the correction for subjectivity, which will be discussed below. If the ratings were given by RVS_1 and RVS_2, then the assessment would not only begin with the words "I believe that…", but would also be intuitive due to the attempt to include in the assessment its own intentions and hidden elements, from the point of view of the assessing RVS. Such assessments could not be given by RVS_3: most likely, RVS_3 would be based on a set of motives, actions and goals underlying the procedure as criteria. But given the generality of the criteria, two estimates cannot arise in the table. Such a table could only be presented by RVS_4, which for one reason or another began to study its opponents. Suppose she wants to understand not just the degree of cohesion expressed in strong ties, but the ability to act as a single whole, i.e. no longer as RVS_1 and RVS_2, but as RVS ("1", "2"). There is also a comparison tool here, but this tool is no longer just a means of analysis, but an independent system, as real as the elements themselves that comprise it. The attitude towards this third system is expressed by the estimates given by RVS_4 in Table 6.

The most significant assessments are similarity assessments. The similarity of motives is assessed as (02; 04). It follows from this that the chances of breaking unity are higher for RVS_1 - 8 out of 10, or 0.8, while RVS_2 demonstrates a greater danger of unity - 0.4. Comparing the chances and risks by category, it is easy to find that the maximum risk lies in the unity of goals (RQ = 1.0), and the maximum chance lies in the unity of motives (P(A) = 0.8), from which it follows that the probability of coherence behavior of RVS_1 and RVS_2 is not as high as it might seem - 0.45.

The initial simulation, based on all previous considerations, is as follows (Fig. 2):

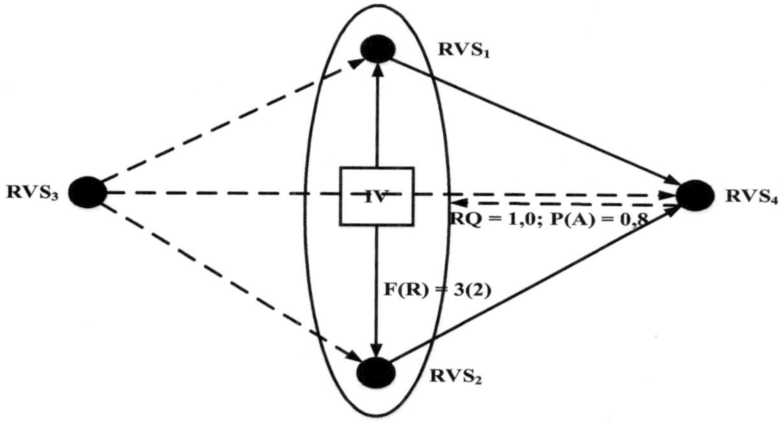

Fig. 2. Graphic representation of the RVSs interaction network.

3 Conclusion

The presented concept of communication of rational-value systems has three dimensions, or levels: the level of ideas, the level of calculations and the level of practical application. This article presents the second level to a greater extent and the first and third to a lesser extent. In view of this, the concept requires repeated clarification, discussion and search for possible applications. Empirical research, using the theory of rational systems as a starting point, will significantly clarify, expand, or, conversely, narrow the scope of practical application of this theory.

The concept of rational-value systems is one of the rational systems theory components. On the one hand, this indicates the possibility of meaningful expansion of the study (description and analysis of the interaction of recursive-sensory, isomorphic indeterministic and rational-indeterminate systems), on the other hand, the continuation of the search for different ways of representing the levels of calculations and applications. In turn, the level of ideas in the theory of rational-value systems is fixed by the following provisions: firstly, this concept is a statement of computable pluralism for rational aspects of interaction. The author presents one of the options for representing the computability level, and this level can be represented in many different ways that may not contradict each other. Secondly, there is an obvious bias towards a psychological description of the interaction of rational systems, but it does not strictly follow from this that the theory is more suitable for studying the behavior of people, citizens, individuals, etc. due to the fact that the rational-value system refers to a method of self-organization as such. Thirdly, the basic component in the communication process is experience, which introduces analysis into the continuum of "certainty-uncertainty" interaction and thereby forms unique strategies and methods of communication. It must be assumed that it is experience, or the modeling block, that will serve as the starting point in describing the types of rational-value systems interaction.

It is also worth noting the fact that the article attempts to open a discussion about the "single whole" - one of the most important paradoxes of systems theory. The paradox lies in the compatibility of the incompatible: "one" means "indivisible", i.e. "not divisible into parts," while "whole," on the contrary, implies "consisting of parts." The paradox is significant because its correspondent meaning is obvious and the coherent meaning is obscure. In subsequent studies, it is also necessary to raise this issue, approaching work that will be entirely devoted to it.

References

1. Kondratenko, K.S.: Elements of the rational-value systems theory. Bulletin of Tomsk State University. Philosophy. Sociology. Political science **459**, 113–118 (2020)
2. Kondratenko, K.S.: Cybernetic philosophy of digital public governance: modeling recursive sensory systems. In: Proceedings of the international conferences on ICT, society and human beings 2022, Web based communities and social media 2022 and e-health 2022 (July 19 - 21, 2022), pp. 51–58. IADIS Press, Portugal, Porto (2022)
3. Kondratenko, K.S.: Indetermination, isomorphism, sustainability: a systemic model of the political process in the context of digital transformation. Polis. Political Studies **3**, 146–164 (2023)
4. Kondratenko, K.S.: Network philosophy of artificial rationality: effects of interaction of multi-level systems. Part 1. Abyss (Questions of philosophy, political science and social anthropology) **3**(25), 92–101 (2023)
5. Kondratenko, K.S.: Network philosophy of artificial rationality: effects of interaction of multi-level systems. Part 2. Abyss (Questions of philosophy, political science and social anthropology) **4**(26), 128–136 (2023)
6. Tikhomirov, O.K.: Structure of mental activity. Moscow University Publishing House, Moscow (1969)
7. Tikhomirov, O.K., Babaeva, Yu.D., Berezanskaya, N.B. et al.: Development of the activity approach in the psychology of thinking. In: Voiskunsky, A.E., Zhdan, A.N., Tikhomirov, O.K. (eds.) Traditions and prospects of the activity approach in psychology: A.N. Leontyev school. Smysl, Moscow, 191–234 (1999)
8. Bratus, B.S.: Moral consciousness of the individual. Knowledge, Moscow (1985)
9. Leontyev, D.A.: Psychology of meaning: nature, structure and dynamics of semantic reality. Smysl, Moscow (2003)
10. Ivkov, N.N.: Analysis of psychological studies of the problem of development of the semantic sphere of personality and its achievement of maturity. World of Psychology **1**, 188–201 (2014)
11. Popova, V.I.: Value-semantic communication, or how to achieve mutual understanding in the educational activities of a teacher. Problems of Modern Pedagogical Education **63–3**, 114–117 (2019)

12. Artyukhova, I.S.: Educational discourse as a system of value-semantic communication of subjects of the educational process. Development of Modern Education: Theory, Methodology and Practice **1**(7), 56–59 (2016)
13. Kahneman, K.: Thinking, fast and slow. Penguin, New York (2012)
14. Frankl, V.: Psychotherapy and existentialism. Simon and Schuster, New York (1967)
15. Deutsch, K.W.: The Nerves of government: models of political communication and control. The University of Toronto Law Journal **16**(1), 265–290 (1965)
16. Kahneman, D., Slovik, P., Tversky, A.: Decision making under uncertainty: Rules and biases. Publishing House Institute of Applied Psychology "Humanitarian Center", Kharkiv (2005)
17. Smithson, M.: Psychology's ambivalent view of uncertainty. In: Bammer, G., Smithson, M. (eds.) Uncertainty and risk. multidisciplinary perspectives. Earthscan Risk in Society Series, London (2008)
18. Dekel, Ed., Siniscalchi, M.: Epistemic game theory. In: Young, P., Zamir, Sh. (eds.) Handbook of Game Theory with Economic Applications, pp. 619–702. Elsevier B.V. (2015)
19. Greco, V., Roger, D.: Coping with uncertainty: the construction and validation of a new measure. Personality Individ. Differ. **31**, 519–534 (2001)
20. Ladouceur, R., Gosselin, R, Dugas, M.J.: Experimental manipulation of intolerance of uncertainty: a study of a theoretical model of worry. Behavior research and therapy **38**, 933–941 (2000)
21. Saaty, T.: Relative measurement and its generalization in decision making: why pairwise comparisons are central in mathematics for the measurement of intangible factors - The Analytic hierarchy/Network process. RACSAM (Review of the Royal Spanish Academy of Sciences, Series A, Mathematics) **102**(2), 251–318 (2008)
22. Myakinnikov, S.P.: Toward the definition of the concept "single whole": the position of postholism. Bulletin of the Vyatka State University **2**(132), 50–62 (2019)

Multimodal Prompts in AI-Assisted User Interface Design: How Many Words a Picture is Worth?

Danila Vologdin and Maxim Bakaev(✉)

Novosibirsk State Technical University, Novosibirsk, Russia
vologdin.2019@stud.nstu.ru, bakaev@corp.nstu.ru

Abstract. The progress in the development of generative models encouraged automated creation of user interfaces (UIs) based on textual prompts. Our study investigates the advantages of using multimodal prompts, which combine text and images, in AI-assisted UI design. In particular, we explored how more thorough textual descriptions compare to supplementation of shorter ones with style-defining pictures, wireframes, or screenshots of real interfaces. The 84 UIs that we generated with 3 different services have been evaluated by two professional UI/UX designers. Their positive feedback suggests that multimodal prompts can result in UI prototypes that have reasonably high Aesthetics, Level of Detail and Utility for the designers. Quantitative analysis demonstrated that the UIs generated with multimodal prompts received significantly higher mean evaluations: by 50.9% for Stable Diffusion 1.5, by 40.5% for KreaAI (which received the highest evaluations overall) and by 9.1% for UI/UX LoRA. The effect of the image type was somehow unexpected: better results (by 43.6% for KreaAI and by 32.4% for Stable Diffusion) were obtained with simpler wireframes (mock-ups) than with more detailed screenshots of real existing UIs. The results of our study might be of interest to HCI researchers and UI/UX practitioners who seek to incorporate AI technologies into UI design process.

Keywords: generative models · human-computer interaction · user interface design · prompt engineering

1 Introduction

Designing a user interface (UI) is one of the main tasks in a software product development, since it is through the UI that interaction between a human and a computer occurs. This task can be quite time-consuming, but recent advances in generative models – AI/ML models designed to generate new data similar to what they were trained on – have shown the potential to automate the process. Generation of UIs from textual or multimodal prompts is relatively novel, but have arrived even before the advent of Large Language Models [1]. Recent advances in Deep Learning (DL) allow the models to generate UI sketches, which are of potential utility in the overall design process. However, so far they largely fall short of creating the final versions of UIs, which would consider the software product usage context, appropriate content, etc.

M. Bakaev et al. (Eds.): IMS 2024, CCIS 2534, pp. 216–227, 2026.
https://doi.org/10.1007/978-3-031-96177-9_18

The concept of a "text-to-image" generative model is that its user makes a text prompt, and a DL model that is trained to create images from words and phrases, returns one or more images that are supposed to represent what the user wrote in the prompt. The advantage of prompts is that they allow anyone, even an untrained person (i.e., a non-expert), to work with DL models, although some researchers note that this mode of interaction requires prohibitively high literacy from the users [2]. Still, natural language is a common way for humans to communicate ideas, and prompts are in a way related to the "thinking out loud" strategy that people employ when solving complex problems.

With all these advantages considered, it should be noted that for most end users writing effective textual prompts is a matter of trial and error [3], as it requires specialized skills: both in prompt engineering and in the domain. Moreover, composing an exhaustive description for a sophisticated UI is hard even for an expert, since it would require accurate and comprehensive description of the sizes and positions of UI elements, their styling, colors, as well as the overall layout, and many other aspects. The volume of such an exhaustive description for a today's web UI can be estimated as 10s Kbytes (derived from the compressed HTML + CSS size, not even considering the interactive JS and the content), whereas a compressed visual representation of a web UI has the order of Mbytes [4]. We presume that along the purely textual prompts approach and with limited "understanding" of the context, generative AI would be largely limited to creating rough sketches of UIs. These can be useful in the ideation stage, but human intervention would still be required to finalize the design [5].

Meanwhile, the challenges described above could be overcome by providing extra information to the model in some other form. One of the key advancements in the field has been the introduction of multimodal prompts that combine text and images. Presumably, providing a mockup image or an example of an existing UI can provide the model with much more context and save the user a considerable amount of the prompt engineering time. Based on this motivation, this paper addresses the following research question: "Can an image supplied with a prompt to a generative model compare with a long and thorough textual prompt, in terms of the generated UI quality?". This exploration of multimodal prompts' feasibility in AI-assisted UI design has been inspired by the classic adage that "a picture is worth a thousand words" and the title of the infamous paper [6]. By examining the impact of different modalities on aesthetic impression, level of detail, and utility in a design workflow, we aim to uncover the true value of each element in enhancing the user experience.

The remainder of our paper is organized as follows. In Sect. 2, we briefly over-view the state-of-the-art with generative models – particularly, their application in the UI/UX design workflow. In Sect. 3, we describe the experiment in which we selectively prompted 3 existing generative services (Stable Diffusion 1.5, UI/UX LoRA and KreaAI) to create 84 UIs for 7 different domains and tasks. The UIs then were assessed by 2 professional UI/UX designers on the scales of aesthetic impression, level of detail, and utility in a design workflow. In Sect. 4, we present statistical analysis of the data collected in the experiment. In the final section of the paper, we summarize and discuss our findings, specify the limitations of the current study, and outline prospects for further research.

2 Methods and Related Work

2.1 Advancements in Generative Models

The two principal generative tasks in GUI creation, for which frontend developers and UI/UX designers seek AI-based support, are ideation (mostly done with mockups and prototypes) and the actual design [7]. Recent advancements in AI yielded scalable models capable of high-quality image generation from textual prompts, such as generative adversarial networks (GANs) [8] and latent diffusion models like Stable Diffusion (SD) [9]. In a GAN, the generator neural network (NN) creates candidate images that are not part of the original image dataset, while the discriminator NN tries to distinguish these "fake" images from the ones it was trained on. SD is a generative model of another type, which use Gaussian noise to encode an image and noise predictor along with a noise subtraction process to reconstruct the image. Currently, diffusion models have generally surpassed the mainstream GANs in their generative abilities [10]. But even though the models have achieved a whole-image understanding, the key challenge has been region-specific comprehension within complex images when accuracy is crucial, such as in UIs [11]. All in all, these models excel in ideation, but do not help that much in the final UI design. The output images might be blurry, fuzzy, but most importantly they do not fully correspond even to a detailed textual prompt, whereas small faults that can be well overlooked in general images, are essential for proper usage of artifacts in general and human-computer interaction (HCI) in particular.

The above considerations have encouraged the exploration of different model input types provision and multi-modal contexts. Recent studies have shown that providing a multimodal context such as an image improves the reasoning ability of Large Language Models (LLMs) [12]. Moreover, multimodal LLMs outperform baseline generation models on tasks with longer and more complex language [13]. However, it is yet to be discovered how multimodal prompts affect the generated result compared to the expanded and thoroughly engineered text-only prompt. Moreover, many of the today's AI-driven generative tools have clunky prompt-driven interfaces [14], so the introduction of multimodal prompts could improve not just their usefulness, but also their usability.

2.2 The Practicing Designers' Workflow

In order to provide a theoretical background for the study, we ought to describe UI/UX designers' process of creating an interface [15]. First of all, they search for images related to the domain and seek inspiration from existing UI designs or prototypes. After the initial ideation, the designers start sketching initial concepts for the UI design and extract the base UI components. Sketches help in visualizing the structure and flow of the interface. The next step is wireframing, when designers create low-fidelity representations of the UI using basic shapes and figures, and then they move onto creating interactive prototypes (usually with a design tool like Figma) and several thoroughly rendered UI layouts. This stage involves incorporating visual elements, text fonts and color palettes, and results in interactable mockups. After several iterations with the stakeholders and possibly evaluations with experts, a frontend developer implements the UI based on the design and user testing takes place. The designers who participated in our study (see 3.2. Subjects) have emphasized that the ideation and quick creation of several mockups are crucial stages in the design process. Having gathered ideas and considered different mockups, they say, the implementation in Figma is not a problem. This further reinforces the urgency of our study, since a considerable share of automation tools for UI designers focus on the relatively straightforward implementation part [7].

2.3 The Image Generation Models

In our study, we employed three different generative models (offered in the corresponding online services):

1. The mainstream *Stable Diffusion 1.5*. Figure 1 presents an example of a UI image generated by the model with a simple textual prompt "A website layout, a baking club website with the cookies in the middle, name of the store on top, greenish colors".
2. The specifically trained for UI/UX image generation *UI/UX LoRa*, published on the Open-Source Generative AI web service "Civit AI" [16]. It was based on Low-rank Adaptation architecture (LoRA) [17] and the Stable Diffusion 1.5. The model was selected specifically for the reason that the outputs of pretrained diffusion models are inherently constrained by their training corpus and it sometimes even directly copies the data. Figure 2 presents a generated UI image example for the same textual prompt.
3. *KreaAI*, which can transform text descriptions into visuals instantly, whilst allowing sketching in the real-time. This model is the closest one to a real-life scenario of designer's workflow, allowing them not only to generate images but also to move the UI components on the service's website instantly affecting the generated image. Figure 3 presents a generated UI image example for the same textual prompt.

3 The Experiment Description

3.1 Procedure and Material

The prompts were constructed in a specific way with the focus on positions and colors of the UI components and required illustrations since these are the most important details, as emphasized by designers. Especially, we provided extra clarifications for long prompts, such as setting the whole style of image, color palette and resolution level. For instance, to generate a detailed coffee shop website UI we wrote the following text prompt: "*Coffee shop website layout featuring a sidebar on the left with a list of coffees, a top navbar with a list of links, and a round cup of coffee in the center. Detailed, digital illustration with a cozy indoor lighting style, designed by top artists in the field. Cinematic aesthetic with a focus a usability of the user interface. Resolution set to 4k for optimal viewing experience*".

In total, we generated UIs for 7 different domains and tasks:

1. Coffee shop UI
2. Pokemon game UI
3. Baking club UI
4. Car shop UI
5. Online school UI

Fig. 1. A UI image generated by Stable Diffusion 1.5.

6. User profile settings page UI
7. Availability planner UI

For the multi-modal prompts in our study, three wireframe images were created by hand and four images of already existing UIs were manually collected. The examples for these two types of images are provided in Fig. 4. Then, for each of the 7 tasks we would generate 4 = 2*2 UIs: 1) with long or short prompts, 2) without an image or with an additional input image (i.e. with a multimodal prompt, containing either a wireframe image or real UI images). For every condition, three different generative models would be utilized (KreaAI, Stable Diffusion 1.5 (SD 1.5), UI/UX LoRA), which resulted in 84 = 7*4*3 generated UIs.

3.2 Subjects

Since the evaluation of the quality of UI image generation is a challenging problem, particularly due to the subjective nature of the UI quality concept, we considered it important to ask seasoned professionals to evaluate the UIs in our study.

Two professional UI/UX designers voluntarily participated in the evaluation process for each generated UI using a dedicated survey form. The first designer was male, 31 years old, with over 6 years of experience, and the second one was female, 25 years old, with 3 years of experience. They both worked for a software company that develops UIs for the customers in oil-production industry.

Fig. 2. A UI image generated by UI/UX LoRA.

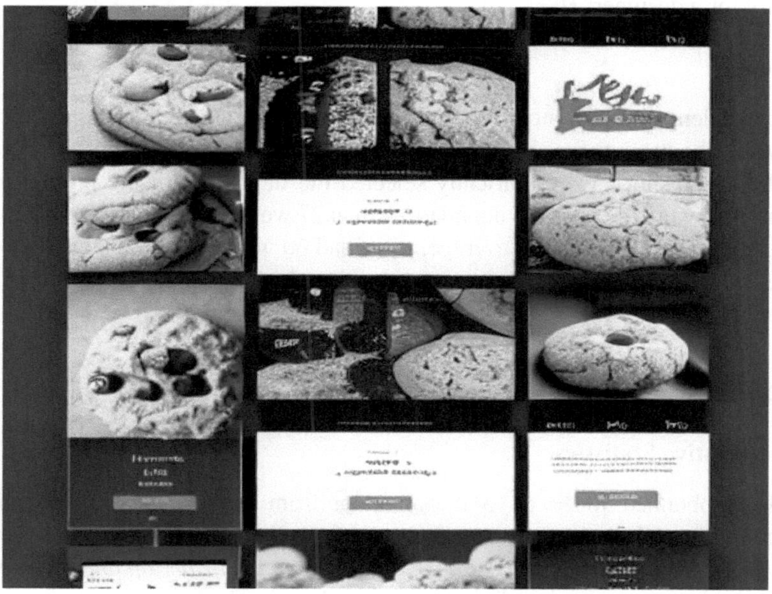

Fig. 3. A UI image generated by KreaAI.

Fig. 4. Examples of the input images: a wireframe (left) and a real UI (right).

The designers performed the evaluation of each generated UI using a dedicated survey form. Specifically, they had three aspects to consider: the generated UI elements' positioning and color styling in UI (aesthetics), quality of image and each one of the UI components (detalization) and overall utility for the designers' workflow. Working independently, each designer would provide his or her evaluation of the UIs as scores from 0 (less) to 10 (more) along the following 3 scales:

- Aesthetic impression: *A*
- Level of detail: *D*
- Utility for a designer: *H*

3.3 Design

The independent variables (nominal) were the *Prompt Length* (short or long), the *Image Presence* in the prompt (yes or no), and the input *Image Type* (a simple wireframe or a real UI screenshot). We empirically selected the threshold for the prompt lengths: short prompts were the ones having no more than 27 words (162 characters), while long prompts had over 27 words (on average, these had 60 words or 380 characters).

The dependent variables were the designers' evaluations of the UIs per the 3 scales: *A, D,* and *H.*

4 Results

4.1 Descriptive Statistics

In total, we obtained 504 = 84*3*2 evaluations from the designers for the generated UIs. An output of KreaAI (the textual prompt for was: "*A coffee shop website layout with a sidebar with a list of coffes on the left and the navbar on top and the round cup or coffee in the center top down*") is provided in Fig. 5. The UI on the left received the highest score in our study (A: 8; D: 10; H: 10), yet the UI obtained with same prompt without an image (right) have obtained considerably lower evaluations from the same designer (A: 4; D: 9; H: 1).

Fig. 5. Best evaluated UI with image (left) and without image (right).

In Table 1, we present descriptive statistics (means and standard deviations) for the dependent variables per the different levels of the independent variables that reflect the prompt length and the usage of the image (the highest values for each scale and condition are highlighted).

All pairwise correlations (Kendall's tau-b) between the scales were significant ($p < 0.001$), the highest being the one between A and D scales ($\tau_{84} = 0.643$). The moderately high correlations suggest that the scales in our study are meaningful.

Next, we sought to examine if there was a difference due to the type of image used in multimodal prompts: a simple wireframe or a real UI. In Table 2, we present descriptive statistics per the different levels of the respective independent variables.

4.2 Effect of the Prompt Attributes

To check the statistically significant differences in the dependent variables due to the Prompt Length and Image Presence, multivariate analysis of variance (MANOVA) was performed for each of three services used for the UI generation, assuming $a = 0.05$. The results of the analysis are provided in Table 3, with significant differences highlighted in bold.

The two-way MANOVA suggests that Prompt Length only significantly affected the H scale, and the evaluations of the utility for a designer in our experiment were actually **higher** for short (mean = 3.52) rather than for long prompts (mean = 2.83). This unexpected result might be an artifact of the data obtained for the SD 1.5 model – the only one that demonstrated the significance.

Meanwhile, the effect of Image Presence was clearly significant, especially so for the *H* scale ($p < 0.001$). For LoRA however, no statistically significant differences were found at all. Overall, the analysis suggests that the UIs generated with images (i.e., from multimodal prompts) tended to get considerably better evaluations from the designers than without images (A: 3.98 vs. 3.5; D: 4.44 vs. 3.69; H: 4.15 vs. 2.20).

Table 1. Descriptive statistics for the designers' evaluations of the generated UIs (with or without an image).

Service	Prompt			
	Long, with image (n = 21)	Long, no image (n = 21)	Short, with image (n = 21)	Short, no image (n = 21)
KreaAI	A: 4.85 (1.51) D: 6.14 (1.41) H: 4.86 (1.14)	A: 4.14 (1.49) D: 5.00 (1.22) H: 2.36 (1.57)	A: 5.28 (1.80) D: 6.07 (0.79) H: 5.71 (1.88)	A: 4.50 (2.16) D: 4.93 (2.19) H: 2.50 (1.73)
SD 1.5	A: 3.64 (1.06) D: 4.21 (1.55) H: 3.28 (1.28)	A: 3.21 (1.65) D: 3.14 (1.24) H: 1.36 (0.55)	A: 3.92 (1.13) D: 4.58 (0.67) H: 4.57 (1.13)	A: 3.00 (1.35) D: 3.21 (1.60) H: 2.07 (1.54)
LoRA	A: 3.07 (1.17) D: 2.86 (1.18) H: 2.92 (0.93)	A: 3.21 (2.02) D: 2.92 (1.59) H: 2.21 (1.29)	A: 3.21 (1.31) D: 2.79 (1.07) H: 3.57 (1.39)	A: 2.92 (1.45) D: 2.92 (0.89) H: 2.71 (1.28)
Avg	A: 3.82 (1.42) D: 4.40 (1.91) H: 3.69 (1.37)	A: 3.52 (1.71) D: 3.69 (1.61) H: 1.98 (1.23)	A: 4.14 (1.62) D: 4.48 (1.60) H: 4.61 (1.68)	A: 3.48 (1.77) D: 3.69 (1.81) H: 2.42 (1.48)

Table 2. Descriptive statistics for the designers' evaluations of the generated UIs (wireframe or real UI screenshot).

Service	Prompt			
	Long, with wireframe (n = 9)	Long, with real UI (n = 12)	Short, with wireframe (n = 9)	Short, with real UI (n = 12)
KreaAI	A: 5.83 (1.25) D: 6.50 (1.80) H: 6.67 (1.04)	A: 4.25 (1.55) D: 4.88 (1.03) H: 4.50 (0.82)	A: 6.33 (1.61) D: 6.50 (0.50) H: 7.67 (0.58)	A: 4.50 (1.68) D: 5.12 (1.65) H: 4.25 (1.65)
SD 1.5	A: 5.00 (0.50) D: 4.50 (1.32) H: 4.50 (0.86)	A: 3.25 (1.19) D: 4.00 (1.87) H: 2.62 (1.25)	A: 4.83 (0.58) D: 4.67 (0.58) H: 5.83 (1.25)	A: 3.87 (1.11) D: 4.00 (0.91) H: 4.37 (1.31)
LoRA	A: 2.17 (0.58) D: 2.17 (0.77) H: 3.33 (1.90)	A: 3.75 (1.04) D: 4.37 (1.25) H: 3.12 (1.11)	A: 2.00 (0.50) D: 2.00 (0.50) H: 3.17 (0.29)	A: 4.12 (0.85) D: 3.38 (1.03) H: 4.25 (1.50)
Avg	A: 4.33 (1.82) D: 4.39 (2.21) H: 4.83 (1.87)	A: 3.75 (1.23) D: 4.08 (1.44) H: 3.41 (1.28)	A: 4.39 (2.10) D: 4.39 (2.01) H: 5.55 (2.08)	A: 4.16 (1.17) D: 4.17 (1.35) H: 4.29 (1.36)

4.3 Effect of the Image Type

In Table 4 we present the results of MANOVA for the effect of different image types on the dependent variables (only UIs generated from the prompts with images were considered in this analysis, n = 42).

Table 3. The MANOVA results for the prompt attributes.

Service	Prompt Length	Image Presence	Interaction
KreaAI	A: $F_{1,24} = 0.347$, $p = 0.561$ D: $F_{1,24} = 0.016$, $p = 0.901$ H: $F_{1,24} = 0.675$, $p = 0.419$	A: $F_{1,24} = 1.266$, $p = 0.271$ D: $F_{1,24} = 4.118$, $\mathbf{p = 0.053}$ H: $F_{1,24} = 22.069$, $\mathbf{p < 0.001}$	A: $F_{1,24} = 0.002$, $p = 0.957$ D: $F_{1,24} = 0.000$, $p = 1.000$ H: $F_{1,24} = 0.344$, $p = 0.562$
SD 1.5	A: $F_{1,24} = 0.005$, $p = 0.943$ D: $F_{1,24} = 0.184$, $p = 0.671$ H: $F_{1,24} = 4.983$, $\mathbf{p = 0.035}$	A: $F_{1,24} = 1.841$, $p = 0.187$ D: $F_{1,24} = 5.908$, $\mathbf{p = 0.022}$ H: $F_{1,24} = 24.432$, $\mathbf{p < 0.001}$	A: $F_{1,24} = 0.250$, $p = 0.621$ D: $F_{1,24} = 0.081$, $p = 0.777$ H: $F_{1,24} = 0.406$, $p = 0.529$
LoRA	A: $F_{1,24} = 0.015$, $p = 0.902$ D: $F_{1,24} = 0.006$, $p = 0.938$ H: $F_{1,24} = 1.491$, $p = 0.233$	A: $F_{1,24} = 0.015$, $p = 0.902$ D: $F_{1,24} = 0.054$, $p = 0.817$ H: $F_{1,24} = 2.819$, $p = 0.106$	A: $F_{1,24} = 0.138$, $p = 0.713$ D: $F_{1,24} = 0.006$, $p = 0.938$ H: $F_{1,24} = 0.023$, $p = 0.880$
Avg	A: $F_{1,80} = 0.111$, $p = 0.739$ D: $F_{1,80} = 0.008$, $p = 0.925$ H: $F_{1,80} = 4.737$, $\mathbf{p = 0.032}$	A: $F_{1,80} = 1.957$, $p = 0.165$ D: $F_{1,80} = 3.921$, $\mathbf{p = 0.050}$ H: $F_{1,80} = 37.880$, $\mathbf{p < 0.001}$	A: $F_{1,80} = 0.217$, $p = 0.642$ D: $F_{1,80} = 0.009$, $p = 0.925$ H: $F_{1,80} = 0.563$, $p = 0.455$

Table 4. The MANOVA results for the Image Type (only for multimodal prompts)

Service	Prompt Length	Image Type	Interaction
KreaAI	A: $F_{1,10} = 0.200$, $p = 0.664$ D: $F_{1,10} = 0.029$, $p = 0.868$ H: $F_{1,10} = 0.369$, $p = 0.557$	A: $F_{1,10} = 4.154$, $p = 0.068$ D: $F_{1,10} = 4.198$, $p = 0.067$ H: $F_{1,10} = 20.423$, $\mathbf{p = 0.001}$	A: $F_{1,10} = 0.022$, $p = 0.884$ D: $F_{1,10} = 0.029$, $p = 0.867$ H: $F_{1,10} = 1.023$, $p = 0.335$
SD 1.5	A: $F_{1,10} = 0.198$, $p = 0.666$ D: $F_{1,10} = 0.014$, $p = 0.909$ H: $F_{1,10} = 5.604$, $\mathbf{p = 0.039}$	A: $F_{1,10} = 6.905$, $\mathbf{p = 0.025}$; D: $F_{1,10} = 0.679$, $p = 0.428$ H: $F_{1,10} = 6.549$, $\mathbf{p = 0.028}$	A: $F_{1,10} = 0.590$, $p = 0.460$ D: $F_{1,10} = 0.014$, $p = 0.909$ H: $F_{1,10} = 0.102$, $p = 0.755$
LoRA	A: $F_{1,10} = 0.056$, $p = 0.817$ D: $F_{1,10} = 0.025$, $p = 0.878$ H: $F_{1,10} = 0.443$, $p = 0.521$	A: $F_{1,10} = 17.848$, $\mathbf{p = 0.002}$ D: $F_{1,10} = 5.995$, $\mathbf{p = 0.034}$ H: $F_{1,10} = 0.369$, $p = 0.556$	A: $F_{1,10} = 0.381$, $p = 0.551$ D: $F_{1,10} = 0.025$, $p = 0.877$ H: $F_{1,10} = 0.805$, $p = 0.391$
Avg.	A: $F_{1,38} = 0.232$, $p = 0.633$ D: $F_{1,38} = 0.006$, $p = 0.939$ H: $F_{1,38} = 2.471$, $p = 0.124$	A: $F_{1,38} = 0.676$, $p = 0.416$ D: $F_{1,38} = 0.237$, $p = 0.629$ H: $F_{1,38} = 6.961$, $\mathbf{p = 0.012}$	A: $F_{1,38} = 0.135$, $p = 0.714$ D: $F_{1,38} = 0.006$, $p = 0.939$ H: $F_{1,38} = 0.022$, $p = 0.881$

The two-way MANOVA results suggest that Image Type had significant effect in most of the conditions: *H* for KreaAI; *A, H* for SD and *A, D* for LoRA ($p < a$). It is worth noting that the simpler image type, wireframes, resulted in **higher** average evaluations than the real UI images (A: 4.36 vs. 3.96; D: 4.39 vs. 4.13; H: 5.19 vs. 3.85) for all models except for LoRA. For Prompt Length and the factors' interactions, we did not find any statistically significant differences in the designers' evaluations for any conditions except for *H* for SD.

5 Discussion and Conclusions

Our paper reports a pilot study aimed on analyzing the feasibility of supplying an image to the textual prompts in UI generation task. We prompted 3 GenAI models: KreaAI, Stable Diffusion 1.5, and UI/UX LoRA to output 84 UI images that were subsequently evaluated by 2 practicing designers on the scales of aesthetics (A), level of detail (D) and usefulness (H).

Our finding is that UIs generated from multimodal prompts have obtained better evaluations from the designers, A: + 14.3%; D: + 20.3%; H: + 88.6%. Meanwhile, the increase of the textual prompts' length (by 250% on average) did not have a significant positive effect, with or without an image. The latter finding rather contradicts the conventional wisdom of prompt engineering for image generation, which encourages more detailed prompts for better quality of the models' output. Further research is needed to clarify whether this is merely an artifact of the prompts in our study, or a genuine difference in prompt engineering for generating UIs. However, it can be concluded that an image was "worth" more than about 35 words in our study.

Another somehow unexpected finding was that images with less complexity and detail (wireframes) have yielded better results than more sophisticated screenshots of real existing UIs. The effect was notable for A: + 10.1% and D: + 6.3%, but also for the utility for a designer scale: H: + 34.8%. Interestingly, the effect was the opposite only for LoRA UI/UX, which did benefit from the real UI examples, but still produced the output that generally received inferior evaluations.

Of the three GenAI models we employed, KreAI's outputs have obtained the highest evaluations from the designers, for almost all conditions and scales. Another notable finding is that LoRA, although being a specialized model in UI/UX, did not benefit from the multimodality of the prompts, and also obtained the evaluations that were among the lowest. In other words, in our study general-purpose AI models (KreaAI and SD 1.5) have demonstrated advantages in UI generation.

Among the limitations of our study is the relatively small size of the dataset and the modest number of expert evaluators, who were not randomly selected. They both responded with a positive feedback about using the GenAI services for the design process, but it is not generally the case for the entire community of UI designers. Also, the choice of the website domains and of the scales for the evaluation were not entirely rooted in literature.

However, already we believe that our findings might be of interest to HCI researchers and practitioners dealing with UI generation. Some additional qualitative findings from our study that we recommend as prompt engineering take-aways are:

- explicitly indicate the domain (e.g., a coffee shop website);
- specify the positions of UI components and their type (e.g., navbar, sidebar, etc.);
- include the desired colors of the UI elements in the prompt;
- provide a simple sketch as a multimodal prompt to the model if you have one.

References

1. Huang, F., et al.: Creating User Interface Mock-ups from High-Level Text Descriptions with Deep-Learning Models. In: arXiv preprint arXiv:2110.07775 (2021)
2. Nielsen, J.: The Articulation Barrier: Prompt-Driven AI UX Hurts Usability, UX Tigers blog, https://www.uxtigers.com/post/ai-articulation-barrier. Last accessed 13 March 2024
3. Dang, H., et al.: How to prompt? Opportunities and challenges of zero-and few-shot learning for human-AI interaction in creative applications of generative models. In: arXiv preprint arXiv:2209.01390 (2022)
4. Boychuk, E., Bakaev, M.: Entropy and compression based analysis of web user interfaces. In: Web Engineering: 19th International Conference, ICWE 2019, Daejeon, South Korea, June 11–14, 2019, Proceedings 19, pp. 253–261. Springer International Publishing (2019)
5. Brie, P., Burny, N., Sluÿters, A., Vanderdonckt, J.: Evaluating a large language model on searching for GUI layouts. In: Proceedings of the ACM on Human-Computer Interaction, 7(EICS), pp. 1–37 (2023)
6. Dosovitskiy, A., et al.: An image is worth 16×16 words: Transformers for image recognition at scale. arXiv preprint arXiv:2010.11929 (2020)
7. Bakaev, M., et al.: A Taxonomy of User Behavior Model (UBM) Tools for UI Design and User Research. In: International Conference on Web Engineering, pp. 236–244. Springer Nature Switzerland, Cham (2023)
8. Bleichner, A., Hermansson, N.: Investigating the usefulness of a generative AI when designing user interfaces. Master thesis (2023)
9. Robin, R., Andreas, B., Dominik, L., Patrick, E., Björn, O.: High-resolution image synthesis with latent diffusion models. In: Proceedings of the IEEE/CVF Conference on Computer Vision and Pattern Recognition, pp. 10684–10695 (2022)
10. Malik, S., et al.: Reimagining Application User Interface (UI) Design using Deep Learning Methods: Challenges and Opportunities. In: arXiv preprint arXiv:2303.13055 (2023)
11. Cai, M., et al.: Making large multimodal models understand arbitrary visual prompts. arXiv preprint arXiv:2312.00784 (2023)
12. Zeng, X., Gao, Z., Ye, Y., Zeng, W.: IntentTuner: An Interactive Framework for Integrating Human Intents in Fine-tuning Text-to-Image Generative Models. In: arXiv preprint arXiv: 2401.15559 (2024)
13. Koh, J.Y., Daniel, F., Russ, R.: Generating images with multimodal language models. In: Advances in Neural Information Processing Systems 36 (2024)
14. Nielsen, J.: UX Needs a Sense of Urgency About AI, UX Tigers blog, https://www.uxtigers.com/post/ux-urgency-ai. Last accessed 22 March 2024
15. UxPin blog: UX Workflow – How to Create and Improve Yours, https://www.uxpin.com/studio/blog/ux-workflow-guide/. Last accessed 10 March 2024
16. Civitai website: UI/UX LoRA model, https://civitai.com/models/98715/ui-ux-lora-sd-15-and-sdxl. Last accessed 05 March 2024
17. Hu, E.J., et al.: Lora: Low-rank adaptation of large language models. In: International Conference on Learning Representations (2021)

Interactive Systems & Information Society Technologies: Interactive Systems and Language Models

Can GPT Technology Overcome the Techno-Linguistic Bias in Machine Translation?

Galina Kedrova(✉) and Sergey Potemkin

Lomonosov Moscow State University, Moscow, Russian Federation
kedr@philol.msu.ru

Abstract. Techno-linguistic bias in machine translation can occur when a machine translation system is trained on one language or text type, leading to inaccurate translations in other languages or text types. This can happen due to variations in training data representation or the presence of language-specific terminology and concepts. The implications of techno-linguistic bias are significant, especially for low-resourced languages, endangered languages, and dialects. Machine translation systems must take into account the characteristics of different languages and dialects during training to avoid inaccurate translations that could harm the preservation and transmission of cultural heritage and linguistic traditions. It is crucial to develop machine translation systems that cater to the diversity of languages and dialects, providing accurate and respectful translations for all users. We propose a method for assessment of techno-linguistic bias in MT and GPT-based services using a multilingual parallel corpus.

Keywords: Techno-linguistic bias · Machine translation · Multilingual parallel corpus · Chat GPT · phraseology

1 Introduction

The possibility of global communication, regardless of language, is becoming more feasible due to the rapid development of linguistic technologies in recent years. These technologies include universal translation tools and digital resources on the internet for number of languages, underrepresented, small languages and dialects as well. Bilingual and multilingual machine translation, natural language processing, and speech recognition projects are actively developing in this direction for various kinds of multi-lingual communication.

Recently, new computer-aided technologies for communication in virtual digital space, such as intelligent (neural) machine translation (NMT) [1] and Large Language Model (LLM) [2] technologies, have given a new impetus to the study of the problem of computer-supported translator's practice.

However, it should be noted that both NMT and Large Language Models (LLMs) such as GPT-4 have the potential to introduce various kinds of techno-linguistic bias into their responses due to the selection of training data and/or availability of the bilingual and

M. Bakaev et al. (Eds.): IMS 2024, CCIS 2534, pp. 231–239, 2026.
https://doi.org/10.1007/978-3-031-96177-9_19

multilingual translation dictionaries and vocabulary datasets. Researchers persistently report on different types of biases, including demographic biases, cultural biases, linguistic biases, temporal biases, confirmation biases, and ideological and political biases, manifested in the production of large language models and machine translation tools [3].

It has been observed that the issue of techno-linguistic bias in artificial intelligence modeling algorithms restricts their availability and performance to only a small percentage of the world's most commonly spoken languages – the English language primarily. However, this problem has not been adequately addressed in the available literature [4].

1.1 Techno-linguistic Bias: Causes and Consequences

The paper "Diversity and Language Technology: How Techno-Linguistic Bias Can Cause Epistemic Injustice" [5] discusses this phenomenon and its ethical and epistemological implications in detail. In the paper Paula Helm gives the following definition of techno-linguistic bias: "Techno-linguistic bias is observed when the technology, by design, represents, interprets, or processes content less accurately in certain languages than in others, thereby forcing speakers of the disadvantaged language to simplify or adapt their communication, (self-)representation, and expression when using that technology to fit the default incorporated in the privileged language." [5: 9].

A technical-linguistic bias is evident in a resource or tool when it cannot accurately represent or process the language it is applied to. This issue is particularly noticeable in machine translation programs, even those that use neural machine translation technologies and large language models. Techno-linguistic bias in machine translation can cause inaccurate translations when a system is designed or trained on a specific language or text type. This is because the training data may not be uniformly represented in different languages or may contain terminology that is not commonly used in other languages. It is critical therefore to consider language and context specifics when using a machine translation system to avoid generating translations that are inappropriate for the purpose of communication. If necessary, manual correction of the translation should be performed.

It was hypothesized that the same problem would occur translating texts by LLM such as Chat GPT. The paper [6] examines the use of generative pre-trained transformer (GPT) models in machine translation. The evaluation of GPT models includes translation quality, the impact of cueing strategies, robustness to domain switching, and document-level translation. The experiments were conducted on a variety of languages, including high- and low-resource languages, as well as non-English translations. The study found that GPT models achieve high translation quality for high-resource languages, but have limitations for low-resource languages. Additionally, the study revealed the challenges that GPT models face when dealing with underrepresented languages. However, the hybrid approaches that combine GPT models with other translation systems are supposed to improve translation quality.

It is widely acknowledged that biases in language models can arise from various factors, including training data, algorithms, labeling and annotation, product development decisions, and policy decisions [7]. These biases can have a significant impact on the information generated and disseminated by these tools and models and may even lead to unconscious or intentional misrepresentation of information. It is crucial thus to consider the potential ethical and cultural distortions that computer-based machine translation tools and large language models can introduce in cultural and educational projects. A further consequence is that the automatic translation system has the capacity to create and impose certain stereotypes on the user or content that disregard the cultural context in which communication or learning occurs.

Currently the scientific community is carrying out several comparative studies of translating strategies and the capabilities of different automated translating tools. It is supposed that the results could improve the adaptability and cultural awareness of all available automated translation tools. The dominant hypothesis is that better translation could be achieved by developing translation technologies combining the efficiency and speed of NMT and LLM (ChatGPT) with the cultural sensitivity, linguistic flexibility, and domain expertise demonstrated by professional human translators [8]. We tested this hypothesis through assessment of techno-linguistic bias in MT and GPT-based services using a multilingual parallel subcorpus of translations of A.P. Chekhov's works in the Russian National Corpus (https://ruscorpora.ru).

Linguistic technologies are crucial in addressing the issue of bias in modern AI tools used in various fields that require information mining and knowledge generation procedures. Although there are many unsolved problems in this area, researchers have noted as primary challenge the lack of sufficiently representative bi-lingual and multilingual parallel corpus resources, orthography variation in some languages, complexity of the morphological analysis, and other low-resourced languages description technologies. [9] It is our contention that parallel corpus technologies have the potential to facilitate the incorporation of a vast array of linguistic data, including data from underrepresented and minor languages and dialects, into the training database of large language models.

1.2 Parallel Bilingual and Multilingual Corpora as Resource Data

Nowadays, more and more parallel bilingual and multilingual corpus resources become essential tools for translation work and translation research. They offer valuable material for understanding translation strategies and contribute to the development of translators' competencies. Computerized corpora of texts are of great scientific interest because they provide an opportunity to conduct an experimental study of language functioning. This allows for the identification of which words, expressions, grammatical constructions, and discourse types are actually used (or have been used) by native speakers at different times, how often they are used, and for what purposes. Computerized corpora of translated fiction and non-fiction texts are currently one of the primary sources for experimental research into the features of the target language, as well as one of the main resources for translator training [1].

The translation of literary texts is one of the most difficult cases in the line, for there are the most problematic issues and unsolved problems in this type of translation. Since the goal of the literary translation is the maximum possible transfer of the author's intention ensuring adequacy of the emotional and aesthetic impact of the original and translated text, one of the main tasks of the translator is to prevent the formation of semantic and emotional gaps, or cohesive shifts in the foreign reader's perception [10]. All those elements of a foreign language text that are nationally specific elements of the culture in which the text was created could be the sources of such gaps. These elements are strange and incomprehensible for the recipient belonging to a different culture [11]. Realia, which refers to culturally specific vocabulary, is widely recognized as one of the main challenges in translating fiction. However, the translation of phraseological phrases, phraseological combinations, and idioms is much less studied than the translation models of the so-called non-equivalent lexicon, which are well-documented in dictionaries of established interlingual correspondences.

Improving bilingual and multilingual phraseological dictionaries is urgently needed, which can be achieved by utilizing the results of parallel translation corpora studies. Comparison of translation options with bilingual and multilingual parallel corpora of literary works makes it possible to explore the strategies used by the translators when translating phraseological units and phraseological compounds, to assess the success or failure of these strategies, to analyze in detail the reasons of omission or substitution while translating certain lexical unit and phraseological construction which leads to gaps in the translated text. Based on the results obtained, it will be possible to develop some standardized models for the transfer of phraseological units and phraseological compounds between different languages. Thus, corpus resources of all types should become an integral part of training databases for all applications that use large language model algorithms.

2 Materials and Method

For the purposes of this study, the extraction of phraseological units and phraseological compounds in a parallel (comparable) corpus of translations of A.P. Chekhov's works into foreign languages was carried out. We used a specially developed program of marking phraseological units in the author's text based on the "Large Phraseological Dictionary of the Russian Language" by E.N. Telia [12], and identifying their translation equivalents in the aligned texts of translations. The algorithm for the study of translation equivalents includes the following procedures: identifying cases of omission / transformation of a phraseological unit or phraseological compound in the translated text, and analysis of possible causes for a lacuna / transformation; description and classification of translation models used in the translation of phraseological units, practical recommendations on the use of the results obtained while training translators. The multilingual concordances of translations of phraseological units and phraseological phrases were obtained and subjected to functional-semantic analysis.

The objective of the current experiment was to test the hypothesis that techno-linguistic bias is present in modern computer-assisted translation tools, specifically those based on NMT and LLM models, and to assess the degree of bias observed across the different tools. The experiment evaluated the quality of automatic translation provided by the leading machine translation systems and freely available GPT resources. DeepL (https://www.deepl.com), Google Translate (https://translate.google.com), and Yandex Translator (https://translate.yandex.ru), as well as ChatGPT (https://chatgpt.org/chat), Yandex.GPT (https://yandex.ru/project/alice/yagpt), GIGA:Chat (https://developers.sber.ru/gigachat) were tested for their ability to translate the culturally significant Russian text 'The cook's wedding' by A.P. Chekhov, which has been translated into multiple languages by professional translators in the 'Project Gutenberg' database (https://www.gutenberg.org/) and incorporated into multilingual parallel corpus of works by A.P. Chekhov, which is currently being developed at the Faculty of Philology of Lomonosov Moscow State University.

3 Results and Discussion

This paper analyzes the translation results of the fragment from the short story 'The cook's wedding' by A.P. Chekhov 'Да на что тебе молодой? С лица, дура, воды не пить… Выходи, вот и всё!' (Eng. 'what do you want a young man for? Handsome is as handsome does… Marry him and that's all about it') provided by human translators and the leading machine translation systems, in comparison with the translations provided by some GPT resources, both Russian and international ones.

Proposition 2 in this fragment contains a Russian phraseological expression с лица не воду пить (literal translation: not to drink water from the face). This phraseological unit has proven difficult to convey meaning in another language. In the dictionary of Sophia Lubensky, the phraseology is defined as follows: "С ЛИЦ´А НЕ В´ОДУ ПИТЬ [saying] physical attractiveness is not important (usu. Said when choosing a plain looking husband or wife): $\simeq$ beauty is only skin-deep; handsome is as handsome does; pretty is as pretty does; looks aren't everything" [13:293].

Table 1 presents the human translations for the Russian phraseological unit 'с лица не воду пить' (literal translation: 'not to drink water from the face') in various languages.

Table 1. Translations of the idiom 'с лица воды не пить' ('not to drink water from the face') by human translator.

Russian original text	English	French	Italian
Да на что тебе молодой? С лица, дура, воды не пить… Выходи, вот и всё! ("Кухарка женится"/"The cook's wedding")	He has not reached his fortieth year; and what do you want a young man for? Handsome is as handsome does… Marry him and that's all about it!	Quel besoin as-tu d'un jeune homme? Sotte, ce n'est pas la beauté qui fait le bonheur (1)… Marie-toi; ne cherche pas plus loin! (1) Mot à mot: Ce n'est pas l'eau d'un visage que l'on boit. (Tr.) (Translation into English by Google: What do you need of a young man? Stupid, it is not beauty that makes happiness (1)… Get married; look no further! (1) Word for word: It is not the water of a face that one drinks. (tr.))	E che te ne fai d'un giovane? La faccia, sciocca, non ti dà da bere (5). (5) Proverbio russo. (Translation into English by Google: And what do you do with a young man? His face, silly, does not give you a drink (5). (5) Russian proverb.)

The analysis of translation strategies in our corpus revealed the methods used to convey the meaning of phraseologies and phraseological word combinations that are frequently found in Chekhov's works. As we see from Corpus' results search presented in the table, the best translation strategy is to find an identical phraseological unit, although the number of such correspondences is very limited. If such matches are not available, the next best solution is to find an equivalent phraseological unit (Eng. 'Handsome is as handsome does'; Fr. 'ce n'est pas la beauté qui fait le bonheur'). In certain contexts, such as a language game based on the literal meaning of a phraseological unit, it may be necessary to translate on the 'word-to-word' basis and explain the phrase (It. 'La faccia, sciocca, non ti dà da bere' (5). (5) Proverbio russo. – Eng. 'His face, silly, does not give you a drink' (5). (5) Russian proverb). Eliminating a phraseological unit (lexical gap, or lacunar strategy) is minimally effective and does not fulfill the communicative task, though there are multiple cases of the phraseology omission in translated texts. Although it must be admitted that the majority of omissions of Russian phraseological units in translated texts are observed, according to the corpus, in translations of Chekhov into less common languages. Thus, the Norwegian translation ignores the phraseological unit in the original text, therefor its meaning is lost in the translated phrase: 'Og hva skal du med en ung mann. Gift deg med ham og bli ferdig med det!' - Eng. 'And what are you going to do with a young man. < … > Marry him and get it over with').

Table 2 presents the translations of the test phrases generated by the selected MT systems.

Table 2. Translations of the idiom 'с лица воды не пить (not to drink water from the face)' by MT.

Russian original text	DeepL	Google Translate	Yandex Translator
Да на что тебе молодой? С лица, дура, воды не пить… Выходи, вот и всё! ("Кухарка женится"/"The cook's wedding")	Why should you be young? Don't drink water from your face, you fool! Come out, that's all!	What do you need young for? Don't drink water off your face, you fool… Come out, that's all!	What do you need a young man for? Don't drink water from your face, you fool… Come out, that's all!

When comparing the translation variants of phraseological expressions provided by human translators to those given by machine translation systems, it is evident that the primary translation strategy of the former is to search for idioms that are equivalent in meaning to the original. No online MT resource can match the accuracy of a human. This is exemplified by the translation of the phraseological expression 'С лица, дура, воды не пить' (Eng: 'Don't drink water off your face') in A.P. Chekhov's story 'The Cook's Wedding'. Though the key phrase has been translated differently by machine translation systems, such as DeepL, Google Translate, and Translate.Yandex.ru, all of those translations were more or less literal word-for-word translations and therefore all of them completely lack any meaning. It is only a human translator could accurately translate this phrase with the English idiom 'handsome is as handsome does', or the French phraseological equivalent 'ce n'est pas la beauté qui fait le bonheur' (Eng. 'It is not beauty that creates happiness').

The same task has been offered to several GPT resources based on the AI model. As it is known that texts generated by LLM system strongly depend on the prompts' structure, we asked the GPT services to generate answer to two types of questions: (1) 'Translate into English + Russian text', and (2) 'Translate into English from Russian like you are human translator + Russian text'. Table 3 presents both translations of the test phrases generated by the selected LLM systems.

Table 3 presents the translations of the test phrases generated by the selected MT systems.

Table 3. Translations of the idiom "с лица воды не пить (not to drink water from the face)" by LLM.

Russian original text	Yandex.GPT.API	ChatGPT	GIGA: Chat
Да на что тебе молодой? С лица, дура, воды не пить… Выходи, вот и всё! ("Кухарка женится"/"The cook's wedding")	1. Why do you need a young one? It's not like you'll drink water from his face, fool. Just marry him, and that's all! 2. Why do you need a young one? It's not like you're going to drink from his face, fool! Marry him, that's all!	1. Why do you need a young man? You're not getting any younger… Come on, that's enough! 2. And what would you do with a young one? Don't judge by appearances, you fool… Just go out, that's all!	1. Why should you be young? Don't drink water from your face, fool! Just get out, that's all! 2. And why do you need a young one? You can't drink water from her face, you fool… Come out, that's all there is to it!

A comparison of the translation options for phraseological expressions provided by humans and by LLM systems reveals that neither of the latter employs the translation strategy typically employed by professional translators. This indicates that the LLM systems do not use corresponding English idioms in an adequate manner to convey the meaning of a phraseological unit. Nevertheless, the extent of techno-linguistic bias observed across the various LLM tools may vary. The GPT Chat provides the closest meaning, while Yandex Chat also translates the test phrase accurately. Giga Chat offers a more formal and literal translation, but it contains factual errors. However, the results of the translation performance of systems based on large language models demonstrate considerable potential for improvement in comparison to machine translation systems, including those that employ neural machine translation algorithms.

4 Conclusion and Recommendations

To enhance translation quality and achieve competitive results for languages with ample digital resources, it is proposed to adopt hybrid approaches based on the widening of the training resource base onto multilingual parallel corpora. The implementation of this approach would enhance the capabilities of both MT systems based on neural machine translation (NMT) models and natural language processing algorithms that utilise large language models (LLM) based on Generative Pre-trained Transformer (GPT) technology. Further combination of these approaches may be considered to represent a significant advancement in global digital communication, regardless of the language used. Currently, a new large-scale project, known as the 'Metaverse' or 'Metauniverse' [14], is also actively developing similar approaches to achieve this goal.

The results of the experiment indicate that the techno-linguistic bias is currently a significant factor in the translation output of all three MT systems tested (DeepL, Google Translate and Yandex Translator). However, while performing the same task, the AI systems demonstrated greater efficacy in the translation strategies employed (though not equal to the human translator). This suggests that through further expansion of the training base of large language models with multilingual parallel corpora resources, it will be possible to eliminate the majority of issues counterproductive for effective communication across languages.

Given the challenges outlined previously in relation to the use of AI technologies in various fields that require the generation of information and knowledge, it is crucial to utilise linguistic technologies that facilitate the incorporation of all types of language data and an extensive range of language resources, including bilingual and multilingual corpora of literary texts, into training bases for large language models. Furthermore, recent progress has been made in developing similar technologies for digitally documenting underrepresented languages, endangered ones, as well as dialects.

In the future, the integration of systems based on large language models such as GPT (Generative Pre-trained Transformer) and MT systems will likely progress in several directions. These include the development of more efficient and accurate methods for training language models, as well as improving their ability to understand context and generate natural language without losing meaning. To ensure the universal applicability of these resources, it is crucial to address the potential issues of bias and the equitable access to them. Other potential areas of development include advanced dialogue systems, expanded multi-language capabilities, and integration with other AI technologies, such as computer vision and speech recognition.

References

1. Gaspari, F., Almaghout, H., Doherty, S.: A survey of machine translation competences: Insights for translation technology educators and practitioners. Perspectives **23**(3), 333–358 (2015)
2. Yan, H., Liu, Y.L., Jin, L.W., Bai, X.: The development, application, and future of LLM similar to ChatGPT. Journal of Image and Graphics **28**(9), 2749–2762 (2023)
3. Ferrara, E.: Should chatgpt be biased? challenges and risks of bias in large language models, arXiv preprint arXiv:2304.03738 (2023)
4. Spennemann, D.H.R.: ChatGPT and the Generation of Digitally Born "Knowledge": How Does a Generative AI Language Model Interpret Cultural Heritage Values? Knowledge **3**, 480–512 (2023). https://doi.org/10.3390/knowledge3030032
5. Helm, P., et al.: Diversity and Language Technology: How Techno-Linguistic Bias Can Cause Epistemic Injustice, arXiv e-prints, arXiv: 2307.13714 (2023)

6. Hendy, A., et al.: How Good Are GPT Models at Machine Translation? A Comprehensive Evaluation, ArXiv, abs/2302.09210 (2023). https://doi.org/10.48550/arXiv.2302.09210
7. Lin, Z.: Why and how to embrace AI such as ChatGPT in your academic life. R. Soc. Open Sci. **10**, 230658 (2023). https://doi.org/10.1098/rsos.230658
8. Jiang, Z., Lv, Q., Zhang, Z.: Distinguishing Translations by Human, NMT, and ChatGPT: A Linguistic and Statistical Approach, arXiv preprint arXiv:2312.10750 (2023)
9. Mager, M., et al.: Neural Machine Translation for the Indigenous Languages of the Americas: An Introduction, arXiv e-prints, arXiv: 2306.06804 (2023)
10. Blum-Kulka, S.: Shifts of Cohesion and Coherence in Translation. In: House, J., Blum-Kulka, S. (eds.) Interlingual and Intercultural Communication: Discourse and Cognition in Translation and Second Language Acquisition Studies, Tübingen, Germany: Narr, (Tübinger Beiträge zur Linguistik 272), pp. 17–35 (1986)
11. Sorokin, Y.A., Markovina, I.Y.: An attempt to in the systematize linguistic and cultural lacunae: Methods and methodological aspects: Lexical units and organization of the structure of the literary text. Kalinin, pp. 35–52 (1983)
12. The Big Phraseological Dictionary of Russian Language. AST-Press, Moscow (2006)
13. Lubensky, S.: Russian-English dictionary of idioms. Yale University Press, Russian-English Dictionary of Idioms (2014)
14. Doğan, T.E.T.: Translating and interpreting in the Metaverse: potential opportunities and challenges. RumeliDE J. Lang. Literat. Stud. **35**, 1589–1604 (2023)

Word Recognition Efficiency Among Adolescences with Visual Dyslexia: An Accessibility Study in Russian

Alexandra Burdyna[1(✉)], Yana Nikonova[1], and Svetlana Alexeeva[2]

[1] Saint Petersburg State University, St. Petersburg 199034, Russia
burdyna@yandex.ru

[2] Saint Petersburg State University, 6th Line of Vasilievsky Island 11D, 199034 St. Petersburg, Russia

Abstract. Dyslexia is a common reading disorder, often characterized by slow or inaccurate word recognition. Inappropriate typography design may pose an additional challenge for struggling readers, particularly when visual impairments contribute to their difficulties. One crucial aspect of typography is the choice of typeface. Previous studies examining dyslexia-friendly typefaces in Latin and Cyrillic scripts yielded inconclusive results, with participants' visual skills remaining unassessed.

This study aimed to address this gap by recruiting adolescents in Grades 8–11 exhibiting signs of visual and nonvisual dyslexia. We tested three typefaces in Russian: the dyslexia-friendly LexiaD, the default font for Google applications, Roboto, and the widely used Times New Roman found in textbooks. This was done in a lexical decision task that primarily reflects the speed of word recognition. Participants were tasked with identifying, via key presses, whether presented letter strings were real Russian words or pseudowords, with their reaction times measured.

The findings showed that in the nonvisual subgroup words in LexiaD were recognized slower than in Roboto and Times New Roman, the difference between control fonts were insignificant. However, adolescents with visual dyslexia showed no significant difference between Times New Roman and LexiaD, with Roboto being identified as the most effective font.

These results suggest that inclusive typography features should be tested, taking into account dyslexia subtypes. We do not recommend using Times New Roman in digital texts for struggling readers in Russian; instead, Roboto may be a better option.

Keywords: inclusive typography · dyslexia · typeface

1 Introduction

Accessibility is a broad concept that spans across different areas of life, including communication, architecture, and services. It ensures that individuals, regardless of their abilities or limitations, can access and participate in various aspects of society. When

M. Bakaev et al. (Eds.): IMS 2024, CCIS 2534, pp. 240–249, 2026.
https://doi.org/10.1007/978-3-031-96177-9_20

it comes to the digital realm, Web Accessibility specifically focuses on making online content and services accessible to everyone, including those with disabilities.

Web Accessibility encompasses a range of measures aimed at ensuring that websites, applications, and digital content are usable and understandable by all users, regardless of any disabilities they may have. This includes considerations for people with visual, auditory, motor, and cognitive impairments, among others. By implementing Web Accessibility standards, developers and designers can create online experiences that are inclusive and barrier-free.

One group that often faces challenges when using digital platforms is individuals with dyslexia. Dyslexia is a learning disorder that affects reading and language processing abilities. People with dyslexia may struggle with tasks such as reading, writing, and spelling, despite having normal intelligence. When it comes to web content, individuals with dyslexia may encounter difficulties due to issues such as poor information structure, complex language, and inadequate text formatting [11, 21].

To address the needs of users with dyslexia and ensure their equal access to online information, it's essential for developers and designers to consider dyslexia-friendly design principles. This may involve using clear and legible fonts, avoiding excessive use of complex language, providing sufficient spacing between lines and paragraphs, improving website navigation, incorporating multimedia elements to enhance understanding, etc. [11, 22].

While many guidelines seem to be universally applicable, particularly in terms of using clear language and maintaining coherent website structure, recommendations for text presentation may vary based on the script being used. For example, in the Russian language, which uses Cyrillic script, 73% (24 out of 33) of lowercase letters lack ascenders/descenders, while in standard Latin script, this proportion is only 50% (13 out of 26). This discrepancy can impact word readability, potentially resulting in some words appearing monotonous and the text feeling looser[1]. Font selection can help mitigate some of these readability challenges.

Hence, our study aimed to evaluate the readability of several fonts among individuals with dyslexia using Cyrillic script—a script known to be somewhat more intricate than Latin script. Furthermore, font readability was assessed while considering two distinct dyslexia profiles (Sect. 2).

2 Dyslexia

Dyslexia is a neurobiologically rooted reading disorder, characterized by difficulties in both accurate and fluent reading. These challenges often arise from a deficiency in the phonological aspect of language, and they are typically unexpected given an individual's age and intellectual capacity. Secondary effects may include difficulties in reading comprehension, resulting in limited exposure to reading materials. Consequently, this limitation can potentially hinder the acquisition of vocabulary and knowledge about the world [16].

[1] https://typejournal.ru/en/articles/Cyrillic-Letterforms-Development.

According to the International Dyslexia Association, dyslexia affects approximately 15% to 20% of the global population, resulting in around 700 million individuals worldwide [16]. Given that the modern world is hardly adapted to the needs of this condition, individuals with dyslexia, who already experience significant difficulties in processing text, develop additional problems. Among them are low self-esteem, social isolation, and underperformance in other areas of activity [14]. This underscores the importance of developing specific interfaces that enhance text perception and accessibility.

As mentioned earlier, most individuals with dyslexia primarily struggle with phonological processing. However, within the broader dyslexic population, there exists a specific subgroup that experiences visual impairments, making it challenging to process text visually [15]. For instance, while reading, letters may interchange, vanish, be substituted with similar-looking characters, or appear blurred; lines could overlap or be skipped [27].

For these individuals with dyslexia, we believe that typographic text appearance, particularly font selection, plays an important role.

2.1 Typeface Guidelines for People with Dyslexia

The most readable, popular, and widely used fonts by people with dyslexia are considered to be Arial, Comic Sans, Verdana, Tahoma, Century Gothic, Georgia, Trebuchet, Calibri, and Open Sans. Most of these fonts are sans-serif, which individuals with dyslexia find easier to read due to the absence of detailed serifs. Serif fonts tend to be more complex and harder to process [6, 11, 12]. Additionally, it's advised to avoid using small text sizes (less than 12 pt) and italic font styles as they can further impair readability [6, 11, 19, 21].

Meanwhile, specialized fonts have been developed for people with dyslexia. These include Open Dyslexic[2], Dyslexie[3], Read Regular[4], Sylexiad[5], and EasyReading[6]. Most of them support Latin characters and are characterized by increased spacing between letters/words/lines and unique shapes for visually similar letters.

The results of testing the most popular dyslexia-friendly fonts (Open Dyslexic, Dyslexie), using perceptual methods among a group of people with dyslexia did not reveal a significant difference in reading speed between words and text in specialized and standard fonts [18, 23, 26, 28]. However, two points should be noted. Firstly, participants were exposed to specialized fonts for the first time, so unfamiliarity may have hinder the positive effect of the dyslexia-friendly typeface design. Secondly, the testing was conducted without considering subtypes of dyslexia. Our study aims to elaborate on the second point by exploring Russian, a language whose script may impose additional challenges on text readability (see Introduction).

---

[2] https://opendyslexic.org/about#.

[3] https://dyslexiefont.com.

[4] http://www.readregular.com/english/intro.html.

[5] https://www.sylexiad.com.

[6] https://www.easyreading.it/en/.

3 The Present Study

Previously, we presented examples of fonts specifically designed for individuals with dyslexia, tailored for the Latin script. Similarly, fonts have been developed for the Cyrillic script, including EasyReading Cyrillic[7], Antidyslexia[8], Adys[9], Dyslexic FZF [17], OpenDyslexic Cyrillic[10] and LexiaD [1]. This study will focus on the LexiaD font.

The LexiaD font (see Fig. 1) is distinguished by increased spacing between letters, words, and lines. These features are suggested as recommendations for creating dyslexia-friendly interfaces that enhance text readability. Furthermore, LexiaD lacks serifs and maintains proportional spacing—key characteristics that align with guidelines, including those proposed by the BDA [8]. Additionally, LexiaD offers another advantage: it enables dyslexic individuals with visual impairments to improve text accessibility by ensuring that similar Cyrillic letters are easily distinguishable from each other. This aspect aims to reduce the occurrence of letter substitution errors resulting from letter template similarities or identical letter features.

Table 1. The Russian alphabet in LexiaD, Roboto and Times New Roman

Font	The Russian alphabet
LexiaD	Аа Бб Вв Гг Дд Ее Ёё Жж Зз Ии Йй Кк Лл Мм Нн Оо Пп Рр Сс Тт Уу Фф Хх Цц Чч Шш Щщ Ъъ Ыы Ьь Ээ Юю Яя
Roboto	Аа Бб Вв Гг Дд Ее Ёё Жж Зз Ии Йй Кк Лл Мм Нн Оо Пп Рр Сс Тт Уу Фф Хх Цц Чч Шш Щщ Ъъ Ыы Ьь Ээ Юю Яя
Times New Roman	Аа Бб Вв Гг Дд Ее Ёё Жж Зз Ии Йй Кк Лл Мм Нн Оо Пп Рр Сс Тт Уу Фф Хх Цц Чч Шш Щщ Ъъ Ыы Ьь Ээ Юю Яя

Previously, the LexiaD font underwent testing in several readability studies involving both dyslexic and non-dyslexic individuals [1, 3-5], using eye tracking methodology. However, the outcomes remain inconclusive:

- LexiaD demonstrated a positive impact on feature extraction (but a negative effect on lexical access and text integration) compared to the unfamiliar but standard PT Sans font, among primary school children with and without dyslexia when reading digital texts.
- It exhibited an advantage in text integration (but a disadvantage in lexical access, with no significant difference in feature extraction) compared to the unfamiliar but standard PT Serif font among primary school children with and without dyslexia during digital reading.
- LexiaD displayed an advantage in feature extraction but only after participants became accustomed to it (with no significant difference in lexical access, text integration, or global reading speed) compared to Arial, a popular sans serif font, among adolescents with and without dyslexia during digital reading.

[7] https://www.easyreading.it/en/.

[8] https://www.facebook.com/ProstoSlovoApp/.

[9] https://adysfont.com/en/.

[10] https://opendyslexic.org/about#.

- It showed a disadvantage in global reading speed compared to Roboto, an increasingly popular modern Arial-like font, among adolescents and adults without dyslexia when reading printed text.
- There was no significant difference in global reading speed compared to Times New Roman, a common serif font, among adolescents and adults without dyslexia when reading printed text.

However, none of these studies evaluated visual skills in the dyslexic group. Addressing this gap, our present study selects dyslexic participants both with and without signs of visual dyslexia. Participants undergo a lexical decision task, primarily reflecting the speed of lexical access (recognition of individual words). This task entails classifying letter strings as either words or nonwords by pressing keys, with reaction latencies measured. Importantly, conducting this experiment only requires a computer, simplifying the technical and logistical aspects of the project.

As control fonts, we chose Roboto and Times New Roman (see Table 1). Both fonts are familiar to participants, with Roboto being the default font for Google applications and Times New Roman commonly used in Russian language and literature textbooks. Moreover, Roboto previously demonstrated a clear advantage over LexiaD (but for participants without dyslexia).

Thus, we hypothesize that the LexiaD font would outperform the control fonts in word processing speed among participants with visual dyslexia, while familiar control fonts would have an advantage in the group without signs of visual dyslexia.

3.1 Method

Participants

The study involved 23 Russian-speaking adolescents in Grades 8–11, aged 14–17 (average age = 15;8 years; 10 girls), who exhibited signs of dyslexia as identified by a qualified speech therapist. The same speech therapist categorized participants into visual and non-visual groups based on their oral reading errors and a visual processing test where they identified partially depicted objects. Out of these, 10 participants displayed signs of visual impairments, while 13 did not.

All participants underwent an intelligence test using the Raven's Progressive Matrices, with their results conforming to established age norms [10].

Ethical approval was obtained from the ethical committee of Saint Petersburg State University (protocol No. 115-02-7). Informed consent was provided by both parents and participants, with the option to withdraw from the study at any point.

Materials and Procedure

To investigate the primary hypothesis regarding the font's impact on word recognition speed, we conducted a lexical decision task. Initially, we selected 75 high-frequency and 75 low-frequency Russian words from the StimulStat database [2], with low-frequency words having an instances per million (ipm) score below 5, and high-frequency words scoring above 80. These words were five or six characters long. Additionally, we generated 150 pseudowords for the experiment by maintaining the syllabic structure of each real word. Thus, there were a total of 300 stimuli.

The lexical decision task was implemented using the PsychoPy software on the experimenter's computer. Each trial started with a fixation cross appearing on the screen for 500 ms, followed by a letter string. The letter string remained on the screen until the participant's response. Participants were instructed to determine whether the letter sequence represented a real Russian word. They responded by pressing the "K" key for a real word or the "F" key for a pseudoword. Reaction times were registered.

The experiment comprised three blocks, each consisting of 100 stimuli (50 words and 50 pseudowords). The stimuli in each block were presented in one of the three fonts studied (Roboto, LexiaD, or Times New Roman). Font order was randomized between blocks for each participant. The vertical letter size of the stimuli remained consistent across all fonts, and the distribution of words and pseudowords between blocks was randomized for each participant.

4 Analysis and Results

4.1 Analysis

We analyzed correct responses to words using mixed linear models in the R environment (the *lmerTest* package). The dependent variable was reaction time, while the independent variables were font (Roboto, LexiaD, Times New Roman), participant group (with visual difficulties / without visual difficulties), and their interaction. Random effects included participant and word intercepts. The dependent variable was entered into the model in transformed form ($-1000/rt$) to meet the assumption of residual normality. Sliding contrast was used for fixed effects, allowing comparison between neighboring levels.

26 low-frequency words was recognized by fewer than 65% of participants; hence, reactions to these words were excluded from the analysis. Prior to statistical analysis, outlier reactions were removed in two steps. First, extremely long reactions (over 5500 ms) and short reactions (less than 350 ms) were excluded. Second, thresholds of $\pm$ 2.5 standard deviations from the mean were calculated for each participant, and reactions outside these thresholds were discarded. In total, we excluded 4.2% of reactions. The analysis included 933 measurements for the group with visual difficulties and 1365 for the group without visual difficulties.

4.2 Results

Figure 1 presents the mean word reaction times in the lexical decision task for each participant subgroup.

Linear mixed modeling revealed that high-frequency words were processed faster than low-frequency ones ($b = 0.27$, $SE = 0.02$, $t = 13.27$, $p < 0.001$). This well-established effect validates our data. Regarding fonts, overall, there was no significant difference between LexiaD and Times New Roman ($b = 0.02$, $SE = 0.02$, $t = 0.94$, $p = 0.345$), while LexiaD yielded slower processing times compared to Roboto ($b = 0.07$, $SE = 0.02$, $t = 4.02$, $p < 0.001$).

More importantly, we identified a significant interaction between font and participant subgroup ($\chi2(2) = 22.71$, $p < 0.001$) when comparing models with and without the interaction based on maximum chi-square likelihood estimates (using the

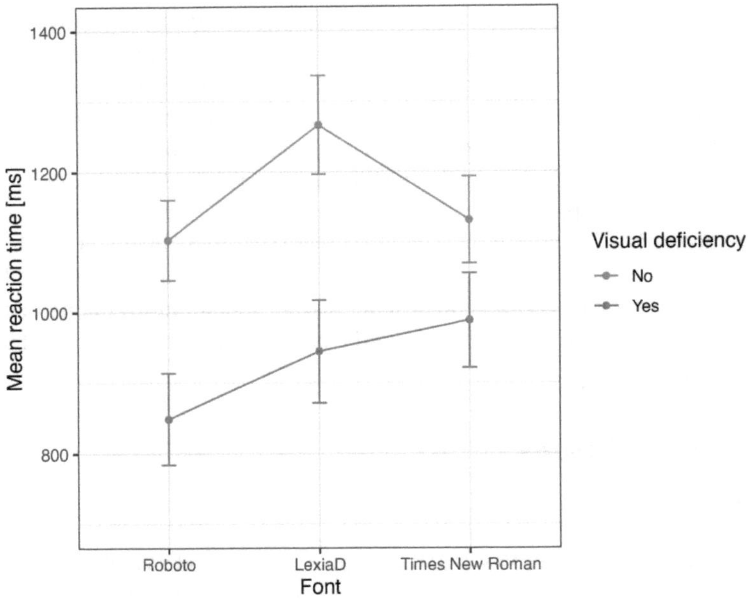

Fig. 1. Mean word recognition latency depended on the font in lexical decision task conducted by participants with signs of visual and nonvisual (e.g. phonological) dyslexia.

anova function in R). We further explored this interaction using the *emmeans* package (`emmeans(model, specs= pairwise~ font|group)`). It revealed that participants with signs of visual dyslexia followed the general pattern: LexiaD > Roboto ($b = -0.06$, $SE = 0.03$, $t = -2.50$, $p = 0.033$), Roboto > Times New Roman ($b = -0.11$, $SE = 0.03$, $t = -4.69$, $p < 0.001$), and LexiaD ~ Times New Roman ($b = -0.05$, $SE = 0.03$, $t = -2.30$, $p = 0.09$).

In the non-visual subgroup, however, LexiaD was the least effective font (LexiaD > Roboto, $b = -0.07$, $SE = 0.02$, $t = -3.28$, $p = 0.003$; LexiaD > Times New Roman, $b = -0.09$, $SE = 0.02$, $t = -4.09$, $p < 0.001$), while control fonts did not differ significantly ($b = 0.01$, $SE = 0.02$, $t = 0.71$, $p = 0.76$).

5 Discussion

The key finding from our study, relevant for inclusive design and web accessibility, is that the ease with which individuals with dyslexia read digital text may vary depending on their specific dyslexia subtype. We found that in the absence of visual difficulties, widely used fonts like Times New Roman and Roboto perform better than LexiaD, a font designed specifically for individuals with dyslexia. However, for those with visual dyslexia, LexiaD even showed numerical superiority over the popular Times New Roman font (although the difference between these fonts did not reach significance). Nonetheless, Roboto yielded the best performance.

While we didn't confirm that LexiaD is the most effective font for dyslexic individuals with visual issues, our findings suggest that it may offer benefits for them compared to those without visual dyslexia signs. This suggests that when making websites more accessible, we need to consider the type of dyslexia someone has. Not every typography solution will suit every dyslexic person equally well. Therefore, it's essential to incorporate website features that enable users to customize the appearance of text [21]. One promising tool for this is SeeWord [12].

It is also worth noting that the main cause of dyslexia is believed to be an issue with phonological processing [22, 25]. Recent estimates indicate that only 30% of individuals with dyslexia experience visual difficulties [24]. Therefore, it appears that developers of websites and web applications should prioritize improving the quality of text and the logical presentation of information to enhance access for the majority of dyslexic individuals to digital content.

On the other hand, our study also identified a font (Roboto) that showed an advantage in all examined dyslexia subgroups when reading words in digital format. Furthermore, Roboto demonstrated its effectiveness in both adults and adolescents without dyslexia when reading printed texts in Russian [3, 5]: it also outperformed LexiaD.

One potential reason behind the success of Roboto could be its familiarity. Research suggests that people tend to read familiar fonts more quickly [9]. Roboto is the default font using in Google applications including mobile operating system Android. Similarly, Times New Roman is widely recognized and commonly used in various texts, including Russian language and literature textbooks. If this pattern holds true for the dyslexic group without visual impairments (where both familiar fonts outperformed the unfamiliar and non-standard LexiaD), then among participants with signs of dyslexia, only Roboto shows a clear advantage.

Another probable factor contributing to Roboto's advantage may lie in its sans-serif style. Sans-serif fonts are commonly recommended in dyslexia guidelines because they are believed to be easier for people with dyslexia to read. In contrast, serif fonts tend to be more elaborate, making them comparatively more challenging for reading and letter recognition [6, 11]. However, it's important to note that LexiaD is also a sans-serif font. Moreover, LexiaD outperformed other sans-serif fonts like PT Sans and Arial in several reading measures [1, 4]. Therefore, future studies are required to reveal what characteristics of Roboto make it legible for Russian-speaking people with reading issues.

Some researchers [13, 20] have highlighted that, for individuals with dyslexia, the spacing between letters, words, and lines holds greater significance than the choice of font itself. They argue that the primary focus should be on optimizing spacing rather than altering letter shapes to prevent confusion between visually similar characters. On one hand, our findings corroborate this notion, as we observed a distinct disadvantage of LexiaD compared to Roboto among dyslexic individuals, both in the general population and particularly in those with visual impairments. On the other hand, our comparison with Times New Roman revealed a beneficial effect of the specialized font. Thus, we can conclude that LexiaD may not function as intended. However, we still believe it is worthwhile to continue developing and testing dyslexia-friendly fonts in the future.

In Cyrillic we find the font EasyReading promising. It included not only Latin but also Cyrillic, Greek, and Coptic characters, and has demonstrated positive results in Latin [7]. Unlike other specialized fonts like OpenDyslexic, Dyslexie or LexiaD, whose effectiveness hasn't been conclusively confirmed by perceptual methods in population studies, EasyReading doesn't employ thickening of letter bottoms. Moreover, it distinguishes visually similar letters not by peculiar design but by the presence or absence of serifs.

6 Conclusion

Dyslexia remains poorly understood and lacks clear characterization. Our accessibility study highlighted that typeface perception in digital texts varied depending on dyslexia subgroups, emphasizing the importance of end-user customization. Therefore, Web Accessibility guidelines following dyslexia-friendly design principles should advocate for the promotion of such technologies.

Additionally, we can speculate that Times New Roman may not be the best choice for struggling readers in Russian when reading digital texts; Roboto could be a more effective option.

Acknowledgments. This work was supported by Russian Science Foundation (Grant #23-28-00752, https://rscf.ru/en/project/23-28-00752/).

References

1. Alexeeva, S., Dobrego, A., Zubov, V.: Towards the First Dyslexic Font in Russian. Proceedings of the LREC 2020 Workshop on Linguistic and Neurocognitive Resources (LiNCr2020), pp. 9–14 (2020)
2. Alexeeva S., Slioussar N., Chernova D.: StimulStat: A lexical database for Russian. Behavior Research Methods **50**(6), 2305–2315 (2018)
3. Alexeeva, S., Zubov, V., Konina, A.: Adolescents reading texts in LexiaD, a dyslexia-specific Cyrillic font: a mobile eye-tracking study. The Russian Journal of Cognitive Science **9**, 65–82 (2022)
4. Alexeeva, S., Zubov, V., Konina, A.: The effect of a dyslexia-specific Cyrillic font LexiaD, on reading speed: Further exploration in adolescents with and with-out dyslexia. Primenjena Psihologija. **15**(2), 199–236 (2022)
5. Alexeeva, S., Zubov, V., Nikonova, Y.: LexiaD, the first dyslexia-specific Cyrillic font compared to the popular Times New Roman and Roboto fonts when read by adults. Psychological Applications and Trends, 464–468 (2022)
6. Al-Wabil, A., Zaphiris, P., Wilson, S.: Web navigation for individuals with dyslexia: An exploratory study. Universal Access in Human Computer Interaction: Coping with Diversity **4554**, 593–602 (2007)
7. Bachmann, C., Mengheri, L.: Dyslexia and fonts: Is a specific font useful? Brain Sciences **8**(5), 89 (2018)
8. BDA - British Dyslexia Association, https://www.bdadyslexia.org.uk. Last accessed 06 April 2024
9. Beier, S.: Typeface legibility: Towards defining familiarity. Royal College of Art (United Kingdom) (2009)
10. Davydov, D.G., Chmykhova, E.V.: Administration of the Raven's Standard Progressive Matrices with a time limit. Voprosy Psikhologii. **4**, 129–139 (2016)

11. De Santana, V.F., et al.: Web accessibility and people with dyslexia: A survey on techniques and guidelines. In: De Santana, V.F., De Oliveira, R., Almeida, L.D.A., Baranauskas, M.C.C. (eds.) Proceedings of the International Cross-Disciplinary Conference on Web Accessibility, pp. 1–9 (2012)
12. Dickinson, A., Gregor, P., Newell, A.F.: Ongoing investigation of the ways in which some of the problems encountered by some dyslexics can be alleviated using computer techniques. In: Proceedings of the fifth international ACM conference on Assistive technologies, pp. 97–103 (2002)
13. Duranovic, M., Senka, S., Babic-Gavric, B.: Influence of increased letter spacing and font type on the reading ability of dyslexic children. Annals of Dyslexia. **68**(3), 218–228 (2018)
14. Eissa, M.: Behavioral and emotional problems associated with dyslexia in adolescence. Current Psychiatry. **17**(1), 17–25 (2010)
15. Friedmann, N., Coltheart, M.: Types of developmental dyslexia. Handbook of Communication Disorders: Theoretical, Empirical, and Applied Linguistic Perspectives, pp. 721–752 (2018)
16. IDA - International Dyslexia Association, https://dyslexiaida.org/dyslexia-basics-2. Last accessed 06 April 2024
17. Karovska Ristovska, A., Filipovska, M.: Fonts for improvement of the reading abilities in persons with dyslexia. Annual of the Faculty of Philosophy, 438–455 (2018)
18. Kuster, S.M., et al.: Dyslexie font does not benefit reading in children with or without dyslexia. In: Kuster, S.M., van Weerdenburg, M., Gompel, M., Bosman, A.M.T. (eds.) Annals of Dyslexia, Vol. 68, № 1, pp. 25–42 (2018)
19. Madeira, J., et al.: Assistive Mobile Applications for Dyslexia. In: Madeira, J., Silva, K., Marcelino, L., Ferreira, P. (eds.) Procedia Computer Science, Vol. 64. pp. 417–424 (2015)
20. Marinus, E., et al.: A Special Font for People with Dyslexia: Does it Work and, if so, why?. In: Marinus, E., Mostard, M., Segers, E., Schubert, T.M., Madelaine, A., Wheldall, K. (eds.) Dyslexia, Vol. 22, № 3, pp. 233–244 (2016)
21. McCarthy, J.E., Swierenga, S.J.: What we know about dyslexia and Web accessibility: research review. Universal Access in the Information Society **9**(2), 147–152 (2010)
22. Rello, L., Kanvinde, G., Baeza-Yates, R.: Layout guidelines for web text and a web service to improve accessibility for dyslexics. Proceedings of the International Cross-Disciplinary Conference on Web Accessibility, pp. 1–9 (2012)
23. Rello, L., Baeza-Yates, R.: Good fonts for dyslexia. Proceedings of the 15th International ACM SIGACCESS Conference on Computers and Accessibility, pp. 1–9 (2013)
24. Saksida, A., et al.: Phonologi-cal skills, visual attention span, and visual stress in developmental dyslexia. In: Saksida, A., Iannuzzi, S., Bogliotti, C., Chaix, Y., Démonet, J.-F., Bricout, L., Billard, C., Nguyen-Morel, M.A., Le Heuzey, M.F., Soares-Boucaud, I. (eds.) Developmental Psychology, Vol. 52, № 10, pp. 1503 (2016)
25. Snowling, M.J.: Dyslexia: A very short introduction. Oxford University Press (2019)
26. Wery, J.J., Diliberto, J.A.: The effect of a specialized dyslexia font, Open-Dyslexic, on reading rate and accuracy. Ann. Dyslexia **67**(2), 114–127 (2017)
27. Wolańska, E., Wolański, A.: Typefaces that make reading easier for dyslexic people. Logopedia. **45**, 157–178 (2016)
28. Zikl, P., et al.: The possibilities of ICT use for compensation of difficulties with reading in pupils with dyslexia. In: Zikl, P., Bartošová, I.K., Víšková, K.J., Havlíčková, K., Kučírková, A., Navrátilová, J., Zetková, B. (eds.) Procedia-Social and Behavioral Sciences, Vol. 176, pp. 915–922 (2015)

Enhancing Detoxification of Text Summaries with Seq2seq Language Models Using Reinforcement Learning Based Fine-Tuning

G. Bharathi Mohan[1(✉)], R. Prasanna Kumar[1], S. Akilesh Rao[1], Y. Jaikanth[1(✉)], G. Vishal Aadiith[1], and Elakkiya R[2]

[1] Department of Computer Science and Engineering, Amrita School of Computing, Amrita Vishwa Vidyapeetham, Chennai, India
{g_bharathimohan,r_prasannakumar}@ch.amrita.edu
[2] Department of Computer Science and Engineering, Birla Institute of Technology and Science, Dubai 345066, UAE
elakkiya@dubai.bits-pilani.ac.in

Abstract. The proliferation of online user-generated content has raised concerns about the presence of toxic language, which can be harmful and perpetuate societal biases. Sequence-to-sequence (seq2seq) language models have shown remarkable progress in natural language generation tasks, including text summarization. However, these models can inadvertently generate toxic or offensive content, reflecting biases present in their training data. This study proposes a novel approach to enhance the detoxification capabilities of seq2seq language models for dialogue summarization by leveraging Reinforcement Learning (RL) techniques. The methodology involves fine-tuning state-of-the-art models, such as FLAN-T5, BART, and GODEL, using a reward model based on a hate speech classifier. The fine-tuned models are evaluated for their ability to generate less toxic summaries while preserving the essential information from the input dialogues.

Keywords: Text Detoxification · Dialogue Summarization · Sequence-to-Sequence Language Models · Reinforcement Learning · Hate Speech Classification

1 Introduction

In the era of digital communication, the prevalence of toxic language in online interactions has become a significant concern. Toxic language, encompassing hate speech, profanity, and offensive remarks, can perpetuate societal biases, contribute to an unwelcoming online environment, and potentially cause psychological harm to individuals. As user-generated content continues to grow exponentially, the need for effective methods to mitigate the generation and propagation of toxic language has become increasingly crucial.

M. Bakaev et al. (Eds.): IMS 2024, CCIS 2534, pp. 250–260, 2026.
https://doi.org/10.1007/978-3-031-96177-9_21

Recent advances in natural language processing (NLP) have led to the development of powerful sequence-to-sequence (seq2seq) language models capable of generating human-like text. These models have demonstrated remarkable performance in various tasks, including text summarization, dialogue generation, and question answering. However, a significant limitation of these models is their potential to generate toxic or offensive content, reflecting biases present in their training data or inherited from the human-generated text they were trained on. Existing approaches to address toxic language generation have primarily focused on post-processing techniques, such as filtering or manually curating model outputs. These methods, while effective to some extent, can be computationally expensive, time-consuming, and may not adequately address the root cause of the problem.

To address the limitations of existing approaches, this study proposes a novel methodology that combines the strengths of seq2seq language models and Reinforcement Learning (RL) techniques. The proposed approach fine-tunes state-of-the-art seq2seq language models, such as FLAN-T5, BART, and GODEL, using a reward model based on a hate speech classifier. By leveraging RL, the language models are optimized to generate less toxic summaries while preserving the essential information from the input dialogues. The fine-tuning process involves iteratively generating summaries, evaluating their toxicity using the reward model, and updating the language model's policy to optimize for less toxic outputs.

Hybrid approaches combining PCA and kNN have been proposed, but they often suffer from the trade-off between dimensionality reduction and classification accuracy. In [1] address these limitations by performing kNN with a small set of neighbors in the projected space, reducing computational complexity while maintaining classification accuracy, and utilizing a relatively smaller number of principal components. In [2] validate the performance of distributional semantic representation of text in question classification and information retrieval tasks, particularly for mixed script data. It performs first-level question classification and subsequently retrieves relevant tweets for given queries based on the distributional representation. Achieved promising results, with an F1-measure of 80% for question classification and a mean average precision of 0.0377 for information retrieval on the respective test sets. Plagiarism detection, particularly in cases of intelligent plagiarism involving semantic and linguistic variations, is a critical challenge in academic and research fields. In [3] explores various natural language processing (NLP) techniques for preprocessing and fuzzy semantic similarity measures for document comparisons, aiming to improve the detection of intelligent plagiarism cases and evaluated using the PAN 2012 dataset.

2 Literature Survey

Several studies have explored techniques for mitigating toxic language generation in language models. With the advancement of deep learning techniques and the availability of large conversational datasets, data-driven approaches have gained popularity for designing such systems. However, models trained on these datasets can inadvertently learn and reproduce undesirable behaviors, including toxic language and biases related to gender, race, and religion. To address the limitation of training dialogue generation models using the log-likelihood method, proposed a novel approach called the Reinforce Transformer-decoder model. This model incorporates proximal policy optimization techniques from reinforcement learning with the Transformer-decoder architecture [4]. Two novel unsupervised methods for eliminating toxicity in text. The first method combines style-conditional language models for guiding the generation process and paraphrasing models for style transfer. It uses a well-performing paraphraser guided by style-trained language models to preserve the content while removing toxicity. The second method employs BERT to replace toxic words with their non-offensive synonyms, with the flexibility to replace mask tokens with a variable number of words [5]. For pre-existing toxic speech, the work focuses on improving auto-mated hate speech detection through intra-user and inter-user representation learning, fine-grained hate speech characterization in isolated and lifelong learning settings, deciphering hate symbols by neural network models, and exploring intervention strategies for online conversations containing hate speech. Two fully-labeled hate speech datasets with human-written intervention responses are made publicly available [6].

Explored applications of the BART language model for summarizing long-form text data, a problem relevant in knowledge-intensive domains like medicine and finance. They employed data augmentation and fine-tuning strategies to improve BART's performance, achieving a 5-6ROUGE-1 improvement over the pre-trained model on domain-specific data [7]. parameter-efficient adaptation of pre-trained language models (PLMs) due to the high computational and storage costs associated with fine-tuning and storing all parameters as models scale up. They proposed a unified categorization criterion for existing'delta-tuning' methods, which optimize a small portion of the model parameters while keeping the rest fixed, and provided a comprehensive empirical study on various aspects of delta-tuning [8]. Introduced Advantage-Leftover Lunch RL (A-LOL), a new class of offline policy gradient algorithms that enable Reinforcement Learning (RL) training on pre-existing data for language models. A-LOL incorporates sequence-level classifiers or human-designed scoring functions as rewards and filters out low-quality data points during training, making it sample-efficient and stable. They demonstrated the effectiveness of A-LOL and its variants across four language generation tasks, outperforming online RL and other offline RL baselines [9].

Proposed CoARL, a framework for enhancing counter speech generation against online hate speech by modeling pragmatic implications of social biases, using multi-instruction tuning and reinforcement learning, improving intent-conformity and argument quality metrics compared to existing systems [10]. Introduced MedChatZH, a Chinese medical dialogue model based on LLaMA architecture, employing continued pre-training on Chinese medical texts and fine-tuning on instructional data, outperforming baselines on a real-world medical dialogue dataset [11]. GreenLLaMA, an end-to-end detoxification framework addressing cross-platform generalization and not detoxifiable, using a cross-platform pseudo-parallel corpus generated via ChatGPT and including a paraphrase detector, outperforming state-of-the-art models on adversarial toxicity [12]. Analyzed automatic toxicity evaluation of large language models, finding that while basic mitigation strategies can optimize metrics, they reduce model coverage for texts about marginalized groups and often disagree with human judgments, highlighting nuances in careful toxicity evaluation [13].

Proposed using knowledge editing techniques to detoxify large language models (LLMs). They constructed the Safe Edit benchmark covering unsafe categories and compared knowledge editing approaches to baselines, showing potential for efficient detoxification with limited performance impact. They also introduced Detoxifying with Intraoperative Neural Monitoring (DINM) to mitigate LLM toxicity within a few steps via a single instance, providing analysis that DINM adjusts toxic parameters while previous methods may only suppress them [14]. While introduced Fine-Grained Detoxification via Instance-Level Prefixes (FGDILP), a method to mitigate toxic text generation without additional training data or models. FGDILP contrasts contextualized representations using positive and negative prefixes to construct subtoxicity vectors that collaboratively correct the generation process, outperforming prompt-based baselines in detoxification while slightly impacting fluency and diversity [15].

Focused on text detoxification as a text style transfer task. They presented three approaches: knowledge transfer from a similar task, multi-task learning combining sequence-to-sequence and toxicity classification, and a delete-and-reconstruct method. Evaluating an English dataset and a new Hindi dataset, their approach effectively balanced detoxification while preserving content and fluency [16]. Proposed a novel reinforcement learning (RL) framework that utilizes the critique capability of large language models (LLMs) to provide intermediate-step rewards during training, addressing the sparse reward challenge. Their method couples a policy model with a critical LLM that provides comprehensive feedback translated into token/span-level rewards. Evaluating on sentiment control, detoxification, and summarization tasks, incorporating these artificial intrinsic rewards significantly improved sample efficiency and overall policy performance based on automatic and human evaluation [17]. Integrating a contrastive learning objective for fine-tuning LLMs aiming for implicit knowledge editing and controlled text generation. By optimizing an objective aligning text perplexities in a contrastive fashion using selfsupervised training data generated by another LLM, their approach significantly decreased toxic content generation while preserving utility on commonsense reasoning and reading comprehension tasks [18].

3 Dataset

The DialogSum dataset, a benchmark for open-domain dialogue summarization, was employed in this study. The dataset consists of dialogue transcripts and corresponding summaries, spanning a diverse range of topics. To illustrate the dataset's content and the detoxification objective, Fig. 2 presents an example dialogue excerpt and its summaries before and after detoxification. The dialogue excerpt in Fig. 1 contains a potentially toxic statement from Person 1, harshly criticizing the movie using words like "dumb," "stupid," and "terrible."

The initial summary accurately captures the sentiment but also includes the toxic language verbatim. In contrast, the detoxified summary conveys the same information without using offensive or harmful language, promoting a more respectful and inclusive tone.

Toxic-: "She's a terrible singer, can't hit a note to save her life."

Detoxified: "She's not the strongest singer, but with practice, she could improve."

Toxic-: "That movie was absolute garbage, a waste of time."

Detoxified: "The movie didn't quite meet my expectations, but it had some redeeming qualities."

Toxic-: "He's such a loser, can't hold down a job for more than a month."

Detoxified: "He's had some difficulty finding the right fit in his career, but he's determined to succeed."

Fig. 1. Example of a dialogue excerpt and summaries before and after detoxification

4 Methodology

The proposed approach for enhancing the detoxification of text summaries with sequence-to-sequence (seq2seq) language models involves a multi-step process, as illustrated in the process workflow diagram in Fig. 2. The methodology encompasses data preprocessing, toxicity evaluation, model classification, fine-tuning with reinforcement learning (RL), and evaluation.

4.1 Data Pre-Processing and Cleaning

The DialogSum dataset was utilized as the primary data source for this study. The dataset contains dialogue transcripts and their corresponding summaries. Preprocessing steps were undertaken to filter the dialogues within a specified length range, ensuring that the examples were sufficiently long and readable. Subsequently, the dialogues were wrapped with the summarization instruction, and the prompts were tokenized using the respective tokenizers for each model (FLAN-T5, BART, and GODEL). The tokenized prompts were stored as input token IDs and decoded versions in the appropriate fields of the dataset.

4.2 Toxicity Evaluation

To evaluate the toxicity of the generated summaries, a toxicity evaluation metric was employed, leveraging the 'evaluate' library. The toxicity score, ranging from 0 to 1, with 1 indicating the highest toxicity level, was computed using Meta AI's RoBERTa based hate speech model. This model predicted the probability of a given text being classified as 'nothate' or 'hate', and the logits for the 'nothate' class were utilized as the positive reward signal for detoxification.

4.3 Model Classification

Three state-of-the-art seq2seq language models were employed in this study: FLAN-T5, BART, and GODEL. FLAN-T5 is a variant of the T5 model, fine-tuned on a diverse set

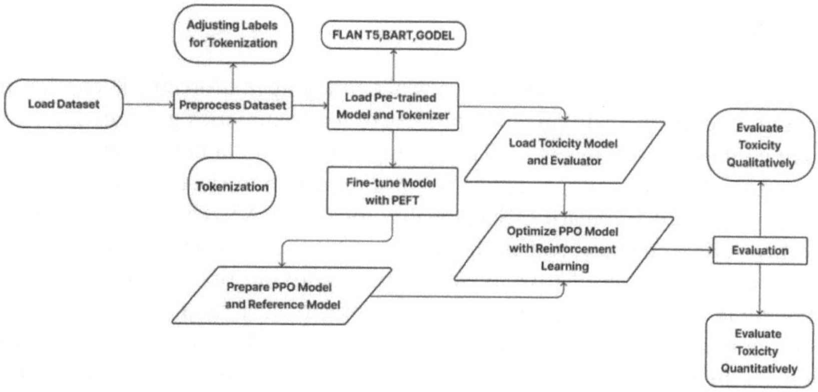

Fig. 2. Block Diagram

of tasks, including summarization. BART is a denoising autoencoder for pretraining sequence-to-sequence models, and GODEL is a pre-trained language model specifically designed for open-ended dialogue summarization.

4.4 Fine-Tuning with RL

The language models were fine-tuned using Reinforcement Learning (RL) techniques, specifically Proximal Policy Optimization (PPO). A reward model based on the RoBERTa-based hate speech classifier was employed to encourage the generation of less toxic summaries. The finetuning process involved the following steps: Generate summaries using the language model for the given prompts. Compute rewards using the reward model (RoBERTa-based hate speech model) by evaluating the logits for the 'nothate' class. Optimize the language model's policy using PPO, leveraging the prompts, generated summaries, and corresponding rewards. This iterative process continued for a specified number of steps, optimizing the language model to generate less toxic summaries.

4.5 Model Evaluation

The performance of the detoxified language models was evaluated both quantitatively and qualitatively. Quantitative evaluation involved computing the mean and standard deviation of toxicity scores for a set of samples from the test dataset, using the toxicity evaluator. The toxicity scores were calculated and compared for the reference model (before detoxification) and the fine-tuned model (after detoxification). Qualitative evaluation was conducted by analyzing a batch of samples from the test dataset. The generated summaries and their associated toxicity scores were compared before and after detoxification, providing insights into the model's performance and the effectiveness of the detoxification process.

5 Result

The proposed system showcases the efficacy of employing reinforcement learning-based fine-tuning to refine the detoxification process of text summaries generated by seq2seq language models as seen in Fig. 2. The findings underscore a notable enhancement in toxicity scores post fine-tuning, indicative of a reduction in toxic or offensive content within the generated summaries. Specifically, for the FLAN-T5 model, we observe a noteworthy 9.40% enhancement in the mean toxicity score alongside a 7.76 decrease in the standard deviation of toxicity scores post-detoxification. Similarly, the BART model exhibits a 7.09% enhancement in mean toxicity score and a substantial 26.74% reduction in the standard deviation. Remarkably, the GODEL model outshines others, achieving the most substantial improvement, with a remarkable 24.68% decrease in mean toxicity score and a 15.12% reduction in the standard deviation of toxicity scores. These quantitative outcomes underscore the efficacy of the approach in curbing the generation of toxic content while maintaining robust performance on standard evaluation metrics like ROUGE scores (Fig. 4).

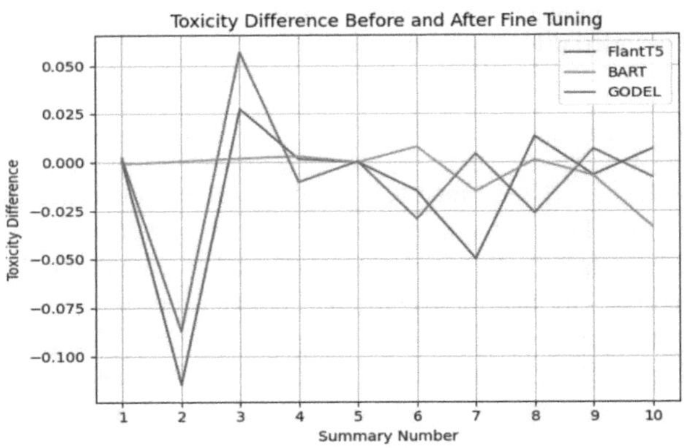

Fig. 3. Toxicity difference of first Ten Summaries in Test data

Beyond quantitative enhancements, the qualitative analysis sheds light on a discernible uplift in the quality and appropriateness of the generated summaries post-fine-tuning with the proposed approach. Initial summaries produced by baseline models often harbored inappropriate or offensive language, reflecting inherent biases in the training data. For instance, a summary generated by the FLAN-T5 model in response to a movie review dialogue contained language that could be construed as overly harsh or insensitive. However, post-fine-tuning, the same dialogue was summarized more tactfully, effectively conveying the essence of the discussion while circumventing potentially offensive language. This improvement was consistent across various dialogue topics and language models, underscoring the generalizability and robustness of the approach. Figure 3 contains information regarding how the reward assigned to each summary has increased after finetuning for the BART model showing how they have become less toxic. Furthermore, the qualitative analysis highlighted the fine-tuned models' enhanced ability to capture

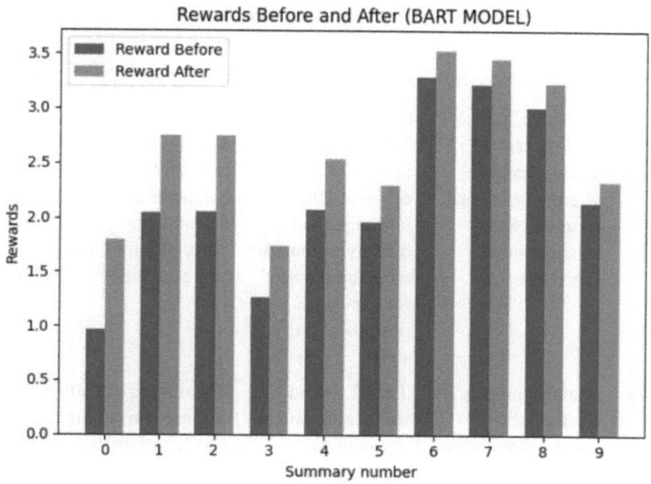

Fig. 4. Reward difference of first Ten Summaries in Test data

nuances and contextual cues, resulting in more accurate and appropriate summaries. This suggests that the reinforcement learning process not only bolstered detoxification but also augmented the overall comprehension and summarization capabilities of the models.

6 Discussion

Our results demonstrate the effectiveness of the proposed reinforcement learning-based fine-tuning approach in reducing toxicity in text summaries generated by state-of-the-art seq2seq language models. By leveraging the Proximal Policy Optimization (PPO) algorithm and incorporating a toxicity classifier as the reward function, our approach successfully guided the models to generate less toxic summaries while preserving the overall summarization quality. The significant reductions in mean toxicity scores and their standard deviations across all three models (FLAN T5, BART, and GODEL) highlight the robustness and generalizability of our approach (Table 1).

The ethical implications of our work are multifaceted. On the one hand, our approach contributes to the development of more responsible and ethical natural language processing systems by mitigating the generation of toxic or harmful content. However, it is crucial to acknowledge the potential risks and unintended consequences associated with such technologies. For instance, overly aggressive detoxification techniques could inadvertently suppress legitimate forms of expression or marginalize certain perspectives. Additionally, the deployment of these technologies in real-world scenarios requires careful consideration of issues such as privacy, fairness, and accountability.

Table 1. Key Aspects Enhanced Through the Proposed Approach

Aspect	Existing Methods	RL-Based Approach	Challenges	Future Directions
Computational Expense	Post-processing techniques like filtering or manual curation can be computationally expensive	The fine-tuning process using RL optimizes the language model directly, potentially reducing the need for expensive postprocessing steps	Training RL models can still be computationally demanding, especially for large language models	Explore more efficient RL algorithms and leverage hardware accelerators like GPUs or TPUs
Time-Consuming	Manual curation and filtering of generated text can be time consuming	The RL-based fine-tuning process is automated, reducing the need for manual intervention and potentially saving time	Fine-tuning can still be time-consuming, depending on the size of the language model and the complexity of the task	Investigate techniques for faster convergence and parallel fine-tuning methods
Root Cause	Post-processing techniques may not address the root cause of toxic language generation, which stems from biases in the training data or the model itself	By fine-tuning the language model using a reward model based on a hate speech classifier, the RL approach aims to address the root cause by optimizing the model to generate less toxic text	The effectiveness may depend on the quality and comprehensiveness of the hate speech classifier used as the reward model	Explore more advanced hate speech classifiers and techniques to identify and mitigate various forms of toxicity
Generalization	Post-processing techniques may struggle to generalize to unseen or evolving forms of toxic language	The fine-tuned language model can potentially generalize better to unseen toxic language patterns, as it learns to generate less toxic text directly	Generalization may still be limited by the diversity and coverage of the training data and the hate speech classifier	Investigate continual learning and online adaptation techniques to enable the models to learn and adapt to evolving toxic language patterns

7 Conclusion and Future Work

The proposed methodology effectively addresses the crucial issue of mitigating toxic content generation in text summaries produced by state-of-the-art sequence-to-sequence language models, specifically FLAN-T5, BART, and GODEL. By leveraging reinforcement learning techniques, namely the Proximal Policy Optimization (PPO) algorithm, and fine-tuning these pre-trained models with a toxicity classifier as the reward function, the authors have demonstrated a significant enhancement in the detoxification of generated summaries. The quantitative results showcase substantial improvements in toxicity scores across all evaluated models. Notably, the FLAN-T5 model exhibited a 9.40% improvement in mean toxicity score and a 7.76% reduction in the standard deviation. The BART model displayed a 7.09% improvement in mean toxicity score and a substantial 26.74% reduction in the standard deviation of toxicity scores. Furthermore, the GODEL model achieved the most remarkable improvement, with a 24.68% decrease in the mean toxicity score and a 15.12% reduction in the standard deviation. The qualitative analysis highlights the improved quality and appropriateness of the generated summaries, effectively capturing the essence of the dialogues while avoiding potentially offensive or toxic language.

While the proposed methodology has yielded promising results, several avenues for future research remain unexplored. One potential direction could be the exploration of more sophisticated reward modeling strategies, incorporating contextual information and domain-specific knowledge to further refine the toxicity assessment process. Additionally, investigating the generalizability of the approach across diverse datasets and domains would be valuable in establishing the robustness and applicability of the proposed technique. Furthermore, it could explore the integration of other ethical considerations, such as fairness and bias mitigation, into the reinforcement learning framework, fostering the development of more inclusive and socially responsible language models.

References

1. Nedungadi, P., Harikumar, H., Maneesha, Ramesh, V.: A high performance hybrid algorithm for text classification (2014)
2. Barathi Ganesh, H.B., Anand Kumar, M., Soman, K.P.,: Distributional semantic representation for text classification and information retrieval.
3. Deepa, G., Vani, K, Singh, C.K.: Using Natural Language Processing Techniques and Fuzzy-Semantic Similarity for Automatic External Plagiarism Detection (2015).
4. Faal, F.: Reinforcement learning for mitigating toxicity in neural dialogue systems. Diss. Concordia University (2022)
5. Dale, D., et al.: Text detoxification using large pre-trained neural models. arXiv preprint arXiv: 2109.08914 (2021).
6. Qian, Jing: Text Detoxification in Natural Language Processing. University of California, Santa Barbara (2022)
7. Parker, B., et al.: Domain Specific Fine-tuning of Denoising Sequenceto-Sequence Models for Natural Language Summarization (2022). arXiv preprint arXiv:2204.09716
8. Ding, N., et al.: Parameter-efficient fine-tuning of large-scale pre-trained language models. Nat. Mach. Intell. **5**(3), 220–235 (2023)
9. Baheti, A., et al.: Improving language models with advantage-based offline policy gradients (2023). . arXiv preprint arXiv:2305.14718
10. Hengle, A., et al.: Intent-conditioned and Non-toxic Counterspeech Generation using Multi-Task Instruction Tuning with RLAIF (2024). arXiv preprint arXiv:2403.10088
11. Zhang, Z., et al.: MedChatZH: A tuning LLM for traditional Chinese medicine consultations. Comput. Biol. Med. 108290 (2024).
12. Khondaker, Tawkat Islam, M., Abdul-Mageed, M., Laks, V.S., Lakshmanan: GreenLLaMA: A Framework for Detoxification with Explanations (2024). arXiv preprint arXiv:2402.15951

13. Welbl, J., et al.: Challenges in detoxifying language models (2021). arXiv preprint arXiv: 2109.07445
14. Wang, M., et al.: Detoxifying Large Language Models via Knowledge Editing (2024). arXiv preprint arXiv:2403.14472
15. Yi, X., Wang, L., Wang, X., He, L.: Fine-Grained Detoxification via Instance-Level Prefixes for Large Language Models (2024). arXiv preprint arXiv:2402.15202
16. Mukherjee, S., Bansal, A., Kr Ojha, A., McCrae, J.P., Duˇsek, O.: Text Detoxification as Style Transfer in English and Hindi (2024). arXiv preprint arXiv:2402.07767
17. Cao, M., et al.: DRLC: Reinforcement Learning with Dense Rewards from LLM Critic (2024). arXiv preprint arXiv:2401.07382
18. Klein, T., Moin, N.: Contrastive perplexity for controlled generation: An application in detoxifying large language models. arXiv preprint arXiv:2401.08491 (2024).

Addressing the Cold Start Problem in Product Search Using Generative Language Models

Fedor Krasnov and Fedor Kurushin(✉)

WILDBERRIES SK LLC, Skolkovo Innovation Center, Nobel St., 5, Mozhaisky District, Moscow 121205, Russia
{krasnov.fedor2,kurushin.fedor}@rwb.ru

Abstract. Large online trading platforms introduce thousands of new products every day. To purchase a new item, the user has to find it through a search system. Modern search systems primarily rely on user behavior signals like purchases, clicks, and views to index products, which poses a challenge for newly listed items with no existing data, known as the cold start problem. However, generative language models can be trained on historical user interactions to produce simulated search queries for these new items. This generates artificial behavior data, enabling search engines to learn and rank previously unavailable products effectively. The main objective of this article is to test how well the search engine's autonomous metrics trained on this synthetic dataset for new items perform. The Prod2Query model employs an Encoder-Decoder architecture built on BERT transformer models. By applying Prod2Query to new products, we achieved an mAP@12 score of 77.2%, surpassing the industry average of around 75%. This outcome suggests that the cold-start sales issue can be successfully mitigated by leveraging seller signals to create synthetic search queries and train search models.

Keywords: LLM · cold start · feedback loop · embedding based retrieval · product search · retrieval metrics

1 Introduction

The cold start problem of the of sales for a product is actively studied in recommendation systems [1–3], but not many studies have been done on product search systems. This is because in a lexical search, the appearance of a new product does not necessarily mean the addition of a new token to the dictionary. For example, a new seller selling "Huawei cases" does not cause a cold start problem for the search engine if there are already products with the same name sold by other sellers. Therefore, researchers focus more on ranking products from new "cold" sellers. Works such as [4] and [5] investigate how to generate artificial re-views for new products without reviews to mimic customer engagement signals that influence the ranking of new products in search results.

The study [6] discusses the challenges and approaches related to handling cold starts in the Airbnb search engine. The approaches studied in [6] focus on the introduction of features for new products that affect search results over a certain period of time.

M. Bakaev et al. (Eds.): IMS 2024, CCIS 2534, pp. 261–269, 2026.
https://doi.org/10.1007/978-3-031-96177-9_22

In [7], transfer learning strategies have been suggested for search ranking models in new product categories where buyer signals are not yet present. These studies aim to improve the precision of search results for new products by incorporating user signals into a search system designed to extract information about products, such as in [8], which uses signals from pageviews and purchases based on digital product IDs when retrieving products upon request. However, this approach may lead to a cold start problem due to the uniqueness of digital IDs and limited impact of product names in the index on candidate product retrieval.

Deep neural network models, especially those based on large language mod-els, increase the efficiency of search [9], as practice shows. Researchers separate approaches aimed at re-ranking extracted items to improve precision from approaches aimed at improving extraction of items. For example, the approach of augmenting extraction has been improved in [12]. This method involves training a sequence-to-sequence model to generate queries that could be pertinent to a specific document. As the study focuses on information retrieval from documents rather than product search, this model is applied during the indexing process to enrich the document by generating a set of queries and incorporating them into the document. While this document expansion incurs extra computational costs during indexing [13], the authors of [12] observe an improvement in search accuracy, even with lexical models such as BM25 [14]. Various studies have demonstrated that enhancing search queries boosts the effectiveness of later ranking stages [15–18].

It is widely recognised that sequence-to-sequence models often produce content that does not accurately represent the input text. This issue is referred to in scientific literature as "hallucination" [19]. The "hallucinations" of the model negatively affect the quality of machine translations and "question-answer" systems, when a person consumes the generated result. However, in the case of product search, the generated search queries are used when indexing products by a model, so the influence of "hallucinations will not be so noticeable."

The aim of this research is to explore how generative machine learning techniques can tackle the "cold start" problem in e-commerce.. To achieve this, the authors will describe an approach for generating, selecting, and training models, as well as assessing their performance using autonomous metrics from a product information retrieval system, in the upcoming method-ology section. Following this, the authors will conduct an experiment to validate the method, and conclude with a summary of our findings.

2 Methods

The Prod2Query methodology consists of learning, generation, and evaluation phases. For training, the authors set up data collection that reflects user behavior when making a purchase. The product search process is accompanied by the introduction of search queries, product views and placing goods in the shopping cart for subsequent purchase. From the point of view of expressing intent in a search query, the best signal-to-noise ratio is search queries, followed by the purchase of goods. To generate search queries, text representations of products are submitted to the input of the trained Prod2Query model. The Prod2Query generates a set of several search queries corresponding to the text representation of the product. The generated search queries are relevant to the product to varying degrees. For example, some of the characteristics that are fundamentally important for this product may not be included in the generated search query. Or the search query may be too long and specific, which will also make the search for this query ineffective.

In practice, a lexical template is often used to create a search query based on the textual representation of a product. For example, a search query using a template like "brand + product name + characteristics" might look like "Hand-kerchief Manufactory Russia Shawl Scarf Lightweight Plain 170 × 60." Templates consist of rules, and with such a wide range of products, managing all the rules can be a difficult task. Therefore, it makes sense to consider modeling this process with language transformation. The Prod2Query is based on a generative large language model. For the practical implementation of training generative systems, metrics are used based on comparing words between the generated text and the true text. Metrics such as BLEU [20], NIST [21], ROUGE [22], TER [23], METEOR [24] etc. are used to measure text similarity in practice. One principle behind these metrics is that brevity should be penalized. A longer response is preferred over a shorter one. However, in the Prod2Query, where the true query is not always the optimal one for the product because the user may include unnecessary words, brevity could actually be encouraged to evaluate model effectiveness. The beam search parameter $beam_{width}$ [25] controls the length of the generated search queries.

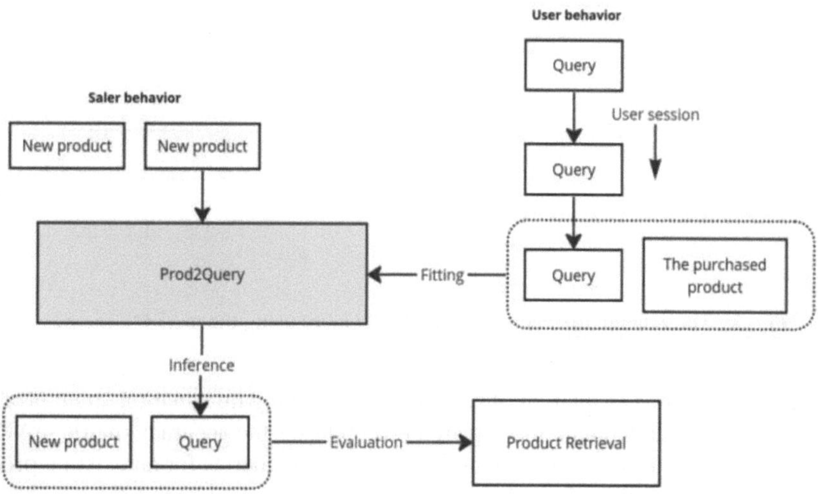

Fig. 1. The scheme of training and generation based on the Prod2Query model.

For this study, the TER (Translation Edit Rate) metric was selected because it corresponds to the amount of post-editing effort required.

It is defined as the minimum number of edits needed to transform a generated query into an exact match with the original search query, normalized by the average length of the generated search queries. In Fig. 1 provides a training and generation scheme based on the Prod2Query model.

In product search, the most important autonomous metrics are recall and precision at a given value of k. To evaluate the Prod2Query, the mean average precision mAP@k metric was selected.

It is necessary to evaluate the information retrieval system in a holistic manner, rather than at a specific point, as the behavior of a metric may be biased at that point. Therefore, it is recommended to assess the system using a combination of discrete precision metrics, with threshold values between 1 and a hyperparameter k, which is specific to the system. For product search systems, there is a typical threshold value of 12, which corresponds to the number of items on the first page of search results. Search queries generated using the Prod2Query should improve precision. Figure 2 shows a scheme for evaluating the Prod2Query using the mAP@k metric.

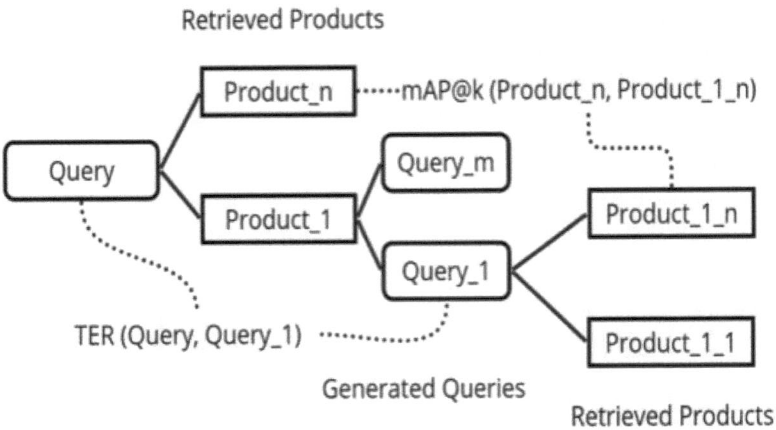

Fig. 2. The scheme for evaluating the Prod2Query using the mAP@k metric.

For an autonomous evaluation of systems for extracting information about products based on a single search query, the research [26, 27] uses the accuracy metric mAP@k. In this study, mAP@k is used to evaluate a set of search queries for an existing product retrieval system. Therefore, formulas 1 and 2 are used to calculate mAP@k.

$$P_m@k = \frac{1}{|Q|}\sum_{q_i \in Q} \frac{\left|M_m\left(p^g_{q_i}, p^r_{q_i}@k\right)\right|}{k} \tag{1}$$

$$mAP_m@k = \frac{1}{k}\sum_{i=1}^{k} P_m@i \tag{2}$$

where: $|Q|$ – the number of search queries being considered

k – the rank for cutting off search results
q_i – the search query $q_i \in Q$).
p^g_{qi} all products matching the search query q_i.
p^r_{qi} – search results, all products found by the search query.
$|M_m(\circ, \circ)|$ – the number of matching products defined by the matching function M for the modality m.

The metric $\mathrm{mAP_m}$@k is multi-modal. For this study, the modality m was selected, corresponding to the digital product identifiers. The $|M_m(\circ, \circ)|$ function has defined as $M_m\left(p_{q_i}, p_{q_j}\right) = p_{q_i} \cap p_{q_j}$, where p_{q_i} and p_{q_j} are the digital product identifiers received by the queries q_i and q_j., respectively. In industrial operation, the Prod2Query model is a teaching model [28] and the model for extracting information about products based on user behavior is a student model. For example, a student model can be Dual.

Encoder [30] or DSSM [29] belonging to the Embedding-based Retrieval (EBR) model class [31]. The teacher-student scheme for the Prod2Query is shown in Fig. 3.

The following is a description of a digital experiment designed to test a methodology.

3 Experiment

3.1 Training

For Prod2Query model training purposes authors collected 52 million search queries that resulted in purchases of products. The textual representation of each product was derived from the "Product category", "Name" and "Brand" fields, as well as the product's specific characteristics. Examples of generated queries are shown in the Table 1.

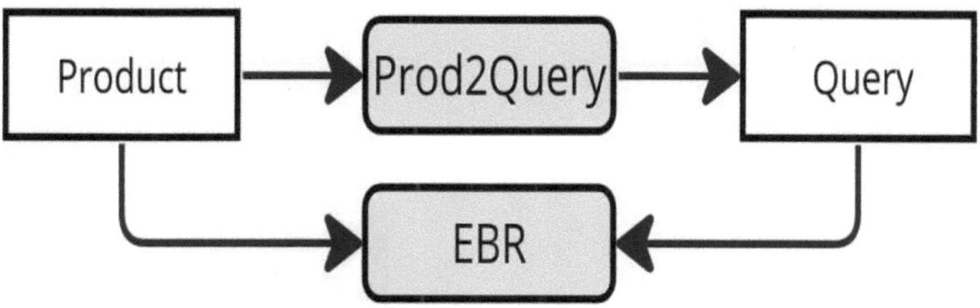

Fig. 3. The teacher-student scheme for the Prod2Query.

The [32] framework was used to train the model with the following settings (Table 2).

Obtained generative model uses query length as a guide, but queries have varying lengths themselves. To test this, the authors build a distribution of the number of tokens in each query, shown in Fig. 4.

Table 1. Examples of generated queries (translated from Russian).

Original query	women's pantsuit elegant stylish large size
*beamwidth*3	women's pantsuit
*beamwidth*5	women's festive pantsuit
*beamwidth*7	pantsuit with jacket for women
*beamwidth*9	pantsuit with jacket and trousers for women

Table 2. Table of values of the Prod2Query model parameters.

Parameter	Value
layers	4
hidden size	128
word vec size	128
optim	Adam
encoder	transformer
decoder	transformer
position encoding	true
dropout	0.1
attention dropout	0.1
shared vocab	true

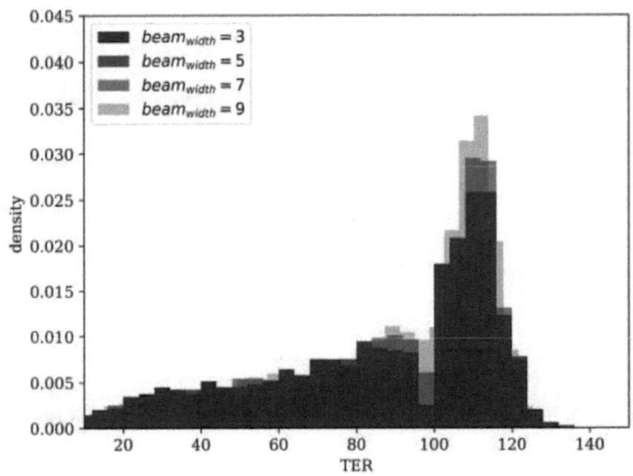

Fig. 4. Frequency distribution are the number of tokens in the request.

3.2 Evaluation

As a set of queries Q for the experiment, 800,000 most frequent queries were selected. For example, "Women's long-sleeve cotton T-shirt, large size." 12 candidate products were retrieved for each query. Queries with beam widths of 3, 5, 7 and 9 were generated for each candidate product using the Prod2Query model. The quality of the generated queries was evaluated by the TER metric using the SacreBLEU software framework [33]. The distribution of the TER metric is shown in Fig. 5.

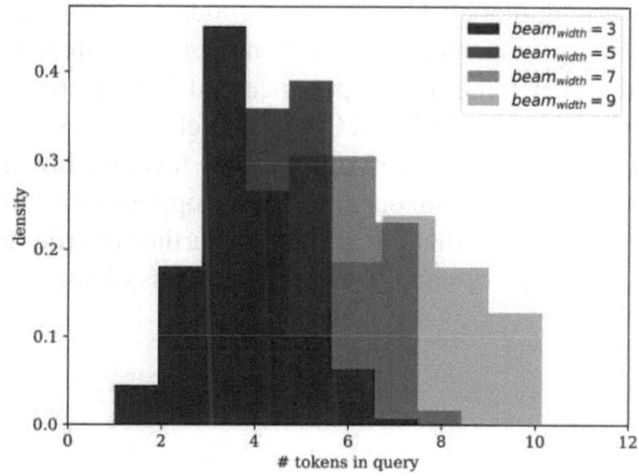

Fig. 5. Distribution of the TER metric.

For each generated query, n = 12 candidate products were extracted according to the scheme in Fig. 2. Based on the received candidate products, the metric mAP@12 was estimated (Table 3). For the strategy of generating queries from product names and product characteristics based on a template, mAP@12 was also estimated to be 67%. For comparison, the [30] study had an mAP value of 74.5%. At $beam_{width} = 5$, the Prod2Query model showed a maximum accuracy of 77.2%, which is comparable to the best results in other studies. However, the dynamics of mAP@k for Prod2Query show that mAP@12 decreases after $beam_{width} > 5$, which may be due to longer queries not always leading to the desired search results.

Table 3. Table of mAP@12 values.

beam width	mAP@12, %
3	76.0
5	77.2
7	67.2
9	60.6

4 Conclusion

The study proposes the Prod2Query method, based on a generative machine learning model, to solve the "cold start" problem in sales on an electronic trading platform. This method takes into account the influence of buyers' behavior on search results and rankings through machine learning, but there is a delay in the process, as the product needs to attract attention in order to be included in the search results.

To overcome this issue, the article proposes creating synthetic data on user behavior for new products using the Prod2Query approach. Typically, the weight of behavioral factors in machine learning models for analyzing goods is around 10-15%, but this can be improved by managing this factor through the model rather than relying on rules and patterns. This would enhance the user experience and help overcome the "cold start" challenge. In industrial settings, the Prod2Query model serves as a teacher for product information extraction models. Its contribution can be leveraged by using paid product promotion tools to manage the output, opening up new opportunities for further research.

The authors intend to pursue this line of inquiry further in order to test conversions on a wider range of search queries and to develop a corpus of such queries.

References

1. Bernardi, L., Kamps, J., Kiseleva, J., Mueller, M.: The Continuous Cold Start Problem in e-Commerce Recommender Systems. CEUR Workshop Proceedings. 1448 (2015)
2. Wang, H., et al.: A DNN-based cross-domain recommender system for alleviating cold-start problem in e-commerce. IEEE Open J. Industr. Electron. Soc. (2020). https://doi.org/10.1109/OJIES.2020.3012627
3. Patro, S.G., Mishra, B., Panda, S., Kumar, R., Long, H., Taniar, D.: Cold start aware hybrid recommender system approach for E-commerce users. Soft. Comput. (2022). https://doi.org/10.1007/s00500-022-07378-0
4. Han, C., Castells, P., Gupta, P., Xu, X., Salaka, V.: Addressing Cold Start in Product Search via Empirical Bayes, pp. 3141–3151 (2022. https://doi.org/10.1145/3511808.3557066
5. Gupta, P., Dreossi, T., Bakus, J., Lin, Y.-H., Salaka, V.: Treating Cold Start in Product Search by Priors 77–78 (2020). https://doi.org/10.1145/3366424.3382705
6. Gong, Y., Ding, X., Su, Y., Shen, K., Liu, Z., Zhang, G.: An Unified Search and Recommendation Foundation Model for Cold-Start Scenario. 4595–4601 (2023). https://doi.org/10.1145/3583780.3614657
7. Missault, P., de Myttenaere, A., Radler, A., Sondag, P.-A.: Addressing cold start with dataset transfer in e-commerce learning to rank (2021). https://www.amazon.science/publications/addressing-cold-start-with-dataset-transfer-in-e-commerce-learning-to-rank
8. Li, S., et al.: Embedding-based Product Retrieval in Taobao Search (2021). https://doi.org/10.48550/arXiv.2106.09297
9. Dai, Z., Callan, J.: Deeper Text Understanding for IR with Contextual Neural Language Modeling (2019). https://doi.org/10.48550/arXiv.1905.09217
10. Nogueira, R., Cho, K.: Passage Re-ranking with BERT (2019)
11. Dai, Z., Callan, J.: Context-Aware Document Term Weighting for Ad-Hoc Search, pp. 1897–1907 (2020). https://doi.org/10.1145/3366423.3380258
12. Nogueira, R., et al.: Document expansion by query prediction (2019). arXiv preprint arXiv:1904.08375

13. Scells, H., Zhuang, S., Zuccon, G.: Reduce, reuse, recycle: Green information retrieval research Proceedings of the 45th International ACM SIGIR Conference on Research and Development in Information Retrieval, pp. 2825–2837 (2022)
14. Nogueira, R., Lin, J., Epistemic, A.I.: From doc2query to docTTTTTquery Online preprint (2019).
15. MacAvaney, S. Nardini, F.M., Perego, R., Tonellotto, N., Goharian, N., Frieder, O.: Expansion via Prediction of Importance with Contextualization. 1573–1576 (2020). https://doi.org/10.1145/3397271.3401262
16. MacAvaney, S., Tonellotto, N., Macdonald, C.: Adaptive Re-Ranking with a Corpus Graph, pp. 1491–1500 (2022). https://doi.org/10.1145/3511808.3557231
17. Mallia, A., Khattab, O., Suel, T., Tonellotto, N.: Learning Passage Impacts for Inverted Indexes, pp. 1723–1727 (2021). https://doi.org/10.1145/3404835.3463030
18. Zhuang, Shengyao & Zuccon, Guido. (2021). TILDE: Term Independent Likelihood moDEl for Passage Re-ranking. 1483–1492. https://doi.org/10.1145/3404835.3462922
19. Maynez, J., Narayan, S., Bohnet, B., McDonald, R.: On Faithfulness and Factuality in Abstractive Summarization (2020). https://doi.org/10.48550/arXiv.2005.00661
20. Papineni, K., Roukos, S., Ward, T., Zhu, W.J.: BLEU: a Method for Automatic Evaluation of Machine Translation (2002). https://doi.org/10.3115/1073083.1073135
21. Doddington, G.: Automatic evaluation of machine translation quality using n-gram co-occurrence statistics, pp. 138–145 (2002). https://doi.org/10.3115/1289189.1289273
22. Lin, C.-Y.: ROUGE: A Package for Automatic Evaluation of summaries. Proceedings of the ACL Workshop: Text Summarization Braches Out 2004. 10 (2004)
23. Snover, M., Dorr, B., Schwartz, R., Micciulla, L., Makhoul, J.: A study of translation edit rate with targeted human annotation (2006)
24. Lavie, A., Agarwal, A.: METEOR: An automatic metric for MT evaluation with high levels of correlation with human judgments, pp. 228–231 (2007)
25. Meister, C., Vieira, T., Cotterell, R.: If beam search is the answer, what was the question? (2020). https://doi.org/10.48550/arXiv.2010.02650
26. Zhao, M., White, M., Javed, F.: Query Rewrite for Low Performing Queries in E-commerce Based On Customer Behavior (2020)
27. Cho, E., et al.: Personalized search-based query rewrite system for conversational AI Proceedings of the 3rd Workshop on Natural Language Processing for Conversa-tional AI, pp. 179–188 (2021)
28. Cui, J., et al.: Knowledge distillation across ensembles of multilingual models for low-resource languages, pp. 4825–4829 (2017). https://doi.org/10.1109/ICASSP.2017.7953073
29. Huang, P.S., et al.: Learning deep structured semantic models for web search using click through data. In: Proceedings of the 22nd ACM international conference on Information & Knowledge Management, pp. 2333–2338 (2013)
30. Nigam, P., et al.: Semantic Product Search, pp. 2876–2885 (2019). https://doi.org/10.1145/3292500.3330759
31. Huang, J.T., et al.: Embedding-based retrieval in facebook search Proceedings of the 26th ACM SIGKDD International Conference on Knowledge Discovery & Data Mining, pp. 2553–2561 (2020)
32. Klein, G., Kim, Y., Deng, Y., Senellart, J., Rush, A.: OpenNMT: Open-Source Toolkit for Neural Machine Translation (2017). https://doi.org/10.48550/arXiv.1701.02810
33. Post, M.: A Call for Clarity in Reporting BLEU Scores (2018). https://doi.org/10.48550/arXiv.1804.08771

Interactive Systems & Information Society Technologies: Human-Computer Systems in Biomedicine

A Comprehensive Analysis of Computer-Aided Techniques: The Future of Gastric Cancer Diagnosis

S. P. Aarathy(✉) and K. S. Ravichandran

Department of Mathematics, School of Physical Sciences, Amrita Vishwa Vidyapeetham, Coimbatore, India
cb.ps.p2asd22009@cb.students.amrita.edu,
ks_ravichandran@cb.amrita.edu

Abstract. Despite significant advancements in the field of medicine, Gastric Cancer (GC) continues to pose a major global health challenge and is currently recognized as the fifth leading cause of cancer-related lethality. The prognosis of the GC is heavily reliant on the staging of the cancer, underscoring the importance of early detection. Traditional diagnostic methods, such as histopathological examination by trained pathologists, are time-consuming and subjective. However, in the rapidly evolving landscape of medical image analysis, cutting-edge technologies like deep learning and computer vision, including techniques such as endoscopy, confocal laser endomicroscopy, magnification endoscopy with narrow-band imaging, chromoendoscopy, and AI-based image analysis, are making significant advancements. These innovations hold great promise for enhancing the accuracy of gastric cancer diagnosis. Nonetheless, a major challenge persists: the scarcity of relevant datasets presents obstacles to computer-aided diagnosis. This review underscores the significance of computer-aided diagnosis in the timely identification and clinical assessment of stomach cancer (SC), focusing on the promising field of histopathological image analysis (HIA) within this broader context. We explore deep-learning techniques, address the challenges associated with dataset scarcity, and discuss potential innovations to overcome this hurdle. Building upon existing research, this review contributes to our understanding of and strategies for improving the detection of gastric cancer, bridging the gap between traditional diagnostic methods and innovative image analysis techniques. This review aims to comprehensively examine the current landscape, highlight significant challenges, conduct a detailed analysis of state-of-the-art technologies, and propose potential directions for future research.

Keywords: Gastric Cancer · Stomach Cancer · Diagnosis · Image Analysis · Endoscopy · Deep Learning · Narrow-Band Imaging · Histopathology

M. Bakaev et al. (Eds.): IMS 2024, CCIS 2534, pp. 273–284, 2026.
https://doi.org/10.1007/978-3-031-96177-9_23

1 Introduction

The fight against Gastric Cancer (GC) or Stomach Cancer is expected to witness significant progress shortly, with several promising research studies and innovative treatments in the pipeline. However, it remains a major global health challenge that requires continuous efforts and collaboration from medical professionals, researchers, and policymakers worldwide. Gastric cancer originates from the mucosal layer within the stomach. It is a form of cancer characterized by the uncontrolled growth of malignant cells within this vital organ. The prognosis of this disease depends on the cancer stage, which can vary from localized lesions to lymph node involvement or metastasis. Unfortunately, GC often remains asymptomatic in its early phases, leading to delayed diagnoses. Worldwide, around 990,000 individuals are diagnosed with gastric cancer every year, and approximately 738,000 deaths are linked to this illness 3. GC ranks as the fifth most prevalent cancer globally 1 and is also the fifth-highest contributor to cancer-related mortality 2. GC predominantly impacts older individuals, with the average age of diagnosis being 68 years 3. Approximately 60% of yearly diagnosed cases of SC occur in individuals aged 65 and above 3. Additionally, men have a greater lifetime risk of developing GC compared to women3.

While stomach cancer is not as widespread in the US, it is still a major health issue in other areas, particularly in East Asia. New GC cases in the US have declined by approximately 1.5% annually over the past ten years 7. This positive trend is linked to factors such as decreased intake of salted and smoked foods and a decrease in Helicobacter pylori (H. pylori) infections, a major contributor to stomach cancer 5. GC often conceals its presence through subtle symptoms. These may include indigestion, bloating, or mild discomfort in the early stages. These nonspecific signs hinder timely detection.

As the disease progresses, symptoms become more pronounced. Unexplained weight loss, persistent abdominal pain, vomiting, and blood in the stool or vomit signal advanced gastric cancer 6. The predominant form of stomach cancer is adenocarcinoma, making up over 90% of all instances globally. It originates in the mucosa, or inner lining of the stomach. Gastrointestinal stromal tumor (GIST) is a relatively uncommon neoplasm of the stomach, accounting for a small fraction of cases, and can exhibit either a benign or malignant behavior. Gastric lymphoma is less common than adenocarcinoma and begins in immune system cells within the stomach walls. 7. Early identification of cancer is vital for improving outcomes in GC. EGC is cancer curbed to the mucosa or submucosa, with a higher survival rate than advanced GC. Detecting early-stage GC significantly improves survival rates compared to cases diagnosed at advanced stages. However, EGC is often asymptomatic and difficult to detect by conventional endoscopy.

Cancer diagnosis involves a series of tests and procedures to determine whether a person has cancer and to identify the specific type. Molecular biology techniques are essential in the analysis of genetic and molecular alterations in cancer cells, enabling the identification of specific mutations and changes that inform treatment strategies. Blood chemistry tests measure the substances released into the blood by organs and tissues, and abnormal levels can indicate cancer. Imaging modalities, such as CT scans, X-rays, MRI, PET scans, and ultrasounds, are utilized for the visualization of internal anatomical structures. 8.

Endoscopy, chromoendoscopy, magnification endoscopy with narrow-band imaging, and confocal laser endomicroscopy are some of the most integral image analysis techniques used in this regard. Endoscopy allows for visualizing the stomach's interior, providing an initial understanding of the patient's condition. Magnification endoscopy offers a closer examination of the mucosal patterns, providing more detailed information on the patient's condition. Narrow-band imaging enhances blood vessel visibility, chromoendoscopy uses dye to improve pattern visibility, and confocal laser endomicroscopy allows for real-time microscopic imaging of affected areas. A biopsy involves removing a sample of tissue or cells from an affected area, which is essential for cancer diagnosis. It undergoes HIA - the study of microscopic tissue changes caused by diseases. These images, obtained by staining tissue samples, serve as benchmarks for identifying tumors. The collected sample is examined by pathologists under a microscope to identify cancerous cells and determine the type of cancer. In recent years, the development of high-throughput tissue banks and digitized histological studies has facilitated the application of computer-aided image analysis for cancer detection through the utilization of histological tissue patterns.

The field of medical image analysis has seen remarkable growth and transformation with Computer-assisted diagnosis (CAD) over the past decade. The combination of deep learning and AI is revolutionizing diagnostic capabilities and patient outcomes for gastric cancer. For instance, we can identify specific chromatin textures in cancerous cell nuclei, which may indicate certain genetic abnormalities. Several difficulties exist in this field, including complex clinical presentations, limited training data, and large image dimensions. CAD techniques (using DL-Convolution Neural Network) identify and measure characteristics of interest, but they face challenges such as limited accessible datasets, diverse cancer subtypes, lack of standardized metrics, and the need for clinical validation. One way to improve classification and segmentation is by leveraging CNN activation features from models trained on natural images (e.g., ImageNet), as these features transfer well to other images. CNNs outperform expert-designed features [9, 11].

This paper explores the relationship between deep learning methods and medical imagery for early gastric cancer detection and aims to contribute to the ongoing discussion by synthesizing research findings. By examining a variety of papers, this article provides insights into evolving methodologies, challenges, and potential solutions for timely and accurate diagnoses.

2 Literature Review

In recent years, computer-aided diagnosis (CAD) techniques have been applied to histopathology images of gastric cancer using various methods and datasets. The inception of CAD was initiated in the first half of the 1990s, coinciding with the rise of digital mammography for breast cancer detection through mammograms [10]. The integration of CAD into routine clinical practice has made it a major research subject in medical imaging and diagnostic radiology.

2.1 Datasets

First, The studies that are prevalent in the present scenario use datasets that are collected from medical universities, hospitals, clinics, the American Cancer Association, and other clinical data. The publicly available data are as follows:

- TCGA Stomach Cancer Data: This dataset contains processed RNA-seq gene expression data obtained from 415 gastric tumor samples. The dataset covers information for 20502 genes.29
- Gene Expression Omnibus (GEO) Gastric Cancer Data Set: This dataset contains processed Illumina microarray gene expression data obtained from 300 gastric tumor samples. The dataset covers information for 20515 genes.36
- Gastric Histopathological Sub-size Image Database (GasHisSDB): This publicly available histopathological images dataset contains 245,196 tissue case images. The database contains 3 sub-size classes: 80 X 80, 120 X 120, 160 X 160. [12, 22, 34]

2.2 Histopathological Image Analysis (HIA)

Histopathological image analysis is critical for early diagnosis of gastric cancer. Numerous research endeavors have been dedicated to crafting computer-aided detection (CAD) systems aimed at refining the accuracy and objectivity of analyzing gastric histopathological images. These systems leverage deep convolutional neural networks, trained with meticulously annotated whole-slide images at the pixel level, to achieve notable sensitivity and specificity in detecting gastric cancer 20. Moreover, the integration of handcrafted features with CNNs has been explored, enhancing the representation of local contour and rotation characteristics of pathological tissues, thereby improving the performance in identifying early lesions of gastric cancer 21. In summary, these studies underscore the potential of HIA and CAD systems in supporting pathologists with the early diagnosis and precise diagnosis of gastric cancer.

Latest Trend: Deep learning(DL) is a major trend in histopathological image analysis as it can extract intricate features from extensive amounts of data. It has proven to deliver superior performance in segmentation, classification, detection, and representation tasks. Other methods, such as multimodality size reduction algorithms and feature extraction techniques, have also been employed to reduce dimensionality and improve classification accuracy in histopathological stomach image analysis. 22.

In 2021, Lee et al. 19, introduced a DL framework tailored for analyzing histopathological images at the single-cell level. Utilizing the TCGA-Head and Neck Squamous Cell Carcinoma (HNSCC) dataset comprising 500 images, research employs a novel cell segmentation method based on Mask R-CNN and a cell classification method based on ResNet-50. Impressively, the segmentation method achieves a Mean Average Precision (map) of 0.87, while the classification method attains an accuracy of 0.94. The paper also explores challenges and opportunities associated with single-cell analysis, including data quality, augmentation, cell heterogeneity, interactions, and spatial transcriptomics.

Naik et al. [11] introduced an integrated framework for analyzing breast cancer histopathological images, integrating image processing techniques and supervised ML algorithms. They achieved notable accuracy rates, with the Random Forest algorithm standing out with an impressive 98.2% accuracy for benign and 98.3% accuracy for malignant cancer. In 2023, Atabansi [17] and colleagues conducted a comprehensive study of Transformer models applied in various histopathological tasks, comparing them with convolutional neural networks. They discussed the strengths, weaknesses, and challenges of these methodologies, including data scarcity, interpretability, and integrations with other modalities.

Gastric Cancer Images: In research focused on Gastric Histopathology Image Analysis, there has been notable advancement in leveraging advanced computational methods to enhance diagnostic capabilities. This progress holds the promise of significantly improving the accuracy and effectiveness of diagnoses in this domain. Deep learning has emerged as a major trend in histopathological image analysis, offering superior performance in various tasks such as segmentation, classification, and detection. These advancements include the integration of Transformer models and multimodality size reduction algorithms. Additionally, researchers have combined different types of deep learning models and techniques, resulting in even more precise analysis.

In 2018 Kim et al. 27 introduced a two-phase deep learning framework for automatically detecting GC in whole slide images (WSIs). To overcome limited dataset challenges, they prioritized collecting region-level labels to reduce labeling time. Their method, focusing on biopsy screening, utilized 90 cases for development and 548 cases for testing. Utilizing InceptionV3 architecture for region-level inference, their approach achieved outstanding accuracy(92.5%) in classifying Normal, Tubular Adenoma (TA), and Cancer tissues. The subsequent slide-level inference utilizes the probability map generated at the region level, incorporating features calculated for WSI classification through a random forest classifier. The method showcased exceptional proficiency in the classification of TA, highlighting its sensitivity to subtle abnormalities. The study calls for further validation with diverse datasets from multiple laboratories to solidify its applicability in varied clinical scenarios.

Sevcan et al.22 a study conducted in 2021 proposed a method for classifying. Their method uses a combination of a novel algorithm for size reduction called EEHOG and alternative approaches to dimensionality reduction such as MDS, LLE, Sammon mapping, Isomap, Laplacian eigenmaps, SNE, and t-SNE. The results show that using the EEHOG + ODRM size reduction method outperforms the ODRM method. Moreover, the accuracy achieved by the Multilayer Perceptron (MLP) classifier surpassed that of the RF classifier. The highest accuracy result was achieved with the EHOG_EEHOG + LLE_MLP method, which reached 98.14%. On average, the MLP classifier achieved accuracy results of 89.57%, while the RF classifier achieved 84.49%.

The paper by Shiliang Ai et al. 15 published in 2021 focuses on CAD techniques for SC histopathological image analysis (HIA). The dataset used in this study comprises 560 HE-stained pathological images of GC. The authors generated a large dataset of 231,000 instances using various data enhancement methods. They discuss specific methods like the HOG-LDA-ANN method for GC images and the comparison of feature reduction methods (LBP-MDS-ANN and LBP-LLE-ANN), providing insights into the intricacies of the proposed techniques.

Waddingham et al.14 developed a clinical-grade artificial intelligence (AI) system for diagnosing gastric histopathology. The system utilizes a deep convolutional neural network(CNN) and was trained on 2,123 pixel-level annotated whole slide images(WSI).

The AI system achieved impressive accuracy rates of 94.4% for gastric cancer detection and 86.9% for gastric cancer subtyping. The sensitivity rates were also high at 95.6% and 88.9%, respectively. These results suggest that AI systems are substantive tools for improving the accuracy and efficiency of gastric cancer diagnosis.

In 2021, Hu et al. 23, introduced the GasHisSDB dataset to address the paucity of publicly accessible gastric histopathology images for the computer-aided GC diagnosis. While emphasizing its utility for the automated diagnosis of SC, the paper underscores the dataset's significance for weakly supervised learning, containing 245,196 tissue case images Traditional ML and DL methods were used to evaluate classifier performance on GasHisSDB, revealing discrepancies over time. However, it is noted that the paper lacks a detailed analysis of classifier performance, potential biases in data collection, and the dataset's limitations in representing the full diversity of gastric cancer cases.

Haiqing et al. 24 in 2022 focuses their study on utilizing graph-based features within CAD systems for classifying histopathological images of SC. The study compares various segmentation methods, such as Level-Set, watershed, Otsu thresholding, SegNet, and Trans-U-Net segmentation, utilizing the U-Net segmentation approach. Additionally, the study evaluates different classifiers, including RBF SVM, k-nearest Neighbour, Linear SVM, AN Network, VGG16, Random Forests, and Inception-V3. The results indicate that U-Net segmentation, graph-based feature extraction, and RBF SVM classifier exhibit optimal outcomes with 94.29% accuracy in gastric cancer cell classification. The study highlights the significance of graph-based features in gastric cancer diagnosis and emphasizes appropriate segmentation and classifier choices in achieving accurate results.

The paper 35 of 2022 proposes a novel approach for classifying gastric cancer histopathological images. The Local-Global Feature Fuse Network for Gastric Histopathological Image Classification (LGFFN-GHI) model integrates Pvt-Tiny networks and ResNet18 to capture both global and local features from microscopic gastric tissue images, enhancing the efficiency of disease diagnosis. Experiments were conducted on the GasHisSDB dataset, and the model achieved an accuracy of 96.814%, outperforming baseline methods by significant margins. The model shows high precision, recall, and specificity, along with a strong F1 score and MCC compared to traditional deep learning models. The ROC curve analysis indicates a high AUC, demonstrating the model's accuracy in classifying gastric cancer pathology images. Overall, LGFFN-GHI's fusion of local and global features has the potential to improve gastric cancer diagnosis through HIA.

The recent study by Yong et al. 13 (2023) proposed a deep ensemble learning model. Building on the work of Wang et al., who previously suggested ensemble-based approaches for detecting GC, the study evaluates their performance on the publicly available GasHisSDatabase. The ensemble models prove highly effective, achieving state-of-the-art detection accuracy, particularly notable in the 160 × 160 pixels sub-database where a remarkable 99.20% accuracy is attained. The use of ensemble models allows for faster detection and potentially higher patient survival rates. The research emphasizes the deep ensemble learning models' advantages in HIA for stomach cancer, highlighting their superior detection accuracy and potential benefits for patient outcomes.

2.3 Pathological Analysis

In the paper by Sreeranganathan et al.,37. Presents a research on the advancement and evaluation of cetuximab (CET MAb)-conjugated docetaxel-loaded γ-polyglutamic acid (γ-PGA) nanoparticles (CET MAb-DOCT-γ-PGA Nps) for the targeted approach for treating EGFR-overexpressing GC. The paper involves using pathological images obtained through in vivo optical imaging techniques, specifically employing the FOBI imaging system, to track the distribution and accumulation of these nanoparticles in a gastric cancer xenograft model. The nanoparticles were prepared using ionic gelation and further conjugation, and their characterization involved dynamic light scattering and scanning electron microscopy for size determination and surface charge. Results indicated that the targeted nanoparticles showed enhanced tumor accumulation and improved pharmacokinetic profiles compared to non-targeted nanoparticles and free docetaxel, leading to superior anticancer efficacy in reducing tumor volume and weight. However, the study faced challenges in optimizing the nanoparticle size and surface properties to maximize targeting efficiency and minimize off-target effects.

In 2017, Oikawa et al., 25 introduced a new computerized analysis system that can help with the pathological diagnosis of GC. The system was trained with gastric tissue samples and showed comparable accuracy in detecting malignancies when compared to expert pathologists' conventional diagnosis. This novel computer-assisted pathology system can be advantageous for quality control and screening, and it also provides support for histological diagnosis. The system has the potential to be extended to other carcinomas and can contribute to developing more objective grading systems and staining analysis systems. They suggested the advancement of more immunohistochemical staining systems, objective grading systems, and fluorescent-stained image analysis systems.

In 2020, Liu B et al.26 presented a study that used deep learning technology to identify gastric cancer in magnified (20 ×) Gastric Pathological Section Images (GPSI) with high proficiency. The study introduced a Multistage Attention Module (MSA-DenseNet) to a novel DenseNet architecture to focus on gastric features and extract more semantic information about cancer. To train the model, a 121-layer DenseNet16 as the backbone architecture was used, including an attention module to enhance gastric features. The study results showed that the model achieved state-of-the-art performance on a test dataset, with a remarkable F1 score of 0.9947 and ROC AUC of 0.9976. The high recall (0.9929) indicates a robust sensitivity to positive samples. Comparing the model's performance with other models, such as VGG16, ResNet-50, and XCeption, demonstrated that MSA-DenseNet outperformed in F1-score and AUC.

Huang et al. 16 developed two CNN models, GastroMIL and MIL-GC, to diagnose gastric cancer and assess patient prognosis. The models were trained on a dataset of 871 GC patients from RHWU, TCGA, and NHGRP cohorts. GastroMIL achieved a high performance in distinguishing malignant from normal tissues with AUCs nearly 1.000, while MIL-GC showed good performance in predicting overall survival with C-index of 0.728 and 0.671. Although the study's retrospective nature and variation in survival times between cohorts are acknowledged limitations, the research contributes to the digital pathology field and highlights the potential of DL models for GC diagnosis and prognosis prediction. Compared to previous studies, which often relied on endoscopy or radiologic technology and had smaller sample sizes from single centers, this study stands out for its use of extensive datasets from multiple cohorts and validation using external independent data. The study's webpage provides a user-friendly interface that facilitates automated GC diagnosis and survival estimation, which could prove particularly valuable in regions with a shortage of pathologists and enhancing the accuracy of junior pathologists' diagnoses. This has implications for personalized treatment strategies in clinical practice.

2.4 Endoscopic Image Analysis

In 2019, Zhu et al., [29] investigated using a CNN-CAD system to accurately predict the depth of invasion in patients with GC. Based on the ResNet50 structure, the CNN-CAD system was trained to categorize invasion depth into two groups: within the mucosa (P0) or beyond the submucosa (P1). Findings reveal that the CNN-CAD achieves an accuracy of 89.16%, surpassing both experienced and junior endoscopists in terms of accuracy and specificity. The system's ability to swiftly assess invasion depth, coupled with its heightened accuracy, suggests its potential clinical usefulness in screening patients for endoscopic resection. The research in Hu et al., [33] demonstrated a significant contribution to medical diagnostics by developing a CAD model called the Endoscopic GC Model (EGCM) using deep learning and magnifying endoscopy narrow-band imaging (ME-NBI). They trained and tested EGCM on 1777 ME-NBI images from 295 studies across three hospitals. They utilized the VGG-19 architecture for EGCM development. The model achieved high AUC scores of .808 and .813 in the internal and external test groups, respectively, performing comparably to senior endoscopists and better than junior ones. The study's multicenter design enhances the findings' generalizability. However, EGCM made errors in diagnosing some cases, mostly due to small cancerous areas blending with normal tissue or specific conditions like erosive gastritis.

The proposed method [32] addresses missed diagnoses caused by reliance on operator experience by using a deeper-shallower feature (DSF) enhancement module to effectively combine low-level and high-level features. The method also incorporates a bottom-up path feature fusion (BUF) module and a channel-wise attention (CA) module for accurate prediction. The model demonstrates substantial enhancements over standard models, achieving F1-scores of 63.34%, 90.65%, and 89.95% on ETIS-Larib, Kvasir, and the authors' endoscopic dataset, respectively, indicating improved detection accuracy. The method adopts the SSD framework, leveraging VGG16 as a feature extractor and incorporating additional convolutional layers.

In their recent study, Minggui Liu et al.32 presents an enhanced method for detecting gastric cancer using DL. The authors improved an existing detection method called Single Shot MultiBox Detector (SSD) by adding new features. They introduced a recurrent feature pyramid network (RFPN) to better understand image features and a feature fusion module (FFM) to combine different types of features. They added a segmentation branch to better detect small lesions, which are signs of early-stage cancer. Visual analysis confirmed the method's effectiveness in accurately detecting small cancerous lesions, which are crucial for early diagnosis. In their 2021 publication, Jiang et al. [30] presented findings indicating that AI-supported endoscopy outperforms traditional methods in detecting early gastric cancer. The analysis examined 16 chosen articles, revealing that AI-assisted endoscopy obtained an AUC of 0.96, with 86% sensitivity and 93% specificity in early gastric cancer detection. AI also showed promising results in discerning the depth of cancer invasion, particularly when trained on larger datasets. Narrow-band imaging (NBI) demonstrated better sensitivity compared to White Light Endoscopy (WLE) images.

3 Future Directions in Gastric Cancer Diagnosis and Image Analysis

Recent research indicates substantial improvements in diagnostic capabilities for gastric cancer detection due to advancements in computer vision and deep learning technologies. CAD, particularly with DL techniques like CNNs, has shown notable progress in analyzing histopathological images, augmented by Transformer models and deep ensemble learning. Despite data scarcity challenges, resources like TCGA and GasHisSDB hold promise for advancing research in this domain. Future research should prioritize integrating multimodal data, including histopathological images and clinical data, to enhance the reliability and precision of CAD systems. Emphasizing the interpretability of DL models in HIA could foster trust among clinicians. Investigating the real-time diagnostic capabilities of CAD systems for endoscopic images is imperative for expediting clinical decision-making. Prospective studies validating CAD system performance across diverse clinical settings are pivotal for ensuring efficacy in real-world scenarios.

In addition to existing research priorities, future directions should consider the development of standardized protocols and benchmarks for evaluating AI systems in gastric cancer diagnosis. Establishing common evaluation metrics and datasets will enable more consistent and comparable assessment of AI performance across different studies and clinical settings. The integration of AI with emerging technologies like augmented reality and robotics could enhance diagnostic procedures. AI-driven overlays in augmented reality can highlight areas of concern during examinations. Additionally, the impact of AI on healthcare economics should be studied to ensure cost-effectiveness and resource allocation. Addressing these additional areas can further solidify the part of AI in improving GC analysis and treatment outcomes.

4 Conclusion

Recently, technological advances, especially in computer vision and DL, offer significant promise for enhancing diagnostic capabilities in detecting gastric cancer. CAD has made remarkable progress, leveraging DL techniques like CNNs and integrating transformer models and deep ensemble learning, thus improving detection accuracy. Despite challenges related to data scarcity, resources such as TCGA and GasHisSDB provide valuable support for research in this area. AI-based systems show potential in predicting invasion depth and aiding endoscopists in decision-making, but further research and validation are essential in ensuring their reliability and efficacy in clinical practice. The transformative potential of AI-driven approaches underscores the need for continued innovation and collaboration in this field. Encouraging cross-disciplinary collaboration between computer scientists, clinicians, and medical experts is indispensable for crafting comprehensive diagnostic and treatment strategies for gastric cancer. Future research can focus on improving model generalizability, developing novel deep learning architectures, addressing dataset scarcity, enhancing model interpretability, conducting rigorous validation studies, developing clinical decision support systems, and addressing ethical and regulatory considerations. Prioritizing these research areas can lead to significant advancements in gastric cancer diagnosis and image analysis, ultimately improving patient outcomes and reducing associated healthcare expenses.

References

1. Cancer Today (who. int). https://gco.iarc.who.int/today/en/dataviz/bars?cancers=39&types=0&sexes=0&palette=Blues&mode=cancer&group_populations=1&key=total
2. Machlowska, J., Baj, J., Sitarz, M., Maciejewski, R., Sitarz, R.: Gastric cancer: epidemiology, risk factors, classification, genomic characteristics, and treatment strategies. Int. J. Mol. Sci. **21**, 4012 (2020). https://doi.org/10.3390/ijms21114012
3. Karimi, P., Islami, F., Anandasabapathy, S., Freedman, N.D., Kamangar, F.: Gastric cancer: descriptive epidemiology, risk factors, screening, and prevention. Cancer Epidemiol. Biomark. Prevent. **23**(5), 700–713 (2014). https://doi.org/10.1158/1055-9965.EPI-13-1057
4. Stomach (Gastric) Cancer Key Statistics | American Cancer Society. https://www.cancer.org/cancer/types/stomach-cancer/about/key-statistics.html
5. What you should know about stomach cancer – Mayo Clinic Comprehensive Cancer Center Blog. https://cancerblog.mayoclinic.org/2021/11/29/what-you-should-know-about-stomach-cancer/
6. Gastric Cancer Facts and Statistics: What to Know (verywellhealth.com) https://www.verywellhealth.com/gastric-cancer-facts-6385424
7. Tests and Procedures Used to Diagnose Cancer – NCI https://www.cancer.gov/about-cancer/diagnosis-staging/diagnosis
8. Cancer - Diagnosis and treatment - Mayo Clinic https://www.mayoclinic.org/diseases-conditions/cancer/diagnosis-treatment/drc-20370594
9. Histopathology: Definition, Techniques, Results (verywellhealth.com) https://www.verywellhealth.com/histopathology-2252152
10. Mendez, A.J., Tahoces, P.G., Lado, M.J., Souto, M., Vidal, J.J.: Computer-aided diagnosis: automatic detection of malignant masses in digitized mammograms. Med. Phys. **25**(6), 957–964 (1998)
11. Naik, D.A., Mohana, R.M., Ramu, G., et al.: Analyzing histopathological images by using machine learning techniques. Appl. Nanosci. **13**, 2507–2513 (2023). https://doi.org/10.1007/s13204-021-02217-4
12. Ping Yong, M., et al.: Histopathological gastric cancer detection on GasHisSDB dataset using deep ensemble learning. Diagnostics **13**(10), 1793 (2023). https://doi.org/10.3390/diagnostics13101793
13. Waddingham, W., Nieuwenburg, S.A.V., Carlson, S., et al.: Recent advances in the detection and management of early gastric cancer and its precursors. Frontline Gastroenterol. **12**(4), 322–331 (2021). https://doi.org/10.1136/flgastro-2018-101089
14. Shiliang Ai, Chen Li, Xiaoyan Li, Tao Jiang, Marcin Grzegorzek, Changhao Sun, Md Mamunur Rahaman, Jinghua Zhang, Yudong Yao, Hong Li, "A State-of-the-Art Review for Gastric Histopathology Image Analysis Approaches and Future Development", *BioMed Research International*, vol. 2021, Article ID 6671417, 19 pages, 2021. https://doi.org/10.1155/2021/6671417

15. Huang, B., et al.: Accurate diagnosis and prognosis prediction of gastric cancer using deep learning on digital pathological images: a retrospective multicentre study. Biomedicine **73**, 103631 (2021). https://doi.org/10.1016/j.ebiom.2021.103631
16. Rogers, W., Ryack, B., Moeller, G.: Computer-aided medical diagnosis: literature review. Int. J. Biomed. Comput. **10**(4), 267–289 (1979)
17. Atabansi, C.C., Nie, J., Liu, H., Song, Q., Yan, L., Zhou, X.: A survey of transformer applications for histopathological image analysis: new developments and future directions. Biomed. Eng. Online **22**(1), 1–38 (2023). https://doi.org/10.1186/s12938-023-01157-0
18. Lee, K., et al.: Deep learning of histopathology images at the single cell level. Front. Artific. Intell. **4**, 754641 (2021). https://doi.org/10.3389/frai.2021.754641
19. Yihao, Luo. (2019). Combination of Deep and Handcrafted Features Enabling Automated and Accurate Detections of Early Gastric Cancer Lesions in Histopathology Images. Investigation Clinica, 60(4)
20. Song, Z., et al.: Clinically applicable histopathological diagnosis system for gastric cancer detection using deep learning. Nat. Commun. (2020). https://doi.org/10.1038/s41467-020-18147-8
21. Korkmaz, S.A.: Classification of histopathological gastric images using a new method. Neural Comput. Appl. **33**(18), 12007–12022 (2021). https://doi.org/10.1007/s00521-021-05887-x
22. Weiming, H., et al.: GasHisSDB: A New Gastric Histopathology Image Dataset for Computer Aided Diagnosis of Gastric Cancer. arXiv: Computer Vision and Pattern Recognition (2021)
23. Haiqing, Z., et al.: Application of Graph-Based Features in Computer-Aided Diagnosis for Histopathological Image Classification of Gastric Cancer. Digital medicine, abs/2205.08467 (2022). https://doi.org/10.48550/arXiv.2205.08467
24. Oikawa, K., Saito, A., Kiyuna, T., Graf, H.P., Cosatto, E., Kuroda, M.: Pathological diagnosis of gastric cancers with a novel computerized analysis system. J. Pathol. Inform. **8**(1), 5 (2016). https://doi.org/10.4103/2153-3539.201114
25. Liu, B., Zhao, Y., Yang, B., Zhao, S., Gu, R., Gahegan, M.: A gastric cancer recognition algorithm on gastric pathological sections based on multistage attention-DenseNet. Concurrency Comput.: Pract. Experience **33**(10), e6188 (2021). https://doi.org/10.1002/cpe.6188
26. Kim, Y.W., Kim, D.-I., Jung, K.-H.: Detection of Gastric Cancer from Histopathological Image using Deep Learning with Weak Label (2018)
27. Junjun, H., Yujie, J.: Image recognition and diagnosis system of early gastric cancer based on artificial intelligence algorithm. In: 2023 3rd Asia-Pacific Conference on Communications Technology and Computer Science (ACCTCS), pp. 77–81. Shenyang, China (2023). https://doi.org/10.1109/ACCTCS58815.2023.00068
28. Cancer Genome Atlas Research Network: Comprehensive molecular characterization of gastric adenocarcinoma. Nature **513**(7517), 202–209 (2014). https://doi.org/10.1038/nature13480
29. Zhu, Y., et al.: Application of convolutional neural network in the diagnosis of the invasion depth of gastric cancer based on conventional endoscopy. Gastrointest. Endosc. **89**(4), 806-815.e1 (2019). https://doi.org/10.1016/j.gie.2018.11.011
30. Jiang, K., et al.: Current evidence and future perspective of accuracy of artificial intelligence application for early gastric cancer diagnosis with endoscopy: a systematic and meta-analysis. Front. Med. **8**, 629080 (2021). https://doi.org/10.3389/fmed.2021.629080
31. Liu, M., Luo, Z., Cao, D., Lin, D., Su, S., Li, S.: An improved ssd-based gastric cancer detection method. In: Sun, Y., et al. (eds.) Computer Supported Cooperative Work and Social Computing: 16th CCF Conference, Chinese CSCW 2021, Xiangtan, China, November 26–28, 2021, Revised Selected Papers, Part I, pp. 451–459. Springer Nature Singapore, Singapore (2022). https://doi.org/10.1007/978-981-19-4546-5_35

32. Pan, D., Zhang, R., Wang, Y., Feng, H.: Detection of early gastric cancer based on single shot detector with feature enhancement. In: 2020 IEEE International Conference on Bioinformatics and Biomedicine (BIBM), pp. 1091–1095. Seoul, Korea (South) (2020). https://doi.org/10.1109/BIBM49941.2020.9313339
33. Hu, H., et al.: Identifying early gastric cancer under magnifying narrow-band images with deep learning: a multicenter study. Gastrointest. Endosc. **93**(6), 1333-1341.e3 (2021). https://doi.org/10.1016/j.gie.2020.11.014. Epub 2020 Nov 26 PMID: 33248070
34. Li, S., Liu, W.: LGFFN-GHI: a local-global feature fuse network for gastric histopathological image classification. J. Comput. Commun. **10**, 91–106 (2022). https://doi.org/10.4236/jcc.2022.1011007
35. Cristescu, R., Lee, J., Nebozhyn, M., Kim, K.M., et al.: Molecular analysis of gastric cancer identifies subtypes associated with distinct clinical outcomes. Nat. Med. **21**(5), 449–456 (2015)
36. Sreeranganathan, M., Uthaman, S., Sarmento, B., Mohan, C.G., Park, I.K., Jayakumar, R.: In vivo evaluation of cetuximab-conjugated poly(γ-glutamic acid)-docetaxel nanomedicines in EGFR-overexpressing gastric cancer xenografts. Int. J. Nanomed. **12**, 7165–7182 (2017). https://doi.org/10.2147/IJN.S14352

Diagnosis of Alzheimer's Disease Using Machine Learning and Deep Learning: A Study

B. Reshma(✉) and K. S. Ravichandran

Department of Mathematics, School of Physical Sciences, Amrita Vishwa Vidyapeetham, Coimbatore, India
reshmab2002@gmail.com, ks_ravichandran@cb.amrita.edu

Abstract. Alzheimer's disease is a neurological disorder that is progressive and primarily affects memory and other cognitive functions. According to the studies conducted by World Health Organization, or WHO, "over 55 million individuals worldwide suffer from dementia and that around 10 million new cases are recorded each year". Furthermore, accounting for 60–70% of dementia cases, Alzheimer's disease is the most frequent cause of the condition. To effectively treat Alzheimer's disease (AD), a precise diagnosis is essential, especially in the early stages when preventive actions can be performed to lessen the irreversible impairment of the brain. The traditional methods of diagnosing Alzheimer's disease, such as clinical evaluations, medical history analysis, cognitive assessments, and brain imaging, have limitations, including delayed detection of symptoms, subjective interpretation, and invasive procedures. The recent discoveries in neuroimaging, biomarkers, deep learning, and machine learning algorithms have created novel opportunities for early detection and improved diagnostic accuracy. The main objective of the paper is to review some of the important literature on Alzheimer's disease and gain insight into how deep learning and machine learning can aid in the timely identification of the condition.

Keywords: Alzheimer's Disease · Dementia · Deep Learning · Machine Learning · neuroimaging

Abbreviations

HC	Healthy Control
NC	Normal Control
AD	Alzheimer's disease
MCI	Mild Cognitive Impairment
sMCI	Stable MCI
cMCI, FMCIc	Convertible MCI
MCInc	Nonconvertible MCI
LMCI	Late MCI
EMCI	Early MCI
MoD	Moderate dementia
MID	Mild dementia

M. Bakaev et al. (Eds.): IMS 2024, CCIS 2534, pp. 285–296, 2026.
https://doi.org/10.1007/978-3-031-96177-9_24

VMD	Very mild dementia
ND	Non-Dementia
SAMC	South Asian Medical Center
KVHS	Korean Veterans Health Services
TL	Transfer learning

1 Introduction

Alzheimer's disease (AD) is a neurological disorder that causes cerebral degeneration, resulting in memory impairment and the gradual decline of cognitive functions. AD is a major reason of dementia and is usually seen in the senior population above the age of 65 [1]. AD is marked by the loss of neuronal connections in the human brain because of the accumulation of abnormal protein structures called "plaques" and "tangles" [2]. These plaques consist of insoluble deposits of Abeta peptide.

The progression of AD is represented by three stages, namely early-stage AD (mild), Middle-stage AD (moderate), and Late-stage AD (severe). In the mild stage, the individual might function independently but may feel as if having memory failures. The moderate stage is the most prolonged and symptoms are more pronounced in this stage as damage in brain cells makes it difficult for the person to perform tasks without assistance. In the severe stage, the symptoms are acute and the individual loses the ability to respond to their surroundings [3].

The early indications of AD include difficulty in recollecting recent events or conversations, misplacing items, exhibiting poor judgment, experiencing difficulty in decision-making, having trouble completing routine tasks, difficulty in problem solving, and confusion about time or location [4]. As the disease progresses the patients tend to develop confusion and encounter difficulty in recognizing family and friends, alongside developing confusion. Hallucinations, delusions, and paranoia can also emerge. In the advanced stage, patients become bedridden and reliant on others for essential care.

Over 55 million of the population are detected with dementia, out of which 60–70% of them have AD [5]. About, 10 million people are reported with AD every year. Alzheimer's disease lacks a cure or definitive treatment, but with appropriate care and interventions, we can slow down its progression. Early detection of the disease can help in starting early care and medication which can help in improving the lifestyle of the patient and decelerate the advancement of the disease. Therefore, there is a necessity to develop innovative methods for the detection of AD at an early stage and assist in implementing preventive medical interventions early on to prevent additional brain damage.

The most prominent feature of AD is the progressive shrinkage of the brain, which begins in key regions associated with the disease and gradually extends throughout the entire cortical region. These evident changes in brain structure occurred well in advance of notable cognitive decline, suggesting a possibility for early detection of AD. AD would have already seriously damaged brain tissue by the time mental health deterioration is documented, which is a major component of the standard diagnostic techniques for AD. The recent developments in neuroimaging, biomarkers, machine learning, and deep learning have created novel opportunities for early detection [6]. These neuroimaging techniques offer the potential to mitigate the abnormal degradation of brain tissue, cut healthcare expenses, and improve treatment outcomes. Researchers are exploring techniques to detect AD at an earlier stage using neuroimaging techniques.

Structural Imaging techniques can be utilized for the early detection of AD as it provides insights into the brain's anatomy, making it possible to identify cerebral atrophy. Magnetic Resonance Imaging (MRI) and Computed Tomography (CT) are the basic structural imaging techniques. MRI creates detailed brain images by using a strong magnet and radio waves. It is highly beneficial in AD research, as even the slightest changes in brain structure can be identified, including shrinkage of the entorhinal cortex and hippocampus, which are early indications of the disease. In contrast, CT scans produce cross-sectional brain images by using X-rays. CT scans can reveal substantial atrophy and assist in eliminating other possible causes of dementia but it is not as effective as MRI in identifying the initial cerebral changes related to AD.

Functional imaging techniques are methods used to assess cerebral activity by observing changes in glucose metabolism, oxygen utilization, or blood flow. Three common functional imaging techniques are PET, SPECT, and fMRI (functional MRI). PET involves injecting a tiny amount of a radioactive tracer, known as a radiopharmaceutical, into the bloodstream. This tracer emits positrons, which are detected by the PET scanner. As the tracer travels to different parts of the brain, it accumulates in regions with increased metabolic activity or specific molecular targets, such as receptors or neurotransmitters. By measuring the distribution of the tracer, PET can create three-dimensional images of brain activity. In Alzheimer's research, SPECT is valuable for assessing variations in blood flow and evaluating the integrity of specific cerebral systems, such as the cholinergic system. Unlike PET and SPECT, Functional Magnetic Resonance Imaging (fMRI) does not use radioactive tracers. Instead, it depends on the magnetic properties of hemoglobin in blood to indirectly measure brain activity. When a particular brain region becomes active, it requires more oxygenated blood. This leads to variations in blood oxygenation level-dependent (BOLD) signals, which can be detected by an MRI scanner. By measuring these signal changes, fMRI can create maps of brain activity with high spatial resolution. In AD research, fMRI is used to investigate alterations in brain connectivity, activation patterns, and functional networks, providing insights into the underlying pathophysiology of the disease. [7]. In recent times, researchers and academics have exhibited keen attention to employing computer-assisted machine learning (ML) and deep learning (DL) methods to analyze and predict various diseases by leveraging medical data.

In this paper, we systematically examine relevant research conducted in recent years that explores AD using MRI data and employs ML and DL methodologies across diverse Alzheimer's disease datasets.

2 Alzheimer's Disease Detection

2.1 Dataset

Advancements in Alzheimer's prediction research have been significantly facilitated by the accessibility of open-source databases. This section explores the prominent open-source databases utilized for studying AD and developing robust predictive models.

- *Alzheimer's Disease Neuroimaging Initiative (ADNI)* [8]: ADNI is an open-source dataset used for the majority of the research works considered in this study. ADNI dataset was released in 2004 under the supervision of Michael W. Weiner. ADNI database consists of data including clinical, genetic, MRI images, Positron Emission Tomography (PET) images, and Biospecimens. ADNI has dependable clinical data and images that can be used to develop models for predicting AD.
- *Open Access Series of Imaging Studies (OASIS)* [9]: The OASIS datasets, created by the Knight ADRC and managed by central.xnat.org, provide open access to a large database of brain imaging and processed imaging data that covers a wide range of demographics, cognitive abilities, and genetic backgrounds. The most recent releases are versions OASIS 3 and OASIS 4.
- *Minimal Interval Resonance Imaging in Alzheimer's Disease (MIRIAD)* [10]: The MIRIAD dataset comprises volumetric MRI brain scans of 46 individuals with Alzheimer's and 23 healthy elderly participants.
- *Australian Imaging, Biomarker & Lifestyle (AIBL)* [11]: In 2006, the AIBL study began with a group of 1112 people who were over 60 years old, to examine the aging process, cognitive decline, and neurodegenerative diseases like Alzheimer's disease.

Additional datasets mentioned were collected specifically for research purposes, distinct from pre-existing datasets by the authors.

2.2 Machine Learning Approaches for Early Diagnosis of Alzheimer's Disease

In 2010, R. Chaves et al. [12] presented a method of using association rule mining to identify connections between attributes in pre-processed datasets to detect AD as early and effectively as possible. The authors focused specifically on three-dimensional regions of interest (ROIs) in the brain and established these ROIs by analyzing the voxels of each image and estimating activation with a specific threshold. The study used a SPECT dataset with 97 instances, 54 of which were AD patients and 43 of which were normal controls. The authors compared their method to other techniques such as VAF, PCA-SVM, and GMM-SVM, and found that their method had a classification accuracy of 95.87% (with 100% sensitivity and 92.86% specificity) and reduced computational costs compared to other methods.

In 2011, they [13] conducted further research on characterizing perfusion patterns in SPECT images of healthy individuals. They analyzed a large image database to replicate the knowledge of medical professionals. Using a dataset from ADNI, including 97 participants, they compared their findings with other techniques such as PCA-SVM and GMM-SVM. Their analysis resulted in an accuracy of 94.87%, with sensitivity at 91.07% and specificity at 100%, which was achieved by minimizing class imbalances. However, the data analyzed were unproven, and potential missing values were not addressed. Also in 2012, they [14] introduced a mining technique that uses association rule mining on discriminant regions that are identified through pre-processed SPECT and PET imaging modalities. The dataset consisted of 97 participants, with 42 healthy controls and 55 AD patients. The method was compared to other techniques such as PCA-SVM and VAF-SVM, and it demonstrated superior performance, obtaining 92.78% accuracy for SPECT, and 91.33% accuracy for PET. The study addressed class imbalance, but it did not discuss missing values.

In 2014, Veeramuthu et al. [15] developed a computer-aided diagnosis (CAD) tool designed to help with decision-making around brain abnormalities. The authors advocated preprocessing of PET datasets, including spatial and intensity normalization. Fisher discriminant ratio (FDR) was used to perform feature extraction to identify regions of interest (ROIs) and classify instances as normal if the number of verified rules extracted surpassed a final threshold; otherwise, the image was classified as indicative of AD. The model gave an accuracy of 91.33% with 82.67% sensitivity, and 100% specificity and in 2015, Zhang et al., [16] proposed a novel CAD system that uses eigenbrains and ML to accurately detect AD patients and AD-related cerebral regions from MR images. The process of extracting information from MR brain images involves choosing important slices from volumetric data using a method called maximum inter-class variance (ICV). Eigenbrain sets are created for each individual, and the most significant eigenbrain is identified using Welch's t-test (WTT). Finally, kernel SVMs are trained using particle swarm optimization to accurately predict Alzheimer's. The study focuses on distinguishing between AD and normal control (NC) subjects using brain imaging data. Discriminant regions were identified based on coefficients of the MIE with values higher than the 0.98 quantile. The proposed model achieved an high accuracy for the polynomial kernel.

In 2020, Afreen Khan et al. [17] Introduced an automated classification system aimed at identifying information patterns. It presents a comprehensive ML pipeline consisting of five stages, namely Data pre-processing, Data segregation, modelling, model prediction, performance metrics, each with various sub-levels. The study involved analyzing 343 MRI sessions of MRI brain images from 150 subjects using the OASIS database. Three scores were used to assess this study: MMSE (mini-mental state examination), CDR (clinical dementia rating), and ASF (atlas scaling factor). The highest classification accuracy of 86.84% was demonstrated by the Random Forest (RF) classifier during performance evaluation. In 2022, Diogo et al. [18] developed a comprehensive method that detects MCI and AD using ML and structural MRI. Three binary classifiers were involved, each trained on seven distinct classifiers. The classifiers were evaluated using ADNI and OASIS databases to determine their generalizability across different imaging protocols and datasets. The results showed an accuracy of 90.6% and MCC of 0.811 for HC vs MCI. The hippocampal was the most influential feature in the classification decisions.

In 2023, Rashni Biswas et al., [19] proposed a multi-class classification system to diagnose AD. The system uses MRI to measure anatomical regions like the hippocampus, white and grey matter. Demographic data, like age, gender, and MMSE score, are used as input for various machine learning algorithms to detect AD and evaluate its severity. The proposed method's effectiveness is evaluated using the OASIS and the ADNI dataset. The maximum accuracy of 99% was obtained for white matter volume using the OASIS dataset with Random Forest. For the ADNI dataset, an accuracy of 92% was obtained for the gradient boost classifier using both white matter volume and fusing all three volumes. For both datasets, an accuracy of 91% was obtained using gradient boost.

2.3 Deep Learning Approaches for Early Diagnosis of Alzheimer's Disease

The progress in the field of DL and the remarkable performance of various DL models have motivated researchers to use deep learning algorithms for neuroimaging data. This section delves into the recent developments in early AD diagnosis using deep learning. Jyothi Islam et al., [20] developed a model motivated by the Inception-V4 network with modified Inception B and C modules to accept MRI data. They have used the publicly available OASIS dataset. To prevent overfitting of data, data Augmentation techniques such as reflection and scaling have been applied. 5-fold cross-validation has been applied as the dataset is small. They have achieved an accuracy of 73.75%.

Chong-Yaw Wee et al., [21] has employed a graph-CNN that distinguishes between individuals with MCI and AD by integrating cortical thickness and geometry data. A graph-based convolutional neural network was trained on 3089 MRI scans from the ADNI-2 cohort and then evaluated for its ability to predict AD in both the ADNI-1 cohort and a separate Asian cohort. High classification accuracy of 85.5% was shown for CN vs. AD. Hongming Li et al., [22] developed a DL model to predict the progression of MCI subjects to AD using MRI images. The model can extract relevant features from the hippocampal MRI and the extracted features are used for the prediction of the progression of MCI subjects to AD using the LASSO regularized Cox regression model. They obtained data from AIBL study of Aging (435 subjects) along with ADNI. The accuracy of the model was evaluated using a concordance index on testing subjects, which was 0.762 on ADNI and 0.781 on AIBL.

Zhang et al., [23] introduced a multi-modal deep learning modal having two convolutional neural networks, independent of each other, whose consistency is assessed by correlation analysis. Neuroimaging data and the clinical and neuropsychological assessment results are combined to provide a more accurate diagnosis. They have obtained the data from the public database ADNI. The proposed technique obtained 88.25% accuracy for the diagnosis of MCI vs CN, Also, Simeon Spasov et al., [24] developed a deep learning architecture integrating dual learning alongside a specialized layer designed for 3D separable convolutions to identify MCI patients who have a high probability of developing AD within the next 3 years. The DL techniques used in this study incorporate input measures such as structural MRI, demographic information, genetic data, and neuropsychological data relating to the APOe4 gene. They have used the ADNI dataset comprising 785 subjects. The model produced an accuracy of 86%.

Silvia Basaia et al., [25] utilized single, cross-sectional structural MRI scans in their experiments. They employed a CNN on three-dimensional T1-weighted images from the ADNI dataset to predict individuals who have a risk of developing AD from MCI or remain stable (MCI-c). The study also included participants recruited from their institute. The CNN was evaluated in distinguishing between normal/healthy controls (HC), AD patients, stable MCI (MCI-s), and MCI converters (MCI-c), achieving the highest accuracy in differentiating between HC and AD. The CNN displayed a 75% accuracy in discriminating between patients with MCI-c and MCI-s.

Jain et al., [26] proposed a mathematical model PFSECTL based on transfer learning to classify Alzheimer's as AD, CN, and MCI. Feature extraction is done using pre-trained VGG-16 architecture. The dataset used for the study is the ADNI. The proposed method obtained high accuracy. Ekin Yagis et al., [27] introduced a 3D VGG variant convolutional network model to classify AD. They have used ADNI and OASIS datasets. The ADNI dataset's T1-weighted images have been processed to align them with a standard T1-weighted template using the SyN method, resulting in a standardized structure for all the data. Additionally, skull stripping was performed to remove non-brain tissues. The resulting resolution of the aligned images was 1 mm. Following alignment, a brain mask specific to the standard space has been utilized to exclude extracranial tissues from each volume. For the OASIS dataset, they utilized data that had already undergone gain-field correction. The proposed model with a 5-fold CV obtained an accuracy of 73.4% and 69.9% on the ADNI and OASIS datasets, respectively. Dan Pan et al., [28] combined CNN and ensemble learning to develop a classifier to classify between AD and HC, MCIc (Individuals with MCI who are likely to convert to AD) and HC, and MCIc and MCInc (Individuals with MCI who are not likely to convert to AD). Multiple CNN models were trained for each binary classification task using coronal, sagittal, or transverse MRI slices, and subsequently merged into a unified ensemble. The ADNI dataset was utilized and findings indicated accuracy rate of 0.84 in distinguishing AD vs HC.

Rahma Kadri et al., [29] analyzed the OASIS dataset by fine-tuning various convolutional neural networks, namely VGG16, ResNet152, AlexNet, and DenseNet. Additionally, they have introduced a unimodal Alzheimer's prediction method employing the EfficientNet network, which addresses key shortcomings of existing convolutional neural networks. The preprocessing steps were image resizing. Results indicate an accuracy of 79% using VGG16, 92% using ResNet, 93% using DenseNet, and an impressive 96% accuracy using the EfficientNet model. Also, Gargi Sharma et al. [30] utilized eight transfer learning models, namely DenseNet-169, MobileNet-V2, ResNet-101, Inception ResNet-V2, Inception-V3, VGG-16, VGG-19, and ResNet-50 to classify AD. The dataset contains 6400 brain MRI scans. Transfer learning model VGG-16 gave an accuracy of 98% and precision of 98.01% which was better compared to other models, and Ahila A et al. [31] have developed a computer-aided diagnosis (CAD) system using a 2D CNN that can differentiate between normal controls (CN) and AD patients. The model has an input layer, 2 subsampling layers, 3 convolutional units, a dropout layer, a fully connected layer, and a smooth max layer. The proposed method evaluated 855 18FDG-PET images, comprising 635 NC and 220 AD patients, with 96% accuracy, and Atif Mehmood et al. [32] utilized transfer learning and tissue segmentation of MRIs to isolate gray matter tissue for early AD detection. This approach eliminated the need for a large amount of annotated data while training. A pre-trained VGG architecture was used for transfer learning and analyzed a dataset of 300 subjects from the ADNI dataset, classified into four groups – normal control (NC), late MCI, early MCI, and AD. The study obtained 98.73% accuracy in differentiating AD vs NC.

Suriya Murugan et al., [33] proposed A DEMNET (DEMentia NETwork) for identifying four different stages of Dementia. They introduced a novel CNN architecture with a reduced number of parameters. They applied the Synthetic Minority Oversampling Technique (SMOTE) analysis. Their experimentation involved datasets comprising 6400 MR images. Additionally, they conducted a five-way classification on 1296 images from the ADNI, covering AD, MCI, EMCI, LMCI, and HC. They attained an accuracy of 95.23% and 85% with and without SMOTE, respectively.

Peixin Lu et al., [34] incorporated transfer learning and contrastive learning to build a two-stage model to improve the specificity of features in MCI. The model was pre-trained on publicly available medical image data using a 3D CNN architecture and then fine-tuned using contrastive learning. The study utilized the ADNI dataset to assess various Med3D pre-trained CNN backbones, including ResNet-50, ResNet-34, ResNet-18, and ResNet-101. The model obtained an accuracy of 82%. Maysam Orouskhani et al. [35] employed a deep triplet network that uses a VGG-16-based model to detect AD by examining brain MR images. The model classifies the disease into four different stages, including, MID, MoD, and ND. To overcome the limited sample sizes and improve accuracy, the network employs a conditional loss function. The OASIS dataset was utilized for training and testing the model, and it achieved an accuracy of 99.41%. Modupe Odusami et al. [36] developed ResNet18 and DenseNet121 deep CNNs that automatically extract randomized deep features from brain functional networks in MRI. These architectures produce concatenated deep features, which are then utilized for 3-way, 4-way, and 5-way classifications of MR images. A dataset comprising 7509 images obtained from the ADNI is utilized.

Bing Yan Lim et al., [37] developed a method for categorizing 3D T1-weighted brain sMRI images into different classes, including MCI, CN, and AD. They utilized the ADNI dataset to train and test their models. The team tested three models: VGG-16, ResNet-50, and a custom-built CNN. They built a new densely connected classifier on top of the pre-trained VGG-16 and ResNet-50 convolutional bases which was utilized for feature extraction, to conduct the classification. While testing, the VGG-16 model outperformed the other models. Sheng Liu et al., [38] a new method was proposed utilizing 3D deep convolutional neural networks to analyze structural MRIs. ADNI and the NACC (National Alzheimer's Coordinating Centre) dataset were utilized. The DL model outperformed the volume or thickness model, obtaining an AUC of 85.12 when differentiating between CN with either MCI or mild Alzheimer's dementia subjects. The DL model was also found to be significantly faster and more effective in forecasting, but this was not the case for the ApoE4-positive group among NACC.

Geneedy et al., [39] presented a shallow CNN model that uses 2D T1-weighted MRI for two types of classifications. The first classification, global, which includes Normal versus MCI and MCI versus AD. Second classification, local, including Stratify MCI into VMD, MD, and MoD. The proposed architecture consists of an input, an output, and several designed units. The study employed five 2D convolutional units, each with a 2D max-pooling layer. OASIS dataset was used and the proposed approach obtained a higher accuracy of 99.68%.

3 Results and Discussion

Throughout several years, numerous models based on ML and DL techniques have been created to detect AD in its initial stages. In this section, we have consolidated all the papers discussed in the previous section and presented them in a tabular form (Table 1).

Table 1. Methods utilizing deep learning to identify Alzheimer's disease

Author	Model	Classification	Dataset	Accuracy
Jyothi Islam et al., [20]	Inception-V4	MoD vs MID vs VMD vs ND	OASIS	73.75%
Chong-Yaw Wee et al., [21]	spectral graph -CNN	CN vs AD	ADNI	85.8% (CN vs AD)
Hongming Li et al., [22]	CNN	HC vs AD, MCI vs AD	ADNI, AIBL	90% 92.9%
Zhang et al., [23]	CNN	AD vs CN, AD vs MCI	ADNI	98.47% (AD vs CN), 88.20% (AD vs MCI)
Simeon Spasov et al., [24]	3D-CNN	HC vs AD, MCI vs AD	ADNI	100% (HC vs AD), 86% (MCI vs AD)
Silvia Basaia et al., [25]	3D-CNN	HC vs AD	ADNI	99.2% (HC vs AD)
Silvia Basaia et al., [25]	3D-CNN	HC vs AD	ADNI	98.2% (HC vs AD)
Jain et al., [26]	CNN	AD vs CN vs MCI	ADNI	95.73% (AD vs CN vs MCI)
Yagis et al., [27]	3D CNN	HC vs AD	ADNI, OASIS	73.4% (ADNI), 69.9% (OASIS)
Dan Pan et al., [28]	CNN - EL	AD vs HC, MCIc vs HC,MCIc vs MCInc	ADNI	84% (AD vs HC), 79% (MCIc vs HC)
Rahma Kadri et al., [29]	CNN and TL	MoD vs MID vs VMD vs ND	OASIS	92% (ResNet), 79% (VGG16)
Gargi Sharma et al., [30]	Transfer learning	MoD vs MID vs VMD vs ND	Kaggle	98% (VGG 16), 97.11% (VGG19)
Ahila et al. [31]	CNN	HC vs AD	ADNI	96%
Atif Mehmood et al., [32]	CNN with Transfer learning	HC vs AD, HC vs LMCI	ADNI	98.73% (HC vs AD), 89.17% (HC vs LMCI),
Suriya et al., [33]	2D CNN DEMNET	MID vs MoD vs ND vs VMD	Kaggle	95.23%
Suriya et al., [33]	2D CNN DEMNET	AD vs MCI vs EMCI vs LMCI	ADNI	84.83%
Peixin Lu et al., [34]	3D CNN	MCI vs AD	ADNI	82%
Maysan Orouskami et al., [35]	Deep triplet Network	ND vs MID vs MoD vs VMD	OASIS	99.41%
Modupe Odusami et al., [36]	ResNet18 and DenseNet201	AD vs MCI vs EMCI vs LMCI vs HC	ADNI	98.86% (5 way), 93.06% (4 way), 98.21% (3 way)
Bing Yan Lim et al., [37]	CNN,VGG16, ResNet	MCI vs AD vs CN	ADNI	72.70% (CNN), 78.57% (VGG16),
Sheng Liu et al., [38]	3D CNN	CN vs MCI vs AD	ADNI	87.59% (CN vs rest), 89.21% (AD vs rest)
Sheng Liu et al., [38]	3D CNN	CN vs MCI vs AD	NACC	85.12% (CN vs rest)
Geneedy et al., [39]	CNN	ND vs MID vs MoD vs VMD	OASIS	99.68%

4 Conclusion

In this study, recent research endeavors focusing on utilizing DL and ML techniques on MRI scans have been examined for the early detection of AD from MCI. Various ML classifiers such as RF, GB, and DL models including 2D/3D CNN, ResNet, DenseNet,

VGG, and Deep Polynomial Networks for AD detection. A significant volume of research has utilized ML, DL and MRI to differentiate between Healthy Controls (HC) and AD, resulting in notably high accuracies. However, our study indicates that the classification accuracy scores for MCI versus AD for early detection using deep learning have consistently been lower compared to HC versus AD. This disparity arises because progressive MCI exhibits similar traits to AD in contrast to HC, thus necessitating more robust deep learning models for discrimination. The integration of multi-modalities has the potential to enhance detection accuracies. Nevertheless, there are relatively few papers available on multi-modality approaches utilizing deep learning for early AD detection. This limited exploration could be attributed to the inherent capability of deep learning to automatically extract relevant features from input images without requiring explicit pre-processing or feature selection. Consequently, integrating other clinical data such as PET scans, genetic information, or cognitive test results can pose challenges. However, multi-modal learning offers the advantage of incorporating diverse perspectives and has the potential to significantly improve diagnostic classification accuracies. Therefore, it warrants further exploration and investigation on a broader scale.

References

1. Shamrat, F.M.J.M., et al.: AlzheimerNet: an effective deep learning based proposition for alzheimer's disease stages classification from functional brain changes in magnetic resonance images. IEEE Access **11**, 16376–16395 (2023). https://doi.org/10.1109/ACCESS.2023.3244952
2. Korolev, I.O.: Alzheimer's disease: a clinical and basic science review. Med. Student Res. J. **4**(1), 24–33 (2014)
3. Alzheimer's Association, Stages of Alzheimer's. https://www.alz.org/alzheimers-dementia/stages
4. Uddin, K.M.M., Alam, M.J., Anawar, J.-E., et al.: A novel approach utilizing machine learning for the early diagnosis of Alzheimer's disease. Biomed. Mater. Dev. **1**(2), 882–898 (2023). https://doi.org/10.1007/s44174-023-00078-9
5. Dementia https://www.who.int/news-room/fact-sheets/detail/dementia
6. Juganavar, A., Joshi, A., Shegekar, T.: Navigating early alzheimer's diagnosis: a comprehensive review of diagnostic innovations. Cureus **15**(9), e44937 (2023). https://doi.org/10.7759/cureus.44937
7. Neuroimagingtechniques: https://openmedscience.com/brain-imaging-in-alzheimers-disease-techniques-advancements-and-challenges/
8. ADNI: https://adni.loni.usc.edu/data-samples/access-data/
9. Open Access Series of imaging Studies (OASIS): https://www.oasis-brains.org/#data
10. MIRIAD: https://www.ucl.ac.uk/drc/research-clinical-trials/minimal-interval-resonance-imaging-alzheimers-disease-miriad
11. AIBL: https://aibl.org.au/about/
12. Chaves, R., et al.: Effective Diagnosis of Alzheimer's Disease by Means of Association Rules. In: Graña Romay, M., Corchado, E., Garcia Sebastian, M.T. (eds.) Hybrid Artificial Intelligence Systems, pp. 452–459. Springer Berlin Heidelberg, Berlin, Heidelberg (2010). https://doi.org/10.1007/978-3-642-13769-3_55
13. Chaves, R., Górriz, J., et al.: Efficient mining of association rules for the early diagnosis of Alzheimer's disease. Phys. Med. Biol. **56**(18), 6047 (2011)

14. Chaves, R., Ramírez, J., Górriz, J.M., Illán, I.A.: Functional brain image classification using association rules defined over discriminant regions. Pattern Recognit. Lett. **33**(12), 1666–1672 (2012). https://doi.org/10.1016/j.patrec.2012.04.011
15. Veeramuthu, A., Meenakshi, S., et al.: A new approach for Alzheimer's disease diagnosis by using association rule over PET images. Int. J. Comput. Appl. **91**(9), 9–14 (2014)
16. Zhang, Y., et al.: Detection of subjects and brain regions related to Alzheimer's disease using 3D MRI scans based on eigenbrain and machine learning. Front. Comput. Neurosci. **9**, 66 (2015). https://doi.org/10.3389/fncom.2015.00066
17. Khan, A., Zubair, S.: An improved multi-modal based machine learning approach for the prognosis of Alzheimer's disease. J. King Saud Univ. – Comput. Inform. Sci. **34**(6), 2688–2706 (2022). https://doi.org/10.1016/j.jksuci.2020.04.004
18. Diogo, V.S., Ferreira, H.A., Prata, D., et al.: Early diagnosis of Alzheimer's disease using machine learning: a multi-diagnostic, generalizable approach. Alz Res Therapy **14**, 107 (2022). https://doi.org/10.1186/s13195-022-01047-y
19. Biswas, R., Rolant Gini, J.: Multi-class classification of Alzheimer's disease detection from 3D MRI image using ML techniques and its performance analysis. Multimed. Tools Appl. **83**(11), 33527–33554 (2023). https://doi.org/10.1007/s11042-023-16519-y
20. Islam, J., Zhang, Y.: A novel deep learning based multi-class classification method for Alzheimer's disease detection using brain MRI data. In: Zeng, Y., et al. (eds.) Brain Informatics: International Conference, BI 2017, Beijing, China, November 16-18, 2017, Proceedings, pp. 213–222. Springer International Publishing, Cham (2017). https://doi.org/10.1007/978-3-319-70772-3_20
21. Wee, C.-Y., Liu, C., Lee, A., Poh, J.S., Ji, H., Qiu, A.: Cortical graph neural network for AD and MCI diagnosis and transfer learning across populations. NeuroImage: Clin. 23, 101929 (2019). https://doi.org/10.1016/j.nicl.2019.101929
22. Li, H., Habes, M., Wolk, D.A., Fan, Y.: A deep learning model for early prediction of Alzheimer's disease dementia based on hippocampal magnetic resonance imaging data. Alzheimer's & Dementia **15**(8), 1059–1070 (2019). https://doi.org/10.1016/j.jalz.2019.02.007
23. Zhang, F., Li, Z., Zhang, B., Du, H., Wang, B., Zhang, X.: Multi-modal deep learning model for auxiliary diagnosis of Alzheimer's disease. Neurocomputing **361**, 185–195 (2019). https://doi.org/10.1016/j.neucom.2019.04.093
24. Spasov, S., Passamonti, L., Duggento, A., Liò, P., Toschi, N.: A parameter-efficient deep learning approach to predict conversion from mild cognitive impairment to Alzheimer's disease. Neuroimage **189**, 276–287 (2019). https://doi.org/10.1016/j.neuroimage.2019.01.031
25. S. Basaia, et al.: Automated classification of Alzheimer's disease and mild cognitive impairment using a single MRI and deep neural networks. NeuroImage: Clin. **21**, 101645 (2019). https://doi.org/10.1016/j.nicl.2018.101645.
26. Jain, R., Jain, N., Aggarwal, A., Jude Hemanth, D.: Convolutional neural network based Alzheimer's disease classification from magnetic resonance brain images. Cognit. Syst. Res. **57**, 147–159 (2019). https://doi.org/10.1016/j.cogsys.2018.12.015
27. Yagis, E., Citi, L., Diciotti, S., Marzi, C., Workalemahu Atnafu, S., Seco De Herrera, A.G.: 3D Convolutional Neural Networks for Diagnosis of Alzheimer's Disease via Structural MRI (2020)
28. Pan, D., Zeng, A., Jia, L., Huang, Y., Frizzell, T., Song, X.: Early detection of Alzheimer's disease using magnetic resonance imaging: a novel approach combining convolutional neural networks and ensemble learning. Front. Neurosci. **14**, 259 (2020). https://doi.org/10.3389/fnins.2020.00259
29. Kadri, R., Tmar, M., Bouaziz, B.: Alzheimer's disease prediction using EfficientNet and fastai. In: Qiu, H., Zhang, C., Fei, Z., Qiu, M., Kung, S.-Y. (eds.) Knowledge Science, Engineering

and Management: 14th International Conference, KSEM 2021, Tokyo, Japan, August 14–16, 2021, Proceedings, Part II, pp. 452–463. Springer International Publishing, Cham (2021). https://doi.org/10.1007/978-3-030-82147-0_37
30. Sharma, G., Vijayvargiya, A., Kumar, R.: Comparative assessment among different convolutional neural network architectures for Alzheimer's disease detection. In: 2021 IEEE 8th Uttar Pradesh Section International Conference on Electrical, Electronics and Computer Engineering (UPCON), Dehradun, India, pp. 1–6 (2021). https://doi.org/10.1109/UPCON52273.2021.9667607
31. Ahila, A., Poongodi, M., Hamdi, M., Bourouis, S., Rastislav, K., Mohmed, F.: Evaluation of neuro images for the diagnosis of Alzheimer's disease using deep learning neural network. Front. Public Health **10**, 834032 (2022). https://doi.org/10.3389/fpubh.2022.834032
32. Mehmood, A., et al.: A transfer learning approach for early diagnosis of Alzheimer's Disease on MRI images. Neuroscience **460**, 43–52 (2021). https://doi.org/10.1016/j.neuroscience.2021.01.002
33. Murugan, S., et al.: DEMNET: a deep learning model for early diagnosis of alzheimer diseases and dementia from MR images. IEEE Access **9**, 90319–90329 (2021). https://doi.org/10.1109/ACCESS.2021.3090474
34. Lu, P., Hu, L., Zhang, N., Liang, H., Tian, T., Lu, L.: A two-stage model for predicting mild cognitive impairment to Alzheimer's disease conversion. Front. Aging Neurosci. **14**, 826622 (2022). https://doi.org/10.3389/fnagi.2022.826622
35. Orouskhani, M., Zhu, C., Rostamian, S., Zadeh, F.S., Shafiei, M., Orouskhani, Y.: Alzheimer's disease detection from structural MRI using conditional deep triplet network. Neurosci. Inform. **2**(4), 100066 (2022). https://doi.org/10.1016/j.neuri.2022.100066
36. Odusami, M., Maskeliunas, R., Damaševičius, R.: An intelligent system for early recognition of Alzheimer's disease using neuroimaging. Sensors. **22**, 740 (2022). https://doi.org/10.3390/s22030740
37. Lim, B.Y., et al.: Deep learning model for prediction of progressive mild cognitive impairment to Alzheimer's disease using structural MRI. Front. Aging Neurosci. (2022). https://doi.org/10.3389/fnagi.2022.876202
38. Liu, S., Masurkar, A.V., Rusinek, H., et al.: Generalizable deep learning model for early Alzheimer's disease detection from structural MRIs. Sci. Rep. **12**, 17106 (2022). https://doi.org/10.1038/s41598-022-20674-x
39. El-Geneedy, M., El-Din Moustafa, H., Khalifa, F., Khater, H., AbdElhalim, E.: An MRI-based deep learning approach for accurate detection of Alzheimer's disease. Alexandria Eng. J. **63**, 211–221 (2023). https://doi.org/10.1016/j.aej.2022.07.062
40. Kumar, A., Ramachandran, M., Gandomi, A.H., Patan, R., Lukasik, S., Soundarapandian, R.K.: A deep neural network based classifier for brain tumor diagnosis. Appl. Soft Comput. **82**, 105528 (2019). https://doi.org/10.1016/j.asoc.2019.105528

Advancements and Applications of 3D Bioprinted Scaffold in Diabetic Wound Healing

Arindam Kolay[1(✉)], Trishna Paul[2], and Ravindra Pal Singh[1]

[1] NIMS University Rajasthan, Jaipur 303121, India
kolayarindam2012@gmail.com
[2] BITS Pilani, Pilani Campus, Rajasthan 333031, India

Abstract. Wound healing presents a significant challenge in healthcare, particularly in cases of diabetic wounds, chronic wounds, burns, and tissue defects. Conventional wound healing methods often fall short in addressing complex wounds, highlighting the urgent need for innovative approaches. In current years, 3D bioprinting has appeared as a promising technology with vast potential in tissue engineering and regenerative medicine. The capability to precisely deposit biomaterials and cells layer by layer offers unprecedented control over scaffold design and composition, making it particularly suitable for creating customized scaffolds tailored to individual patient needs. This review explores the recent advancements and applications of 3D bioprinted scaffolds in diabetic wound healing. We discuss various biological materials used for scaffold fabrication, containing natural polymers, synthetic polymers, and hybrid constructs, emphasizing their bio-compatibility, mechanical properties and degradation kinetics. Additionally, we examine the incorporation of biologically active molecules, growth factors, and stem cells into bioprinted scaffolds to enhance the wound healing processes such as cell proliferation, angiogenesis, and tissue regeneration. Even with the numerous advancements in this sector up to this point, it is still difficult to handle the intricacy of the tissue with the present manufacturing techniques. A review of the characteristics, parameters, and formulations of bioinks are included, along with the current bioprinting techniques. Ultimately, a range of instances and developments in the subject are presented, along with their limits and future directions. Scaffolds are a 3D fabrication that may be used as a template for cell growth and regeneration, avoiding infections and speeding up the diabetic wound healing process.

Keywords: Wound healing · 3D bioprinting · scaffold · skin tissue engineering · tissue regeneration

1 Introduction

Over the last two decades tissue engineering has become increasingly important in restoring injured tissues and organs. Skin, the body's largest organ and outermost layer, has seen significant advancements in wound healing through tissue engineering and regeneration [1]. Efforts to improve 3D bioprinting have led to more detailed structures

M. Bakaev et al. (Eds.): IMS 2024, CCIS 2534, pp. 297–309, 2026.
https://doi.org/10.1007/978-3-031-96177-9_25

resembling natural tissues. Various printing technologies and settings are pivotal in this progress, with additive manufacturing enabling the creation of tissue-like structures. It offers automation and precision in integrating live cells and biomolecules, surpassing conventional methods in skin regeneration [1, 2]. Bioinks, crucial for 3D bio-printing in tissue engineering and wound healing, consist of naturally occurring polymer hydrogels like cellulose, hyaluronic acid, alginate, chitosan, and collagen. Synthetic-based biopolymers are also used to enhance structural mechanics. Bioinks require specific characteristics similar as bio-printability, mechanical reliability, bio-compatibility, biodegradability, less-toxicity, bio-availability, and fidelity post-printing [1, 3]. Moreover, because they directly affect the immune system responses following the implantation of the bioprinted scaffolds, the choice and supply of live cells are top priorities when creating the bioink [4]. Thus, it is preferable to co-cultivate dominant skin cells (fibroblasts, keratinocytes, and melanocytes) for skin and tissue bioprinting structures. This is critical that the bioprinted tissue or organs maintains normal biological functions at all times, including the ability for cell migration and rate of proliferation [5]. The viscoelastic properties of bioinks affect both printability and cell behavior within the matrix. Skin bioprinting has gained popularity, attracting investment from large corporations. The global 3D bio-printing demand for live human tissues and organs is projected to reach USD 2,846.3 million by 2027, with segments for research and clinical applications. Clinical products including tissues, skins, bones, cartilages and blood vessel printing. The uses of 3D bioprinting for skin regeneration and diabetic wound healing began in 2009, with a significant increase in published papers by 2019 and 2020 [6]. Upgradations in 3D bio-printers and bio-materials, coupled with increasing demands in pharmaceutics, cosmetics, and surgery, project a 19.8% compounding annual growth rate (CAGR) for skin bioprinting from 2019 to 2024 [7]. 3D printing technology promises precise design, multiple bioink use, and interconnected porosity, making it ideal for skin scaffold development [8]. Wound healing is a complex process aiming to restore tissue integrity and function, but challenging wounds like large defects and severe burns often hinder this process. Traditional treatments often prove insufficient, underscoring the need for innovative therapeutic approaches [9]. 3D bioprinting is revolutionizing tissue engineering, allowing exact deposition of bio-materials and cells to creates complicated structures resembling native tissue. Customized treatments can be specialized to individual patient requires, prior to superior clinical consequences [9, 10]. The use of 3D bioprinted scaffolds shows promise in wound healing by mimicking tissue environments, promoting cell growth, and controlling chemical release. They utilize various biomaterials and incorporate bioactive compounds to enhance healing. Scaffold architecture influences cell behavior, with challenges in repeatability and scalability being addressed. Ultimately, 3D bioprinting could revolutionize wound care and regenerative medicine.

We provide an in-depth review of the latest advancements in 3D bioprinted scaffolds for diabetic wound healing in this study. We explore various biomaterials used in scaffold fabrication, including synthetic materials, natural polymers, and hybrid structures, emphasizing their mechanical behaviour, biocompatibility, and bio-degradation rates. Additionally, we investigate the addition of biological active compounds, growth factors and stem cells into bioprinted scaffolds to improve diabetic wound healing and tissue regeneration. Furthermore, we analyse the role of scaffold architecture in regulating cell responses and tissue remodelling in the wound microenvironment, emphasizing the importance of pore size, porosity, and mechanical cues in promoting angiogenesis, cell infiltration, and extracellular matrix deposition. We further address the difficulties and limitations of 3D bio-printing technology, such as issues with repeatability, scalability, and regulatory compliance, and propose solutions to overcome these obstacles hindering clinical use.

2 Different 3D Printing Technology

3D printing technology enables the creation of customized framework with precise internal micro-architecture and high resolution. Various 3D printing methods are used to fabricate structural scaffolds for tissue reconstruction, each with its benefits and limitations. In tissue engineering, 3D bioprinting techniques fall into two main categories: those unable to print living cells directly into the structure (such as LDM, SLS, SLA, and FDM) and those utilizing live cells in bioinks for cellular bioprinting. These bioprinting techniques can be grouped into four classes: extrusion-based, droplet-based, laser-based, and stereolithography-based bio-printing [11, 12]. Several different 3D printing technologies are currently utilized in various industries, including healthcare and bioprinting. Each technology has its unique advantages, limitations, and applications. Here are few of the prominent 3D bio-printing technologies (Fig. 1):

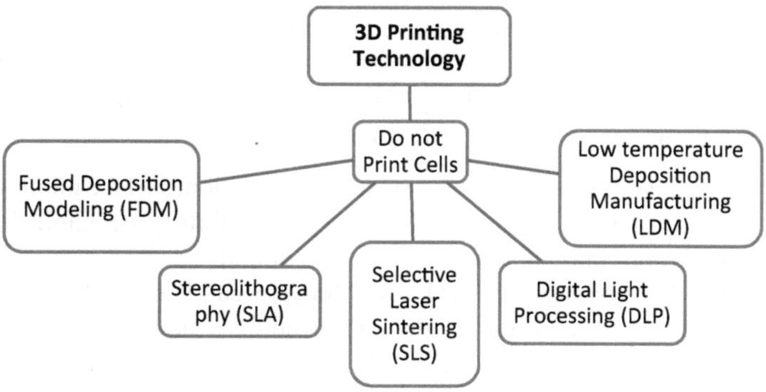

Fig. 1. The 3D bioprinting classification [3D printing technology which don't print cell]

2.1 Fused Deposition Modeling (FDM)

Fused Deposition Modeling is a well-known 3D printing technique, extrudes thermoplastic filaments via a heated nozzle, solidifying layer by layer to create objects. It's extensively used in tissue engineering, including diabetic wound healing, for scaffold preparation. Here's how FDM can be utilized in scaffold fabrication for this purpose:

Material Selection: FDM employs thermoplastic components, such as polylactic acid (PLA), polycaprolactone (PCL), or poly (lactic-co-glycolic acid) (PLGA), which are biocompatible and suitable for tissue engineering purposes. These components can be loaded with biological active agents, growth factors, or antimicrobial components to improve diabetic wound healing properties [1, 3].

Design Considerations: Scaffold design is crucial for tissue regeneration, and FDM enables for the formation of complicated geometries based on CAD models. Parameters like pore size, porosity, and surface roughness can be optimized to promote cell infiltration, vascularization, and tissue integration.

Controlled Porosity: FDM allows for precise control over scaffold porosity by adjusting printing standards such as layer thickness, infill density, and raster scan angle. Porous scaffolds support nutrient and oxygen diffusion, waste excision, and cell migration, which are crucial for supporting cell viability and tissue repair in diabetic wounds [1].

Integration of Bioactive Agents: FDM enables the incorporation of biological active agents, such as cell growth factors or antimicrobial peptides, directly within the scaffold material. These kinds of agents can be encapsulated within the polymer matrix or loaded onto the scaffold surface to encourage wound healing, reduce inflammation, and avoid infection.

Patient-specific Design: FDM supports for the fabrication of patient specific scaffolds designed to the size and shape of the diabetic wound. By utilizing medical imaging data, CAD models can be generated to design scaffolds that precisely fit the wound area, optimizing tissue regrowth and wound resolution outcomes [1].

Cell Seeding: After scaffold fabrication, cells can be seeded onto the scaffold surface or incorporated into the printing material during the fabrication process. This enables the creation of cell-laden scaffolds that promote cell proliferation, extracellular matrix deposition, and tissue regeneration within diabetic wounds.

Post-processing: Post-processing phases such as sterilization, surface modification, and coating can be performed to enhance scaffold biocompatibility, mechanical properties, and functionality before implantation into diabetic wounds.

By leveraging the versatility of FDM technology, researchers can fabricate scaffolds with tunable properties and tailored architectures to address the specific challenges associated with diabetic wound healing, ultimately promoting improved wound closure and tissue regeneration outcomes.

Advantages: FDM printers are relatively affordable and can produce robust, functional prototypes and parts [1].

Limitations: Limited resolution and top layer finish relative to other technologies. Not suitable for printing complex geometries with intricate details.

2.2 Stereolithography (SLA)

Stereolithography or SLA employs a UV laser to exclusively cure liquid photopolymer resin layer by layer, stiffening it into the desired shape. It's a popular 3D bio-printing technology used in scaffold preparation for tissue engineering, including applications related to diabetic wound healing. Here's how SLA can be used for scaffold fabrication:

High Resolution Printing: SLA is known for its high resolution and clarity, enabling for the fabrication of intricate and detailed scaffold structures with accurate control over feature size and geometry. This capability is beneficial for creating scaffolds with complex architectures that thoroughly mimic the native tissue micro environment.

Biocompatible Materials: SLA utilizes biocompatible photopolymer resins that solidify under ultraviolet (UV) light exposure. Suitable for tissue engineering, these resins may comprise acrylates, methacrylates, or other biocompatible monomers promoting cell attachment, proliferation, and differentiation [3].

Tailored Material Properties: SLA resins offer versatility in mechanical properties, including stiffness and elasticity. Researchers can tailor these properties for diabetic wound healing by adjusting resin composition to provide adequate support and flexibility.

Precise Control over Porosity: SLA enables the construction of scaffolds with controlled porosity, distribution, and interconnectivity. This accurate control over scaffold porosity allows intended for optimization of nutrient diffusion, waste removal, and cell infiltration within diabetic wounds, fostering tissue regrowth and wound healing.

Incorporation of Bioactive Agents: SLA resins can integrate biological active molecules like growth factors or antibiotics to improve scaffold bioactivity. These agents, encapsulated within the resin or immobilized on the scaffold surface, promote cell behavior, modulate inflammation, and prevent infection in diabetic wounds [1, 9].

Multi-material Printing: Certain SLA printers support multi-material printing, enabling the creation of composite scaffolds with varied properties. In diabetic wound healing, this feature can be used to design scaffolds with gradient structures or localized delivery of bioactive agents, enhancing wound healing outcomes.

Post-processing Options: SLA-printed scaffolds may require post-processing stages such as cleaning, sterilization, and top layer modification to improve biocompatibility, remove residual uncured resin, and enhance cell-material interactions before implantation into diabetic wounds [7].

Overall, SLA technology provides accurate control over scaffold design, material qualities and bioactive agent incorporation, offering a promising approach for fabricating scaffolds tailored to the particular needs of diabetic wound healing.

Advantages: High resolution, excellent surface finish, and ability to produce intricate details [1].

Limitations: Limited choice of materials, higher cost compared to FDM, and post-processing steps may be essential to remove uncured resin.

2.3 Selective Laser Sintering (SLS)

Selective Laser Sintering or SLS utilizes a high-voltage laser to selectively fuse powdered materials like nylon or metal layer by layer, forming a solid structure. It's a 3D printing technology used for scaffold preparation in tissue engineering, including diabetic wound healing. Here's how SLS can be used for scaffold fabrication:

Powder-based Printing: SLS selectively fuses powdered materials layer by layer with a high-powered laser, creating intricate scaffold structures without requiring support structures, thanks to the unsintered powder's inherent support during printing.

Biocompatible Powder Materials: SLS can utilize biocompatible powder materials like polycaprolactone (PCL), poly (lactic-co-glycolic acid) (PLGA), or polyethylene glycol (PEG), providing flexibility in scaffold design to match the mechanical support and degradation kinetics required for diabetic wound healing [1, 3].

High Porosity and Interconnectivity: SLS enables the fabrication of highly porous scaffolds with interlinked pore networks, essential for promoting cell penetration and tissue regeneration in diabetic wounds.

Graded Porosity and Density: SLS can produce scaffolds with varying porosity and density, offering spatial control over mechanical properties and bioactive agent release. This capability allows for mimicking the hierarchical structure of native tissues, enhancing wound healing in diabetic patients.

Incorporation of Bioactive Agents: SLS-printed scaffolds can integrate biological active molecules, growth factors or pharmaceutical substances to support tissue regeneration and wound healing. These agents can be incorporated into the scaffold during printing or post-processing, enabling targeted delivery to the wound site [2].

Patient-specific Design: SLS medical technology enables for the fabrication of patient-specific scaffolds customized to the size, shape and contours of diabetic wounds. By utilizing medical imaging data, customized scaffolds can be designed to precisely fit the wound site, promoting optimal tissue integration and wound healing outcomes.

Post-processing Options: SLS-printed scaffolds may require post-processing phases such as cleaning, sterilization, and surface alteration to improve biocompatibility and enhance cell-material interactions before implantation into diabetic wounds.

In summary, Selective Laser Sintering (SLS) presents numerous advantages for scaffold fabrication in diabetic wound healing, providing precise control over scaffold architecture, porosity, and bioactive agent integration. These capabilities position SLS as a promising technology for crafting scaffolds tailored to the exact needs of diabetic wound healing.

Advantages: No need for support structures, capability to print complicated geometries, and a wide range of substances including thermoplastics, metals and ceramics [1].

Limitations: Higher equipment cost, rough surface finish, and limited resolution compared to SLA.

2.4 Digital Light Processing (DLP)

Digital Light Processing or DLP's use of a UV light source enables precise curing of photopolymer resin layers, allowing for the creation of detailed structures. This technology is versatile and applicable to tissue engineering, including diabetic wound healing, due to its capability to fabricate complex three-dimensional scaffolds. Here's how DLP can be utilized for scaffold fabrication:

High Resolution Printing: DLP provides high-resolution printing, allowing for intricate scaffold designs with precise architectural control. This capability is crucial for mimicking native tissue microenvironments and promoting tissue regeneration in diabetic wounds.

Biocompatible Photopolymer Resins: DLP uses biocompatible photopolymer resins that solidify under light exposure. These resins assist cell attachment, proliferation and differentiation producing them suitable for tissue engineering applications.

Tailored Material Properties: DLP resins offer customizable mechanical properties, allowing researchers to tailor scaffold characteristics for diabetic wound healing, ensuring adequate support and flexibility.

Precise Control over Porosity: DLP provides accurate control over scaffold porosity, optimizing nutrient diffusion and cell infiltration for enhanced tissue regeneration in diabetic wounds.

Incorporation of Bioactive Agents: DLP resins can incorporate bioactive molecules to enhance scaffold bioactivity, promoting cell behavior and aiding wound healing in diabetic patients [3].

Multi-material Printing: Some DLP printers support multi-material printing, enabling the creation of composite scaffolds with varied properties. This feature can be used for diabetic wound healing to design scaffolds with gradient structures or targeted delivery of bioactive agents, enhancing wound healing [14].

Post-processing Options: DLP-printed scaffolds may require post-processing phases such as cleaning, sterilization and surface alteration to improve biocompatibility, remove residual uncured resin, and enhance cell-material interactions before implantation into diabetic wounds.

In summary, Digital Light Processing offers several advantages for scaffold preparation in diabetic wound healing including high resolution printing, exact control over scaffold construction and porosity and the ability to incorporate bioactive agents. These capabilities make DLP a promising technology for fabricating scaffolds designed to the particular requirements of diabetic wound healing applications.

Advantages: Faster printing speed compared to SLA, high resolution, and good surface finish [1].

Limitations: Limited choice of materials, higher cost compared to FDM, and potential for resin waste due to the vat-based printing process.

2.5 Low Temperature Deposition Manufacturing (LDM)

Low Temperature Deposition Manufacturing or LDM is a 3D printing innovation ideal for processing temperature-sensitive materials like certain polymers and biomaterials used in tissue engineering. It allows the fabrication of structures at less temperatures compared to traditional methods, making it suitable for scaffold preparation. LDM can offer several advantages:

Biocompatible Material Processing: LDM allows the use of biocompatible materials that may degrade or lose their properties at high temperatures. This enables the fabrication of scaffolds using temperature-sensitive biomaterials such as hydrogels, bioactive ceramics, and biodegradable polymers.

Cell Viability: Lower processing temperatures in LDM help preserve the viability of encapsulated cells within the scaffold. This is crucial for maintaining the functionality of seeded cells and promoting tissue regeneration in the scaffold after implantation.

Precise Control: LDM technology provides precise control over scaffold architecture and feature resolution allowing the construction of complex framework with tailored features. This enables the design of scaffolds with specific pore sizes, interconnectivity, and geometries optimized for tissue regeneration.

Multi-material Printing: Some LDM systems support multi-material printing, allowing the incorporation of multiple materials within the scaffold structure. This capability can be used to build composite scaffolds with gradient characteristics or localized delivery of bioactive agents, enhancing their effectiveness in promoting wound healing and tissue regeneration [1, 3].

Patient-specific Design: LDM technology facilitates the fabrication of patient-specific scaffolds tailored to individual anatomical requirements. By utilizing medical imaging data, customized scaffolds can be designed to precisely fit the wound site, promoting better integration and wound healing outcomes.

Post-processing Options: LDM-printed scaffolds may need post-processing phases such as sterilization, surface modification and coating to improve biocompatibility and enhance their performance before implantation into diabetic wounds [11, 12].

In summary, Low Temperature Deposition Manufacturing offers several advantages for scaffold preparation in tissue engineering applications, including diabetic wound healing. Its ability to process temperature-sensitive biomaterials while maintaining cell viability and providing exact control over scaffold architecture creates it a promising technology for fabricating scaffolds tailored to the particular needs of diabetic wound care (Fig. 2).

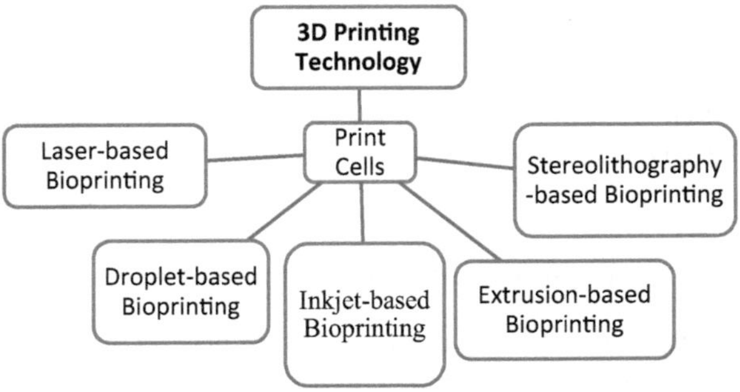

Fig. 2. The 3D bioprinting classification [3D printing technology which print cell]

3 Different 3D Printing Technology [Print Cell]

3D bioprinting is a cutting-edge technology that includes the layer-by-layer deposition of living cells, biomaterials and bioactive molecules to build complex 3D structures that mimic native tissues or organs. This technology contains immense potential for various purposes in regenerative medicine, drug discovery and personalized healthcare.

3.1 Laser-Based Bioprinting

Laser-based bioprinting offers accurate control over cell placement and biomaterial deposition, creating high-resolution tissue constructs. It minimizes shear stress on cells and is ideal for sensitive biomaterials, promising for tissue engineering, drug screening, and personalized medicine [6, 16].

3.2 Droplet-Based Bioprinting

Droplet-based bioprinting creates precise structures with high resolution and cell viability by depositing bioink droplets. Its versatility makes it suitable for various biomaterials and cell types, crucial for applications like drug screening and regenerative medicine [1, 3].

3.3 Inkjet-Based Bioprinting

Inkjet-based bioprinting layers bioinks with living cells, offering speed, precision, and scalability. Its non-contact nature minimizes cell stress, ideal for delicate types and bioactive substances. Promising for tissue modeling, drug screening, and regenerative medicine, it advances both research and therapy [2, 3].

Advantages: Capability to print with multiple materials at the same time, including cells and biomaterials, allowing the fabrication of tissues and organs [17].

Limitations: Obstacles related to cell viability, resolution and limited control over tissue architecture compared to other bioprinting technologies.

3.4 Extrusion-Based Bioprinting

Extrusion-based bioprinting layers bioink through a nozzle, providing versatility, high cell viability, and customizable properties. Precise control allows intricate structures, and multiple bioinks enable complex tissues. Promising for regeneration, organ-on-a-chip, and personalized medicine, it advances research and therapy.

Advantages: Versatility in printing various biomaterials and cells, relatively low cost, and scalability [1, 4].

Limitations: Limited resolution compared to inkjet-based bioprinting, potential for shear stress-induced cell damage during printing, and challenges in achieving precise control over cell distribution.

3.5 Stereolithography-Based Bioprinting

Stereolithography-based bioprinting utilizes UV laser to polymerize photosensitive bioinks, enabling high-resolution structures with precise geometry. It supports diverse biomaterials, fostering intricate scaffold architectures resembling native tissues. This method accommodates several cell types and biological active molecules, reducing mechanical stress on cells. With employment in tissue engineering, regenerative medicine and drug discovery, it advances both research and clinical therapies [1, 3] (Fig. 3).

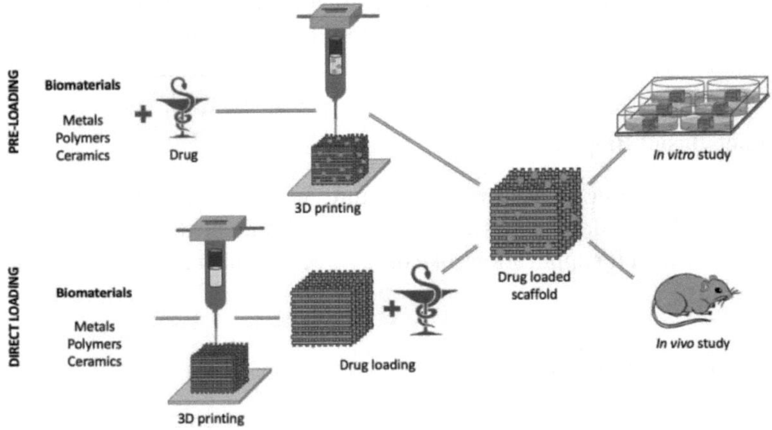

Fig. 3. Schematic format summarizing pre-loading and direct loading 3DP porous substrate construction for in vitro and in vivo drug delivery applications [3].

4 Printer Software's

As 3D bioprinting technology has advanced, computer-aided project software like UG, CATIA, or ProE are used to model structures. An ST-format file is transported to the 3D printing system to manage the printing process. Bioprinting includes three main stages: pre-processing, processing, and post-processing [18]. Pre-processing calculates planned elements and converts imaging data into a bioprinting blueprint. Processing includes creating and producing the bioprinted tissue, while post-processing prepares the tissue for use. Specialized software like AutoCAD and SOLIDWORKS is used throughout these stages [1, 20].

5 Bioinks for 3D Printing Technology

Bioinks are vital for 3D bioprinting, enabling the creation of complex structures mimicking natural tissues. These formulations help cell growth and tissue development, but the scarcity of suitable materials has prompted research into novel bioinks [19]. Various additive manufacturing techniques, including inkjet, extrusion, and lithography-based methods, aim to address this challenge by incorporating specific rheological and physical properties required for effective printing in tissue engineering [4, 5].

6 Applications of 3D Printed Scaffold for Diabetic Wound Healing

3D printed scaffolds hold significant promise for diabetic wound healing due to their capability to provide tailored structural support, mimic the extracellular matrix (ECM) of tissues and support cell adhesion, proliferation, and differentiation [3]. Here are several key applications of 3D bioprinted scaffolds in diabetic wound healing:

Customized Wound Dressings: 3D printing offers tailored wound dressings for diabetic ulcers, featuring precise fit, porous structures for improved gas exchange, moisture management, and controlled release of bioactive agents to support wound healing [1, 15].

Biologically Active Scaffolds: Bioactive 3D printed scaffolds for wound dressings can contain growth factors, antimicrobial agents, or other molecules to enhance healing in diabetic wounds by promoting angiogenesis, tissue regeneration, and infection mitigation [12].

Cell-seeded Constructs: Cell-seeded 3D scaffolds promote diabetic wound healing by integrating cells for tissue regeneration. MSCs, keratinocytes, fibroblasts, and endothelial cells enhance angiogenesis, collagen production, and re-epithelialization.

Mechanical Support and Protection: 3D printed scaffolds offer tailored mechanical support for diabetic wounds, reducing infection risk and trauma while supporting tissue regeneration [1, 3].

Patient-specific Implants: 3D bioprinted patient-specific implants can aid in closing chronic diabetic wounds, leveraging precise fitting and tailored design for improved integration and healing [13].

Drug Delivery Systems: 3D printed scaffolds can act as localized drug delivery systems for diabetic wound healing, offering controlled release of therapeutic agents to the wound site, enhancing efficiency while minimizing systemic side effects [21].

Overall, 3D bio-printed scaffolds offer a versatile system for personalized and effective wound management in diabetic patients, addressing the complex challenges associated with reduced wound healing in this population. Ongoing research in scaffold design, biomaterial selection, and cell incorporation strategies continues to advance the field toward the development of innovative therapeutic solutions for diabetic wound care.

7 Conclusion

In conclusion, 3D bioprinted scaffolds show great promise for addressing challenges in diabetic wound healing. These customizable structures provide support, encourage tissue regeneration and aid wound healing for diabetic patients. Advanced bioprinting techniques allow precise control over scaffold architecture, porosity and bioactive agent incorporation, mimicking the native extracellular matrix and facilitating angiogenesis. Personalized treatment approaches can be achieved by incorporating patient-specific factors. While further research is needed to optimize scaffold design and functionality, 3D bioprinted scaffolds provide a promising avenue for accelerating diabetic wound healing and improving patient outcomes. Continued innovation and collaboration are essential for advancing these therapeutic solutions in clinical settings.

References

1. Antezana, P.E., et al.: The 3D bioprinted scaffolds for wound healing. Pharmaceutics **14**(2), 464 (2022). https://doi.org/10.3390/pharmaceutics14020464
2. Li, X., et al.: 3D-printed biopolymers for tissue engineering application. Int. J. Polym. Sci. **2014**, 1–13 (2014)
3. Limongi, T., Susa, F., Allione, M., di Fabrizio, E.: Drug delivery applications of three-dimensional printed (3DP) mesoporous scaffolds. Pharmaceutics **12**(9), 851 (2020). https://doi.org/10.3390/pharmaceutics12090851.PMID:32911620;PMCID:PMC7558976
4. Hospodiuk, M., Dey, M., Sosnoski, D., Ozbolat, I.T.: The bioink: a comprehensive review on bioprintable materials. Biotechnol. Adv. **35**, 217–239 (2017)
5. Groll, J., et al.: A definition of bioinks and their distinction from biomaterial inks. Biofabrication **11**, 013001 (2019)
6. Koch, L., et al.: Laser printing of skin cells and human stem cells. Tissue Eng. Part C Methods **16**, 847–854 (2010)
7. D Bioprinting Market by Component (3D Bioprinters (Microextrusion, Inkjet, Laser), Bioink (Natural, Synthetic, Hybrid)), Material (Hydrogel, Living Cells), Application (Skin, Drug Research), End user (Biopharma, Academia)-Global Forecast to 2024
8. Zhang, B., Song, J.: 3D-printed biomaterials for guided tissue regeneration. Small Methods **2**, 1700306 (2018)
9. Suamte, L., Tirkey, A., Jayasekhar Babu, P.: Design of 3D smart scaffolds using natural, synthetic and hybrid derived polymers for skin regenerative applications. Smart Mater. Med. **4**, 243–256 (2023)
10. Guo, S.A., DiPietro, L.A.: Factors affecting wound healing. J. Dent. Res. **89**(3), 219–229 (2010)
11. Murphy, S.V., Atala, A.: 3D Bioprinting of tissues and organs. Nat. Biotechnol. **32**, 773–785 (2014)
12. Zhang, X., Zhang, Y.: Tissue engineering applications of three-dimensional bioprinting. Cell Biophys. **72**, 777–782 (2015)
13. Intini, C., et al.: 3D-printed chitosan-based scaffolds: an in vitro study of human skin cell growth and an in-vivo wound healing evaluation in experimental diabetes in rats. Carbohydr. Polym. **199**, 593–602 (2018)
14. Ng, W.L., Qi, J.T.Z., Yeong, W.Y., Naing, M.W.: Proof-of-concept: 3D bioprinting of pigmented human skin constructs. Biofabrication **10**, 025005 (2018)
15. Do, A.-V., Khorsand, B., Geary, S.M., Salem, A.K.: 3D Printing of scaffolds for tissue regeneration applications. Adv. Healthc. Mater. **4**, 1742–1762 (2015)
16. Schiele, N.R., Corr, D.T., Huang, Y., Raof, N.A., Xie, Y., Chrisey, D.B.: Laser-based direct-write techniques for cell printing. Biofabrication **2**, 032001 (2010)
17. Vikram Singh, A., et al.: The Adoption of Three-Dimensional Additive Manufacturing from Biomedical Material Design to 3D Organ Printing. Appl. Sci. **9**, 811(2019)

18. Soman, P., Chung, P.H., Zhang, A.P., Chen, S.: Digital microfabrication of user-defined 3d microstructures in cell-laden hydrogels. Biotechnol. Bioeng. **110**, 3038–3047 (2013)
19. Bishop, E.S., et al.: 3-d bioprinting technologies in tissue engineering and regenerative medicine: current and future trends. Genes Dis. **4**, 185–195 (2017)
20. Tottoli, E.M., Dorati, R., Genta, I., Chiesa, E., Pisani, S., Conti, B.: Skin wound healing process and new emerging technologies for skin wound care and regeneration. Pharmaceutics **12**, 735 (2020)
21. Ishack, S., Lipner, S.R.: A review of 3-dimensional skin bioprinting techniques: applications, approaches, and trends. Dermatol. Surg. **46**, 1500–1505 (2020)

Interactive Systems and Information Society Technologies: Human-Computer Systems in Industry and Economy

Visualizing Quantum Machine Learning Concepts: A Unity 3D Approach

Mohamed Fawaz Ariff(✉) and B. Vijayakumar

Department of Computer Science, Birla Institute of Technology and Science Pilani, Dubai Campus, Dubai, UAE
{f20200059,vijay}@dubai.bits-pilani.ac.in

Abstract. This paper presents a novel method for visualizing quantum machine learning concepts using Unity 3D, aimed at enhancing comprehension and engagement in this burgeoning field. Through animated simulations, fundamental principles of quantum computing are elucidated, showcasing their synergy with machine learning algorithms. Leveraging the robust capabilities of Unity 3D, dynamic 3D animations vividly illustrate complex quantum phenomena like superposition and entanglement. The implementation phase involves the scripting of interactive features, empowering users to explore and manipulate visualizations interactively. By integrating animation, interactivity, and user engagement, this approach offers a unique and immersive learning experience, fostering deeper insights into the intricate realm of quantum machine learning. Through this innovative methodology, the paper aims to bridge the gap between theoretical concepts and practical understanding, paving the way for broader adoption and advancement in quantum machine learning education and research.

Keyword: Quantum Machine Learning · Quantum Computing · Quantum Algorithm · Animation

1 Introduction

The fusion of quantum computing and machine learning has emerged as a transformative force, promising unprecedented advancements in fields ranging from cryptography to drug discovery. However, the abstract nature of quantum concepts presents a significant barrier to understanding for both novice learners and professionals. In response, this paper proposes a novel approach to elucidate the concepts of Quantum Machine Learning (QML) through the usage of Unity 3D, a versatile game development platform. By utilizing the Unity's immersive visualization capabilities, simulations and dynamic animations, the paper aims to bridge the gap between theoretical concepts and practical understanding.

Compared to other software and game engines, Unity 3D stands out for its versatility and ease of use, particularly in educational applications. Unlike Unreal Engine, which is known for its highfidelity graphics but has a steeper learning curve, Unity offers a more accessible development environment and is compatible on most devices. While software

M. Bakaev et al. (Eds.): IMS 2024, CCIS 2534, pp. 313–322, 2026.
https://doi.org/10.1007/978-3-031-96177-9_26

like Blender excels in 3D modeling and animation, it lacks the interactive capabilities essential for creating engaging educational experiences. Additionally, specialized educational software often lacks the flexibility and cross-platform support that Unity provides, limiting their accessibility and adaptability. Unity's real-time rendering, comprehensive asset store, and user-friendly interface makes it a superior choice for developing interactive educational tools which can effectively convey complex concepts like quantum machine learning.

1.1 Objective and Scope

The objective of this paper is to explore the feasibility and effectiveness of utilizing Unity 3D software as a platform for visualizing and understanding quantum machine learning concepts, and to demonstrate the potential educational benefits of such visualizations. The scope of this paper encompasses an in-depth examination of key quantum machine learning concepts, including superposition, entanglement, quantum circuits, and quantum algorithms, with a focus on their visualization within the Unity 3D environment. Through a series of interactive simulations and animations, the paper aims to elucidate these abstract concepts in a visually engaging manner. Additionally, this paper will evaluate the educational impact of utilizing Unity 3D, assessing its effectiveness in enhancing comprehension, retention, and engagement among students and educators alike.

1.2 Motivation

The motivation behind this paper stems from the vital need to bridge the gap between the abstract nature of quantum mechanics and the practical applications of machine learning. Quantum machine learning holds immense promise for revolutionizing industries ranging from healthcare to finance. However, understanding the intricate concepts of quantum phenomena and machine learning algorithms poses a significant challenge for learners. Traditional methods of teaching and visualization often fall short in conveying these complex ideas effectively. Hence, there is a compelling need for innovative approaches that can provide intuitive insights into the interplay between quantum mechanics and machine learning.

2 Literature Survey

2.1 Overview of Quantum Computing

In regular computers, information is stored as bits, which are either 0's or 1's. But in quantum computers, information is stored in quantum bits, or qubits, which can be both 0 and 1 at the same time thanks to a phenomenon called superposition [1]. This allows quantum computers to perform many calculations simultaneously, making them potentially much faster and more powerful than classical computers for certain tasks [2]. Additionally, qubits can be entangled, meaning the state of one qubit is dependent on the state of another, enabling even more complex computations. Some of the basic Quantum Computing concepts are: -

1) Qubit: Quantum bits, or qubits, are the building blocks of quantum computing, similar to bits in regular computers. However, unlike bits which can only be in one state at a time (0 or 1), a qubit can exist in multiple states at once. Despite this, the amount of information a qubit can hold is the same as a single bit in classical computing.
2) Superposition: It means that a qubit can exist in a combination of states simultaneously, like both 0 and 1 at the same time. This allows us to store more information with fewer qubits. For example, with just one qubit, we can store the equivalent of two classical bits. This scales exponentially: for every additional qubit, we can double the amount of information stored.
3) Entanglement: It is a remarkable phenomenon in quantum mechanics where the properties of qubits become intertwined, resulting in a loss of individuality for each qubit. This means that the state of one qubit is inherently linked to the state of another, regardless of the physical distance between them. Even if the qubits are separated by vast distances, changes in one qubit instantaneously affect the other, creating a strong correlation between them.
4) Quantum Gates: They are like instructions in quantum computing, helping transform the state of qubits from one state to another. When we apply a quantum gate, we expect the total probability of all possible outcomes to remain the same. This ensures that the probability amplitudes of all possible states add up to one. Quantum gates are reversible, meaning we can undo their effects.

2.2 Quantum Machine Learning

In recent years, the field of machine learning has experienced significant growth, driven by the exponential increase in available datasets [3]. Machine learning aims to empower computers to perform tasks autonomously, without explicit programming [4]. Its applications span diverse domains, from predicting protein structures and discovering drugs [5] to detecting black holes and analyzing waves. However, the escalating size of datasets presents challenges. Moore's Law which observes that the number of transistors in a computer chip doubles approximately every two years, is reaching its limits, indicating that conventional computational methods may struggle to handle these vast datasets.

Quantum machine learning (QML) is the intersection of machine learning and quantum computing. QML along with quantum computers can handle data at unprecedented speeds compared to traditional computers [6]. It involves implementing algorithms on quantum systems, enabling computer programs to learn and improve through experience. The two major quantum algorithms are explained below:-

5) Grovers Algorithm: Grover's algorithm serves as a foundational component in numerous machine learning algorithms. Many complex problems, such as the K-Means clustering or the Traveling Salesman Problem, involve searching for specific elements within datasets. Inefficient search algorithms can significantly impact the overall performance of these machine learning algorithms. NP-Complete problems, including these examples, are characterized by their complexity, where solving them becomes increasingly time-consuming as the dataset size grows [7].

While classical algorithms typically take linear time (O(n)) to locate a match within a dataset of n values, Grover's algorithm achieves the same task on a quantum computer in only square root time. In machine learning, it's especially useful for optimization problems, where finding the minimum is crucial. Grover's algorithm utilizes a quantum oracle, a unitary operator, to verify if the searched result is correct by identifying items smaller than a threshold value. It repeats this process multiple times to pinpoint the correct solution. Overall, Grover's algorithm's speedup makes it a valuable subroutine in many machine learning algorithms.

6) Harrow-Hassidim-Lloyd (HHL) Algorithm: The HHL Algorithm is a prominent quantum algorithm known for its capability to accelerate various machine learning techniques. Serving as a fundamental subroutine, it excels in solving systems of linear equations. Linear systems are prevalent in science and engineering fields, making the HHL algorithm highly valuable. Its exponential speedup compared to classical methods enables efficient data processing, numerical calculations, and applications in quantum machine learning models such as support vector machines, linear regression, and recommendation systems [8].

3 Problem Description

The complex and abstract nature of quantum machine learning concepts presents a significant challenge for learners and educators alike. Traditional methods of teaching and visualization often struggle to convey these intricate ideas effectively. As shown in the Data Flow Diagram below in Fig.1, learners are faced with the daunting task of understanding quantum phenomena such as superposition, entanglement, and quantum circuit operations through static diagrams and textual descriptions alone. Without dynamic and interactive visualizations, comprehension of these concepts may remain limited, hindering the development of a deeper understanding and appreciation for the potential applications of quantum machine learning.

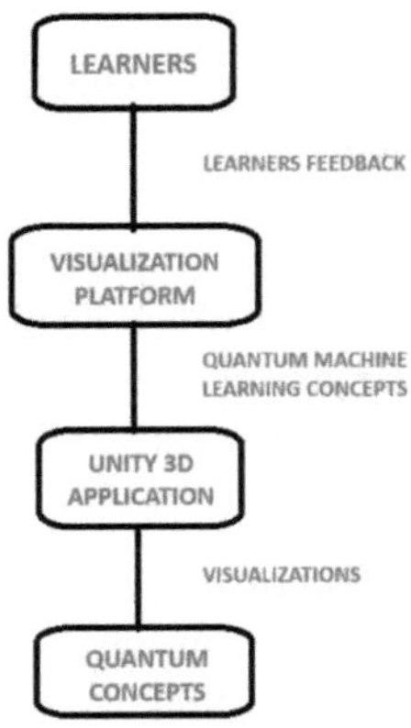

Fig. 1. Data Flow Diagram

In this Data Flow Diagram, learners interact with the Visualization Platform, which utilizes Unity 3D to create dynamic visualizations of Quantum Machine Learning Concepts. These visualizations help learners understand complex concepts more effectively.

Additionally, learner feedback may flow back into the system, allowing for iterative improvements in the visualizations to better meet the needs of learners.

4 Experimental Setup

4.1 Unity 3D Application

Unity 3D is a powerful cross-platform game engine and development environment used for creating interactive 2D and 3D experiences. Its intuitive interface, extensive features, and flexibility makes it a superior choice for educational purposes. It provides a dynamic and immersive learning environment where students can engage with interactive simulations and visualizations, which will result in deeper understanding of complex concepts [9].

The intersection of quantum computing and machine learning has got significant attention for its potential to revolutionize various industries. However, understanding and visualizing the complex concepts underlying quantum machine learning can be challenging. In response to this challenge, the use of Unity3D software emerges as a powerful tool for creating immersive and interactive visualizations.

By utilizing Unity 3D, users can bridge the gap between theoretical knowledge and practical understanding, facilitating deeper insights into the complex interplay between quantum mechanics and machine learning algorithms.

Animations and visualizations serve as indispensable tools for elucidating complex concepts. Through animated simulations, concepts such as superposition, entanglement, and quantum circuit operations can be visualized in a way that transcends traditional static representations [10].

4.2 Microsoft Visual Studio

Microsoft Visual Studio is a comprehensive integrated development environment (IDE) utilized for programming of animations and other interactive tasks with unity 3D. With the extensive suite of tools and features, Visual Studio streamlines the coding process, facilitates debugging, and enhances project management. The integration of Microsoft Visual Studio with Unity 3D provides a powerful environment for C# programming, the primary scripting language used in Unity development.

Visual Studio offers advanced code editing capabilities, including syntax high- lighting, code completion, and error checking, enabling to write clean and efficient C# scripts for Unity projects. Additionally, Visual Studio's debugging tools allow for seamless identification and resolution of code errors, ensuring smooth development workflows. Furthermore, Visual Studio facilitates efficient project management within Unity environments.

By combining Unity 3D's animation capabilities with C# scripting in Visual Studio, dynamic and informative visualizations can be created that aid in un- derstanding intricate QML principles, such as superposition, entanglement, and quantum algorithms like Grover's and HHL algorithms.

5 Design and Implementation

5.1 Implementation in Microsoft Visual Studio

The pseudo code shown in Fig. 2 is responsible for the transition from one scene to another. This code is sourced from the project's demonstration model. A Cross-fade transition style is used here and the script is written in Unity's C# language in Microsoft Visual Studio. The sceneLoader class contains several member variables, including transition, which represents an Animator component responsible for handling transition animations between scenes, and transitionTime, a float variable indicating the duration of the transition effect. The Update() function, a built-in Unity method, is called every frame and checks for user input. In this case, it detects if the left mouse button is pressed down using Input.GetMouseButtonDown(0). When triggered, it calls the LoadNextScene() function.

```
DECLARE class sceneLoader
    DECLARE transition of type Animator
    DECLARE transitionTime of type float

    FUNCTION Update()
        IF left mouse button is pressed down THEN
            CALL LoadNextScene()
        END IF
    END FUNCTION

    FUNCTION LoadNextScene()
        CALL StartCoroutine(LoadScene(SceneManager.
        GetActiveScene().buildIndex + 1))
    END FUNCTION

    FUNCTION LoadScene(sceneIndex)
        SET transition trigger to "Start"
        WAIT for transitionTime seconds
        Load scene with index sceneIndex
    END FUNCTION
END class
```

Fig. 2. Pseudo Code

The LoadNextScene() function initiates the scene loading process by starting a coroutine called LoadScene(). This coroutine takes an integer parameter sceneIndex, which specifies the index of the scene to be loaded. It retrieves the index of the current active scene and increments it by one to load the next scene in the build order. Within the LoadScene() coroutine, the transition animation is triggered by setting the trigger parameter of the transition Animator component to "Start". The coroutine then waits for a specified duration, determined by the transitionTime variable, using yield return new WaitForSeconds(transitionTime). After the delay, the SceneManager.LoadScene() function is called to load the scene with the specified index, effectively transitioning to the next scene in the sequence.

5.2 Implementation in Unity 3D

The animation flow-chart designed in the animator tab as shown in Fig. 3 is used for transitioning from one scene to another. This snapshot of the animator controller is taken from the project's demonstration model. Here, the cross-fade transition script is implemented between the CrossFade_End and CrossFade_Start. The Animator tab in Unity is used for creating and managing complex animation sequences and state transitions within a game or application. Within this tab, the visualization and organization of the animation logic is done using a flowchart-like interface, known as the Animator Controller. Here, individual animation states are represented as nodes, interconnected by transitions that define the conditions for switching between states. By dragging and connecting these nodes, animation behaviors can be tweaked, incorporating blending, layering, and parameter-driven transitions to achieve desired effects.

The Fig. 4 shows the settings and animation pane for transition between scenes. This snapshot of the animator settings is taken from the project's demonstration model. In Unity's Animator Controller, transitions define the flow between animation states, allowing for smooth and controlled movement between different actions or behaviors. These transitions are configured with various settings, including conditions that must be met for the transition to occur, such as parameter values or triggers. Additionally, transition settings can be adjusted to control the timing and blending of animations, ensuring seamless transitions between states. By fine-tuning these settings, dynamic and responsive animations can be created that enhance the realism and fluidity of gameplay experiences.

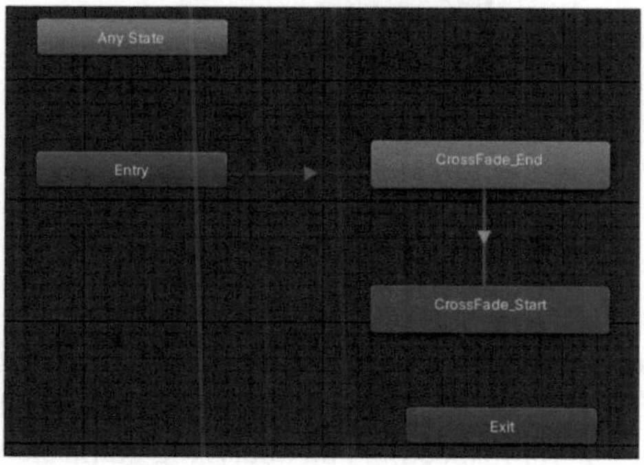

Fig. 3. Animator Controller

The Fig. 5 displays the Scene Creation using canvas. The snapshot of the scene creation is taken from the project's demonstration model. In Unity, creating scenes within a canvas to represent slides involves designing individual canvas elements, such as images, text, and UI buttons, to visually represent each slide. Each slide is typically organized as a separate canvas object within the Unity Editor, allowing for easy manipulation and arrangement. These canvas elements are then scripted to transition between slides based on user input or predefined triggers, creating a seamless slideshow experience.

The Fig. 6 displays the Game View of a scene which is sourced from the project's demonstration model. The Game View in Unity provides a real-time preview of the game or application as it will appear to users. This viewport displays the scene currently being edited in the Unity Editor, which allows to observe the creations in action and test gameplay mechanics, visual effects, and user interactions. By simulating the game

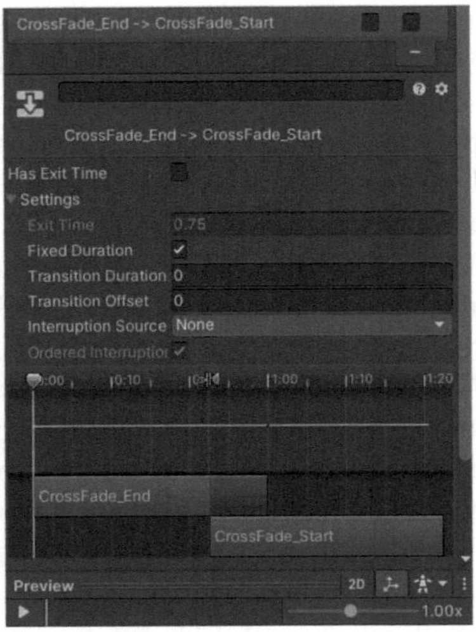

Fig. 4. Animator Settings

Fig. 5. Scene Creation

environment in the Game View, designs can be iterated rapidly, settings can be adjusted and changes can be made while instantly seeing the results. Additionally, the Game View also has various tools for inspecting and analyzing game elements, such as camera perspectives, lighting effects, and physics interactions, enabling developers to ensure a polished experience for users.

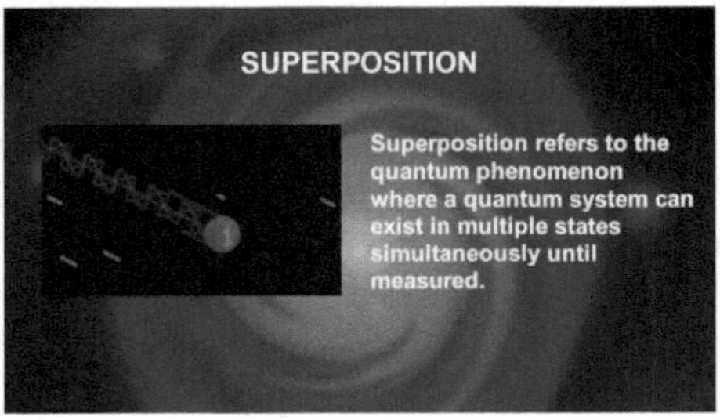

Fig. 6. Game View

6 Discussion and Future Work

The proposed approach of using Unity 3D for visualizing quantum machine learning concepts offers several educational benefits, including enhanced comprehension and engagement through interactive simulations. However, there are notable limitations to this method. First, the complexity and theoretical nature of quantum phenomena may not be fully captured by the visualizations, potentially leading to oversimplification of certain concepts.

Another significant limitation is the current inability to demonstrate the programming and execution of specific QML algorithms, such as Grover's algorithm and the HHL algorithm, within the Unity 3D environment. These algorithms involve intricate quantum gate operations and require a detailed representation of quantum circuits and state evolution, which are challenging to accurately simulate and visualize in a game development platform primarily designed for 3D graphics and user interactions.

Furthermore, the computational resource requirement for rendering detailed 3D animations can be demanding on hardware, potentially limiting accessibility for users with less powerful systems. Future work should aim to address these limitations by incorporating more sophisticated quantum simulations, improving user interface design to accommodate different levels of user expertise, optimizing performance to ensure broader accessibility, and exploring ways to integrate programmable quantum algorithms to provide a more comprehensive learning tool.

7 Conclusion

The Unity model was showcased to a group of students to evaluate its interactivity and educational value. During the demonstration, students were able to use keyboard keys and mouse clicks to navigate through the Unity game engine, exploring various quantum machine learning concepts in an interactive 3D environment. This hands-on experience allowed students to actively engage with the content, enhancing their understanding and observation. The interactive nature of the model facilitated an immersive learning experience, enabling students to visualize complex quantum phenomena dynamically. Feedback from the students indicated that the ability to control and interact with the simulations significantly improved their comprehension.

In conclusion, the utilization of Unity 3D for visualizing Quantum Machine Learning (QML) concepts presents a promising approach to enhancing under- standing and engagement in this cutting-edge field. The usage of animation and visualization capabilities has created an immersive and interactive experiences that facilitates the comprehension of complex QML principles, such as superposition, entanglement, and quantum algorithms like Grover's and HHL algorithms.

Furthermore, the integration of Microsoft Visual Studio with Unity 3D for C# programming offers a robust development environment, enabling the implementation of dynamic and informative visualizations. Through custom scripts and coroutines, interactive simulations could be created, allowing users to explore QML concepts in a hands-on manner.

References

1. Jhanwar, A., Nene, M.J.: Enhanced machine learning using quantum computing. In: 2021 Second International Conference on Electronics and Sustainable Communication Systems (ICESC), pp. 1407–1413. Coimbatore, India (2021). https://doi.org/10.1109/ICESC51422.2021.9532638
2. Sood, V., Chauhan, R.P.: Archives of quantum computing: research progress and challenges. Arch. Computat. Methods Eng. **31**, 73–91 (2024)
3. Sarker, I.H.: Machine learning: algorithms, real-world applications and research directions. SN Comput. Sci. **2**, 160 (2021)
4. Sood, S.K., Agrewal, M.: Quantum machine learning for computational methods in engineering: a systematic review. Arch. Computat. Methods Eng. **31**, 1555–1577 (2024)
5. Mana, S.C., Kalaiarasi, G., Yogitha, R., Helen, L.S., Senthamil Selvi, R.: Application of machine learning in healthcare: an analysis. In: 2022 3rd International Conference on Electronics and Sustainable Communication Systems (ICESC), pp. 1611–1615. Coimbatore, India (2022). https://doi.org/10.1109/ICESC54411.2022.9885296
6. Valdez, F., Melin, P.: A review on quantum computing and deep learning algorithms and their applications. Soft. Comput. **27**, 13217–13236 (2023)
7. Roy, A., Pachuau, J.L., Krishna, G., et al.: Applying Grover's algorithm to implement various numerical and comparison operations. Quantum Stud.: Math. Found. **11**(2), 291–306 (2024). https://doi.org/10.1007/s40509-024-00323-w
8. Alchieri, L., Badalotti, D., Bonardi, P., et al.: An introduction to quantum machine learning: from quantum logic to quantum deep learning. Quantum Mach. Intell. **3**, 28 (2021)
9. Akcaoglu, M., Dogan, S., Hodges, C.B.: Real coding and real games: design and development of a middle school curriculum using unity 3D. TechTrends **66**, 931–937 (2022)
10. Nofal, E.: Studying User Experience in Architectural Education Using Unity Game Engine. In: Ibrahim, A., Mohamed, M.A.A., Fekry, M. (eds.) Man and Place. ARCH + DESN 2023 (2024)

Optimizing Battery Management Through AI Based Virtual Assistant in Electric Vehicles

Anubhav Agrawal[1], Ananya Aggarwal[1], Aditya Rastogi[1], Ranbir Singh[1], and Pradeep Kumar Arya[2](✉)

[1] BML Munjal University, Gurugram, Haryana, India
[2] Bennett University, Greater Noida, Uttar Pradesh, India
pradeeparya25@gmail.com

Abstract. The recent developments in the field of energy and technology have altered the transportation sector in numerous ways. One of the significant changes is the emergence of Electric Vehicles (EVs). The push for eco-friendly mobility has emphasized the role of EV batteries in ensuring performance and sustainability. This research paper emphasizes the pressing need and relevance of well-maintained electric vehicle batteries, especially with reference to critical parameters such as State of Charge (SoC), and State of Health (SoH). The paper explores the integration and potential of AI based virtual assistant in transforming battery management. The AI-driven virtual assistant helps in predicting the State of Charge and State of Health, as well as forecasting energy consumption along with assessing the battery's recyclability. It also incorporates voice-controlled insights, and propagates real-time charge information along with recommending nearby charging stations, and provides advise on the optimal charge time. The research aims to explore the significant role of incorporating AI virtual assistant in enhancing battery performance for electric vehicles. The advantages from these advancements are expected to play a key role in the establishment of a more efficient and sustainable electric transportation system.

Keywords: Electric Vehicles · Battery Management · Artificial Intelligence · State of Charge · State of Health

1 Introduction

In recent years, there has been an increased awareness of the adverse impacts of climate change, including rising global temperatures, extreme weather events, and the depletion of natural resources. Understanding the major reasons behind these issues is essential for combating their destructive impact. While industries are primary in the terms of carbon-dioxide release activities, accounting for 21.3% of the share to the environmental destruction, it is the transport sector that stands out, as 24% of the carbon-dioxide emissions are due to vehicles [1]. Recognizing the pushing need for the change, since the situation is worse daily with natural resources and man-made elements extinguishing, the governments and organizations have recognized the urgent need for change and are seeking sustainable solutions to address this pressing concern [2]. At the forefront of this

M. Bakaev et al. (Eds.): IMS 2024, CCIS 2534, pp. 323–337, 2026.
https://doi.org/10.1007/978-3-031-96177-9_27

transformation are Electric Vehicles (EVs), which are well-known for being the next-generation mode of sustainable transportation [3]. The journey towards widespread EV adoption has been marked by innovation, perseverance, and a steadfast commitment to environmental stewardship.

The idea of Electric Vehicle began with the recognition of the detrimental effects of traditional internal combustion engine vehicles on air quality and public health [4]. As cities struggle with increasing air pollution and many built new emission regulations every year, the development of an alternative clean source of transportation grows as a necessity. Electric Vehicle is a revolutionary concept that promises to revolutionize the way we think about transportation [5].

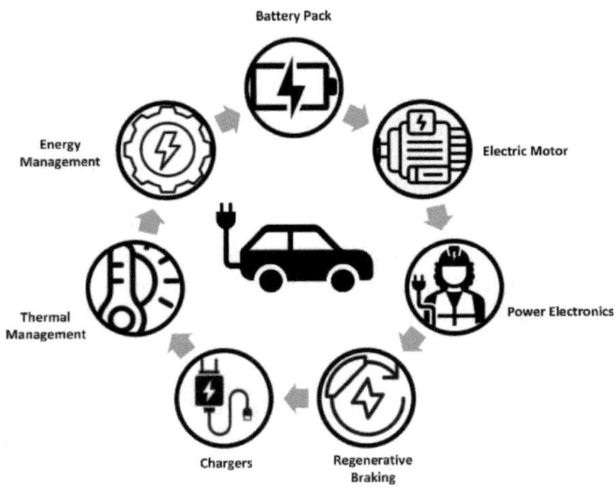

Fig. 1. Process Involved in a Battery Management System

Figure 1 illustrates the integral components of electric vehicles (EVs), pivotal in advancing their efficiency and sustainability. At the core of EV technology lies the battery pack, serving as the fundamental energy reservoir. This pack stores the electrical energy imperative for propelling the vehicle's electric motor. Linked to the battery pack is the electric motor, pivotal in converting electrical energy into mechanical force, thus facilitating the vehicle's forward motion. The motor's efficiency and power output significantly influence the EV's acceleration and overall performance. Operating in conjunction with the electric motor is the power electronics system, regulating the seamless flow of electrical energy among various components such as the motor, battery, and ancillary systems [6]. Supplementary to these components are onboard chargers, thermal management systems, and energy management software, collectively fine-tuning efficiency, bolstering safety, and refining user experience in EV operation [7].

Nonetheless, it is the EV battery that emerges as the hallmark of modern engineering prowess, serving as the primary energy source propelling these vehicles towards a sustainable future. Unlike conventional vehicles fueled by gasoline or diesel, EVs rely on electricity stored in batteries to power electric motors, propelling the vehicle forward without any tailpipe emissions. Battery Management Systems (BMS) play a pivotal role in maintaining the optimal performance and longevity of EV batteries.

A battery's operations consist of monitoring, optimization, and control of components. These functionalities are controlled by the BMS [8]. Metrics such as SoC, SoH and Remaining Useful Life (RUL) assist in an efficient battery management and use, which further ensure an enhancement in its lifespan. BMS can help in providing efficient operations for an electric vehicle by managing the charge and discharge cycles of the battery, taking several external factors into consideration such as temperature changes and overcharging.

BMS is of a greater use, but the overall operation of the BMS can be ensured using predictive algorithms that would further tune the accuracy of the system in estimating critical battery parameters. These estimations within parameters assist in real-time monitoring, prediction of SoC, SoH, RUL and overall energy consumption within the battery. A review presented by the authors in [9] shows the importance of foundational predictive algorithms in the state estimation for SoC, SoH and RUL which further highlight the accuracy in battery parameter predictions. [10] shows an integration of big data analytics, which further assist in the management of data derived from electric vehicles and further optimize its operations. These help in energy consumption predictions and monitoring of battery health, ensuring better life and reliability. In [11, 12], the authors have derived the importance of SoH within a vehicle battery.

Algorithms such as RNN, SVM, LSTM and ANN have been used to enhance the efficacy of SoH and RUL predictions. [13] have highlighted the challenges that can be faced while making estimations using algorithms for SoC, SoH and RUL. These also take into consideration several factors such as environmental factors and technical parameters. AI, cloud-computing, IoT, blockchain and other advanced technologies have been fundamental in outlining the concepts for battery modelling, metric predictions and highlighting different challenge within them. [14] discusses a possibility of using these technologies and integrating them with the concept of digital twins (DT) and use it for different purposes such as charging and overall battery load balancing.

BMS can also be integrated with data-driven methods and sensors with high precision to develop hybrid models and methods to improve the accuracy within predictions. These methods also help in the optimization of battery management systems. [15, 16] talks about the integration of AI-based approaches for ensuring a longer life and safety within battery management systems. These also enhances the overall system reliability by making the system capable of analyzing the complex data patterns, identify anomalies and optimize the overall battery performance in real-time. The authors of this paper have developed the concept of an AI-Based Virtual Assistant that can be used for the predictions made for SoC, SoH and RUL, which could be further used to optimize battery performance. Table 1 provides insights of the research contributions that have been made in the field of battery management systems and predictive algorithms for electric vehicles. It shows the methodologies, techniques and results published in studies [17–21] highlighting approaches adopted to enhance battery performance and health.

Table 1. Literature Review of the Recent Advancements within the field

Citation	Year	Features involved in Effective Battery Management in Electric vehicles							Description
		Battery State of Charge (SoC) Monitoring	Battery State of Health (SoH) Monitoring	Battery Thermal Management	Battery Charging Optimization	Predictive Maintenance	Energy Harvesting Integration	User Behaviour Analysis	
[17]	2020		✓		✓				Explores AI-based strategies for battery manufacturing and management to enhance longevity
[18]	2019				✓	✓			Investigates machine learning techniques for battery management in electric vehicles
[19]	2023	✓			✓				Focuses on utilizing AI and IoT for smart battery management in electric vehicles
[20]	2022	✓		✓		✓	✓		Presents a comprehensive review of battery design. Thermal management, and AI application in battery management systems for electric vehicles
[21]	2020	✓			✓			✓	Proposes an advanced AI-based Battery Management System utilizing FPGA acceleration

In this paper, the authors have proposed an AI-Based Virtual Assistant that has been built according to the requirements specified for electrical mobility and its battery optimization. This assistant uses advanced machine learning algorithms to predict battery metrics such as SoC, SoH and RUL which further assists in optimizing the battery management. The assistant-based battery management system is using features such as internal resistance of the battery, temperature, voltage, cycle count and other factors to increase the level of prediction made and would further provide important information to the user. The system can monitor and analyze these metrics to offer recommendations for charging schedules, usage patterns and maintenance procedures which enhance the battery efficiency and life. The assistant provides the user with their vehicle's charging status, find nearby EV charging stations and also contain voice-controlled actions for a seamless user experience. The assistant aims to enhance the driving experience and further improve the efficiency and sustainability of electrical mobility. In the next section, the authors have talked about the EV Battery Management System and their operations in detail. The subsequent sections discuss the development and role of an AI-based Virtual Assistant in battery optimization, the proposed methodology for the integration of an electric vehicle battery management system and AI-based Virtual Assistant and presenting the results obtained from this framework.

2 Electric Vehicle Battery Management System

An Electric Vehicle Battery Management System (BMS) consists of several key components, each one of which plays a pivotal role in ensuring the ideal performance, safety, and life of the battery pack. Understanding these components is important for working on the complexities of how a BMS operates. The primary components of an EV BMS are:

- **Battery Monitoring Unit (BMU):** The BMU is responsible for monitoring the SoC, SoH, SoF, and other key parameters of individual cells within the battery pack. It collects data from cell voltage, temperature sensors, and current sensors to estimate the overall condition of the battery pack.
- **Cell Balancing Circuit:** In a battery pack, disparities in cell characteristics can lead to imbalances, which can cause some cells to charge or discharge faster than others. The cell balancing circuit ensures constant charging and discharging across all cells by managing the redistribution of energy among them.
- **Temperature Monitoring and Thermal Management:** Temperature sensors used within the battery modules monitor the temperature of individual cells and the overall pack. The BMS uses this data to implement thermal management strategies such as active cooling or heating to prevent overheating or overcooling.
- **Safety System:** The BMS integrates various safety features to prevent dangerous conditions such as overcharging, over-discharging, short circuits, and thermal runaway. It continuously monitors battery parameters and executes protective measures.
- **State Estimation and Control Algorithms:** Advanced algorithms are used within the BMS to accurately estimate the SoC, SoH, and other applicable parameters of the battery pack based on the collected data. These algorithms apply mathematical models and predictive analytics to optimize charging and discharging strategies while considering various factors such as temperature, current, voltage, and aging effects. The SoC is an important indicator of the current energy level stored in the battery relative to its maximum capacity. The SoH reflects the overall condition and longevity of the battery. It provides insights into potential failures, maintenance requirements, and RUL. SoH is influenced by battery chemistry, temperature management, charging patterns, and operating conditions as shown in Fig. 2.

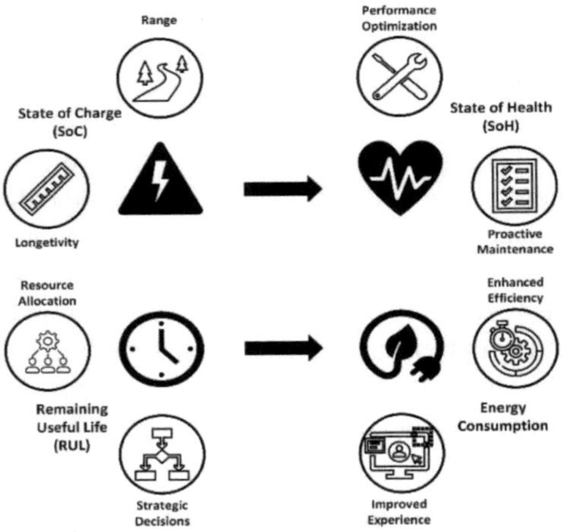

Fig. 2. Components of State Estimation and Control Algorithms

- **Communication Interface:** The BMS includes communication interfaces, such as Ethernet, or wireless protocols like Bluetooth or Wi-Fi, to facilitate communication with other vehicle systems, external charging infrastructure, and remote monitoring systems.

The integration of these components within the BMS plays a synergistic role in ensuring optimal performance of the battery pack in electric vehicles [22]. Figure 3 highlights the architecture of a battery management system consisting of different units that are involved in the efficient operation of the framework. In the next section, integration of AI technology into the BMS is proposed to develop an AI virtual assistant that will leverage machine learning algorithms to enhance predictive maintenance in EVs.

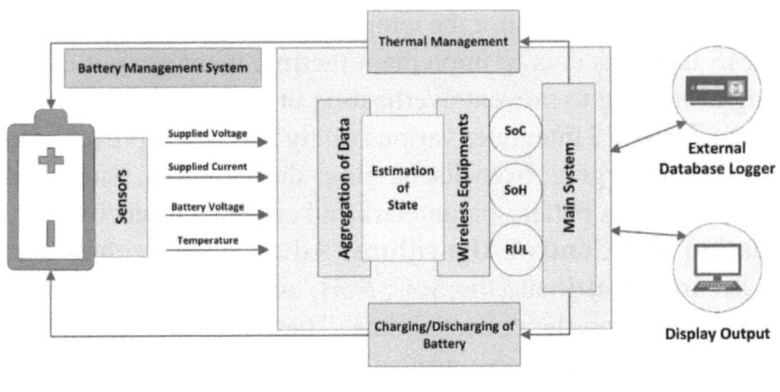

Fig. 3. Architecture of a Battery Management System

3 AI-Based Virtual Assistance for Battery Management in Electric Vehicles

The integration of AI into EV BMS represents a significant advancement in the realm of electric vehicle technology. This integration revolutionizes the management of battery systems along with opening new possibilities for the enhancement of efficiency, reliability, and user experience. Figure 4 discusses various features of an AI Virtual Assistant based Battery Management System.

Fig. 4. Features of an AI-Virtual Assistant for Battery Management

These features help in enhancing the user experience and help in the development of an efficient framework. Figure 5 depicts the framework that has been proposed by the authors in this research for the optimization of battery management within electric vehicles.

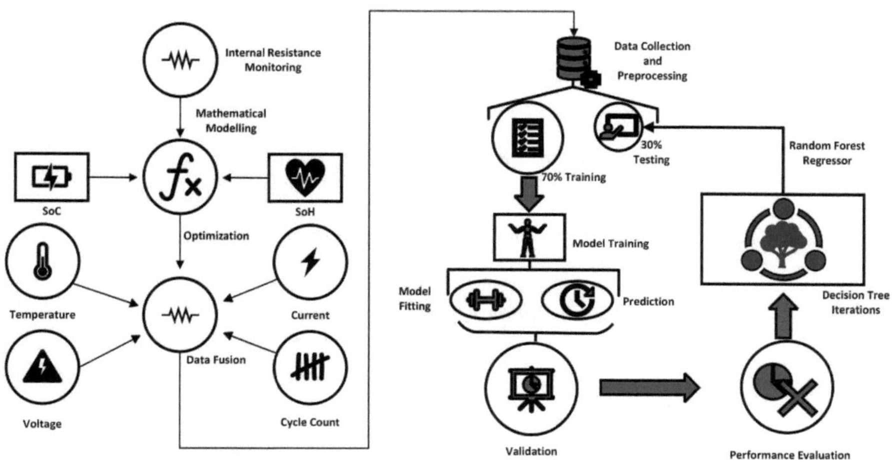

Fig. 5. Designed Framework for Optimized Battery Management

Predictions within a battery related to different parameters are done using Coulomb Counting as in Eq. (1) and Kalman Filtering as shown in Eq. (2).

$$SoC_t = SoC_{t-1} + \frac{1}{Q_{rated}} \int_{t_{start}}^{t_{end}} i(t)dt \tag{1}$$

$$SoC_t = SoC_{t-1} + K_t \cdot (v_t - SoC_{t-1}) \tag{2}$$

The AI Virtual Assistant for optimizing battery management within an electric vehicle is a framework which will utilize advanced technologies to enhance the overall efficacy of a battery in an electric vehicle to increase the SoC and decrease the intensity of the decrement within the SoH. It also includes the usage of factors that are involved in managing an efficient BMS. These features include current flowing in and out of the battery, voltage across the battery, temperature, cycle count and internal resistance of the battery.

$$SoC(t) = State\ of\ Charge\ in\ time\ t$$

$$\Delta SoC = Change\ in\ State\ of\ Charge\ over\ time\ t$$

$$SoH(t) = State\ of\ Health\ at\ time\ t$$

$$\Delta SoH = Decrement\ in\ State\ of\ Health\ over\ time\ t$$

$$I = Current\ flowing\ in\ and\ out\ of\ the\ battery$$

$$V = Voltage\ across\ battery\ terminals$$

$$N = Cyclecount$$

$$T = Temperature\ of\ the\ battery$$

$$R = Internal\ Resistance\ of\ the\ battery$$

$$k_1 = Coefficient\ of\ efficiency\ and\ capacity\ of\ the\ battery.$$

$$k_2 = Temperature's\ Constant$$

3.1 Proposed Mathematical Model for SoC and SoH

Equation (3) refers to the SoC at any specific time 't' which is equal to the sum of SoC at time t and the overall change in SoC during that time.

$$SoC(t+1) = SoC(t) + \Delta SoC \tag{3}$$

The difference of SoC is formulated as a function of the flow of current within the battery and voltage across its terminals and shown in Eq. (4).

$$\Delta SoC = f(I, V, t) \tag{4}$$

$$0 \leq \Delta SoC \leq 100$$

According to Ohm's law, the flow of current is directly proportional to the voltage across the terminals and inversely proportional to the internal resistance of the battery. This is shown in Eq. (5).

$$V = IR \tag{5}$$

Further, using Faradays Law, change in SOC is shown in Eq. (6).

$$\Delta SoC = k_1 \cdot I \cdot \Delta t \tag{6}$$

Taking temperature's influence over the battery performance and efficiency, Eq. (7) highlights the overall function.

$$\Delta SoC = f(I, V, t)$$

$$\Delta SoC = k_1 \cdot k_2(T) \cdot I \cdot \Delta t = f(I, V, t) \tag{7}$$

Hence, the overall equation for State of Charge can be represented as in Eq. (8):

$$SoC(t+1) = SoC(t) + f(I, V, t)$$

$$SoC(t+1) = SoC(t) + (k_1 \cdot k_2(T) \cdot I \cdot \Delta t) \tag{8}$$

State of Health (SoH) refers to the repeated charge and discharge cycles of a battery. Every time an EV battery is charged and operated causing discharge, the SoH decrements by a particular value dependent upon factors such as cycle count, internal resistance, and temperature stress. Equation (10) deduces a relationship between SoH and the cycle count.

$$SoH(t+1) = SoH(t) + \Delta SoH \tag{9}$$

$$0 \leq \Delta SoH \leq 100$$

$$\Delta SoH = k_3 \cdot N \tag{10}$$

$$k_3 = Cyclecount\,factor$$

High temperature accelerates the overall degradation process of a battery. To analyze this, SoH can be derived as a function of temperature as shown in Eq. (11):

$$\Delta SoH = k_4 \cdot T \cdot k_3 \cdot N \tag{11}$$

Internal resistance is also a decisive factor to be considered for evaluating the optimization within an electric vehicle battery. Higher internal resistance leads to increased heat generation and inefficiencies within the battery. Equation (12) and (13) depicts a relationship between SoH and internal resistance of the battery.

$$\Delta SoH = k_4 \cdot T \cdot k_3 \cdot N \cdot k_5 \cdot (R) = f(N, T, R) \tag{12}$$

$$SoH(t+1) = SoH(t) + (k_4 \cdot T \cdot k_3 \cdot N \cdot k_5 \cdot (R)) \tag{13}$$

Equations (8) and (12) account various factors that affect the efficiency of an electric vehicle battery and reduce the efficacy of the BMS if not considered. The proposed model was tested over a certain set of data. Random Forest Regressor technique was applied over the model to gain insights about the overall performance and efficiency of the model. Figures 6 and 7 highlight the decision trees with iterations till a maximum depth of 3 levels, produced for the SoC and SoH predictions.

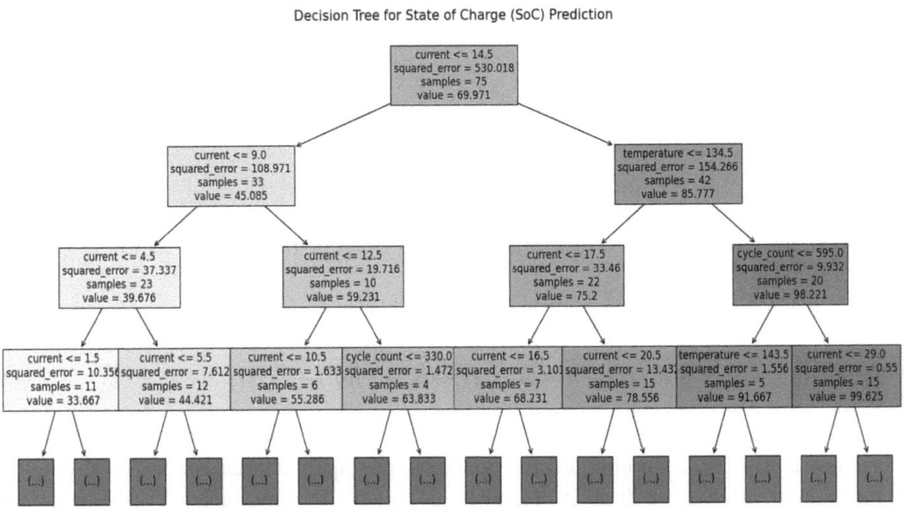

Fig. 6. Decision Tree for SoC Optimization

In the decision tree, each leaf node represents a different feature that was taken into consideration while predicting the value of a particular variable. Multiple iterations lead to more accurate predictions. Both SoC and SoH have been predicted using the model and the decision trees have been generated. The decision tree obtained for SoC consisted of 9 levels, whereas for SoC, the decision tree obtained consisted of 11 levels.

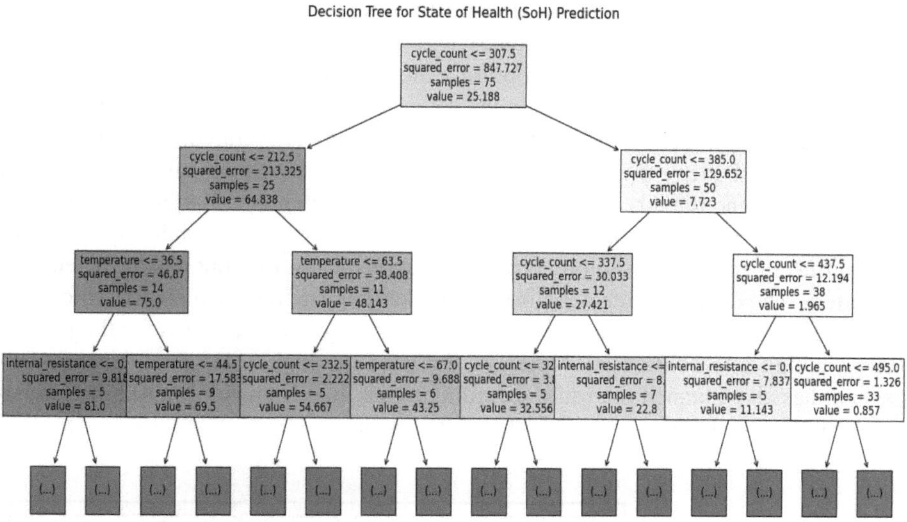

Fig. 7. Decision Tree for SoH Optimization

4 Results and Discussions

AI Virtual Assistant for battery management within electric vehicles is a concept that will assist in the maintenance of the battery management system and will further enhance the efficacy of the system. In the last section, the authors derived a relationship framework for the efficient prediction and overall optimization of the SoC and SoH for an EV BMS. In this section, the integration of an AI Virtual Assistant and this framework has been discussed and highlighted. Figure 8 highlights the confusion matrices which depict the dataset recorded and the times when the framework efficiently managed to predict the correct SoC and SoH. The framework achieved an overall accuracy of around 89% in predicting the optimal SoC and an accuracy of 86% in predicting the SoH for the battery within the electric vehicle.

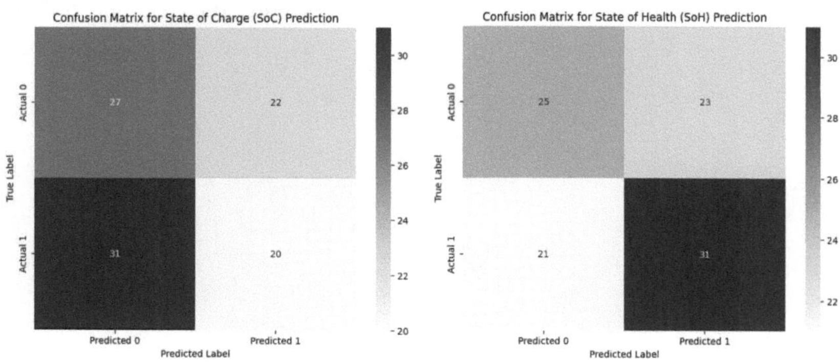

Fig. 8. Confusion Matrices for SoC and SoH Prediction

The AI Virtual Assistant integrated within the system uses this framework to identify and predict the SoC and SoH for the battery within the EVs. The virtual assistant records every form of data possible to further optimize the prediction and the overall efficiency of the battery management system within the vehicle. This includes planning a trip where the efficiency of the battery further increases considering the overall distance and charge of the vehicle's battery and considering the estimated time of arrival as specified by the user. Such functionality of the AI Virtual Assistant integrated Battery Management System has been highlighted in Fig. 9, where the user provides certain input and the assistant take decisions based on certain predictions about the route and efficiency of the battery. The decided route contains an EV charging station at a distance which may be reached within the next 23 min, so that the vehicle could be charged for the journey further, taking into consideration the low SoC and the high SoH of the battery. This assistant has also planned the route according to the time frame of 1 h 30 min that has been provided by the user to the AI Virtual Assistant.

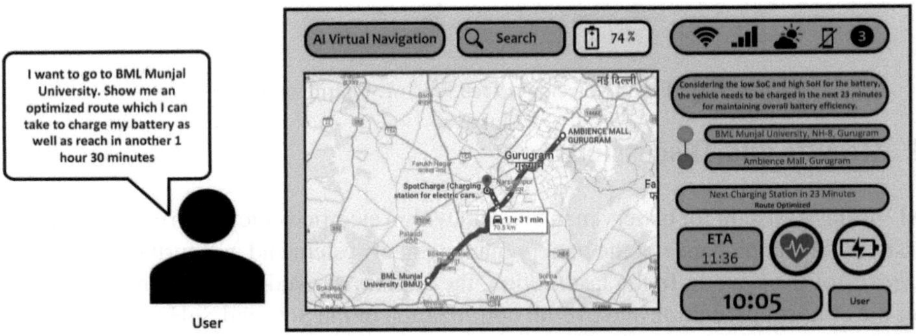

Fig. 9. Route Optimization using the AI Virtual Assistant

This assistant further records data that can be used to make further predictions. This includes the total distance the vehicle has been driven, the efficiency of the battery, average daily mileage, and the charge capacity. Figure 10 highlights the metrics that were recorded using the AI Virtual Assistant for predicting the SoC and SoH in this case.

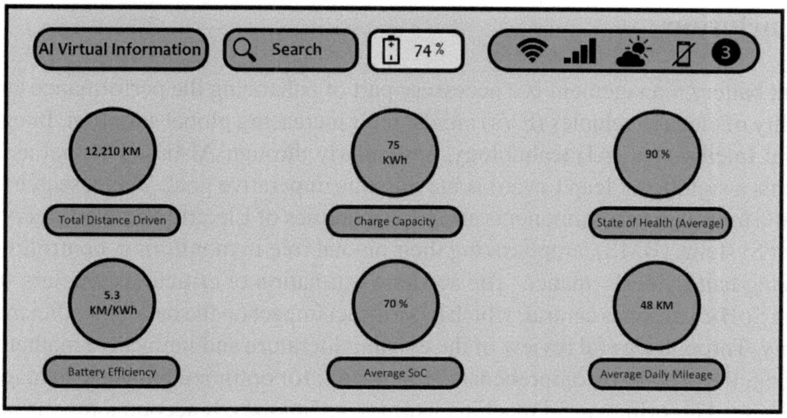

Fig. 10. Recorded Metrics for SoC and SoH Prediction

This is how the framework, and the modelling assists in the SoC and SoH prediction of the battery within the electric vehicles using the proposed AI Virtual Assistant. The overall accuracy of the framework can also be visualized using the regression analysis as done in Fig. 11. The analysis explains the positioning of data points from the SoC and SoH prediction collected data over the regression line produced by the framework. The overall minimal error depicts the increased accuracy and efficiency of the framework and provide insights into the prediction of SoC and SoH of the battery of an electric vehicle.

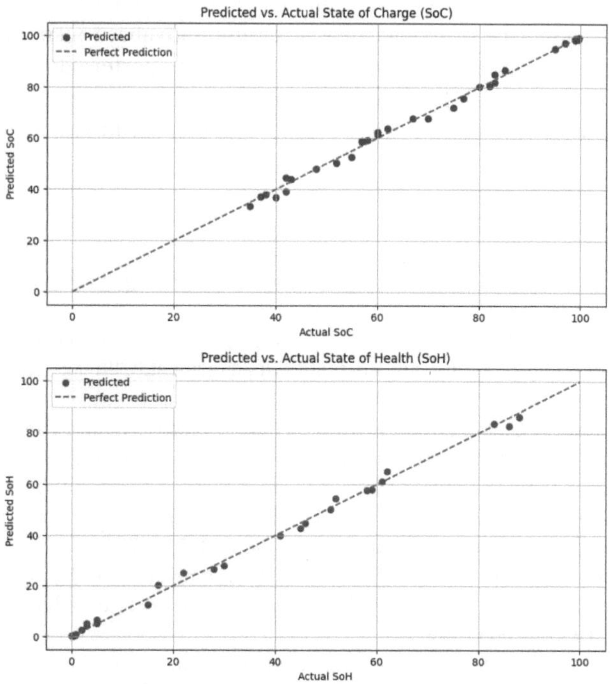

Fig. 11. Regression Analysis for SoC and SoH Prediction

5 Conclusion

Efficient battery management is a necessary part of enhancing the performance and sustainability of electric vehicles (EVs) amidst their increasing global adoption. Integrating Artificial Intelligence (AI) technology, particularly through AI-based virtual assistant, represents a significant leap toward achieving this imperative goal. This research underscores the multifaceted components and functionalities of Electric Vehicle Battery Management Systems (BMS), emphasizing their pivotal role in monitoring, controlling, and optimizing battery performance. The accurate estimation of critical parameters such as SoC and SoH emerges as central, which has a direct impact on the battery's efficiency and longevity. Through careful review of the existing literature and innovative mathematical modelling, the proposed comprehensive framework for optimizing battery management uses advanced algorithms and machine learning techniques. It accounts for various factors including current flow, voltage, temperature, cycle count, and internal resistance, aiming to predict SoC and SoH precisely. The integration of an AI-driven virtual assistant further enhances battery management effectiveness by providing real-time insights, personalized recommendations, and an ideal user experience. It also helps in user assistance for the optimization of charging schedules, planning routes with charging stations, and carefully addressing maintenance needs which further results in maximizing the battery efficiency and longevity. The results validate the effectiveness of the proposed framework and AI virtual assistant, with an overall accuracy of around 89% in predicting SoC and 86% in predicting SoH. This showcases promising potential in enhancing the overall efficiency and reliability of electric vehicle battery management. The transformative potential of AI-based virtual assistant in revolutionizing battery management for electric vehicles cannot be overstated. By leveraging advanced technologies and predictive analytics, this approach not only improves battery performance but also significantly contributes to establishing a more sustainable and efficient electric transportation ecosystem, thereby paving the way for a cleaner and greener future.

References

1. Moomaw, W.R.: Industrial emissions of greenhouse gases. Energy Policy **24**(10–11), 951–968 (1996)
2. Radović, V., Iglesias, I.: Extreme weather events: Definition, classification, and guidelines towards vulnerability reduction and adaptation management. Climate Action, pp. 464–476. Springer International Publishing, Cham (2019)
3. Rubino, L., Capasso, C., Veneri, O.: Review on plug-in electric vehicle charging architectures integrated with distributed energy sources for sustainable mobility. Appl. Energy **207**, 438–464 (2017)
4. Nichols, B.G., Kockelman, K.M., Reiter, M.: Air quality impacts of electric vehicle adoption in Texas. Transp. Res. Part D: Transp. Environ. **34**, 208–218 (2015)
5. Sovacool, B.K., Hirsh, R.F.: Beyond batteries: An examination of the benefits and barriers to plug-in hybrid electric vehicles (PHEVs) and a vehicle-to-grid (V2G) transition. Energy Policy **37**(3), 1095–1103 (2009)
6. Shen, M., Gao, Q.: A review on battery management system from the modeling efforts to its multiapplication and integration. Int. J. Energy Res. **43**(10), 5042–5075 (2019)

7. Naseri, F., et al.: Digital twin of electric vehicle battery systems: Comprehensive review of the use cases, requirements, and platforms. Renewable and Sustainable Energy Reviews **179**, 113280 (2023). ISSN 1364-0321, https://doi.org/10.1016/j.rser.2023.113280
8. Karmawijaya, M.I., Nashirul Haq, I., Leksono, E., Widyotriatmo, A.: Development of Big Data Analytics Platform for Electric Vehicle Battery Management System. 2019 6th International Conference on Electric Vehicular Technology (ICEVT), pp. 151–155. Bali, Indonesia (2019). https://doi.org/10.1109/ICEVT48285.2019.8994013
9. Surya, S., Rao, V., Williamson, S.S.: Comprehensive review on smart techniques for estimation of state of health for battery management system application. Energies **14**, 4617 (2021). https://doi.org/10.3390/en14154617
10. Wang, W., et al.: Application of digital twin in smart battery management systems. Chinese Journal of Mechanical Engineering **34**(1), 57 (2021)
11. Li, Y., et al.: Data-driven health estimation and lifetime prediction of lithium-ion batteries: a review. Renewable and Sustainable Energy Reviews **113**, 109254 (2019). ISSN 1364-0321, https://doi.org/10.1016/j.rser.2019.109254
12. Gou, B., Xu, Y., Feng, X.: State-of-health estimation and remaining-useful-life prediction for lithium-ion battery using a hybrid data-driven method. IEEE Trans. Veh. Technol. **69**(10), 10854–10867 (2020). https://doi.org/10.1109/TVT.2020.3014932
13. Liu, K., Wei, Z., Zhang, C., Shang, Y., Teodorescu, R., Han, Q.-L.: Towards long lifetime battery: AI-based manufacturing and management. IEEE/CAA Journal of Automatica Sinica **9**(7), 1139–1165 (2022). https://doi.org/10.1109/JAS.2022.105599
14. Das, K., Kumar, R.: Electric vehicle battery capacity degradation and health estimation using machine-learning techniques: a review. Clean Energy **7**(6), 1268–1281 (2023). https://doi.org/10.1093/ce/zkad054
15. Wu, B., et al.: Battery digital twins: Perspectives on the fusion of models, data and artificial intelligence for smart battery management systems. Energy and AI **1**, 100016 (2020)
16. NaitMalek, Y., et al.: On the use of machine learning for state-of-charge forecasting in electric vehicles. 2019 IEEE international smart cities conference (ISC2). IEEE (2019)
17. Li, J., et al.: Methods and applications for Artificial Intelligence, Big Data, Internet of Things, and Blockchain in smart energy management. Energy and AI **11**, 100208 (2023)
18. Murugan, M., et al.: Thermal management system of lithium-ion battery packs for electric vehicles: An insight based on bibliometric study. Journal of Energy Storage **52**, 104723 (2022)
19. Karras, K., et al.: A hardware acceleration platform for AI-based inference at the edge. Circuits, Systems, and Signal Processing **39**(2), 1059–1070 (2020)
20. Ouyang, Q., et al.: Cell balancing control for lithium-ion battery packs: A hierarchical optimal approach. IEEE Transactions on Industrial Informatics **16**(8), 5065–5075 (2019)
21. Rallabandi, S., Isaac Selvaraj, R.V.: Advancements in Battery Cooling Techniques for Enhanced Performance and Safety in Electric Vehicles: A Comprehensive Review. Energy Technology, 2301404
22. Pop, V., et al.: State-of-the-art of battery state-of-charge determination. Measurement Science and Technology **16**(12), R93 (2005)

Bytes to Bucks, Review of Technology in High-Speed Stock Markets

Abhishek Kumar[1], Ritesh Rastogi[1], Aditee Mattoo[1], Ankur Chaudhary[1], and Pradeep Kumar Arya[2(✉)]

[1] Noida Institute of Engineering and Technology, Greater Noida, UP 201306, India
aditeemattoo@niet.co.in

[2] School of Computer Science Engineering and Technology (SCSET), Bennett University, Greater Noida, UP 201306, India
pradeeparya25@gmail.com

Abstract. The landscape of financial markets is evolving every day. In this ever-evolving field, algorithm trading has emerged as a transformative force, it has reshaped the execution of transactions at the speed of microseconds. Modern markets require high-performance hardware, reconfigurable components like FPGAs and GPUs for parallel processing, and an optimized software architecture to handle an extremely large amount of transactional data within microseconds. This study delves into the pivotal role of technologies such as low latency, advanced algorithms, and efficient design patterns, examining advancements in hardware and software, network infrastructure, data processing capabilities, and trading algorithms. This study traces the progression from manual, non-digital trading methods to the integration of computer science in the mid-20th century, marking the conceptual beginnings of algorithmic trading to the modern high-speed markets executing millions of transactions per second. The paper concludes with various insights into future trends, highlighting the potential role of AI, ML, and blockchain to enhance decision-making capabilities and transparency among the participants, along with security, respectively. The adaptability to dynamic changes in technology, economics, and regulations is emphasized as crucial for sustained success in the dynamic field of low-latency algorithmic trading.

Keywords: Algorithmic trading · High-frequency trading (HFT) · Low latency · financial markets · Technology · Trading strategies · Quantitative analysis · Artificial intelligence (AI) · Machine learning (ML)

1 Introduction

In today's financial world, driven by constant technological advancements, wealth is created and lost in the blink of an eye. Algorithmic trading is a method of using computer algorithms to make financial transactions and has become the basis of modern trading strategies [1]. The viability of an algorithmic transaction hinges on the importance of low latency, where milliseconds can mean the difference between profit and loss. As the importance of speed increases in the financial world, the ability to do business

M. Bakaev et al. (Eds.): IMS 2024, CCIS 2534, pp. 338–350, 2026.
https://doi.org/10.1007/978-3-031-96177-9_28

quickly and effectively becomes more important [2]. Some significant developments include the transition from manual to computerized trading systems, the adoption of high-speed networking technologies such as fiber optics, the design of low-latency hardware and software architectures, and the implementation of sophisticated algorithmic trading strategies that use advanced data processing and machine learning techniques. Market participants are focusing on using technology to analyze and trade within milliseconds, leading to the spread of algorithmic trading. This article covers the historical development of algorithmic trading and highlights the important role of technology in the results. The implementation of low latency stimulates the development of many ideas and technologies and promotes competition among business people. Low latency has become the key to capturing business opportunities and diversifying business strategies. The research examines the fundamentals of algorithmic trading, examining advances in hardware, software, network infrastructure, data processing, and trading algorithms. It traces the progress from manual, non-digital trading methods to the integration of computer science in the mid-20th century, marking the beginning of the concept of algorithmic trading.

The rest of this research paper delves into many facets of algorithmic trading, beginning with a detailed review of the financial markets in Sect. 2. Section 3 examines several algorithmic trading tactics, including trend following, mean reversion, statistical arbitrage, pair trading, and market creation. Section 4 investigates the crucial role of low latency in algorithmic trading, with subsections covering its impact on trade execution speed and efficiency, slippage minimization, and risk management enhancement. Section 5 focuses on high-frequency trading (HFT), highlighting significant aspects such as unmatched speed and huge transaction volume before discussing its influence on market liquidity, pricing, efficiency, and price discovery. Section 6 delves into the technical aspects of algorithmic trading, including high-performance hardware, FPGAs, GPUs, and software optimization design. Section 6.2 delves further into software architectural concerns, including the examination of code optimization approaches for latency reduction, which is discussed in Sect. 7. In Sect. 8, we discuss how algorithmic trading profitability is fueled by the combination of human skill and algorithmic technology. Finally, Sect. 9 brings the research to a close by summarizing significant results and insights and suggesting a future framework that incorporates numerous design patterns and optimization approaches to make it easier to construct and implement high-performance algorithmic trading strategies.

2 Landscape of the Financial Marketplace

Financial markets have changed a lot over time. It has evolved from traditional trading centers to modern, computerized stock exchanges. Originally based on a face-to-face marketplace, in the mid-20th century, the combination of computer science, mathematics, and finance transformed the economy through algorithmic strategies [3]. Financial markets facilitate the exchange of assets such as stocks, bonds, and currencies among various participants, such as investors, traders, brokers, and exchanges [4]. However, major market participants have remained somewhat similar, which include retail investors, institutional investors, and market makers [5, 6]. The markets encompass primary markets for new security issuances and secondary markets for trading existing securities, the below figure (see Fig. 1) shows the relationship between market participants and markets. Figure 1 displays two markets: the primary market, where corporations issue new securities to raise cash from investors, and the secondary market, where existing securities are traded among investors. It depicts the movement of funds from investors to firms in exchange for securities in the primary market, as well as securities trading and share buybacks between investors and corporations in the secondary market. The figure depicts firms as issuers, capital demanders, and investors as capital suppliers.

The origins of algorithmic trading can be traced back to the 1960s, with the creation of models such as the Capital Market Pricing Model (CAPM) and Black-Scholes for asset and option pricing [8, 9]. Pioneers used mathematical techniques for trading strategies using trading patterns and arbitrage opportunities. Advances in computing power, electronic trading, and data availability have contributed to the growth of algorithmic trading. Strategies such as high-frequency trading have emerged that take advantage of ultra-low latency. Multiple quantitative models support automated operations such as trend-following, statistical arbitrage, and market-making.

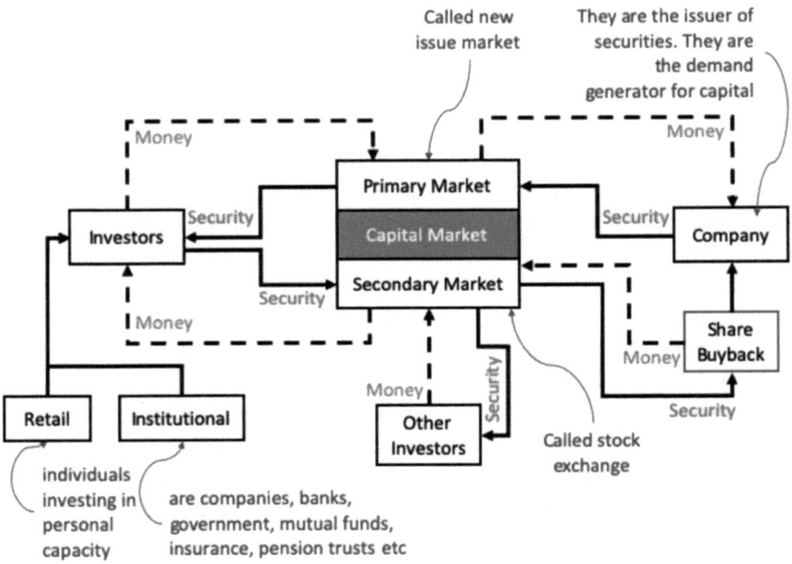

Fig. 1. Relationship between market participants [7].

The algorithmic market is growing rapidly and the market is expected to reach $31.3 billion by 2030, growing at a Compound Growth Rate (CAGR) of 12.73 [10]. Algorithm trading impact spans efficient execution, risk management, price discovery and overall market quality across the financial ecosystem.

3 Algorithm Trading Strategies

Algorithmic trading uses pre-computed instructions to trigger the buying and selling of financial instruments [11]. It uses mathematical models, data analysis, and high performance to perform tasks in milliseconds, reduce costs, and increase performance [12]. The shift from manual to algorithmic trading represents a revolution driven by advances in computing power, instant access to data, and complex algorithms. It gives birth to many ideas.

Trend-following Strategies Use indicators such as moving averages to identify trends in order to identify and engage with ongoing price movements [13, 14].

Mean Reversion Strategies Mean taking advantage of temporary deviations from past price patterns to enter a position where the price is above or below a high [14, 15]. Statistical arbitrage is an important practice for identifying and trading asset errors [16].

Market-Making Strategies Provide liquidity by continuously quoting bid and ask prices. Algorithms automate liquidity provision based on real-time data. Actively managed strategies also include inventory management to capitalize on accurate price predictions [17–20].

Key benefits of this algorithmic strategy include speed, reduced costs, elimination of bias, and the ability to monitor and process multiple transactions and data streams simultaneously. However, risks include potential technical failures, liquidity crunches, and exacerbating volatility during market disruptions [21].

4 Low Latency in Algorithm Trading

In algorithmic trading, low latency refers to the minimum lag or delay between the initiation and execution of a trade. Latency is a measure of the time taken for data to travel from the source (such as a trader's algorithm or a trading platform) to the destination (exchange or market), which affects the speed at which transactions are processed across the markets [22]. Low latency is an important aspect of algorithmic marketing because it directly affects the efficiency, effectiveness, and competitiveness of your marketing strategy. The importance of low latency lies in its role in ensuring accurate time in the market. In algorithmic trading, where decisions are made in split seconds, minimizing delays in the processing, transmission, and execution of trading orders is paramount. Timing precision ensures that trading strategies can quickly exploit market opportunities and respond quickly to fluctuating conditions while executing orders at the most favourable prices [23, 24].

Low latency has a direct impact on the speed and efficiency of trade execution. In the fast-paced world of business finance where prices change rapidly, the ability to execute transactions quickly provides a competitive advantage. Algorithms are designed to run with low latency so they can capture business opportunities as they arise, thus doing the most effective work at the best price. The faster the activation, the lower the risk of negative costs during transfer [24].

Slippage is the variance between the expected value and the actual value of the transaction. Slippage can affect profitability [25]. Low latency plays an important role in reducing slippage by ensuring orders are closed as close to their expected value as possible. Quick orders reduce the risk of market volatility, help complete entry and exit points, and finally reduce the impact of slippage on the market.

Reduced latency helps better manage algorithmic trading risk. Low latency enables timely responses to changes in the business and facilitates the implementation of risk assessments. Improved control of the trading system helps investors operate better in a volatile market by improving overall risk management.

5 High Frequency Trading

High-frequency trading (HFT) is one of the algorithmic products that demonstrate rapid execution of large orders in a short period of time [26]. High-frequency trading systems use advanced algorithms and technology (such as high-speed data) to make secondary trading decisions. The latency of these systems is usually measured in microseconds or milliseconds. The main purpose of frequent trading is to use small variable costs and unprofitable trading to make a profit. The main feature of high-frequency trading is its unparalleled performance speed. High-frequency trading systems are designed to process large trading data and execute trades at a speed not possible with traditional trading. This speed advantage allows many companies to gain a competitive advantage by doing business faster than other market participants, thus gaining an advantage over time in business. Another feature of frequent trading is the execution of large transactions in a short time. High-frequency trading strategies involve placing and canceling orders quickly, thus encouraging high trading volume. Product frequency is often measured in millions or millions per day to indicate the frequency and scale at which these strategies work [18].

An important difference between high-frequency trading and traditional algorithmic trading is their time horizon. While traditional algorithmic trading can operate on a time scale of minutes to hours, HFT operates on a micro to millisecond scale. High-frequency trading focuses on taking advantage of short-term trading and their strategies are adjusted to complete the trade as quickly as possible [27]. The high frequency nature of trading may have a more direct impact on market performance and prices than algorithmic trading strategies. Rapid posting and cancellation of orders from the market can often affect the market, leading to product and price fluctuations [18]. This has led to a debate about the potential impact of HFT on economic stability and fairness of market access. High-frequency trading increases the efficiency of financial transactions by processing information and executing transactions quickly [28, 29]. The speed and integration of new information makes it easier to find value to ensure the property reflects the most up-to-date information. This functionality benefits the wider industry by providing timely cost information.

6 Technology in Algorithm Trading

Technology plays a pivotal role in the success of algorithmic trading, with its critical significance highlighted in achieving low-latency objectives. The ability to process massive volumes of information at fast speed, make split-second decisions, and execute trades rapidly are all reliant on cutting-edge technological components. Efficiency and speed are paramount in algorithmic trading. Technology ensures that trading systems can execute orders with precision, responding swiftly to market changes, and minimizing delays in the entire trading process. This efficiency is not only a competitive advantage but also fundamental to the profitability of algorithmic trading strategies [30].

6.1 High Performance Hardware

High performance hardware is essential for low latency systems in algorithmic trading. Advancements in processors, memory, and storage are crucial to handle data intensive operations. The speed and processing power of the hardware directly impact the speed of data analysis, decision making, and ultimately trade execution [31].

FPGA. A Field programmable gate array is an IC that can be designed to perform a function for a specific application. It has thousands of doors. FPGA has become very popular in the VLSI field. Write FPGA code using languages such as VHDL and Verilog. FPGAs are reconfigurable hardware components used in low-latency systems. They offer the advantage of hardware-level optimization, allowing traders to customize hardware to specific algorithmic needs. The reconfigurability of FPGAs allows rapid implementation of algorithms at the hardware level [32, 33].

GPU. A graphics processing unit (GPU) is a dedicated electronic unit designed to perform computer graphics and photography (such as on video cards or built into motherboards, mobile phones, computers, workstations, and game consoles). After the design began, it was discovered that GPUs were useful for calculations that were not included in the comparison due to their parallel nature. GPUs play an important role in parallel processing in the algorithmic market. Their ability to manage multiple parallel operations simultaneously increases the computing power of the business, enabling rapid analysis and decision-making [34].

6.2 Software Optimization

Optimized software is equally vital for algorithmic trading systems. The design of algorithms and coding practices must prioritize speed and efficiency. Software that can quickly analyze market data to implement complex strategies are essential. Optimized software interface with hardware is also required for rapid execution. Since the focus of software in High performance computing is on speed and efficient execution, software design pattern focusses on speed rather than code reusability and structure [24, 35]. Further subsections discuss about various design patterns.

LMAX Disruptor. The LMAX Disruptor is designed for low-cost messaging, resolving conflicts and challenging traditional messaging in challenging environments such as financial markets. Its main innovation is the pre-engagement ring, which eliminates friction and memory. While producers broadcast and write inputs to the buffer, consumers wait for a specific partition to ensure the data is consistent. Memory barriers enable exchange between producers and consumers. A key benefit is batch processing, where customers can complete multiple entries, thus increasing throughput and reducing latency. This separation of producer and consumer roles makes it easier to work on clear responsibilities and interactions between events. Figure 2 below (see Fig. 2) depicts a producer-consumer structure for efficient data exchange. The Producer creates data and claim sequences from the Entry Factory by writing data with a Claim Strategy. When there are no available sequences, the Consumer utilizes a Wait Strategy to wait for them. It reads data from accessible sequences using Read Data from Sequence. The RingBuffer allows data flow between the Producer and Consumer. This approach optimizes the producer-consumer data flow by leveraging adjustable sequence management, waiting, and data buffering mechanisms.

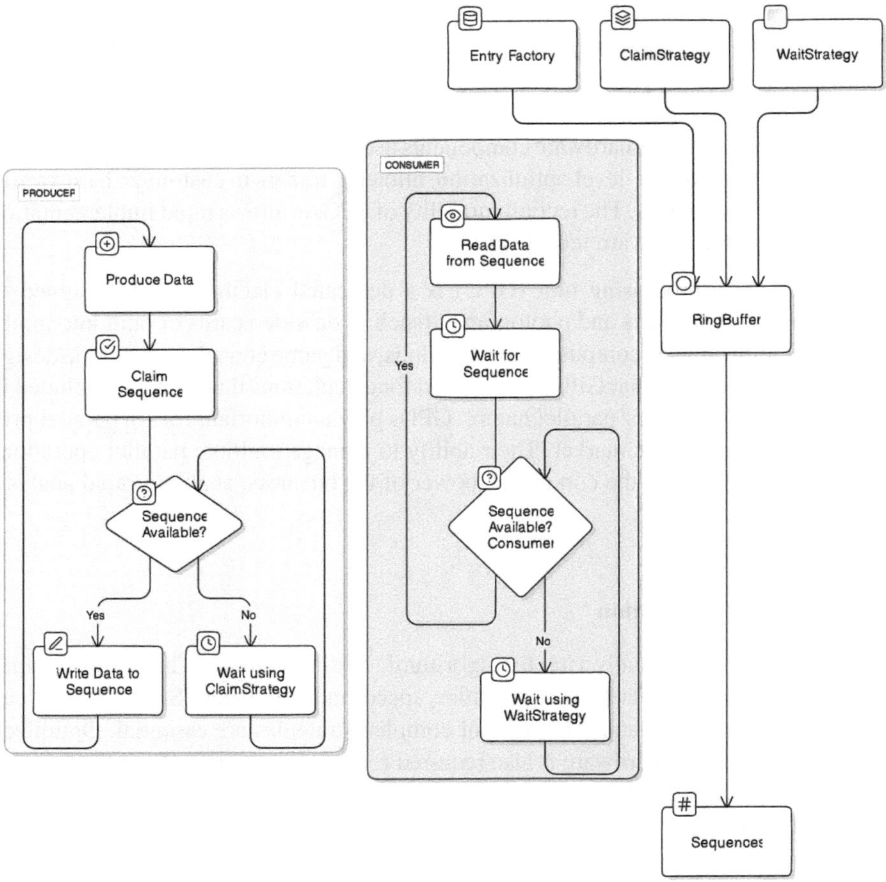

Fig. 2. UML of disruptor framework [36].

Overall, LMAX Disruptor offers lower latency and greater flexibility compared to queuing, making it more capable of meeting messaging needs. However, for many developers this comes with trade-offs such as pre-allocation of memory and potential complexity [36, 37].

Code Optimization Techniques. In the relentless pursuit of speed and efficiency, programmers constantly seek ways to push their code to the limit. This quest becomes even more critical in resource-constrained environments or real-time applications where milliseconds matter. This sub-section discusses programming techniques that exists to help squeeze the most performance out of the code. Let's delve into some key strategies that can significantly enhance program's speed and responsiveness.

Cache Warming. Data is sent to the CPU cache before it is needed to reduce memory access time and increase the response time of tasks [38].

Dispatch at Compile Time. Through procedures such as template specialization or function overloading, improved code paths are selected at compile time built on type or value, evading runtime dispatch and premature optimization choices [36].

Constexpr. The calculation of constexpr characters is assessed at compile time, ensuring stable balance and efficiency by eliminating runtime evaluation [39].

Short Circuiting. Logical instructions stop evaluation when the goal is established, reducing unnecessary calculations and possibly refining performance [39].

Unsigned vs Signed. Ensuring consistent signedness in evaluations evades conversion related performance problems and sustains effective code implementation [39].

Float and Double. Consistent use of float or double types in calculations avoids implicit type conversions, probable loss of precision, and slower performance [36].

Branch Prediction and Reduction. Accurately predicting results from branches allows code to be executed, reducing penalties for incorrect branches and improving performance [36].

Slowpath Removal. Optimization techniques are designed to reduce the application of less successful methods and thus improve overall performance [36, 40].

SIMD. Single Instruction Multiple Data (SIMD) speeds up vector and matrix calculations by allowing a single instruction to run on several elements concurrently [41].

Prefetching. Determining how to load information into the cache beforehand can help reduce data retrieval latency, especially in memory applications [42].

Lock Free Programming. Utilizes atomic processes to accomplish concurrency without the use of locks, thus removing the overhead and possible deadlocks related with lock-based synchronization [36, 43, 44].

Inlining. Combines the body of a function at each point the function is called, reducing function call overhead and aiding additional optimization by the compiler [36, 39].

7 Evaluating Code Optimization Techniques for Latency Reduction

The aim of this study is to investigate the effect of various optimization techniques on reducing latency in C++ programs. Appropriate code was written for this study and the Google Benchmark library was used to measure the execution time of the application with and without any optimization method. Research approaches include cache warm-up, dispatch at Compile time, constexpr, short-circuiting, unsigned and signed integers, use of floating-point and double-precision data types, branch approximation and reduction, slow path removal, SIMD instructions, and prefetching.

The following Table 1 below shows the significant improvements achieved using this optimization technique. More importantly, the constexpr method shows the largest reduction in latency, with a 91.31% reduction in the time to complete one iteration. Cache warming has also proven to be effective, reducing latency by 90.42%. Other techniques such as short-circuiting, and SIMD instructions reduce the latency from 29.21% to 53.24%. Techniques such as gradually removing and selecting unsigned and signed numbers have a small impact but contribute to overall improvement. These findings highlight the importance of using optimization techniques in C++ applications.

Table 1. Impact of optimization techniques on reducing latency.

Programming Techniques	Time without Technique(ns)	Time with Technique (ns)	Percentage Change in Time (%)
Cache Warming	268685127	25734044	90.4222
Dispatch at Compile time	2.67	1.89	29.2135
Constexpr	2.74 (per iteration)	0.238 (per iteration)	91.3139
Short circuiting	12501273900 (8192 iteration)	5845912631 (8192 iteration)	53.2375
Unsigned vs signed	0.332(unsigned)	0.273(signed)	17.7711
Float and Double	22.4	14.5	35.26786
Branch Prediction and Reduction	7.54	4.71	37.53316
Slowpath Removal	28168	24645	12.5071
SIMD	22.357	10.727	52.0195
Prefetching	8225823	6311310	23.27442

8 Human Oversight in Algorithmic Trading Systems

Profitability in algorithmic trading stems from a combination of human and technological talents. The data flow diagram (see Fig. 1) depicts this partnership, in which human roles and algorithms work together to make educated decisions and benefit from trading. The Strategy Developer develops effective algorithms based on business expertise, while the Data Scientist assures their integration with reliable market data. The Algorithm implements these tactics quickly for data-driven judgements.

Human monitoring is crucial. The Analyst checks algorithm performance, discovers flaws, and recommends enhancements. This iterative technique enables for ongoing response to market changes. The Trade Executor executes deals using algorithms, but the Risk Manager manages risks using human judgement. The Compliance Officer enforces regulations and ethical standards while emphasising the importance of human governance.

Effective communication channels facilitate the flow of thoughts and data, resulting in a more unified decision-making environment. This synergy combines human knowledge and algorithmic efficiency to enable lucrative trading. As a result, success in algorithmic trading is determined by the interplay of human expertise and computational power, assuring ethical behaviour, risk management, and market flexibility.

Figure 3 below (see Fig. 1) displays the series of interactions in an algorithmic trading system that makes trade decisions. Information is exchanged by key players such as the trader, data source, risk advisor, portfolio, trade manager, risk manager, and regulator. The process consists of the Trader initiating a trade request, risk assessment based on data inputs, portfolio evaluation, trade execution while assuring regulatory compliance through the Risk Manager, and communication between components along the flow.

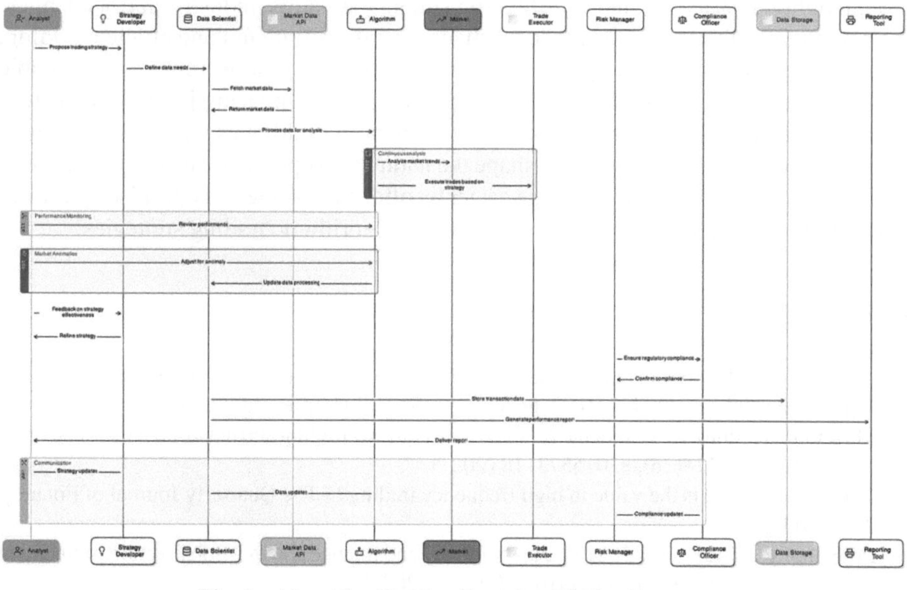

Fig. 3. Algorithm Trading Decision Making Process.

9 Conclusion and Future Work

Algorithmic trading has clearly altered the financial landscape, transforming the market into a high-speed, data-driven environment in which low latency is critical for success. This study investigated several code optimisation strategies and their influence on lowering latency in C++ programmes, which is a critical component of algorithmic trading systems. The findings show that using optimisation techniques like as constexpr, cache warming, short-circuiting, SIMD instructions, and dispatch at compile time can result in considerable performance gains. These approaches have proved to be beneficial in reducing execution time and improving overall system efficiency, emphasising the need of using proper optimisation algorithms in algorithmic trading applications.

As we progress towards a revolutionary future, fascinating technologies like artificial intelligence and machine learning have enormous promise for further developing algorithmic trading systems. Self-learning algorithms promise to transcend previous models, reveal hidden patterns, and make faster judgements than ever before. Furthermore, blockchain technology's capacity to provide transparency and security through the use of "smart contracts" is an exciting line of investigation. To enable the adoption of these cutting-edge technologies while maintaining optimal performance, we propose creating a complete framework that combines numerous design patterns and optimisation methodologies. This framework would allow users to focus on implementing their strategy logic rather than worrying about the complexities of code optimisation.

While technology's revolutionary potential continues to reshape the structure of commercial finance, dangers like flash crashes and algorithmic bias must be addressed through tighter restrictions and coordination among regulators, industry, and academics. By encouraging ethics, adjusting to legal changes, and assuring fair and efficient trading, we can pave the path for a future in which algorithmic trading remains a valuable tool for entrepreneurs and multinational corporations. This amazing journey is far from finished, and the next chapter promises to be even more exciting as we see technology's revolutionary potential continue to reshape the nature of corporate finance. The proposed framework intends to make this change easier by offering a stable and optimised platform for creating and implementing high-performance algorithmic trading strategies.

References

1. Aldridge, I.: High-Frequency Trading: A Practical Guide to Algorithmic Strategies and Trading Systems, pp. 2–4, 9–10. John Wiley & Sons, Incorporated (2013)
2. Musciotto, F., Piilo, J., Mantegna, R.N.: High-frequency trading and networked markets. Proc. Natl. Acad. Sci. **118**(26), e2015573118 (2021)
3. Cartea, A.: Where is the value in high frequency trading? ´ The Quarterly Journal of Finance, 2–4 (2011)
4. Lothian, J.R.: The internationalization of money and finance and the globalization of financial markets. J. Int. Money Financ. **21**(6), 699–724 (2002)
5. Hasbrouck, J.: Empirical Market Microstructure: The Institutions, Economics, and Econometrics of Securities Trading. Oxford University Press (2007)
6. Menkveld, A.J.: High-frequency trading and the new-market makers. Journal of Financial Markets **16**(4), 712–740 (2013)
7. Relationship between market particiapants. (n.d.). GETMONEYRICH. https://getmoneyrich.com/wp-content/uploads/2010/01/Financial-Market-Capital-market.png
8. Madani, S., Atmadjaja, Y.V.I., Purnomo, E.: Analysis of decision making investment in shares of non-bumn banking companies using the capital asset pricing model (CAPM) method. International Journal of Economic, Business, Accounting, Agriculture Management and Sharia Administration (IJEBAS) **4**(1), 325–333 (2024)
9. Fwaga, C., Mukuna, W.O., Olwamba, L.O.: Mathematical investigation of option pricing using black-scholes-merton partial differential equation with transaction cost. J. Adv. Math. Comp. Sci. **39**(4), 1–9 (2024)

10. Global Algorithmic Trading Market Size, Share Forecast 2021–2030. (n.d.). Spherical Insights. https://www.sphericalinsights.com/reports/algorithmic-trading-market
11. Hendershott, K., Jones, C., Sager, A.: Algorithmic trading: What it is and why it matters. The Journal of Portfolio Management **37**(4), 22–31 (2011)
12. Aldridge, I.: High-Frequency Trading: A Practical Guide to Algorithmic Strategies and Trading Systems. John Wiley & Sons (2013)
13. Addy, W.A., Ajayi-Nifise, A.O., Bello, B.G., Tula, S.T., Odeyem, O., Falaiye, T.: Algorithmic Trading and AI: A Review of Strategies and Market Impact. World J. Adv. Eng. Technol. Sci. **11**(1), 258–267 (2024)
14. Solanki, J.: Getting Started with Algorithmic Trading Strategies. Admirals (2023). https://admiralmarkets.com/education/articles/automated-trading/algorithmic-trading-strategies-guide
15. Wu, B., Lyu, B., Gu, J.: Weighted Multivariate Mean Reversion for Online Portfolio Selection. In: Joint European Conference on Machine Learning and Knowledge Discovery in Databases, pp. 255–270. Springer Nature Switzerland, Cham (2023)
16. Arbitrage Strategies: Understanding Working of Statistical Arbitrage. Quantitative Finance & Algo Trading Blog by QuantInsti (2023). https://blog.quantinsti.com/statistical-arbitrage/
17. Waelbroeck, H.: Order flow as a control system. Journal of Financial Markets **12**(4), 441–464 (2009)
18. Hendershott, T., Jones, C.M., Menkveld, A.J.: Does algorithmic trading improve liquidity? J. Financ. **66**(1), 1–33 (2011)
19. Brogaard, J., Hagströmer, B.: Liquidity supply across multiple trading venues. Journal of Financial Markets **18**, 108–131 (2014)
20. Harris, T.: Liquidity in financial markets. Cambridge University Press (2003)
21. Jumadinova, J., Dasgupta, P.: A Comparison of Different Automated Market-Maker Strategies (2010)
22. Clapham, B., Haferkorn, M., Zimmermann, K.: The impact of high-frequency trading on modern securities markets: an analysis based on a technical interruption. Bus. Inf. Syst. Eng. **65**(1), 7–24 (2023)
23. A. (2023, July 10). Trading at light speed: designing low latency systems in C++ - David Gross - Meeting C++ 2022. Electronic Trading Technology. https://sissoftwarefactory.com/blog/trading-at-light-speed-designing-low-latency-systems-in-c-david-gross-meeting-c-2022/
24. A. (2023, December 5). Best Practices on HFT low-latency software. Electronic Trading Technology. https://sissoftwarefactory.com/blog/best-practices-on-hft-low-latency-software/
25. Nagy, P., Powrie, J., Zohren, S.: Machine learning for microstructure data-driven execution algorithms. Handbook of Artificial Intelligence and Big Data Applications in Investments **8**, 100 (2023)
26. Chugh, Y., Agrawal, S., Shetty, Y., Guruprasad, M.: Algo-Trading and its Impact on Stock Markets. Int. J. Res. Eng. Sci. Manage. **7**(3), 48–55 (2024)
27. Harrison, M.: Essays in high frequency trading and market structure, Doctoral dissertation. University of East London (2023)
28. Kirilenko, A., Kyle, K., Samadi, S.: The impact of high-frequency trading on market quality. The Review of Financial Studies **24**(6), 2012–2051 (2011)
29. Kirilenko, A.N., Kyle, A.S.: The flash crash: A study of market microstructure. Journal of Finance **60**(5), 1989–2014 (2005)
30. Khadelwal, N., Jain, A.: Effect of Technology Innovations toward High-Frequency Trading (HFT) in Equity
31. Ali, A., et al.: Speed vs. efficiency: A framework for high-frequency trading algorithms on FPGA using Zynq SoC platform. Alex. Eng. J. **96**, 1–14 (2024)
32. Boutros, A., Betz, V.: Field-Programmable Gate Array Architecture. In Handbook of Computer Architecture, pp. 1–47. Springer Nature Singapore, Singapore (2023)

33. Evans, H.: In Pursuit of Ultra-Low Latency: FPGA in High-Frequency Trading, p. 4. https://www.velvetech.com/blog/fpga-in-high-frequency-trading/. Accessed: 4 June 2023
34. Kehinde, T.O., Chung, S.H., Chan, F.T.: Benchmarking TPU and GPU for Stock Price Forecasting Using LSTM Model Development. In Science and Information Conference, pp. 289–306. Springer Nature Switzerland, Cham (2023)
35. A. (2022, September 11). How do I design high-frequency trading systems and its architecture. Part II. Electronic Trading Technology. https://sissoftwarefactory.com/blog/how-do-i-design-high-frequency-trading-systems-and-its-architecture-part-ii/
36. Bilokon, P., Gunduz, B.: C++ design patterns for low-latency applications including high-frequency trading (2023). arXiv preprint arXiv:2309.04259
37. Thompson, M.: Lmax disruptor: High performance alternative to bounded queues for exchanging data between concurrent threads, 6–32 (2011)
38. Weller, D., et al.: Latency critical workload acceleration in financial applications. ACM SIGARCH Computer Architecture News **41**(5), 42–43 (2013). pages 10
39. Stroustrup, B.: An overview of c++. in: Proceedings of the 1986 sigplan workshop on object-oriented programming, 7–18, 4–20 (1986)
40. CppCon. CppCon 2017: Carl Cook "When a Microsecond Is an Eternity: High Performance Trading Systems in C++", 2–18. https://www.youtube.com/watch?v=NH1Tta7purM&t=1227s. Accessed: 4 June 2023
41. Asaduzzaman, Md., Khan, L.: Optimizing simd code generation: a new approach. Int. J. High Perform. Comp. Appl. **21**(4), 481–491 (2007). pages 21
42. Zhong, W., Chang, W.: A performance study of cooperative prefetching for the disk cache of a proxy server, 44–60, 8
43. Anderson, T.E.: The performance of spin lock alternatives for shared-memory multiprocessors. IEEE Transactions on Parallel and Distributed Systems **1**(1), 6–16 (1990). pages 22
44. McKenney, P.E., Slingwine, J.D.: Read-copy update: Using execution history to solve concurrency problems. In: Parallel and Distributed Computing and Systems, pp. 509–518 (1998). pages 22

Effective Pre-processing of Datasets by Removing Anomalies with OptiContamFinder on Isolation Forest for Stock Market forecasting and Nowcasting

Jayaraman Kumarappan(✉) and Elakkiya R

Department of Computer Science, Birla Institute of Technology and Science Pilani, Dubai International Academic City, Dubai 345055, UAE

jramans@gmail.com

Abstract. Effective stock market forecasting and nowcasting requires effective data collection pre-processing. Traditional methods are often unable to identify and remove abnormalities, which be able to have a noteworthy impact on predictive model presentation. Current limitations of pre-processing stock market datasets require appropriate methods for correcting anomalies in an appropriate manner, resulting in low model performance In this case, researchers propose a different approach so detecting and extracting anomalies in stock market data sets efficiently using OptiContamFinder is proposed. Abnormalities, such as extreme changes can distort the underlying assumptions and correlations in the data, reducing the accuracy of the prediction model. To address these limitations, develop OptiContamFinder, which enables anomaly detection with Isolation Forest. This method excels in reducing anomalies by generating random forests of isolated trees and identifying remote areas with short path lengths. OptiContamFinder improves anomaly detection by striking a balance between anomaly removal and data preservation by providing optimization options for determining contamination thresholds. The entire process consists of gathering historical stock market data, cleaning and identifying important characteristics, normalizing or scaling the features, and using OptiContamFinder to discover and remove anomalies. After pre-processing, the predictive models are trained and tested against acceptable performance metrics. By implementing both nowcasting and forecasting for the pre-processing of stock market anomaly detection shows pre-processed accuracy of 85% and 88%. By successfully detecting and cancelling anomalies, OptiContamFinder prolongs forecasting models, resulting in better forecasts of stock price movements using python.

Keywords: Stock market forecasting · Anomaly detection · OptiContamFinder · Isolation Forest · Nowcasting

1 Introduction

Financial risk frameworks are essential for measuring and controlling financial risk within the background of financial risk management. Their findings and risk assessments can support decision-making and guarantee adherence to regulations [1]. Risk prediction

M. Bakaev et al. (Eds.): IMS 2024, CCIS 2534, pp. 351–370, 2026.
https://doi.org/10.1007/978-3-031-96177-9_29

methods and the utilization of their outcomes are therefore fundamental to managing finances. Time series data represents a range of markets-specific risk characteristics generally make up the data. The existence of abnormalities in datasets like this is a major challenge. When a portion of the data series behaves significantly differently from the other portion of the series over time, it is referred to be anomalous [2]. The stock market is regarded as the most important and active segment of financial institutions and consumers. Financial articles and data on trends have been regarded as the major factors in market trend forecasting. Most organizations rely on high-performance computational tools to forecast market trends using sentiment scores and stock technical data. These forecasts are used to filter both positive and negative emotions in equities, allowing investors to make informed selections. Thus, the modelling and analysis procedure for news stories is highly important to produce correct forecasts. Organizations can gain market prominence by attracting the attention of an increasing number of investors. Consider the following scenario: an investor possesses 100 stocks, but he or she is unable to identify the top positive and negative trends stocks according to corporate announcements or technical data [4].

Stock exchanges are unpredictable and may alter over time; the relationship between social media and stock market data undoubtedly evolves with time [5]. A great variety of strategies have been developed in the literature for determining and predicting the connection between stock attributes and financial time series data. These strategies apply to both structured and quantitative databases. Traditional methods utilize a variety of market analytical and statistical analysis tools to forecast stock market sentiment [6]. Share prices in the stock market can be influenced by a wide range of events, including business news and political news. Stock markets may be viewed as dynamic systems; the relationship among social media and stock market data is undoubtedly changing with time. Choosing time-varying behaviour into consideration may result in greater accuracy since correlations that fluctuate over time may now be included. This is especially beneficial for predicting stock movements using social media data because no time-invariant connection can be predicted [7]. For instance, a tight credit search keyword may not be as relevant in months. Expecting that a steady correlation for an extended period is most likely to contribute to improper assessment of the data once it is no longer valuable or ignore data from previous where useful data may be offered [8].

Nowcasting is the 'forecasting' of a financial system's present or recent collective condition. It may be done either at the start of enhancing "flash" predicts in a National Statistical Agency, which would have been based on conclusions from the irregular arrival of highly separated measures, or by an outside organization using more frequent available information, such as polls, to improve offered particles, or both. Everyone will primarily concentrate on the former, discussing how recent advances in modelling and forecasting might boost the accuracy and timing of initial information releases [9]. Techniques based on establishing the status of an economy from an array of data sources, which means "high-frequency estimates" of important aggregates are continually available, are presented. Some of the challenges and techniques discussed here apply to both systems. Everyone refers to any technique that integrates additional information when producing current aggregate data, rather than just gathering observed breaks down, like forecasting [3].

Nowcasting, referred to as the forecast of the current moment, very near the future, and very recent past, is fundamentally a Big Data challenge since it requires monitoring a large number of macroeconomic time frames with varying frequencies, release dates, and data abnormalities. The 3 Vs of "volume, velocity, and variety," which define Big Data, are vital in nowcasting [10]. Not only have macroeconomic datasets grown exponentially in bulk, but macro econometricians have developed strategies to cope with complicated settings with an enormous amount of factors relative to the number of observations since their inception. Furthermore, numerous strategies have been developed to utilize, efficiently and in immediate time, the speed of macroeconomic series, At last, the data used for nowcasting are accessible at different frequencies and vary significantly in regards to their sources (e.g., hard data vs soft data that comes from qualitative data like surveys and polls) and precision [11].

Forecasting has relied extensively on referred to as regular macroeconomic information releases, one of the most well-known instances being the US Bureau of Labour Statistics' Employment Situation Report, released on the first Friday of every month. This report includes information on agricultural payroll jobs, average hourly earnings, and other summary labour market statistics [12]. Because the majority of the economy moves in lockstep through the business cycle, positive developments for the labour market often help the whole economy. In addition to labour market information, forecasting models usually incorporate building spending, (non-)manufacturing states, retail sales, pricing indices, and other conventional macroeconomic data. The Federal Reserve Bank of New York provides a notable example of nowcasting employing a dynamical model that includes thirty-six predictors of various frequencies for more information.

Effective data set pre-processing is essential in stock market forecasting and nowcasting, as successful forecasting depends on the quality and integrity of investment data Traditional pre-processing methods often fail to detect and eliminate anomalies well, and severely hamper predictive model performance. These anomalies, which include large value spikes to the wrong data points, pose a significant challenge to obtain reliable estimates and can distort trends and correlations appearing in the data, reducing the accuracy and usefulness of predictive models [13]. Algorithms that can efficiently handle anomaly detection and removal are urgently needed to improve the accuracy of stock market forecasts Despite the shortcomings of traditional pre-processing methods, this paper presents a different approach using OptiContamFinder, a separation forest algorithm-based tool high -Well known for its ability to extract anomalies from dimensional datasets, the isolation forest is the foundation of the anomaly detection capability of OptiContamFinder. Isolation Forest excels at detecting anomalies that vary significantly after the majority of the data.

OptiContamFinder improves the anomaly detection method by adding optimization functions for determining the contamination threshold, resulting in a delicate equilibrium between anomaly removals and data retention. The primary purpose of this research is to overcome the limitations of current pre-processing approaches in stock market forecasting and nowcasting. OptiContamFinder as an anomaly detection and removal method, increase the precision and dependability of prediction models in capturing the complex dynamics of stock price fluctuations. This study aims to enhance the advanced financial dataset pre-processing methods by employing a complete approach that includes data collecting, cleaning, feature selection, and OptiContamFinder. The aim is to provide financial sector stakeholders with more powerful and informed choices for traversing the complexity of analysing stock markets and trading methods.

The main contributions of this work are as follows:

1. OptiContamFinder uses the anomaly detection method to take advantage of Isolation Forest's ability to rapidly extract anomalies in high-dimensional datasets, minimizing operator intervention.
2. OptiContamFinder offers optimization features to determine contamination thresholds, between anomaly detection and data protection, which is critical for preserving useful information in a dataset.
3. By completing detection for anomalies, OptiContamFinder improves forecasting algorithms for stock market forecasting and nowcasting, resulting in more accurate forecasts of stock price movements.
4. This research adds to the advances in pre-processing data sets, enabling more reliable and informed choices in stock market research and investment strategies.

The paper is organized as follows: Sect. 2 discusses related works on anomaly detection and pre-processing for stock market datasets. Section 3 gives the problem statement, the limits of current pre-processing technologies for a successful approach to anomaly identification and elimination. Section 4 describes the entire technique for using OptiContamFinder to pre-process stock market data, including data collection, cleaning, feature selection, and anomaly identification. Section 5 displays the results of using the proposed technique to improve the accuracy of stock market forecasting and nowcasting. Section 6 summarises the discussions of the suggested methodology. Section 7 summarises the important findings, discusses possible future study topics, and emphasizes the importance of the work in enhancing pre-processing approaches for financial information.

2 Related Works

New mathematical and technical ideas that have become presently leading advances in the information economy, including the Internet of Things, ubiquity technological advances, and Ubicomp, encourage the establishment of new infiltration pathways which could have an immediate effect on everyday life for individuals. This is in addition to advancements in the instruments and techniques employed for launching newer cyber-attacks, significantly increases the amount of cyber threats to the data culture. As a consequence, developing and improving technologies to assist security experts in avoiding and identifying attacks has grown as an essential part of cybersecurity. Particularly, detection systems for intrusions are currently an indispensable tool for supplying services via the web. Yet such devices have drawbacks, including false positives and immediate data analysis, which need them to be operated within monitoring. Since a consequence, frameworks and techniques have to be developed to offer appropriate assessment of the information produced by these gadgets. Larriva-Novo et al. [14] provides an innovative data processing process that utilizes a novel distributed computer system for big data sets such as UGR'16. Furthermore, the study looks at the use of machine learning techniques to improve the adaptability and effectiveness of the proposed preparatory processing framework. As a consequence, the invention works effectively on desktops. Finally, the suggestion shows that decision tree approaches are more suitable for training a machine learning model with a large dataset than a multi-layered the perceptron neural network. A drawback of the proposed architecture is that techniques for deep learning, such as MLP, are inappropriate for massive data sets, necessitating improvements for distributed platforms that use Apache Spark libraries.

Faraz et al. [15] Auto encoder long short-term memory (AE-LSTM) networks are used by Faraz et al. [15] to predict the closing price of the stock market one at a time. In order to integrate technical assessment with neural network techniques, the raw dataset's characteristics include synthesizers and financial indicators. One method for eliminating noise from indexes of securities is the wavelet-based treatment. The technique of z-score is also employed to identify abnormalities within the dataset. The auto encoder gets trained first to accurately reflect the data. In order to anticipate the stock index's ultimate price, the encoder then gathers features and sends them across the network of LSTM. Utilizing the previous forecasts, the system then generates the subsequent ones. Analysts examine the proposed technique through a series of fake experiments using the Standard and Poor's 500 (S&P 500) stock market index. The average return (AR), root mean square error (RMSE), and mean absolute error (MAE) are the outcomes parameters. The data demonstrate that the recommended forecasting-by-prediction technique trumps the generative adversarial network (GAN) for daily improved closing price prediction. In daily price prediction, the recommended AE-LSTM method is less accurate than GAN for stock market approximately price prediction.

The characteristics and parameters that affect the use of machine learning methods' out-of-sample performance are determined by Azevedo et al. [16] using information collected from a globally distributed dataset consisting of about 1.9 billion stock-month anomaly events between 1980 and 2019. A straightforward combination of components (the baseline factor benchmark) is significantly outperformed by the vast majority of analyzed models, which display noteworthy monthly value-weighted (long-short) returns of about 1.8–2.2%. Most significant long-short investment outcomes are achieved using machine learning-driven aggregate predictors, despite transaction costs of up to 300 basis units. Through a comparative analysis of 46 distinct algorithmic learning models, it was determined that the approaches exhibiting the highest return predictability are those utilizing the feed-forward neural network learning or composite classifiers. These models prolong rolling windows, employ an elastic net to reduce features, and utilize % ranked returns as their aim. The nonlinear structures yield important results in a variety of classic asset pricing models, exposing inefficiencies in the marketplace and challenging accepted notions of asset pricing in global marketplaces. This analysis has a limitation in that, although highlighting the importance of relationships that are nonlinear within the factor zoo and their impact on the global asset pricing, it also draws attention to the potential effects of data removing and excessive overfitting. Future research should attentively address these issues to prevent false outcomes and mistaken interactions. Furthermore, the complexity of computational machine learning algorithms may make it difficult for operators to appropriately implement successful trading strategies based on those findings, even if they beat the models and reveal possible shortcomings in prices.

Every day, the size of data provided by users on public media microblog sites like Twitter and Reddit grows exponentially, providing academics with unique chances to analyse financial markets from fresh viewpoints. The 2021 meme stock frenzy brought together social media-savvy stock traders and investors. During the COVID-19 lockdowns, retail investors discussed investing plans on social media channels such as Reddit, which contributed significantly to this hysteria. These retail investors conducted their stock trades using platforms such as Robinhood. Cruz et al. [17], Machine learning techniques are being used to anticipate pricing variations in two meme stocks: GameStop ($GME) and AMC Entertainment ($AMC). Two sentiments evaluations based on everyday public discussions regarding the shares on Reddit are joined with 85 other fundamental and technical indicators to generate a set of characteristics for artificial intelligence algorithms. This is demonstrated that by properly picking a mix of memes based on a stock's basic parameters, physical indications, and internet opinion evaluations, it is possible to estimate the stock's following days ending price. Furthermore, using an anomaly detection approach and everyday Reddit discussions on a meme stock, potential market players can be spotted. One disadvantage is the possibility of bias or noise in Reddit contributions, which may affect the accuracy of anomaly identification and study of online sentiment's influence on price movement.

The state of the global financial system is steadily improving. For example, the US stock market both influences and acts as a "barometer" of the global economy. Analysing data related to the US marketplace is therefore crucial, especially the data mining process for irregular data. Although the use of data mining has yielded a number of study findings in the world of finance, a reliable research methodology for the analysis of time-series data related to stock market anomalies has not yet been established. Wang et al. [18] employ data attributes and actual results of the stock market anomalies. The separated point identification strategy, which depends on densities and distance, is used to analyze the obtained aberrant data in order to extract implicit useful information. Data mining tools are used to find abnormal data in stock market data. Nonetheless, this work provides a modified the process for unpredictability information and applies its ideas to the world of data mining in order to address the limitations of traditional data mining methods for dealing with anomalies in the stock market that includes undetermined factors, i.e., errors caused by various human factors. For the US financial sector anomaly, a crude entropy-based data mining technique is developed. At last, a quantitative evaluation of the technique is performed. The results of the experiments indicate that the rough entropy-based data mining method presented in this study is effective in identifying irregular oscillations in historical data related to the stock market. One drawback is that data mining methods that employ basic entropy could have trouble being able to fully capture and understand the intricacy of irregularities in the US share market.

The expansion of computational and technical concepts in the information society has resulted in an increased frequency of cyber risks, demanding advances in cybersecurity technologies. To address these problems, researchers have proposed a variety of solutions, including innovative pre-processing methods for intrusion detection systems that use distributed computing infrastructures and machine learning approaches. Furthermore, efforts have been undertaken to combine technical evaluation with deep learning approaches for stock market prediction, with positive outcomes in terms of accuracy and efficiency. Yet, obstacles remain, including the appropriateness of algorithms using deep learning for large-scale datasets and the possibility of bias in social media sentiment evaluation. Despite these disadvantages, developments in machine learning models as well as data mining algorithms provide prospects for enhancing cybersecurity and comprehending complicated phenomena such as stock market anomalies, opening the path for future study and practical uses in these sectors.

3 Problem Statement

The pre-processing approaches for stock market forecasting frequently fail to adequately identify and remove abnormalities from datasets [14]. These anomalies, like excessive price changes or incorrect data points, can differ the fundamental trends and correlations in the data, resulting in poor model performance. Conventional methodologies may struggle to distinguish between actual market movements, resulting in wrong predictions and untrustworthy traits for traders and shareholders [19]. Manual anomaly identification procedures are time-consuming and subjective, with limited scalability and resilience when dealing with enormous amounts of data [16]. The demand for enhanced anomaly detection algorithms that can rapidly pre-process stock market information to improve the precision and dependability of forecasting models [18]. This study provides to solve current challenges in stock market data pre-processing by proposing OptiContamFinder, a tool based on the Isolation Forest algorithm. OptiContamFinder is an automated and optimized anomaly detection solution that successfully identifies and removes anomalies from datasets with minimum user involvement. OptiContamFinder improves predictive model by eliminating the Isolation Forest algorithm's capacity to identify anomalies based on shorter path distances in random forests, resulting in a more accurate description of market dynamics. OptiContamFinder's optimization skills for the contamination threshold allow for a finer balance between anomaly elimination and data preservation, improving the whole pre-processing procedure for stock market forecasting and nowcasting. This study gives the area of financial information analysis by offering a revolutionary methodology that tackles the limits of standard pre-processing procedures, boosting the accuracy and dependability of stock market forecasts.

4 Enhanced Pre-processing of Stock Market Data Using OptiContamFinder for Improved Forecasting and Nowcasting

The main way to obtain and pre-process historical stock market data is to use OptiContamFinder, a special application based on the Isolation Forest algorithm. After collecting the data, the dataset is organized and feature is selected to identify objects an importance of prediction. OptiContamFinder is then used to detect and automatically remove anomalies, leveraging Isolation Forest's abnormal filtering capabilities. The features change the presence of contaminants, and uses the same approach to anomaly prevention and data protection. Following pre-processing, multiple forecasting models are developed using the pre-processed data, and their efficacy is assessed using relevant criteria. The current study aims to improve the dependability and accuracy of forecasting techniques by introducing OptiContamFinder, an automated and optimized solution for identifying anomalies in stock market data pre-processing, which will result in more effective financial data analysis and stock market forecasts. Figure 1 depicts the proposed stock market data pre-processing for anomaly discovery, forecasting, and nowcasting.

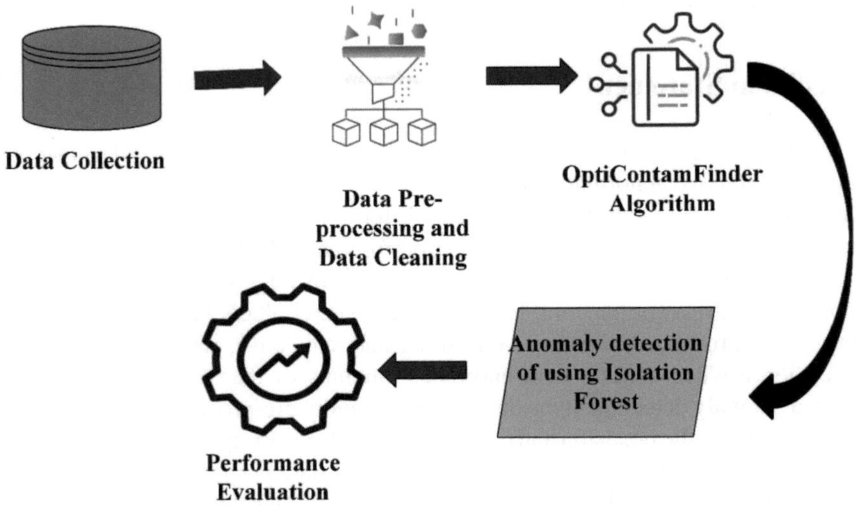

Fig. 1. Stock Market Data for Anomaly Detection Forecast and Nowcast

4.1 Data Collection

Sources of Financial Data

The quantity and significance of the data utilized in the study are important to the effectiveness of utilizing machine learning to analyse stock market trends. This section will explore the financial data sources used to anticipate stock market trends. Historical stock price data is a valuable resource for understanding historical market activity. Daily or intraday stock price data was collected from credible financial data companies including Bloomberg, Yahoo Finance, and Alpha Vantage. This data comprises open, high, low, and close prices, trade volumes, and, in certain cases, modified closing prices [20]. GDP growth, rates of unemployment, and inflationary statistics are all economic indicators that have an impact on the overall status of the economy and, by extension, on the stock market. To guarantee precise and up-to-date information, economic data was acquired from central banks, government agencies, and economic research groups.

4.2 Data Pre-processing

Gathering information is an important step in ensuring that the data is reliable and ready for machine learning analysis. It involves several stages, including feature engineering, normalization, and data cleansing.

4.2.1 Data Cleaning

Data cleaning is important to remove inconsistencies, mistakes, and outliers that may mislead the analysis. The research used the following data-cleaning techniques:

Handling Missing Data: The efficacy of a model can be significantly impacted by missing data. Depending on the kind of data, values that were missing were calculated using average computation, forward-fill, or backward-fill methods.

Outliers Identification and handling: Outliers were identified using statistical approaches as well as subject expertise. To reduce the possible negative impacts of outliers on the evaluation, they were either deleted or adjusted.

Data Integrity Tests: Everyone performed integrity checks to ensure the correctness of the data. This included screening for duplicate entries, maintaining consistency among datasets, and guaranteeing that data quantities were within the anticipated ranges.

4.2.2 Data Normalization

Normalization is used to convert data to a similar scale and avoid characteristics with higher values from dominating the study. The following normalization approaches were used:

Min-Max Scaling: By subtracting the lowest value and splitting by the range of values, the data may be rescaled to [0, 1].

Z-Score Standardisation: To ease convergence, many models' data was normalized to 0 as a mean and 1 as a standard deviation.

4.2.3 Feature Engineering

Feature engineering is the procedure of developing new features from already acquired data or altering existing data to enhance model performance. Lag characteristics, which reflect temporal interdependence, are an important part of time series analysis, Moving averages that capture movements and trends in stock price data and indicators of technology have been computed to give additional insight into the condition of the market, such as the Moving Average of Convergence Divergence and Relative Strength Index. The data prepared undergoes thorough data preparation before being used in machine learning models. The cleansed and engineered dataset forms the basis for training and assessing models for forecasting stock market trend research.

4.3 Anomaly Detection Using Isolation Forest

The Isolation Forest is an autonomous anomaly identification method that assumes abnormalities are rare and exhibit anomalies features values that differ from the norm. This is a tree-structured approach for isolating every situation in a collection. Because the abnormalities are infrequent and unique, they congregate towards the tree's root. The typical points are located at the lower end of the tree.

The Isolation Forest method creates an ensemble of trees based on a provided a set of training information. The dataset contains anomalies, which are examples with short average path lengths on these trees. To construct the Isolation Forest, first pick the number of isolation trees in the forest [21]. The isolation tree is then created using the procedures listed below:

1. Randomly select n examples from the training datasets.
2. Randomly choose one element to divide on.
3. Choose a split value at randomly from a distribution of even numbers that runs from the least quantity to the maximum value of the feature given in Step 2.

Steps 2 and 3 are performed repeatedly until all n occurrences of the randomly selected samples have been separated in the isolation tree's leaf nodes. In this manner, the anomalies will need fewer random divisions to be isolated in leaf nodes, resulting in a reduced predicted route length from the root nodes to the leaf node.

Assume there are n occurrences in a dataset, and $h_0(x)$ is the path length for instances x. The path lengths $h_0(x)$ is then normalized to the mean path length $c(n)$. . Because the isolation trees possess a similar architecture to the Binary Search Tree (BST), determined that the value of $c_0(n)$ in Eq. (1) is the same as the path length of an unsuccessful BST search. They computed the values of $c_0(n)$ using the following equations, where $H_0(i)$ the harmonic number, which may be approximated by is $ln(i)' + 0.5772156649$ (Euler's constant):

$$c_0(n) = 2H_0(n-1) - \left(\frac{2(n-1)}{n}\right) \tag{1}$$

For a dataset with n occurrences, the anomaly scores for every point of data x is determined as follows in Eq. (2):

$$s_0(x, n) = 2^{-\left(\frac{E(h_0(x))}{c_0(n)}\right)} \tag{2}$$

$E(h_0(x))$ is the mean of $h_0(x)$ across a set of isolation trees. When a data point's anomalous score approaches one, it is more inclined to be a problem. On the opposite hand, an anomaly level closer to zero indicates that the data point is more normal.

4.4 OptiContamFinder Algorithm

OptiContamFinder is software that detects and removes contaminated elements from outstanding performance genomics data sets, ensuring the quality and relevance of biological data. It involves approach so performing sequence comparisons against a reference database, statistical analysis to detect discrepancies, including modifiable user-defined variables, and subsequent filtering of potentially contaminating sequences is supported by OptiContamFinder the accuracy of genomes and metagenomics analysis to a great extent, and provides particularly important findings in areas such as microbiome analysis, where contamination can also affect the testing of results.

The OptiContamFinder method enhances the anomaly discovery performance of the Isolation Forest method by improving the contamination criteria. The method starts at the beginning, defining contaminated values to be evaluated and also setting performance objectives such as precision, recall, and F1 scores and then evaluating iteratively on a pre-processed dataset deforestation process and fixed pollution price. An anomaly score is calculated for each data point, and tags are assigned using a cut-off from a contamination criterion. Then, performance is evaluated using metrics such as precision, recall, and F1 scores that are obtained from the sum of similarity scores and compared with ground truth. To increase efficiency, pollutant factors are optimized based on the study's findings and changed within the available area. The best contaminant value for anomaly detection is one that maximizes key performance metrics while maintaining accuracy and recall. The OptiContamFinder method, written in programming languages like Python, R, or MATLAB, includes pre-processing cycles for stock market data analysis. This continuous strategy, combined with data collection and model training, enhances the detection abilities of the forest separation method, leading to more precise and trustworthy anomaly detection endpoints.

5 Results

The effectiveness of OptiContamFinder, researchers found a significant improvement in the performance of predictive models for stock market forecasting. By successfully detecting and removing the anomalies, OptiContamFinder made these models longer, resulting in more accurate predictions of stock price movements Optimization options provided by OptiContamFinder, especially in terms of contamination threshold and anomaly a removal and data storage in balancing anomaly removal with data retention, achieve improvement. Additionally it contributed to improved efficiency by generating random forests of isolation trees which identified outliers with short path lengths Overall, the use of OptiContamFinder in pre-processing stock market datasets demonstrated its predictive capabilities model accuracy and reliability increase revealed. Major limitations of the methods were addressed to dataset pre-processing.

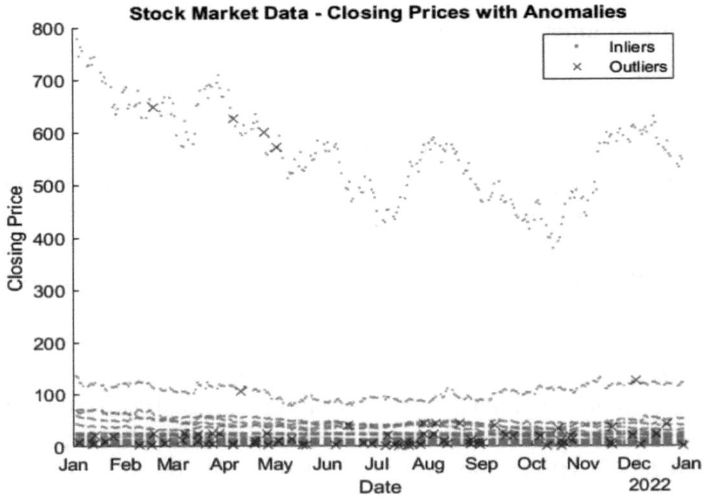

Fig. 2. Stock Market Closing Prices with Anomalies

Figure 2 depicts a graph of stock market closing prices, as well as some abnormalities. Anomalies are data points that differ greatly from the normal or anticipated distribution. They may suggest extraordinary occurrences or market shifts that have an impact on stock values. The graph illustrates that there were several irregularities in the months of March, April, and May 2021, which might be attributed to the COVID-19 epidemic and its influence on the world economy. The graph also illustrates that closing prices have usually climbed over time, with a high in January 2022. This might indicate that the stock market has rebounded from the crisis and hit a new high. But there are certain outliers in January 2022 that may signal volatility in the markets or unpredictability.

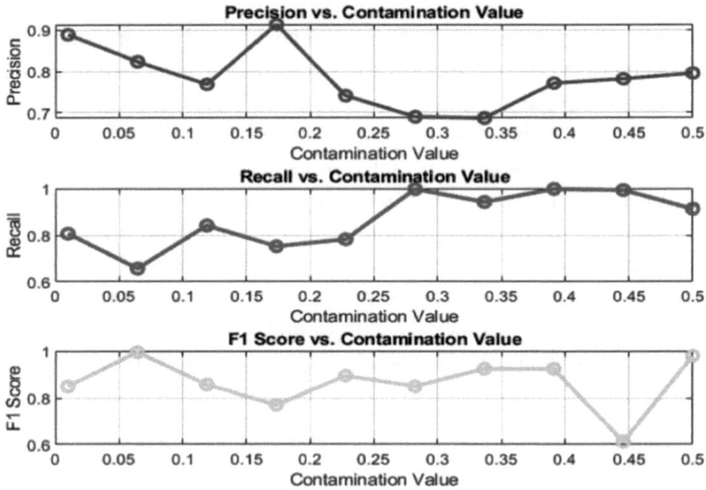

Fig. 3. Different Metrics with Different Amount of Data Contamination.

Figure 3 is a series of three graphs demonstrating how different metrics alter with varying amounts of records trash. Contamination refers to the proportion of outliers or abnormalities in data. Outliers are data points that differ considerably from the normal or anticipated distribution. Precision falls as contamination rises, which means that the outlier identification method gets less accurate as the number of outliers in the data grows. Recall is reasonably steady across all contamination levels, indicating that the outlier identification approach can identify the majority of true outliers regardless of their fraction in the data. The F1 Score is a U-shaped curve, which means that the outlier identification approach performs effectively when there are either very few or very many outliers in the data.

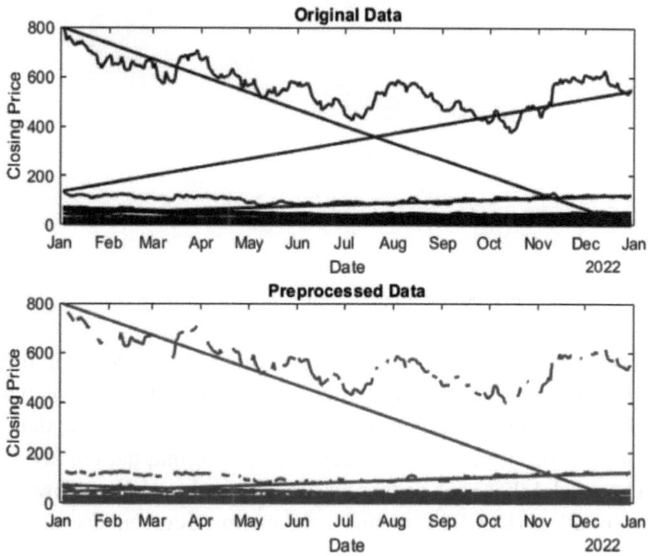

Fig. 4. Difference between Original and Pre-processed Data

Figure 4 shows the difference between original and pre-processed data. The graphs show the closing price of some item or stock over a year, from January to January 2022. The original data is more volatile, meaning that it has more fluctuations and variations. The pre-processed data is smoother, meaning that it has less noise and more consistent trends. This can make it relaxed to classify patterns, correlations, or anomalies in the data.

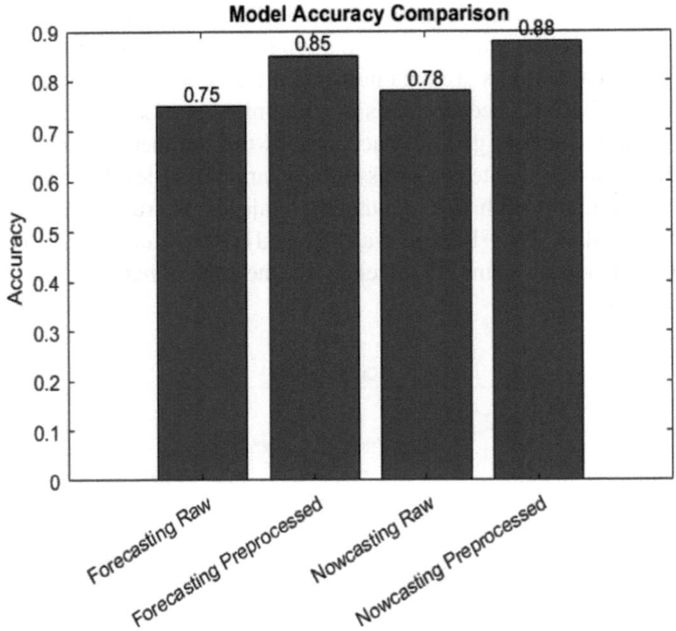

Fig. 5. Comparison of Model Accuracy

Figure 5 shows the accuracy comparison of different models for forecasting and now casting. Forecasting is the task of predicting future events based on past data, while nowcasting is the task of estimating current events based on real-time data. The models are either raw or preprocessed, meaning they use the original data or some transformed version of it. The model that uses preprocessed data and performs now casting has the highest accuracy of all, at 0.88. This means it can estimate current events very well based on real-time data.

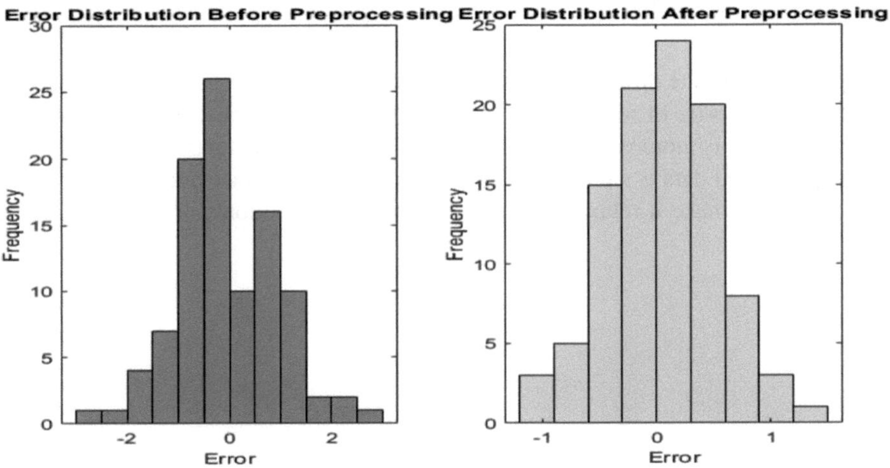

Fig. 6. Histogram of Error Distribution Before and After Pre-Processing

Figure 6 is histogram of fault distribution before and after pre-processing. The left histogram has a wider range of error values, while the right histogram has a narrower range of error values around zero. This means that pre-processing has made the model more accurate and less prone to errors. The left histogram has a higher variance of error principles, sense that the model is more inconsistent and unpredictable. The right histogram has a lower variance of error values, significance that the archetypal is more stable and reliable.

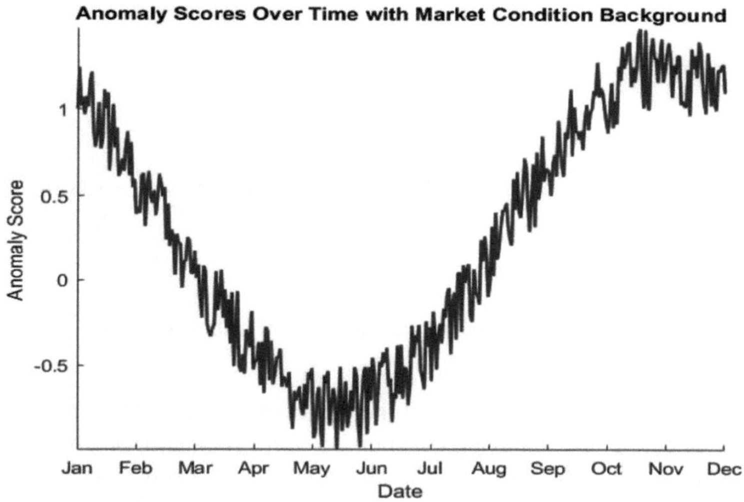

Fig. 7. Anomaly Scores Change Over Time with Diverse Marketplace

Figure 7 shows how anomaly scores variation over time with diverse marketplace.Anomaly scores are a measure of how unusual or abnormal a data point is compared to the expected pattern. The higher the score, the more anomalous the data point is. The graph also shows the background color indicating the market condition, such as normal, volatile, or crisis. The anomaly scores tend to be higher when the market condition is volatile or crisis, indicating more uncertainty and unpredictability in the data. The anomaly scores reach their lowest point in June, when the market condition is normal, indicating a stable and consistent pattern in the data. The anomaly scores peak in November, when the market condition is crisis, indicating a sudden and drastic change in the data.

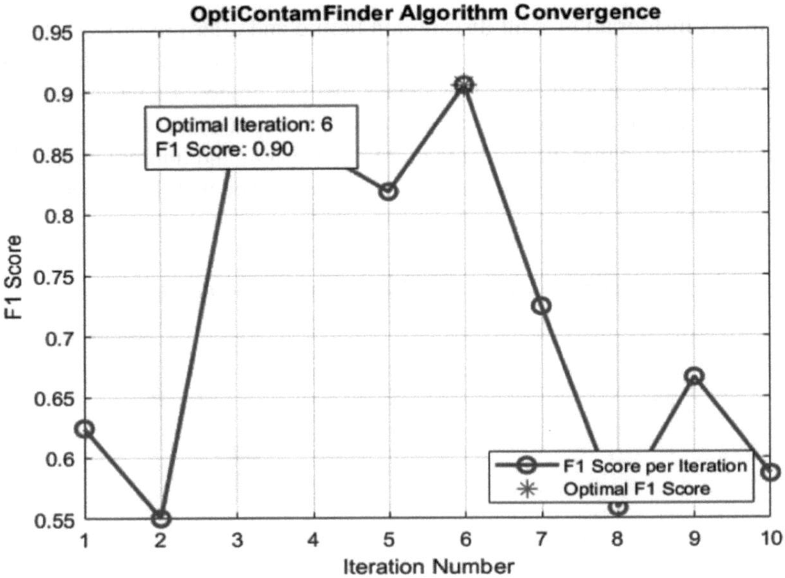

Fig. 8. Convergence of the OptiContamFinder Algorithm

Figure 8 showing the convergence of the OptiContamFinder Algorithm, which is a method for detecting and removing contamination in genomic data. The graph shows how the F1 Score, which is a measure of accuracy, changes with different iterations of the algorithm. The optimal iteration is 6, where the F1 Score reaches 0.90, meaning that the algorithm correctly identifies 90% of the contaminated and non-contaminated samples. The graph also shows that after iteration 6, the F1 Score drops slightly, indicating that the algorithm starts to over fit the data and lose generalization ability. Therefore, the graph suggests that the OptiContamFinder Algorithm should stop at iteration 6 to achieve the best performance.

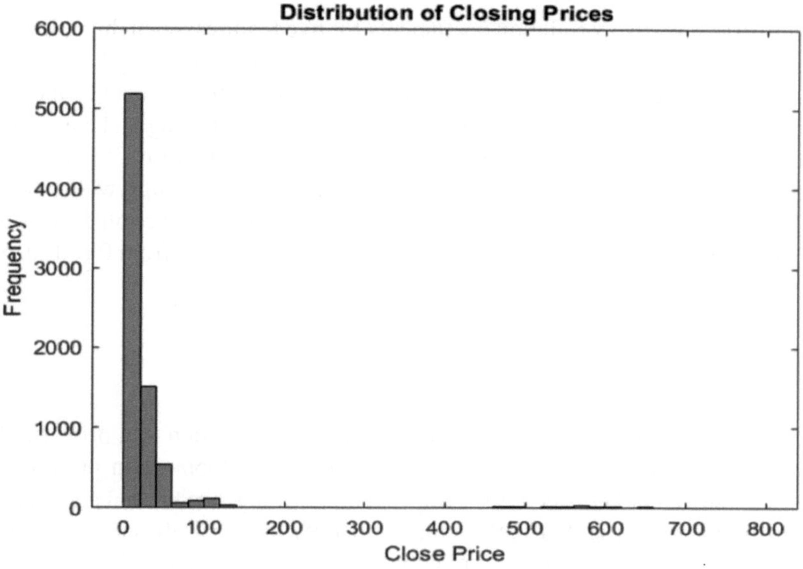

Fig. 9. Histogram Distribution of Closing Prices

Figure 9 displays the distribution of closing prices in a stock market. It does not immediately give information on anomaly detection, forecasting, or now casting. The x-axis symbolizes "Close Price" and ranges from 0 to 800. The y-axis denotes "Frequency" and ranges from 0 to 6000. For near prices ranging from 0 to 100, a very tall bar stretches up to almost 5500 times. A shorter bar has a frequency of around 1000 for near prices between 100 and 200. Most closing prices range between 0 and 200.

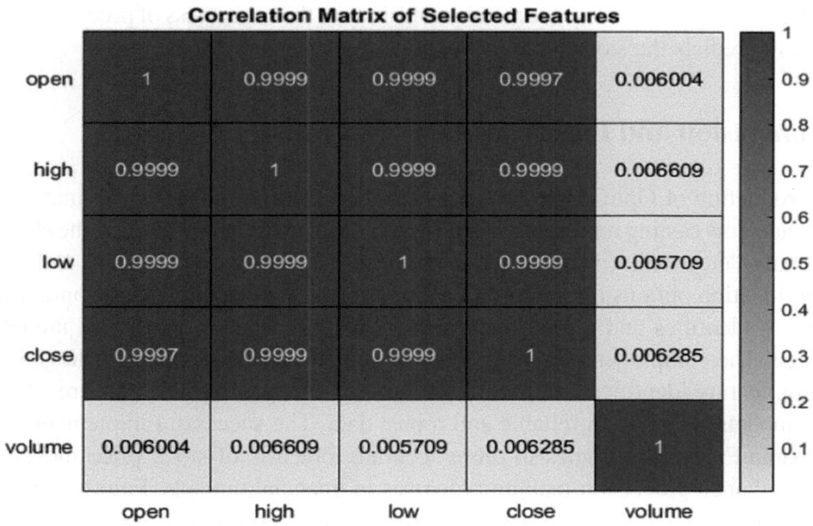

Fig. 10. Correlation Matrix of Selected Features

Figure 10 shows the correlation coefficients for five features: open, high, low, close, and volume. Each cell has a numerical value that represents the strength and direction of the association between the associated pair of attributes. The diagonal elements' values are near to one, suggesting strong positive connections. Off-diagonal elements have significant positive connections with 'open', 'high', 'low', and 'close'. The correlations for 'volume' are substantially smaller, indicating poor relationships with other variables. The cells are color-coded according to their values, with darker blue suggesting a higher positive association. The color scale on the right side goes from 0 to 1, denoting correlation strength.

6 Discussions

The utilization of OptiContamFinder, a unique anomaly detection tool primarily based on the Isolation Forest algorithm, gives a substantial development in pre-processing strategies for stock marketplace forecasting and now casting. Traditional pre-processing strategies frequently struggle to efficaciously identify and cast off anomalies that can drastically obstruct the accuracy of predictive ways. OptiContamFinder addresses this venture by means of leveraging the strengths of the Isolation Forest algorithm to successfully isolate anomalies inside stock marketplace datasets. By generating random forests of isolation trees and identifying outliers with shorter path lengths, OptiContamFinder excels at detecting anomalies such as excessive price changes or incorrect data points that could distort underlying patterns. The optimization options provided by OptiContamFinder for determining the contamination threshold enable a balanced approach between anomaly removal and data retention, ensuring that important information is preserved while anomalies are effectively removed. This pre-processing method, which encompasses facts collecting, cleansing, feature identity, normalization, and anomaly removal with OptiContamFinder, units a solid basis for education forecasting techniques. This identifies and eliminates anomalies contribute to the robustness of predictive model, accurately predicts the stock price movement.

7 Conclusion and Future Work

The introduction of OptiContamFinder as a pre-processing tool for stock market forecasting and now casting represents a significant advancement in addressing the challenge of anomaly detection in financial datasets. The Isolation Forest algorithm and providing optimization options for determining contamination thresholds, OptiContamFinder effectively identifies and removes anomalies that could distort predictive model performance. The comprehensive pre-processing pipeline, which includes data gathering, cleaning, feature identification, normalization, and anomaly removal, ensures that predictive models are built on reliable and robust data. The successful implementation of OptiContamFinder contributes to more accurate forecasts of stock price movements, thereby enhancing decision-making processes in financial markets. Future work could focus on several avenues for further improvement and exploration. Firstly, the performance of OptiContamFinder could be evaluated across a broader range of financial datasets and compared against existing anomaly detection techniques to assess its generalizability and effectiveness in different market conditions. Additionally, research could delve into enhancing the scalability and efficiency of OptiContamFinder to handle larger and more complex datasets, considering the high-frequency trading environment and the increasing volume of financial data generated daily. Integrating OptiContamFinder into more predictive modelling frameworks, such as machine learning ensembles or deep learning architectures, could potentially enhance its predictive capabilities and further improve forecasting accuracy. The application of OptiContamFinder beyond stock market forecasting to other domains with similar data characteristics, such as crypto currency markets or macroeconomic indicators, could uncover new insights and opportunities for anomaly detection and predictive modelling. Overall, the development and refinement of OptiContamFinder represent a promising direction for advancing the field of financial data analysis and forecasting.

References

1. Toma, A., Dedu, S.: Quantitative techniques for financial risk assessment: a comparative approach using different risk measures and estimation methods. Procedia Econ. Finance **8**, 712–719 (2014)
2. Crépey, S., Lehdili, N., Madhar, N., Thomas, M.: Anomaly detection in financial time series by principal component analysis and neural networks. Algorithms **15**(10), 385 (2022)
3. Maguluri, L.P., Rengaswamy, R.: An efficient stock market trend prediction using the real-time stock technical data and stock social media data. Int. J. Intell. Eng. Syst. **13**(4), 316–332 (2020). https://doi.org/10.22266/ijies2020.0831.28
4. Xu, H., Pang, G., Wang, Y., Wang, Y.: Deep isolation forest for anomaly detection. IEEE Trans. Knowl. Data Eng. **35**(12), 12591–12604 (2023). https://doi.org/10.1109/TKDE.2023.3270293
5. Alshdaifat, E., Alshdaifat, D., Alsarhan, A., Hussein, F., El-Salhi, S.M.F.S.: The effect of pre-processing techniques, applied to numeric features, on classification algorithms' performance. Data **6**(2), 11 (2021)
6. Hilal, W., Gadsden, S.A., Yawney, J.: Financial fraud: a review of anomaly detection techniques and recent advances. Expert Syst. Appl. **193**, 116429 (2022)
7. Wambura, S., Huang, J., Li, H.: Robust anomaly detection in feature-evolving time series. Comput. J. **65**(5), 1242–1256 (2022)
8. Mehtab, S., Sen, J.: A time series analysis-based stock price prediction using machine learning and deep learning models. Int. J. Bus. Forecast. Mark. Intell. **6**(4), 272–335 (2020)
9. Cao, Y.: Application of machine learning algorithms in financial market risk prediction. In: The 2021 International Conference on Machine Learning and Big Data Analytics for IoT Security and Privacy, pp. 161–168. Springer International Publishing, Cham (2022). https://doi.org/10.1007/978-3-030-89508-2_21
10. Sonar, P., KishorJagad, P.: Financial institutions and their role in the development and financing of small individual projects. NeuroQuantology **20**(10), 2333 (2022)
11. Bhadkamar, A., Bhattacharya, S.: Tesla Inc., stock prediction using sentiment analysis. Australas. Account. Bus. Finance J. **16**(5), 52–66 (2022)
12. Saeed, M.M., Saeed, R.A., Abdelhaq, M., Alsaqour, R., Hasan, M.K., Mokhtar, R.A.: Anomaly detection in 6G networks using machine learning methods. Electronics **12**(15), 3300 (2023)

13. Thaseen, I.S., Mohanraj, V., Ramachandran, S., Sanapala, K., Yeo, S.-S.: A hadoop based framework integrating machine learning classifiers for anomaly detection in the internet of things. Electronics **10**(16), 1955 (2021)
14. Larriva-Novo, X., Vega-Barbas, M., Villagra, V.A., Rivera, D., Alvarez-Campana, M., Berrocal, J.: Efficient distributed preprocessing model for machine learning-based anomaly detection over large-scale cybersecurity datasets. Appl. Sci. **10**(10), 3430 (2020)
15. Faraz, M., Khaloozadeh, H., Abbasi, M.: Stock market prediction-by-prediction based on autoencoder long short-term memory networks. In: 2020 28th Iranian Conference on Electrical Engineering (ICEE), IEEE, pp. 1–5 (2020)
16. Azevedo, V., Kaiser, G.S., Mueller, S.: Stock market anomalies and machine learning across the globe. J. Asset Manag. **24**(5), 419–441 (2023)
17. Cruz, R., Kinyua, J., Mutigwe, C.: Analysis of social media impact on stock price movements using machine learning anomaly detection. Intell. Autom. Soft Comput. **36**(3), 3405–3423 (2023). https://doi.org/10.32604/iasc.2023.035906
18. Wang, G., Miao, J.: Design of data mining algorithm based on rough entropy for us stock market abnormality. J. Intell. Fuzzy Syst. **39**(4), 5213–5221 (2020)
19. Ayesha, S., Hanif, M.K., Talib, R.: Overview and comparative study of dimensionality reduction techniques for high dimensional data. Inf. Fusion **59**, 44–58 (2020)
20. Anwar, A., Patil, A.A., Choudari, S., Chetna, C., Kiran, C.S.: Machine learning insights for stock market trend identification. Int. J. Intell. Syst. Appl. Eng. **12**(10s), 567–575 (2024)
21. Laskar, M.T.R., et al.: Extending isolation forest for anomaly detection in big data via K-means. ACM Trans. Cyber-Phys. Syst. TCPS **5**(4), 1–26 (2021)

Author Index

M. Bakaev et al. (Eds.): IMS 2024, CCIS 2534, pp. 371–372, 2026.
https://doi.org/10.1007/978-3-031-96177-9

FSC
www.fsc.org
MIX
Papier aus verantwortungsvollen Quellen
Paper from responsible sources
FSC® C105338

If you have any concerns about our products,
you can contact us on
ProductSafety@springernature.com

In case Publisher is established outside the EU,
the EU authorized representative is:
Springer Nature Customer Service Center GmbH
Europaplatz 3, 69115 Heidelberg, Germany

Printed by Libri Plureos GmbH
in Hamburg, Germany